# 797,885 Books

are available to read at

www.ForgottenBooks.com

---

Forgotten Books' App
Available for mobile, tablet & eReader

ISBN 978-1-330-63955-9
PIBN 10086030

This book is a reproduction of an important historical work. Forgotten Books uses state-of-the-art technology to digitally reconstruct the work, preserving the original format whilst repairing imperfections present in the aged copy. In rare cases, an imperfection in the original, such as a blemish or missing page, may be replicated in our edition. We do, however, repair the vast majority of imperfections successfully; any imperfections that remain are intentionally left to preserve the state of such historical works.

Forgotten Books is a registered trademark of FB &c Ltd.
Copyright © 2015 FB &c Ltd.
FB &c Ltd, Dalton House, 60 Windsor Avenue, London, SW19 2RR.
Company number 08720141. Registered in England and Wales.

For support please visit www.forgottenbooks.com

# 1 MONTH OF FREE READING

at

www.ForgottenBooks.com

By purchasing this book you are eligible for one month membership to ForgottenBooks.com, giving you unlimited access to our entire collection of over 700,000 titles via our web site and mobile apps.

To claim your free month visit:

www.forgottenbooks.com/free86030

\* Offer is valid for 45 days from date of purchase. Terms and conditions apply.

# Similar Books Are Available from
# www.forgottenbooks.com

**A Study of English Words**
by Jessie Macmillan Anderson

**How to Write Clearly**
Rules and Exercises on English Composition, by Edwin Abbott

**Grammar of the English Sentence**
by Jonathan Rigdon

**Mistakes Writing English, How to Avoid Them**
by Marshall T. Bigelow

**A Higher English Grammar**
by Alexander Bain

**Words and Sentences**
by Harry Stuart Vedder Jones

**McGraw-Hill Handbook of English**
by Virginia Shaffer

**Better English for Speaking and Writing**
A Series of Three Books, by Sarah Emma Simons and Clem Irwin Orr

**The Old and Middle English**
by Thomas Laurence Kington Oliphant

**Advanced Course of Composition and Rhetoric**
by G. P. Quackenbos

**Everyday English, Vol. 1**
by Franklin T. Baker

**A Guide to Good English**
by Robert Palfrey Utter

**An Outline of English Phonetics**
by Daniel Jones

**Course in General Linguistics**
by Ferdinand de Saussure

**A Concise Etymological Dictionary of the English Language**
by Walter W. Skeat

**Pure English**
A Treatise on Words and Phrases, or Practical Lessons in the Use of Language, by Fred H. Hackett

**English Pronunciation for Foreigners**
by Sarah Jan Barrows

**Linguistic Change**
An Introduction to the Historical Study of Language, by E. H. Sturtevant

**An Improved Grammar of the English Language**
by Noah Webster

**The Excitement of Verbal Adventure, Vol. 1**
A Study of Vladimir Nabokov's English Prose, by Jürgen Bodenstein

# CONTENTS

|  | PAGE |
|---|---|
| INTRODUCTION . . . . . . . . | vii |
| BIBLIOGRAPHY . . . . . . . . | lxxix |
| SELECT EXTRACTS FROM 'NOTES AND QUERIES': | |
| The Third Series (1866–1867) . . . . . | 1 |
| The Fourth Series (1868–1873) . . . . | 31 |
| The Fifth Series (1874–1879) . . . . . | 81 |
| The Sixth Series (1880–1885) . . . . . | 129 |
| The Seventh Series (1886–1891) . . . . | 212 |
| The Eighth Series (1892–1896) . . . . | 316 |
| INDEX . . . . . . . . . . | 403 |

# ERRATA AND ADDENDA.

P. xvi. l. 14.   *For* 1870 *read* 1860.

P. lvii. l. 6 from bottom.   *For* are *read* is.

P. lxiii. l. 21.   *For* Wilhelm Grimm *read* Jacob Grimm.

P. lxvi. l. 3 from bottom.   Dr. Bosworth continued to hold the rectory of Water Stratford for some time after 1858.

P. 26, last line but one.   *For* Lambert *read* Lambeth.

P. 135, line 9 from bottom.   For *Rock* read *Lock*.

APPENDIX, p. 393: on "Cambridge and the Cam."  DR. CHANCE has kindly drawn my attention to the important fact that he had already arrived at similar conclusions to those here printed, at a much earlier date. His first article on the subject appeared some twenty-seven years ago, in the pages of the *Athenaeum*; and he also contributed valuable notes on the subject to *N. and Q.*, 4 S. iv. 401, and 8 S. ii. 429. I willingly admit that his articles on the subject were both earlier and more complete; and I regret that, to my loss, I overlooked them.

He gave authorities for the intermediate spellings *Grant-bridge*, *Gran-bridge*, *Gante-bridge*, and *Cranta-bridge*, which I failed to find; and suggested that the change from *Gr* to *C* (initial) was due to a confusion between the old forms of *Cambridge* and *Canterbury*. See the *Cambridge Review*, Nov. 19, 1896; and *N. and Q.*, 8 S. x. 430.

*A Student's Pastime.*

# INTRODUCTION

—◆◆—

Now that my attention has been definitely given to the study of English for more than thirty years (to say the least), it is high time for me to consider the question of venturing to reprint some of my scattered utterances on the subject.

A good friend of mine once asked me—'How came you to think of studying English?' The fact that such a question was possible suggests that to do so is an uncommon course; and this is certainly the case, extraordinary as the assertion may seem to the foreigner. Under the circumstances, perhaps a few personal details are allowable.

The book entitled *Men of the Time* correctly gives the day of my birth as November 21, 1835; five years before that of the Princess Royal, as she was once called, on the same day. The place of it was Mount Street, Park Lane; but, from the age of two to somewhere about fourteen, we lived at Perry Hill, Sydenham, at that time quite in the country; and certainly a boy brought up (in holiday-time) in the country has much to be thankful for. It was then that I acquired, by help of various opportunities, some acquaintance with the dialects of West Kent, London, and Essex. But the speech which became most familiar to me was that of South Shropshire, where I had many relatives, and which I often visited in company with my parents. My mother once knew the dialect well, and occasionally exemplified it. This explains why Miss Jackson's *Shropshire Word-book*, of which I read all the proof-sheets, was dedicated to myself; and why the lamented authoress, but lately dead, made me a present of the copyright of the work. The result is that the *English Dialect Dictionary* will be able to make very free use of it; and this is a point of some moment, as the work in question is one of the best of its kind.

It will be understood that I shall only mention such details as bear more or less directly upon my friend's question. It is of small interest to give the names of the five schools with which I was connected, but I will mention two of them. During part of the time when I was at King's College School, in the Strand, it was my singular fate to have for my class-master the Rev. Oswald Cockayne, well known to students as a careful and excellent Anglo-Saxon scholar, perhaps one of the best of those of his own date. He was an excellent and painstaking teacher, and it was, I believe, from him that I imbibed the notion of what is known as scholarship. In after life, it was my good fortune to know him personally, and I always experienced from him the greatest kindness and readiness to help. After his death, I acquired some of his books, including his well-known and useful work entitled *Anglo-Saxon Leechdoms*, and some of his carefully executed transcripts. His transcript of Ælfric's *Lives of the Saints*, in particular, has often proved useful.

One of his chief objects was the preparation of a new Anglo-Saxon Dictionary, a work which he undertook because he was dissatisfied with the first edition of Bosworth, which is, in fact, little more than a translation of **Lye** and **Manning**. At the time of his death, he had actually completed, on clearly written slips, the letters A to E; and these came into my hands with the other papers. By that time, the new edition of Bosworth had already advanced to F, so that they were not available for collation. Nevertheless, I sent them to Professor Toller, in the hope that they may afford some materials for a Supplement; and I may add that I have since bought a copy of Somner's *Dictionary* containing a considerable number of MS. references. These are added in a most delicate handwriting resembling print, a handwriting obviously adopted on account of the difficulty of writing upon the old paper, which is by no means well sized. Notwithstanding this change in the style of the handwriting, I cannot doubt that these references are Cockayne's own, and should some day deserve attention.

The last school that received me was that of Sir Roger Cholmeley at Highgate, founded in the reign of Elizabeth, in 1565. The three years which I spent there was a time of much profit and pleasure; the head-master being then the Rev. John Bradley Dyne. It was in the year of the Great Exhibition of 1851 that I obtained as a prize a copy of Steevens and Malone's *Shakespeare*; and this edition was, at any rate, good enough for purposes of common use. The glossary, of course, has no references, but it was an amusement to supply them for myself.

It was at this school that I gained some notion of the excellence of English literature. For it was customary to give us occasional scraps of it, on which to exercise our skill by translating them into Greek and Latin verse. Probably it is by the same curious and circuitous course that boys still have English authors brought under their notice. However this may be, it is certain that no portion of our literature was ever explained to me at any of my five schools. It was then considered as a thing altogether apart from our ordinary curriculum, and only to be seriously

## INTRODUCTION.

regarded when in the privacy of our own homes during holidays. And what an astounding fact this now seems to me to be! If we really possess, as many think, one of the finest literatures in the world, why are not boys informed of its value, and why are they not shown how to approach it with profit to themselves? There is only one thing yet more extraordinary, viz. the total disregard of the history of the English language. All we knew of its etymology was that many English words are derived from Latin and Greek; but I doubt if even our masters could have told us the history of such common words as *home* or *ransom*.

But there were some gleams of light accorded us, which were by no means devoid of benefit. There was a school library, and one of its possessions was a glorious copy of Spenser. He must have felt rather solitary, from the dearth of brother-poets around him; but doubtless, his isolation has long ago been remedied.

Our head-master had one somewhat uncommon idea, which savoured, as it has always seemed to me, of great wisdom. Instead of invariably requiring us to turn English poetry into Latin verse, he sometimes gave us pieces of Latin poetry to turn into English verse; a change which was delightful and refreshing. The English verse was usually poor enough, but the attempt to produce it was stimulating and valuable. And he did more than this; for our usual holiday-task, in the longest holidays, was to produce an English poem of 200 lines on a given theme. I can conscientiously say that such tasks did me a great deal of good, and the advantages of it are obvious, namely these. In the first place, a boy who has done English verses at school soon gets to understand what genius he has in that direction. If he finds it to be very small, he has learnt a most valuable lesson, viz. to refrain, when he comes of age, from publishing a volume of 'poems.' This alone is a gain both to himself and to the public.

Again, the frequent habit of writing 'verses' is a most valuable introduction to the art of writing prose. The verse-writer soon forms a habit of considering what words will best suit the idea which he wishes to express; so that when he has, for example, a letter to write, he does not feel quite all abroad. This is a benefit to his correspondent as well as to himself.

Moreover, the experiment produced one result which was probably unexpected. One of my schoolfellows actually exhibited the true poetic faculty, and his short life was full of promise of much excellence. This was Philip Stanhope Worsley, scholar of Corpus Christi College, Oxford; whose splendid translation of Homer's *Odyssey* into Spenserian stanzas has met with a fair meed of admiration. He afterwards attempted a translation of the *Iliad*, which he did not live to complete; it was completed, as is well known, by Professor Conington. One of my treasures is his small volume of *Poems and Translations*, published in 1863. It is probably little known, but it contains some beautiful lines.

> 'Who once hath chosen the ranks of right,
>   With clenched resolve by his choice to stand,
>  Saves a people oft in their own despite,
>   And loveth wisely his native land.'

I am thankful to say that, in my time, there were few (if any) 'open' scholarships. Instead of being 'crammed' at school for the special purpose of being examined, we honestly earned our scholarships by hard work at college during our 'first year'; the year which some freshmen now think they can easily afford to despise. For myself, I had the special advantage of residing in Cambridge before entering college at all; my private tutor, in mathematics, being the Rev. Harvey Goodwin, afterwards Bishop of Carlisle. It is not many years since I again met the bishop at Ely, on which occasion I reminded his lordship of his former helpfulness, when he replied with that geniality which made him so attractive—'Well, do you know I had quite forgotten it!' immediately adding, to my intense surprise—'I wish you'd teach *me* something!' And it turned out that he, at any rate, knew my books. He also spoke feelingly of the great interest which his deceased brother used to take in Anglo-Saxon; this brother being Charles Wycliffe Goodwin, formerly fellow of Catharine Hall, and editor of *The Life of St. Guthlac.*

This year of preparation for college was not wholly given to mathematics. English literature was, at all times, a delightful change and recreation; and I gained at least one special advantage at this time, from a careful and systematic study of the glorious *Faerie Queen*. I was never, to use Macaulay's phrase, 'in at the death of the Blatant Beast,' for the simple reason that he never was slain, but is still alive; as the curious reader may discover for himself, unless he is aware of the fact already. Moreover, the Blatant Beast appears in the Sixth Book, not at the end of the extant portion of the poem; for we must not ignore the two splendid cantos on Mutability.

I early formed the habit of endeavouring to study poets by the perusal of the texts themselves, rather than by judging of their merits from accidental scraps as presented in books of extracts. I do not mean to say that in the case of Byron, for example, one is bound to read *Marino Faliero* and *Sardanapalus* along with the rest at the first time of reading; but it is surely best to examine a considerable portion of his works at the same time, and there is no reason for neglecting *Lara* after perusing *The Giaour*. Some poets, like Keats and Campbell and Milton and Longfellow, wrote nothing that one would like to miss; and it is no bad plan to extend one's domain of English poetry so as to include such works as Cary's *Dante* and Fairfax's translation of *Tasso*. It does not take much longer to read the *Paradise Regained* than a second-rate three-volume novel; and, for my part, I prefer the poem. I am aware that others are of a different opinion.

It will thus be seen that, in my case, a love of our splendid literature was early formed, and at no time required any external stimulus. But this does not explain how I came to take a special delight in the linguistic and philological side of it, whilst revelling in its appeals to the imagination. Some are tempted to suppose that a critical examination of language is likely to interfere with the romantic element. I have never found it so in any appreciable degree; and I sometimes suspect that those who decry philology want to make us believe, with the fox, that the grapes are sour. Why are we to be debarred from examining a poet's language because his words are sweet and his descriptions entrancing? That is only one more reason for weighing every word that he uses. As to the charge sometimes made against philologists, that they have no real love for literature and are incapable of tracing the indebtedness of one writer to another, it is all pure assumption, cunningly put forward for the purpose of decrying philology. The philologist, on the contrary, has the larger view, and can see the value both of the language and of the ideas; but there are some critics who care nothing for the language, and prefer to regard our great masters with but one eye.

It so happens that I can even now remember how my attention was drawn to our earlier writers. As in the case of many others in my time, one of my lesson-books was Mrs. Markham's *History of England*; and I was of course attracted, as many others have been, by the 'Conversations' which she appended to her historical chapters. The Conversation on the reign of Richard II is one of special interest, containing as it does, a mention of 'Chaucer, the father of English poetry,' and a quotation comprising a pretty description of a morning, which you will find intelligible.

> 'The busy lark, the messenger of day,
> Saluteth with her song the morning gray;
> And fiery Phebus riseth up so bright
> That all the orient laugheth at the sight,
> And with his beamès drieth in the *grevès*
> The silver droppès hanging on the levès.'

And when her son Richard wants to know what *greves* means, Mrs. M. informs him that it is the same as *groves*. Next, this good lady tells us something about Langland, 'who wrote a very severe satire against persons of all professions, called the *Vision of Piers Plowman*, which, for the insight it gives into the manners of the times, is a very valuable relic.' Asked, if it is as difficult to understand as Chaucer's poetry, she replies : ' You will find it more so.' She then gives some idea of what is meant by 'alliterative' poetry, and selects for our instruction the following extract [1]·

> 'I found there
> A hall for a high king, a household to holden,
> With broad boards abouten, y-benched well clean ;
> With windows of glass wrought as a church,
> And chambers with chimneys, and chapels gay.'

Young as I then was, these quotations haunted me ; and I well remember making an internal resolution that, if ever I lived to grow up, I would desire better acquaintance with the originals, little dreaming that it would be my good fortune to edit both of the works which the extracts represent, as well as the *Vision of Piers Plowman*, which, as we are here told, is certainly 'a very valuable relic.'

Nor was this all. The words 'holden' and 'abouten' and 'y-benched' seemed so quaint, that their forms irresistibly invited further consideration. Why and when did

---

[1] It is not from *Piers Plowman*, but from *Pierce Plowman's Crede*, by a different author.

people say 'abouten,' and what did they mean by the prefix *y-* in 'y-benched'? These were problems to be seriously considered; they could not be beyond human discovery, and discovered they must some day be!

Hence it was that, throughout my college life, classics, mathematics, and theology were my more serious studies, whilst Chaucer, and Spenser, and Shakespeare were an unfailing resource in many an hour of leisure. My future was, as I then supposed, to be spent in the obscurity of a country curacy, and our great writers could be safely depended on for affording excellent companionship on a rainy day.

I had come to Cambridge because I was supposed to have 'a turn' for mathematics; and the next question was the choice of a college. Taking counsel with a very old friend and schoolfellow, at that time an undergraduate of Peterhouse, and being desirous of entering a college which should be large enough for forming acquaintances, and not so large as to overwhelm me with competition, he suggested that Christ's College would probably suit me; and the advice was gratefully received.

No loyal student, whose affection for his own college is sincere and ineradicable, will blame me for entertaining the pious belief that it is a college of the highest merit. Milton and Darwin are great names; and even in my own time good men were not altogether lacking. It was a treat to hear Charles Stuart Calverley, more familiarly known by his own chosen title of 'C. S. C.,' accompany himself on the pianoforte whilst singing his 'Italian' songs. If perchance a line of *La donna è mobile* slipped his memory, its place was readily supplied by any other words that would suit the scansion, such as 'mezzo soprano,' or 'la piano forte,' or the English phrase 'mili potaato'; and even such a word as 'celery' sounded like Italian when the *c* before the *e* was duly pronounced like the *ch* in *chin*. With John Robert

Seeley, historian and true patriot, I was well acquainted; not only during his latter years at college, but to the end of his useful life; and none could wish for a more amiable or gentle companion. I remember the time when he began to study German seriously; we even read *Faust* together.

Other friends were Sir Walter Joseph Sendall, now Governor of Cyprus; Sir Walter Besant, a familiar name throughout England's wide dominions; Dr. John Peile, our much-revered Master of the college; and John Wesley Hales, Professor of English Literature in King's College, London. But this is not the place for dwelling on such recollections.

I was elected to a Fellowship at Christ's College, on the same day with Hales, in July, 1860; shortly after which my college career came to an end. The time came for my ordination, and in December of the same year I became curate of East Dereham, in the centre of Norfolk, where the first two years of my married life were happily spent. In the north aisle of the parish church is the tomb of the poet Cowper, and in the hall of one of the principal houses in the market-place I was shown the veritable sofa which gave occasion to his *Task*. It was easy to acquire a good deal of the Norfolk dialect; indeed, it surprised me to find how very well known some of the dialect words were to most of the townspeople. Nearly every one seemed to know what was meant by 'haining' a hedge, and could distinguish between a 'dor' and a 'hodmandod.'

On February 27, 1861, I ventured to give a popular lecture at East Dereham, 'On the Origin and Progress of the English Language.' It was received with some favour, and, with a few alterations, appeared in all the glory of print. This little pamphlet of forty pages, now (happily) no longer procurable, was the beginning of a long series of works on the same subject, some of which, for the present at least, are useful to students. I find, on reference, that it opens with words which, in 1861, were almost prophetic :—

'Any one who is a little acquainted with the history of philology in England must, I think, be aware that the state of that science at the present time is very different from what it was only a few years ago. We live in an age, not of progress merely, but of rapid progress.'

I make no apology for transcribing a few more sentences from this extinct 'work' :—

'It is to be hoped that the foolish custom of making out forced and far-fetched derivations has gone by; nothing is learnt by it, because the meaning is not thereby simplified.'

'It is clear that English grammar depends upon that of Anglo-Saxon almost wholly.' (This, by the way, was clean contrary to the prevalent idea in schools.)

'Our grammar has become simplified in some points, and rendered puzzling in others. We never know, for instance, whether we ought to say *he sang* or *he sung*[1]; but, according to Saxon usage, we ought to conjugate the tense thus :— *I sang, thou sungest, he sang; we, ye,* or *they sung*. Whence we see that the two forms are not to be used indifferently, but vary according to the pronoun that precedes them.'

'Most of our older grammars ignore Saxon so completely that they are of little use except for the mere beginner.'

'It was owing to a want of knowledge of Anglo-Saxon that Dr. Johnson, in his *Dictionary*, committed some of those astounding blunders which were so ably and numercifully exposed by Horne Tooke in that brilliant, curious, but by no means reliable book[2] which he capriciously named *The Diversions of Purley*. He points out, for

---

[1] This very problem was again brought under my notice last year (1895).

[2] The book is, practically, obsolete; but it did good service in its time. Many of its principles are right; but the examples are faulty and cannot be trusted. Nevertheless, I revere the author's memory.

instance, a statement of Dr. Johnson's, according to which one meaning of the word *down* is "a valley"; the truth being that it always means precisely the opposite, viz. "a hill," or perhaps, more strictly, an exalted table-land; and for a very sufficient reason—that it is merely the modern form of the Anglo-Saxon word *dūn*, which means *a rolling hill, down,* or *dune.*'

'There is, however, a better way of studying English than by having recourse to dictionaries and grammars; and this is, to read some good standard author of the Elizabethan period, such as Shakespeare or Spenser or Bacon, and to observe in them all the phrases which strike a modern reader as peculiar. Such peculiar phrases should be carefully noticed, and, if possible, remembered; after a while, the reader will find himself gradually enabled to account for and explain some of them; and then he will have made a considerable advance; . . . so may he come at last to be able to read and understand Chaucer, of whom Spenser says, that he is "a well of English undefiled."

'The knowledge of older English that may thus be readily acquired will be of far greater service in explaining modern English than any laborious search in dictionaries. Besides, one thus kills two birds with one stone; whilst acquiring some knowledge of old English, one is reading books that are worthy of being read for their own sake; and it is by far the more interesting method.

'But what is of still more importance than an acquaintance with languages, is a habit of careful observation. The chief aim should be to try and understand *every word* that occurs in common passages of standard authors. Few but those who have looked into the matter with a little care, can have any idea of the utter misconception that often prevails [1]

---

[1] Remember, this applies to 1861; since which a great deal has happened.

as to the meaning of some common passages even in Shakespeare.' [I here quoted the famous passage from the *Tempest*, Act iv, ending—'leave not a *wreck* behind,' as it was then usually cited.] ... 'Only imagine the absurdity of talking about "a baseless fabric of a vision," or "an unsubstantial pageant faded," leaving behind them *a wreck!* ... Such blunders often arise thus:—Shakespeare uses some word which, though common in his day, is now nearly obsolete, or quite so. Thereupon comes some editor who, not understanding such a word, makes what he calls a conjectural emendation. ... Shakespeare wrote "racke," or, as we should now spell it, "rack"; upon which Horne Tooke remarks: "Rack is a common word, and ought not to be displaced because the commentators know not its meaning"; and he adds, with brilliant but bitter sarcasm—"If such a rule for banishing words were adopted, the commentators themselves would, most of them, become speechless!" ... What makes the wrong reading the more remarkable is that *rack* occurs elsewhere in Shakespeare, always in the sense of "drifting vapour"; see *Hamlet*, ii. 2. 506; *Antony*, iv. 14. 10; *Sonn.* 33. 6 [passages which were quoted at length]. But the most lamentable effect of this false reading remains to be told. The passage is inscribed upon Shakespeare's tomb in the Poets' Corner in Westminster Abbey, and, as may be verified by inspection, this mistaken reading is there adopted! The monument was erected in A.D. 1740; and it is exactly the kind of blunder we should expect to be made by the critics of the reign of George the Second. Considering how Englishmen venerate Shakespeare, it is not a pleasant fact to meditate upon, that on his public monument his words have been quoted incorrectly.'

After two years had been spent at East Dereham, we left that place, with much regret, to be nearer to relatives in London. My next curacy was, consequently, at Godalming, in the midst of much charming and picturesque scenery.

The church has lately undergone a much-needed transformation, and is no longer remarkable for an almost incredible ugliness. The lower part of the central tower has been much lightened in appearance; it was formerly an almost solid mass, with a low tunnel cut through the centre, whereby to reach the chancel from the aisle. On the north side of the chancel is the memorial tablet of Owen Manning, S.T.P., editor of Lye's *Anglo-Saxon Dictionary* in 1772. He is described on the title-page of that work as 'Canon. Lincoln. Vicarius de Godelming, et Rector de Peperharow in Agro Surreiensi.'

The neighbourhood was beautiful, but the climate proved unsuitable; and at last an alarming attack, of a diphtheritic character, totally unfitted me for clerical work and rendered a long rest absolutely necessary; and I thus found myself, in the end of 1863, at the age of twenty-eight, in the desolate condition of finding my chosen career brought to a sudden end, without any idea as to my future course, and even without much prospect of ever again rendering any help to my fellow-creatures, which (I can truly say) has always been my object as regards this present world.

Man proposes, but God disposes. I have never doubted that the work of a country clergyman is work of the noblest kind, with abundant opportunities for unobtrusive helpfulness, especially if he is not wholly dependent on having to eke out his subsistence by some form of additional labour. With such honest Christian work I could have been well content, and I had no ambition beyond it.

But I can now believe that I was meant to labour in a different field. Each man has his appointed task; and I have long since loyally accepted the educational duty of endeavouring to instil into the minds of Englishmen the respect in which they ought to hold their noble literature and their noble language, and the desirability of fighting against all the forms of error that beset the study of these invaluable treasures. Every true scholar is in some degree a missionary; he must hold fast to that which is good without wavering, and spare no pains to allure men to the reception of the truth.

A period of enforced idleness soon gave rise to a wish for some form of employment; and I could think of nothing better than to return to Cambridge. In October, 1864, I was appointed a mathematical lecturer at my own college, and I occasionally took a few pupils; but this left me a good deal of leisure time.

After some inquiry, I could not find that any one in Cambridge had any very accurate or extensive knowledge of Anglo-Saxon; and the idea occurred to me that, as it was obviously a useful study and in a fair way of becoming one of considerable importance, it would be a good plan to take up the subject seriously. It is fair to say that I formed this resolve with the sincere intention of assisting in the promotion of English scholarship, without any idea that it would afterwards fit me for doing work as a professor; for no one could then foresee that Dr. Bosworth would, in 1867, provide means for founding a Professorship of Anglo-Saxon [1].

It is now time to consider the history of the Philological Society's *Dictionary*, with which I have, indirectly, been much concerned.

At a meeting of the Philological Society of London, held on January 7, 1858, it was resolved—'that, instead of the *Supplement* to the standard English Dictionaries, then in the course of preparation by the Society's Unregistered Words Committee, a *New Dictionary of the English Language* should be prepared under the authority of the Philological Society.'

The work was placed in the hands of two Committees, the one, Literary and Historical, consisting of the Very

[1] The money was left to accumulate for over ten years; so that the actual establishment of the Professorship was put off till 1878.

Rev. the Dean of Westminster (Dean R. C. Trench), F. J. Furnivall, Esq., and H. Coleridge, Esq., Secretary; the other, Etymological, consisting of H. Wedgwood, Esq., and Professor Malden. Soon after, Mr. Coleridge and Mr. Furnivall were appointed editors of the *Dictionary*.

The practical results of the work of these Committees were remarkable. They soon discovered that, in both these departments, there was room for a great deal to be done.

Let us first consider the historical evidence. None could doubt that our linguistic treasures were abundant, but a great number of them existed only in manuscript, or had never been printed in any accessible form. The sumptuous editions for the Maitland and Roxburghe clubs were beyond the means of students; and it has lately been ascertained that some of the editors were not remarkable for any close acquaintance with their subjects.

The publication, in 1859, of Herbert Coleridge's *Glossarial Index* to the printed English Literature of the Thirteenth Century was timely and useful; but the practical result of it was to render it clearer than ever that the commencement of the publication of the *Dictionary* at too early a date would be disastrous, and would only demonstrate how little was known, from a philological point of view, of many of our most valuable literary monuments.

There was only one course to be taken. The MSS., especially of the thirteenth and fourteenth centuries, had to be printed at a reasonable price, and such of them as had only been edited in an expensive form, had to be printed over again. With this end in view, and at the urgent request of Dr. Morris, Mr. Furnivall started the Early English Text Society in 1864, with a goodly list of subscribers at a guinea apiece; and he had to look about for patriotic editors, who were willing to do the editing gratis, if the Society would pay for the printing.

The Society was extremely fortunate in its first editor. This was Dr. Richard Morris, who had already edited, for the Philological Society, a small book entitled *Liber Cure Cocorum*, as well as a more important one, viz. Hampole's *Pricke of Conscience*. Morris was gifted with a remarkable activity of mind and swiftness of comprehension, an excellent memory, and an unusual capacity for mastering minute grammatical details. In his preface to the *Pricke of Conscience*, he described, with great precision[1], the peculiarities of the Northumbrian or Northern English Dialect; and thus laid the foundation of a more accurate study of Middle English. In his preface to *Early English Alliterative Poems* (the Text Society's first volume), he brought out the peculiarities of the dialect and grammar of the West Midland district; and in 1867, viz. in the first edition of his *Specimens of Early English*, he clearly made out the chief characteristics of the three main dialects, Northern, Midland, and Southern. The results of his work are now common property, and almost every beginner of the study of Middle English is perfectly familiar with facts which, in 1866, were quite unknown. Every such student ought to know, further, what a debt of gratitude he owes, for this and many other lessons, to Richard Morris.

At any rate, let me acknowledge, with all thankfulness, how much I learnt from him. His *Specimens of Early English* was, in my eyes, of such great value, that I could not rest till I had provided it with a new Glossarial Index and furnished the author with such notes and small emendations as it was in my power to offer. With these he

---

[1] Morris's work was founded on a minute investigation of Middle-English poems. An earlier worker in the field was the Rev. Richard Garnett, who contributed an article on the 'Local Dialects of England' to the *Quarterly Review*, in Feb. 1836, and several papers to the *Philological Society's Transactions* in 1844-5. These were afterwards reprinted in Garnett's *Philological Essays*, edited by his son in 1859.

was so well satisfied that he practically put the book into my hands, and allowed my name to be added to the title-page. I also prepared an additional volume, containing extracts from our literature from 1394 to 1579; and, at a subsequent period, Morris produced a third volume, ranking as the *first* of the three in chronological order, as it contains 'Specimens' from 1150 to 1300. And even this was not all; for the idea afterwards occurred to me that the very numerous references given in these three books of 'Specimens' ought certainly to be registered under one alphabet; an idea which was taken up by my friend Mr. A. L. Mayhew, of Oxford, and made the foundation of the still more comprehensive volume entitled *A Concise Middle-English Dictionary*, edited by Mr. Mayhew and myself.

But Morris's work for the English Text Society extended far beyond his first very useful volume. It is to him that we are also indebted for an accessible reprint[1] of *Sir Gawayne and the Grene Knight* (1864), a poem of great merit, written by the same unknown hand that wrote those edited in his first volume; a *Metrical Paraphrase of the Books of Genesis and Exodus* (1865), a poem written about 1250; the very valuable prose work by Dan Michel of Northgate, known as *The Ayenbite of Inwit, or Remorse of Conscience*[2], dated 1340, and the chief source of our knowledge of the dialect of Kent; two series of *Early English Homilies* of the thirteenth century (1867-8, and 1873); *Legends of the Holy Rood* (1871); *An Old English Miscellany* (1872); the long religious poem known as the

---

[1] It had previously been edited by Sir Frederic Madden, one of the few of the earlier editors whose work was remarkable for true scholarship and accuracy. His edition of Layamon's *Brut* is also excellent; and he was joint-editor of the splendid Oxford edition of Wycliffe's Bible.

[2] Previously edited by the Rev. J. Stevenson.

*Cursor Mundi* (begun in 1874); *The Blickling Homilies*, from a MS. dated 971 (1874–1880); and a new edition of Chaucer's *Boethius*, from the two best MSS. (1868). No student can afford to neglect these justly esteemed editions by Dr. Morris, if he wishes to have a correct notion of the state of the English language in the thirteenth century.

The Early English Text Society being thus well started on its long and useful career, Dr. Furnivall, who has throughout been the chief source of the energy expended upon it and has himself edited considerably more than a dozen of its publications, began to cast about for more editors. My name was mentioned to him as that of one who was fond of Early English and had some leisure; and the result was that I was entrusted with the duty of re-editing a poem of no great value, entitled *Lancelot of the Laik*, formerly edited by the Rev. Joseph Stevenson for the Maitland Club in 1839. My objection, that I was unable to read a MS., was over-ruled on the grounds, first, that the sole MS. was always at hand in the Cambridge University Library; and secondly, that I could learn.

My first inspection of the MS. was not reassuring; in fact, any one who can thoroughly master a Scottish MS. of the end of the fifteenth century is in a fair position to be not easily daunted by MSS. of an earlier date. But there was a teacher at hand such as few men ever had. To this day I can remember the smile of amused satisfaction with which the MS. was brought to me by our justly celebrated librarian, Henry Bradshaw by name, of King's College. I much suspect that he thought he had extinguished me; indeed, after puzzling over the first page for a couple of hours, I was not conscious of having advanced beyond some twenty lines; and so retreated for that time. But as I gradually gained the courage to maintain that, if the MS. was right, the printed copy was sometimes wrong, Bradshaw became interested, authoritatively confirmed all my emendations, and never failed to give me his most valuable aid, in every case of doubt and difficulty, from that day forward till that which brought me the unexpected and startling news that my kind teacher and most sincere friend had died of a disease of the heart.

The announcement, in my preface to *Lancelot*, published in 1865, that the Maitland Club edition contained some strange errors—it must have been printed from a faulty transcript without any subsequent collation—created, at the time, quite a nine-days' wonder. It showed, at any rate, that the editors for the Early English Text Society really aimed at a reasonable accuracy; and it was urged that it was incumbent upon me to take up some more important work. In particular, a new edition of *Piers Plowman* was suggested, for which purpose it was necessary to examine all the available MSS. The generous help afforded me on this occasion is a thing to be remembered. A particular passage of the poem was selected by Dr. Furnivall, and transcripts of this passage came to hand from many helpers; from Dr. Furnivall himself, from the Rev. H. O. Coxe, Bodley's Librarian, and from Mr. W. Aldis Wright; whilst other aid was forthcoming from many quarters. Mr. (now Dr.) E. A. Bond gave his opinion as to the age of some of the MSS.; and, at a later date, MSS. were either lent or shown to me by the Earl of Ilchester, the Duke of Westminster, Mr. Henry Yates Thompson, and Lord Ashburnham. Not the least pleasant of my experiences were some valuable hints sent me by Mr. Thomas Wright, who had made a very useful edition of this great poem on his own account.

And so it came to pass that I began editing this poem in 1866, and only finished the last page of the General Introduction in 1885. A complete edition of the three principal texts, together with a sufficient reproduction of the Notes and Glossary, was reprinted by the Clarendon Press in 1886.

My work upon this edition of *Piers Plowman* suggested to me the idea of endeavouring to print or reprint, in due course, all the Early English poems that have come down to us in the form of alliterative verse without rime. This intention was never wholly fulfilled, but I nevertheless made considerable progress in this direction. The poems of this character edited by me were *Pierce the Ploughman's Crede*, the fragmentary *Romance of Joseph of Arimathea* (from the Vernon MS.), *Richard the Redeless* (by the author of *The Vision of Piers Plowman*); the short piece which I have called *The Crowned King*; *William of Palerne*; *The Romance of Alexander and Dindimus*; and the *Wars of Alexander*. Nearly all these poems are of considerable service to the lexicographer owing to the abundance in them of unusual, dialectal, and obsolescent words. By the difficulties which they thus frequently present I was especially attracted.

Most of these poems belong to the fourteenth century, and I was thus led to a special study of the language of this period, so that it has long been as familiar to me (as far as such a result is possible) as the language of the present day. I shall always be glad of having had a main hand in the editing and interpretation of three great authors of this period, viz. John Barbour, William Langland, and Geoffrey Chaucer. Future editors may do better; but my work will never (I hope) become quite superfluous.

It will now readily be understood that the foundation of the Early English Text Society was the first outcome of the desire of the Philological Society to provide for the publication of the *New English Dictionary*. But there were other results, of much importance for the study, which should be briefly mentioned.

The next result was this. We had (nearly?) all been

taught at school to pronounce Latin like modern Victorian English, a statement which ought to seem ludicrous, but is rather to be accounted as a lamentable disgrace. Consequently, it came natural to us to pronounce Early English after the same extraordinary and chaotic fashion. Neither did the evil stop there; for when I began the study of Anglo-Saxon, I knew no better than to pronounce the *i* in the A. S. *rīdan* like the *i* in the modern English *ride*; whereas, like the *ī* in Latin, Icelandic, Swedish, Danish, French, Spanish, Portuguese, Italian, Greek, and Russian, it was pronounced like the *i* in *machine*.

It was obvious that this would never do. It was useless to produce texts unless we could correctly pronounce the words which they gave us; and it was fortunate that the highly complex problem of the study of our old pronunciation was undertaken by the two men who were most competent to deal with it, as being intimately acquainted with the actual pronunciation of many languages. In England, men often 'spring up wherever they are wanted, capable of ruling, of conquering, of mastering difficulties[1]'; and the two men who mastered this particular difficulty were Alexander John Ellis and Henry Sweet. The great work by the former on *Early English Pronunciation*, and the *History of English Sounds* by the latter, have made it abundantly clear that our pronunciation has suffered many and startling alterations from time to time, and most of these changes can now be approximately dated. Anglo-Saxon was written with letters which were Celtic adaptations from the Latin alphabet, and the pronunciation of Anglo-Saxon did not greatly differ from that of Latin. Early English was respelt by Anglo-French scribes, but their pronunciation was much the same, so that it made no great difference. The vowel-sounds used by Chaucer were much

---

[1] J. R. Seeley; in *Literary Remains of C. S. Calverley*, p. 113

the same as those used by his great Italian cotemporaries, Dante, Petrarch, and Boccaccio. It was not till after 1400 that most of the new vowel-sounds began to arise which have been developed, in course of time, into those which we now use. The difference, in some cases, is very great; so that it is indeed difficult for any one who is inexperienced in our older literature to realize that our *a* in *dame* was once the French *a* in the French *dame*; that our *e* in *deity* was once the French *é* in *déité*; that our diphthongal *i* in *silence* was once the French *i* in *silence*; and that our diphthongal *ou* in *doubt* was once the French *ou* in *doute*. Yet such statements as these ought to be self-evident; we cannot even conceive that a Norman noble could have pronounced *dame, deity, doubt,* and *silence* with the modern English vowels.

The conclusions obtained by the labours of Ellis and Sweet have had far-reaching consequences. Englishmen are awaking to the value of phonetics generally. It is hardly too much to say that the study of etymology, in England, has been quite revolutionized by the use of newer and surer methods, based upon the careful observations of sounds and of the method of representing them by symbols. The student who understands the history of English sounds can no longer put up with the old and slovenly neglect of the history of the sounds in Latin and Greek; he awakes to the facts that language is a living thing, and that the spoken tongue is full of information as regards the written representation of it; he learns to listen to what he hears around him, and to make mental notes of the many varieties of pronunciation which are, literally, always in the air. In this way the subject of his study is quickened into full and active life; forms that are written down in old manuscripts by hands that are now mere dust may be, and continually are, illustrated, as by a revealing flash, by the chance word of an unknown stranger; and if the problems presented by the subtle changes in sounds are almost endless, we have at the same time a never-failing supply of undoubted facts ever filling the air around us, asking only for recognition, for memory, and for record. The position of learners is one of highest hope. There was a time when Greek accents were mere unmeaning marks, to be set over certain syllables because it was unreasonably esteemed a sign of scholarship (!) to do so; but to-day they are being severely scrutinized, for they tell us which syllable received the pitch, and afford much valuable information as to the way in which each word was sounded.

We now come to another matter altogether, though it has a close relationship to English philology, viz. the utility of a knowledge of our modern English dialects. In compiling the vocabulary of words admitted into the *New English Dictionary*, it was often extremely difficult to know where to draw the line. It has sometimes happened that a word which in olden times may fairly be said to have been in general use, or at any rate, in use over a large area, is now only heard in some provincial dialect, being unknown to nearly all the inhabitants of the rest of England; and, on the other hand, a word which was once used, as it would seem from the evidence, in one dialect only, has now become familiar to everybody. It follows from this that the collection of provincial words is absolutely necessary for completing the material with which the lexicographer has to deal; and hence Mr. Ellis and others suggested the establishment of an English Dialect Society. A letter written by Mr. Aldis Wright to *Notes and Queries* in March, 1870, was particularly explicit as to this necessity, and contained the ominous warning that 'in a few years it will be too late.'

Being deeply impressed with the incontrovertible truth of this statement, and finding that still the work could not be done till some one would definitely undertake the trouble of performing all the duties of an honorary secretary, I at last resolved to follow Dr. Furnivall's example, and to write the necessary prospectus for the formation of such a society. This was the beginning of the English Dialect Society, established in 1873, and commencing with a Bibliographical List of works written in English dialects, or directly concerned with the same. The Society is now (in 1896) still in existence, and in the course of its career has issued no less than seventy-six parts or numbers, including some highly valuable special glossaries, such as those of Mr. Elworthy (West Somerset), Mr. F. K. Robinson (Whitby), Messrs. Nodal and Milner (Lancashire), Mr. C. Clough Robinson (Mid Yorkshire), Mr. E. Peacock (Lincolnshire), and many more, for which I must refer the reader to the Society's list. Indeed, the work already accomplished is so considerable that we have arrived, as it were, in sight of land, and can contemplate the probable extinction of the Society in a not very distant future without any great anxiety. We are already beginning to gather together all the material; and, under the able editorship of Professor Wright, a general *English Dialect Dictionary* is already in the press. We may fairly hope for the completion of this truly national work in the course of another eight years.

As the publications of the Early English Text Society were specially designed, from the outset, for the use of future lexicographers, most of them were accompanied with glossaries, more or less complete, giving very copious and exact references to the passages which contain the harder words. But it was soon felt that something like a general *Dictionary of Middle English* was much needed, in order to exhibit results collected from many various sources. The two chief Dictionaries of this character were both undertaken, in the first instance, by Germans; we are much indebted, in this respect, to Dr. Francis Henry Stratmann, of Krefeld, and to Dr. Eduard Mätzner, of Berlin.

The first edition of Dr. Stratmann's *Dictionary of Middle English* was not wholly satisfactory. It was open to three objections, from a practical point of view. In the first place, the meanings assigned were too briefly given, and frequently rendered unintelligible by the use of provincial English words which represented the old word as to form, but not always as to sense. Secondly, many words were given under twelfth-century forms, without any recognition, in the alphabet, of forms with more usual spellings. And thirdly, which was worst of all, the author at first devoted himself solely to the explanation of words of Germanic origin, thus leaving the highly important Anglo-French element almost unrepresented. The third and latest edition, in a much improved form, was published in 1878, and an extensive supplement was issued in 1881; but in 1884 the author died. At the suggestion of Dr. Furnivall, the copyright of the work was purchased by the Clarendon Press, and all the materials, including the author's collections for a new edition, were placed in the hands of Mr. Henry Bradley. With almost incredible industry and perseverance, Mr. Bradley reconstructed the whole work, removing the above-mentioned obvious defects and largely increasing the vocabulary. The new edition (technically, the fourth) appeared in 1891, and is a book which every serious student of historical English keeps within easy reach, as a matter of course. A mere glance at this volume affords almost instantaneous proof that the Early English Text Society was not established in vain, and was founded none too soon.

The second *Middle English Dictionary*, by E. Mätzner, was originally planned as an accompanying glossarial volume to the *Altenglische Sprachproben*, or *Specimens of Early English*, issued by Mätzner and Goldbeck in 1867-9. But the work grew under the author's hands, till at length he formed the ambitious design of including in it references to all the chief works existing in our Middle English Literature.

It was, from the first, a better planned book than that of Stratmann. The explanations are fuller, the quotations more extended, and the vocabulary more complete; at the same time, the forms chosen as normal ones are such as very frequently occur. It had but one drawback, but that proved to be a very great one. The scale on which it was planned was such that the author could not complete it, though he lived till over eighty years of age, and was at work upon it almost to the last. The eleventh and last part appeared in 1891; and the last word discussed in it is the verb *makien*, to make. Whether it is in contemplation to continue this great work any further, I am unable to say.

It thus appears that, in the quarter of a century which elapsed between 1857 and 1882, an enormous advance had been made towards providing the *New English Dictionary* with better materials. It must further be borne in mind that, during all this period, hundreds of readers had been employed in making suitable extracts from thousands of books; and the precaution had been taken of requesting all the readers to write out their extracts on one side only of a half-sheet of ordinary note-paper, so that they might be duly sorted out in alphabetical order and tied up in bundles for ready reference. In this way several tons in weight of most valuable materials have been accumulated by the united efforts of a small army of workers; and though it frequently happens that, owing to imperfections in the work or a want of legibility, a given extract has to be re-compared with the source whence it was originally taken (causing much delay and trouble in the case of works that are difficult of access), yet the references alone are of infinite service, as without them the work would have remained impossible of execution in any satisfactory manner. And when all things are taken into account, viz. the establishment during this period of the Early English Text Society and of the Chaucer Society by Dr. Furnivall, and of the

English Dialect Society—the numerous editions of previously unprinted MSS. which have appeared not in England only, but also in Germany and America—the numerous re-editions of pieces that had previously been edited in an unsatisfactory or insufficient manner—the splendid success of Dr. Ellis and Dr. Sweet in recovering the almost lost history of our pronunciation—and the hearty co-operation of so many readers in preparing useful extracts—it may be doubted whether any similar enterprise was ever carried out with such sustained vigour and so much practical success. It is also of great importance to observe that, during the same period, very great advances have been made, especially in Germany, in the study of comparative grammar.

So far, I have spoken mainly of the historical side of the development of our venerable and venerated language. It remains to add a brief account of what has been done from a purely etymological point of view.

I have no space here to explore a subject which would, I think, prove to be of great interest, viz. the history of the progress of English etymology, beginning (let us say) with Minsheu and Blount and Skinner, and so onwards to Bailey and Johnson, with an occasional excursus on the wonderful vagaries of Richard Verstegan and the Rev. G. W. Lemon, and others like unto them. Let us begin at once with much more recent times.

It must be remembered that English, considered as to its vocabulary, is as a great river derived from many rills. Setting aside such words as have been adopted from sources of less importance, we may confine our attention, at the outset, to three streams which supplied us more copiously than others, viz. the Old English (including Scandinavian), the Anglo-French or Anglo-Norman, and the 'classical,' which includes Latin and Greek. Ever since the period of the Renaissance, to the end of the last century, and even later, abundant attention has been bestowed upon the third of these, almost as if it were all-sufficient and all-important, whilst the other two have been treated with an indifference that has often savoured of contempt. No man is a 'scholar' unless he can account for the spelling and etymology of *system*; but he is not expected to know anything of the history of such words as *home* or *ransom*, which are at once of earlier introduction and in much more extended use. It is difficult to conceive of anything more perverse.

The publication, in 1659, of Somner's *Anglo-Saxon Dictionary* was (or rather might have been) a great step in advance; but Skinner, in 1691, failed, for the most part, to make any satisfactory use of it, owing to his want of knowledge of the grammar and phonetic laws of the oldest stage of English. Dr. Johnson trusted much to the guidance of Skinner, so that but little progress was possible.

Just at the beginning of the present century appeared the remarkable work by Horne Tooke entitled *The Diversions of Purley*. In this the author assailed the etymologies in Johnson with much smartness and pitiless logic; showing, with great force, the value of Anglo-Saxon and Mœso-Gothic in questions relating to words of native origin, and opening the way to a better appreciation of our old expressions. Unfortunately, however, he was led to the construction of two most grotesque and crazy theories; the one, that conjunctions are derived from verbs in the imperative mood; and the other, that substantives ending in *-th* are formed from the third person singular of indicatives! And so it has come to pass that his book is obsolete, though it may still be read with pleasure by a student who is curious as to the history of the study of our language.

It was necessary to mention this work of Horne Tooke, in order to explain the singular phenomena presented by Richardson's *Dictionary*, of which a new edition appeared, in two fine quarto volumes, as late as 1863. This great work has two chief features, viz. its etymologies and its quotations. As regards the latter, its excellence and copiousness are surpassed by the great *New English Dictionary* only; indeed, we owe to Richardson the valuable habit of making a free use of our older authors. But when we come to investigate his etymologies, we find that he has not only adopted Tooke's theories, but carried them out with a boldness of invention that almost surpasses belief. Thus he expressly selects, for our approval and admiration, his account of the verbs *till* and *tell* (which happen to be unrelated), by repeating it complacently in his Preface: 'Again, to *tell* and to *till* are the same word, and mean to *lift*, to raise. To *till* with the plough is to *raise* (sc. the ground) with it. To *tell* with the tongue is to *raise* (sc. the voice) with it.' And all this, because Tooke had a fancy of deriving these words from the Latin *tollere*; which, by Grimm's Law, is impossible.

It soon became clear that this kind of roundabout reasoning, if reasoning it can be called, enabled anybody to derive any one word from any other, if only a case could somehow be made out; and the method had the inherent weakness of satisfying no one but the particular inventor of the guess. There was no stability or finality about such a process, and another one had to be resorted to.

It has already been remarked that Mr. Wedgwood was one of the committee appointed by the Philological Society to look after etymologies. To this circumstance we owe the highly ingenious and suggestive *Dictionary of English Etymology* written by my fellow-collegian Hensleigh Wedgwood, late-Fellow of Christ's College, Cambridge; which was undertaken at the urgent solicitation of Dr. Furnivall, the Society's honorary secretary. The second edition, revised and enlarged, appeared in 1872, and the third edition in 1878. The Introduction, containing an essay on the Origin of Language, is of great interest, as the author maintains, with much skill and abundant illustrations, the theory that language took its rise from the imitation of natural sounds and cries and from expressive interjections, in opposition to the theory of Max Müller that linguistic roots are 'phonetic types produced by a power inherent in human nature,' whatever that may mean.

The theory here advocated by Wedgwood is (as I believe) right in the main, and I may refer the reader to the treatment of it by Whitney and Sweet. Unluckily, it influenced the author far too much in his account of various words; for in many cases the forms in use are too modern or too much altered from their primitive shape for us to be still able to trace how they first arose. In the case of the verb *to plunge*, for example, Wedgwood's statement that its origin, 'like that of *plump*, is a representation of the noise made by the fall,' is purely fanciful; for it is merely borrowed from the F. *plonger*, answering to the Low Latin type \**plumbicare*, a derivative of *plumbum*, lead; see the account of the F. word in Littré and Diez.

It will be found, in fact, that several of Wedgwood's articles refer us to imitative types, where it is very doubtful if any such imitation was really intended. There is much in the book that is very useful, but the treatment of words of native origin leaves much to be desired. It is surprising that the word *home* should be referred to *ham-let*, and treated as if the *a* in the A.S. *hăm* (printed *ham*) was a short vowel. So under *horn*, we are referred to the 'Goth. *haurn*, Lat. *cornu*, Bret. *corn*, Gr. κέρας, Heb. *keren*'; without any mention of the A.S. *horn* as being the actual source. Very little regard is paid to the length of vowels, and the historical method is hardly pursued at all. There is no scientific treatment of the consonants, nor any recognition of the phenomena which are formulated and summarized in the convenient canon known as 'Grimm's Law.'

Briefly, Wedgwood's *Etymological Dictionary*, though it represents an enormous advance beyond the methods employed by Skinner and Richardson, is sadly deficient in scientific method, and could not be regarded as approaching finality.

The first English etymological dictionary in which the scientific treatment of language is sufficiently recognized was written, as might have been expected, in Germany; and remains to this day, owing to the excellence of its method, a reasonably good authority. This is the *Etymologisches Wörterbuch der englischen Sprache* by E. Müller, of which the first edition was published at Cöthen in 1865, and the second and much improved edition at the same place in 1878. This is a thoroughly good and sound work; and the author took the precaution of consulting the best authorities then available. The chief English works to which he refers are the dictionaries by Johnson, Richardson, Webster (with the etymologies revised by Dr. Mahn), Worcester, and Wedgwood; but he also availed himself of the excellent works by German authorities, such as Grimm, Koch, Fiedler, Mätzner, and Stratmann. The results are presented in a brief but usually accurate form, so that most of the articles require little or no correction. But it does not seem to be much known or much used in England, owing, I suppose, to the fact that the text is written in German.

The mention of the second edition of E. Müller's *Dictionary* has already brought us on to the year 1878. Meanwhile, the preparations for the *New English Dictionary* had been much advanced, and there seemed good hope that in a few years more, the time would have arrived for commencing to print and publish it. At this stage, the idea occurred to me that, as Wedgwood's work had been printed in advance as a contribution to the labour of furnishing the etymologies, and at the same time did not present the results in a well-assorted form, it would be helpful for some one to attempt to revise the whole of it, in a form more available for immediate use. I had the temerity to undertake this important task myself, having then hardly arrived at the age when one ceases to be infallible; and I began to bethink me of the improvements that could be made; and I took particular note of what seemed to be the more obvious defects in the existing dictionaries.

As I cannot explain the state of the case more clearly than I have already done in the Preface to the first edition (in 1882) of my *Etymological Dictionary*, I make no apology for citing a considerable portion of it here. Few people read a preface to a dictionary printed in a quarto form; so that it will probably be new to most of my readers·—

'The present work was undertaken with the intention of furnishing students with materials for a more scientific study of English etymology than is commonly to be found in previous works upon the subject. It is not intended to be always authoritative, nor are the conclusions arrived at to be accepted as final. It is rather intended as a guide to future writers, showing them in some cases what ought certainly to be accepted, and in other cases, it may be, what to avoid. The idea of it arose out of my own wants. I could find no single book containing the facts about a given word which it most concerns a student to know, whilst, at the same time, there exist numerous books containing information too important to be omitted. Thus Richardson's *Dictionary* is an admirable store-house of quotations illustrating such words as are of no great antiquity in the language, and his selected examples are the more valuable from the fact that he in general adds the exact reference. Todd's *Johnson* likewise contains numerous well-chosen quotations, but perhaps no greater mistake was ever made than that of citing from authors like Dryden or Addison at large, without the slightest hint as to the whereabouts of the context. But in both of these works the etymology is, commonly, of the poorest description; and it would probably be difficult to find a worse philologist than Richardson, who adopted many suggestions from Horne Tooke without enquiry, and was capable of saying that *hod* is "perhaps *hoved, hov'd, hod,* past part. of *heafan,* to heave." It is easily ascertained that the A. S. for *heave* is *hebban,* and that, being a strong verb, its past participle did not originally end in *-ed.*

'It would be tedious to mention the numerous other books which help to throw such light on the *history* of words as is necessary for the right investigation of their etymology. The great defect of most of them is that they do not carry back that history far enough, and are very weak in the highly important Middle English period. But the publications of the Camden Society, of the Early English Text Society, and of many other printing clubs, have lately materially advanced our knowledge, and have rendered possible such excellent books of reference as are exemplified in Stratmann's *Old English Dictionary* and in the still more admirable but (as yet) incomplete *Wörterbuch* by Eduard Mätzner. In particular, the study of phonetics, as applied to Early English pronunciation by Mr. Ellis and Mr. Sweet, and carefully carried out by nearly all students of Early English in Germany, has almost revolutionized the study of etymology as hitherto pursued in England. We can no longer consent to disregard vowel-sounds as if they formed no essential part of the word, which seems to have been the old doctrine; indeed, the idea is by no means yet discarded even by those who ought to know better.

'On the other hand, we have, in Eduard Müller's *Etymologisches Wörterbuch der englischen Sprache,* an excellent collection of etymologies and cognate words, but without any illustrations of the use or history of words, or any indication of the period when they first came into use. We have also Webster's *Dictionary*, with the etymologies as revised by Dr. Mahn, a very useful and comprehensive volume; but the plan of the work does not allow of much explanation of a purely philological character.

'It is many years since a new and comprehensive dictionary was first planned by the Philological Society, and we have now good hope that, under the able editorship of Dr. Murray, some portion of this great work may ere long see the light. For the illustration of the *history* of words, this will be all-important, and the etymologies will, I believe, be briefly but sufficiently indicated. It was chiefly with the hope of assisting in this national work, that, many years ago, I began collecting materials and making notes upon points relating to etymology. The result of such work, in a modified form, and with very large additions, is here offered to the reader. My object has been to clear the way for the improvement of the etymologies by a previous discussion of all the more important words, executed on a plan so far differing from that which will be adopted by Dr. Murray as not to interfere with his labours, but rather, as far as possible, to assist them. It will, accordingly, be found that I have studied brevity by refraining from any detailed account of the *changes of meaning* of words, except where absolutely necessary for purely etymological purposes. The numerous very curious and highly interesting examples of words which, especially in later times, took up new meanings will not, in general, be found here; and the definitions of words are only given in a very brief and bald manner, only the more usual senses being indicated. On the other hand, I have sometimes permitted myself to indulge in comments, discussions, and even suggestions and speculations, which would be out of place in a dictionary of the usual character. Some of these, where the results are right, will, I hope, save much future discussion and investigation; whilst others, where the results prove to be wrong, can be avoided and rejected. In one respect I have attempted considerably more than is usually done by the writers of works upon English etymology. I have endeavoured, where possible, to trace back words to their Aryan roots, by availing myself of the latest works upon comparative philology. In doing this, I have especially endeavoured to link one word with another, and the reader will find a perfect network of cross-references enabling him to collect all the forms of any given word of which various forms exist; so that many of the principal words in the Aryan languages can be thus traced. Instead of considering English as an isolated language, as is sometimes actually done, I endeavour, in every case, to exhibit its relation to cognate tongues; and as, by this process, considerable light is thrown upon English by Latin and Greek, so also, at the same time, considerable light is thrown upon Latin and Greek by Anglo-Saxon and Icelandic. Thus, whilst under the word *bite* will be found a mention of the cognate Latin *findere*, conversely, under the word *fissure*, is given a cross-reference to *bite*. In both cases, reference is also made to the root BHID; and, by referring to this root (No. 240, on p. 738), some further account of it will be found, with further examples of allied words. It is only by thus comparing all the Aryan languages together, and by considering them as one harmonious whole, that we can get a clear conception of the original forms; a conception which must precede all theory as to how those forms came to be invented. Another great advantage of the comparative method is that, though the present work is nominally one on *English* etymology, it is equally explicit, as far as it has occasion to deal with them, with regard to the related words in other languages; and may be taken as a guide to the etymology of many of the leading words in Latin and Greek, and to all the more important words in the various Scandinavian and Teutonic tongues.

'I have chiefly been guided throughout by the results of my own experience. Much use of many dictionaries has shown me the exact points where an enquirer is often baffled, and I have especially addressed myself to the task of solving difficulties and passing beyond obstacles. Not inconsiderable has been the trouble of verifying references. A few examples will put this in a clear light.

'Richardson has numerous references (to take a single case) to the *Romaunt of the Rose.* He probably used some edition in which the lines are not numbered; at any rate, he never gives an exact reference to it. The few references to it in Tyrwhitt's *Glossary* and in Stratmann do not help us very greatly. To find a particular word in this poem of 7700 lines is often troublesome; but, in every case where I *wanted* the quotation, I have found and noted it. I can recall several half-hours spent in this particular work.

'Another not very hopeful book in which to find one's place, is the *Faerie Queene.* References to this are usually given to the book and canto, and of these one or other is (in Richardson) occasionally incorrect; in every case, I have added the number of the stanza.

'One very remarkable fact about Richardson's *Dictionary* is that, in many cases, references are given only to obscure and late authors, when all the while the word occurs in *Shakespeare.* By keeping Dr. Schmidt's comprehensive Shakespeare *Lexicon* always open before me, this fault has been easily remedied.

'To pass on to matters more purely etymological. I have constantly been troubled with the vagueness and inaccuracy of words quoted, in various books, as specimens of Old English or foreign languages. The spelling of " Anglo-Saxon " in some books is often simply outrageous. Accents are put in or left out at pleasure; impossible combinations of letters are given; the number of syllables is disregarded; and grammatical terminations have to take their chance.

Words taken from *Ettmüller* are spelt with *ä* and *œ*; words taken from *Bosworth* are spelt with *æ* and *é*[1], without any hint that the *ä* and *œ* of the former answer to *æ* and *é* in the latter. I do not wish to give examples of these things; they are so abundant that they may easily be found by the curious. In many cases, writers of "etymological" dictionaries do not trouble to learn even the alphabets of the languages cited from, or the most elementary grammatical facts. I have met with supposed Welsh words spelt with a *v*, with Swedish words spelt with *æ*, with Danish infinitives ending in *-a*[2], with Icelandic infinitives in *-an*, and so on; the only languages correctly spelt being Latin and Greek, and commonly French and German. It is clearly assumed, and probably with safety, that most readers will not detect mis-spellings beyond this limited range.

'But this was not a matter which troubled me long. At a very early stage of my studies, I perceived clearly enough that the spelling given by some authorities is not necessarily to be taken as the true one; and it was then easy to make allowances for possible errors, and to refer to some book with reasonable spellings, such as E. Müller, or Mahn's *Webster*, or Wedgwood. A little research revealed far more curious pieces of information than the citing of words in impossible or mistaken spellings. Statements abound which it is difficult to account for except on the supposition that it must once have been usual to *manufacture* words for the *express purpose* of deriving others from them. To take an example, I open Todd's *Johnson* at random, and find that under *bolster* is cited "Gothic *bolster*, a heap of hay." Now the fragments of Gothic that have reached us are very

---

[1] Usually also printed *æ*, without the accent. I suspect that *é* is seldom provided for.

[2] Todd's *Johnson*, s.v. *Boll*, has 'Su. Goth. *bulna*, Dan. *bulner*.' Here *bulna* is the Swedish infinitive, whilst *bulner* is the first person of the Danish present tense. Similar jumbles abound.

precious but very insufficient, and they certainly contain no such word as *bolster*. Neither is *bolster* a Gothic spelling. *Holster* is represented in Gothic by *hulistr*, so that *bolster* might, possibly, be *bulistr*. In any case, as the word certainly does not occur, it can only be a pure invention, due to some blunder; the explanation "a heap of hay" is a happy and graphic touch, regarded in the light of a fiction, but is out of place in a work of reference.

'A mistake of this nature would not greatly matter if such instances were rare; but the extraordinary part of the matter is that they are extremely common, owing probably to the trust reposed by former writers in such etymologists as Skinner and Junius, men who did good work in their day, but whose statements require careful verification in this nineteenth century. What Skinner was capable of, I have shown in my introduction to the reprint of Ray's *Glossary* published for the English Dialect Society. It is sufficient to say that the net result is this; that words cited in etymological dictionaries (with very few exceptions) cannot be accepted without verification. Not only do we find puzzling mis-spellings, but we find actual fictions; words are said to be "Anglo-Saxon" that are not to be found in the existing texts; "Gothic" words are constructed for the mere purpose of "etymology"; Icelandic words have meanings assigned to them which are incredible or misleading; and so on of the rest.

'Another source of trouble is that, when real words are cited, they are wrongly explained. Thus, in Todd's *Johnson*, we find a derivation of *bond* from A. S. "*bond*, bound" Now *bond* is not strictly Anglo-Saxon, but an Early English form, signifying "a band," and is not a past participle at all; the A. S. for "bound" being *gebunden*. The error is easily traced; Dr. Bosworth cites "*bond*, bound, ligatus" from Somner's *Dictionary*, whence it was also copied into Lye's *Dictionary* in the form: "*bond*, ligatus, obligatus, *bound.*" Where Somner found it, is a mystery indeed, as it is absurd on the face of it. We should take a man to be a very poor German scholar who imagined that *band*, in German, is a past participle; but when the same mistake is made by Somner, we find that it is copied by Lye, copied by Bosworth (who, however, marks it as Somner's), copied into Todd's *Johnson*, amplified by Richardson into the misleading statement that "*bond* is the past tense [1] and past participle of the verb *to bind*," and has doubtless been copied by numerous other writers who have wished to come at their etymologies with the least trouble to themselves. It is precisely this continual reproduction of errors which so disgraces many English works, and renders investigation so difficult.

'But when I had grasped the facts that spellings are often false, that words can be invented, and that explanations are often wrong, I found that worse remained behind. The science of philology is comparatively modern, so that our earlier writers had no means of ascertaining principles that are now well established, and, instead of proceeding by rule, had to go blindly by guesswork, thus sowing crops of errors which have sprung up and multiplied till it requires very careful investigation to enable a modern writer to avoid all the pitfalls prepared for him by the false suggestions which he meets with at every turn. Many derivations that have been long current and are even generally accepted will not be found in this volume, for the plain reason that I have found them to be false; I think I may at any rate believe myself to be profoundly versed in most of the old fables of this character, and I shall only say, briefly, that the reader need not assume me to be ignorant of them because I do not mention them. The most extraordinary fact about

[1] *Bond* is a form of the *past tense* in Middle English, and indeed the sb. *bond* is itself derived from the grade of *bindan* found in the A. S. pt. t. *band*; but *bond* is certainly not 'the past participle.'

comparative philology is that, whilst its principles are well understood by numerous students in Germany and America, they are far from being well known in England, so that it is easy to meet even with classical scholars who have no notion what "Grimm's Law" really means, and who are entirely at a loss to understand why the English *care* has no connexion with the Latin *cura*, nor the English *whole* with the Greek ὅλος, nor the French *charité* with the Greek χάρις. Yet for the understanding of these things nothing more is needed than a knowledge of the relative values of the letters of the English, Latin, and Greek alphabets. A knowledge of these alphabets is strangely neglected at our public schools; whereas a few hours carefully devoted to each would save scholars from innumerable blunders, and a boy of sixteen who understood them would be far more than a match, in matters of etymology, for a man of fifty who did not. In particular, some knowledge of the vowel-sounds is essential. Modern philology will, in future, turn more and more upon phonetics; and the truth now confined to a very few will at last become general, that the vowel is commonly the very life, the most essential part of the word, and that, just as pre-scientific etymologists frequently went wrong because they considered the consonants as being of small consequence and the vowels of none at all, the scientific student of the present day may hope to go right, if he considers the consonants as being of great consequence and the vowels as all-important.

'The foregoing remarks are, I think, sufficient to show my reasons for undertaking the work, and the nature of some of the difficulties which I have endeavoured to encounter or remove.'

However far my performance has fallen short of my intentions, it was encouraging to find that my *Etymological Dictionary* supplied to some extent a real want, and was very well received. Indeed, I have more than once been informed that some of the articles are quite readable, owing, no doubt, to the historical information which they contain, or to the curious changes of form which they record.

As regards method, at any rate two great improvements were made; the former of these has relation to chronology, the latter to the exact source of a word's origin.

The value of chronology is insisted upon throughout. We cannot rest satisfied with any account of a word that does not give at least some approximate notion of the date when it first came into use. This is the first step towards tracing its source; and the truth of this is so obvious that no more need be said. The *New English Dictionary* assumes the necessity of this principle in every case.

The other improvement was in the attempt to discriminate the *exact* source of a word's origin. I am not aware that this had ever been attempted before, though the utility of doing so was explicitly asserted by Trench in his First Lecture upon 'English Past and Present,' in his account of 'The English Vocabulary.' We want to know, in every case, whether the word is native or foreign. If it be adapted from French, we again want to know the source whence the word found its way into that unoriginal language; and the like, in other cases. By taking notes of this kind in every case, it became possible to compile, for the first time, long lists showing the comparative influence upon English of various foreign languages. Another great practical advantage is that these lists can be studied and corrected by specialists, or by books which treat of special languages. The list of Malay words, for example, can be revised by help of a Malay dictionary, or by help of some one who can speak the language, without the trouble of going through the whole Dictionary in order to pick them out.

The preparation for press of this rather ambitious work occupied four years; and it would have occupied a much longer time if I had not made some previous preparation for work of this character, and if, on the other hand, I had exercised fuller research in some cases of unusual difficulty. I am ready to confess, with all candour, that it seemed to me more necessary that the work should be completed within a somewhat short time than that it should be delayed too long. The publication, soon afterwards, of a second edition enabled me to correct some of the more obvious errors; and several more corrections and additions have been made, from time to time, in the successive editions of the epitome called *A Concise Etymological Dictionary*.

With all its errors, the work has been of much use. The references are numerous and not often incorrect; and, though many were taken from Richardson and Stratmann and Morris, a considerable number of them were due to my own reading. Many of the etymologies are more correct than in most of the preceding works of a similar character, and point out the immediate sources of words with a greater degree of exactness.

One test of comparative success is imitation; and of this form of compliment the work has had its fair share. Most of the Dictionaries which have appeared since 1882 have borrowed from it more or less.

The increased interest now shown in etymological study of a stricter and more scientific kind is best shown by the books that have appeared of late years in foreign languages. Foremost among these is the excellent *Etymologisches Wörterbuch der deutschen Sprache* by Friedrich Kluge, Professor in the University of Jena. In Dutch, we have not only the *Etymologisch Woordenboek der Nederlandsche Taal* by Dr. Johannes Franck, of Bonn, but also the *Beknopt Etymologisch Woordenboek*, by J. Vercoullie, of Ghent. Others are the *Dansk Etymologisk Ordbog*, by E. Jessen, printed at Copenhagen, in 1893; the *Vocabolario Etymologico Italiano*, by F. Zambaldi; and the *Greek* and *Persian Etymological Dictionaries*, by Dr. Prellwitz and

## INTRODUCTION.

Paul Horn respectively. These and other recent works on the subject, several of which are of much value, have greatly contributed to help the more advanced student. The highest place is taken by the valuable and erudite *Grundriss der vergleichenden Grammatik der Indogermanischen Sprachen*, by Karl Brugmann, completed in 1893.

I now return to the history of the *New English Dictionary*, for which so much preparation had thus been made, both directly and indirectly. The net result was that a work which, in 1858, could not have been safely commenced, was, in 1878, being seriously considered. Twenty years of faithful work of various kinds had made a great difference. A fairly complete history of the whole movement is given in the *Transactions of the Philological Society*, the most interesting portion of it being from the year 1879 onwards. In that year, Dr. Murray had been elected President of the Society, in recognition of the fact that he had definitely undertaken the editorship of the Dictionary; and on May 16, he delivered the Presidential Address, which dealt with the subject at length. On the preceding March 1, the contracts between the Society, the Delegates of the Clarendon Press, and the Editor were signed. 'A fortnight before that day,' says Dr. Murray, 'I had commenced the erection of an iron building, detached from my dwelling-house, to serve as a *Scriptorium*, and to accommodate safely and conveniently the materials. This has been fitted up with blocks of pigeon-holes, 1,029 in number, for the reception of the alphabetically arranged slips, and other conveniences for the extensive apparatus required. On Lady Day, when I was joined by my assistant, Mr. S. J. Herrtage, I received from Mr. Furnivall some ton and three-quarters of materials which had accumulated under his roof as sub-editor after sub-editor fell off in his labours. . . . One or two of the letters are in excellent order and really sub-edited, in a true sense of the word. This refers to F, K, parts of C and R[1]; in a less degree to A, E, N, parts of O and U; of others of the letters it may be said that the slips have received *some* amount of alphabetic arrangement; of one or two unhappily I have to report that they are in primitive chaos.'

In 1880 Dr. Murray reported that 'during the year our readers have risen to the number of 754.... Altogether 1,568 books have been undertaken, of which 924 have been finished.' A most interesting feature of this report is the notice of the great help received from America. Among American readers he names 'three to whom we are pre-eminently obliged'—the Rev. J. Pierson, of Ionia, Michigan, 'our first helper in the States,' who has also sent in 7,650 quotations from important sixteenth and seventeenth century works; Prof. G. M. Philips, of the University, Lewisburg, Pennsylvania, and Dr. Henry Phillipps, of Philadelphia. The same report gives many interesting details as to particular words beginning with A.

In 1881, the editor again reported excellent progress. The number of readers had then risen to upwards of 800, and the total number of authors represented in the Reference Index was 2,700. 'In the alphabetical arrangement of the old slips, we are in sight of the end, only W remaining to be put in order.' Much careful sub-editing of various letters had been accomplished. By way of example, it may be noted that the division of the meanings of the verb *Set*, and the attempt to put them in satisfactory order, had occupied a sub-editor for over forty hours.

In 1882, the editor was able to report that 'the *Dictionary*

---

[1] The material for this letter was, at one time, entrusted to myself, and I found it in tolerably good order. Mr. Cornelius Payne had prepared a portion, as if for press, down to the word *Ravel*, or thereabouts. I finished *Ra*, and began *Re*, but the pressure of editorial work made it impossible for me to proceed; and I soon relinquished the responsibility.

is at last really launched, and some forty pages are in type.' From that time the work proceeded without further interruption; and the first part, from the beginning of A down to *Ant*, appeared in 1884. In 1888, Mr. Henry Bradley, whose excellent edition of Stratmann's *Middle-English Dictionary* has been already mentioned, was appointed joint-editor. He has finished E and a large portion of F, whilst Dr. Murray, having completed A–C, is engaged upon the latter part of D. So that now, in 1896, it is a great satisfaction to think that more than a quarter of this monumental work has already appeared, and to remember the old days when it was brought home to its well-wishers that a great number of MSS. had still to be edited, or else edited anew, before it could reasonably be commenced.

Now that I have traced the outlines of the history of the great *Dictionary*, and shown how the endeavour to provide for it worthy materials led to the formation of the English Text Society and the printing of many previously inedited MSS.; and how the impulse thus given to the historical study of our own language originated many other collateral movements, such as the foundation of the English Dialect Society, and the Chaucer and Shakespeare Societies, the phonetic researches of Dr. Ellis and Dr. Sweet, the compilation of the *Middle-English Dictionaries* by Stratmann and Mätzner, and a greatly increased and more rational interest in the study of English etymology; it may, perhaps, be allowed me to return to matters more personal.

The training which I gained by the editing of Middle-English texts proved particularly beneficial; chiefly because I thus came to learn the spelling of the fourteenth century from MSS. written during that period. Knowledge of old texts, as derived at second-hand from printed texts, is a very poor thing in comparison with that obtained from the MSS. themselves. From the MSS. themselves it is possible to learn, precisely and accurately, the character and origin of such mistakes as the scribes sometimes perpetrate, as well as the sources of such peculiar fancies as some editors, either consciously or unconsciously, adopt. It is often easy, for one who is thus familiar with all (or most) of the causes of error, to see through and correct the blunders of the editor who is new to his trade, viz. by help of the ability to recognize forms, which the editor, even with the MS. before him, could not decipher. Of this many instances could be given, from the marginal notes in some of my books, or they may be found in my paper on *Ghost-Words*. By way of specimen of editorial ingenuity of this character, I may cite one from my Notes to *Piers the Plowman*, C. ix. 2. In that passage we find the expression *half acre*, meaning a small plot of ground, about half an acre in size. The same expression occurs in *Gammer Gurton's Needle*, Act i. sc. 2, where 'Tom Tankard's cow' is described as 'flinging [i. e. capering] about his *halfe aker*, fisking [flourishing] with her tail.' But unluckily, when Mr. Hazlitt reprinted this play in Dodsley's collection, the expression appeared as *halse aker*, by the usual confusion between $f$ and the long $s$ ($f$); and he was consequently much exercised to find an explanation. At last he was driven to suggest that it must be an error for *halse anker*, because 'a *halse* or *halser* was a particular kind of cable'; to which a tail might, conceivably, be likened. The point is, of course, that even this gratuitous alteration gives little more sense than before. Moreover, '*his*' refers to 'Tom'!

I have frequently been asked how I managed to turn out so much work, and to edit so many texts. The answer is, simply, that it was done by devoting to them nearly all my spare time, and that of spare time I had abundance, having not much else to do. It is astonishing how much can be done by steady work at the same subject for many hours every day, and by continuing the same during most months in the year. It is also necessary to be an enthusiast, working with an ever-present hope of doing something to increase our knowledge in every available direction. Then the merest drudgery becomes a sincere pleasure; and, if any one would learn what drudgery means, let him make glossaries, and *verify the references.*

Of making many glossaries I have had much experience; on which account I here presume to explain how it may best be done[1]

The best way is to make a note of every word that requires explanation on a *separate slip* of paper, with a reference to the place where it occurs. I keep the slips *in the order in which the words occur in the book*, and afterwards go over each one again separately, adding the part of speech and the sense (unless this has already been done), at the same time *verifying the references* and making sure that the sense is correct. Then, and *not till then*, the slips are all sorted into alphabetical order; after which, I go over them once more, collecting the references from *several* slips on to *one*, where necessary, putting all the information together, and sometimes adding etymologies where required. The rejected slips can be thrown away; the rest go to press without rewriting. This is the best plan, but very few will believe it; most people try to put down the words, in approximately alphabetical order, in a note-book kept wholly for the purpose. But the attempt will assuredly break down or lead to trouble, if the text is of any great length.

It is, of course, absolutely necessary that the slips should all be exactly of the same shape and size. My favourite size is that of a slip five inches and three-quarters long, and two inches and a quarter wide. The number of them is of no consequence. For example, the original number

[1] This method is copied from a note at p. lxvi of my General Preface to *Piers the Plowman*.

of slips for the Glossarial Index in the sixth volume of Chaucer's *Works* considerably exceeded 30,000; and even when a large number had been weeded out and thrown aside, there were so many left that, when piled one upon the other, the whole *depth* of them was quite two inches over *nine feet*. And the result is decidedly useful.

My work of editing and explaining texts began, as has been said, in 1864, and had been continued (of course without payment) for fourteen years when, in 1878, I had the honour to be unanimously elected the first Professor of Anglo-Saxon in Cambridge on the foundation of Dr. Bosworth[1]; a most gratifying result, as it was precisely the post which I most coveted, so that I thus attained the very summit of my ambition. The kindness of the friends who furnished me with testimonials on that occasion is a thing not to be forgotten; and one of my chief treasures is a small volume in which all the original letters then sent me are bound together. Opening it, I find the autograph signatures of some who, alas! are no longer with us—such as Professor J. S. Brewer (of King's College, London), the Rev. H. O. Coxe (Bodley's well-known and much-regretted Librarian), Dr. Ellis, Professor Freeman, Professor Morley, Dr. Morris, Dr. Swainson (Norrisian Professor of Divinity), Dr. Small of Edinburgh, the Archbishop of Dublin (better known by the name of Richard

[1] I am careful to say 'the first . . . on the foundation of Dr. Bosworth.' For it is a matter of history, that a Professorship of Anglo-Saxon was established in Cambridge by Sir Henry Spelman more than two centuries ago. The first Professor on his foundation was Abraham Whelock, who had previously been elected the first Professor of Arabic in 1632, on the foundation of Sir Thomas Adams. Whelock published his edition of the Anglo-Saxon version of *Beda's History* in 1644; and was succeeded in the chair by William Somner, whose *Dictionary* and text of *Ælfric's Grammar* were published at Oxford in 1659. But the professorship came to an end during the civil wars, when the Spelman family were no longer in a position to continue this useful benefaction.

Chenevix Trench), Professor Stephens of Copenhagen, Professor Ten Brink of Strassburg, Dr. Stratmann of Krefeld, and Professor Zupitza of Berlin. Of the many others who are still living I will say no more than that it is delightful to experience from nearly all of them, even up to the present time, most ready sympathy and kindly help whenever difficulties arise.

The chief result of my promotion has been that the work which was before a pleasure only has now become, at the same time, a duty. And perhaps no man is more fortunate than one whose self-chosen occupation has become his allotted task.

Another piece of exceptional good fortune was my election to a Professorial Fellowship at my own college, in 1883; for it was the fortune of some professors to be elected to fellowships at colleges with which they had no previous connexion; a fate which I did not much desire. My dear friend, Sir John Seeley, Regius Professor of History, had obviously a prior claim; but he had been promptly secured by Gonville and Caius College, for which wise choice I have always been grateful.

Considering that Anglo-Saxon is not a subject in very great request, it might very easily have happened, especially at the beginning of my professional work, that I might some day be prepared to lecture, and might find no one to listen. Curiously enough, this has never actually happened; in every year there have been some two or three at least who, for some reason or other, have wanted instruction. And in 1886, a new Tripos for Medieval and Modern Languages was established, in which candidates have the opportunity of choosing English as one of their subjects, if they are so minded; and for those who choose it a fair knowledge of Anglo-Saxon is, of course, essential. Hence the work in this department has become regular and constant, and is likely, we may hope, to remain so.

The known gentleness of the courteous reader will excuse a few more notes; they are not intended to claim merit, but to inform and encourage others.

As far back as 1865, I gave £100 to found a small prize, at Christ's College, for the encouragement of English literature. The candidates are usually examined in a selected piece of Middle-English, a couple of Shakespeare's plays, and some third subject, such as Sidney's *Apology for Poetry*. Small as the prize is, it has been a considerable success, inasmuch as it has been gained, in some years, by men of some mark. I may instance, for example, Dr. J. S. Reid, well known as a classical scholar, Professor Gardner of Oxford, Sir J. W. Bonser, Chief Justice of Ceylon, and Mr. I. Gollancz, Editor of the *Temple Shakespeare*.

Shortly after the death of Charles Darwin, a memorial fund was raised among the members of Christ's College, of which I had the honour to be treasurer. After paying for an excellent portrait, by Ouless, which now adorns the college-hall, a small sum was left which, it was thought, might be gradually expended in giving occasional prizes for natural science. As it seemed to me a pity that this design should, in the course of a few years, come to a sudden end, I again gave £100, in 1888, to make the prize permanent.

My chief anxiety, in connexion with the University of Cambridge, has been, for some years past, the establishment of a University Lectureship in English. For more than ten years, we have had University Lecturers in French and German, each of whom is in the receipt of £200 a year; but when the endeavour was made, in 1889, to secure a Lecturer in English at half that stipend, no funds were any longer available for the purpose, owing to the impossibility of meeting ever-increasing needs upon an ever-diminishing income. In this dilemma, I could think of nothing better than to appeal to the generosity of the public in general, and wrote a letter to *The Times* to that effect. To this appeal I received precisely one answer, but it made a good beginning. The late Mr. S. Sandars, a well-known benefactor to Cambridge on many occasions, at once offered the sum of £50; and adding this to a promise of £100 from Mr. Mocatta, I was encouraged to proceed. A splendid gift of 200 guineas came from the Company of Merchant Taylors, fifty guineas from the Company of Mercers, £100 from the Master of Trinity Hall, and another 200 guineas from an 'anonymous donor.' The result has been the appointment, in March, 1896, of Mr. Gollancz as the Lecturer, at the modest stipend of £50 per annum; and it is at least somewhat of a triumph to find that the importance of the subject has at last found some sort of public recognition.

One of my most delightful experiences has been my connexion with the University of Oxford, as it has led to my finding there many sincere friends. When I first had to visit the Bodleian Library for the purpose of consulting MSS., I found (notwithstanding many kindnesses) that my evenings were often spent alone; and I found it depressing to be, practically, a stranger. Some years ago, it was possible for a Cambridge M.A. to take an *ad eundem* degree at Oxford without joining any college; but there was not much to be gained by this, in the case of one not usually resident there. Under the new statutes, it is necessary for one who seeks this degree to join a college, which is a much better arrangement. The college of my choice was Exeter, which proved a very happy one; and I went through what I believe to be a wholly unique experience; at least, I have never heard of a similar case. The Oxford University statutes require a term's residence in the case of one who, besides seeking the M.A. degree, also desires to become a full member of Convocation;

and though I had no object in desiring this privilege in itself, I was glad of an opportunity of seeing something of the Oxford life. One of the fellows of Exeter who happened to be for a while abroad kindly lent me his rooms, and I duly completed my term's residence in college with much satisfaction. The kindness which I there experienced, and the opportunities thus given me of making friends, proved a very great advantage; and now it is a most pleasant change to visit Oxford rather frequently, and to find myself among many friends in that famous University; in fact, I am quite at home there, finding all the attractions of a student's life, without any responsibility in the way of lecturing or otherwise. It is a good thing for a student of one university to know something of the ways of the other, without actual migration; and I rather wonder that the idea is not more frequently entertained. The chief reason against it is to be found in the detestable arrangement whereby the London and North-Western Railway compels every traveller to spend three hours over a journey that might be completed in little more than two. An enforced wait of three-quarters of an hour or so at the cheerless Bletchley station is decidedly unaccommodating and ruthless; and there can be little doubt that this is the chief cause that keeps the two Universities apart.

The reader who has, by this time, had enough of my own doings may perhaps be interested in a few remarks about other people.

The revival of the study of Anglo-Saxon in the present century was largely due to Benjamin Thorpe and John Mitchell Kemble. Thorpe's editions of the *Anglo-Saxon Chronicle* and of the *Ancient Laws and Institutes of England* are well-known and useful books; he also gave us an edition of *Cædmon* in 1832, of the *Codex Exoniensis* in 1842, of the *Homilies of the Anglo-Saxon Church* in 1844–46, and of *Beowulf* in 1855; besides issuing a translation of Rask's

*Anglo-Saxon Grammar* and a good selection of short pieces entitled *Analecta Anglo-Saxonica*. The student who desires a complete account of Anglo-Saxon studies will find it all in Dr. Wülker's *Grundriss zur Geschichte der angelsächsischen Litteratur*, published at Leipzig in 1885.

To Kemble we owe an edition of *Bēowulf* in 1833, which reached a second edition in 1835, and was followed by a translation, with notes and a glossary, in 1837; a collection of Anglo-Saxon charters, in six volumes, known as the *Codex Diplomaticus Ævi Saxonici*; the poetry of the *Codex Vercellensis*, 1843-56; and the *Dialogue of Salomon and Saturn*, 1848. He also wrote the esteemed historical work known as *The Saxons in England*, published in two volumes in 1849. The latest work which he undertook, on behalf of the University of Cambridge, was an edition of all the known MSS. of the Anglo-Saxon, Northumbrian, and Mercian versions of the four Gospels; but at the time of his death, in the spring of 1857, the portion actually completed did not reach much beyond the beginning of the twenty-fifth chapter of St. Matthew. The small portion of this Gospel thus left unfinished was completed by Charles Hardwick in 1858; and there the matter rested for more than ten years. After this lapse of time, the Syndics of the Pitt Press, being unwilling that the work should be abandoned, entrusted me with the task of continuing the work; and I was able gradually to complete it, issuing the Gospel of St. Mark in 1871, that of St. Luke in 1874, and that of St. John in 1878. After this, I was permitted to bring out a second and revised edition of St. Matthew's Gospel in 1887; and all four Gospels can now be obtained in a single quarto volume, which is a convenient form for use.

*I was never so fortunate as to meet with Thorpe or Kemble, but I heard something about the latter from Mr. Thomas Wright, whom I met frequently. Kemble had taken his B.A. degree in 1830, at Trinity College, Cambridge, a year later than Archbishop Trench. In 1834 Kemble, being then well versed in Anglo-Saxon, was anxious to impart some of his knowledge to his fellow-collegians, and designed an ambitious course of twenty lectures, of which he issued a printed prospectus, twenty pages long, interleaved with blank paper for the convenience of such as were disposed to take notes [1]. When the day appointed for the first lecture came, he duly donned his cap and gown, and appeared in the lecture-room which the college had assigned for the purpose. But where was the audience? There was precisely one person present, Thomas Wright by name, at that time (I believe) an undergraduate of the same college. As this one hearer evidently meant business, the lecture was duly delivered. But when, on the second occasion, the same thing happened again, notwithstanding that the main subject of the lecture was the poem of *Bēowulf*, and that one of the things noted in the Syllabus was the 'arrogance and ignorance of Mr. Ritson,' which ought in itself to have drawn a crowd of hearers, Kemble could stand it no longer, but invited his young friend to come to his own rooms, and discuss the subject freely over a tankard of beer. And certainly that undergraduate had a pleasant experience, and considered himself more than usually fortunate. Wright's extraordinary industry is shown most clearly by the fact that the mere enumeration of his books fills a whole column of small print in the *English Encyclopaedia*; a large number of them being especially concerned with Anglo-Saxon and Middle-English. I remember him as a quiet but cheery old gentleman, who more than once stayed with me when he came to Cambridge

---

[1] I possess a copy of this syllabus. It bears, on the title-page, the following :—*History of the English Language. First, or Anglo-Saxon Period.* By J. M. Kemble, Esq., A.M., Trinity College, Cambridge: printed for J. and J. J. Deighton, Trinity Street, 1834.

lxii        *INTRODUCTION.*

to consult MSS. He had sharp quick eye-sight, and wrote a very legible hand at a quite unusual pace; he used to say of himself that he was 'pretty quick,' and perhaps he trusted to his quickness a little too much in later years, as some of his errors of reading are somewhat surprising. His encyclopaedic literary knowledge of many various subjects, especially antiquarian, was very remarkable. We were excellent friends, with a common interest in Middle-English and in things relating to Shropshire[1].

I possess a copy of a small work entitled *Bibliothèque Anglo-Saxonne*, par F. Michel (Paris, 1837). This is a catalogue of the chief works printed before that date that relate to Anglo-Saxon studies. But it is especially remarkable for the Letter by Kemble to M. Francisque Michel, which occupies the first forty-three pages. This is an excellent outline of the general history of the study, containing several remarks of interest. Thus, in a note at p. 24, he pursues his quarrel with Ritson's work with much energy. He declares that Ritson's print of *The Frere and the Boy* contains sixty-four mistakes, and that in his print of *The King and the Barker*, there are 140 errors in the course of 128 lines. 'Yet this man dared to run down and persecute Warton! It is now beginning to be felt, that it was not Warton's inaccuracy which moved Ritson's bile: oh, no! it was the unhappy fact that Warton was a fellow of a college, a scholar, a gentleman, and a Christian, to no one of which titles Ritson had the slightest claim.' Of Horne Tooke, Kemble asserts that 'he was barbarously ignorant

[1] He had a favourite dialect story, which I fear has often done duty under various forms. Seeing a peasant at work in a field abounding with mole-hills, he pointed to them, saying—'My good man, what be those?' The reply was, of course, 'they bin ŏŏnty-tumps!' 'But, pray, what do you mean by ŏŏnty-tumps?' 'Why, ŏŏnty-tumps bin the tumps as the ŏŏnts maken.' 'But what do you mean by ŏŏnts?' 'I think yo' mun be a fool; the ŏŏnts bin the things as maken the tumps!'

of all the Teutonic tongues; and owes what reputation he has enjoyed solely to a happy knack of outbullying his opponents upon subjects with which he and they were alike conversant.' 'Sharon Turner's *History of the Anglo-Saxons*, 1801,' is 'a learned and laborious work; yet in all that relates to the language and the poetry of our forefathers, often deficient, often mistaken.' 'Sir F. Palgrave's *Anglo-Saxon Commonwealth*, 1832, cannot be too highly valued, as a clear and learned exposition of the Saxon polity. Nevertheless one must, as a philologist, quarrel with Sir Francis for false etymology. As long as he is at work with his Latin or Saxon charters, he reads them well and no man can more safely be followed; but set him once upon a bit of etymology, up go the heels of his hobby, and down comes Sir Francis into the mire, no better informed, as it appears, than most of his English predecessors have been, respecting the true form and power of many words[1].'

But the most valuable contribution made by Kemble to the study of Anglo-Saxon was that he was the first to call attention to the value of scientific philology, as illustrated by the great German scholar, Jacob Grimm. 'The system of this scholar,' he says, 'which can henceforth alone form the basis of any philosophical study of the Teutonic tongues, rests upon two propositions: (1) that the roots of these languages, their methods of declension, conjugation, and derivation, are common to them all; and (2) that each language, according to fixed laws of its own, differences[2] the common element.' He gives two excellent examples of Grimm's methods. He first quotes 'mægða

[1] It is but too true. Sir Francis was one of those who thought that any sound-changes could take place in any direction and to any extent. Thus in the preface to his *History of the Anglo-Saxons*, p. xiii, he argues that *bet* is merely another form of *wager*! *Bet*, he tells us, is derived from *bad*; and it appears that, by *bad*, he means A. S. *bād*, a pledge, with long *a*!

[2] We should now say—'differentiates.'

hōse' from *Bēowulf*, l. 924, an expression of which the meaning was quite unknown till Grimm pointed it out. The word *hōse* occurs nowhere else in A.S.; yet, by the method of comparison, the solution is easy. For, just as the A. S. *gōs*, 'a goose,' answers to the G. *Gans*, it is clear that the A. S. *hōs* answers to the M. H. G. *hans* (mod. G. *Hanse*) and the Goth. *hansa*, 'a company.' Accordingly, 'mægða hōse' simply means 'with a company of maidens.' Next, he illustrates Grimm's law (which requires that a Latin *p* should be represented in English by *f*) by pointing out that the A. S. word corresponding to the Lat. *palma* is precisely the A. S. fem. sb. *folm*, meaning the palm of the hand, or the hand itself. We have indeed adopted the word *palm* in English, but it is merely the Latin form, not the native one.

Speaking of his edition of *Bēowulf*, in 1833, Kemble claims that, in that book, he was the first who ever attempted, in England, 'to separate the long from the short sounds, upon a philosophical principle of analogy and the authority of MSS.'; and felt himself justified accordingly in 'claiming favour for errors.' Finally, he concludes this interesting 'Letter' with words of hope:—'From the activity which *all at once* appears to prevail among the Saxonists of England, there is hope that we may make some important advances, and escape the reproach, at present too well deserved, of suffering foreigners to outstrip us in acquaintance with our native tongue. *Surely, while we have all the MSS., it cannot be right that they should have all the knowledge.*'

These are words of encouragement that may well be laid to heart. Dr. Sweet's useful *Anglo-Saxon Reader*, and, still better, his accurate edition of *The Oldest English Texts*, well exemplify how much can be done by a scholar who knows what he is about. Perhaps the most unexpected result of modern times is the extension of Anglo-Saxon studies to the continent of America. But whatever progress may be made in the future, we must not forget that the Englishman who first vindicated the importance of the application of philological principles to the study of English was certainly JOHN MITCHELL KEMBLE.

I have good reason to remember very well the Rev. Oswald Cockayne, because, as I have already said (at p. viii), he was my class-master at King's College School. It will readily be understood that he did not teach me Anglo-Saxon, but Latin and Greek. He was an excellent teacher, and I profited by his instruction sufficiently to obtain the first prize in the Lower Third form. It must have been some twenty years before we again met, and discussed the subject in which we had a common interest. I was even able to afford him, occasionally, some humble assistance by consulting for him some of the precious MSS. in the library of Corpus Christi College, Cambridge. His knowledge was very extensive and extremely accurate; and it was fortunate that the peculiarly difficult task of editing the *Leechdoms, Wortcunning, and Starcraft of Early England* fell into such able hands. His own copy of this work is now in my possession, and I observe in vol. i. just a few minute corrections, of no real consequence; such as, for example, that at p. 156, in the fourth line from the bottom, the word 'wæstme' is written, in the MS., with the usual short *s*, and not, as printed, with a long one. His love of exactness led him to the use of the 'Anglo-Saxon' type, which is rightly now discarded as being needless and clumsy. Another objection is that some letters are liable to be confused; for I observe in the same volume, at p. 74, l. 12, the curious word 'þyrte,' translated by 'wort,' where it is obvious that the first letter was intended for a *w*. A misprint of this kind is of course extremely rare in any of his books, as he was obliged to watch such letters very closely.

A very characteristic book of his is that entitled, *The*

*Shrine: A Collection of Occasional Papers on Dry Subjects.* My copy of it, presented by the author, ends abruptly at p. 208; but I am not aware that it ever went any further. The corrections for Bosworth's *Dictionary*, at pp. 1–11 and 23–28, have proved of service. One very curious criticism is that wherein Mr. Cockayne accuses Dr. Bosworth of making the sb. *dūst*, 'dust,' masculine. It is undoubtedly marked with '*m.*' in the smaller Dictionary of 1848; but this may well be due to a misprint, seeing that it is marked '*n.*' in the first edition of the larger work, printed ten years earlier.

It was once my fortune to hear Mr. Cockayne preach a sermon without notes, and I was much struck with his eloquence of expression. His language had the classic elegance of the well-read scholar, and approached more nearly to the style of Johnson than I should have expected. He told me that he preferred to preach extempore, as he disliked the labour of writing down the discourse; and there was certainly no need for him to do so.

I can well recall the tall and upright figure of Dr. Bosworth, founder of the Professorship which I now hold, and author of two Anglo-Saxon Dictionaries. He was born in Derbyshire, more than a century ago, in 1789, and educated at Repton, Aberdeen, and Trinity College, Cambridge. In 1817 he became vicar of Little Horwood, in Buckinghamshire, and in 1823 he published the work entitled *The Elements of Anglo-Saxon Grammar*. In 1829 he was appointed British Chaplain in Holland, where he acquired a knowledge of Dutch, in which he was able to converse fluently. In 1840 he became vicar of Waith in Lincolnshire; and in 1857 rector of Water Stratford, Bucks., where he remained but a short time, being appointed Rawlinsonian Professor of Anglo-Saxon at Oxford in 1858. His larger *Anglo-Saxon Dictionary*, published in 1838, when he was

## DR. JOSEPH BOSWORTH.

chaplain at Rotterdam, was, at that date, a very useful book. It was largely a translation of the *Dictionary* by Lye and Manning, with some additions and alterations, and is a much more convenient book to handle than the two folio volumes that preceded it. Still more useful, for many students, was the cheaper *Compendious Anglo-Saxon Dictionary* published in 1848. But the dictionaries published in Germany by Ettmüller in 1851, and by Leo in 1872-7, as well as the extremely exhaustive *Glossary* of the poetical A. S. literature by Grein in 1861-4 rendered it necessary for him to prepare a new edition, on a fuller plan. When my edition of St. Mark's Gospel in the Anglo-Saxon and Northumbrian versions was published by the Pitt Press in 1871, the Syndics of the Press sent a copy of it to Dr. Bosworth, who, in his reply (dated Dec. 15, 1871) acknowledging the present of the book, made an interesting allusion to the work upon which he was then engaged. He was glad to find that the readings of all the MSS. were presented to the reader at once, and observed that—'instead of having the trouble of referring to the MSS. or the various books in which some of them are printed, I find, at once, all I want to quote in my large *Anglo-Saxon Dictionary* preparing for the Clarendon Press, on which I and my amanuenses are employed at least seven hours a day.' He was working at the *Dictionary* up to the very last; and at his death, which took place on May 27, 1876, had finally revised the first 288 pages of the work, down to the word *firgen-strēam*. It was some time before it was possible to make preparations for the continuation of the work; but it was at last undertaken by Professor Toller, of Manchester, who completed Part II (down to *hwistlian*) in 1882, Part III (to *sār*) in 1887, and Part IV, section 1 (to *swithrian*) in 1892; so that we may reasonably hope for the completion of this important work at no very distant date

Dr. Bosworth once told me how he made a considerable

lxviii                    *INTRODUCTION.*

sum of money in a very simple way. There was formerly a stupid fashion in vogue of writing Greek Grammars in Latin. I have now before me the one which I used at school—*Graecae Grammaticae Rudimenta in usum scholarum*—printed at Oxford in 1849. As this, naturally enough, appeared to him a useless piece of tyranny on the part of pedagogues, he brought out a *Greek Grammar* containing very similar information, the text of which was entirely written in perfectly plain English, such as every schoolboy could understand; and he had his reward in an enormous sale.

Dr. Bosworth will always be remembered by a grateful University for his liberal gift, in 1867, of the sum of £10,000, which, after accumulating till it produced £500 per annum provided the stipend of the Elrington and Bosworth Professorship of Anglo-Saxon. The reason for the founder's adoption of this title is easily discovered. The doctor was thrice married, and the name of his second wife, who had herself been previously married, was Mrs. Elrington. She took much interest in the study of Anglo-Saxon, and we find, from a remark in Dr. Bosworth's edition of *Orosius* (p. lxii), that she assisted him in collating the manuscript readings of that work. If I rightly interpret the following extracts from the *Gentleman's Magazine*, her maiden name was Anne Margaret Elliot.

'Married, Dec. 13, 1828. At St. Margaret's, Westminster, Lieut. Col. Elrington, of the 3rd Guards, to Anne Margaret, second daughter of John Elliot, Esq., of Pimlico Lodge.'

'Died, July 6, 1842. Sarah, wife of Dr. Bosworth, at Quorn, Derbyshire.'

'Died, Nov. 26, 1842. At Berkley Square, John Hamilton Elrington, late Lieut.-Col. Scots Fusilier Guards.'

'Married, Dec. 8, 1853. At Leckhampton, Cheltenham, the Rev. J. Bosworth, D.D., F.R.S., to Anne Margaret, widow of Col. Hamilton Elrington' (*Gent. Mag.*, March, 1854).

Another good friend of mine was Miss Georgina Jackson,

authoress of the *Shropshire Glossary*, one of the very best of its kind. After many years employed in collecting dialect words, some of which were acquired when travelling in a third-class railway-carriage on a market-day, she consulted me—then a total stranger to her—as to the best method of preparing her work for press. I recommended the use of slips—each slip to be of the size of a half-sheet of note-paper—a suggestion which she adopted. I also took occasion to recommend the use of 'glossic,' or, at any rate, of some fixed mode of representing sounds by symbols. At this she at first rebelled, on the grounds that it was quite unintelligible to her, and that she could never acquire it. I could only reply that it was worth while to acquire either that system or something like it; at the same time alluding to the difficulty of discussing sounds through the medium of writing. At once, with characteristic decision, she started from Chester for Cambridge, to discuss the matter personally; whereupon ensued a long and amusing argument, conducted on both sides with due spirit and vigour. Being very anxious to render her work as useful as possible, she soon found that 'glossic' was not so very difficult, and that it could be adapted to the Shropshire pronunciation with sufficient accuracy for practical purposes. She then had an interview with Dr. Ellis, with the most satisfactory results; and the end of it was that he described her investigation of the dialect-sounds as 'perhaps the most searching that has been made.' It was quite a treat to hear her give the sounds which I had so often myself heard in the neighbourhood of Corve-dale. Her favourite story was that of Betty Andrews, of Church Pulverbatch. Betty was going in a market-train from Hanwood to Shrewsbury, and while talking with her usual rapidity, was thus addressed by a man who was her fellow-traveller:—'Wy, Missis, I should think as yo' mun a 'ad yore tongue iled [oiled] this mornin' afore yo' started.' 'No, indeed, Sir,' said Betty, 'I hanna;

fur if it 'ad a bin īled it ŏŏd never a stopped. No danger¹!'

Miss Jackson became a sad invalid in her later years, being confined to one room and often to bed for long periods, and suffering much pain; but she bore her trials with much courage and even cheerfulness, and at all times took much interest in English dialects and etymology.

It has always been a great pleasure to me to welcome English scholars to Cambridge; and to find that they are not unfrequently attracted here. The manuscript treasures of the University library and of Corpus Christi College are an inducement to them to visit us; and it is a great privilege for us to meet them. It is thus that I became personally acquainted with many scholars from Germany; such as Professors Ten Brink, Zupitza, Kölbing, Schröer, Koch, and Brandl; and with Professors Child, Bright, Cook, and several others, from America. Zupitza was one of the most kindly and delightful of companions, a great enthusiast in his subject, and an excellent teacher. As a critic, he possessed a faculty of too great rarity, in that he could detect an error and set one right without causing even the slightest annoyance. We all know how prone are critics, in general, and especially, perhaps, the German critics, to give the impression that they like seeing the victim wince while they forcibly stick in the pin. To Professor Child belongs, as I believe, the honour of being one of the first to show that England could learn from America in matters relating to the philology of our common language. His wonderful essays on the Language of Chaucer and on the

---

[1] In glossic—'Wi Mis·is, ei shud thing·k uz yoa mun a ad· yoa·r' tung·g ei·ld dhis maur·'nin ufoa·r' yoa staa·r'tid.' 'Noa indee·d Sur, ei an·u fur' if it ad· u bin ei·ld it ŏŏd nev·ur' u stop·t. Noa· ·dei·nju'r'!' The use of *yoa* for *you*, of *mun a* for *must have*, of *an·u* for *have not*, and the total loss of initial *h*, are very characteristic of Shropshire. And as for 'no danger,' i.e. not at all likely, it is quite the usual way of concluding a reply.

Language of Gower laid the foundation of nearly all that we have learnt as to the grammar and metre of these poets; and any one who examines his splendid collection of English Ballads will marvel at the erudition he displays with regard to all the numerous ballads that are found among Teutonic peoples.

Perhaps the most remarkable sign of the times is the recognition of English philological studies at the universities by the conferring of honorary degrees. I can recall three examples at Cambridge within recent years. I have seen Stephens, of Copenhagen, Zupitza, of Berlin, and Alexander John Ellis, all presented, in different years, for the honorary degree of Doctor of Letters in the Senate House. The last of these cases is the most striking, as the degree was conferred upon one who was himself a Cambridge man. Dr. Ellis, of Trinity College, took his B.A. degree as sixth wrangler, as far back as 1837, and was at the head of the second class in the classical tripos in the same year; but, owing to certain theological restrictions then in vogue he was never elected a fellow of any college, nor even took the M.A. degree. Fifty-three years later, in 1890, he was made a Litt. D.; an honour which he did not long survive.

---

Account of the Extracts in the Present Volume.

The present volume is entirely occupied with selected extracts from the articles contributed by me at various times to the well-known weekly periodical entitled *Notes and Queries*.

As these amount to several hundred, and many of them relate to questions which were chiefly of interest at the moment, or give results which have since found their way into books, it became necessary to make a selection. The number of articles which are omitted because the suggestions which they expressed have been disproved, is very small.

On the other hand, a considerable number of etymologies have been here reprinted, notwithstanding their appearance in later works, because I had much to do with their enunciation or explanation, and their appearance in *N. and Q.* has become a matter of history.

I may note, for example, that the etymology of *Carfax* was suggested to me by the perusal of the French MS. of *Melusine*, and has since been adopted in all the newer dictionaries. The etymology of *puzzle* was put together from certain examples of the word in Lydgate and Skelton. The etymology of *spawn* came out of *Walter of Biblesworth*. The right explanation of *talon* and *pounce* is in the *Book of Hawking*. The full explanation of the prefixes *to-* and *all-to-* was due to collation of the usages of many English writers. *Lammas* was explained by King Ælfred; and the provincial word *ollands* by Ray. The first clear light as to the origin of *nuncheon* came from Mr. Riley; following in whose trace the true explanation was given by Mr. Walford, and at a later time, but independently, by myself. Our use of *atone* is due to imitation of a French idiom. *Sparable* is a modern spelling of *sparrow-bill*; and *wag* is short for *wag-halter*. *Hogs-head* was formerly *ox-head*, whatever may have been the reason for so naming it. I found the etymology of the provincial words *aund*, *reckan*, and *wicks* (of the mouth) in the *Icelandic Dictionary*. Before we can explain *hugger-mugger*, we must know that the older spelling is *hoder-moder*. All these things, and many more like them, prove that there is no royal road to etymology; it is simply a matter of pure research, conducted in accordance with very careful study of the phonetic changes that have taken place in our language from time to time.

Besides preserving here many illustrations of difficult words, such as *caddy, cap-a-pie, beef-eater, bernar, blake-beryed, bydand, carminative, gist,* and many others of a like kind, I have brought together, from almost countless sources, illustrations of phrases of interest, such as *key-cold, as dead as a doornail, a year and a day, by hook or by crook, a baker's dozen, exceptio probat regulam,* and others like them; all gathered by the simple process of diving into all kinds of books of all periods. In fact, one never knows whence help may come; Anglo-Saxon, Anglo-French, Middle-English, and Elizabethan texts all abound with possibilities for the discovery of 'origins,' for those who have the courage to attack them. I found, for example, the true etymology of *dismal*[1] in the catalogue of the MSS. in the Glasgow Library; and I am not aware that it has, till lately, been given anywhere else; though it was duly pointed out by M. Paul Meyer, who made the catalogue.

In reading such old texts, there is no reason for confining one's attention to the language only; nor have I ever omitted to learn from them whatever else I could there find. Hence the reader may find here discussions on several literary points of some interest, such as the Middle-English accounts of the Seven Ages of man, of the creation of roses, of Cain's jaw-bone, and of the story of 'the pound of flesh.' The *Jackdaw of Rheims* is illustrated by the *Knight de la Tour,* and the *Lay of Havelok* by the poems of Robert of Brunne. There are some remarkable parallelisms of expression between Chaucer's *Troilus* and his *Knightes Tale*; and the passage in *Piers the Plowman* about Lucifer's seat in the north can be illustrated from the Vulgate version of the Bible and from Milton's *Paradise Lost.* There is no end to the interest to be derived from the study of our splendid literature; and it is just as easy, for a mind not already debilitated by the perusal of magazines,

[1] From A. F. *dis mal,* evil days; whence the common old phrase 'dismal days.' See my note to *Chaucer's Works,* vol. i. poem iii. l. 1206.

to cultivate a taste for the Elizabethan drama as for *Tit-bits* and the *Yellow Book*. All that is needed is to read the former *first*. The works of our best authors form a true 'Pastime of Pleasure,' and are a source of rational recreation; magazines are chiefly good for killing time in hours of intentional idleness.

One of the queerest crazes in English etymology is the love of paradox, which is often carried to such an extent that it is considered mean, if not despicable, to accept an etymology that is obvious. It is of no use to prove, to some people, by the clearest evidence, that *beef-eater* is derived from *beef* and *eater*; or *fox-glove* from *fox* and *glove*; or *offal* from *off* and *fall*; or *garret* from the French *garite*; or the A. S. *hláfmæsse* (Lammas) from *hláf*, a loaf; or *marigold* from *Mary* and *gold*; or *Whitsunday* from *white* and *Sunday*: all this is to them but food for babes, and they crave for strong meat, such as only themselves can digest. Most of these questions are here touched upon; but I only attempt to convince such as are more humble-minded.

Against this desire of seeing 'corruption' in almost every word, I have always waged war; and that is why many of the articles in this volume have a controversial tone. Moreover, it has always seemed to me legitimate to show up the absurdity and crudity of many of these notable ideas; but I have always attacked the ideas, not the persons who utter them. The trouble is, of course, that the originators of the ideas do not like it, and are far too apt to hide the weakness of their case by assuming that they are personally affronted. Surely this is hardly in accordance with common sense. If a man has a good case, he can base it upon facts and quotations; and it is no answer to tell me, when I ask for proof, that it is ungentlemanly to dare to contradict. Moreover, it is very strange, as I have often argued, that it is only in the case of etymology that such tactics are resorted to If the question were one of chemistry, botany, or any form of science, the appeal would lie to the facts; and we should be amazed if any one who asserted that the chief constituents of water are oxygen and nitrogen were to take offence at contradiction. The whole matter lies in a nutshell; if etymology is to be scientific, the appeal lies to the facts; and the facts, in this case, are accurate quotations, with exact references, from all available authors. To attempt to etymologize without the help of quotations, is like learning geology without inspecting specimens; and we may well ask, what good can come of it?

Yet this very absurdity happens. A man sees a piece of quartz for the first time, and writes 'a note' that he has discovered a piece of malachite. This is no unfair description of some of the wonderful crazes which I have often taken upon myself to 'contradict.' Take, for example, my article on *amperzand* at p. 67. It was written to put an end to the extraordinary notion that it is a 'corruption' (oh! this beloved word!) of *and-pussy-and*, 'because' (another very precious word) the symbol (&) suggests a cat sitting well up, and holding up one fore paw. The lowest curl, I believe, was thought to be due to the end of the tail. One wonders where was the inventor's sense of humour.

Here are a few more specimens of pure invention, viz. that *swine* is the plural of *sow*; that *glove* is of Celtic origin; that the Whitby word *gaut*, a narrow lane, is of Hindustani origin; that the phrase 'he *dare* not' is modern, an assertion which was shifted to another one equally baseless, that it does not occur in Elizabethan literature; that *sweetheart* is a 'corruption' of a form *sweetard*, which never existed; that the Latin word *laburnum* is derived from French (!); that, in the phrase 'to set the Thames on fire,' the word *temse* means 'a sieve'; that *offal* is derived from *or-val*, refuse, which is not, in any case, a correct form; that *balloon* is derived from the name of *M. Ballon*, who was a dancing-master (this precious specimen actually appeared in the *Times* newspaper); that *ing* is Swedish (!) for a meadow; and a great many more things of the same kind. For the forgers of these curiosities are not in the least bound by the authority of dictionaries and grammars, but coin words for the nonce with the same freedom as is indulged in by the providers of *canards* for our daily papers. Even good writers make curious mistakes, as the reader will discover. Spenser thought that *yede* was an infinitive mood, with a past tense *yode*. Keats seems to have been under the impression that *darkling* is a present participle; but let us charitably hope that he knew it to be an adverb. Blackmore imagined that the old word *watchet*, signifying 'blue,' is derived from Watchet in Somersetshire. Browning thought that *slughorn* (variant of *slogan*) was a kind of horn that could be blown. Nearly all the world has gone wrong over the interpretation of 'one touch of nature,' owing to a contemptuous disregard of the context.

And then there are the critics! One of them opines that the O. French word *serfs* cannot mean 'stags,' because his limited experience only recognises the spelling *cerfs*. Richardson, in his *Dictionary*, misunderstands Chaucer's *t'apére* (meaning 'to appear'), and enters it to illustrate *taper*. Another critic wants to rewrite a line of Dryden's, because he did not know that *instinct* was, in those days, accented on the second syllable; with many more vagaries of a like kind.

And then there are the editors! Caxton turned the old word *estres* into *eftures*, which has no meaning at all. An editor of *Hudibras* turns *tricker* into *trigger*, because he is unaware that *tricker* is merely a Dutch word anglicized. An editor of Cowper's *John Gilpin* turns *lumbering* into *rumbling*. Crabbe's own son altered *rimpling* to *rippling*. And so the game goes on.

My position has always been, that things of this kind are

not glorious, but sad; not laudable, but discreditable, if not dishonest. And few things have surprised me more, in the course of my experience, than the eager recklessness with which such puerilities are vented, the extraordinary readiness with which they are accepted and applauded, and the tenacity with which they are defended against the clearest exhibition of evidence Paradox and grotesqueness are powerful in their favour, whilst the simple truth is but plain and prosaic. Are we therefore to give way, to let fancy have its free fling, and allow ignorance to revel in its recklessness? I have always maintained that, if truth be simple, it is also instructive, and that only docility promotes progress. Of course I have found mistakes in ideas of my own, but have always thought it wisest to drop such notions like a red-hot coal; which is the teaching of common sense.

Indeed, the very point for which I here contend was well stated by a writer with the signature 'H. de B. H.' in *N. and Q.* 7 S. ix. 442; and I appended some remarks of my own which I here beg leave to quote[1]:

'I am extremely thankful to the author of this article for saying that "people who touch on specialist points should have special knowledge." This is what I have been saying for years with respect to the English language, concerning which floods of untruths are continually being poured out by persons absolutely ignorant of the fact that its study does require special knowledge, and is full of "specialist points"—a phrase, by the way, that is a little awkward. Because I have said this I have been told that I am rude, and it has been plainly hinted that I can be no gentleman. Nevertheless, I shall maintain my position, and I can at once illustrate it by a very clear example from the same number of *N. and Q.* (7 S. ix. 453). We are there told,

[1] From *N. and Q.* 7 S. ix. 495 (1890), in an article headed 'Critical Carelessness.'

under the heading " Heriots," that Coke derives it [heriot] from *here,* " lord," and *geat,* " beste." We thus learn that even so great an authority as Coke was entirely ignorant of the subject concerning which he professed to give information. It so happens that *here* does not mean " lord," neither does *geat* mean " beste." And it is clear, too, that he made yet a third blunder in writing *geat,* when the word to which he meant to refer is *geatu.* *Geat* means a gate !'

It is a pleasure to observe that, in spite of recurring outbreaks, guess-work is no longer adored with that blind admiration which it once evoked. Its ancient glory is waning, and its acceptance is transitory and hesitating; towards which hopeful change in public opinion I claim to have contributed somewhat, by means of the very articles which are here collected and reprinted.

I have only to add that I have contributed a large number of articles, on linguistic and literary subjects, to many other publications besides *Notes and Queries.* If the reception of the present book is sufficiently encouraging, it will be easy to produce another volume, or even two more, of a like kind.

# BIBLIOGRAPHY.

(From *N. and Q.* 8 S. ii. 241 (1892); *with subsequent additions*).

I HOPE there is no harm in my attempting to give some account of my books. I suppose it must be done some day, and I am more likely than another to be able to do it correctly. I begin with books and editions, excluding letters and pamphlets. As many of the editions mentioned below came out in parts, at different dates, it is clearest to adopt a perfectly chronological order, mentioning each part separately, and denoting it by the letters *a, b, c*; different editions I denote by the letters A, B, C :—

1. **The Songs and Ballads of Uhland**: translated from the German. London, Williams and Norgate, 1864. Post 8vo, pp. xxviii 455.

2 (A). **Lancelot of the Laik**: a Scottish Metrical Romance. Re-edited with an Introduction, Notes, and Glossary. (Early English Text Society, No. 6.) London, Trübner and Co., 1865. Demy 8vo pp. lvi, 132. (B) Revised ed., 1870. Pp. lvii, 132.

3 (A). **Parallel Extracts from MSS. of Piers the Plowman** (E.E.T.S., No. 17.) Trübner, 1866. Pp. 24. (B) Second edition, with alterations and additions, 1885. Pp. 34.

4. **The Romance of Partenay, or the Tale of Melusine.** (E.E.T.S. No. 22.) Trübner, 1866. Pp. xix, 299.

5. **A Tale of Ludlow Castle.** A Poem. Bell and Daldy, 1866. Fcap. 8vo, pp. x, 101.

6 (*a*). The Vision of William concerning Piers the Plowman. By Wm. Langland. Part I, or the A-Text. (E.E.T.S., No. 28.) Trübner, 1867. Pp. xliii, 158.

7 (A). Pierce the Ploughman's Crede, with God Spede the Plough. (E.E.T.S., No. 30.) Trübner, 1867. Pp. xx, 75. (B) Revised ed., 1895.

8. The Romance of William of Palerne, or William and the Werwolf; with a fragment of an Alliterative Romance of Alisaunder. (E.E.T.S., Extra Series, No. 1.) Trübner, 1867. Pp. xliv, 328.

9 (A). The Lay of Havelok the Dane. (E.E.T.S., Extra Series, No. 4.) Trübner, 1868. Pp. lv, 159. (B) Re-issued, with Corrections and Additions, 1889. Pp. lxii, 159.

10. A Mœso-Gothic Glossary. (Philological Society.) London, Asher and Co., 1868. Small 4to, pp. xxiv, 341.

11 (A). The Vision of William concerning Piers the Plowman. B-Text; Prologue and Passus i–vii. Oxford, 1869. Extra fcap. 8vo, pp. xlii, 195. (B) Second edition, revised, 1874. (C) Third edition, revised, 1879. Pp. xlviii, 216. (D) Fourth edition, revised, 1886. (E) Fifth edition, revised, 1889. (F) Sixth edition, revised, 1891.

6 (*b*). The Vision of William concerning Piers the Plowman. Part II. or the B-Text. (E.E.T.S., No. 38.) Trübner, 1869. Pp. lvi, 427. N.B. Appended to this part is a Supplement to Part I, pp. numbered 137*–144*.

12 (*a*). The Bruce. By John Barbour. Part I. (E.E.T.S., Extra Series, No. 11.) Trübner, 1870. Pp. 1–256.

13. Joseph of Arimathie; or the Holy Grail; with the Life of Joseph of Arimathea. (E.E.T.S., No. 44.) Trübner, 1871. Pp. xlvii, 100.

14 (A). The Poems of Thomas Chatterton; with an Essay on the Rowley Poems and a Memoir by E. Bell. Bell and Daldy, 1871. 2 vols. fcap. 8vo. Vol. I, pp. cvii, 379; vol. II, pp. xlvi, 346. (B) Re-issued, 1890.

15 (A). Specimens of English, from A.D. 1394 to 1597. Oxford, 1871. Extra fcap. 8vo, pp. xxxii, 536. (B) Second edition, revised, 1879. (C) Third edition, revised, 1880. (D) Fourth edition, revised, 1887, pp. xxxi, 550. (E) Fifth edition, 1890.

16 (*a*). The Gospel according to St. Mark; in the Anglo-Saxon and Northumbrian Versions. Cambridge, 1871. Demy 4to, pp. xxxii, 144.

17 (A). Specimens of Early English, from A.D. 1298 to 1393. By Dr. Morris, and the Rev. W. W. Skeat. Oxford, 1872. Extra fcap. 8vo. (B) Second edition, 1873. Pp. xl, 490. (C) Third edition, 1894.

18. Chaucer's Treatise on the Astrolabe. (E.E.T.S., Extra

Series, No. 16, and Chaucer Soc.) Trübner, 1872. Pp. lxix, 119 (with seven plates).

6 (*c*). **The Vision of William, &c. Part III.**; or the C-Text. Together with Richard the Redeles, and the Crowned King. (E.E.T.S., No. 54.) Trübner, 1873. Pp. cxxviii, 534 (with a facsimile).

19 (A). **Questions for Examination in English Literature**, with an introduction on the Study of English. Bell and Daldy, 1873. Pp. xxvii, 100. (B) Second and revised edition, 1887. Pp. xxx, 110.

20. **Seven Reprinted Glossaries.** (English Dialect Society, No. 1.) Trübner, 1873. Demy 8vo, pp. vi, 112.

16 (*b*). **The Gospel according to St. Luke, &c.** Cambridge, 1874. Pp. xii, 252.

21 (A). **Chaucer : The Prioresses Tale, Sir Thopas, The Monkes Tale, The Clerkes Tale, The Squieres Tale, &c.** Oxford, 1874. Extra fcap. 8vo. (B) Second edition, revised, 1877. Pp. lxxx, 312. (C) Third edition, revised, 1880. Pp. xcv, 316. (D) Fourth edition revised, 1888. (E) Fifth edition, revised, 1891.

22. **Seven Reprinted Glossaries.** (E.D.S., No. 5.) Trübner, 1874. Pp. viii, 92.

12 (*b*). **The Bruce.** Part II. (E.E.T.S., Extra Series, No. 21). Pp. 257–336.

23. **Ray's Collection of English Words not generally used.** Reprinted, with rearrangement and additions, from the edition of 1691. (E.D.S., No. 6.) Trübner, 1874. Pp. xxix, 122.

24. **The Two Noble Kinsmen.** By Shakespeare and Fletcher. Cambridge, 1875. Extra fcap. 8vo, pp xxiv, 159.

25. **Shakespeare's Plutarch.** London, Macmillan, 1875. Crown 8vo, pp. xxii, 352.

26. **Five Original Provincial Glossaries.** (E.D.S., No. 12.) Trübner, 1876. Pp. xiv, 149.

27. **A List of English Words**, the Etymology of which is illustrated by comparison with Icelandic. (Supplement to Vigfusson's *Icelandic Dictionary*.) Oxford, 1876. 4to, pp. iv, 20.

28 (A). **Chaucer : The Tale of the Man of Lawe, The Pardoneres Tale, The Second Nonnes Tale, The Chanouns Yemannes Tale.** Oxford, 1877. Extra fcap. 8vo, pp. xlviii, 275. (B) Second edition, revised, 1879. Pp. xlviii, 282. (C) New edition, revised, 1889. (D) New edition, revised, 1889.

29. **A Bibliographical List of the Works illustrative of the various Dialects of English.** By the Rev. W. W. Skeat and J. H. Nodal. (E.D.S.) Part I, 1873, pp. 1–48, and Part II, 1875, pp. 49–131, by W. W. S.; Part III, 1877, pp. i–viii, by W. W S., pp. 133–201, by J. H. N., inclusive of an Index by W. E. A. Axon.

6 (*d*). **Notes on Piers the Plowman.** *P*art IV, sect. i. (E.E.T.S., No. 67.) Trübner, 1877. Pp. 1-512.

12 (*c*). **The Bruce.** *P*art III. (E.E.T.S., Extra *S*eries, No. 29.) Trübner, 1877. Pp. 337-785.

16 (*c*). **The Gospel according to St. John, &c.** Cambridge, 1878. Pp. xx, 197.

30. **Alexander and Dindimus.** (E.E.T.S., Extra *S*eries, No. 31.) Trübner, 1878. Pp. xxxvi, 93.

31. **Wycliffe's New Testament,** ed. Forshall and Madden. Reprinted, with Introduction and Glossary. *O*xford, 1879. Extra fcap. 8vo, pp. xxiii, 541.

32. **Five Reprinted Glossaries.** (E.D.S., No. 23.) Trübner, 1879. Demy 8vo, pp. viii, 191.

33. **Specimens of English Dialects :** including a Bran New Wark. (E.D.S., No. 25.) Trübner, 1879. Demy 8vo, pp. viii, 222.

34. **Wycliffe's Translation of Job, Psalms, &c.** Ed. Forshall and Madden. Reprinted, with Introduction and Glossary ; *O*xford, 1881. Extra fcap. 8vo, pp. xi, 300.

35 (*a*). **Ælfric's Lives of Saints.** *P*art *I*. (E.E.T.S., No. 76.) Trübner, 1881. Pp. vii and 1-256.

36. **The Gospel of St. Mark in Gothic.** *O*xford, 1882. Extra fcap. 8vo, pp. lxxv, 103.

[36*. *I* was entrusted with the reissue of the following work, to which *I* supplied many references and an index.

**The History of English Rhythms,** by Edwin Guest, LL.D. Ed. by W. W. *S*. London, G. Bell and *S*ons, 1882. Demy 8vo, pp. xviii, 730.]

37. **Fitzherbert's Book of Husbandry.** 1534. (E.D.S., No. 37.) Trübner, 1882. Demy 8vo, pp. xxx, 167.

38 (A). **An Etymological Dictionary of the English Language.** (*P*art I, A-Dor, 1879. *P*art II, Dor-Lit, 1880. *P*art III, Lit-Red, 1881. *P*art IV, Red-Z, &c., 1882.) *O*xford, 1882, 4to, pp. xxviii, 799. (B) *S*upplement to the first edition ; pp. 775-846. *O*xford, 1884, 4to. (C) *S*econd edition, including the *S*upplement. *O*xford, 1884. 4to, pp. xxxii, 844.

39 (A). **A Concise Etymological Dictionary of the English Language.** *O*xford, 1882. Crown 8vo, pp. xii, 616. (B) *S*econd edition, revised, 1885. Pp. xii, 625. (*C*) Third edition, 1887. Pp. xii, 633. (D) *F*ourth edition, 1890. Pp. xii, 633.

40. **The Tale of Gamelyn,** with Notes and a Glossary. *O*xford 1884. Extra fcap. 8vo, pp. xxxix, 64.

6 (*e*). **Notes on Piers the Plowman.** *P*art IV, section ii. (E.E.T.S., No 81.) Trübner, 1884. Pp. lxxvii, and 513-910.

41. **The Kingis Quair.** By King James *I* of *S*cotland. (*S*cottish Text *S*ociety, No. 1.) Edinburgh, 1884. Demy 8vo, pp. lv, 113.

# BIBLIOGRAPHY. lxxxiii

35 (*b*). **Ælfric's Lives of Saints.** Part II. (E.E.T.S., No. 82.) Trübner, 1886. Pp. 257–554.

42. **The Wars of Alexander**; an Alliterative Romance. (E.E.T.S., Extra Series, No. 47.) Trübner, 1886. Pp. xxiv, 478.

43 **Piers the Plowman.** By W. Langland. In three parallel Texts; with Introduction, Notes, and Glossary. Oxford, 1886. In two vols. demy 8vo ; vol. I, pp. viii, 628 : vol. II, pp. xciii, 484.

16 (*d*). **The Gospel according to St. Matthew, &c.** Cambridge, 1887. Pp. xi, 258.

The complete work, in one volume, is entitled, 'The Holy Gospels in Anglo-Saxon, Northumbrian, and Old Mercian Versions, synoptically arranged,' &c. Cambridge, 1871–1887. Demy 8vo. Paged as before.

44 (A). **Principles of English Etymology.** First Series. The Native Element. Oxford, 1887. Crown 8vo, pp. xxxiv, 541. (B) Second and revised edition, 1892. Pp. xxxix, 547.

45. **A Concise Dictionary of Middle English.** By A. L. Mayhew and W. W. S. Oxford, 1888. Crown 8vo, pp. xv, 272.

46. **Chaucer: the Minor Poems.** Oxford, 1888. Crown 8vo, pp. lxxxvi, 462.

12 (*d*). **The Bruce.** Part IV. (E.E.T.S., Extra Series, No. 55.) Trübner, 1889. Pp. i–cv.

47. **Chaucer : the Legend of Good Women.** Oxford, 1889. Crown 8vo, pp. liv, 229.

35 (*c*). **Ælfric's Lives of Saints.** Part III. (E.E.T.S., No. 94.) Trübner, 1890. Vol. II, pp. i–224.

48. **Principles of English Etymology.** Second Series. The Foreign Element. Oxford, 1891. Crown 8vo, pp. xxix, 505.

49. (A) **Chaucer ; the Prologue to the Canterbury Tales.** Oxford, 1891. Extra fcap. 8vo, pp. xvi, 83. (B) Second and revised edition, 1895.

50 (A). **A Primer of English Etymology.** Oxford, 1892. Extra fcap. 8vo, pp. viii, 112. (B) Second and revised edition, 1895.

51. **Twelve Facsimiles of Old English MSS.** Oxford, 1892. Demy 4to, pp. 1–36 ; with twelve plates.

52. **Chaucer's House of Fame.** Oxford, 1893. Crown 8vo, pp. 136.

53 (*a*). **The Bruce.** By John Barbour. Part I. (Scottish Text Society.) Edinburgh, 1893–4. Demy 8vo, pp. 1–351. (*b*) The same ; Part II, 1893–4. Pp. i–viii, 1–431. (*c*) The same ; Part III, 1894–5. Pp. i–xci. N.B. (*c*) and (*a*) make up vol. I ; (*b*) constitutes vol. II.

54. **The Complete Works of Geoffrey Chaucer.** Oxford, 1894. Six vols. demy 8vo. Vol. I.—The Romaunt of the Rose, and Minor Poems; pp. lxiv, 568. Vol. II.—Boethius ; Troilus; pp. lxxx, 506.

Vol. III.—House of Fame ; Legend of Good Women; Astrolabe ; Sources of the Tales; pp. lxxx, 504. Vol. IV.—Canterbury Tales ; Tale of Gamelyn ; pp. xxxii, 667. Vol. V.—Notes to the Canterbury Tales ; pp. xxviii, 515. Vol. VI.—Introduction ; Glossary ; Indexes ; pp. ciii, 445.

55. **The Student's Chaucer.** Oxford, 1895. Crown 8vo, pp. xxiv, 732; with Glossarial Index, pp. 149.

56. **Nine Specimens of English Dialects.** (E.D.S., No. 76.) Oxford, 1895. Demy 8vo, pp. xxiv, 193.

57. **Two Collections of Derbicisms;** by S. Pegge, A.M. Edited by W. W. S. and Thomas Hallam. (E.D.S., No. 78.) Oxford, 1896. Demy 8vo, pp. c, 138.

58. **A Student's Pastime;** being a select series of articles reprinted from *Notes and Queries.* Oxford, 1896. Cr. 8vo, pp. lxxxiv, 410.

59. **The Complete Works of Geoffrey Chaucer.** Vol. VII (supplementary).—Works printed in old editions. Oxford. Demy 8vo. (*In the press.*)

35 (*d*). **Ælfric's Lives of Saints.** Part IV. (E.E.T.S.) Vol. II ; concluding part. (*In the press.*)

# ERRATA.

P. 46, l. 11. For *Libra* read *Liber*.
P. 108, l. 3. For 187 read 1877.
P. 129, l. 10. *For* parables *read* parable.
P. 137, l. 12. *For* ofel *read* ofer.

# A STUDENT'S PASTIME

## FROM 'NOTES AND QUERIES.'

ONE of my earliest contributions to *Notes and Queries* appeared in the Third *S*eries, vii. 407; May 20, 1865. Later contributions can be found in the *Indexes* to the various years, under my name.

I here give a selection from the numerous articles contributed by me to that periodical from the year 1866 onwards. In a few cases, I have slightly altered the wording, but as a rule it is unaltered. In other cases, I give only a portion of the article, when the rest of it is of no general interest.

The articles are, for the most part, arranged in chronological order. The Index at the end of the volume is a sufficient guide to the subjects under discussion.

The reference to '3 S. ix. 379' means Third *S*eries, vol. ix. p. 379; and so in other cases.

### 1. Conrad: derivation of (3 S. ix. 379; 1866).

Of Teutonic origin. From Old High Germ. *Kuon-rát*, i.e. keen (in) counsel. [See *kuoni*, keen, *rát*, counsel, and *Kuonrát* (s.v. *Chuonzo*), in Schade's O. Ger. Dict.] The Ital. *Currado*, in Dante, *Parad.* xv. 139, is borrowed from the German. The Dutch words *koen*, keen or bold, and *raad*, counsel, still strikingly resemble the old *Kuon-rát*.

## 2. English accent thrown back; as in balcony
(3 S. ix. 380; 1866).

The history of the pronunciation of such words as *balcony* is easily explained, and has been often discussed; see, e.g., Marsh's *Lectures on the English Language*, Series 1, p. 531. In almost all such words, the foreign pronunciation comes near the end, as in the Ital. *balcóne*; but when the word becomes thoroughly familiar to us, we throw back the accent, and call it *bálcony*. It is useless, therefore, to protest against *bálcony*, for that this pronunciation will prevail there can be no doubt; and we may therefore as well accept it at once. Thus Robert Browning, writing *later* than Scott and Byron, adopts the newer pronunciation as being more in accordance with *English*, and is right in so doing.

The list of words, the accent of which has been thrown back, is a very long one. I may instance *áspect, prócess, cóntrite, blásphemous, úproar, cóntemplate*, &c.; formerly pronounced *aspéct, procéss, contríte, blasphémous, upróar, contémplate*; nor would it be at all surprising if we soon have to say *décorous* and *sónorous*, badly as these sound to any one acquainted with Latin; for pronunciation is regulated by common custom, not by any consideration of right and wrong. And when an Englishman is in doubt, he throws back the accent as a matter of course.

## 3. Rime v. Rhyme (3 S. ix. 102, 264; 1866).

[In 3 S. ix. 102, I observed, on the spelling *rime*, that I had explained it in a letter to *The Reader*, in February, 1865. After this, I was referred to Jamieson's Dictionary, where I should 'find that *rime* is a word totally inconsistent with any idea of poetic lines' (3 S. ix. 169). Of course I replied that the word *rime* does not occur in Jamieson at all! For such is the fact[1]. I also wrote as follows.]

---

[1] Jamieson merely gives *rind, rhyne, rhyme* as words meaning *rime*, i.e. boar-frost.

## RIME V. RHYME.

I am not surprised that the correctness of the spelling 'rime' for 'rhyme' should be doubted, but I do not think that many readers (especially if they have looked into Shakespeare[1], where the word occurs about forty times) will attribute the 'idea' to *me*! I suppose MR. I. means that the *old* meaning of *rime* had sometimes reference to another kind of verse than that which has chimed couplets, which may be quite true; as it is also true that the A. S. *rīm* generally meant a reckoning or computation. What I mean is, that the authors who assert *rime* to be the true spelling are right. Mr. Marsh has done this most explicitly, in his *Lectures on the English Language*, Series 1, p. 509; the statement, strongly put, also appeared in the *Saturday Review*, Aug. 17, 1861, p. 105; it is also distinctly stated in Ogilvie's *Imperial Dictionary*; and Tyrwhitt uses this spelling throughout his 'Essay on the Versification of Chaucer.' This was whence I first derived the idea, and it has been abundantly confirmed by investigation. Thus the word is spelt *rym* in Havelok the Dane, and in Chaucer; *ryme* in Robert of Brunne, N. Udall, W. Webbe (1586), Skelton, Donne, and Shakespeare; *rime* in Chaucer, Shakespeare, Spenser, and Milton (see particularly Milton's preface to *Paradise Lost*); whilst we find *ryming* in Roger Ascham and Bishop Cosin, and *riming* and *rimer* in Shakespeare. Very many more authors might be cited, but perhaps the following from Shakespeare may suffice:—

'Marry, I cannot shew it in *rime*; I have tried, I can finde no *rime* to ladie but badie, an innocent *rime*; for scorne, horne, a hard *rime*; for schoole, foole, a babling *rime*; very ominous endings.'—*Much Ado about Nothing*, Act V. Sc. 2 (ed. 1623).

It is obvious that this writer believed rime to be *not* 'totally inconsistent with any idea of poetic lines.' The

---

[1] *I* had previously referred to Chaucer and *Spenser*. Of course, the Middle-English spelling is always *rime, rim* (or *ryme, rym*).

intrusion of *h* into the word was doubtless due to confusion with the Greek ῥυθμός; but it should be noted that English is the only language which has admitted this pedantic innovation[1]. Compare A. S. *rím*, Icelandic *ríma*, Dutch *rijm*, German *Reim*, Danish *riim*, Swedish *rim*, French *rime*, Ital. *rima*, Span. and Port. *rima*, Prov. *rim*. [Even Polish has *rym*.]

### 4. Anointed; in a depraved sense (3 S. ix. 422; 1866).

[Murray's *New English Dictionary* has · '*Anoint*: ironically, to beat soundly, to baste. In the North they say humorously "to *anoint* with the sap of a hazel rod."' He then quotes the very passage to which I called attention in 1866.]

I have just met with so singular a use of this word, that I make a note of it at once. In the French MS. Romance of Melusine is an account of a man who had received a thorough and severe beating, which is thus referred to:— 'Qui auoit este si bien *oingt*.' The English version, which I am now editing for the E. E. T. Society, says:—'Which so well was *Anoynted* indede[2]' It is clear that *to anoint* a man, was to give him a sound drubbing, and that the word was so used in the fifteenth century. This, I think, explains all. 'An *anointed* rogue' means either one who has been well thrashed, or who deserves to be. In the latter case, it expresses the opinion and the wish of the speaker.

### 5. Carfax. I (3 S. x. 184; 1866).

Having duly read all I can find in *N. and Q.* about *Carfax*, well known as the name of a place in Oxford, I feel bound to say that none of the derivations proposed for it

---

[1] The insertion of the *h* into the word is not much earlier than 1550.

[2] See the Romance of Partenay, ed. Skeat, 1866, l. 5653; and the note.

seem to me to be properly *proved*, and I therefore venture to propose another which is something more than a guess, as a good deal can be shown in its favour, it being capable of being traced through all its changes. The best of those proposed are *quatre-faces* and *quatre-voies*, the latter being the favourite, and adopted in the Oxford guide-books. But I submit that it remains to be shown that the phrase *quatre-voies* was ever commonly used; *quadrivium* was used in Latin, but was *quartre-voies* used in French? The answer is, no; the word commonly used in Old French was *carrefourg*, and the word still commonly used in French is its modern form, *carrefour*.

Now the history of this word is very much to the purpose. First, let us see what Burguy says of it: he says, '*quarefor*, *quarefort*, carrefour; composé de *quadrifurcum*, propr. quadruple fourche.' This is quite sound; there is no doubt that the Latin root-words are *quatuor* and *furca*. Next, hear Cotgrave; he says, 'Quarrefour: the place in, or part of, a towne whereat four streets meet at a head. Par tous les quarrefours de: Throughout all the four quarters, corners, or streets of'; and this is a good sound explanation. I must now remark that, according to *N. and Q.*, an old spelling for Carfax is 'Carfox,' and I can then trace the word from beginning to end as follows. In MS. Camb. Ll. 2. 5, fol. 41, are the lines—

'A lentree de luxenbourg,
Lieu ny auoit ne *carrefourg*
Dont len neust veu venir les gens,' &c.

In MS. Trin. R. 3. 17, which is a translation of the above Romance of Melusine, we find on fol. 39 the corresponding lines—

'No place ther had, neither *carfoukes* non,
But peple shold se ther come many one[1].'

[1] Printed in the Romance of Partenay, ed. Skeat (E. E. T. S.), 1866; lines 1819-20.

Whence it is easy to see that *Carfox* is a contraction of *Carfoukes*, and from *Carfox* comes, as has been admitted, the modern form Carfax. I propose, therefore, to give up the derivations *quatuor facies* and *quatuor vias*, and to adopt *quatuor furcas*; to suppose, in fact, that the *-fax* or *-fox* answers to the English *forks*. Those who think *voies* the true original have to show how the *k*-sound *got in* to the word; I make the simpler supposition that an *r* has *dropped out*. By way of corollary, it may be noted that the French have *retained* the *r*, but have *dropped* the *k* or *g*: thus they no longer write *carrefourg*, but *carrefour*.

A correspondent has made the curious objection that, at Horsham, *Carfax* means a place where *three* ways meet, and he actually thinks this fatal to the etymology!

Of couse, the idea of *four* was easily lost, but the idea of *crossways*, or *roads meeting*, retained. How would such a person understand Peter's 'passing through all *quarters*' (Acts ix. 32)? Or, we might thus argue that *journal* has no connexion with the Latin *diurnus*, *because* the *London Journal* is published once a *week*. Or again (and this is yet more to the purpose), it may be shown that even *carrefour* may denote, not *four* crossways, but *one* street only. For Froissart uses *le souverain carrefour* to denote *the principal street*; Froissart, vol. iv. c. 28.

[PS. The above etymology is adopted in the *New Eng. Dict.*; and the above passage is there cited. It had previously appeared in my own *Etym. Dictionary*, in 1882.]

### 6. Carfax. II (4 S. iii. 273; 1869).

The word *carfukes* occurs in the *Memorials of London*, ed. Riley, p. 300. I am sorry Mr. Riley reproduces in his note the erroneous notion of a derivation from *quatre faces*, four faces. It is, on the contrary, one more instance which illustrates the true derivation from the Latin *quadrifurcum* (or *quatuor furcas*), as I have explained in *N. and Q.* in the passage to which I here refer; (see p. 4 above). Mr. Wedgwood has adopted my suggestion in the Appendix to his *Etymological Dictionary*, and gives further information concerning the etymology.

### 7. 'As nice as a Nun's Hen' (3 S. x. 215; 1866).

The word *ƒastidious* very nearly expresses the sense of *nice* here. The priest alluded to was *ƒastidious* and mincing in his talk; and, by a sort of pun, was said to be as fastidious and particular as a nun's hen; according to a proverb in the north, which makes a nun's hen to be something peculiarly delicate and pure. The following quotation well exemplifies this:—

'Women, women, loue of women
Make bare purs with some men.
Some be *nyse as a nonne hene*,
Yet al thei be nat soo;
Some be lewde, some all be schreude,
Go schrewes wher thei goo.'

From a poem on 'Women,' appended to the *Wright's Chaste Wife*, ed. F. J. Furnivall (Early English Text Society).

### 8. Rhyme nor Reason (3 S. x. 236; 1866).

Two or three correspondents have already explained that the phrase probably has reference to some poetical attempt which was recommended neither by metre nor meaning. I merely write to 'make a note' that the phrase seems to be of considerable antiquity, and is probably of French origin. In a MS. written before 1500 (Camb. Univ. Ll. 2. 5, fol. 9$^b$.) is the line—

'En toy na *Ryme ne Raison*,'

i. e. there is neither rime nor reason in thee.

[PS. This MS. is the French original of the Romance of

Partenay. The translation does not reproduce the line here quoted. See note to l. 279 of the Romance of Partenay, ed. Skeat, E. E. T. S., 1866; p. 235.]

### 9. Resplend (3 S. x. 258; 1866).

*Resplend* occurs in the following passage:—'He sees Berinthia's modesty *resplend* and shine in her affection.' (Reynolds's *God's Revenge against Murder* (1622), booke ii. hy. vii. p. 57.) I take it to be closely related to the verb *resplendish*, which is not uncommon in early English, as in the following:—'The fame of Ffabius *resplendysshed* and floured after his deth more thanne at that tyme when he lyved.' (Caxton's *Boke of Tulle, Of Old Age* (1481)). *Resplendence* and *resplendent* are common enough, probably owing to their having been used by Milton, as, e. g. in *Paradise Lost*, v. 720, 'in full resplendence,' and ix. 568, 'resplendent Eve.'

### 10. Curious Tradition : Roses (3 S. x. 276; 1866).

May I suggest that there *were no roses* in Paradise? They are, comparatively, quite a recent creation! At any rate, Sir John Maundeville gives the full and true account of their first appearance on earth, and says expressly they were the first 'that euer ony man saughe.' See Southey's fine poem called 'The Rose,' at the head of which the quotation from Maundeville is fully given. But Southey is not true to his original; for, instead of saying that the rose was then seen for the *first* time, he says—

'First seen on earth *since Paradise was lost.*'

Whence it appears that he had also read Milton (see P. L. iv.•256), and had combined his information. The 'rose of Sharon' was only a narcissus. See Smith's *Dictionary of the Bible*, s. v. 'Rose.'

## 11. Caddy (3 S. x. 323; 1866).

The following curious passage in a lately-published work is worth notice, and may perhaps at the same time suggest to W. S. J.[1] an etymology for the word *caddy* :—

 'The standard currency of Borneo is brass guns. This is not a figure of speech, nor do I mean small pistols or blunderbusses; but real cannon, five to ten feet long, and heavy in proportion. The metal is estimated at so much a picul, and articles are bought and sold, and change given, by means of this awkward coinage. The picul contains 100 *catties*, each of which weighs about 1⅓ English pounds. There is one advantage about this currency, it is not easily stolen.'
F. Boyle, *Adventures among the Dyaks*, p. 100.

To the word *catties* the author subjoins a footnote as follows :—

 'Tea purchased in small quantities is frequently enclosed in boxes containing one *catty*. I offer a diffident suggestion that this may possibly be the derivation of our familiar tea-caddy.'

I may add that the use of this weight is not confined to Borneo; it is used also in China, and is (as I am informed) the only weight in use in Japan.

[PS. A note by R. W. W., also printed in *N. and Q.*, contained the information that 'an original package of tea, less than a half-chest, is called in the trade a box, caddy, or catty. This latter is a Malay word—*kati*, a catty or weight, equivalent to 1⅓lb. avoirdupois.'

This etymology was repeated in my *Etym. Dict.*, 1882, and is adopted in the *New Eng. Dictionary.*]

## 12. Expulse (3 S. x. 437; 1866).

*Expulse* is simply the French and old English form of the word *expel*, and is now used but rarely; so that it may be more justly deemed a term of the *past* than of the *future*. I find '*Expulser*, to expulse, expell,' in Cotgrave's *French Dictionary*, editon of 1660; and '*Expulser*, to expulse,' in

---

[1] My dear brother-in-law, since dead.

Nugent's *French Dictionary*, dated 1844. It occurs in Shakespeare (1 Hen. VI. iii. 3. 25) as equivalent to *extirp* :—

> *Charles.* 'Nor should that nation boast it so with us,
>     But be *extirped* from our provinces.
> *Alen.* For ever should they be *expulsed* from *France*;
>     And not have title of an earldom here.'

Nares, in his *Glossary*, also quotes the following :—

> 'He was *expulsed* the senate.'—North's *Plutarch*, p. 499.

And—

> 'If he, *expulsing* King Richard, as a man not meet for the office he bare, would take upon him the scepter.'—*Holinshed*, vol. ii. vv. 8.

But why the writer in *The Guardian* could not use the simpler term *expel*, seems odd; perhaps he may have thought *expulse* more expressive and forcible, from the consideration that, in Latin, *expulsare* is the frequentative form of *expellere*; or, more probably, he was thinking of the French form *expulser*, which is in common use. I may add, that *expulse* is a favourite word with dictionary-makers. I find it in Meadows' Spanish and Italian dictionaries, in Vieyra's Portuguese dictionary, and in the Tauchnitz Dutch and Swedish dictionaries. Both forms, *expeler* and *expulsar*, occur in Spanish, and *expellir* and *expulsar* in Portuguese; but the Italian has *expellere* only, which is counterbalanced by the sole French form, *expulser*.

### 13. French Proverb: 'Grate' (3 S. x. 523; 1866).

MR. B. says that he wants an explanation of *grate* in the phrase 'Tant *grate* chièvre que mal gist,' and suggests that it will be found in Cotgrave. There it is, sure enough; for Cotgrave gives, '*Grater*, to scratch, to scrape, to scrub, claw, rub. *Tant grate la chevre que mal gist* (a proverb applicable to such as cannot be quiet when they are well).'

[PS. The mod. F. form is *gratter*.]

## 14. English without Articles (3 S. xi. 52; 1867).

It is worth noting that Sir William Davenant contrived to write a poem, 'The London Vacation,' almost without the use of articles. In the course of 162 lines, *the* only occurs about four times, and *a* about thrice. The effect is rather odd, as may be seen from this specimen:—

> 'Now wight that acts on stage of Bull
> In scullers' bark does lie at Hull,
> Which he for pennies two does rig,
> All day on Thames to bob for *grig*.
> Whilst fencer poor does by him stand
> In old dung-lighter, hook in hand;
> Between knees rod, with canvas crib
> To girdle tied, close under rib;
> Where worms are put, which must small fish
> Betray at night to earthen dish.'

It may be noted, too, that *grig* here occurs in the sense of *a little eel.* (See 3 S. x. 413.)

## 15. Keycold (3 S. xi. 171; 1867).

Shakespeare speaks of '*key-cold* Lucrece'; and again, we find the line—

> '*Poor key-cold* figure of a holy king!'
> *Richard* III, Act I. Sc. 2.

It may be noted that a similar idea is found in Gower. Compare—

> 'And so it coldeth at min herte
> That wonder is, how *I* asterte (*escape*),
> In such a point that *I* ne deie.
> For certes, there was never *keie*
> Ne frosen is (*ice*) upon the walle
> More inly *cold*, than I am alle.'
> Gower, *Confessio Amantis*, ed. Pauli, iii. 9.

## 16. 'As Dead as a Door-Nail' (3 S. xi. 173; 1867).

That this proverb is old enough, is easily shown. It occurs in the following passages:—

> 'For but ich haue bote of mi bale bi a schort time,
> I am *ded as dore-nail*; now do all thi wille!'
> *William and the Werwolf,* p. 23, l. 628.
>
> 'Thurth the bold bodi he bar him to the erthe
> As *ded as dornayl,* to deme the sothe.'
> *Id.* p. 122, l. 3396.
>
> 'Feith withouten the feet is right nothyng worthi,
> And as *deed as a door-tree,* but if the dedes folwe.'
> *Piers Ploughman,* ed. Wright, p. 26.

For which another MS. (Trin. Coll. R. 3. 14) reads—

> '*F*eith withoute fait is feblere than nought,
> And as *ded as a dorenail,* but ghif the dede folewe';

both of which latter are free translations of St. James's saying, that 'faith without works is dead.'

Sir F. Madden, in his glossary to *William and the Werwolf,* calls it 'a proverb which has become indigenous, but the sense of which it is difficult to analyze'; and I am very much of the same opinion. 'As dead as a *door-tree,*' i. e. as a door-post, is somewhat more intelligible, for the wood of which the post is formed was part of a live tree once. There is then a possibility that such was the original expression, and that the proverb was transferred from the door-post itself to the nails that studded the door, without any very great care as to maintaining the sense of the expression. There are other sayings in the same plight.

[PS. See my note to P. Plowman, B. i. 185 (C. ii. 184), where I also quote from Shak. 2 Hen. IV. v. 3. 125-6.]

## 17. Bernar (3 S. xi. 191; 1867).

In Jesse's *Researches into the History of the British Dog,* I find the following passages :—

'We send you also William *F*itz-R:chard, Guy the huntsman, and Robert de *S*tanton, commanding you to provide necessaries for the same greyhounds and "veltrars," and our dogs "de motis," and brachets, with their *bernars,*' &c.—Vol. ii. p. 27.

'And than shuld ye *beerners* on foot, and ye gromes lede home ye houndes,' &c.—Vol. ii. p. 123.

'And whan ye yemen, *beerners,* and gromes han ladde home ye houndes, and sette hem wel up, and ordeynne water and strawe after yat hem nedeth,' &c.—*Ibid.*

Observing that the learned author is for once somewhat at fault about the meaning and origin of the term, I send you the following note :—

Mr. Jesse says :—

'*Bernars,* qy., bowmen, or huntsmen, from *bersare,* to hunt or shoot.—*Cowel.* Or from *bernage,* equipage, train, &c.—*Cotgrave.*'

But the true meaning is better given in Roquefort. We there find—

'*Berniers,* vassaux qui payoient le droit de *brenage.*'

And again :—

'*Brenage,* redevance en son, que des vassaux payoient d'abord à certains seigneurs pour la nourriture de leurs chiens ; en bas-Lat. *brenagium.*'

And again :—

'*Bren, bran, brenie,* ordure, et du son, ou ce qui reste dans le sas de la farine sassée ; en bas-Bret. *bren,* son.'

It hence appears that a *bernar* might, in modern English, be well named a *branner* ; i. e. a man who provides *bran* for dogs, where by *bran* may be denoted refuse of various kinds, and not only that obtained from husks of corn. Wedgwood, s. v. *Bran,* explains that it means refuse, draff, leavings, ordure ; and instances the Breton *brenn hesken* as meaning refuse of the saw, sawdust. The duty of the *berner* was, no doubt, to feed the dogs; for Mr. Jesse says again :—

' Besides the foregoing, and not included, was the wages of a certain valet ('berner') for the keep of fifteen running-dogs during forty days in Lent.'—Vol. ii. p. 132.

Yet again we read :—

' Mention is made likewise of "the Pantryes, Chippinges, and broken breade," a kind of food which is frequently spoken of about this period.'—Vol. ii. p. 125.

This may be the signification of *bran* in its wider sense.

One more quotation (referring to the 49th year of Henry III) is too important to be omitted :—

'In acquittance of the expenses of Richard de Candevere and William de Candevere going for *bran*,' &c.—Vol. ii. p. 36.

It might easily happen that a person who engaged to provide food for hounds was a man of wealth : for numerous examples of such 'dog tenures,' see the same volume, pp. 41, 42, 43. This perhaps may account for the name being applied to persons of higher station, and I suppose such to have been the origin of the name Berners, of which Juliana Berners and Lord Berners are such bright ornaments.

[PS. This etymology appears in the *New Eng. Dict.*, s. v. *Berner*.]

## 18. Putting a Man under a Pot (3 S. xi. 277 ; 1867).

I have seldom met with a more amazing statement than there is in *Piers Ploughman's Crede*, and I should greatly like to know of something that would corroborate it. The author distinctly asserts that there was a regular system of making away with friars who were not sufficiently active in begging for the good of their house. He says :—

'But[1] (*except*) he may beggen his bred, His bed is y-greithed
  (*prepared for him*) ;
Under a pot he shall be put In a pryvye chambre,
That he shall lyuen ne laste But lytel whyle after.'
                                        Ed. Wright, l. 1247.

This clearly means that a useless friar is *put under a pot*, and that he soon dies in consequence.

The only passage I know of that throws any light on this is also in the *Crede* :—

'For thei ben nere dede ;
And put al in pur clath With pottes on her hedes.'
                                        Id. l. 1222.

[1] The Trinity MS. has 'But.' The printed texts have 'That.'

Now why, I ask, should a pot be put on a man's head when he lies on his death-bed?

[This question remains unanswered.]

### 19. Living (3 S. xi. 286 ; 1877).

Wright's *Provincial Dictionary* gives 'Living, a farm: *Leicestershire.*'

In Norfolk it is a very common word.

A London man might call a person's house and grounds a nice *place*, but a Norfolk man would use the word *living*. In this sense, too, it occurs in Ben Jonson: 'I have a pretty *living* o' mine own too, beside, hard by here·' *Every Man in his Humour*, Act I. Sc. 1 (or 2).

[Nares misses the word. There is no note on it in Wheatley's edition of *Every Man*, Act I. Sc. 2, l. 8. I frequently heard it when residing in Norfolk. I was once told that I seemed to have a nice *living* (i. e. a pleasantly situated house). It seemed to me a queer thing to say to a curate.]

### 20. Two faced Pictures (3 S. xi. 346 ; 1867).

Few things are easier to make. Get two pictures of the same size; cut them vertically into strips half an inch broad; paste the corresponding strips back to back (you will see which these are by trial), and then set them up on their edges in a row from left to right at equal distances of about three-quarters of an inch or an inch apart. Then, if you stand to the left, you see the whole of one picture; if to the right, the whole of the other. If, instead of setting them up above plain paper, you set them up above a third uncut picture, you will see *this one only* by standing *directly in front*; and the double picture thus becomes a treble picture without any increase of difficulty in the construction.

[PS. Now (in 1895) used to advertise 'Sunlight Soap.']

### 21. Christ-cross (3 S. xi. 352 ; 1867).

In *Piers Ploughman's Crede*, l. 1, we find ' *Cros* and curteis Christ this *begynnyng* spede,' where there seems to be an allusion to the prefixing of a cross to the beginning of a piece of writing, especially of an alphabet in a primer ; see Nares's *Glossary*, s. v. Cross-row and Christ-cross-row. Also in a poem, by the Rev. R. S. Hawker, called ' A Christ-cross Rhyme,' we find at the very beginning—

> ' Christ his cross shall be my speed,
> Teach me, father John, to read.'

Now it is to be observed, that in Chaucer's *Treatise on the Astrolabe* occurs the following:—' This border is devided also with xxiii letters, and a *small crosse* aboue the south line that sheweth the xxiiij houres equales of the clocke ' ; and in the diagrams accompanying this in the MSS. we accordingly see a *cross* at the south or *starting-point*, followed by the twenty-three letters of the alphabet, *j, v,* and *w* being omitted. The fact is, that the true use of a cross, in drawing, is to define or mark a *point*, especially a point to start or measure from (there being no more convenient way of defining a point than by thus considering it as the spot *where two short lines intersect*) ; and I believe this to be its simple sole and original use when prefixed to the alphabet in an astrolabe, except that it was also found convenient to increase the number of symbols from the awkward number of twenty-*three* to the very convenient one of twenty-*four*. But it was impossible that it could be used long without reference being supposed to be made to the cross of Christ, and it must soon have been regarded as invoking Christ's blessing upon the commencement of any writing. Hence the term Christ-cross-row, or shortly, cross-row. Archdeacon Nares has another suggestion, that the *cross-row* was probably named from a superstitious custom of writing the alphabet in the form of a cross, by way of charm ; but I prefer the former explanation. He also says, 'the mark of noon on a dial is in the following passage jocularly called the *Christ-cross* of the dial, being the figure of a cross placed instead of xii :—

"*F*all to your business roundly ; the fescue [Lat. *festuca*] of the dial is upon the Christ-cross of noon." '—Puritan iv. 2, *Suppl. to Sh.* ii. 607.

But there is no need to insert the word *jocularly* ; it was natural enough that it should come to be so called.

[See *Christ-cross* and *Cross-row* in the *New Eng. Dictionary*.]

### 22. As right as a trivet : As clean as a whistle (3 S. xi. 361 ; 1867).

These are excellent examples of the way in which proverbs rapidly become obscure when based on something that is a sort of pun upon words. Thus, we use such a word as *deep* in two senses, and we might facetiously call a very astute man 'as *deep* as the Bay of Biscay,' which would be readily intelligible at first, but might easily, by a slight alteration, become almost meaningless. I suppose the same sort of process to have been at work in the case of the two above proverbs. ' The ' rectitude of a trivet ' consists in its *rectangularity* [1]. If that sort of trivet which is placed upon the upper bar of a grate is not accurately made, the kettle that stands upon it will not stand even, but will inconveniently slouch forward or backward. The trivet, to be a good one, must be right-angled, or made 'right and true.' In the next proverb a further stage of corruption of the sense has been reached, the word *clean* being put for *clear*. No sound is more *clear* than that of a whistle ; hence 'as clear as a whistle' is good sense.

[1] [Or, if we take *trivet* in the sense of ' a three-legged support,' the sense is quite clear, in that case also. You cannot make a three-legged stool stand unsteadily.]

But if a man speaks of cutting anything off with perfect smoothness and evenness, he would say he has cut it off *clear* or *sheer*, or *clean*, with equal readiness; and he would probably add the words 'as a whistle' to one phrase quite as soon as to the other, without any great amount of reflection as to the congruity of his speech. Just in the same way, a church is a *safe* place of sanctuary, or may be regarded as *safely* built, secure and ?*fast*; whence arises such a question and answer as the following, which is not uncommon:—'Is he ?*fast* asleep?' 'Aye, as *safe* as a church.' A play upon *words* necessarily leads to a play upon *phrases*. See note on 'as dead as a door-nail,' *N. and Q.*, 3 S. xi. 173.

## 23. Milton's use of the word ' charm.' I (3 S. xi. 382 ; 1867).

The word *charm* is well explained by Wedgwood. The root of it is preserved in the A. S. *cyrm*, loud noise.

Another quotation for it is:—

'Vor thi ich am loth smale foghle
Hit me *bichermit* and bigredeth.'
*Owl and Nightingale*, 280.

It also occurs in one of our Early English Text Society's Books:—

'Tentes, pauilons freshly wrought and good,
Doucet songes hurde of briddes enuiron,
Whych meryly *chirmed* in the grene wood.'
*Romance of Partenay* (ed. Skeat, 1866), p. 37, l. 876;

which is thus explained in the Glossarial Index:—

'*Chirmed*, made a loud noise, chirped loudly, 878. Cf. "*synniga cyrm*, the uproar of sinners"; Caedmon, ed. Thorpe, 145, 17.

"With *charm* of earliest birds"; Milton, *P. L.*, iv. 642. See Forby.'

By 'Forby' I mean 'Forby's *East-Anglian Glossary.*'

[See *Charm* (2) and *Chirm* in the *New Eng. Dictionary*.]

**24. 'Charm.' II** (5 S. vii. 278; 1877).

This word has been often discussed; see, e. g., *N. and Q.*, 3 S. xi. 221, 382, 510. It is a perfectly common English word, used, to my own knowledge, in Shropshire, and is not a Celtic, but an English word, being the A. S. *cirm* (*cyrm*), the hard *c* turning into *ch* as usual. Jamieson has it in his *Dictionary*, with the spelling *chirm*; and though he fails to give the A. S. form, he gives the correct equivalent Dutch verb, viz. *kermen*, to lament. The A. S. substantive is better spelt *cirm*; and Grein, in his A.S. *Dictionary*, s v. *cirm*, gives fifteen examples of its use as a substantive, and six examples of the verb *cirman*, which he rightly compares with O. H. G. *karmian*, to make a noise. The word is perfectly well known, and the supposed 'Gaelic' equivalent is all moonshine; so, too, is a supposed connexion with the Latin *carmen*.

**25. Luther's Distich** (3 S. xi. 449; 1867).

This distich is attributed to Luther by the poet Uhland, who was no bad judge in such matters. See 'Gedichte' von L. Uhland—*Die Geisterkelter*.

The passage runs thus in my translation:—

> 'At Weinsberg, town well known to fame,
> That doth from *wine* derive its name,
> Where songs are heard of joy and youth,
> Where stands the fort, hight "Woman's Truth"
> *Where Luther e'en, 'mid women, song,*
> *And wine, would find the time not long,*
> And might, perchance, find room to spare
> For Satan and an inkhorn there
> (For there a host of spirits dwell);—
> Hear what at Weinsberg once befel!'
> *Songs and Ballads of Uhland,* translated by Skeat, p. 318.

There is a note on the passage by Mr. Platt, at p. 497 of his translation of Uhland's poems. He says:—

'The great Martin Luther was no ascetic. In one of his merry moments he is reported to have written the following couplet, which frequently adorns the margin of the wine-bills, drinking-cups, &c., in houses of glad resort in Germany :—

"Who loves not woman, wine, and song,
Remains a fool his whole life long."

The story of Luther's conflict with the devil, when he put the fiend to flight by throwing his inkstand at him, is well known.'

This, by the way, is precisely how Mr. Pickwick vented his rage upon A. Jingle, Esq., of No-hall, Nowhere.

**26. 'Honi,' its meaning and etymology in the phrase 'Honi soit qui mal y pense'** (3 S. xi. 481; 1867).

This is a common enough word in Old French. Thus we find in Roquefort—

'HONIR (*honier, honnir, hontager, hontir, hounir, hounnir*); mépriser, blâmer, déshonorer, maltraiter, diffamer.'

And in Cotgrave—

'HONNIR. To reproach, disgrace, dishonour, defame, shame revile, curse, or outrage, in words; also, to spot, blemish, pollute, foule, file, defile.'

When we consider how many Teutonic words there are in French, and more especially in Old French, the derivation becomes not far to seek. I take it to be simply allied to the Moeso-Gothic *hauns* (low), which was used as a contrasted word to *hauhs* (high). In Ulfilas's translation of St. Paul's Epistles, we have this well brought out in the following :—'Ni waiht bi haifstai aiththau lausai *hauheinai* ak in allai *hauneinai* gahugdais,' &c.—i. e. 'No whit by strife or empty *haughtiness*, but in all *lowliness* of mind,' Phil. ii. 3; and again, only five verses farther on, we read that Christ '*gahaunida* sik silban,' i. e. humbled himself, where the Greek is ἐταπείνωσεν, and the Latin *humiliauit*. Hence *haunjan* (Greek ταπεινοῦν, Lat. *humiliare*), means 'to make low,' 'to humiliate': whence the meanings given by Cotgrave, 'to reproach, disgrace, dishonour,' &c., follow easily enough. Compare also the German *hohn*, an affront. I do not see why we should quarrel with the commonly-received translation. *Literally*, the phrase means, 'Disgraced be he who thinks evil thereat'; of which 'Evil be to him who evil thinks' is no bad version. Its chief defect is, that it ignores the word *y*

[Strictly, the O.F. *honir* is from the O. H. G. *hōnjan* (see Schade), which is cognate with the Goth. *haun̂jan*. See Diez, s. v. *onire*; cf. F. *honte*.]

**27. Dryden Queries : 'Neyes'** (3 S. xii. 56 ; 1867).

I have not Dryden's plays to refer to, but probably *neyes* means *eyes*. There is an undoubted instance of this in a quotation given in Jesse's *History of the British Dog*, vol. ii., where, at a bear-baiting, the bear is described 'with his two pink *neyes*.' Is not this, by the way, the etymology of the name *Pinckeney*? It is an instance of the 'epenthetic *n*,' so common in old English. In my new edition of *Piers Plowman*, the first volume of which is just ready, the various readings furnish several instances. Thus, in the prologue, l. 42, instead of 'at the ale,' some MSS. have 'at the *nale*,' or 'at *nale*'; and again, in Passus v. l. 115, instead of 'at the *oke* (oak)' most MSS. have 'at the *noke*' or 'atte *noke*.' Hence the explanation of the phrase 'for the nonce,' which simply means 'for the *once*' (A. S. for than ānes), but which so puzzled Tyrwhitt, one of our greatest scholars, that he was driven to conjecture a derivation from the Latin *pro nunc*. The history of this *n* seems to be simply this, that the dative of the article takes the form *than* or *then* in the masculine and neuter in early English... But when the noun following began with a vowel, this *n* was transferred to the beginning of such words; and this transfer took place, not only in the dative case, but often in *all* cases for the mere sake of euphony, so that we not only find 'the neyes' in the dative case, but even in the nominative. Nor did this addition of *n* stop here; we may go a step further, and dismiss the article altogether, and speak of 'two pinke neyes.' To add to the confusion thus introduced, we have numerous instances of the *reverse* process, the *taking away* of an *n*, so that instead of *a nadder*, we now absurdly write *an adder*. See Ulphilas's translation of Luke iii. 7—'kuni nadre,' i. e. O kin of *nadders*, O generation of vipers. Other instances are, *an auger, an umpire*, miswritten for *a nauger* (A. S. *nafegār*), and *a numpire* (O. F. *noumpere*).

[See further in the Remarks on the letter N in my *Etym. Dict.*, at the beginning of N; and my *Principles of Eng. Etymology*, First Series, § 346, 347.]

### 28. Lucifer (3 S. xii. 110; 1867).

I think it should be noted that Lucifer was applied to Satan, in English literature, at least four hundred years before Milton's time, and probably long before that[1]. In some *Early English Homilies*, which Mr. Morris is editing for the Early English Text Society, and the date of which is about 1220–30 A.D., it is stated most explicitly. The book is not yet published, but I quote from a proof-sheet, p. 219:—

'Tha wes thes tyendes hades alder swithe feir isceapan, swa that heo was geboten leoht-berinde': i. e. 'Then was this tenth order's elder very fair shapen, so that he was called light-bearing.'

The context explains that there were originally ten orders of angels; nine of which are angels still, but the tenth order fell from heaven through pride, and their chief's name was Light-bearing, or Lucifer.

So again, in A. D. 1362, Langland wrote:—

'Lucifer with legiouns lerede hit in heuene;
He was louelokest of siht after vr lord,
Til he brak boxsumnes thorw bost of himseluen.'
Langland, *Piers Plowman*, pass. i. l. 109.

That is:—

\* 'Lucifer with his legions learnt it (viz. obedience) in heaven. He

---

[1] It has been so applied 'from St. Jerome downwards.'—Smith's *Dictionary of the Bible*.

was loveliest to look upon, next to our Lord, until he brake obedience, through boast of himself.'

Still more curious is the English form of the name, *Ligber* (A. S. *līg-bær*, flame-bearing), as in the following:—

> '*Ligber* he sridde a dere srud,
> And he wurthe in himseluen prud,' &c.

i. e. 'Ligber, he shrouded him in a noble shroud, and he became in himself proud.'

This I quote from Mr. Morris's *Genesis and Exodus*, l. 271: the date is about 1250 A. D.

No doubt this is all derived from a misapplication of Isaiah xiv. 12. But I think it is worth while to add, in confirmation of this, and by way of further illustration, that we hardly ever find an allusion to Lucifer in early English, without finding, at the same time, a mention of his trying to seat himself in the *north*—a curious perversion of the verse following, viz. Isaiah xiv. 13, which is, in the Vulgate:—

'Qui dicebas in corde tuo : in caelum conscendam, super astra Dei exaltabo solium meum, sedebo in monte testamenti, in lateribus *aquilonis*.'

Compare the Septuagint version—ἐπὶ τὰ ὄρη τὰ ὑψηλὰ τὰ πρὸς βορρᾶν; and the English, 'in the sides of the *north*.'

Thus, even as early as Cædmon, who speaks of Satan as 'like to the light stars,' we find, 'that he west and *north* would prepare structures'; as Thorpe translates it in his edition, at p. 18. So, too, in the *English Homilies*, three lines below the quotation already given; 'and sitte on north[d]ele hefene riches,' i. e. and sit on the *north-part* of the kingdom of heaven. So again in *Genesis and Exodus*, l. 277:—

> ' Min flight—he seide—Ic wile uptaken,
> Min sete *north* on heuene maken.'

So again in some (not in all) of the MSS. of *Piers Plowman*, as, e. g.:—

'Lorde, why wolde he tho, thulke wrechede Lucifer
Lepen on a-lofte in the *northe* syde?'
Langland, *Piers Plowman*, C. ii. 112, ed. Whitaker, p. 18.

In fact, Satan's name of Lucifer, and his sitting in the north, are generally found in company. Even Milton has :—

'At length into the limits of the *north*
They came; and Satan to his royal *seat*
. . . . . .
The palace of great *Lucifer*,' &c.
*Paradise Lost*, v. 755-760.

## 29. Notes on Fly-leaves (3 S. xii. 126; 1867).

At the end of the MS. No. xlv., in University College, Oxford—which contains a copy of *Piers Plowman* in its earliest form—is the following note :—

'Euery man whoes wife wereth a great horse must keep a frenche hood, quod Josua Sl—— in the parlement house.

'Euery man whoes wife wereth a frenche hode must kepe a great horse; all one to hym.

'the kynge was borne thre year after I cam to yᵉ court.
I cam to yᵉ court iij yeer after the king was borne.

'Drinke er you goe ⎱ horse-mylle.
goe er you drinke ⎰ mylle-horse.

If Hunne had nat sued the premunire, he shuld nat haue ben accused of heresie.

'If Hunne had nat ben accused of heresie, he shuld nat have sued the premunire.

'The cat kylled the mouse. Mus necabatur a cato.
'The mouse kylled the cat. Catus necuit murem.
'catus muri mortem egit.
'mus interemit catum.'

All this obviously refers to some member of Parliament who was unfortunate enough to put the cart before the horse, evidently to the great amusement of some hearer who 'made a note' of it.

## 30. Cap-a-pie (3 S. xii. 135; 1867).

*I think your correspondent D. P. S. does very wisely in thus asking for examples of the occurrence of this phrase before proceeding to give his theory of the etymology; for it is not uncommon for etymologists to construct a theory *first*, and look about for facts *afterwards*, and it is this practice which has often brought etymology into contempt. In the present instance, I think the received explanation may stand.

First, by way of examples. The phrase occurs, according to the dictionaries, both in Prescott and Swift. In A. D. 1755 we meet with:—

> 'Armed *cap-a-pee*, forth marched the fairy king.'
> Cooper, *Tomb of Shakspear.*

Tracing back, we come to:—

> 'Armed *cap-a-pie*, with reverence low they bent.'
> Dryden, *Palamon and Arcite*, l. 1765.

There is also another curious instance. In a poem called *Psyche, or Love's Mystery*, by Joseph Beaumont, published in 1651, we have:—

> 'For knowing well what strength they have within,
> By stiff tenacious faith they hold it fast;
> How can these champions ever fail to win,
> Amidst whose armour heaven itself is plac'd.'
> *Pysche*, canto xii. st. 136.

At that time Joseph Beaumont was an ejected Fellow of St. Peter's College, but he lived to be master of the college nevertheless, and half-a-century later this poem attained to a second edition, viz. in 1702. In its second form, the poem was much expanded, so that the above stanza, 136, became stanza 154, and at the same time a variation was made, so that it ran thus:—

> 'How can those champions ever fail to win,
> Who, *cap-a-pe*, for arms, with heaven are drest.'

I have little doubt that many more examples might be found; and now for the etymology.

The received one is, that *cap-à-pied* means from head to foot, and surely it is simply equivalent to the usual French phrase, 'armé de pied en cap,' for which Raynouard gives the quotation:—

'*De pied en cap* s'armera tout en fer.'
Laboderie, *Hymn Eccl.*, p. 282.

The only objection to this seems to be that there is a reversal of the order of the words. But if, leaving the *Langue d'Oïl*, we consult the *Langue d'Oc*, we shall then find the words in the right order, and at the same time establish, as I think, the right explanation beyond a doubt, besides showing that the phrase existed in the *twelfth* century.

In his Provençal Lexicon, Raynouard gives—'CAP, KAP, *s. m.* Lat. *caput*, tête, chef'; and he goes on to explain the phrases *de cap en cap* (from one end to the other); *del cap tro als pes* (from the head to the foot); *del premier cap tro en la fi* (from the first beginning even to the end). The second of these is clearly the one we want, and he gives the following example:—

'Que dol si *del cap tro als pes*.'
Guillaume Adhémar (died A. D. 1190).

This he translates by 'Qu'il se plaint de la tête jusqu'aux pieds.'

When your correspondent says he doubts this explanation, I suspect he is being misled by a French proverb given by Cotgrave, viz. 'n'avoir que la *cape et l'épée*,' which means, 'to have nothing left but your mantle and your sword, to be brought to dependence on your own exertions.' The resemblance between the two phrases *cap-à-pie* (head to foot), and *cape et l'épée* (mantle and sword), is certainly striking, but they seem to be quite distinct nevertheless, and I do not think they can be proved to be otherwise.

[See *Cap-à-pie* in the *New Eng. Dictionary*.]

**31. The Seven Ages of Man. I** (3 S. xii. 145; 1867).

* In a poem entitled *This World is but a Vanyte*, from the Lambeth MS. 853, about 1430 A.D., printed in *Hymns to the Virgin and Christ* (edited by F. J. Furnivall for the

Early English Text Society), at p. 83 we have a very curious comparison of the life of man to the seven times of the day. The number seven is here determined apparently by the *hours* of the Romish Church. Thus, corresponding to matins, prime, tierce, sext, nones, vespers, and compline, which were called in Old English *uhtsang, primesang, undernsang, middaysang, nonsang, evensang, nightsang,* we have the following periods of the day and of man's life:—

1. Morning. The infant is like the morning, at first born spotless and innocent.

2. Midmorrow. This is the period of childhood.

3. Undern (9 A.M.). The boy is put to school.

4. Midday. He is knighted, and fights battles.

5. High Noon (i.e. nones or 9th hour, 3 P.M.). He is crowned a king, and fulfils all his pleasure.

6. Mid-overnoon (i.e. the middle of the period between high noon and evensong). The man begins to droop, and cares little for the pleasures of youth.

7. Evensong. The man walks with a staff, and death seeks him. After this follows the last stanza:—

> '"Thus is the day come to nyght,
>   That me lothith of my lyuynge,
> And doolful deeth to me is dight,
>   And in coold clay now schal y clinge."
> Thus an oold man y herde mornynge
>   Biside an holte vndir a tree.
> God graunte us his blis euerlastinge!
>   This world is but a vanite!'

The resemblance of this to Shakespeare's 'Seven Ages' is curious and interesting.

**32. The Seven Ages of Man. II** (4 S. iv. 303; 1869).

I have already pointed out a description of the seven ages of man in the old poem entitled *This World is but a Vanyte*. I have just come across a paragraph in Arnold's *Chronicle* (ed. 1811, p. 157) which seems worth noting. Arnold is supposed to have died about A. D. 1521 :—

*The vij Ages of Man liuing in the World.*—The first age is infancie and lastith from y⁰ byrth vuto vij. yere of age The ij. childhod and endurith vnto xv. yere age. The iij. age is adholecencye and endurith vnto xxv. yere age. The iiij. age is youthe and endurith vuto xxxv. yere age. The v. age is manhood and endurith vnto l. yere age. The vi. age is [elde][1] and lasteth vnto lxx. yere age. The vij. age of man is crepill and endurith vnto dethe.'

### 33. Notes on Fly-leaves (3 S. xii. 412; 1867).

On the fly-leaf of a Collection of Musical Tunes, by John Dowlande, M.B., in MS. Camb. Univ. Dd. ii. 11 is the following specimen of alliteration :—

'Musica mentis medicina moestae.'

There are also the lines :

```
'Qu     an      di      tris    dul         pa
    os      guis    rus     ti      cedine      vit'
 H      san     mi      Chris   mul         la
```

which have been already discussed in *N. and Q.*, 3 S. x. 414, 503[2]; and also the following, in the same style, which I had not before seen, but which I dare say may be common enough :—

```
         pit     rem     nam     pit         rem
'Qui ca      uxo     poe     ca      atque dolo
         ret     re      na      ret         re.'
```

In one respect these latter verses are the more curious of the two, as they are Leonine verses, wherein *uxorem* and *uxore* rime to *dolorem* and *dolore*.

[Read the lines by taking the first and second lines together—Quos anguis dirus, &c.; and the third and second lines together—Hos sanguis mirus, &c.]

---
[1] A blank space here. *Probably it should be elde,* i. e. old age.

[2] This version is the one which *I* said would be found to be the correct one of these lines.

**34. The word 'All-to.' I** (3 S. xii. 464 ; 1867).

On the subject of 'A Tobroken Word,' I beg to refer Mr. H. to my letter in *The Athenaeum* of October 5. The fact is that, wherever *alto* (in Mid. English) is *apparently* a separate word, it is so by a blunder of an editor. It is common enough in MSS. to separate a prefix from its verb. Any one who has ever seen an Anglo-Saxon MS. knows that the prefix *ge-* is far more often written separately from the word it belongs to, than it is joined to it; and an editor ought to represent this by a *hyphen*, unless, professing to give a facsimile of the MS., he discards hyphens altogether as in Sir F. Madden's excellent edition of *William and the Werwolf*. Hence, the mere fact of *to* or *alto* being written *apart from* the word it belongs to, is not at all surprising: it is only what we expect.

I think it is not quite safe, for the purpose of argument, to assert that 'there is no instance, I believe, of the use of the word *to-troublid*.' I found *two*, in less than two minutes, in the very first book I laid my hands on. I quote from the *Wicliffite Glossary*, where I find 'to-truble, *to greatly trouble*, Ecclus. xxxv. 22, 23 ; *v*. 'al-to-trublist.' This second reference gives: 'al-to-trublist, *extremely afflictest*, Ps. lxxiii. 13 ; *pl.* al-to-trubleden, Dan. v. 6 ; *v*. to-truble.'

I have only to repeat that—

'*All-to*, as equivalent to *all to pieces*, and as separable from the verb, is comparatively modern. As the force of *to* as an intensive prefix was less understood, and as verbs beginning with it became rarer, it was regarded as leaning upon and eking out the meaning of *all*, whereas in older times it was *all* that added force to the meaning of *to*.'

Halliwell, I now find (for I had not noticed it before', says much the same thing :—

'In earlier writers, the *to* would of course be a prefix to the verb, but the phrase *all-to*, in Elizabethan writers, can scarcely be always so explained.'

It is not the only blunder perpetrated by these later writers. Some one of them took to spelling *rime* with an *h*, and produced the word *rhyme*—thus giving a Greek commencement to a Saxon word; and this was thought so happy and *classical* an emendation, that nearly every one has followed suit ever since.

A somewhat wider search through English literature would disclose the not recondite fact, that *all* is used before *other* prefixes besides *to*.

Thus (1) it is used before *a* (I write as it stands in the MS., omitting hyphens) in the line—

'here of was sche al a wondred and a waked sone.'
*William and the Werwolf*, l. 2912.

(2) It is used with the prefix *for*—

'as weigh al for waked for wo vpon nightes,'
*Id.* l. 790.

which should be compared with l. 785 just above, viz.—

'Febul wax he and feynt for waked a nightes.'

(3) It is used before the prefix *bi*; as in

'al bi weped for wo wisly him thought.'
*Id.* l. 661.

Perhaps when *alto* has been *proved*, in *early* English, to be a complete word *in itself*, distinct from the past participle—which, oddly enough, is always found not far off it—we may hope to have an explanation of the words *alfor*, *ala*, and *albi*! But surely, the simpler explanation is that, when the later writers looked on the *to*- as separable, they did so because they knew no better.

[Admirably explained on similar lines, in the *New Eng. Dict.* s. v. *All*, C. 14, 15; p. 227, col. 2.]

### 35. The word 'All-to.' II (3 S. xii. 535; 1867).

May I add two quotations of great importance? The first is—

'*Al to-tare* his a-tir that he *to-tere* might.'
*William and the Werwolf*, l. 3884.

That is, 'he completely tare-in-pieces his attire, whatever of it he could tear-in-pieces.'

And, if this be not thought decisive enough as to the separation of the *al* from the *to*, here is another more decisive still—

> 'For hapnyt ony to slyd and fall,
> He suld sone be *to-fruschyt all.*'
>     Barbour's Brus, ed. Jamieson, p. 207.

That is 'For, if any one had happened to slide and fall he would soon have been broken-in-pieces utterly.'

### 36. Wolwarde. I (4 S. i. 65 ; 1868).

I quite agree with Mr. Addis in thinking Mr. Morris is here, for once, wrong in his explanation of the word, because I do not see how to join *-ward* on to *wol*, so as to make sense. But the explanation *wolwarde*, 'with wool next the body,' satisfies all three quotations, viz. in the *Pricke of Conscience*, in *Piers Plowman*, and in the *Crede*. It is always connected with the idea of penance or of poor clothing. The quotation from the *Pricke of Conscience* is very much to the point :—

> 'And *fast* and *ga wolwarde*, and *wake.*'

Accordingly, when Mr. Addis receives my edition of the *Crede* from the E. E. T. S., he will find in the glossary :—

'"*Wolwarde*, without any lynnen next one's body, *sans chemyse.*" —Palsgrave. To go *woolward* was a common way of doing penance, viz. with the *wool towards*[1] one's skin.'

### 37. Wolwarde. II (4 S. i. 254 ; 1868).

I fail to understand the point of the note by A. H. What is the 'simpler meaning' he suggests? Merely, I suppose, that he thinks *woolward*, in that it means with the *wool towards* one, does not necessarily imply *penance*, and might

[1] [Unless it meant—' with the skin towards the wool.']

be found very comfortable. No doubt of it. But the idea of penance, or poor clothing, was connected with it in early English, though the quotation from Shakespeare shows that it was ceasing to be a penance in his time, and it seems that the common people of Russia at the present day like it. A. H. ought, in all fairness, to read over the passages referred to, *together with the context.* The references are:— Hampole's *Pricke of Conscience,* ed. Morris, l. 3514; Langland's *Vision of Piers Ploughman,* ed. Wright, p. 369 (see p. 497 of the same volume); and *Pierce the Ploughman's Crede,* ed. Skeat, l. 788. Besides these, Halliwell gives *one* more example, and Nares *five,* with an excellent note, that will convince A. H. more than I seem to have done. The example of it in Shakespeare occurs in *Love's Labour's Lost,* Act V. Sc. 2, l. 717.

### 38. Wolwarde. III (4 S. i. 425; 1868).

If A. H. will only take time enough he will find my explanations quite right; and if so, he will not need to be at the trouble of proving them wrong.

Meanwhile, I must comment upon his two new statements. His first is, that there is no allusion to *penance* in the quotation from the *Crede.* Of course this is quite right, for it is in the quotation from *Hampole* that *penance* is implied. Secondly, he thinks that *to go wolwarde* means *to go woolwards.* Certainly not. In the first expression, *wolwarde* is an *adjective*; and he has not distinguished between the endings *ward* and *wards,* which were seldom confounded till recently in English writings. *To go woolward* means *to go about 'with the woolly side in'*; and the verb *to go* is here used, as elsewhere in old English, for *to go about,* much as in the Bible (see Gen. iii. 14). *To go woolwards,* if it ever were to be used (for it never has been), could only mean that which we more commonly express by the phrase—'to go a wool-gathering.'

### 39. 'Rabbit' (4 S. i. 279; 1868).

No doubt F. C. H. is right. Compare the account of the word in Hartshorne's *Salopia Antiqua*, which contains a list of Salopian expressions :—

'RABBIT IT, *phr.* The evidently profane phrase " *Od rabbit it* " is not local. The *Od* in this case is but a corruption of *God*, and the other part of the oath has become changed to its present form from the Old English *rabate, rebate*, which in its turn is altered from the French *rebatre*; Teut. *rabatten*, de summa detrahere.'

*Rebate*, in Old English, means to *drive back, repulse* :—

'This is the city of great Babylon,
Where proud Darius was *rebated* from.'
R. Greene, ' Orlando Furioso,' *Works*, vol. i. p. 34 (ed. 1831).

### 40. Hogshead (4 S. i. 613; 1868).

The great point in etymology—but the lesson will never be learnt—is, that we should be guided by *facts*, and not by *guess*. The guess *hog's-hide* is very ingenious, but against it we must set these facts. The first is, that, in Dutch, the word for a hogshead is *okshoofd*; the second is, that the Swedish is *oxhufvud*; and thirdly, the Danish is *oxehofved*. Hence *hogshead* is a corruption, not of *hog's-hide*, but of *ox-head*. The suggestion *hog's-hide* does not explain things at all; because it leaves the Dutch, Danish, and Swedish words quite untouched; and indeed, if we are to guess at all, *ox-hide* would be, undoubtedly, *half* right. Permit me, then, to put the query in a form more likely to produce a true answer. How comes it that the Swedish word *oxhufvud* means both an *ox's head* and the measure called a *hogshead*? It is clear that an *ox*, not a *hog*, is the animal meant.

### 41. Lister (4 S. i. 547; 1868).

A *Lister* is a *dyer*. Jamieson gives *Lit*, to dye; Isl. *lita*, to dye; Suio-Goth. *lit*, colour. Also *Lidstar*, a dyer. In the Promptorium Parvulorum, we have *Lytyn, litiyn*, or *lytyn*, to dye; and again, *Lytynge* or *littinge* of cloth, i. e. dyeing. Mr. Way, the editor of this book, gives other instances. *Lit* also means dye-stuffs; and to *lit* is sometimes used in Lowland Scotch for to blush deeply, to be suffused with blushes. *Dyer* is used as a surname as well as Lister.

**42. The 'Jackdaw of Rheims'** (4 S. i. 577; 1868).

Many readers must remember the story about the scalded magpie, which the author of the *Ingoldsby Legends* says was told him by Cannon. Hence he adopted the notion about the 'Jackdaw of Rheims,' which he expressed in the line:

'His head was as bald as the palm of your hand.'

It is amusing to compare this with a similar one in *The Knight of La Tour-Landry* (E.E.T.S.), p. 22. This relates how a magpie told a man that his wife had eaten an eel which he was fattening in a pond in his garden for himself and friends. The wife tried to excuse herself by saying the husband had eaten it; but the husband told her he knew better, as he had heard about it from the magpie. In revenge, the lady and her maid plucked the bird's feathers off, saying: 'Thou hast discovered us of the eel.' And ever after, the magpie repeated this to any one whom he saw with a bald head. Surely this is curiously like the conclusion of Cannon's story, as told in the *Memoir of the Rev. F. H. Barham*. [It is, practically, the same story as that in Chaucer's Manciples Tale; respecting the oriental origin of which see my ed. of Chaucer, iii. 501. Chaucer took it from Ovid.]

**43. Walter pronounced as 'Water'** (4 S. i. 595; 1868).

A very early instance is the following:—

'Byhold opon Wat Brut whou [*how*] bisiliche thei pursueden.' *Pierce the Ploughman's Crede*, l. 657.

Here *Wat* is the reading of the Trinity MS., but the British Museum MS. and the early printed edition of 1553 both have *Water*, which represents Walter at full length. The short form *Wat* is spelt without an *l*. Similarly the common Old English word for *fault* is *faute*, and for *assault* is *assaut*.

[This illustrates Shak., 2 Hen. VI. iv. 1. 31–35. My own name as a boy, in Shropshire, was ' our Wat.']

### 44. Gist (4 S. ii. 42 ; 1868 ; curtailed).

The derivation of *gist* is very obvious, being the French word *gîte*, formerly spelt *giste*, a derivative of *gésir* ; Lat. *iacere*, to lie. The *gist* of a thing is the point in law whereon the action *rests*. According to analogy, the pronunciation ought to be with the soft *g* [i. e. as *j*]; and as there is hardly an instance where a soft *g* is hardened, but many of the contrary, there is no sort of excuse for pronouncing it hard [i. e. as *g* in *go*].

### 45. ' Lene ' and ' leue ' (4 S. ii. 126 ; 1868).

I wish to draw attention to the two words *lene* and *leue* as occurring in Chaucer, Piers Plowman, and other poems, which have, as I think, been utterly confused by most editors ; probably, because they can hardly be distinguished in the MSS. In Halliwell's *Dictionary* I find—' LENE, to give. Hence our word *lend*. The editor of *Havelok* absurdly prints *leue*.'

In Morris's *Specimens of Early English*, ed. 1867, at p. 395, we read—'*Lene*, grant. Many editors of Old English works print *leue* (leve, give *leave* to), for *lene*, as if from A.S. *lefan*, to permit ; *lene* is from *lænan*, to give, lend.'

Here, I submit, there is the most dire confusion. The editor of *Havelok* did not act absurdly in printing *leue*, because he had to deal with another word, quite different from *lene* ; and secondly, Mr. Morris, after making the right distinction between the words, proceeds to confound them. But it is proper to add that he now writes to tell me that he has discovered the mistake, and holds the view which I proceed to state.

This is, that Sir F. Madden and Dr. Stratmann, who *do* put a difference between the words, are right; and what I wish to do now, is to show the exact difference between them, and to offer some arguments in place of assertions.

In the first place, all scholars agree in accepting that the old spelling of *lend* is *lene* or *len*, just as the old spelling of *sound* is *soun*. This shows, too, why the past tense and past participle are alike; for *lent* (as the past tense) is contracted from the old past tense *lende*, and *lent* (as the past participle) from the old past participle *lened*; both of which are formed from *len* or *lene*. Now the old meaning of *lene* is to give, deliver, hand over, impart, and it answers to the German *leihen*. None would deny that the following are correct examples of it:—

>'To yeue and *lene* him of his owne good.'
>>Chaucer, *Prol.* 611.
>'That hote cultre in the chymney heere
>As *lene* it me, I have therwith to doone.'
>>Chaucer, *Miller's Tale*, 589.
>'*Lene* me a mark,' quod he, 'but dayes thre.'
>>Chaucer, *Chan. Yem. Tale*, 15.
>'I shal *lene* the a bowr.'—*Havelok*, 2072.

But what Mr. Halliwell appears to deny is, the existence of the verb *leue*; and this is the point to come to.

Dr. Stratmann's account of it is, that *leue* or *leve* is the A.S. *lēfan*, German *erlauben*, to give *leave* to, permit, allow. Now this word in various forms, *lȳfan, lēfan, alȳfan, gelȳfan,* is common enough in Anglo-Saxon, and as *yf* between two vowels had the sound of *v*, it would necessarily produce *leve* in Old English. There are three undoubted examples of its occurrence. Thus, in the *Ormulum*, we have (vol. i. p. 308) the line:

>'Godd allmahhtigg *lefe* uss swa
>To forthenn Cristess wille,'

i.e. 'God Almighty *grant* (or *permit*) us so to further Christ's will.' Here the spelling with *yf* makes the word certain; and to make doubly sure, we have a similar expression in the same volume, at p. 357. But there is a third instance. In Douglas's *Virgil* is the phrase 'Gif us war *lewit*,' which is equivalent to *leuit*, as explained by Jamieson. Here again, the use of the *w* makes the word altogether certain; for *w* has the force of *v* very commonly in Lowland Scotch. The signification of the phrase is—'if it were *permitted* to us.'

That the two words have been so hopelessly jumbled together is no doubt owing to the fact that each can be represented by the verb *to grant*; but it really makes all the difference whether we are speaking of to *grant* a thing to a person, or to *grant* that a thing may happen. 'God *lene* thee grace' means, 'God *grant* thee grace,' where to *grant* is to *impart*; but 'God *leue* we may do right' means, 'God *grant* we may do right,' where to *grant* is to *permit*.

The difference between the two is distinct enough, and the instances of *lefe* in the *Ormulum* render the blunder here protested against quite unjustifiable. Briefly, *lene* requires *an accusative case* after it, *leue* is followed by *a dependent clause*.

And now for the results. The following are true examples of *leue*:—

'God save and gyde us alle and some,
And *leue* this sompnour good man to become.'
Chaucer, *Freres Tale*, 346.

Printed *lene* by Tyrwhitt, and *leene* by Morris.

'Ther he is now, God *leue* us for to meete.'
*Prioresses Tale*, 231.

Printed *lene* by Tyrwhitt and Morris.

'Depardieux'—quod she—'God *leue* all be wele.'
*Troil. and Creseide*, ii. 1212.

38       *PORCELAIN.*

> 'God *leue* hym werken as he can devyse.'
> *Troil. and Creseide*, ii. 7.
> 'God *leue* us for to take it for the best.'
> *Ibid.* v. 1749.

Morris prints *lene*. Moxon prints *leve*, but Tyrwhitt has *lene* in his *Glossary* (*s. v.* 'Leveth'), in all three instances.

The three instances in *Havelok* occur in similar exclamations, in the forms 'God leue,' or 'Crist leue,' and Halliwell need not have called such a spelling absurd. The quotations from the *Ormulum* entirely establish the phrase.

Lastly, by way of a crucial test, take *Pierce the Ploughman's Crede*. I regret that I have, in all four places, printed *lene* in the text. Yet, strictly speaking, there are *two* instances of *lene*, in lines 445, 741; and *two* of *leue*, in lines 366, 573, where the phrase is 'God leue,' etc. And now observe a circumstance that clinches the whole result. In lines 445 and 741 all three copies of the *Crede* have *lene*; but in lines 366 and 573 the best MS. can be read either way; the British Museum MS. has *leve*, and the old printed edition has *leue*, as shown by my footnotes. Surely future editors of Chaucer ought to note these corrections.

Of course I have not taken into consideration here the other senses of the word *leue*, viz. (1) to believe, (2) to leave, and (3) dear. Curiously enough, all these three occur in one line :—

> 'What! leuestow, leue lemman, that i the leue wold?'
> *William of Palerne*, 2358.

### 46. Porcelain (4 S. ii. 155; 1868).

Mr. Wedgwood derives this from 'Ptg. *porcellana*, china ware, said to be so called from the surface being like that of the *porcellana*, a large univalve, commonly known as the tiger-shell, or Venus' shell.' But this does not tell us why the *shell itself* was so named.

In the *Catalogue of the Chinese Collection* exhibited some years ago near Hyde Park Corner, at p. 63, I met with the following remark, which seems worth preserving :—

'Marsden, as quoted by Davis, shows that it [*porcelain*] was applied by the Europeans to the ware of China, from the resemblance of its finely polished surface to that of the univalve shell so named [in Portuguese]; while the shell itself derived its appellation from the curved shape of its upper surface, which was thought to resemble the raised back of a *porcella*, or little hog.'

Thus the word *porcelain* is finally traced back to the Latin *porcus*; just as *porpoise* is the *pork-fish*, and *porcupine* means *spiny pig*.

[See further in Littré, s. v. *porcelaine*; and in the larger edition of my Etym. Dict.]

### 47. Age of the World. I (4 S. ii. 156; 1868).

In *two* MSS. *only* of Piers Plowman, viz. that belonging to Oriel College, Oxford, and one in the Cambridge University Library, marked Ll. 4. 14, are the two following lines, which have reference to the *plenitudo temporis*, the 'fulness of time' of Christ's birth :—

> 'Annis quingentis decies, rursumque ducentis
> Unus defuerat, cum Deus ortus erat.'

My query is, whence did the monks in the fourteenth century derive the idea that Christ was to be born exactly 5199 years after the Creation?

[Answered by myself, in a later number; see below.]

### 48. Age of the World. II (4 S. iii. 203; 1869).

I can now answer my own question, as to why Christ's birth is made to have taken place 5199 years after the Creation. The reckoning is *British*, and is very curious. In *A Chronicle of London*, p. 183, there is a copy of the great tablet which was once hung up in Old St. Paul's, and which contained the curious chronological *?facts* which I here tabulate. (Cf. MS. Harl. 565.)

Destruction of Troy, Anno Mundi 4030.
Building of New Troy, called London, A. M. 4094.
Building of Rome, A. M. 4484.
Christ born, in the 19th year of Cymbeline, A. M. 5199.

Add to these, that Brutus landed at Totness, in Cornwall (it was in Cornwall then), A. M. 4063, where he destroyed, amongst other giants, three who were named respectively Geomagog, Hastripoldius, and Rascalbundy, as we learn from a MS. in the Heralds' College; the one, namely, which contains the original French version of *Havelok*.

### 49. 'Yede,' misused by Spenser (4 S. ii. 199; 1868).

It is strange that no one seems to have remarked the curious blunder made by Spenser respecting the verb *yede*. In yielding to his propensity for archaic diction, he has, in this instance at least, not perfectly learnt his lesson, and fallen into a remarkable grammatical error. *Yede* and *yode* are both, as every student of Early English should know, various forms of the A.S. *ēode*, a past tense without any corresponding present tense, employed with the sense of 'went.' But Spenser, observing the differing forms of the word, came to the extraordinary, yet somewhat logical, conclusion that *yede* must be the infinitive mood, and *yode* the past tense of the same. This did not mislead him as regards *yode*, so that he wrote correctly enough—

'Before them *yode* a lustie tabrere.'
*Shepheard's Calendar*, May, 22.

But, with respect to *yede*, he has erred in at least three places:

'Then badd the knight his lady *yede* aloof.'
*Faerie Queene*, I. xi. 5.
'The whiles on foot was forced for to *yeed*.'
*Ibid.* II. iv. 2.
'But if they with thy gotes should *yede*.'
*Shepheard's Calendar*, July, 109.

Nares gives no instance from any other author beyond

quoting *yede* as a preterite; and it would be curious to know if the mistake really occurs in any other author's works. Spenser certainly did not find it so used by his master Chaucer, nor by any other writer of the fourteenth century.

### 50. A Year and a Day (4 S. iii. 222; 1868).

Perhaps several of your readers, like myself, have felt inclined to smile at the expression, 'a year and a day,' occurring so frequently in old ballads. The words 'and a day' seem so unnecessary. But I now feel inclined to smile at my own want of perception; there is very good reason for the phrase.

If, in a passage of a melody, we wish to rise from one C to the C above, we ascend by the *seven* notes of the scale, C to B, and by *one more*, i.e. we arrive at the *octave*. In the same way, Low Sunday is not said to be seven days after Easter, but is called the *octave*. The phrase 'in a week's time' is felt to be vague; and therefore people say 'this day week.' But this is sometimes expressed in old books by 'in *eight* days,' and a fortnight is sometimes denoted by 'in fifteen days'; cf. Fr. *quinzaine*. Now the period of the *octave* might also be fairly called 'a week and a day,' as well as a period of eight days; and in the same way, *a year and a day* must mean on the 366th day from the present, i.e. on the same day of the month as the present, in next year. The intention of it is to show that not only has a year elapsed, but that the day now spoken of is *the same day of the month as the day before mentioned*. Cf. Exod. xii. 41.

Again, the present 25th of August being a *Tuesday*, the 25th next year will be *Wednesday*; and by that time we shall have advanced not only by a *year* (reckoned by years), but by a *day* (reckoned by days of the week). Here is another reason for choosing the phrase.

[Cf. Chaucer, 'Knightes Tale,' Group A, l. 1850; and my note on the passage.]

### 51. Chronology of Chaucer's 'Knightes Tale'
(4 S. ii. 243; 1868).

After some little trouble, I have arrived at the conclusion that Chaucer has given us sufficient *data* for ascertaining both the days of the month and of the week of many of the principal events of the 'Knightes Tale.' The following scheme will explain many things hitherto unnoticed. I refer to the lines of the Aldine edition, ed. Morris, 1866.

On Friday, May 4, before 1 A.M. Palamon breaks out of prison. For (l. 605) it was during the 'third night of May, but (l. 609) a little *after* midnight.' That it was Friday is evident also, from observing that Palamon hides himself at day's approach, whilst Arcite rises 'for to doon his observance to May, remembryng of the *poynt of his desire.*' To do this best, he would go into the fields at *sunrise* (l. 633), during the hour dedicated to *Venus*, i.e. during the hour after sunrise *on a Friday*. If however this seem for a moment doubtful, all doubt is removed by the following lines:—

> 'Right as the *Friday*, sothly for to telle,
> Now it schyneth, now it reyneth faste,
> Right so gan gery *Venus* overcaste
> The bertes of hire folke, right as *hir day*
> Is gerful, right so chaungeth hire aray.
> Selde is the *Fryday* al the wyke alike.'

All this is very little to the point unless we suppose Friday to be the day. Or, if the reader have *still* any doubt about this, let him observe the curious accumulation of evidence which is to follow.

Palamon and Arcite meet, and a duel is arranged for an early hour on the *day following*. That is, they meet on Saturday, May 5. But, as Saturday is presided over by the inauspicious planet Saturn, it is no wonder that they are both unfortunate enough to have their duel interrupted by Theseus, and to find themselves threatened with death. Still, at the intercession of the queen and Emily, a day of assembly for a tournament is fixed for *'this day fyfty wekes'* (l. 992). Now we must understand 'fyfty wekes' to be a poetical expression for a *year*. This is not mere supposition, however, but a *certainty*; because the appointed day was in the month of *May*, whereas fifty weeks and no more would land us in *April*[1]. Then 'this day fyfty wekes' means 'this day year,' viz. on May 5. Now, in the year following (supposed not a leap-year), the 5th of May would be *Sunday*. But this we are expressly told in l. 1330. It must be noted, however, that this is not the day of the *tournament*, but of the *muster* for it, as may be gleaned from ll. 992-995 and 1238. The tenth hour 'inequal' of Sunday night, or the second hour before sunrise of Monday is dedicated to *Venus*, as explained by Tyrwhitt (l. 1359); and therefore Palamon then goes to the temple of Venus. The third hour after this, the first after sunrise on Monday, is dedicated to Luna or Diana, and during this Emily goes to Diana's temple. The third hour after this again, the fourth after sunrise, is dedicated to Mars, and therefore Arcite then goes to the temple of Mars. But the rest of the day is spent merely in jousting and preparations—

'Al the *Monday* jousten they and daunce' (1628).

The tournament therefore takes place on Tuesday, May 7, on the day of the week presided over by *Mars*, as was very fitting; and this perhaps helps to explain Saturn's exclamation in l. 1811, 'Mars hath his wille.'

Thus far all the principal days, with their events, are exactly accounted for. In what follows I merely throw out a suggestion for what it is worth. It is clear that Chaucer

[1] It turns out that Boccaccio, whom Chaucer here follows, actually uses the expression 'un anno intero,' a complete year.

would have been *assisted* in arranging all these matters thus exactly, if he had chosen to calculate them according to the year *then current*. Now the years (not bissextile) in which May 5 is on a Sunday, during the last half of the fourteenth century, are these : 1359, 1370, 1381, 1387, 1398. Of these five, it is at least curious that the date 1387 *exactly* coincides with this sentence in Sir H. Nicolas's *Life of Chaucer* :—
'From internal evidence it appears that the "Canterbury Pilgrimage" was written after the year 1386.'

### 52. A Baker's Dozen (4 S. ii. 464 ; 1868).

I do not know if the following passage in the *Liber Albus* has been noticed. It occurs at p. 232 of the translation by Mr. Riley :—

'And that no baker of the town shall give unto the regratresses the six pence on Monday morning by way of hansel-money, or the three pence on Friday for curtesy-money; but, *after the ancient manner*, let him give thirteen articles of bread for twelve.'

That is, the retailers of bread from house to house were allowed a thirteenth loaf by the baker, as a payment for their trouble.

### 53. Pied Friars (4 S. ii. 496 ; 1868).

A further investigation has convinced me that my note upon 'Pied Friars,' instead of being wrong, as is now suggested, is perfectly correct [1]. They are not, or at any rate were not originally, the same as the Carmelites. The latter were (not the *Pied*, but) the *White* Friars. The truth is, that we know very little about these Pied Friars. They only had one house in all England, viz. at Norwich, and this only for a time; so that any allusion to them, or account of

[1] My note to l. 65 of *Pierce the Ploughman's Crede*, which mentions the *freres of the Pye*, is : 'They would appear to be not very different from the Carmelites; they were called *Pied Friars* from their dress being a mixture of black and white, like a magpie.'

them, is very difficult to obtain. In Thomas Walsingham's history [ed. H. T. Riley, i. 102], there is an allusion which seems to imply, and probably does imply, that they once had a burial-ground in London; but that, in A.D. 1326, their name, as that of a separate fraternity, was no longer used. In describing the murder by the Londoners of Walter de Stapleton, Bishop of Exeter, he says that the dead body was cast in an old cemetery which had once belonged to the Friars, whom our ancestors used to call 'Pied Friars': 'quod fuerat quondam Fratrum, quos *Freres Pyes* veteres appellabant.' All that is said about them, in the course of the eight large volumes of Dugdale's *Monasticon*, is contained in one short paragraph; and even this is copied from Blomefield's *Norfolk*. It is in the latter work that we at last find some account of them. After describing the church of St. Peter per Mountergate, in Norwich, he says that there was a college at the north-east corner of the churchyard, which was 'first given to the Pied Friars, so named from their habit; and after they quitted it, which was when they were *obliged to join one of the four principal orders*, it came to the Hospital of Bek, in Billingford, in Norfolk.' Blomefield's *Norfolk*, ii. 537; cf. Dugdale's *Monasticon*, viii. 1611.

The only other reference to them that I can discover, is the one already cited in my notes, viz. *Political Poems*, i. 262 · where some *change* is evidently expressed by the words *fuerunt* and *mutati sunt*, though I forget the context at this moment[1]. It will be observed that Blomefield himself is quite at a loss as to *which* of the four orders they joined, but the passage in the *Crede* furnishes evidence that they joined the Carmelites. I may then repeat my original note ·

---

[1] [The lines are:
    'With an O and an I, fuerunt *pyed freres*
      Quomodo mutati sunt, rogo dicat Per[e]s.'
But they throw no special light upon the matter.]

'that they were not very different from the Carmelites.' They were different once, but not at a later period. Their Latin name was 'Fratres de Pica.'

### 54. Genteel Dogs (4 S. ii. 507; 1868).

'Also, to avoid the noise, damage, and strife that used to arise therefrom, it is forbidden that any person shall keep a dog accustomed to go at large out of his own enclosure without guard thereof, by day or night, within the franchise of the City, *genteel* dogs excepted; under pain of paying forty pence, to the use of the Chamber.'

Mr. Riley's note to this passage (*Liber Albus*, p. 389) is that the word *gentilx* may mean 'gentle' or pet dogs of the then known description. But 'gentyll houndes' are such as were kept for hawking and hunting, as 'grayhoundes, braches, spanyellis, or suche other.' See Laurens Andrewe on the Dog, quoted in Mr. Furnivall's *Babees Book*, p. 225.

### 55. 'Ye' for 'The' (4 S. ii. 545; 1868).

The reason why 'y$^e$' is sometimes used for 'the' in old books wherein 'the' is the more usual form, is simply that printers in former times had difficulties about 'spacing out.' When pressed for room, they put 'y$^e$'; when they had plenty of room, they put 'the.' This distinction is made over and over again in Crowley's edition of *Piers Plowman*, printed in 1550. Many people use 'y$^e$' still, but few of those who use it know what it means, as is shown by their pronouncing it *ye*. But the proper pronunciation is *the*, for the *y* is only a corruption of the old *thorn-letter*, or symbol for *th*. In the MS. of Barbour's *Brus*, for instance, *ye*, *yat*, *yair*, *yaim*, *yat*, &c., occur frequently, and are to be pronounced *the*, *thai*, *thair*, *thaim* (them), *that*. The methods of printing the *e* above the line, and of putting 'y$^t$' for *that*, are borrowed from the abbreviations 'þ$^e$' and 'þ$^t$' in MSS. Another common abbreviation is 'þ$^u$' for *thou*, which would be printed 'y$^u$.'

### 56. Coat, a name for the dress of women: is it proper? (4 S. ii. 586; 1868).

There is here no difficulty. Whatever be the ultimate etymology of the word, which is the French *cotte*, Italian *cotta*, German *kutte*, it implies a *covering*. There is no reason for restricting it to male dress, except that it is now customary to do so. We still apply it widely when we speak of a coat of plaster, or of a pony having a rough coat. In early English it is *much more frequently* applied to male than to female attire; but the following are a few examples of the latter use:

'This was her *cote*, and her mantel.'
Chaucer, *Rom. of the Rose*, 459.
'And she hadde on a *cote* of grene.'—*Ibid.* 573.
'How Heyne hath a new *cote*, and his *wif* another.'
*Piers Plowman*, A. v. 91.
'I have put off my *coat*; how shall I put it on?'
*The Bible* (Authorised Version), Sol. Song, v. 3.
'The *cote-hardie* was also worn by the ladies in this reign [Edw. III].'—*British Costume*, p. 133.

The first, second, and fourth examples are given in that excellent book entitled *The Bible Word-Book*. The word *gown* is, on the other hand, very frequently used of *male* attire, as in Chaucer. So also in *Piers Plowman*, ed. Wright, p. 259. And Stow says, anno 1507:—

'The Duke of Buckingham wore a *gowne* wrought of needle-work, and set upon cloth of tissue, furred with sables, the which *goune* was valued at 1500*l*.'

We still have *gownsmen* in plenty.

[See *Coat* in the New Eng. Dictionary.]

### 57. Soc-lamb (4 S. ii. 592; 1868).

According to Halliwell, this term is also used in Sussex. The A.S. *soc* means the act of suction, and the existence of the Germ. *Saugelamm*, Dutch *zuig-lam*, both meaning a *sucking-lamb*, leaves us in no doubt as to the true etymology. Compare *sokerel*, an unweaned child; *souking-?fere*, a foster-brother; *sokeling*, a suckling plant or a young animal. Jamieson also tells us that one of the designations among the vulgar for a simpleton is a *sookin' turkey*.

### 58. The problem of 'the trisection of an angle' (4 S. iii. 94; 1869).

The locus of the points of trisection of any arc which has a *given* chord is an hyperbola, of which the eccentricity is 2, the foci are the ends of the chord, and the directrix is the sagitta of the arc. Hence it follows that the problem cannot be solved *by the ordinary methods of geometry*, i.e. by the rule and compasses *only*. But it is easily solved by constructing the hyperbola, which can be done by tolerably simple means—viz. merely with the aid of a piece of string, a ruler revolving round a fixed end, and a tracing-pencil.

### 59. Monkey (4 S. iii. 183; 1869).

I see no reason for doubting the etymology commonly accepted (as e.g. in Ogilvie and Wedgwood), that *monkey*, though formed with an English suffix, is equivalent to the Italian *monicchio*. It is clearly a diminutive, and the fact that we have the older word *ape* shows that *monkey* is an imported word. The original word is Italian *mona*, an ape; Spanish *mono* (masculine), and *mona* (feminine). We find also Spanish *monillo*, a small monkey; Italian *monna*, *monnino*, *monnone*. The Italian *monna* meant originally mistress, and seems to be a mere abbreviation of *madonna*, my lady; hence it came to mean dame, old woman, &c. The degradation of the term is certainly very great; but there is an exactly parallel instance in the case of the word *dam*, which has been degraded from the Latin *domina*, in French 'notre *dame*,' till it now means only the mother of a racehorse, or of a less important animal.

[Cf. *Monkey* in my larger Etym. Dictionary.]

### 60. Watershed (4 S. iii. 215 ; 1869).

Some time ago there was a discussion about this word in *The Athenaeum*, some of the correspondents of that paper not understanding its derivation. Others, better informed, pointed out that it is simply equivalent to the German *Wasserscheide*, and that to *shed* is still used, locally, in the sense of *parting* the hair. I have little doubt that many quotations might be adduced assigning to *shed* (German *scheiden*) the sense of to *part* or divide. Still, as the word is not very common, it may be as well to note the following, where it is used as a *neuter* verb, meaning to *separate*:—

'The River Don or Dun (says Dodsworth in his Yorkshire collections) riseth in the upper part of Pennystone parish near Lady's Cross—which may be called our Apennines, because the rain-water that falleth *sheddeth* from sea to sea.'
Southey's *The Doctor*, 2nd edition, vol. ii. p. 4.

The exact meaning of *watershed*, I may add, is the *ridge* or elevation which causes the streams of water on either side of it to flow in opposite directions, and so *parts* them asunder.

### 61. Final -e in Early English (4 S. iii. 215 ; 1869).

There is a curious instance of careful spelling in MS. Camb. Univ. Lib. Dd. 1. 17, which shows that the scribes did pay some regard to the final *e* even in alliterative poems, where a syllable more or less in the line is not of much consequence. It is in the passage of *Piers Plowman* (B. xi. 166) which is thus given in that MS. :—

'Or any science vndir sonne, the seuene artz and alle,
But thay be lerned for oure lordes loue, lost is al the tyme.
*Cf.* Wright's ed., p. 212.

Here *all* occurs twice: once in the pl. *alle*, and once in the sing. *al*. In the second place, the scribe had at first written *alle* as before; but on second thoughts, he became aware of his mistake, and destroyed the *le* by placing a point beneath each letter in the usual manner. It evidently made a difference to *him*.

### 62. Roodee (4 S. iii. 228 ; 1869).

The origin of this word [the name of a piece of ground at Chester] has not yet, I believe, been shown, although the Editor pointed out that the old form of the word was *Rood Eye*. The answer is to be found, however, in Mr. Wright's note to his edition of *Piers Ploughman*. (See vol. ii. p. 521.) There was a famous *Rood* or cross at Chester, mentioned by Langland, which stood on an *eye*, or piece of ground surrounded by water. Hence this plot of ground was named *Rood Eye* or cross-island, as explained by Pennant in his *Tour in Wales*, edit. 1778, p. 191. Nowadays this level space is used as a race-course ; the cross has probably disappeared (though its base was to be seen in 1789), and the name made into *Roodee*; and this, owing to the proximity of the river Dee, is again most absurdly corrupted into *Roo-Dee*. In the *English Cyclopaedia* it is thus spelt. No wonder that *Roo* cannot be explained !

### 63. Poetic diction of the Anglo-Saxons (4 S. iii. 268 ; 1869).

The difference between Anglo-Saxon *prose* and Anglo-Saxon *poetry* is best understood by reading a little of both. In poetry, the requirements of alliterative verse tend to render the sentences involved and disjointed. The principal characteristics of our old poetry are, among others, these following.

1. Inversion of the order of words. Example :—
(I only give the translation, not the original)—

'For us it is very right that we the Guardian of the skies, the Glory-king of hosts, with our words praise, in our minds love ' Cædmon ; the opening lines.

2. Insertion of numerous epithets and equivalent ex-

pressions. Thus, in the above, the Lord is called in one line 'the Guardian of the skies,' and in the next 'the Glory-king of hosts.' In one line we have 'with our words praise,' in the next 'in our minds love,' which are parallelisms.

3. An abundance of names for the *same* object. Thus even in the later English, a man is called a *man*, a *freke*, a *renk*, a *segge*, a *burne*, or a *gome*, merely to satisfy the requirements of alliteration. These names are picked out just as required: that is, if the alliteration requires *f*, it is *freke*; if *s*, it is *segge*, and so on. So also in Anglo-Saxon, very numerous are the expressions for a *sword*, or a *ship*, &c.

4. A curious chopping up of sentences into pieces of the same metrical length. Every line being divided into hemistichs by a metrical pause, it will be found that, in many cases, there is a pause in the sense as well as in the sound. This is seen in the specimen given above. 'For us it is very right—that we the Guardian of the skies—the Glory-king of hosts—with our words praise—with our minds love.' We thus get each sentence piecemeal as it were, and it is often necessary to get to the end of each sentence before the drift of it can be even guessed at. These are a few of the points which must strike every reader who peruses but one page of Anglo-Saxon poetry. To appreciate the matter fully, your correspondent should consult Conybeare's *Illustrations of Anglo-Saxon Poetry*, or (which would be far better) steadily make his way through a good long portion of Cædmon or Beowulf. This may be done in part, without a knowledge of Anglo-Saxon, by help of Mr. Thorpe's translations. On Early English Alliterative Poetry of a somewhat later date, see my Essay[1] in vol. iii. of the *Percy Folio* MS., by Hales and Furnivall.

[1] [It is rather obsolete now, and not very correct; but contains some useful information.]

### 64. Did Adam and Eve fall into the Sea?
(4 S. iii. 275; 1869).

Certainly they did so. How they did it, is sufficiently explained by the context of the passage cited. Philip de Thuan carefully explains that the sea means this world, and the miseries of it. They were driven out of Paradise, and into the world of sorrows. This is all that is meant by their falling into the sea. The same idea is found in Langland's *Piers Plowman*, ed. Wright, p. 153; ed. Skeat, B. viii. 40.

### 65. 'Havelok' and Robert of Brunne (4 S. iii. 357; 1869).

Robert Mannyng of Brunne, himself a Lincolnshire man, was probably alive and of sufficient age to compose poetry when the English version of *Havelok* was written in the Lincolnshire dialect. In a passage to which Sir F. Madden has drawn attention, he uses expressions which show clearly (1) that he was well acquainted with *Havelok*, and (2) that it was no work of his own, as might perhaps for a moment be imagined. But that he knew it tolerably well can be verified by internal evidence, which also shows that Robert of Brunne's *Handlyng Synne* was written *after Havelok*; which is precisely in accordance with other evidence. I think the following is a clear example of plagiarism :—

> 'Al þat he þer-fore tok
> With-held he nouth a ferþinges nok.'
> *Havelok*, l. 819.
> 'Plenerly, alle þat he toke
> Wyþhelde he nat a ferþynge noke.'

Robert of Brunne, *Handlyng Synne*, 5811, in Morris' *Specimens*.

This case is so clear that other instances are hardly needed, though I think it very likely that a fair number of such imitations could be found ; and it is very interesting to know where to look for the original of some of Robert's expressions. The word to *swill*, to wash dishes, is *very* rare, both in Anglo-Saxon and Early English. Here is one example of it :—

> 'Ful wel kan ich *dishes swilen*.'
> *Havelok*, 919.

And here is another :—

> 'Pottes and *dysshes* for to *swele*.'
> *Handlyng Synne*, 5828 (Morris).

One of the most curious stories about Havelok is, that a flame was often seen to proceed out of his mouth as he slept. Compare—

> 'Out of hys mouþ me þoghte brak
> A flamme of fyre bryght and clere.'
> *Handlyng Synne*, 5922 (Morris).

Now that I have pointed this out, I dare say some of your readers can multiply instances of similar plagiarism. Observe, too, that the *metre* of the *Handlyng Synne* is precisely the same as that of *Havelok*, although on other occasions Robert wrote in long lines, averaging fourteen syllables.

### 66. Bydand (4 S. iii. 494; 1869).

There is no difficulty in this word: why Halliwell did not explain it, I cannot guess. It simply means *abiding*, i.e. never budging an inch. When Fitz-James said to Roderick Dhu—

> 'Come one, come all! this rock shall fly
> From its firm base as soon as *I*,'

he approved himself to be *bydand*. Cf. Halliwell's quotation—

> 'And ye, Ser Gye, a thousande,
> Bolde men and wele *bydande*,'—

where 'wele *bydande*' means well abiding, unflinching. There is a passage in Langland's *Piers the Plowman* which is very much to the point. Avarice is described as fighting on the side of Antichrist, and is represented as fighting without flinching as long as his bag of money holds out. It runs thus :—

> '"Allas!" quod Conscience, and cryde tho, "wolde Crist of his grace,
> That Coveitise were Cristene ! that is so kene a fighteie.
> And boold and *bidynge*, while his bagge lasteth."'
> Langland's *Piers the Plowman*, (B. xx. 139`, ed. Wright, p. 433.

Some MSS. read *abydynge* in this passage. Our word *staunch* expresses the sense of it tolerably well. The ending *-and* is northern.

[Cf. *Biding* in the *New. Eng. Dict.*]

### 67. An error in Fabyan's Chronicles (4 S. iv. 152; 1869).

There is a singular errör in the dates of the reign of Edward III in *Fabyan's Chronicles*, which seems to have escaped the notice of the editor, Sir H. Ellis, and is of some importance. The year of our Lord is given wrongly during nearly the whole of this reign, and this may easily mislead a reader who trusts to this author. I am referring to the edition of 1811, wherein the reader, by turning to p. 441, will find the entry, 'Anno Domini. MCCCXXX-I; Anno v,' meaning that the *fifth* year of Edward's reign began in the last-mentioned date, viz. 1331 (Jan. 25). But on the next page we have the following entry : 'Anno Domini M.CCCXXXI - Anno Domini M.CCCXXXII; Anno VII,' which is as much as to say that the next year to the *fifth* year was the *seventh*. The *sixth* year, in fact, is simply lost sight of, and the error is continued down to the very end of the reign. One consequence is that the years are wrongly calculated down to the end of the reign; another is, that Edward's reign is made a year longer than it was. He died in the fifty-first year of his reign, having reigned fifty years and about five months; but at p. 487 of Fabyan we have the entry, 'Anno lii.' The regnal years and mayors' years are difficult to arrange, because they began at different times. Fabyan begins the reign by passing over the mayoralty of Chickwell, and calls Betayne the *first* mayor; whereas he was not elected till October, 1327, when Edward had reigned about nine months.

This explains the expression on p. 439—'In the ende of yᵉ firste yere of this kynge Edwarde, & begynnynge of this mayres yere'; where 'this mayre' is Fabyan's *first*, the above-named Betayne. But, if he begins to reckon thus, he should have continued it. By the same reckoning the *fourth* mayor would be elected in the end of the *fourth* year of the king; yet on p. 441 we read—'In this .iiii. mayres yere, & ende of yᵉ *thyrde* yere of thys kynge,' where for *thyrde* we must certainly read *fourth*. In the same way, the battle of Cressy is said to have taken place in the *twenty-first* year of Edward's reign, but it was fought during the *twentieth* (1346). And so on throughout.

By way of further example, let me explain the entry on p. 480. We there find 'Anno Domini. M.CCCLXVIII. John Chychester—Anno Domini. M.CCCLXIX. Anno XLIIII.' This refers, not to the 44th, but to the 43rd year, from Jan. 1369 to Jan. 1370, towards the close of which—viz. in October 1369—Chichester was elected as mayor. Hence the entry, under this year, of the death of Queen Philippa (Aug. 15, 1369). It follows that Chichester was still mayor in April 1370, as is proved also by a notice of him as mayor in that very month and year in Riley's *Memorials of London*, p. 344. Hence follows the complete solution of the date of *Piers the Plowman*. When Langland mentions 1370 as Chichester's year, he is right enough. I have said, at p. xxxii of the preface to text A of the poem, that 'our author seems to be a year wrong.' But I am glad to find that the error lies, not with Langland, but with Fabyan; and the date of the *second* version of the poem is irrefragably proved to be later than 1370. Other indications point to the year 1377 as the date thereof.

### 68. Ennui (4 S. iv. 223; 1869).

I cannot allow that English is unequal to translate this word. Our language, which possesses the fulness of several languages rolled into one, is equal to every emergency; and the more so, if we are allowed to fall back upon words that are obsolescent or provincial. It is from the dulness of translators that the frequent miserable wailing over the inadequacy of English arises. *Ennui* is not so expressive as *dumps*. It means, I suppose, to quote Roget's *Thesaurus*, 'melancholiness, the dismals, mumps, dumps, blue devils, vapours, megrims, spleen'; also weariness, tedium, lassitude, and in fact, *boredom*. Mr. Besant, in his pleasant and scholarly book on *Early French Poetry,* in speaking of the English poems of Charles of Orleans, says:—'What is *newous* thought? The French explains it: it is *pensée ennuyeuse*. I believe this is the only attempt to adopt this word in English, though we want it badly.'

I am certainly a little surprised at this remark, for we actually possess the word *annoyance* from the same root; and so far from *newous* or *noyous* being an uncommon word, and only used by Charles, it is a word that is sufficiently familiar to readers of our older literature. Chaucer has *anoyful,* disagreeable; *anoyous,* with the same meaning; *anoyaunce,* grievance; *noyous,* troublesome; whilst Langland not only uses the verb *noyen,* to plague, but actually has the very word *anoy* or *noy,* used as a substantive, which is exactly equivalent to *ennui* in form, and very nearly so in meaning. Even Spenser has the word, and uses it so as to bring out with much clearness the meaning which we now attach to it (*F. Q.* i. 6. 17):—

'For griefe whereof the lad n'ould after joy,
But pynd away in anguish and *selfewild annoy*.'

What better epithet for it than *selfwilled*?

And again, Spenser say (*F. Q.* ii. 9. 35):—

> 'But other some could not abide to toy,
> All plesaunce was to them griefe and *annoy*.'

This is just what happens to those who suffer from *ennui*; they cannot 'abide to toy.' If, then, neither *mumps*, nor *dumps*, nor *boredom* be considered sufficiently near to *ennui* to represent the true force of it, there can be no objection to reviving the English form of the word, viz. *annoy*. As for the amazing number of English words which can be used to translate a single French one, is there not Cotgrave's *Dictionary*?

### 69. Chaucer Parallels: 'The Knightes Tale' and 'Troilus and Cressida' (4 S. iv. 292; 1869).

Since, in both these works, Chaucer was to some measure indebted to the same poet, Boccaccio, it is not unreasonable to suppose that they were composed[1] nearly at the same time. The following parallels seem to point to the same result. I believe their number might be increased. The references are to the Aldine edition [and to my own]:—

1. '*And forth he ryt*: ther [n]is no more to telle.'
    K. T. 116 (A. 974).
  '*And forth she rit*, ful sorwfully, a pas.'
    Tr. v. 60.
2. ' *Thurgh girt with many* a grevous *blody wounde*.'
    K. T. 152 (A. 1010).
  ' *Thorwgh gyrt with many* wyde and *blody wounde*.'
    Tr. iv. 599 (627).
3. ' *That* never, *for to deyen in the payne*.'
    K. T. 275 (A. 1133).
  ' *That* certein, *for to deyen in the peyne*.'
    Tr. i. 674.
4. 'And *lowde* he *song ayens* the sonne *scheene*.'
    K. T. 651 (A. 1509).
  'Ful *lowde song ayein the* moone *shene*.'—*Tr.* ii. 920.

[1] [This refers, of course, to the first draught of the Knightes Tale. called Palamon and Arcite.]

5. 'He may go *pypen in an ivy leef.*'—*K. T.* 980 (A. 1838).
'*Pipe in an ivy leefe*, if that the leste.'—*Tr.* v. 1433.
6. 'As soth *is sayd*, eelde hath gret avantage,
In eelde is bothe wisdom and usage;
*Men may the* eelde *at-renne*, but *nat at-rede.*'
*K. T.* 1589 (A. 2447).
'Your sire is wis, and *seyde is* out of drede,
*Men may the* wise *at-renne*, and *nought at-rede.*'
*Tr.* iv. 1427 (1456)
7. 'To *maken vertu of necessite.*'—*K. T.* 2184 (A. 3042).
'Thus *maketh vertu of necessite.*'—*Tr.* iv. 1558 (1586).
And in *Sq. Ta.* ii. 247 (F. 593).

### 70. Serfs (4 S. iv. 302; 1869).

There is no reason why *serfs* may not mean *stags* without any alteration to *cerfs*. I suppose it to be a parallel case to a passage in the French prose romance of Alexander—'Nas tu pas veu par plusieurs fois que ung [lyon] meit à la fuite grant quantite de *serfz*?'

To this passage the French editor appends a note—

'On reconnait là les idées provenant de la superiorité si marquée de la chevalerie, au moyen âge, sur les *serfs* et sur les vilains.'

This is a delicious blunder, when it is remembered that the parallel passage in the Latin version is 'an nescis quod unus leo multos *cervos* in fugam vertit?' and the Greek version has ἐλάφους. See the passages quoted at length in my edition of William of Palerne (E. E. T. S.), p. 240.

### 71. 'Rue with a difference' in 'Hamlet' (4 S. iv. 559; 1869).

In explaining Shakespeare's phrases, I think that many commentators refine too much. If he indeed 'had in his mind' all the intricate allusions he is said to have had, his mind must have been even greater than most of us grant it to have been. In Ophelia's speech—'there's rue for you; and here's some for me; we may call it herb-grace on Sundays; O, you must wear your rue with a difference'—

there is no difficulty if we do not force the words 'with a difference' into some 'heraldic' phrase. It merely means this: 'I offer you rue, which has two meanings; it is sometimes called *herb of grace*, and in that sense I take some for myself; but, with a difference of meaning, it means *ruth*, and in that respect will do for you.' This explanation is not mine; it is Shakespeare's own.

> 'Here did she fall a tear; here, in this place,
> I'll set a bank of *rue*, sour *herb of grace*;
> *Rue*, even for *ruth*, here shortly shall be seen,
> In the remembrance of a weeping queen.'
> *Richard* II, Act iii. Sc. 4.

[The fact is, there is a play upon words. There are *two* distinct words, both spelt *rue*. *Rue*, the herb, is from O.F. *rue*, which Cotgrave explains by '*rue*, herb grace'; and this is from Lat. *ruta*. But *rue*, the verb, is English; A. S. *hrēowan*.]

Some wrongly explain the word *crants* by *garlands*, whereas it is a garland, in the singular number. Long notes have been written about it, but no one seems to have noticed that Shakespeare not only understood the word, but knew it to be singular. Otherwise he would hardly have used the name of *Rosenkrantz* as that of one of his characters. What need of search for explaining a word which is under one's nose all the while? Surely *Rosenkrantz* is a rose-garland.

### 72. 'Jeresgive,' a mistake for 'Yeresgiue'
(4 S. v. 74; 1870).

I am much obliged to MR. T. for his quotation; the explanation is not difficult. It is the old English ȝeresȝiue, which may be represented by *yeresyiue* or *yeresgiue*, but not by *jeresgiue*, as the letter ȝ may be denoted by *y* or *g*, but not by *j* (except in German). It is a *year's-gift*, i.e. an annual donation, or new-year's gift; or, in common parlance, a Christmas-box. The first part of the word is the genitive case of *year*; the latter part is the A.S. *gifu*, G. *gabe*, a gift. It occurs in *Piers the Plowman*, iii. 99 (ed. Skeat, Clarendon Press Series, p. 27) :—

'Ignis devorabit tabernacula eorum qui libenter accipiunt munera, &c.
'Amonge this lettered ledes this latyn is to mene,
That fyre shal falle, and brenne al to blo askes
The houses and the homes of hem that desireth
Yiftes or yeresyyues bi cause of here offices.'

That is to say, Langland explains the text (Job xv. 34) by the phrase :—

'Among these learned people this Latin signifies, that fire shall fall, and burn all to blue ashes the houses and homes of them that desire gifts or *yeresyiues* by reason of their offices.'

The word is duly explained in my Glossary.

### 73. The Sun: its Gender (4 S. v. 75; 1870).

The statement of E. H. A. that he has never seen the sun used of the feminine gender, except in the works of Mede, is exceedingly amusing. The difficulty would rather be to find any instance of its being masculine in any English writer from the time of the author of *Beowulf* to nearly the end of the fourteenth century. I at once give a couple of examples, viz. : 'the sonne gaf hire litht' (the sun gave *her* light), Layamon's *Brut*, ed. Madden, l. 7239; and 'the sonne gan louke *her* lighte in *her-self*' (the sun locked up her light within herself, or was eclipsed), *Piers the Plowman*, ed. Skeat, B. xviii. 243. My 'B-text' of Langland's *Piers the Plowman*, containing the latter quotation, is now being published.

In our early writers the sun is feminine, and the moon masculine. The question is rather, what are the earliest instances of the contrary? According to Dr. Bosworth's edition, we find the moon masculine in the Old English version of St. Matt. xxiv. 29, which he dates at about A. D. 995, but feminine in Wycliffe's version, A. D. 1389.

**74. The Sangreal, or Holy Grail** (4 S. v. 251; 1870).

That *Sangreal* should be a corruption of *sang real* is such a very obvious derivation, that it will possibly always find acceptance; although it is always safe to regard popular etymologies with suspicion, and the more so if they were constructed in medieval times. As in all other cases, we must have some regard to chronology; and I believe it will be found that the word *graal* existed long before the idea of prefixing the epithet *san* was at all common, and consequently long before the corrupt etymology *sang real* was thought of. The history of the word is given at pp. 102, 378 of tom. 1er of *Les Romans de la table ronde*, by M. Paulin Paris (see also the word *gradale* in Ducange). The many difficulties about the word are there carefully discussed. See also the edition of *The History of the Holy Graal,* edited by Mr. Furnivall for the Roxburghe Club, at the end of the first volume of which the original early French version of the romance was reprinted. At l. 2653 of this romance the question is asked by some sinful men, 'and what is the name of the vessel?' The answer being—

> Qui a droit le vourra nummer
> Par droit Graal l'apelera';

where the prefex *san* or *saint* is not used.

The most ancient notice of the word is certainly to be found in Helinandus, who was a Cistercian monk in the abbey of Froidmond, in the diocese of Beauvais, and died either in 1219 or 1223. His works are printed in vol. ccxii. of Migne's *Cursus Patrologiæ.* The passage is a curious one, and worthy of a corner in *N. and Q.*

'Anno 717. Hoc tempore, cuidam eremitæ monstrata est mirabilis quædam visio per angelum, de Sancto Josepho, decurione nobili, qui corpus Domini deposuit de cruce; et de catino illo vel paropside in quo Dominus cœnavit cum discipulis suis; de qua ab eodem eremita descripta est historia quæ dicit[ur] *Gradal*. *Gradalis* autem vel *gradale* dicitur gallice scutella lata et aliquantulum profunda in qua preciosæ dapes cum suo jure [*gravy*] divitibus solent apponi, et dicitur nomine *graal*,' &c.

The word *Gradale* sometimes means a service-book containing the responses, &c., sung before the steps (*gradus*) of the altar; but in the sense of an open platter, it is said to be allied to *cratella*, the diminutive of *crater*, and four whole pages are devoted to a consideration of it in Roquefort's *Glossaire de la Langue romane*.

I have no space to plunge into a long explanation of the shape of the vessel, or to decide whether it ought to be called a *cup* or a *dish*—it is safest to call it a *vessel*. Spenser calls it holy *grayle* (*F. Q.*, b. ii. c. x. st. liii).

As for the combination *sang real*, it is used in Old English as well as in French, but much more commonly in the sense of *royal* than of *true blood*. I give two examples :—

'Alle with taghte men and towne in togers sulle [? fulle] ryche,
Of *saunke realle* in suyte, sexty at ones.'
      *Morte Arthure* (ed. Perry), l. 178.
'He came of the *sank royall*,
That was cast out of a bochers stall.'
    Skelton, *Why Come ye not to Court*, l. 490.

Considerations as to space render this a very imperfect notice of the word.

75. 'Cry Bo to a Goose' (4 S. vi. 221; 1870).

I doubt the coincidence of this phrase with that of saying '*Bee* to a battledore.' This latter expression means rather to be possessed of elementary knowledge, to have learnt the rudiments. A hornbook, which was originally a flat board with a handle, with a piece of horn in front, was shaped something like a *battledore*, and was at times so named. (See the cut of one in Chambers's *Book of Days*, i. 47.) To be able to say B when B was pointed to in the hornbook, was called 'to say B to a battledore,' or sometimes 'to know B from a battledore,' the words *to* and *from* in these phrases being nearly equal to *at the sight of*, or *as exhibited upon*. The phrase means, proverbially, to be possessed of a knowledge of the alphabet, &c., as already said.

### 76. The Siege of Metz (4 S. vi. 296; 1870).

It is perhaps not generally known that Metz was once besieged by King Arthur. It was defended by the Duke of Lorraine; some of whose men complained that he had defrauded them of their pay, and urged him to treat for peace. The Duke refused, and charged Arthur's knights upon a dromedary. Arthur's knights assaulted the city, throwing down stone steeples and most of the inns. At last the city surrendered, and Arthur (to quote Mr. Perry's words) 'provides for the government of Lorraine, which he had conquered.' See the long account in *Morte Arthure* (ed. Perry, 1865, for the Early English Text Society), pp. 71-91. The whole passage is very curious.

### 77. Peas or Pease? (4 S. vi. 139; 1870).

The explanation of this word ought to be well known. It is not a plural at all, but a singular noun, the plural of which ought to be *peasen*, sometimes misspelt *peason*, as in Nares. It is the A.S. *pisa*, Lat. *pisum*; cf. Ital. *pisello*. In Mid. English it is *pese* in the singular, *pesen* in the plural, as a few extracts will show.

'*Pese*, frute of corne.—*Pisa*.'—*Prompt. Parvulorum*, ed. Way, p. 395.

'The vaunting poets found nought worth *a pease*.'
Spenser, *Shep. Cal.*, Oct. 69.

'He poureth *pesen* upon the hacches slidre.'
Chaucer, *Leg. G. W.*, Cleop. 69.

See also the numerous examples in Nares, s. v. *Peason*.

In Langland's *Vision of Piers the Plowman*, edited by me, in the Clarendon Press Series, the word is fully

64 CHATTERTON'S KNOWLEDGE OF ANGLO-SAXON.

explained in the Glossary. Langland's scribe uses *pees* in the singular, and both *pesen* and *peses* in the plural. The French *pois* and Welsh *pys* also show clearly that the final *s* is not inflexional. In composition we find the words *peascod*, *pease-porridge*, where *peas* or *pease* is still the singular noun; cf. the Mid. Eng. *pese-codde* used by Langland. Thus the *e* in *pease* is merely a relic of the old spelling *pese*; but when, in process of time, this final *e* was dropped, the word *peas* came to be regarded as a plural, and the *singular* word *pea* was invented by some one 'with a turn for grammar[1]'; just as the words *alms* and *riches*, once singular nouns, are beginning to be used as plurals, and only await the touch of genius to develop the singulars *alm* and *rich*.

### 78. Chatterton's knowledge of Anglo-Saxon
(4 S. vii. 278; 1871).

In the paper written by Rowley on the 'Rise of Painting in England in 1469,' and communicated by Chatterton to Walpole, are several Anglo-Saxon words. Most of these are used wrongly; but if we rightly explain them, and tabulate them in alphabetical order, they are as follows :—

*Aad*, a heap.
*Adronct*, drowned.
*Adrifene* (*fatu*), embossed (vessels).
*Æcced-fæt*, an acid-vat, vessel for vinegar.
*Æsc*, a ship; lit. an ash.
*Æðellice*, nobly.
*Afægrod*, coloured, adorned.
*Afgod*, an idol.
*Agrafen*, engraven.
*Ahrered*, reared up.

It thus appears that Rowley was possessed of an Anglo-Saxon dictionary (the earliest was printed in 1659), and he only

---

[1] Beau Brummel said that he 'once ate *a pea*,' a saying which has often been quoted for its imagined brilliancy.

succeeded in acquiring some knowledge of the language as far as AH. Chatterton's letter on 'Saxon Achievements,' printed in Southey's edition, vol. iii. p. 89, exhibits precisely the same singular result. He there explains the words *Aadod, Afgod, Afgodod, Afraten, Amezz*, with the addition of *Thunder-flægod*. The last of these he explains by 'thunder-blasted,' but he has mistaken *ƿ* for *s*. The word which suggested this notion to him is *Thunder-slæge*, a clap of thunder. The exception in Rowley's letter is *Heofnas*, which he uses for the colour *azure*. This is how he came by it; he looked into Bailey, and found '*Azure*, blue (in heraldry),' &c., and again '*Azure*, the sky or firmament.' This suggested the idea of *heaven*.

He then found that Bailey gives *heafian* as the derivation of the word. This led him to look into an Anglo-Saxon dictionary, and he accordingly found *heofon*, pl. *heofenas*, and he adopted the plural as quainter-looking. *Afraten* is either miscopied from '*Afsetan*, to appoint, design,' or simply made up from the heraldic word *fret*. *Amezz* is miscopied from '*Amett*, decked, adorned.' It thus appears that Chatterton knew no more Anglo-Saxon than he might have picked up in an hour from a glossary, and was unable to distinguish between *s* and *ƿ*, and probably misread other letters also.

[PS. Chatterton is known to have used Benson's Anglo-Saxon Vocabulary, printed in 1701. It is a miserable compilation, made from Somner's Dictionary.]

### 79. 'By Hook or by Crook' (4 S. viii. 133; 1871).

This proverb is at least a century older than Skelton's time. It occurs in the works of Wyclif. See Mr. Arnold's new edition of Wyclif's *English Works*, iii. 331. On the very next page is the proverb about 'turning the cat in the pan,' which Bacon has also in his *Essays* : see Essay xxii, 'On Cunning.'

### 80. Chaucer's 'Man of Lawes Tale' (4 S. viii. 201; 1871).

It may be interesting to note that the events narrated in the *Man of Lawes Tale*, and in Gower's *Confessio Amantis*, lib. ii. (where the same story occurs), may be connected more or less with the date A. D. 580 or thereabouts. Gower gives the name of the Emperor of Rome as Tiberius Constantinus. A Latin note in the MSS. of Gower refers to Pelagius as pope. The son of Constance is Maurice, afterwards emperor. Constance marries Ælla, king of Northumbria. The name of the constable's wife, Hermegyld, may have been suggested by the so-called martyrdom of the Visi-Gothic prince St. Hermenegild[1]. The following are the dates:—

Tiberius II, emperor (not of Rome, but of the East), A. D. 578.

Succeeded by Maurice of Cappadocia, A. D. 582.

Pelagius II, pope, A. D. 578–590.

Ælla of Northumbria, A. D. 560–588.

Martyrdom of St. Hermenegild, A.D. 584, or 586.

Thus the story has a certain consistency, but is open to the objection that Tiberius, reigning only four years, could hardly have been succeeded in 582 by his own grandson, born (according to Chaucer) later than 578.

### 81. English Prepositions (4 S. viii. 241; 1871).

I observe that in some remarks upon the word *partake* (the accuracy of which, by the way, I do not admit) your correspondent C. A. W. says:—

> '*I* wish there was a good treatise upon English prepositions, their individual significance, their significance in composition, and their power of modifying meaning when used in connection with verbs.'

Permit me to refer him to Mätzner's *Englische Grammatik*,

---

[1] [So spelt in Alban Butler's *Lives of the Saints*, under April 13. Better *Hermengild.*]

wherein, to take but one example, the word *of* is discussed at the length of *forty pages* of close type, with quotations (to the number of several hundreds) from English writers of every date, from Layamon to Dickens. (See part ii. p. 222.) English prepositions are also treated of in Koch's *Gramm. der engl. Sprache*, in Diefenbach's *Gothic Glossary*, in March's *Anglo-Saxon Grammar*, &c.; but the grammars by Mätzner and Koch give the most copious examples from English authors. There is plenty of information to be obtained by those who will seek for it, and who will remember that philology has made some advances since the days of Dr. Johnson.

## 82. Portress (4 S. viii. 271; 1871).

I do not think this is a very rare word. A much earlier example than the one in Milton is the following:—

> 'And fayre Observaunce, the goodly *portres*,
> Did us receyve with solempne gladnes.'
> Stephen Hawes, *Pastime of Pleasure*, cap. xxxiii. st. 26.

## 83. Amperzand (4 S. viii. 468; 1871).

[In reply to the guess that it was originally *and-pussy-and*, and that its shape (&) suggests a cat sitting up, and raising one fore-paw!]

This word has been explained long ago. It is merely a corruption of *And-per-se-and*, which means that the character &, standing by itself (Lat. *per se*), spells 'and.' The old lady who pronounced it 'and-pussy-and' came much nearer to the old pronunciation than the modern spelling does. It does not follow that it is therefore derived from a pussy-cat. As for the shape of it, I have nowhere seen an explanation. Yet it is not far to seek; it is merely a rough and ready way of writing the Latin word *et*. How this is so I cannot here show without a diagram; but any one may see it repeatedly occurring in the Rushworth MS. at Oxford, or in any tolerably Old Latin MS. The shape of the character has, in fact, no more to do with a cat than the etymology has. Why should the English language be selected as the 'corpus vile' on which to make such unmeaning experiments? Any one who should derive the Latin *vicus*, a street, from *via*, a way, and *causa*, a cause, whence a *cause-way*, a street, would not get a hearing. But in *English* etymology (so low is the general level of English scholarship), grotesqueness seems to be especially aimed at.

The phrase *per se* is not confined to this character only. The letter A was often called the *A-per-se* because it can constitute a whole word when standing alone. From its position at the head of the alphabet, the *A-per-se* became a proverbial symbol of excellence. It was said of Melusine:—

'She was a woman A-per-se, alone.'
*Romans of Partenay*, ed. *S*keat, l. 1148.

In Old English MSS., any letter which constituted a word in itself, as A, I, O, and even E (Old English for *eye*), was frequently written with a point before and after it; to isolate it, as it were. Examples may be seen in the Vernon MS. at Oxford.

As another example of guessing etymology I may refer to *prise*, a word which also received attention in the last number of *N. and Q.*, and was said to be short for *upraise* (!). It is merely the French *prise*, which denoted an advantageous way of seizing a thing, as explained by Cotgrave two centuries and a half ago; from which we have developed a word *prise*, to seize with advantage, to force by leverage. The root is the Latin *prehendere*.

### 84. 'Blakeberyed' in Chaucer (4 S. x. 222; 1872).

This word presents a difficulty, as is well known; and occurs once only, viz., in the lines where the Pardoner says, in his prologue or preamble:—

## 'BLAKEBERYED' IN CHAUCER.

> '*I* rekke neuere, whan that they been beryed,
> Though that hir soules goon a *blakeberyed.*'
> Six-Text Edition, ed. Furnivall, C. 405, p. 316.

The obvious meaning is—'I care not a whit, after people are buried, what becomes of their souls.' The only question is, as to the *literal* meaning. We know, first of all, that when Chaucer uses identical sounds in place of a rime, he invariably takes care that the words denoted by those sounds shall differ in meaning. Thus *seke* (to seek), in the seventeenth line of his Prologue, rimes with *seke* (sick) in the line following, because the word *seke* is used with different meanings. Hence we know, at the outset, that the word *blakeberyed* has nothing to do with *burying*; and the suggested explanation 'buried in black' (which gives no good sense after all) falls through. When we consider further that *blakebery* means simply a *blackberry*, we are driven to suppose that *goon a blakeberyed* means 'go a black-berrying,' which is simply a phrase for 'go where they list'; just like to 'go a wool-gathering,' or to 'go pipen in an ivy leef' (*Knightes Tale*, l. 980).

The only difficulty is in the construction; we have to find instances in which 'go' is used with words ending in *-ed*; and it is because I have met with this construction that I write the present note. For, if no examples could be furnished, the explanation would remain a mere guess, and valueless, as such guesses generally are; but now that other examples have been found, the guess becomes, I venture to think, a certainty. The instances are these:—

1.
> 'Hye treuthe wolde
> That no faiterye were founde: in folk that *gon abegged.*'
> Piers the Plowman (C-text, pass. ix. 136);
> see Whitaker's edition, p. 135.

Here three MSS. read *a-begged* or *abegged*; one has *a-beggyd*, another *abeggeth*, and a sixth *and beggen*. No one can doubt that *gon abegged* has here the meaning of *go a-begging*.

2. 'In somere for his slewthe: he shal haue defaute,
And *gon abrybeth* and beggen : and no man bete his hunger.
*Piers the Plowman* (C-text, pass. ix. 244);
see Whitaker's edition, p. 141.

Here two MSS. have *gon abrybeth*, but two others have *gon abribed* or *abribid*; one has *gon abribeth and abeggeth*, whilst another has *gon abribid and a-begged*. So that we have here not only fresh evidence of *gon abegged* for *to go a-begging*, but are introduced to the phrase *gon abribed* for *to go a-bribing*—i. e. to go a-robbing, since *bribe* in Mid. English means to *rob*. No doubt fresh instances of this peculiar construction will be found. I think, too, it can be explained; but the explanation is long, and of less consequence than the ?*fact* of its occurrence.

[The suffix *-ed*, *-eth*, represents A. S. *-að*, *-oð*, in *hunt-að*.]

## 85. Dr. Johnson's Definition of 'Oats' (4 S. x. 309; 1872).

Dr. Johnson's definition of *Oats*, as 'a grain which in England is given to horses, but in Scotland supports the people,' is well known. It is also reported that he declared Burton's *Anatomy of Melancholy* to have been the only book which ever took him out of bed two hours sooner than he wished to rise. Putting these two things together, it is interesting to observe that something very like the famous definition of 'oats' occurs in Burton. Here is the passage :—

'John Mayor, in the first book of his *History of Scotland*, contends much for the wholesomeness of oaten bread. It was objected to him, then living at Paris, in France, that *his countrymen fed on oats and base grain, as a disgrace.* . . . And yet Wecker (out of Galen) *calls it horsemeat, and fitter for juments* [beasts of burden] *than men to feed on.*'—*Anatomy of Melancholy*, Part I., sec. 2, mem. 2, sub-sec. 1.

## 86. '-mas' (4 S. x. 397; 1872).

The ending *-mas* in Christmas, Lammas, Michaelmas, Martinmas, &c., is the A. S. *mæsse*, Ger. and Dan. *messe*,

Swed. and Icel. *messa*; and the most probable account of it is, that it is from Lat. *missa*. Grein explains A. S. *mæsse* as the mass, or the festival on which high mass is said. We find also A. S. *mæsse-dæg*, a festival; *mæsse-æfen*, a vigil before a festival; *mæsse-bōc*, a mass-book, &c. In the rubrics to my A. S. edition of St. Mark's Gospel, we find that the passage beginning at Mark vi. 17 is to be read on 'sancte iohannes mæssan,' i. e. on the festival of St. John the Baptist; and the passage beginning at Mark viii. 27 is to be read on 'sancte petres mæsse-dæge,' on the festival of St. Peter. The occurrence of the single *s* in *-mas* is really due to the loss of the final *e* in Old English. Thus *richesse* has been cut down to *riches*, not *richess*, probably on account of the accent being thrown back. Lammas is certainly the A. S. *hlāf-mæsse* or loaf-mass, a festival of first-fruits on the 1st of August.

### 87. -mas: Lammas (4 S. x. 521; 1872).

After working for many years at English etymology, I am well aware of the doubtfulness of many derivations that have been proposed. But of the derivation of Lammas no one who cares to look at the authorities can have the slightest doubt; it is merely the modernized spelling of the A. S. *hlāf-mæsse*, and its sense is *Loaf-mass*. The difficulty of supposing that first-fruits should have been offered on the 1st of August vanishes on examination. A couple of loaves made of new corn could as easily be made *before* the general harvest as after it; it would not be necessary that they should be eatable loaves, and they may have been made of any small quantity of new corn that could be obtained, whether properly ripened or not. But, however this may have been, the testimony of our old authors is most express. Not only was the 1st of August called *hlāf-mæssan dæg*, but the 7th was actually named 'Harvest,' irrespective of the fact that the real harvest must frequently have been much later[1]. This we know on the best possible authority, viz. the so-called *Menologium*, or Metrical Calendar of the Months, wherein we read that 'bringeth Agustus yrmentheodum hlāf-mæssan dæg; Swā thæs hærfest cymth ymb ōther swylc, būtan ānre wanan, wlitig wæstmum hladen; wela byth geyped fægere on foldan,' i.e. 'August brings to all men the *loaf-mass day*; so afterwards, *harvest* comes about another such space (of seven days) later, wanting one day; fair (harvest), laden with fruits; abundance is fairly manifested upon the earth.' In the next sentence, by way of making sure that Lammas-day is the *first*, and 'Harvest' the *seventh* of the month, we are told that three days later is Lawrence's day; and this we know to be the *tenth*. See Grein, *Bibliothek der Angelsächsischen Poesie*, vol. ii. p. 4.

The word also occurs in Ælfred's translation of *Orosius*, where we are told that Octavianus defeated Antonius and Cleopatra 'on thǣre tīde [Calendas] Agustus, and on thām dæge the wē hātath *hlāfmæssan*'; i.e. on the Calends of August, on the day which we call *loaf-mass*; where *Calendas* is a reading taken from the older, or Lauderdale MS. This battle, by the way, is not the sea-fight of Actium; for that is mentioned in the next sentence, and we know that it occurred on the 2nd of September, B.C. 31. See Dr. Bosworth's edition of *Orosius*, p. 113.

But in the A. S. Chronicle, under the date A.D. 1009, we get various spellings of the word in the MSS. Where two of them have *æfter laf-mæssan*, a third has *æfter hlammæssan*, which enables us to state confidently that the internal change from *fm* to *mm* must have been made before the

---

[1] [The precession of the equinoxes makes some difference. The sun entered Aries on March 12 in Chaucer's time, but the vernal equinox is now some eight days later. Four centuries earlier than Chaucer, it was some six days earlier; giving a difference of nearly a fortnight between 993 and 1893. Harvest in the tenth century may have been (nominally) two weeks earlier than now.]

time of Stephen, as this MS. ends with the year 1154, and the events of Stephen's reign seem to have been written down at the time. In later authors the word occurs more than once; see the quotations given for *lammasse* from Robert of Gloucester and Robert of Brunne in Richardson's *Dictionary*. The word occurs also in many later authors.

To show that harvest was expected to take place by Lammas-time, I need but quote a well-known passage in *Piers the Plowman*, B-text, vi. 291 :—

> 'And bi this lyflode we mot lyue til *lammasse tyme*,
> And, bi that, I hope to haue *heruest* in my croft.'

It is thus clearly traced from early times through the successive spellings *hlafmæsse*, *(h)lafmæsse*, *hlammæsse*, *lammasse*, down to *lammas*. It were to be wished that all our English words could be traced as easily. See the article on *Lammas* in Chambers's *Book of Days*. The suggestion that *lammas* is from *Vinculamass* is obviously a guess, and nothing more. I have never seen the latter expression in any Old English MS., and should be much surprised to meet with it. I may add, that *harvest* was not generally used in so restricted a sense as it is in the *Menologium*.

**88. Tying a knot in a handkerchief** (4 S. xi. 53; 1873).

There is an early allusion to a similar practice in the *Ancren Riwle* (ed. Morton, p. 396), written about A.D. 1230 :—'Mon knut his kurtel uorte habben þouht of one þinge; auh ure louerd, uor he nolde neuer uorgiten us, he dude merke of þurlunge ine bo two his honden': a man ties a knot in his girdle, to remember a thing; but our Lord, in order never to forget us, made a mark of piercing in both His hands. *Kurtel* is more correctly written *gurdel* in the Cotton MS.

### 89. Suppression of *s* in the Genitive (4 S. xi. 79; 1873).

The tolerably common usage here referred to is explained and exemplified in Morris's *Historical Accidence*, p. 102, sect. 100; and in Abbott's *Shakespearian Grammar*, 3rd ed. p. 356, sect. 471. A very common example of the suppression of *s* to avoid too much sibilation occurs in the phrase 'for conscience sake,' sometimes written with an apostrophe at the end of *conscience*, though the apostrophe is hardly needed. We find 'for al Conscience caste,' i. e. 'for all Conscience's contrivance,' in *Piers the Plowman*, B-text, pass. iii. l. 19. Observe also 'for goodness sake,' Psalm xxv. 7; and 'righteousness sake,' Isaiah xlii. 21.

### 90. Galoches: a Term for Unattached Students (4 S. xi. 112; 1873).

It would appear from Cotgrave's *French Dictionary* that the idea of admitting unattached students to the universities is not a new one. In former times they were termed 'galoches' or 'galloches' (the word being spelt with one or two *l's* indifferently). The following are the quotations explaining the words:—

'*Galoche*, f. : A woodden Shoe, or Patten, made all of a piece, without any latchet, or tie of leather, and worne by the poor Clowne in winter.'

'*Galloches*, m. : Schollers in Universities, admitted of no Colledge, but lying in the Towne, and being at liberty to resort unto what (publike) readers or lectures they please : tearmed thus, because, in passing in the streets, they commonly weare galloches.'

### 91. 'To hell a building' (4 S. xi. 392; 1873).

The verb *hell* is more often spelt *hele* in Old English, being the A. S. *helan*, to cover, hide, cognate with the Latin *celare*, and therefore related to the latter syllable in *conceal*. It was once so common that we may expect to find it in many parts of England still. Thus, Halliwell gives *hele* as a Devonshire word, with the sense of to roof or slate, to earth up potatoes, cover anything up; *hellier*, a thatcher or tiler, he marks as West of England; *hiling*, a covering, occurs in the Chester Plays. He also cites *hull*, a covering, shell, and *hullings*, husks, but without assigning their locality. The verb *hyllen*, to cover, is in the *Promptorium Parvulorum*, which is Norfolk. With the spelling *hele*, it is used by John of Trevisa, a Cornishman. *Hull*, a shell, is in Atkinson's *Cleveland Glossary*, which is Yorkshire. The verb was used also by Barbour and Gawain Douglas. It must have been once in common use in almost every district from Cornwall to Scotland, and probably survives locally in many counties. This can only be ascertained by consulting all the various extant county glossaries.

### 92. English Dialects ( S. xi. 385 ; 1873).

It certainly would be a good plan to make a new list of books in the English dialects, as supplementary to that published some years ago by Mr. Smith. Instead, however, of sending occasional notes to *N. and Q.* about such works, how much better it would be if some one would undertake to receive *all* such notes, with a view to their publication in *N. and Q.*, when a considerable number of them, enough to fill a page at least, has been accumulated! If the editor approves, this may easily be done[1]; and failing any one else, I am ready to undertake the work of receiving and arranging the titles of the works in question. What is wanted is that we should have the correct titles, the authors' names (when known), the date and place of publication, &c. A very brief description of the drift of each book would be useful, but all wandering talk and irrelevant remarks

---

[1] We highly approve of our valued correspondent's suggestion, and gladly accept his kind offer. All communications, therefore, on this subject should be addressed to the Rev. W. W. Skeat, Cintra Terrace, Cambridge.—Ed. *N. and Q.*

would, of course, be rigidly suppressed. The best way of collecting titles is to adhere strictly to the *indispensable* rule, that everything must be written lengthways—on *one* side only of *half-a-sheet* of *note-paper* of the ordinary size. I subjoin a title as a specimen :—

'Laycock, Samuel. Lancashire Songs. London: Simpkin and Marshall, 1866; pp. i-vi, 1-77. Contains 20 Songs, in various metres, in a Lancashire dialect.'

If we can also, in the same way, accumulate a list of all works in MS. upon this subject, it will be a great gain : as also a list of workers who really understand the subject. All this must be done before a complete provincial glossary can be made. Some years ago, when this subject was discussed, Mr. Ellis very properly insisted that some uniform spelling, such as Glossic or Palaeotype, should be employed ; but the result was, that the whole scheme fell through. Palaeotype is not likely to be understood by those who have made no special and careful study of it ; and, if employed *incorrectly*, is worse than useless. The only practical plan seems to be for each word-collector to use his own method of recording sounds (for which he should certainly employ Glossic, if he can, or most of the Glossic symbols, or at least give an account of his own system of spelling according to the pronunciation given by Walker or Webster), and then the Glossic or Palaeotype spelling can be inserted afterwards, between brackets, by some one who understands it. The following rules ought also to be strictly observed by word-collectors :—

1. Avoid etymology ; leave it to those who have made it a special study. Strive rather to record the *words themselves*, with their meanings ; add also scraps of *real* (not invented) talk, to illustrate the occasional uses of the words.

• 2. Put down *everything* that is not in standard English. To miss a word current in Shropshire, *because* it is *also* used in Herefordshire, is an utter mistake ; indeed, many good lists have been ruined this way. Words can always be *struck out*, but they are hard to *put in*. Accordingly, the locality of every word should be noted, without stopping to ascertain if it is *peculiar* to that locality. Other rules can be supplied to those who apply for them.

[A second letter on the same subject appeared in *N. and Q.* 4 S. xi. 406, on May 17 of the same year.

These letters led to considerable results, tending to establish the English Dialect Society, which was started in 1873, and (in 1895) is still vigorous.

The first publication of the Society was 'A Bibliographical List of the Works that have been published, or are known to exist in MS., illustrative of the various dialects of English; compiled by members of the E. D. S., and edited by the Rev. W. W. Skeat and J. H. Nodal. London: Trübner, 1873–7.']

### 93. Tennyson: 'All the swine were sows' (*The Princess*) (4 S. xi. 346; 1873).

It seems hard that Tennyson should be accused of an error on the ground that '*swine* is the plural of *sow*'; an assertion of which no proof is offered. In English it is certainly not the case; the A.S. *swīn* was a collective neuter noun, commonly used as a plural; but it could also be used as a singular. See the example in Bosworth's *Dictionary*, in which *swīnes* is used as the genitive singular, meaning *of a pig*; the gen. pl. was *swīna*, as in *swīna heord*, a herd of swine. Another example of the singular is in *Swīnes-hæfed*, now *Swineshead*, in Huntingdonshire; whilst the adjective *swīnen*, like the modern *swinish*, is derived from *swine* as distinct from *sow*. In German, the sing. is *Schwein*, and the pl. *Schweine*; cf. also the Dutch *zwijn*, Icel. *svín*, &c. But *sow* is the A. S. *sugu*, which is not even of the same gender with *swine*, being a *feminine* noun, like the G. *Sau*, and Icel. *sȳr*. The plural of *sugu* would be *suga*; in German the plural has two forms, *Säue* and *Sauen*. I may here also correct the singular error in a new grammar edited by Dr. Smith, viz. that *kine* is contracted from *cowen*, for which eccentric form no authority is cited. The A. S. *cū*, a cow, made its plural in the form *cȳ*, by vowel-change; the Mid. Eng. *kin* was formed from *cȳ* by adding the plural ending *-en*, whence *ky-en* or *kīn*; the final *-e* is a modern addition.

**94. 'Much' in the sense of 'Great'** (4 S. xi. 220; 1873).

Instances of *much* used in the sense of *great* are probably common. Thus, every Shropshire man must know of *Much* Wenlock, as distinguished from *Little* Wenlock. Three examples of this use of the word in English poetry at once occur to me :—

(1). 'A *muche* mon, me thouhte, lyk to myselue.'
*Piers the Plowman*, A. ix. 61.

From which interesting allusion we gather that the author of the poem was a *big* man, as regarded his stature.

(2). 'The *muckle* devil blaw ye south.'
Burns—*Author's Earnest Cry.*

(3). 'Rise, lass, and mak a clean fireside,
Put on the *muckle* pot.'
Mickle—*There's Nae Luck about the House.*

Besides which, the common surname, *Mitchell*, simply stands for *mickle*, i.e. a tall or big man; cf. Lat. *magnus*, &c. Observe that one quotation is from *Mickle!*

**95. 'Exceptio probat regulam'** (4 S. xi. 197; 1873).

I wish to point out that the phrase 'Exceptio probat regulam' involves no mistake, and is a maxim of perfectly sound sense. It means, 'The exception tests the rule,' a maxim of the highest value in all scientific investigations. The older English equivalent, 'The exception proves the rule,' had once the same signification, the use of *prove* for *test* being familiar to all readers of the Bible; as, e. g., in the wise advice of St. Paul that we should 'prove (i.e test) all things,' so that we may know how 'to hold fast that which is good.' Unhappily, the expression, 'The exception proves the rule,' has become meaningless to all who forget that it is an old, not a modern expression; and perhaps no really wise saying has ever been so frequently taken to mean utter nonsense. Every one who reflects for an instant must see that an exception does not prove, but rather tends to invalidate, a rule. It tests it, and we hence obtain one of three results: either (1) the exception can be perfectly explained, in which case it ceases to be an exception, and the rule becomes, in relation to it, absolute; or (2) the exception resists all explanation, because the rule itself is wrong; or (3) the exception resists explanation, not because the rule itself is wrong, but because the power to explain the exception fails, from a lack of sufficient knowledge.

In like manner, the proverb, 'The more haste, the worse speed,' is now often taken to mean, 'The more haste, the worse haste,' which is but harsh, and tends to nonsense. But, when we remember that *speed* really meant *success* in Old English, the sense becomes 'The more haste, the worse success,' which is a perfectly wise and sensible saying. So also 'God speed the plough' does not mean 'God hasten the plough,' but 'God prosper the plough.'

In the proverb 'God sends the shrewd cow short horns,' *shrewd* means mischievous or ill-tempered, not clever or intelligent.

In the proverb 'Handsome is as handsome does,' *handsome* means *neat*, with reference to skilfulness of execution, not beautiful in the usual modern sense. In 'Good wine needs no bush,' the *bush* is well known to be that which was tied to the end of an ale-stake.

In 'To buy a pig in a poke,' we have the old spelling of *pouch*, with the sense of *bag*.

And of course there are numerous other examples of the perfectly general rule, that all our proverbs have come down to us from olden times, and must be interpreted according to the sense of words in old, not in modern English.

### 96. Briga (4 S. xii. 457; 1873).

[N.B. This article is a skit upon the usual methods employed by guessing etymologists. Many readers, I believe, took it quite seriously!]

At the last reference W. B. traces a large number of English words from *briga*, which he says is from the root *earth*. Has he really secured the *right root*? Surely all the words which he mentions, and many more, are rather to be referred to the Latin *terra*. Thus *plough* and *breeches*, which he instances, are obviously not from *earth*, but from *terra*, as a little reflection will show. From *terra* would come *terrare*, to *tear* the earth (our English *tear*), and by the well-known interchange of *p* with *t* (cf. Gk. *tessares* with Æol. *pisures*) we get a dialectal form *perrare*, also to till the earth, whence *perratum* or *pratum*, a meadow, Eng. *prairie*. By the usual shifting of *r* (as in *bird*, from Old Eng. *brid*) we get *preare*; and, by the common change of *r* into *l*, *pleare*, a word adopted by the Anglo-Saxons as *pleogan*, to till; and hence our *plough*. From the same root, *pleogan*, come *play* and *ply*, and the adjective *pliant*. So, too, with *breeks* (*braccæ*). The compound word *terri-braccæ*, breeches to protect from the earth or soil, is the obvious origin of our *supposed* nautical word *tarry-breeks*, or, by loss of the first part of the word, *breeks*. The liability of these to *tear* (the connexion of which word with *terra* has been already shown) gives the verb to *break*, as also the substantive *brick*, literally *broken* pieces of earth. Just as we find *bacca* written for *vacca*, in Old Latin, we may suppose *breeks* to become *vreeks*, whence the Southern-English *vrock*, our standard English ?*frock*. By loss of *f*, comes the German *Rock*, also meaning coat, the garment which covers the *ridge* or back, since in Old English *rugge* often occurs with the sense of *back*.

*Rock* is clearly the same as *rug* or *rag*, also used for covering the body. All these, it will be observed, are obviously from the Latin *terra*. Then, again, the earth was regarded as an object of mystery or wonder, whence our *terror*; as, also, *terrier*, lit. the scarer, the dog who *terrifies* or scares the sheep. The English *drag* is known to be cognate with Lat. *trahere*; but this is a shortened form of *ter-rahere*, lit. to drag or draw along the ground; so that from the same root, *terra*, come also such words as *drag* or *draw*, *trail*, and, by loss of *t*, *rail* (*rails* still are laid along the *earth*); and by loss of *r*, *ail* or *ale* (made from the produce of *the earth*); by loss of *a*, *ill* (from the effects produced by ale), and so on. It is especially curious to see how W. B., not remembering the Latin *terra*, has failed to solve the word *Albion*. Granting that *Albion* is, as he says, from *arb*, heights, he must allow that *arb* or *arp* is merely a metathesis of the *pra* in *pratum*, the connexion of which with *terra* has been shown above. This is verified by observing the Latin *arbor*, lit. the fruit of the earth, just as our *tree* (Old Eng. *tre*) is short for *terre*, the old spelling of *terrae*, the genitive case of *terra*. I have thus shown that *tree*, *Albion*, *ill*, *ale*, *drag*, &c., are all from the Latin *terra*, and I am prepared to derive from this prolific root, not merely all the words which W. B. mentions, but *every word in our language*; so that, instead of referring all our words to a *few* roots, I would refer them all to *one* root, and that root is the Latin *terra*, and not the Armenian *ard*. If W. B. is serious, I am sure that my derivations are quite as convincing. But, alas, that English etymology should ever, in these days, be trailed through the dirt after such a fashion.

## 97. Why Adam means North, South, East, and West (5 S. i. 305; 1874).

In the *Dialogue of Solomon and Saturn*, ed. Kemble, p. 178, is the following singular passage :—' Tell me, whence was the name of Adam formed? *Answer.* I tell thee, of four stars. Tell me, how are they called? *Answer.* I tell thee, *Arthox, Dux, Arotholem, Minsymbrie*' (I give here Kemble's translation, instead of the Anglo-Saxon original, because it answers my purpose quite as well).

These names have never been explained, to my knowledge, and I confess that I never expected to know what they mean. There are no stars with such names.

But in the *Cursor Mundi*, ed. Morris, p. 42, is a passage, equally hopeless as it stands, to this effect:—' Hear now the reason of his name, why he was called *Adam*. In this name are laid four letters, that are derived from the four ways; so that *Adam* is as much as to say, as East, West, North, and South.' It is obvious that the initials of these words do *not* make up Adam in *English*.

The two passages, both unintelligible in themselves, completely explain each other; for, though these words do not spell Adam in English, they do so *in Greek*. Here, then, is the answer to the riddle; the 'four stars' is a mistake for the four 'quarters,' and the words, apparently so mysterious, are merely Arctos, Dusis, Anatole, Mesembria; ἄρκτος, δύσις, ἀνατολή, μεσημβρία. Moral: never *guess*, but wait for fresh information to turn up.

### 98. Shakespeare's Name (5 S. ii. 444; 1874).

What is meant by saying that 'Fewtarspeare is, doubtless, a local surname,' I cannot understand. Just as Shakespeare means a man who shakes a spear, just as Breakspear means one who breaks a spear, so Fewtarspeare means one who *fewtars* or *feutres* a spear, i. e. who lays it in rest.

'His *speare* he *feutred*, and at him it bore.'
F. Q. iv. 5, 45.

I do not see why English etymology should be considered a fit subject for such unintelligent guess-work.

[With Shake-spear and Fewtar-speare, cf. Wag-staff. I once saw the name Shake-shaft over a shop door at Lichfield.]

### 99. 'Otherwhiles' (5 S. ii. 435 ; 1874).

Certainly this word is nothing new. See Dr. Stratmann's *Old English Dictionary* (which correspondents should consult for themselves), where these references are given. *Otherwhile*, Layamon, 1. 7062 ; *Reliquiae Antiquae*, vol. i. p. 110 ; Robert of Gloucester, p. 100 ; *other hwule*, Ancren Riwle, p. 82 ; *other hwiles*, another reading, at the last reference. Besides which, I may add a reference to *Piers the Plowman*, B. xix. 99.

### 100. 'A Stick of Eels' (5 S. ii. 52 ; 1874).

The following quotation furnishes an answer to the query, how much is a *stick*?

'A *stick* of fish, a term applied to eels when strung on a row, " sic dicta, quod trajecta vimine (quod *stic* dicimus) connectabantur"; Spelman. A *stica* consisted of 25 eels, and 10 *sticæ* made a *binde*; Glanv. lib. ii. c. 9.'

This is a note by Sir F. Madden, reprinted in my edition of *Havelok the Dane*, s. v. *Stac*, in the Glossarial Index, p. 144.

### 101. English Etymology in 1875. (From a note upon 'Fangled' in *N. and Q.* 5 S. iii. 310.)

This brings me to the great principle to which I wish to draw attention, viz., that the publications of the Early English Text Society, the investigations of Mr. Ellis, the strictly scientific methods pursued at the present day in Greek and Latin etymology, and other similar aids, are fast tending to revolutionize, none too soon, the whole study of English etymology. I have great hope that we pioneers have done real good ; and that the next generation of philologists, applying to English the same strictly scientific methods as have already been applied to Latin and Greek, will make a clean sweep of the thousand and one ludicrous guesses with which even the best of our dictionaries are still encumbered, and will unhesitatingly reject, as useless lumber, all that is of the nature of guess-work, all that cannot be supported by ample, or, at any rate, by sufficient evidence. If in this process some of my work is swept away with the rest, I can fully forgive, by anticipation, those who weigh it and find it wanting. Etymology is, in fact, not a personal matter at all; if an etymology rests *merely* on the basis that so-and-so suggested it, it is rotten and useless; and I entirely repudiate the notion, so extremely common even in our best periodicals, that etymology is a mere system of bad puns, and that anything may be 'derived' from anything else, provided there is some 'apparent' outward likeness between the forms compared.

**102. The suffix -ster in English. I** (5 S. iii. 371; 1875).

See, on this suffix, Marsh's *Lectures on the English Language*, ed. Smith, 1862, pp. 207, 208, and the note at p. 217; Mätzner's *Eng. Gram.* i. 434; Loth's *Eng. Gram.* p. 309; Koch's *Eng. Gram.* iii. 47; and Morris's *Historical Outlines of English Accidence*, p. 89. The accounts given by Marsh and Koch are much more satisfactory, in my opinion, than that given by Dr. Brewer. The assertion that '*-ster* is not a female suffix at all, and never was'(?), argues a very slight acquaintance with our older literature. Granting that it was not exclusively so, and that, in the fourteenth century, the distinction between *-er* and *-ster* was not always well preserved, there are quite enough examples extant to show that the termination was very often used as a feminine suffix, and that, too, by evident design. Several examples will be found at the references cited above, to which I add the following. Lye and Manning's *Anglo-Saxon Dictionary* gives the following examples:—

'*Fithelere*, fidicen,' as distinguished from '*fithelstre*, fidicina';

*hearpere*, a harper, as distinguished from *hearpestre*, a female harper; *hoppere*, a dancer; *hoppestre*, a female dancer; *sangere*, a singer; *sangestre*, a female singer; *sēamestre*, a sempster; *tæppere*, a male tapster; *tæppestre*, a female tapster; *webba*, a male weaver; *webbestre*, a female weaver.

To some of these words references are given, and they may be found in Ælfric's *Glossary*, printed at the end of Somner's *A.-S. Dictionary*, and in another copy of the same, to be found in the Bodley MS. Junius 77; see also the MSS. of Ælfric's *Glossary* described by Wanley. Bosworth's *Dictionary* also gives *cennestre*, genitrix; *crencestre*, a female weaver; *lǣristre*, a female teacher; *myltestre*, meretrix (which occurs in the A.-S. version of Lev. xix. 29; Gen. xxxviii. 15; and Matt. xxi. 31). Many more examples will be found in the books cited above.

But in order to establish the case, one example is quite sufficient. We find, then, in the A.-S. version of the Gospels that the word *witega* occurs repeatedly in the sense of prophet. Thus, in St. Mark i. 2, we have, 'Swā āwriten is on þæs *witegan* bēc isaiam,'—as it is written in the book of the prophet Isaiah. But when it is intended to express the idea of prophetess instead of prophet, the feminine termination is duly added, as in St. Luke ii. 36, 'And Anna wæs *witegystre*, fanueles dohtor,'—and Anna was a prophetess, the daughter of Phanuel.

**103. The suffix -ster in English. II** (5 S. iii. 449; 1875).

It is quite true, at the same time, though it has long been notorious, that the termination *-ster* in a great many instances lost its feminine force, and, in some instances, never had that force at all. This was simply due to course of time, and probably in some measure to confusion with the Old French ending *-stre*, as seen in Chaucer's *idolastre* or *ydolastre*, in the sense of *idolater*. But we have had something like this before; see *N. and Q.* 1 S. vi. 409,

568 ; 3 S. iv. 350 ; especially the article at the first of these references.

Each word has its separate history, and should be kept apart from the rest; the chronology is, in each case, of the highest importance. There are some words, such as *bakester*, which appear in Anglo-Saxon, cf. A. S. *bæcestre*; there are others, such as *punster*, which are of modern formation; and there are others again, such as *lobster*, *holster*, which are not properly personal substantives at all. To show how necessary it is to take words separately, I will instance *lobster*. It is clear that A. S. *loppe*, a flea, North-Eng. *lop*, meant a *leaper*; and it is probable that the A. S. *loppestre* was made to match it, with the same signification of *leaper*, but with no very definite idea of gender, merely by way of giving the word a sort of sense. The alternative spelling *lopust* (for *loppestre*) makes it highly probable that the word was merely a vulgar adaptation of the Lat. *locusta* or *locusta marina*, as suggested in Mahn's Webster, in Wedgwood, and in E. Müller. Cf. *crayfish*, from *écrevisse*.

### 104. A Feat in Swimming (5 S. iv. 186 ; 1875).

In connexion with Captain Webb's achievement, recent as it is, it is well worthy of notice that the notion of swimming for a very protracted time is to be found, with full particulars, in the very oldest piece of writing which exists in the English language; proving, as I think, that our English race has always been familiar with the exercise. In the poem of Beowulf is a long and full account of the swimming match between Beowulf and Breca. I fear the description is exaggerated, as it tells us that these two athletes swam side by side for *five days*, whilst 'the ocean boiled with waves, with winter's fury'; or whilst, in the words of the original, 'geofon ȳthum wēol, wintres wylme.' At the end of the five days, says Beowulf, 'unc flōd tōdrāf,' the flood drave us two asunder; after which he met with some thrilling adventures, attacking and killing several sea-monsters with his sword, and (amongst the rest) slaying 'niceras nigene,' i. e. nine nickers, or water-demons; and finally he landed on the shores of Finland. The whole account in Thorpe's edition of *Beowulf*, pp. 35-40, is worth referring to. And I think we may congratulate our gallant countryman that, though he was unfortunately stung by a jelly-fish, he was not under the necessity of slaying nine nickers, nor of remaining, as Beowulf is *said* to have done, for more than *seven* days in the water.

### 105. Comets (5 S. iv. 146 ; 1875).

Milton has—
    'Like a *comet burn'd*
 That fires the length of Ophiuchus huge
 In the *Arctic* sky, and from his horrid hair
 Shakes *pestilence* and *war*.' —*P. L.* ii. 708.

In *Batman uppon Bartholome*, lib. viii. c. 32, we read that—

'*Cometa* is a starre beclipped with *burning* gleames, as Beda doth say, and is sodeinly bred, and betokeneth changing of kings, and is a token of *pestilence*, or of *war*, or of winds, or of great beate ... and they spread their beames toward the *North*, and never towards the West.'

With the phrase, 'changing of kings,' cf. *Paradise Lost*, i. 597, 598—
    'And with fear of change
 Perplexes monarchs.'

### 106. 'Tetter' (5 S. iv. 126 ; 1875).

The word is in *Hamlet*, i. 5. The German form *Zittermal* shows that *tetter* is a *Low* German (English or Dutch) form of the same word. Cf. A. S. *teter*.

'*I*mpetigo, Zerua and Zarua, called of the Greekes Lichen, of some Lichena. There are two kinds, the viscous scab and watrie is called a Ringworme, the other is a drye *Tettar*: this is infectious, and is soone taken by lyeing in an vncleane bedde. The drye scabbe commeth of melancholy, the wet commeth of putrified fleame and corrupt bloud.'—*Batman uppon Bartholome*, Addition to lib. vii. c. 49.

**107. 'Spit white'** (5 S. iv. 106; 1875.)

Falstaff says, ' If it be a hot day, and I brandish anything but a bottle, I would I might never *spit white* again.' This means, of course, 'be in perfect health again.' See the Addition to lib. vii. c. 29 of *Batman uppon Bartholome* (ed. 1582, fol. 97), where all kinds of spittle are described with reference to health :—' If the spettle be white viscus, the sickenesse commeth of fleame; if black ... of melancholy ... The whitte [*sic*] spéttle not knottie, signifieth *health.*'

[Dr. Schmidt, in his admirable Shakespeare Lexicon, observes—' Nares adduces some passages from contemporary writers to prove that to spit white was thought to be the consequence of intemperance in drinking; but he has forgotten to ascertain the colour of other people's spittle.' The remark is just; but our ancestors did not go by facts, but by opinions; and the above extract shows that there was a notion that people could spit ' black.' I leave my note as I wrote it, though it excited some derision; I know not why.]

**108. Cicero speaking Greek** (5 S. iv. 266; 1875).

' *Cassius.* Did Cicero say anything?
  *Casca.* Ay, he spoke Greek.'
                                          *Julius Caesar*, i. 2. 281.

Compare the following :—

' Wherefore when he [Cicero] came to Rome, at the first he proceeded very warily and discreetly, and did vnwillingly seeke for any Office, and when he did, he was not greatly esteemed: for they commonly called him the *Grecian* and *scholer*, which are two words which the Artificers (and such base Mechanicall people at Rome) have euer readie at their tongues' end.'—North's *Plutarch*, 'Life of Cicero,' ed. 1612, p. 861 ; see the whole passage.

[This note afterwards appeared in Mr. W. Aldis Wright's

edition of *Julius Caesar*, published in 1878. But of course Mr. Wright observed the coincidence for himself.]

### 109. Treenware (5 S. iv. 331; 1875).

Without doubt the explanation of *treenware* by 'earthen vessels' is, at least etymologically, incorrect. Of course, it ought to mean 'wooden vessels.' But the explanation occurs in *both* the early editions of Ray's Collection, and it hardly seemed to me to be worth a note. It is possible, after all, that Ray noted correctly the use of the word as current *in his own day*, for nothing is more common than a change of meaning in English words in course of time. Names are often retained long after the things which they denote have suffered alteration. Thus, a *tureen* (formerly *terrene*) means a vessel made of earth; but for all that, people do not hesitate to talk of a '*silver* soup-tureen,' for the simple reason that the vessels which were once made of earth are now often made of silver. Similarly, the name of *treenware* may very well have been continued in use long after the vessels themselves had ceased to be invariably of wood.

I add a good example of *tre* in the old sense of *wood*. In Trevisa's *Description of Britain* (*Specimens of English*, ed. Morris and Skeat, p. 239) we have a description of a petrifying well that turnéd wooden things into stone:—
'Thar ys also a pond that turneth *tre* into yre [*iron*], and [*if*] hyt be ther-ynne al a yer [*year*]; and so tren [*pieces of wood*] buth yschape [*are made*] into whestones' [*whetstones*].

### 110. 'Nuncheon.' I (5 S. iv. 366; 1875).

The etymology of this word is a puzzle of long standing[1]. The guess-work writers have long ago made the desperate

---

[1] It had been solved, previously and independently, by Mr. Walford; see the next article.

attempt to connect it with *noon-shun,* because (note the 'because,' that marks the work of your guesser) labourers *shun* the heat of *noon* when they eat their *nuncheon.* But of course it is obvious that the labourer does not shun the noon itself, but only the heat of it. When the etymology of a word is unknown, there is but one thing to do, viz. to wait in patience till the light comes. In this case the first ray of light came when Mr. Riley printed his valuable and well-edited *Memorials of London.* We there find, at p. 265:

'These donations for drink to workmen are called in Letter-Book G, fol. iv. (27 Edw. III), *nonechenche,* probably "noon's quench," whence the later *nuncheon* or *luncheon.*'

This half solves the difficulty, as it gives the old form of the word; but the suggestion of *quench* is rather too much of a wrench. The reader of Middle English may here recognize the word *schenche,* meaning a drink; and the verb *schenchen* (A. S. *scencan*), to pour out drink. Cf. G. *schenk,* a cup-bearer, in English a *skinker*; and *schenken,* to *skink,* or pour out liquor. Thus *nonechenche* simply means the *noon-drink,* with the implied sense of its being poured out and carried round in fixed quantities, in accordance with the skinker's known duties. Thus *nuncheon* is merely *noon-skink,* with the usual palatalisation of the *k* to *ch* which so abounds in English. When *nuncheon* lost all meaning, popular etymology, always at work to corrupt, desperately confused it with the *lump* of bread instead of the cup of drink, thus producing the absurd *luncheon,* which has so baffled all inquirers.

[Similarly, the A. S. *nōn-mete,* M. E. *nōnmete, nonmet,* i. e. noon-meat, is now the Southern prov. E. *nammet, nummet,* a luncheon. See *nuncheon* and *luncheon* in my *Etym. Dict.,* larger edition.]

111. 'Nuncheon.' II (5 S. iv. 398; 1875).

It is evident, from Mr. Skeat's note, that he was not aware that the same etymology of the word *nuncheon* had been given by me, about twenty-five years ago, in the *Proceedings of the Bury and Suffolk Archaeological Institute*. I have not the volume by me, but I believe it was in vol. i. p. 180. It will there be seen to be probable that the word *noonscench* came to mean something to eat, as well as something to drink, between meals.

W. S. WALFORD, F.S.A.

112. 'Nuncheon.' III (5 S. iv. 434; 1875).

I am glad to know that Mr. Walford had already solved this word, and cheerfully accord to him whatever merit attaches to the first enunciation of the truth concerning it. I had noted it some years ago, independently, but omitted to publish the result.

Mr. K. has made a curious mistake; for his parallel does not hold. He thinks that *chenche* is put for *quench*, because we find *church* put for *kirk*. With a slight amendment I accept his reasoning, and admit that I do not see how *chenche* can come out of *quench*, because I am quite sure that *church* is not a corruption of *quirk*. *Chenche* is an instance of that common substitution of *ch* for *sh* or *sch* with which all readers of Early English manuscripts must be familiar.

There was not only the term *nonechenche* for *noon-drink*, but *none-mete* for *noon-meat*, or noon-eating. See Halliwell's *Dictionary*. The Spanish words cited by Mr. Peacock are hardly to the point. Mere resemblances prove little, and it is far more likely that *luncheon* was an extension of the provincial-English *lunch*, meaning a lump, than that our labourers took to talking Spanish.

The Spanish word *loncha*, meaning a slice of meat, not

a lump of it, was suggested by Minshew, and rejected by Richardson; and rightly, in my opinion.

**113. 'Awn'd,' 'Aund'** (5 S. iv. 384; 1875).

In Halliwell's excellent *Dictionary* is the following entry:—

'*Awn'd*, ordained; Yorksh. Kennett (MS. Lansd. 1033) gives the example—I am *awn'd* to ill luck, i.e. it is my peculiar destiny or fortune.'

In Ray's *Glossary of North Country Words* is the entry:

'*Aund*, ordained; forsan per contractionem. I am *aund* to this luck; *i.e.* ordained.'

In reprinting Ray's collection for the English Dialect Society I added the note, by way of protest against such a guess, that '*aund* being short for *ordained* is out of the question.' I now 'make a note' that the true etymology has appeared.

Mr. Atkinson, in his *Cleveland Glossary*, has the right idea. He connects the word with the 'O. N. *audid*,' meaning thereby the Icelandic *auðit*. But if any one who consults Cleasby and Vigfusson's *Icelandic Dictionary* will (after finding *auðit* on p. 31) just turn over the leaf and examine the word *auðna*—to be ordained by fate—he will find there all that he wants. He will also find that the verb *auðna* is a derivative of the substantive *auðr*, fate, of which the Old Swedish form was *öde*. This is the very result which Mr. Atkinson suspected. I have merely supplied the missing link in the chain of his evidence. [This provincial word is not in the *New Eng. Dict.*]

**114. 'Vant'** (5 S. iv. 455; 1875).

With respect to the suggestion that *vant* may have been 'a stupid churchwarden's spelling of *font*,' I would suggest that this peculiar spelling might have been due to the fact of the churchwarden's being familiar with the dialect of his county. Perhaps he may even have been familiar with

English literature. The spelling is not new, but may be found in Robert of Gloucester, who wrote in 1298. In Hearne's edition of that poet we find (under the word 'vonge' in the Glossary) this note: 'To *vang*, in some parts of England, is even now used for "to answer at the font as godfather," particularly in Somersetshire, where Mr. Somner, in his *Dictionary*, observes that the country people have this expression "he vanged to me at the vant," i. e. "in baptisterio pro me suscepit."' It is instructive to find that, in some cases, this substitution of *v* for *f* has been accepted as standard English. The word *fitches* (A. V. Isa. xxviii. 25; Ezek. iv. 9) has been supplanted by the South-country form *vetches*. The word *fat* (Joel ii. 24; iii. 13), with its derivative *winefat* (Isa. lxiii. 2; Mark xii. 1), has been ousted by the Kentish [or Dutch] form *vat*, with the derivative *winevat*, probably owing to the influence of the hop interest. We all use *vixen* (for *fixen*) as the feminine of *fox*. The word *fane* (A. S. *fana*) is now spelt *vane*. Milton turned *fans* into *vans* (*P. L.* ii. 927). Shakespeare wrote *vade* for *fade* (Sonnet 54). But I do not allow that these poets were 'stupid.'

## 115. Glove (5 S. iv. 409; 1875).

The notion that *glove* is of Gaelic origin is easily shown to be out of the question. Dr. Mackay knows, as well as I do, that there is no such word in Gaelic as *ceillamh* with the sense of *glove*; or if there is, perhaps he will kindly give us the *reference to the passage in which he has found it*. The Gaelic for *glove* is *lamhainn*, from *lamh*, a hand. There is no mystery about the Gaelic words *ceill* or *lamh*. The first is cognate with the Latin *celare*, A. S. *helan*, and, in the form *hele*, is still one of the commonest of our dialectal words. If we had wished to express the idea in English, we could have said *hele-hand*, or *helland*, without taking the slightest trouble to search for the Gaelic equivalent. The derivation of *glove* from the Icelandic *glófi* is, again, just one of those mistakes which are made by those to whom chronology is of no importance ; for it just so happens that the borrowing has been in the other direction, and that the Icelandic *glófi* was borrowed from England. I know of nothing so useless as the attempt that is made by so many to 'derive' English words from some other language. Are there, I would ask, *no* native words? Must we never rest till we have chased every word to death, and are we to write ourselves down as a nation whose language has not *a single native word in it?* Nothing can be clearer than that *glove* is a word of our own. We can boast the oldest monument in all Teutonic literature (the Mœso-Gothic fragments being excepted), viz. the poem of Beowulf. And in this poem we find the word 'glōf'; see Thorpe's edition, p. 140, l. 4177. How could the word *glōf* have been known in Anglo-Saxon, if, as Dr. Mackay pretends, it was a corruption of a compound Gaelic word, of which I can find no proof that it existed, till it pleased our Gaelic friend to coin it ? I think writers would do well to let English etymology alone unless they can take pains with their chronology, and can condescend to give quotations in place of inventions.

It is quite a mistake to suppose that Gaelic is the only language that lends itself to a system of verbal quibbles. When once we begin to *coin* etymologies, any language will serve the turn. For every Gaelic etymology that Dr. Mackay can invent, I can easily invent one in some other tongue that will look quite as well. Take, for instance, *glove*, and try a Sanskrit dictionary. I do this, and find at once that *kalāpa* means a quiver or case; see the *Mahábhárata*, 3, 11454. Suppose it pleased me to say that *glove* is an obvious corruption of *kalāpa*? The change from one form to the other is not very violent, and the change in meaning is conceivable. Or again, if we try Greek, we at once light upon καλύπτειν, to hide or cover. Or again, the Icelandic *làfi*, the palm, comes as near to *glove* as the Gaelic *lamh* does. But I am very strongly of opinion that this sort of guessing is (or ought to be) out of date, and that it is high time for those who propose 'derivations' to propose them in a credible form.

### 116. 'Ghauts.' I (5 S. iv. 456; 1875).

Beyond all question, the Whitby *gaut* is a mere variation of *gote*, a drain. Cf. Icel. *gjóta*, Dan. *gyde*, a narrow lane, and see '*gote* or water-schetelys, *goote* or water-schedyllys, *aquagium, sinoglocitorium,*' in *Prompt. Parv.* Another form of the word is *gut*, a channel; every Cambridge rowing man knows whereabouts on the Cam to find 'The Gut.' The root is the A. S. *gēotan*, to pour, cognate with the Greek χέειν. Much more might be added, but perhaps it will suffice to learn the lesson that *ghaut*, as a mis-spelling of *gaut*, furnishes an additional instance of the absurdity whereby *gost* has been turned into *ghost*, and *gastly* and *agast* into *ghastly* and *aghast*. It is odd that *g* should be unable to run alone in all cases.

[The *Whitby Glossary* (E. D. S.) gives '*Gauts* or *Gotes*; see *Gooats*.' Also '*Gooats* or *Gotes*, openings or slopes from the streets to the water-side. Spelt *goutes* in Camden.']

### 117. 'Ghauts.' II (5 S. v. 114; 1876).

C. S. G. confidently affirms that *ghaut* cannot be another form of *gote* or *gut*, because the latter form *always* means a canal or drain for water, and has no other signification. I commend to his consideration the following instance, which I found in almost the first book I consulted, viz. Richardson's *Dictionary* :—

'You pass a narrow *gut* between two stone terrasses, that rose above your head, and which were crowned by a line of pyramidal yews.'—Walpole, 'On Gardening.'

Will C. S. G. seriously contend that *gut* in this passage means a channel for water?

When we find in Icelandic the word *gjóta*, a narrow lane, taking the same form as *gjóta*, to pour; when we find in Danish *gyde*, a narrow lane, again taking the same form as *gyde*, to pour, what is the use of going to India[1] for an explanation that can be had from Denmark?

I suppose that the spelling *ghaut* (of course it should be *gaut*) originated with some one else who had learnt a little geography at school, and *chose to spell it so.* It looks as if it originated with some one ignorant of Anglo-Saxon, Icelandic, and Danish. What is the authority for it?

### 118. Writer's Errors (5 S. v. 206; 1876).

As the phrase 'clerical errors' has by some been deemed ambiguous, I would point out that it can be avoided by saying 'errors of the scribe,' or 'errors of the writer,' or simply 'writer's errors.' To say that such or such a mistake was due to 'a writer's error,' or to an 'error in writing,' is intelligible enough, and is distinct from an author's error on the one hand, and from a printer's error, or error of the press, on the other. I have seen 'scribal error' used, but the adjective sounds, to me, rather clumsy.

I was reminded of this by having just discovered one of the oddest writer's errors I ever remember to have seen. I had occasion to quote the text, from 1 Tim. vi. 10, that 'the love of money is the root of all evil[2],' and just as I was writing it out, some noise called off my attention. On looking again at the MS. I found, to my great surprise, that, instead of 'money,' I had inadvertently written 'woman.' I am glad the quotation did not go to press in that remarkable form.

[1] I. e. the *G*hauts, from the Hindustani *ghāt*
[2] In my note on the *T*itle of the Pardoneres *T*ale.

### 119. Alliterative Poetry (5 S. v. 224; 1876).

Many of your readers who are aware that much of our early poetry is alliterative may be at a loss where to find an easy example of the force and swing of it. I have ventured to throw together the following lines by way of specimen, in imitation rather of the fourteenth and fifteenth centuries than of the earlier examples. All that the reader need observe is that there are commonly three emphatic syllables in a line which begin with the same letter. To these syllables a special stress may be given, and the result is a metre of a rough but forcible character, by no means unsuited to the genius of the language. If the stress falls upon initial vowels, the vowels need not be the same; and, in fact, are most often different. It will be understood that the subject is chosen in accordance with the national character of the metre.

#### An Englishman's Song.

A curse on the croakers who cowardly prattle
How England is aging to abject abasement,
No longer a leader, no law to the nations!
Though foul birds defile thus the nest that defends them,
The hearts of our heroes beat high in their yearning,
Where dangers are densest. to dash to the onset!
Sweet Peace let us prize, with her pleasures and treasures,
Nor ween to wage wars of a wanton aggression;
Ever firm for defence, not defiant in folly,
Yet weighing with wisdom the words that we utter,
As conscious, though calm, that our counsels are heeded.
We rest, but we rust not: once roused into action,
The life of the old land will leap up in earnest,
With prayers to the Prime Source of progress in goodness,
With trust in the triumph of truth, though it tarry,
And woe to the workers of wicked devices!
The hate of all harm that is hostile to justice
Still steels us to sternness and steady endeavour.
Unfolding the flag that is feared by oppressors,
We dare to the death, never daunted by evil,
Still foremost in fighting where Freedom leads onward!

### 120. Chronology of English (5 S. v. 302; 1876.)

With the editor's permission, I propose to contribute, occasionally, some remarks on the chronology of English, not by way of proposing anything new, but of tabulating what is old, in a more accessible form than heretofore. Our etymology is, perhaps, in want rather of a Kepler than Newton.

One of the most important matters is the date of the introduction of French words. Dr. Morris has given us a most important list of words introduced into English from French before A.D. 1300, at p. 337 of his *Historical Outlines of English Accidence*, but I find it wants to be recast into an alphabetical form before it can be *easily* used. I now attempt a first instalment of such work, in a form that seems to me more convenient.

*List I.*—French words in the *Saxon Chronicle*, with their dates (I have verified both spellings and dates, and added the modern forms): Cuntesse (countess), 1140. Curt (a court), 1154. Dubbade (dubbed as a knight), 1086. Emperice (empress), 1140. Justise (justice), 1137. Miracles, 1137. Pais (peace), 1135. Prisun (prison), 1137. Priuiligies (privileges), 1137. Processiun, 1154. Rentes (rents of lands), 1137. Standard, 1138. Tresor (treasure), 1137. Tur (tower), 1140.

I am surprised to find that Dr. Morris has omitted the word *charity*. This occurs in the true Old French form, viz. *carited*, in 1137. It ought decidedly to be included in the list; so ought *castel*[1] (castle), 1053, 1069, 1075; and *serfis* (service), 1070. Repeated in the shortest form we here have authority for these words:—castle, charity, countess, court, dub, empress, justice, miracle, peace, prison, privilege, procession, rent, service, standard, treasure, tower.

---

[1] *Castel* is of French origin, according to *K*luge, though it occurs in the A. S. *G*ospels.

*List II.*—French words in *Old English Homilies*, ed. Morris, first series. This volume contains several pieces, and the lists of French words in each are given separately by Dr. Morris. For convenience, I throw all into one list, with symbols to give the references, which are to the *pages* of the volume. The pieces are:—'Lambeth Homilies,' before 1200, denoted by *l. h.*; 'An Orison of our Lord,' about 1220, *o. ld.*; 'An Orison of our Lady,' *o. ly.*; 'A Lofsong (Hymn of Praise) of our Lady,' *l. ly.*; 'A Lofsong of our Lord,' *l. ld.*; 'Soul's Ward,' *s. w.*; 'Wooing of our Lord,' *w. l.*

The words are these, omitting some which I shall discuss afterwards. I have verified the spellings, added the meanings, and, in one or two places, corrected the references:—

    Abandun (in subjection), o. ld., 189.
    Asottie (to besot), l. h., 17.
    Beastes (beast's), w. l., 277.
    Blanchet (fine wheaten flour), l. h., 53.
    Buffet (both as vb. and sb.), w. l., 281.
    Buffetunge (buffeting), l. ly., 207.
    Cachepol (catchpoll), l. h., 97.
    Calenges (2 p. s. challengest), w. l., 275.
    Chaumbre (chamber), w. l., 285.
    I-cheret (pp. lit. cheered, i.e. having the appearance), s. w., 257.
    Cherite (charity), o. ly., 199; l. h., 69.
    Cherubine (cherubim), o. ly., 191.
    Ciclatune (a rich stuff, mentioned in Chaucer's *Sir Thopas*, o. ly., 193.
    Clerk, l. h., 133.
    Crune (crown, sb.), w. l., 281.
    Cruneth (crowns), Crunede (crowned, pt. t.), s. w., 247; l. h., 129.
    Crununge (crowning), l. ly., 207.
    Cunestable (constable), s. w., 247.
    Cunfessurs (confessors), s. w., 261.
    Cunfort (comfort), o. ld., 185.
    Cunig (coney, rabbit; cf. O. F. *conil*), l. h., 181.
    Debonairte, w. l., 269, 275; Deboneirschipe, w. l., 275.
    Delit (delight, sb.), o. ld., 187.

Derennedes (2 p. didst fight out; Chaucer's *dereyne* or *darrayne*), w. l., 285).
Dol (sorrow), w. l., 285.
Druri (love-token), w. l., 271.
Druth (love), w. l., 269.
Eise (ease), w. l., 287.
Erites (heretics), l. h., 143.
Ermine, l. h., 181.
Ewangeliste, l. h., 81; l. ld., 209.
*F*als (false), o. ld., 185.
*F*lum (river, Lat. *flumen*), l. h., 141.
Font (in fon-stan *for* fontstan, i. e. font-stone), l. h., 73.
Fou (yellow, Fr. *fauve*), l. h., 181.
Fructe (fruit), l. h., 7.
*G*entile (gentle), Gentiller, Gentileste, w. l., 273.
*G*race, l. ly., 207; s. w., 255; w. l., 275.
Hardi (bold, hardy), w. l., 271.
Jugulere (juggler), l. h., 29.
*K*eiser (emperor), pl. Keiseres, w. l., 271; s. w., 261.
Krune (crown, sb.), o. ly., 193; see Crune.
I-kruned (crowned), o. ly., 193.
Large (liberal), w. l., 271; l. h., 143.
Largesce (liberality), w. l., 269.
Lechurs (lechers), l. h., 53.
Lettres (letters), w. l., 283.
Liureisun (delivery, award), l. h., 85.
Mealles (malls, mallets), s. w., 253.
Manere (manner), l. h., 51.
Medicine, o. ld., 187 [*not* 185].
Meister (master), l. h. 41; Meistre, s. w., 247; Meoster s. w. 257.
Meistreth (mastereth), s. w., 247.
Meosure (measure), s. w., 247; Mesure, 255.
Merci, l. h., 43; l. ld., 209.
Merciable (merciful), l. ld., 211.
Mesaise (misease), w. l., 279.
Noble, w. l., 273.
Noblesce (nobility), w. l., 269.
Obedience, l. ld., 213.
Offrien (to offer), l. h., 87; I-offred (offered), 87.
• Orison, see Ureisun.
Paie (v. to pay, satisfy), w. l., 285.
Palefrai (palfrey), l. h., 5.
Paradise, o. ly., 191, 193; Parais, l. h., 61.

## CHRONOLOGY OF ENGLISH. 101

Passiun, l. h., 119; l. ly., 205; w. l., 275.
Piler (pillar), w. l., 281.
Pouerte (poverty), l. h., 143.
Poure (poor), w. l., 277; Pourere (poorer), 277.
Praie (sb. prey), w. l., 273.
Prei (pray thou), w. l., 287.
Preoouin (to prove), s. w., 249.
Prince, w. l., 281.
Pris (price, praise), l. ly., 205.
Prisun (prisoner, not prison), w. l., 273.
Priuete (privity), o. ld., 185.
Processiun, l. h., 5 [*not* 3].
Prophete, l. h., 5.
Prud (proud), l. h., 5; pl. *prude*, l. h., 143; *prude* (pride), l. ly., 205.
Psalm, Psalter; see Salm, Saltere.
Ribauz (ribalds), w. l., 279.
Riche, l. h., 53; Richere, w. l., 271.
Robbedes (didst rob), w. l., 273; I-robbet (pp. robbed), s. w., 247.
Rubbere (robber), l. h., 29 [*not* 19]; Rupere, l. h., 29.
Sabeline (sable, fur), l. h., 181.
Sacrement, l. ly., 207; pl. Sacremens, l. h., 5.
Sacreth (consecrates), l. ly., 207; I-sacred, l. ld. 209.
Salm (psalm), l. h., 73.
Saltere (psalter), l. h., 7 [*not* 5]; Sauter, l. h., 155; Sawter, l. ld., 215.
Salue (salvation), o. ld., 187.
Salui (to save), o. ld., 189; Unsauuet (unsaved), o. ld., 187; Sauuin (to save), 187.
Schurges (scourges), w. l., 283.
Seinte (saint), l. h., 131.
Semblant (semblance), s. w., 247.
Seraphine (seraphs), o. ly., 191.
Sermonen (vb. to discourse), l. h., 81.
Seruise (service), o. ly., 193.
Seruunge (serving), l. ld., 215; Of-seruunge (deserving), 215; Un-ofserued (undeserved), 215.
Sottes (sots), l. h., 29.
Spuse (spouse), w. l., 277; Spus-had (matrimony), l. h., 143.
Treitur (traitor), w. l., 279.
Tresor (treasure), s. w., 247; Tresur, 247.
Tresun (treason), w. l, 279.
Trones (thrones), s. w., 261.

*T*urnen (to turn), l. ld., 213; A-turnet, s. w., 257.
Ureisun (orison), o. ld., 183; Ureisuns, l. h., 51.
Warant (sb. warrant, guard), l. ld., 211.

This list does not include the following, which seem to me to be mistaken or uncertain. *Carpe* (to speak), w. l., 287; possibly from Lat. *carpere*, but proof of it in *French* is wanting; there is an Icelandic *karpa*, to boast, brag. *Elmesse* (alms), clearly A. S. *ælmesse*, introduced long before this, and found in the A. S. version of the Gospels. *Messe* (mass) is A. S. *mæsse*; *Munt* (mount) is A. S. *munt*, both used long ere this. *Munek, Munuch* (monk), A. S. *munuc*, direct from *monachus*. *Ocquerne* (a squirrel), l. h., 181; which is A. S. *acwern*. *Strete*, which goes back to the time of the Romans in England... On the other hand, I would insert *chatels* (chattels, wealth), w. l., 271.

I repeat the list, partly modernized, marking by italics the words in the *Chronicle*, and by a dagger those that are obsolete:—

Abandon, assot, beast, blanchett†, buffet, *castle*, catchpoll, challenge, chamber, *charity*, chattel, cheer, cherubim, ciclatoun†, clerk, comfort, coney, confessor, constable, crown, crowning, debonair, delight, darraynet†, doolt†, drutht†, drury†, ease, ermine, evangelist, fals, flum†, font, fout, fruit, gentle, grace, hardy, juggler, keiser†, large, largesse, lecher, letter, livreison†, mall (mallet), manner, master, measure, medicine, mercy, merciable†, misease†, noble, noblesse†, obedience, offer, orison, palfrey, paradise, passion, pay, pillar, poor, poverty, pray, prey, price, prince, *prison*, privity, *procession*, prophet, proud, prove, psalm, psalter, ribald, rich, rob, sable (fur), sacret, sacrament, saint, save, scourge, semblant†, seraphin, sermon, serve, *service*, sot, spouse, throne, traitor, treason, *treasure*, turn, warrant.

* Lists like these, I venture to think, give us a surer footing in attempting to make our way amidst the difficulties that attend English etymology.

**121. 'As drunk as mice'** (5 S. v. 314; 1876).

The explanation is very simple. A mouse is a small animal, and it takes very little to make him extremely drunk. The phrase is familiar to readers of Chaucer. See his *Knightes Tale*, l. 402; and my note on the same.

**122. 'Buft' and 'Miff'** (5 S. vi. 114; 1876).

*Buft* is a mere variation of *buff*, to stammer, which is duly entered in the *Herefordshire Glossary*. In the east of England we have *buffle* and *boffle* with the same meaning. Hence the familiar *buffer*, a stammerer, or secondarily, a bungler. Lydgate has *buffard*, with the sense of foolish fellow. All these terms are in Halliwell. Cf. O. Fr. *bufer*, to puff, and our own *puff*. Chaucer uses *buf* to denote the sound of eructation. The verb *to buff* also means to strike with a rebound, whence a *buffet* (a blow) and the railway *buffer*.

*Miff*, a tiff, is common in many counties. It is entered in Halliwell as known to various dialects, but is omitted in the *Herefordshire Glossary*.

**123. 'Mill' in the sense of 'Conflict'** (5 S. vi. 186; 1876).

The word *mill* is generally regarded as a slang term, but it was not always so. It is a contraction of the old Lowland Scottish *mellè* or *mellay*, a conflict, fight, battle, which was merely borrowed from the Old French *meslee*, signifying (1) a mixture, (2) a fray. In other words, *mill* is still in use in the refined form *mêlée*. Jamieson gives the verb *mell*, to intermeddle, to join in battle, showing the shortened form of it. In Barbour's *Bruce* (vii. 622 in my edition) it is said that Clifford and Vaux came to blows, and that they *maid a melle*, or in other words, 'had a *mill*.' The derivation is, accordingly, from the Lat. *misculare*, which is from *miscere*. In a fray, the combatants are sometimes considerably 'mixed up.'

Perhaps I ought to add that, at school, at a time when it was generally believed that all English was derived from Greek and Latin, we were taught to regard *mill* as a shortened form of the Greek ἄμιλλα; and even to this day there are many whose only notion of etymology is, that any connexion suggested by a mere jingle of sound is superior to all historical investigation.

### 124. 'Edyllys be' (5 S. vi. 209; 1876).

After just ten years, I think I have hit upon a possible, perhaps a probable, solution of this phrase, which seems hitherto to have baffled every one. It occurs in Mr. Furnivall's *Babees Book*, p. 22, note 14, where a tract for teaching children courtesy is thus entitled. One title of the tract is *The Lytylle Childrenes Lytil Boke*, and the other is given by the line, 'Lernythe thys boke that ys called *Edyllys be.*' My view of the matter is that it means 'these be secrets,' and thus the phrase means no more than 'learn these secrets which will teach you true courtesy.' This idea pervades the whole tract. I proceed to show how it is possible for the word *edyllys* to mean 'secrets,' though I should be prepared to maintain that the word is not very correctly applied, but only used, in a freak, by a writer who scarcely knew the true sense of a word which, even in the fifteenth century, was obsolescent. Even if my solution be incorrect, it will teach something by the way, and afford some corrections for the dictionaries.

The A. S. *hȳdels* means a hiding-place. It is not very common, perhaps, but regularly derived from *hȳdan*, to hide. It occurs in the Rushworth MS. of the Northumbrian Gospels, where the phrase 'speluncam latronum' (Mark xi. 17) is glossed by 'cofa *vel* hydels ðeafana,' a cove or a hiding-place of thieves. Upon this I would observe as follows:—

1. Mr. Wedgwood, in his long article on *cove*, ignores

the A. S. *cofa*, which, however, is cited by Mahn and E. Müller.

2. In Lye's *Dictionary* the reference for *cofa* is wrongly given as 'Mat. xi. 17.' For 'Mat.' read 'Mk.'

3. In Bosworth's *Dictionary* the reference is still more wrongly given as 'Mat. xi. 1.'

4. The word *hȳd-els* belongs to the set of substantives with the suffix *-els*, on which see March's *A.-S. Grammar*, p. 120. Other examples are:—*rǣdels*, a riddle; *metels*, a dream; *byrigels*, a sepulchre; and others, for which see Koch, *Englische Grammatik*, iii. 44.

5. The ending in *s* is deceptive; such words are easily mistaken for plurals, just as *eaves* is often mistaken for a plural. Yet the plural *eveses* occurs in *Piers the Plowman*, B. 17. 227.

6. Mr. Halliwell, in his *Dictionary*, has fallen, I think, into the trap. He gives *hidel* as a singular substantive, though it is quite an improper form, and the sole example which he offers is a sentence saying that 'they went and helde thame in *hidils*,' i. e., in a hiding-place. See several more examples in Stratmann, *s. v. hudels*, which is the form which the word takes in the *Ancren Riwle*.

7. Hence, naturally enough, as the word became obsolescent, the false form *hidel* or *hiddel* arose, with a false plural *hideles* or *hiddelis*. Of this there is an example in Barbour's *Bruce* (bk. v. l. 306, of my edition), where Sir James Douglas is said to have lurked 'in hyddilis and in preuatè,' that is, in hiding-places and in privacy. Here *-is* is the usual Lowland Scottish plural ending, used as a false interpretation of the *s* in the A. S. suffix *-els*.

8. The word *hiddel* being once thus manufactured, the sense of it had to be modified. It was then supposed to mean 'a secret.' The proof is in the existence of the adverb *hiddil* or *hidlins*, used in the sense of secretly, whilst the men of Perthshire and Fife developed the verb *to hiddle*,

in the sense of to conceal or keep secret. For these words see Jamieson's *Dictionary*.

9. I conclude that, *hiddil* being thus at length falsely formed, and supposed to mean 'a secret,' the word *hiddilis* would, of course, at times mean 'secrets.' The dropping of the *h* would give *idillis* or *ydyllys*, from which the change to *edyllys* is easy enough. We have just such changes in the case of the A. S. *yrnan*, to run, which is spelt *irnen*, *urnen*, *eornen* (all three), in Layamon, and *ernen* in the *Castle of Love*, l. 730, whilst the *h* appears in the Somersetshire form *to hirn*.

10. If it be granted that *edyllys* can mean secrets, there is little difficulty in *edyllys be* being used to mean 'these be secrets.'

[I find no reference to *edyllys* in the *New Eng. Dictionary*. Cf. *hidel-like*, secretly, in Genesis and Exodus, 2882; and see *hudels* in Stratmann.]

### 125. 'Wicks' of the Mouth (5 S. vi. 271; 1876).

I would beg leave to recommend that all who are in search of information concerning provincial English words should consult Halliwell's *Dictionary*. I have long observed that it is very rarely that words are inquired about which are not to be found there. In the present case, '*Wikes*, the corners of the mouth,' is duly inserted therein.

The word was noted by Ray more than two hundred years ago. See the reprint of Ray's *Collection* in the English Dialect Society's publications, p. 74.

Thoresby, in 1703, made the note, '*Wawks, the*, or corners of the mustachios.' This is also reprinted in the same volume, p. 108.

In Bailey's *Dictionary*, ed. 1735, is the entry, *The wikes of the mouth*, the corners of the mouth, N. C.'; where 'N. C.' means 'North Country.'

Brockett, in the first edition of his *North Country Words*, in 1825, has '*Wiks, wicks*, corners; as, the *wiks* of the mouth. Su.-Goth. *wik*, angulus.'

I find it also in Grose's *Glossary*, ed. 1790; in the *Teesdale Glossary*, 1849; in Mr. Atkinson's *Cleveland Glossary*; in the *Whitby Glossary*, where it is also spelt *weaks*; and I suppose it may be found in half a dozen other books, as it is not likely that a glossary of Northern English would omit it.

The word is Scandinavian, viz. Icel. *vik*; Old Swedish *wik*, a corner; Dan. *mund-vig*, the corner of the mouth. It is closely related to a verb which is represented by the Icel. *vikja*, to turn, to recede; cf. G. *weichen*, Gk. εἴκειν.

### 126. Fen: Fend (5 S. vi. 412; 1876).

The exclamation 'fen placings' is short for 'I fend placings,' i.e. I forbid them. *Fend* is used for *defend* in Middle English (see Halliwell); and *defend* in olden times often meant to forbid. In place of *fen*, some boys say 'fain;' hence the unmeaning expression, 'fain I,' used to signify 'I decline that.' It really stands for 'I forbid you to choose me.'

### 127. The phrase 'He dare not.' I (5 S. vii. 173; 1877).

I wish that correspondents who are zealous for the purity of English would learn a little about the matter before proceeding to lay down the law. The phrase 'He *dare* not' (though, perhaps, going out of fashion) is of course quite right. *Dare* is one of the verbs which use an old past tense for a present, and 'he *dares*' is, grammatically, as bad as 'he *mays*,' or 'he *cans*,' or 'he *shalls*.' This fact is perfectly familiar to any one who has ever seen an old English MS. of any value or age. The appearance of 'he dares' in a thirteenth-century or even in a fourteenth-century MS. would brand it as a forgery, just as poor Chatterton thought that *its* was good fifteenth-century English. The phrase 'He dear' occurs in *Beowulf*, l. 684, which I do not think could have been written by 'one of the Kingsleys' [who was credited with inventing *he dare*].

**128. The use of 'Dare.' II** (5 S. vii. 371 ; 187).

I think our good friend C. S. need not have repeated his protest, because all readers of English can judge for themselves, and I hope the time is coming when students really will do so, and then questions like the present will cease to be a matter of opinion at all. He now appeals to the facts, as is quite right ; only, unluckily for him, the facts are the other way.

It is needless to prove this, for it has been already admitted. His first protest against the use of *dare* was due to the fact that he supposed it to be *modern*. He now objects to it because it has been shown to be *old*. The admitted fact is that it is *both*. The statement that '*dares, dared*, and *durst* have been used, and used exclusively, by good English writers for the last two or three centuries' is a mere mistake. *Dare* has also been used, as we all know (for we have all read the Bible, Job xli. 10, and Shakespeare), as well as the other forms, but not quite so freely, because authors have probably been a little afraid of it[1]. Before making any wild statements, C. S. should have looked at his Shakespearian grammar, and he would have found 'But this thing *dare* not,' quoted from *The Tempest*, iii. 2. 63, with the remark that *dare* is 'stronger than dares.' Dr. Abbott quotes an excellent example of the indiscriminate use of *dare* and *dares* from Beaumont and Fletcher, *Faithful Shepherd*, iii. 1 :—

> 'Here boldly spread thy hands; no venomed weed
> *Dares* blister them, no slimy snail *dare* creep.'

[1] I find it *in the first book I open* ·
> 'And scarce an arm *dare* rise to guard its head.'
>                                            Byron, *Corsair*, c. ii.
> 'And who *dare* question aught that he decides.'
>                                            *Id.*, c. i. st. 8.

As to the present use of the word, we might learn something from the dialect of our peasantry. Surely no countryman uses 'he dares'; at least, I have never heard it. But I can certify that I have heard, 'He dar'n't do it,' and, 'He dus'n't do it' (which, like 'I dus'n't do it,' is for 'durst not,' i. e. would not dare, the past tense subjunctive), at least a score of times; and I suppose the experience of others is much the same.

If the appeal is to the facts, let us abide by the facts. Now the facts are that the modern usage admits of 'he dare not,' and 'he dares not,' both in the present tense; and of 'he durst not' and 'he dared not,' both in the past tense. Only, as is often the case when there are double forms, these are being gradually differentiated, and will some day be used differently. Already 'he dared not' is beginning to be used more with reference to *direct* assertions, and 'he durst not' with respect to hypotheses. See Mätzner, *Eng. Grammatik*, vol. ii. pt. 2, p. 4. If your correspondent really means, as I suspect he does, that *dare* is going out of fashion, and will, if no longer wanted in indirect clauses, probable become obsolete, then I quite agree with him. But it is a very different way of putting the matter; and it is well to remember that all 'protests' are perfectly useless, and are so much effort thrown away. The language will go its own way, and the effect of critical dicta upon it has at all times been ridiculously small, except, perhaps, in a few cases; of which I can, however, recall none.

I hope it will be every day better understood that our plain duty is, before we criticize, to study the phenomena and to investigate the history. The notion that the study of Old English has nothing to do with Modern English is becoming obsolescent, and it will be a good thing when it is obsolete. But let me not be misunderstood to mean that the study of Old English is all-sufficient. I mean nothing less. We must study *Old* English, *Middle* English, *Modern*

English, and *Dialectal* English, all with equal care, and range over the whole literature of *every date*, if we would wish our remarks to be worth reading. I am very sorry if, by the expressions used by C. S., he thinks I have answered him unfairly; for the study of English can make its own way, and needs not to be supported by any rudeness. I think, if my remarks be read again, it will be seen that the plainness of speech was no more than was fairly suited to the occasion. I do not see on what principle assertions are to be respected, when they are made in direct violation of historical facts. And for myself, I can promise that, when shown to have made an error, I will own it quite as frankly as I point out errors elsewhere.

**129. Chaucer's Prologue, l. 152; Tretys** (5 S. vii. 291; 1877).

The commentators on Chaucer have certainly taken small pains about explaining the reading *tretys*, which is perfectly right, *streyt* being but a gloss on it. Surely it is rather rash to pronounce a word in Chaucer to be wrong, *without even so much as glancing at Tyrwhitt's ' Glossary' to see whether it occurs elsewhere!* I do not say that the particular translation of the *Romaunt of the Rose* which we possess is Chaucer's version [1], but I do say that the word *tretys* occurs twice in it—ll. 1016, 1216; and that Tyrwhitt gives the references. Here are the passages:—

> 'As whyt as lily or rose on rys,
> Her face gentil and *tretys*.'

> 'Her nose was wrought at point devys,
> For it was gentil and *tretys*.'

Here we have *tretys* applied to a nose. We see that it is accented on the second syllable; also, it rimes with *rys*

---

[1] [I now say that Fragment A of the *Romaunt* (ll. 1-1705) really *is* Chaucer's own; and both the quotations for *tretys* here cited occur within it.]

(Mid. Eng. for *bough*, and pronounced as Mod. Eng. *rees*); and again with *devys*. We also see that *nose*, properly a dissyllable, was pronounced (occasionally, at least) almost as a monosyllable, the final *e* being very light; see l. 123 of the *Prologue*. The word *tretys* is really common enough in Old French, which students of Middle English might study to some advantage. Roquefort gives *seven spellings* of it, and a quotation from the *Roman de Gerard de Nevers*. And Bartsch, in his *Chrestomathie Française*, has, ' *Traitis*, doux, joli, bien fait, süss, niedlich, hübsch,' giving explanations both in French and German, to show that he at least knows the word well. Instances in Bartsch are given at pp. 122, 178, 190:—

'Plaint et sospir, qui d'amor vienent,
Sont molt *traitis*, pres del coer tienent.'
*Roman d'Eneas.*
'Membres orent bien fais, vis formés et *traitis*.'
*Roman d'Alixandre.*
'Clere ot le face, le vis *traitis* asés.'
*Huon de Bo deaux.*

Thus it was specially used as an epithet of the features. I think this may suffice for the present, though of course many more examples of so common a word may easily be found. My experience of the Chaucer MSS. is this, that when the Ellesmere, Hengwrt, and Cambridge MSS. agree, it is fifty to one that they are right. It is not a question of the *number* of the MSS. that give the reading, but of their *value*. The Harleian MS., beautifully written as it is, really exhibits several inferior readings; and the Lansdowne MS. is a very poor one.

### 130. Sweet-heart (5 S. ix. 111; 1878).

The origin of this phrase is much earlier than O. W. T. supposes. It is due to Chaucer, and to his great influence. In *Troilus and Creseide*, bk. iii. l. 988, we have, ' Lo ! *herte mine !*' In the next stanza is ' my *dere herte*'; and, lastly, in l. 1173, the phrase, '*swete herte* myn, Creseide.'[1] The talk about its derivation from *swetard*[2] is all sheer invention, and we may draw two morals : (1) that Chaucer has been neglected by the authorities; and (2) that some etymologies are too clever to be true. Ingenuity is the sworn foe of true philology.

### 131. Buckles on Shoes (5 S. ix. 433; 1878).

There are numerous examples of buckles on belts or girdles. Thus we have 'the bocle of the gerdle' (*Ayenbite of Inwit*, ed. Morris, p. 236). As to buckles on shoes, they were certainly used in the fourteenth century. There is a well-known line in Chaucer, alluding to St. Mark, i. 7, 'Ne were worthy vnbokele his galoche' (*Squieres Tale*, C. T. Group F, 555). Wyclif uses the word *thwong*, i. e. thong, not buckle.

### 132. 'Sparling' (5 S. x. 392 ; 1878).

A *sparling* or *sperling* is a kind of small fish ; some say a smelt. The word occurs in *Specimens of English*, ed. Morris and Skeat, p. 90, l. 48. The cognate German form is *Spierling*; but the Dutch has *spiering*. The root is uncertain. The G. *sperling*, meaning a sparrow, is a different word (see Kluge). A moment's reflection will show that the Fr. *éperlan* stands for an Old Fr. *esperlan*, which is merely the Teutonic word in a French dress. To derive the English from the French word is impossible ; the stream runs the other way.

### 133. Embezzle, its etymology (5 S. x. 461 ; 1878).

[I wrote a long article on this word, which was only partially right. It is a compound from the verb *to bezzle*, for

---

[1] [Not the only quotation; *swete herte* occurs in Chaucer very many times.]

[2] [No one pretends to have found a quotation for this imaginary form.]

which see the *New Eng. Dictionary*. But it was frequently regarded (as I endeavoured to show) as being connected with *imbécil*, which we now pronounce *imbecile*. I subjoin the quotations, which give some idea of the way in which it was formerly used.]

Some of the chief quotations for this word are the following :—

> 1. 'These wicked wretches, these houndes of hell
> As I have told playn here in this sentence,
> Were not content my dere love thus to quell,
> But yet they must *embesile* his presence,
> As I perceive, by covert violence;
> They have him conveyed to my displeasure,
> For here is left but naked sepulture.'
> *Lament of Mary Magdalen*, st. 39.

In this fifteenth-century poem, often printed in Chaucer's works to fill up the place of his lost poem, entitled *Origenes upon the Maudeleyne*, Mary laments that the soldiers have *embezzled*, i. e. *taken away*, the body of her Lord.

> 2. 'I concele, I *embesyll* a thynge, I kepe a thing secret. I *embesell*, I hyde or consoyle [*read* conseyle], *Je cele*. I *embesyll* a thynge, or put it out of the way, *Je substrays*. He that *embesylleth* a thyng intendeth to steale it if he can convoye it clenly.'—Palsgrave's *French Dict.*, temp. Hen. VIII.

Observe that here to *embezzle* is *not* to steal, but to prepare to steal. It means, then, to *take away* or *put aside*, with the intention of filching.

> 3. '*Embler*, to steal, filch, lurch, pilfer, nim, purloin, *imbezel*, convey away.'—Cotgrave's *French Dict.*
> 4. *Imbeseled* is used as equivalent to 'conveyed out of the waye.'—Brende, *Quintus Curtius*, fol. 275.
> 5. '*Imbessedled* and conueighed away underhand.'—North's *Plutarch*, p. 358 (Richardson).
> 6. 'Without any concealment or *imbezling*.'—Milton, *Observations on Peace with the Irish*.

These examples show the modern sense, nearly; but the following are more curious :—

7. 'Of this full well thou art resolude [resolved]
       before *K*yng Tullie gan
   So tyrannous a monarchie
       *imbécelyng* freedome, than,
   By vertues spray, the basest borne
       might be the noblest man.'
                   Drant, tr. of Horace, *Sat.* i. 6, ll. 8-11.

*Imbecelyng* is weakening, detracting from; there is nothing answering to it in the Latin.

8. '*T*hose wryng and wrest the meaner sorte
       whose myndes and tongues are free,
   And so *imbécill* all theyr strengthe
       that they are naught to me.'
                   Drant, tr. of Horace, *Sat.* i. 5.

9. 'This is *imbeselynge* and diminyshe [diminution] of their power and dominion, many landes and people falling from them.'—Udall, *Revelation*, c. 16.

10. 'Princes must ... be guardians of pupils and widows, not suffering their persons to be oppressed, or their states *imbecilled.*'—Bp. *T*aylor, *Holy Living*, c. iii. s. 2, subsect. 8.

11. 'It is a sad calamity that the fear of death shall so *imbecill* man's courage and understanding.'—Bp. *T*aylor, *Holy Dying*, c. iii. s. 7, subsect. 1.

Hence also to *imbezzle* means to diminish from one's *own* substance by squandering it away, just as much as it means to diminish from the store of *others* by taking things to oneself; this is because the true sense is merely to diminish, without reference to the manner of it.

12. 'What, when thou hast *embezel'd* all thy store?'
                   Dryden, *Persius*, Sat. vi.

13. Religion 'will not allow us to *embezzle* our money in drinking or gaming.'—Sharp, vol. 1. ser. 1.

**PS. to 133**; added in *N. and Q.* 5 S. xi. 30.

A friend has kindly sent me a good new quotation. He writes: In a letter from Reginald (afterwards Cardinal) Pole to Henry VIII, dated July 7, 1530, he speaks of the consultation of divines at Paris in the king's 'great matter,' and says it was 'achieved' according to the king's purpose.

The adverse party, he adds, use every means to *embecyll* the whole determination, that it may not take effect. See *Letters and Papers, Foreign and Domestic, of the Reign of Henry VIII*, ed. Brewer, vol. iv. pt. iii. p. 2927. Another friend tells me that he has often heard the word *imbecile* accented *imbécile*, which is to the purpose.

### 134. Gorilla (5 S. xi. 205; 1879).

It is well known that this word occurs in the *Periplus* or Circumnavigation of Hanno the Carthaginian. As the book may not be known to some readers, I make a note of the passage. The original treatise, written probably in Punic, is lost, but a Greek translation has come down to us, from which a Latin translation was also made. The treatise is a very short one, and the passage about the gorillas occurs just at the end of it. I quote from an edition printed in 1675, which contains both the Latin and Greek translations :—

'Erant autem multo plures viris mulieres, corporibus hirsutae, quas interpretes nostri Gorillas vocabant. [Greek text—ἃs οἱ ἑρμηνέες ἐκάλουν γορίλλας]. Nos persequendo virum capere ullum nequivimus: omnes enim per praecipitia, quae facile scandebant, et lapides in nos conjiciebant, evaserunt. Foeminas tamen cepimus tres, quas, cum mordendo et lacerando abducturis reniterentur, occidimus, et pelles eis detractas in Carthaginem retulimus.'

I. e. there were many more females than males, with their bodies covered with hair, whom our interpreters called gorillas. We could never take a male by pursuing him; for they all got away up the precipices, which they easily climbed, whence they threw stones at us. But we caught three females, which, because they struggled with their captors by biting and tearing, we slew; and having skinned them, we took their skins home to Carthage.

In Smith's *Dictionary* we are told that the *Periplus* was also edited by Falconer in 1797, with an English translation.

### 135. Wappered (5 S. xi. 264; 1879).

The form *wappened* in Shakespeare is an old crux. Without wishing to discuss again what has been already discussed too much, I will merely make a note that I have found either the word itself, or something like it. In Caxton's translation of *Reynard the Fox* (1481), edit. Arber, p. 16, is a description of the sufferings of poor Bruin when beguiled by the fox. All the village came out against him.

'They were alle fiers and wroth on the bere, grete and smal; ye, Hughelyn wyth the croked lege, and Ludolf with the brode longe noose [nose]: they were booth wroth. That one had an leden malle, and that other a grete leden *wapper*; therwyth they *wappred* and al for-slyngred hym.'

I do not remember seeing the remarkable verb to *for-slynger* before. As usual, the suffix *-er* is frequentative, and to *wapper* means to beat continually, from the verb *wap* or *whop*, to beat. *For-slynger* is a similar frequentative of *sling*, with the intensive prefix *for*.

### 136. The word 'Eighteen' in Chaucer (5 S. xi. 503; 1879).

A good deal turns upon Chaucer's spelling of the word *eighteen*, because the dates of the days on which the tales are supposed to be told depend upon the reading in the fifth line of the dialogue prefixed to the *Man of Law's Prologue*. All this I have explained at much length in my notes upon this line and upon l. 3, in the Clarendon Press edition of the *Prioress's Tale*, &c. I have there shown that the abbreviation 'xviij. the' is to be written at length *eightetethe*, and the word has four syllables. Similarly, if Chaucer has the word for eighteen, it must be *eightetene*, in four syllables. I have just found the right line; and here it is, as printed in Tyrwhitt's edition:

## THE WORD 'EIGHTEEN' IN CHAUCER. 117

'Of *eighteen* yere she was, I gesse, of age.'
*Cant. Tales*, l. 3223.

Of course, the reader will exclaim that the word is manifestly a mere dissyllable, or the line cannot be scanned. But if the matter be considered carefully, it will be found that it proves exactly the converse. Turn to any *old* edition, and what do we find?

'Of eightene yere she was of age.'—Ed. 1532.

So also in ed. 1561. Both these editions have the line in this form, in spite of the fact that it will not scan. This is very significant.

Let us now turn to the splendid six-text edition, and consult the best MSS. Five of these have the line thus:—

'Of xviij. yeer she was of age.'

The sixth, the Cambridge MS., has the same reading, but expands 'xviij.' as *eightene*, incorrectly. The Harleian MS., as printed by Wright, has *eyghteteene*, which is perfectly correct; but whether the word is written at length in the MS., or whether Mr. Wright expanded it from 'xviij.', I do not know [1]. It does not much matter, as the form *eighte* is amply justified by the A.S. *eahta*, and the forms *eightetene*, *eightetethe*, by the A.S. *eahtatine*, *eahtateoða*. We may safely conclude that the words *I gesse*, inserted by Tyrwhitt, resting on no respectable authority [2], are to be discarded; also that *eighteen* must, consequently, be expanded into four syllables instead of two; and, lastly, that the reading *eightetethe* in the other passage is amply supported.

It is not a little consolation to find that the old editions of 1532 and 1561 both have *eightene* in the *Man of Law* passage. These old editions are, in fact, of some value;

---

[1] [It is written *at length* in the MS.—'ey3teteene.']

[2] [Really, on *no* authority. 'The words *I gesse* are not in the MSS.'—*Tyrwhitt*.]

they are quite unsophisticated[1], and follow the *words* of the old MSS., without regard to the spelling or scansion. They are, accordingly, unprejudiced witnesses, and deserve attention.

### 137. Hundred (5 S. xii. 24; 1879).

Mr. Wedgwood explains the *hund-* in *hundred* as 'a docked form of *taihun*, ten'; the suffix *-red* being equivalent to A.S. *ræd*, with the sense of 'rate.' This is very nearly right, but we may approach a little closer still. The Gothic *taihunte-hund*, a hundred, is equivalent to 'of tens the tenth[2],' and *hund* is a docked form of *taihund*, tenth, the *ordinal*, not the *cardinal* number. It is equivalent, in fact, to the *-enth* in *tenth*, and to the *-ithe* in *tithe*. It is worth noting that the word is similarly docked in other languages. Thus, Lat. *centum* is short for *decentum*, tenth, an old ordinal form from *decem*, ten; the suffix *-tum* answering to E. *-th* by Grimm's law. Gk. ἑκατόν is for ἑ-κατόν, where -κατόν is for δέκατον, tenth. The Skt. *çata*, a hundred, also appears in the form *daçati*, lit. tenth, from *daçan*, ten. We also find Skt. *daçat*, meaning an aggregate of ten, a decade. The Lithuanian *szimtas*, a hundred, is short for *deszimtas*, tenth. It will be easily seen that there is not merely a docking of the form for *tenth*, but an absolute omission of the form for 'of tens' as well. Thus the Latin *centum* really does duty for *decentorum-decentum*, and so on. It was a very pardonable abbreviation, and arose from dealing with large numbers. Thus the Gothic for 100 is *taihunte-hund*, as above stated; but the Gothic for 200 is simply *twa hunda*, a neut. plural form used as an abbreviation for *twa taihunte-(tai)hunda*, which was naturally found to be too long for practical purposes. The same abbreviation was

---

[1] [Not *quite*, but to a great extent. Thynne actually altered *kyte* to *cur* in l. 1179.]

[2] See Brugmann, iii. § 179 (in the translation).

used for any number of hundreds beyond the first. We thus get a complete solution of the word. Similarly the Gk. -κατόν really stands for δεκάτων δέκατον, and so on. There is practically a loss of a word and a bittock, not of a single letter.

### 138. Sidemen (5 S. xii. 31 ; 1879).

I do not think Mr. Marshall has left much to be said. Surely the etymology from *side* and *man* is quite sufficient. The Latin *assistens* means little else ; it is only 'one who stands (or is) beside.' The absurd attempt to make *sidesmen* stand for *synodsmen* is just one of those fancies which were so abundant in the sixteenth century, when it seems to have been held that all English was derived from Latin and Greek, and that there was no originality in it. We find *side-bench*, *side-board*, and *side-wagh* (i. e. side-wall) all in the Middle-English period. Hence *side-man* is a perfectly consistent and intelligible formation. We need seek no further.

### 139. Division of Words into Syllables (5 S. xii. 42 ; 1879).

It is curious to observe the rules which have grown up for dividing English words into syllables. In practice these rules are ready and convenient enough, and have the great merit of following the rules for pronunciation. In other words, they are usually phonetically correct ; so that there is no reason for altering them. But it may still be worth while to show that, from a purely *theoretical* or etymological point of view, they break down entirely, and constantly contradict the theory of the words' origin. A few examples will make this clear.

The rough-and-ready rule is, I suppose, in practice, this. Begin a new syllable with a consonant rather than a vowel, and if two consonants come together, put the former into one syllable, and the latter into another. I take up a well-known handy edition of *Pickwick Papers*, and I find the following examples in the opening pages :—Impera-tive, explana-tion, unques-tionably, asto-nishment, conti-nued, impu-dence, solilo-quize, peru-sal, pros-perity, fes-tivity, counte-nance, uncer-tain, distin-guished, plea-sure, par-ticle, princi-pals, indivi-dual. I omit others which are less odd. Nearly every one of these is, etymologically and theoreti-cally, misdivided, as may easily appear to a Latin scholar. Even those who know no Latin must perceive that we should never think of writing peru-se (cf. peru-sal), feas-t (cf. fes-tivity), plea-se (cf. plea-sure), par-t (cf. par-ticle), or divi-de (cf. indivi-dual). In many cases, the root or base is cut right in half. Thus, 'continue' and 'countenance' are from the base TEN, 'imputdence' from PUD, 'soliloquize' from LOQ, 'prosperity' from SPE, 'distinguished' from STING, 'principal' from CAP. These examples may serve to remind us that our present rules (doubtless convenient, easy, phonetic, and sufficient) nevertheless frequently pro-duce forms which give no hint as to the true form of the verbal root.

[This requires further explanation. I merely mean that such word-division has nothing to do with *etymology*. From a *practical* point of view, it is right, being based on true phonetic principles, i.e. on the *spoken* language. We really *do* say 'im-pu-dence.' It is only when we take the word to pieces, for etymological purposes, that we at last discover that it is formed from *im-* (for *in*), the base *-pud-*, and the suffix *-ence*. Practice is here one thing, and theory another. The *spoken* language has *pe-ruse* at one moment, and *pe-ru-sal* at another; it rightly regards ease of utterance, and nothing else.]

### 140. 'Warish' (5 S. xii. 238; 1879).

The word *warish* (i. e. to cure) occurs in Chaucer, *Cant. Tales*, 12840 (ed. Tyrwhitt) or C. 906 (ed. Skeat); in *Piers*

*Plowman*, B. xvi. 105 (E. E. T. S.); and in *William of Palerne*, l. 4283 (E. E. T. S.). It is not derived from the French *guérir*, which is a modern word, but from the stem *waris-* of *warisant*, the pres. part. of *warir*, an O. French word of Teutonic origin, represented by *guérir* in the modern language. The O. F. *warir* became *garir*, whence also *garite*, a watch-tower, E. garret. *Garir* became *guarir*, as in Cotgrave, and lastly *guérir*. It is connected, etymologically, with *ware* and *wary*.

### 141. Origin of the word 'Garret' (5 S. xii. 351; 1879).

I do not admit that F. *galetas*, a garret, which is rightly derived by Littré from *Galata*, is the same word as our *garret!* Why should I, or where is there a tittle of evidence to that effect? Littré does not say anything of the kind; he merely says that *galetas* means a garret, not that the *words* are the same. Of course the M. E. *garite* and the F. *galetas* both meant at one time an upper chamber, and they now mean a garret; but this does not *identify* the words—it is only one more proof that similar words are apt to run together. Until Mr. P. can produce historical proof that the words *garite* and *galetas* (which Cotgrave separates, and which Littré and Diez practically separate by assigning different origins to them) were originally identical, his whole case breaks down. If the words be examined, they are not particularly alike. The interchange of *r* and *l* is, of course, common; but *garite* has *i* in the second syllable and terminates in *e*, whilst *galetas* has *e* in the second syllable and terminates in *-as*. Modern philology exacts that vowel-changes should be accounted for.

The old use of the words seem to me frequently different. *Galetas* was, most often, a chamber in a castle or mansion. But *garite*, though afterwards assimilated to *galetas* in use, was a military term, and could be used to mean a watch-tower for sentinels. It occurs in this sense in the *Alexander*

*Romance*, ed. Stevenson, l. 1417. But we do not find *galetas*, so spelt, with the same sense in Early French. And if we did, the difference of form would have to be accounted for. I may add that I find myself not alone in the belief that the proposed identification is a mistake.

### 142. Laburnum (5 S. xii. 416; 1879).

The *Notes on Natural History*, cited by Mr. S., must be an amusing book if it contains many suggestions like that of the derivation of *laburnum* from *l'arc bois*. Once more, for about the tenth time, let me press the value of *chronology* in etymology. How could Pliny, who uses the word *laburnum*, have learnt French before French was invented?

### 143. 'Leer' = Hungry (5 S. xii. 431; 1879).

Certainly *lear* or *leer* means 'empty' in some dialects, as in the excellent Wiltshire song by Akerman of the *Hornet and the Beetle*, cited in the preface to Halliwell's *Dictionary*, 'His bill was shearp, his stomach *lear*.' The Middle-English form is *lere*, as in *Rob. of Gloucester*, ed. Hearne, p. 81. Cf. A.S. *lærnes*, emptiness (Bosworth); O. Du. *laer*, 'voyd, or emptie' (Hexham). The original sense seems to have been 'gleaned,' from A. S. *lesan*, prov. E. *lease*, to glean. So also the O. H. G. *lâre*, empty, G. *leer* from O. H. G. *lesan*, G. *lesen*[1].

### 144. 'Apple-cart' (5 S. xii. 472; 1879).

Brogden did well in claiming this as a Lincolnshire word, as he had no doubt heard it there. But it is more general. I used to hear it in Kent in my earliest days. If a child falls down, you first inquire if he is much hurt. If he is

---

[1] [Suggested in Schade, from *G*rimm. It is just possible, as the pt. pl. stem of A. S. *lesan* was *læs*-. *K*luge suggests a connexion with *G*oth. *las-iws*, weak, which is also possible; moreover, the pt. s. stem of *G*oth. *lisan* (= A. S. *lesan*) was *las*.]

merely a little frightened, you say, 'Well, never mind, then; you've only upset your apple-cart and spilt all the gooseberries.' The child perhaps laughs at the very venerable joke, and all is well again.

I think the expression is purely jocular, as in the case of 'bread-basket,' similarly used to express the body. The body, regarded as a food-carrying machine, is at one time a bread-basket, at another an apple-cart, and so on. It is like expressing growth by the eating of more pudding.

### 145. Locksley Hall (5 S. xii. 471; 1879).

The resemblance of Tennyson's line—'For a sorrow's crown of sorrow is remembering happier things'—to a passage in Chaucer was commented on by Mr. Sala in the *Illustrated London News*, on the 20th of last September. I at once informed him that it was pointed out by Dr. Morris, in 1868, that both Chaucer and Dante alike copied from Boethius, *De Consolatione Philosophiae*, lib. ii. prose 4: 'Sed hoc est, quod recolentem me vehementius coquit. Nam in omni adversitate fortunae infelicissimum genus est infortunii, fuisse felicem.' Chaucer's *prose* translation of this may be seen in Dr. Morris's edition of Chaucer's translation of Boethius, p. 39: 'For in alle aduersitees of fortune the most unsely kynde of contrarious fortune is to han bene weleful.' The same passage is to be found in King Ælfred's translation of Boethius also. He says: 'Thæt is seo mæste unsælth on this andweardan life, thæt mon ærest weorthe gesælig, and æfter thām ungesælig'; i.e. It is the greatest misfortune in this present life, that one be at first happy, and afterwards unhappy.

### 146. 'Halfen dale' (5 S. xii. 455; 1879).

This is not 'a tenure' at all, strictly so speaking. It merely means that So-and-so takes the half. If I were to rent the half of a field, I should be said to rent the 'halfen deal.' *Halfen* or *halven* is nothing but the word *half* with an old case-ending, and *deal* is the old word for part or share. It is the usual old expression for it, and *deal* was a necessary addition at a time when *half* usually meant side; thus the 'right half' of a man was his right side. I have seen the phrase 'halven deal' repeatedly, but can only at present refer to Mandeville's *Travels*, ed. Halliwell, p. 166. *Dale* exactly represents an old (Mid. English) pronunciation of the word which we now spell *deal*, formerly *del*, *deel*, or *dele*.

### 147. Dulcarnon (5 S. xii. 454 ; 1879).

I have explained this word, its etymology, and everything belonging to it at great length, but I forget where; I think in the *Academy*[1]. Briefly to recount the chief points, it comes to this. *Dulcarnon*, or the 'two-horned,' was an epithet of Alexander. It was also applied, in jest, to the forty-seventh proposition of the first book of Euclid, with its two squares sticking up like horns. Hence it meant a difficult problem, the sense in Chaucer. Besides this, the fifth proposition, now called the asses' bridge, was once called 'the putting to flight of the miserable,' or, as Chaucer calls it, 'the flemyng of the wrecches,' which has the same sense. Chaucer has mixed up the two propositions.

### 148. Jamieson's 'Dictionary of the Scottish Language' (5 S. xii. 321 ; 1879).

[*An Etymological Dictionary of the Scottish Language, illustrating the Words in their different Significations, etc.* By John Jamieson, D.D. A new Edition, carefully revised and collated, with the entire Supplement incorporated, by John Longmuir, A.M., LL.D., and David Donaldson, F.E.I.S. Vol. i. (Paisley, Alexander Gardner.)]

---

[1] [Now reprinted in my edition of Chaucer, vol. ii. My article did not appear in the *Academy*, but in the *Athenæum*, Sept. 23, 1871, p. 393; in an unsigned review.]

As to the great value of this work, there can be no doubt. The original edition of 1808 has become very scarce, and it was high time that a reprint should be issued. The incorporation of the supplement is a great boon to the student who consults the volume; he has now only one alphabet to search in, instead of two. This was also one great advantage of the abridged edition published by Nimmo, of Edinburgh, in 1867, which is a most handy and useful volume, giving the words and explanations as in the larger book, but omitting the illustrative quotations and abridging the etymological remarks. Such abridgment, instead of being a loss, was a positive gain; and in this respect the smaller edition is the better book of the two. But the omission of the splendid selection of illustrative quotations was a heavy loss; and on this account we welcome the reprint of the original edition, and wish all success to the undertaking. The reprinting of such a book as Jamieson's *Dictionary* is a serious and difficult task; and the editors may as well at once make up their minds to find that their work will hardly give satisfaction. They have taken what is, perhaps, on the whole, the best course, viz., to alter as little as possible, and they are extremely chary of correcting even the most obvious mistake. Thus, if the book is no great improvement on the original edition, it is at least as good; and even so, it possesses a high and almost unique value. So well known a work needs not that much should be said about it; most students who are moderately acquainted with Northern English must know something as to the quality of Jamieson's work. His copious collection of words, his explanations, and his quotations are all excellent. The only part of the work which is unsatisfactory is his etymology. This was as good as it could be expected to be at that date, but it has now, unfortunately, chiefly only an antiquarian value; and it is some consolation to see what great strides the science of philology has made since the beginning of the present century. His chief avoidable fault was in frequently misspelling or misinterpreting the foreign words which he cited from the dictionaries then in use. In this respect the editors might advantageously correct obvious blunders, and perhaps they may in some cases have done so; but this can hardly be determined without a more searching investigation than we have at present the leisure to make. We are glad to see that they have occasionally consulted the corrections made by Prof. Skeat in his edition of Barbour's *Bruce*, but they do not seem to have done so either from the beginning or sufficiently. Thus the mysterious word *allryn*, which originated in a mere printer's error for *alkyn*, still has a place in the vocabulary, without the slightest hint as to its unauthenticity. The articles on *apayn* and *beleif* are as wrong as ever. The word *belene* is still to be found, without a hint that it is an error for *beleue*. The word *bredis*, though it occurs in Jamieson's own edition of Barbour, is absent from the vocabulary, except in another connexion.

It deserves to be noted that a correspondent, signing himself J. S., in a communication to the *Athenaeum*, March 13, 1869, gave the following list of words not in Jamieson:—Benner-gowan, bulldairy, boose, clabber, cowcracker, flapper-bags, gairy, gorachan, kent, kinvaig, peeveralls, peever, semmit, scuddy, shine, teer, teerers; waebrun, yaws; also spenser, spud, spods, yochel, otter, kyaw. All of these were explained at the same time. If their arrangements permit of it, a fresh supplement of words, due to the industry of the editors themselves, might very well be added at the end of Z. The editors, in fact, promise something of the kind, as they give notice that 'lists of *corrigenda* and *addenda* will be collected as the work proceeds, which, when properly sifted and arranged, will form an interesting and valuable addition to the great work by Dr. Jamieson.' If this means that the etymologies will be corrected, they will certainly not lack material for an extra volume. That the services of Mr. Donaldson have, at rather a late stage of the first volume, been secured by the publisher, augurs well for the success of the work. That he is 'specially qualified for the work' there can be little doubt. The present volume contains 'Dr. Jamieson's original Prefaces, his Dissertation on the Origin of the Scottish Language, a List of the Books referred to or quoted by the Author throughout his Dictionary and Supplement, and the list of original subscribers.' Vol. ii. is promised for March, 1880. The work will be completed in four volumes.

[PS. As here suggested, a fifth and supplemental volume was added, edited by Mr. D. Donaldson, and containing many corrections and additions.]

### 149. 'Wycliffe's New Testament' (5 S. xii. 419; 1879).

[*The New Testament in English, According to the Version by John Wycliffe about* A.D. 1380, *and Revised by John Purvey about* A.D. 1388. Formerly edited by the Rev. J. Forshall and Sir F. Madden, and now Reprinted. (Oxford, Clarendon Press).]

It was a great reproach to England that, till about fifty years ago, no adequate attempt was made to give us a full account of Wycliffe's version of the Bible. But at last the task was undertaken, and some reparation to Wycliffe's memory was made by the thorough way in which the editors set about their work. Certainly the Rev. Josiah Forshall and Sir Frederic Madden deserve to be for ever remembered by English scholars for their patience, industry, and accuracy. For twenty-two years they toiled at the task of examining, classifying, choosing, and editing the MSS. They examined no less than 170 manuscripts, and divided them into two sets. One of these sets they distinguished by the name of the earlier version, principally due to the work of Nicholas de Hereford and John Wycliffe;

the other set gives us the later version, mainly revised by John Purvey. As both of the versions are of much importance, and the variations between them of high interest, they decided on printing both *in extenso*, in parallel columns, selecting for this purpose the best manuscript (or manuscripts) of each class and collating it with numerous others, so as to secure, in each instance, a perfectly accurate text. How often they must have read over the whole Bible in English of the fourteenth century it is not easy to tell; but they must have become more familiar with it than many are with the authorized version at the present day. The result of their labours was published in four splendid quarto volumes in 1850, and has been of great service to English philologists, as well as of great interest to theologians. But the price of the publication, though not a high one when the bulk of it is considered, has placed it beyond the reach of many who would be glad to have it. Accordingly, for the benefit of that increasing class of students who are becoming aware that the Latin grammar alone will never teach English idioms, the Delegates of the Clarendon Press have now issued, in one small inexpensive volume, the whole of the New Testament as it stands in the later version, omitting the critical apparatus of various readings, but with an excellent glossary, abridged from the original one and carefully revised.

The later version was chosen because the English of it is easier, more flowing, and in many respects better; though the earlier one is of more interest from a purely philological point of view. We hope that the success of the venture will be such as to enable the Delegates, at no very distant date, to issue the Old Testament also [1]. A short introduction by Prof. Skeat explains the whole history of the book,

[1] The whole of the Old Testament never appeared; but a subsequent volume was issued, containing Job, the Psalms, the Proverbs, Ecclesiastes, and the Song of Solomon (1881).

gives examples comparing the two versions, explains the methods adopted by the editors, and concludes with remarks upon the language. These remarks discuss the dialect, the pronunciation, the spelling, the alphabet, and the vocabulary; and show how, in some passages, obscurities have arisen which are only to be solved by a comparison with the Latin Vulgate version, from which Wycliffe's translation was made. The reader is thus put in possession of the most material facts necessary for a due appreciation of the text. We here give the parables of the ten virgins, as a specimen of the text itself:—

'Thanne the kyngdoom of heuenes schal be lijk to ten virgyns, whiche token her laumpis, and wenten out ayens the hosebonde and the wijf; and fyue of hem[1] weren foolis, and fyue prudent. But the fyue foolis token her laumpis, and token not oile with hem; but the prudent token oile in her[2] vessels with the laumpis. And whilis the hosebonde tariede, alle thei nappiden and slepten. But at mydnyght a crygh was maad, Lo! the spouse cometh, go ye oute to mete with him. Thanne alle tho[3] virgyns risen[4] vp, and araieden her laumpis. And the foolis seiden to the wise, Yyue[5] ye to vs of youre oile, for oure laumpis ben quenchid. The prudent answeriden, and seiden, Lest peraduenture it suffice not to vs and to you, go ye rather to men that sellen, and bie to you. And while they wenten for to bie, the spouse cam; and tho[3] that weren redi, entreden with him to the weddyngis; and the yate[6] was schit[7]. And at the last the othere virgyns camen, and seiden, Lord, lord, opene to vs. And he answeride, and seide, Treuli Y seie to you, Y knowe you not. Therfor wake[8] ye, for ye witen[9] not the dai ne the our[10].'

## 150. A 'Puzzle' solved (6 S. i. 12; 1880).

It is well known that no adequate solution of the word *puzzle* has ever been offered. I now proceed to solve it. It occurs as a verb in *Hamlet*, iii. 1. 80, and in other passages; but it was originally a substantive. From its familiar use as

[1] Them.      [2] Their.      [3] Those.
[4] Rose, *past tense plural; sing.* roos.
   Yyue, yive, give.      [6] Gate.      [7] Shut.
[8] Watch.      [9] Know, *plural of* woot.      [10] Hour.

a verb it seems to have been regarded as a frequentative form of the verb to *pose*, with the addition of the usual suffix *-le*; such, indeed, is Skinner's explanation, hitherto accepted only because no better one has yet appeared. The connexion with *pose* is right, as indeed our instincts assure us; but the suffix, though long regarded as verbal, is not really so, as will appear. Before proceeding, it is necessary to say a word as to the word *pose* itself. This is usually regarded as an abbreviation of *appose*, and this is true; but we must also go back a step further, and acknowledge *appose* to be an adaptation of *oppose*. To *appose* or *pose* was to propose questions; examples are plentiful, especially in Richardson's *Dictionary*, s.v. 'Appose.' But no such sense is commonly found in the French *apposer* or the Latin *apponere*. The true Latin word is *opponere*, which was a regular term in the schools; see Ducange. The old method of examination was by argument, and the examiner was really an umpire, who decided questions put by an *opponent* to the examinee, so that the old word for *to examine* was also *opponere*. Now it so happened that neat answers were called *apposite* answers; and between the opponent on one side, and the apponent (or neat answerer) on the other, a complete confusion easily arose, at any rate in English, as testified by numerous instances. We thus have, as the right order of things, first to *oppose* in the schools; secondly, to *oppose* or *appose* by asking questions; and finally to *pose*, by putting a hard question to a candidate.

We have numerous words formed from verbs by a suffix *-al*, as in the case of *deni-al*, *refus-al*, and the like. Similarly, a hard question was an *oppos-al*, and this is the word which has now become *puzzle*. The whole of this would be but guess-work if it were not that I have been so fortunate as to find the necessary examples which support and elucidate the solution.

We are really indebted for it to Dyce's *Shelton*, which (I say it advisedly) is one of the best edited books in our literature, and a great credit to the honoured name of Alexander Dyce. The references will be found in that book, at vol. i. p. 367, and vol. ii. p. 304, and here they are :—

'And to pouert she put this *opposayle.*'
Lydgate, *Fall of Princes*, ed. Wayland, sig. B iii. leaf lxvi.

' Made vnto her this vncouth *apposaile*,
Why wepe ye so?'—*Id.*, sig. B v. leaf cxxviii.

'Madame, your *apposelle* is wele inferrid'
(i. e. your question is well put).
Skelton, *Garlande of Laurel*, l. 141.

In this last instance the 'various reading' is *opposelle* (Dyce). In all these cases the sense is a question hard of solution, or, in modern language, a *puzzle*.

[See *Appose* (1) in the *New E. Dictionary*, and *Puzzle* in my (larger) *Etym. Dictionary*. The *Century Dictionary* has adopted this etymology of *Puzzle*, and Dr. Murray confirms my view of *Appose*.]

### 151. A pair of Organs (6 S. i. 82 ; 1880).

There is a note on this in my edition of *Piers Plowman*; see index to the notes. A pair of organs means a set of organ-pipes, i. e. an organ. It is quite a mistake to suppose that a *pair*, in old books, always means two. It usually means a set. Hence a pair of beads, a set of them (Chaucer); a pair of cards, i. e. a pack; a pair of stairs i. e. a flight, whence ' two-pair back.'

### 152. 'Gill' (6 S. i. 102 ; 1880).

In giving a definition of *gill*, I of course followed the usual one in Webster's *Dictionary* and elsewhere. I venture to think that if ST. SWITHIN had taken trouble to consult any ordinary arithmetic-book, or had questioned the nearest child, he would probably have found that 'four gills make one pint.' I cite this, first from Colenso's *Arithmetic*, and secondly from the oral statement of the first child I asked, who gave me that answer. And surely nothing is also better known than that weights and measures differ widely in different parts of England. If, at Whitby, a gill is *half* a pint, I may mention that I have been informed that, in Cambridgeshire, a gallon sometimes means *two* gallons. In Philips, ed. 1706, is this remarkable definition, which defies explanation, except on the hypothesis that a pint is a quart: '*Jill*, the smallest sort of wine measure, the eighth part of an English quart, or half a quarter of a pint.' Of course he meant 'a quarter of a pint' simply.

### 153. 'To hold up Oil' (6 S. i. 118; 1880).

I am most grateful to MR. MAYHEW for his quotation; it makes one more in the set which I have tried to get together. It is certain that 'to hold up oil' or 'to bear up oil' was an old proverbial phrase. It does not mean 'to assent,' but 'to aid and abet,' or 'consent in a flattering way.' It answers very nearly to the modern phrase 'to back a person up.' In the quotation given the sense is, 'Alexander began to boast, and most of his friends backed him up,' or 'bore out what he said.' I have had this phrase under consideration for seven years, and a new instance, like that now furnished, is a great gain. It first came under my notice in editing *Richard the Redeles*, appended to the C-text of *Piers the Plowman*. (See *Rich. Redeles*, iii. 186). We there read that, in the days of Richard II, men did not get promotion for good deeds, but for bragging and flattery, or, as the author puts it, 'for braggynge and for bostynge, and *berynge vppon oilles*, for cursidnesse of conscience, and comynge to the assises.' My note on it is, that it is plainly written in the MS.

I have since found a capital instance in Gower's *Conf. Amantis*, bk. vii. vol. iii. p. 159 :—

> 'For, when he doth extorcion,
> Men shall not finden one of tho
> To grucche or speke there agein,
> But *holden up his oile* and sain,
> That all is well that ever he doth.'

That is, when a king is extortionate, people do not reprove him, but aid and abet him, or flatter him up, or bear him out, and say that whatever he does must be right. And again, at p. 172 of the same, we find that the false prophets told Ahab to go and prosper:

> 'Anone they were of his accorde,
> Prophetes false many mo
> To *bere up oile*; and alle tho
> Affermen that which he hath told.'

In all these instances it is remarkable that the flatterers assure the great man he is perfectly right, though he is really wrong. And this, at any rate, clears up the general sense. We have now four instances of the phrase. If the passage in *Piers Plowman* be examined, it will be found to refer to the practices at the king's court, and practically to Richard himself. In all four passages the reference is to the flatterers who uphold a *king*; in one place it is a nameless king (Gower, iii. 158), and in the other places the reference is, respectively, to Alexander, Richard II, and Ahab. I therefore offer, with all diffidence, the suggestion that the proverb may refer to the anointing of kings with oil at their coronation. 'To hold up oil' or 'to bear up oil' may mean to hold up the sacred vessel containing holy oil, ready to anoint the chosen monarch. The sense is remarkably preserved in the modern English phrase 'to butter a person.'

### 154. Pamphlet (6 S. i. 389; 1880).

The usual etymologies of this difficult word are not very satisfactory. I have found a much earlier example of it than any which I have yet seen mentioned. It occurs, spelt *pamflet*, in the *Testament of Love*, pt. iii., near the end; to be found in Chaucer's *Works*, ed. 1561, fol. 317 back, col. 1. This takes us back at once to about A. D. 1400, and renders it tolerably certain that the word can only be French, whilst the peculiar form *pamf-* can hardly be of any origin but Greek. Taylor, in his *Words and Places*, says· '*Phamphylla*, a Greek lady, who compiled a history of the world in thirty-five little books, has given her name to the *pamphlet*.' Such statements are, in general, to be received with great distrust, and I have met with so many unsupported statements in the same book, that it can hardly be accepted without further search. Such slight search as I have been able to make does, however, greatly strengthen the suggestion. In the first place, her name was not *Pamphylla*, but *Pamphila*, which helps us on. There is a short account of her in Smith's *Dictionary of Biography*. She lived in the reign of Nero, and 'her principal work was a kind of historical miscellany. It was not arranged according to subjects, or according to any settled plan, but it was more like a commonplace-book, in which each piece of information was set down as it fell under the notice of the writer.' She seems to have dealt in anecdotes, epitomes, and short notes; and hence we really have some ground for connecting her name with the *pamphlet*, or short tract on a subject. Moreover, Halliwell cites the form *pamfilet*, though without authority. The phonology of such a derivation is unimpeachable. From the Latin name *Pamphila* (of course of Greek origin) we have a French *Pamfile*, whence the sb. *pamfilet*, a diminutive form to express 'a work by Pamphila,' and, by contraction, the Middle-English *pamflet*. There is a notice of her in Suidas, ed. Wolff; he says that she wrote thirty-three books of historical commentaries, an epitome of Ctesias in three books, and very numerous epitomes of histories and of books of all kinds, 'epitomas historiarum, aliorumque librorum *plurimas*, de controversiis, de rebu; Veneriis, et aliis multis.' This testimony is of importance as showing the *character* of her work. In the *Attic Nights* of Aulus Gellius, translated by Beloe, we find the remark: 'This story is taken from the twenty-ninth commentary of Pamphila,' bk. xv. c. 17. The translator has, indeed, really written *Pamphilas* instead of *Pamphila*, but he corrects himself a few pages further on, saying: 'This remark is from the eleventh book of Pamphila,' bk. xv. c. 23.

In the translation of *Diogenes Laertius*, by C. D. Yonge (in Bohn's Library), at p. 35, we find, in the 'Life of Pittacus,' sect. 3, the remark: 'But Pamphila says, in the second book of his [*read* her] commentaries, that he had a son named Tyrrhaeus,' &c. I conclude that there really is some evidence for the etymology here proposed. We see that the works of Pamphila were of a peculiar character, and that, though now lost, they were once well known and quoted by respectable writers. Any further information as to Pamphila, or an early example of the use of *pamphlet*, or a citation giving the spelling *pamfilet*, would obviously be a gain. [The Lat. acc. pl. *panfletos* occurs in *Richard of Bury*, Philobiblon, c. 8. I can now account for the suffix *-et*. It was an O. F. suffix added to names of treatises. Thus *Isop-et* meant 'a book of Æsop'; whence *pamfil-et* must have meant 'a book by Pamphila.' Precisely so. The *Pam* mentioned in Pope, *Rape of the Lock*, iii. 61, represents F. *Pamfile*, from Lat. *Pamphilus*.]

**155. 'Pimple,' its Etymology** (6 S. i. 414; 1880).

That *pimple* is a nasalized form connected with A. S. *pipligend*, pimply, is the usual explanation, and is probably right (see A. S. *Leechdoms*, ed. Cockayne, i. 234, 266). But it is usual to cite A. S. *pinpel*, a pimple, also. This is an excellent instance of how mistakes are spread. In Ælfric's *Glossary*, ed. Somner, p. 61 (Wright's *Vocab.*, i. 26,

l. 1), is the entry, '*Anabala*, winpel.' This was copied into Lye's *Dictionary*, with a change of *winpel* into *pinpel*, and the explanation that *anabala* (= anabolē) means 'a pustule,' the fact being that it means a mantle, or *wimple*. This has been copied by Bosworth, Ettmüller, Mahn (in Webster), E. Müller, Todd (Johnson's *Dictionary*), Wedgwood, and Worcester. The last calmly alters it to *pimpel*. The verification of references often reveals such things as these.

[The *Century Dictionary* adopts the gist of the above, and explains that *pinpel* is an error].

### 156. Birnam Wood (6 S. i. 434 ; 1880).

Readers of *Macbeth* should note that the story of the moving wood occurs in the *Romance of Alexander* :—

'Interea Alexander, amoto exercitu, appropinquavit se ciuitati Perses, in qua Darius consistebat; Ita vt sublimia loca montium que erant supra ipsam ciuitatem conspiciebat. Alexander autem precepit militibus suis vt inciderent ramos arborum et herbas euellerent, easque inferrent equorum pedibus et mulorum; quos videntes [printed *videntis*] Perses ab excelsis montibus stupebant.'—*Historia Alexandri magni de preliis*, ed. 1490, fol. C 1, back.

The Middle-English version of the *Wars of Alexander* (l. 2850) has :—

'With that comaunds he his knightis to cutte doune belyue Bowis of buskis and braunches of bolis and of lvndis,' &c.

### 157. Railway English (6 S. ii. 84 ; 1880).

The following curious sentence has been for years exhibited as a 'Public Notice' at the Cannon Street Terminus and other stations belonging to the South-Eastern Railway Company:

'Tickets once nipped and defaced at the barriers, and the passengers admitted to the platform, will have to be delivered up to the Company, in the event of the holders subsequently retiring from the platform without travelling, and cannot be recognized for re-admission.'

I hope it is generally understood. It is enough to deter

passengers from travelling at all, to be told that they will 'have to be delivered up to the Company' when once 'admitted to the platform.' The 'holders' of tickets are also, it would appear, holders of passengers. Can anything be more slip-shod?

### 158. Cain's Jaw-bone (6 S. ii. 143; 1880).

'As if it were Cain's jaw-bone, that did the first murder' (*Hamlet*, v. 1. 85). Surely a remarkable expression, but there is no comment on it in the Clarendon Press edition. Compare it with the following tradition: 'Saga me, forhwám stánas ne sint berende? Ic thé secge, forthám the Abeles blód geféol ofer͑stán, thá hine Chain his bróther of-slóh mid ánes esoles cinbáne'; i. e. 'Tell me, why stones are not fruitful? I tell thee, because Abel's blood fell upon a stone when Chain, his brother, slew him with the jawbone of an ass'; *Solomon and Saturn*, ed. Kemble, p. 186. Hence the jawbone was not Cain's *own*. (Cf. *Cursor Mundi*, l. 1073.)

### 159. Whittling (6 S. ii. 193; 1880).

At the last reference we have an extract from Brockett's *Glossary* (for 'Brochett' read *Brockett*). It seems worth while to warn readers (if they will kindly accept the warning) that the etymologies offered by Brockett and Jamieson abound with the most curious errors, and are, in fact, in many instances, learned nonsense. In the present case Brockett tells us that *whittle* is derived from 'Sax. *whytel*, and that probably [!] from Goth. *huet tol*, a sharp instrument.' Now let us investigate this solemn absurdity, and we may learn something by the way.

First, 'Sax. *whytel*' means the alleged A. S. *hwitel* given in Somner's *Dictionary*. Brockett, in altering the spelling from *hw* to *wh*, gives us the measure of his knowledge of Anglo-Saxon: *he had not learnt so much as the alphabet*, or he would have known there is no *wh* in it.

Next, let us take Somner.

The A. S. *hwitel* only means a *whittle* in the sense of 'a white cloth,' such as we now call a *blanket* (from F. *blanc*, white); it is a mere derivative of *white*. Somner knew there was such a modern English word as *whittle*, meaning a knife, and rushed to the conclusion that a *hwitel* must mean a knife. Down went his guess, and people have quoted it ever since, and will do so probably for another century. [Let us hope for better things].

It so happens that the spelling *whittle*, for 'a knife,' is a mere mistake, due to the loss of *th* at the beginning of M. E. *thwitel*, used by Chaucer. The loss of *th* was plainly due to confusion with *whet*, to sharpen, according to which *whittle* was supposed to mean something sharp; and a knife being sharp, that was quite enough for popular etymology. Unfortunately, according to the laws of English Grammar, a *whettle* (for *whittle* would not give the right vowel) could only mean a sharpener, i. e. a whetstone or hone. As to *thwittle*, M. E. *thwitel*, the etymology is rightly given, by Wedgwood and E. Müller, from A. S. *thwītan*, to cut off. Hence the old verb *thwite*, to cut, strong verb (pp. *thwitten*); the sb. *thwit-el*, a cutter, with suffix *-le* of the agent, as in *sickle*, a cutter (from the root SEK, to cut); and the frequentative verb *thwittle*, to keep on cutting, to cut away all the while by little and little, which, as is well known in America, is the real and true sense of that verb. *Thwyte* occurs in Palsgrave.

I call attention to this to show what unsafe guides the old etymologists are, and what a mistake it is to quote them; they knew nothing, and cared less, about grammar or comparative philology, and coined words at pleasure, labelling them with the name of the first language that came to hand. This is exemplified easily enough by Brockett's next statement. Having first treated us to 'Saxon *whytel*,' formed by two mis-spellings from a word given by Somner and wrongly explained, he next presents us with 'Goth. *huet tol*, a sharp instrument.'

This is a piece of humbug, pure and simple. If he means Mœso-Gothic, there is no *hu* (before *e*) in the alphabet; but he really means, I suppose, the common English word *whet*, duly turned into 'Gothic' by a little false spelling. Next, *tol* is not 'Gothic' at all, but only the English *tool*, A. S. *tōl*. So that the alleged etymology merely comes to this, that *whittle* is derived from *whet-tool*. As this would hardly impose on the most credulous if left in plain language, the reader is mystified by finding it turned into *huet tol* (an impossible spelling), after which it is called 'Gothic,' on the chance that the reader will accept it.

This is the kind of etymology with which our old 'authorities' abound, and it was honest in the sense that they believed it themselves. But it is amazing that such guesses should still impose on any one, and it can only be accounted for by supposing that English scholars have paid such attention to Latin and Greek that they have had no time for Gothic or Anglo-Saxon. If a Latin quotation were to appear as 'Crescet amore nummo, quanto ipse pecuniae crescat,' people would be horrified at seeing seven glaring mistakes; but I dare say such a sentence as 'And foregyv ous ura giltum, as wee foregyvum urer giltendas,' might pass muster as an Anglo-Saxon version of a sentence in the Lord's Prayer, although every word but the first is entirely inadmissible in the English of the 'Anglo-Saxon' period.

### 160. Bede's Version of St. John's Gospel
(6 S. ii. 214; 1880).

It is certain that Bede's *version* of St. John's Gospel is lost. It cannot possibly have anything to do with the Northumbrian *gloss* in the Lindisfarne MS., because, as I have already explained, a *gloss* and a *version* are, in strictness, different things, written on totally different principles. A gloss may be called a version, but a version should not be called a gloss.

### 161. 'Sumpter' (6 S. ii. 343; 1880).

The word *sumpter* occurs but once in Shakespeare, *K. Lear*, ii. 4. I have nothing to say against Mr. Wright's excellent note, but I have somewhat to add. It may have meant 'literally a pack-horse' in Shakespeare's time, and this makes sufficiently good sense. But it is worth notice that a *sumpter* was originally not a horse at all, but a man; not a pack-horse, but a baggage-driver. A pack-horse was, in Middle-English, called a *somer* or *summer* (Low Lat. *sagmarius*), but the man who drove the pack-horses was called a *sumpter*, answering to O. F. *sommetier*, 'conducteur de bêtes de somme' (Roquefort). This answers to a Low Lat. type *sagmatarius*. Roquefort also gives, '*Sommier*, bête de somme.' Thus *summer* is pack-horse; *sumpter*, pack-horse driver, or baggage-driver; and *sumpter-horse* is not a pack-horse's horse, but a baggage-driver's horse, and so equivalent to the original *summer*. And this is why we never hear of a *summer-horse*, only of a *sumpter-horse*. In the octosyllabic *King Alisaunder*, edited by Weber, the words are kept quite distinct. Thus, at l. 850, we have:—

'And trussed heore *someris*,
And lopen on beore destreris,'

i. e. and packed their baggage-horses, and leapt on their war-horses; the two kinds of horses being contrasted. At l. 6022 we have:—

'Withowte pages and skuyeris,
Divers gyours and *sumpteris*,'

i. e. not counting (in the number of the army) the pages and squires, and certain guides and baggage-drivers.

I would venture to suggest that the true sense of *baggage-*

*driver* will suit the passage in *K. Lear* even better than that of the supposed sense (not proven) of pack-horse :—

> 'Persuade me rather to be slave and *sumpter*
> To this detested groom.'

[See *Sumpter* in my (larger) *Etym. Dictionary*. The same etymology and a similar explanation of *sumpter* in *K. Lear* are given in the *Century Dictionary*.]

### 162. A Curious Illustration (6 S. ii. 405 ; 1880).

In using Richardson's *Dictionary* it is impossible not to be struck with the singular manner in which illustrations of words are introduced that really have nothing to do with the matter in hand. One of the most whimsical is a quotation from Chaucer's (meaning Henrysoun's) *Testament of Creseide*, which concludes with : ' And in the night she listeth best *tapere*,' i. e. and she is best pleased *to appear* in the night. This is given as a quotation in illustration of the sb. *taper*, explained to mean ' a wax-light.'

[I beg leave to notice here a similar extraordinary misconception. In the *Promptorium Parvulorum*, we have the entry ' A-yen wylle, *Invite*.' This means that the M. E. *ayen wylle*, i. e. against one's will, can be expressed in Latin by *invite*. But a certain editor took *invite* to be an *English* word; hence this extraordinary entry in Cassell's *Encyclopaedic Dictionary* : ' A-yen-wylle, v. t. to invite. (*Prompt. Parv.*).' See that work, vol. i. p. 381, col. 1.]

### 163. ' Wage,' used instead of ' Wages' (6 S. iii. 11 ; 1881).

Both *wage* and *wages* are respectable forms enough, just as are *house* and *houses*, or any other pairs of singular and plural words. I find *wage* in Langtoft (ed. Hearne), p. 319. *Wage* occurs also in the *Promptorium Parvulorum*, and (according to Stratmann) in *King Alisaunder*, 904; Hoccleve,

i. 119; whilst the plural *wages* is in *Piers Plowman*, B. xi. 283. I find Dr. Stratmann's references troublesome, from his tacit alterations of the spellings; on actual reference to *King Alisaunder*, 904, the form turns out to be *gage*, the same word, no doubt, but he should have given it as it stands[1]. As to what is *asserted* in these matters, it will generally be found that the less a man knows about them, the more dogmatic he is; the way to *test* a man's knowledge is to ask him to produce his authorities, and to require of him a quotation or two.

### 164. Æstel (6 S. iii. 14; 1881).

The word is not *æstell*, but *æstel*, with one *l*. It is not plural, but singular, used with the article *ān*, one. There is a note on it in Sweet's edition of Gregory's *Pastoral Care*, p. 473. In an A. S. vocabulary by Ælfric we have, 'Indicatorium, *æstel*' (Wright's *Vocab.*, i. 81, col. 1); and again in Ælfric's *Grammar* (ed. Zupitza), p. 31. Mr. Sweet says it occurs to translate Lat. *stylus* in Ælfric's *Glossary*, but it is not there; except as translating *indicatorium*. It is by no means so easy as seems to be supposed. I cannot see that the W. *estyll*, pl. sb., helps us at all, nor is *estyll* certainly a Celtic word; it seems to be nothing but the Low Lat. *astulae* (Ducange), put for Lat. *assulae*, thin boards.

[The A. S. *æstel* still remains in some obscurity.]

### 165. Culpable Emendations (6 S. iii. 24; 1881).

One of the most grievous things in English literature is that editors and printers are continually altering texts whenever a word occurs that is in the least unusual. It is a little too bad that they should treat readers as children, and always assume that they are at least as stupid as them-

---

[1] [The new edition of Stratmann, edited by Mr. Bradley, corrects a very large number of these eccentricities. But this one has escaped notice.]

selves. I have lately noticed three gross instances of this character, and I think some good might be done by noting more specimens of the same sort. My examples are these, all taken from Richardson's *Dictionary*. In each instance Richardson gives the *correct* reading :—

> 1. 'The postboy's horse right glad to miss
> The *lumbering* of the wheels.'
> Cowper, *John Gilpin*, sixth stanza from end, ed. 1818.

Altered by some blockhead to *rumbling*. Who was the blockhead?

> 2. 'As gilds the moon the *rimpling* of the brook.'
> Crabbe, *Parish Register*, pt. i.

Altered by Crabbe's *own son* to *rippling*. This is indeed a sad instance.

> 3. 'And as a goose
> In death contracts his talons close,
> So did the knight, and with one claw
> The *tricker* of his pistol draw.'—*Hudibras*, pt. i. c. 3.

Altered in Bell's edition, with calm effrontery and without any notice given, to *trigger*. Yet *tricker* had not long been introduced into the language from the Dutch *trekker*, and the later form *trigger* is less correct. The first duty of every editor is to *let his text alone*, unless there is *certainly* a corruption in it. Unfortunately editors often measure their authors by themselves, and think that everything must be corrupt that is not at once obvious to their own understandings. The reason is plain enough. It is less trouble to alter than to investigate, and the chances are considerably in favour of their escaping detection. [Cf. p. 151, l. 9.]

### 166. The Pronunciation of 'er' as 'ar' (6 S. iii. 4; 1881).

As the pronunciation of *er* as *ar* is often discussed, I have collected more than fifty examples of it, as will be seen below.

It ought to be well understood that the change of *er* into *ar* is a real law of pronunciation in our language. In Middle-English *er* was pronounced as in F. *serve*, with a strong trilling of the *r*. It is a universal and well-known law of change in English pronunciation always to suppress the trilling of *r* as much as possible. But this caused a slight change of the vowel sound, so that *er* (as in F. *serve*) became *aa*, as in *baa*, or as in vulgar English *saav* for *serve*.

This law of change has been to some extent interfered with by the spelling, for, whilst uneducated people freely retain this change, the educated classes, who read much, have reduced the pronunciation of *serve* to that now in use by a further change of *aa* to an indistinct vowel-sound with which we are all familiar, and which we indicate by *er*, though the *r* is really silent, being wholly untrilled. We may find *sarve* for *serve* in use as early as in Tyndale; we now pretend to be ashamed of it. *Sarmon* for *sermon* occurs in the fourteenth century.

Opponents of spelling reform are often unacquainted with the history of the language, and are wholly unconscious of the fact that in many words we have already adopted a phonetic spelling. Such is peculiarly the case with words of this class; a large number of them are actually *spelt* with *ar*, so that the law of change is thereby concealed. I now give examples:—

1. The Middle-English word *berne* is now phonetically spelt *barn*; the same is the case with *bernacle*, a barnacle; *herte*, the heart (where the old *e* still lingers); *tere*, tar; *terien*, to tarry; *tern*, a tarn; *perseley*, parsley; *berken*, to bark as a dog; *derk*, dark; *herknen*, to hearken (again the *ea*); *merke*, a mark; *querelle*, a quarrel (pronounced *quorrel*, because the sound of *w* precedes); *smert*, smart; *sterten*, to start; *yerde*, a·yard; *Dertemouthe*, Dartmouth; *kerven*, to carve; *fer*, far; *ferme*, a farm; *wernen*, to warn; *werre*, war; *merren*, to mar; *mersh*, a marsh; *merveile*, a marvel;

*gerner*, a garner; *gernet*, a garnet; *werblen*, to warble; *werpen*, to warp; *serk*, a sark, or shirt. And doubtless more might be added; [as *berme*, barm, yeast; *dernel*, darnel; *gerland*, a garland; *herien*, to harry; *hereberye*, a harbour; *hervest*, harvest; *kerlok*, charlock; *perchemin*, parchment; *pertriche*, partridge, &c.]. In particular note *persone*, a parson; *ferrier*, a farrier; and *werriour*, a warrior.

2. In some words we boldly retain the changed pronunciation in spite of the spelling—I allude to *clerk*, *sergeant*, *Hertford*, and the like.

3. As to many words we are in a state of hesitancy; some people shrink from saying *Darby*, *Barkley*, and from sounding *Kerr* as *Carr*, fearing hostile criticism, and unaware that *Darby* is rather the regular than the exceptional pronunciation. Here in Cambridge we have a *Sherman* who always calls himself *Sharman*, whilst another has *Sharman* over his shop-door. We say *Merchant*, yet *Marchant* occurs as a name. As for the *berberis*, we call it a *barberry*, insinuating a third *r* with a clutch at a new sense in *berry*. We say *fern*, but also *Farnecombe*. *Perilous* also appears as *parlous*.

4. Lastly, when we allow the law of change free play (as among the lower classes, who have not yet adopted the last modern refinements) we shall find plenty of examples, familiar to all of us. Such are *sarve* for *serve*; *sarvant*, *larn*, *sarten* for certain; *varjus* (verjuice), *yarb* (Shropshire for herb), *sarpint*, *starn*, *consarn*, *detarmine*, '*varsity*, '*tarnal*, '*tarnation* (short for '*tarnal* '*nation*), *sarmon*, *varmin*, *marcy*, *narvous*, *Jarmany*; besides many more which our readers can supply for themselves.

It will now, I think, be seen that there are really three pronunciations, in chronological order:—

1. *Er*, as in F. *serve*, with trilled *r*; probably obsolete.

2. *Er*, as in *clerk*, with untrilled *r*; very common, but concealed by a phonetic spelling when we write *Clark*.

3. *Er*, with a modern refined pronunciation, as in the highly polite—'your *servant.*'

### 167. The Pronunciation of 'er' as 'ar' and of 'e' as 'a.' II (6 S. iii. 393 ; 1881).

Surely it will be readily understood that in calling the pronunciation of *er* as *ar* a singular habit of English, I meant that no other modern language uses the written symbol *er* where the pronunciation *ar* is intended. The French words mentioned in Dr. Chance's interesting letter are words in which *ar* is written *ar* according to the pronunciation, and the fact that the *ar* in them corresponds to a Latin *er* is not quite the same thing; we should not say that in the word *almond* we have an instance of the pronunciation of *-ygdalum* as *-ond*. At the same time, I have little doubt that the frequent use of the sound *ar* is partly due to French influence. Certainly *hearth* and Middle English *sterven* belong to the set; *hearth* was formerly *herth*, from A. S. *heorth*; whilst M. E. *sterve* is derived, not from Dutch or German, but from A. S. *steorfan*. [P.S. I have seen, in Old French, the spelling *Harri* for *Henri*; whence E. *Harry*.]

### 168. 'Unked,' i.e. Lonely (6 S. iii. 245 ; 1881).

This common provincial word is seldom cited without the usual 'etymology' being appended. It is always said to be derived from the A. S. *uncwyd*, explained in Bosworth by 'without speech or strife, quiet, solitary; hence the provincial word *unkid*; sine lite, quietus, solitarius.'

It never occurs to the easily satisfied compilers of glossaries who so glibly quote the above (with or without acknowledgment) to verify the matter. The fact is that the word *uncwyd* occurs twice, and that in both cases it means 'without contradiction,' or 'unspoken against,' or 'uncontested'; see Thorpe, *Ancient Laws*, i. 298, l. 9; i. 414,

l. 20; *Laws of Ethelred*, sect. 14; *Laws of Cnut, Secular*, sect. 73. There is not the least pretence for the meaning 'solitary,' and it has nothing in the world to do with *unked*.

The word *unkid* (as it is also spelt) is formed by prefixing *un-* to the M. E. *kid*, known, famous, manifest, &c. *Kid* is the pp. of *kythe*, causal of *kunnen*, to know; so that it is the pp. of the secondary verb formed from *couth*, known. *Unkid* and *uncouth* mean much the same thing, viz. unknown, strange, out of the way; hence the sense of lonely, &c.

### 169. 'Windlestrae' (6 S. iii. 249; 1881).

This common northern word is in Jamieson's *Dictionary*. Bosworth gives us A. S. *windel-streowe*, with an unintelligible reference[1]. *Strae* is straw; and *windel* is a derivative of the verb to *wind*, to twist about, &c. So also we have, in Wright's *Vocabularies*, p. 285, 'Oleaster, *windel-treow*,' where *treow* means tree. Anglo-Saxon botanical names were conferred in the wildest and most confused way, and frequently transferred from one plant to another not particularly resembling it. In the first instance *windel-straw* meant 'straw for plaiting,' and *windel-tree* meant 'tree for basket-work.' I look upon MR. H.'s candid confession of his notion of the word as a valuable aid to the understanding of etymology. He tells us that he had interpreted the word, from his own consciousness, as meaning 'the *wind-strewn* leaves of the forest,' and afterwards found, to his 'intense disgust,' that it meant nothing of the kind. This is precisely what has been going on in the minds of thousands for many centuries, though we can seldom so clearly trace it. Every educated man when he hears a new word is tempted to guess at its etymology, and thence

---

[1] [Easily found, in 1895, by help of Wülker's *Indices*. The reference is to 'Cal[a]mum, *windel-streow*' in the Glossaries, 273. 23, and 369. 4. *Calmum* is the accusative of Lat. *calamus*, Eng. *haulm*.]

deduce its sense. After guessing wrongly, and thus forcing the word into a wrong sense, he probably misuses it accordingly, and a second person uses the word *as newly modified*, and hence the endless corruptions in language. The true rule is *never to guess* at an etymology, but this requires a strength of mind beyond that of most of us.

**170. Hearne's 'Chronicles'** (6 S. iii. 425 ; 1881).

It deserves to be mentioned, as one of the curiosities of literature, that the following notice is almost invariably repeated whenever a copy of Hearne's editions of Robert of Gloucester and of Robert Manning's translation of Langtoft is offered for sale in a second-hand bookseller's catalogue :—' Contains the best Anglo-Saxon Glossaries that have ever been published.'

Of course some one was once weak enough to say this, and it has been repeated ever since. But it is most amusingly unveracious. In the first place, the glossaries are not 'Anglo-Saxon' at all, but register the language of the thirteenth century ; and next, the glossaries are almost valueless, even as regards Middle English. Hearne gives no references, and his explanations are not always correct. We may safely conclude that the difference between English of the tenth and thirteenth centuries is still unappreciated by the many, and that Stratmann's and Mätzner's glossaries of Middle English (the latter, alas ! still incomplete) are unknown, even by name, to a large portion of the book-buying public. Halliwell's *Dictionary* is also far more useful than Hearne's glossaries, though the references in it are but few. Even the glossary to the *Specimens of English* edited by Dr. Morris and myself is more worthy of mention, since it, at any rate, gives references to many thousand passages. [And now, in 1893, even Mayhew and Skeat's *Concise Middle-English Dictionary* is better than Hearne.]

## 171. 'Walking width and striding sidth'
(6 S. iv. 95; 1881).

Whether this phrase is still in common use I cannot say, but it is clearly an amplification of the phrase 'wīde and sīde,' i. e. 'wide and long,' which is so common in Anglo-Saxon poetry. See examples, s. v. 'Sīd,' in Grein's *Glossary*, ii. 442. *Width* refers to the breadth of the garment from side to side; *sidth*, to the length of it. A *side* garment in Middle English commonly meant one that trailed on the ground because over-long.

## 172. The name 'Howard' (6 S. iv. 277; 1881).

Verstegan's book (*On the Restitution of Decayed Intelligence*) is almost worthless; he invents his facts, and had no notion of Anglo-Saxon, which he grossly misrepresents. Surely *Howard* is the same as *haw-ward*, also spelt *haward*. Hayward, another common name, is the M. E. *heiward*. *Haw*, from A. S. *haga*, and *hay* or *hei*, from A. S. *hege*, both mean 'hedge.' The *hayward* was well known in former times, and is constantly alluded to; see *Prompt. Parv.*, p. 234, and my notes on *Piers Plowman*. Sherwood gives both spellings in his index to Cotgrave. 'A *haward* or *hayward*, qui garde, en commun, tout le bestail d'un bourg.' As to *holdward*, I do not believe any such word ever existed till Verstegan coined it. What we want for the etymology of any word is a good collection of illustrative quotations. Any one can theorize more easily *without* the facts; but only the facts can guide us to the truth.

## 173. Bad copy and good printers (6 S. v. 72; 1882).

I have often heard this story (viz. that it is advisable to write badly, in order that a good compositor may be set on to the 'copy'); but never so circumstantially. I think it has probably been repeated rather too often, as it is a standing excuse for bad writers. The morality of it is more than questionable; and it ought surely to be understood, amongst gentlemen, that a writer who *purposely* writes illegibly commits a most cowardly and unjustifiable crime against the unfortunate compositors.

[PS. in 1895. I have always found that the compositors set up my 'copy' admirably; precisely because they appreciate its legibility. The Controller of the Clarendon Press is my witness to this.]

### 174. Clôture (6 S. v. 126; 1882).

The etymology of this word is easy enough, viz. from the O. F. *closture*, Low Lat. *claustura*, the original sense being merely 'an enclosure.' I write this to note a passage in which the word occurs. 'Il deyt enclore la place; et si nuly bestes y entrent par defaute de *closture*,' &c. 'He ought to enclose the place; and if any beasts come in for want of fencing,' &c.—*Year-Books of Edward I*, ed. Horwood, vol. iii. p. 65.

### 175. Turken. I (6 S. v. 165; 1882).

This curious word is noticed in Davies's *Supplementary Glossary*, where the meaning of *furbish* is assigned to it, copied from the *Index to the Parker Society's Publications*. But I have found other instances of it, and have no hesitation in saying that this assigned sense of it is the wrong one. The right sense is 'to turn and twist about,' and it is merely a frequentative form of the O. F. *torquer*, to twist (Cotgrave), which is obviously the Latin *torquere*. Roquefort gives O. F. *torcenouse*, violent; *torcenus*, a tormenting tyrant; *torçonnere*, extortionate; *torquelon*, a torch; all from the same source. I first quote the instance cited by Davies, and then two more which I have found in Gascoigne:—

'His majesty calleth for subscription unto articles of religion; but they are not either articles of his own lately devised, or the old newly *turkened*'; i.e. twisted about (Rogers, *On the Thirty-nine Articles*, p. 24).

'And for the rest, you shall find it [a certain story] now in this second imprinting so *turquened* and turned'; i.e. so twisted about and altered (*Gascoigne's Works*, ed. Hazlitt, i. 5, last line).

'This poeticall license is a shrewde fellow, and couereth many faults in a verse ... and, to conclude, it *turkeneth* [alters] all things at pleasure' (Gascoigne, *Extracts from*, ed. Arber, p. 37).

Mr. Hazlitt calmly alters *turkeneth* to *turneth* (*Works*, i. 505) without a word of comment.

Mr. Davies notes that *turkis* also occurs. And it occurs precisely in the same sense. It is formed from the stem of an O. F. pres. part. *torquiss-ant*, from the verb *torquir*, by-form of *torquer*. Such changes of conjugation are common in French.

'Yet he taketh the same sentence out of Esay, somewhat *turkised*,' i.e. altered or turned about (Bancroft, S*urvey of Pretended Holy Discipline*, 1593, p. 6).

### 176. Turken. II (6 S. xii. 33; 1885).

I have explained that *turken*, a very rare word, means to turn, twist, alter, and that it should rather be *torken*, being ultimately from the Latin *torquere*. And I now find this proved by the occurrence of the word in the fourteenth century. In the *Wars of Alexander*, l. 2967, *he torkans with* means 'he turns [himself] towards.'

[Quoted in *Stratmann*, ed. Bradley, s. v. *turken*, from my edition of the romance. Godefroy has the sb. *torquen*, in the sense of 'necklace.']

### 177. On the supposed Change of a Latin L into U in French (6 S. v. 311; 1882).

I am quite willing to accept DR. CHANCE'S explanation, and I think we ought to be much obliged to him for the care he has taken in this investigation. But I hope I may be allowed to plead that there is still a sense in which the *l* can be said to pass into *u*, viz. that, whereas there was once an *l* between *a* and *i* in *regalimen*, there is now a *u* between the *a* and *m* in *royaume*, the *l* having dropped. This is what I call the practical result, the 'rule of thumb,' and this was all that I meant. DR. CHANCE explains quite clearly that this resultant spelling, as it appears to the eye, does not explain the real nature of the phonetic change, and that consequently to talk of a change of *l* to *u* is philologically misleading. What really happens is, that *al* becomes *aul*, and then *l* drops, giving us *au*, with the result that, to the eye, *l* seems to become *u*. The real secret is that this peculiarity is due to the action of *l* on the vowel; compare the pronunciation of *father* with that of *fall*.

For similar loss of *l* compare *would*, *should*, *calm*, *psalm*, *calf*, &c. Note that *falcon* is an artificial spelling, the M. E. form being *faucoun*.

### 178. Lincolnshire Provincialisms: Rauky
(6 S. v. 353; 1882).

*Rauky* cannot be derived from *raw*, because this does not account for the *k*; and it cannot be derived from the Latin *raucus*, because provincial English words are not Latin, save under exceptional circumstances. It is too bad in these days to go on guessing as if the iniquity of guessing had never been pointed out. *Rauky* is the Norfolk *roky* and the common English *reeky*. The form *reeky*, from A. S. *rēc*, smoke, is English; the forms *rauky* and *roky* are Norse[1]. German substitutes *ch* for *k*; hence German *Rauch*, smoke. English often has the sound of long *e* where German has *au*, as in *beam*, *belief* (*Baum*, *Glaube*), &c. With E. *reek*, as cognate with G. *Rauch*, compare E. *leek*, as cognate with *Lauch*.

[1] [Perhaps. Cf. Swed. dial. *rauk*, smoke (Rietz, p. 546; Norweg. *rok* (Aasen). The *I*cel. form is *reykr* (from a base *rauk-*).]

### 179. Talon. I (6 S. v. 394; 1882).

I think I have solved this problem in my *Etymological Dictionary*. There is evidence that *talon* meant 'bird's claw' in English at least as early as the fourteenth century. The English version of *Mandeville's Travels* tells us that a griffin 'hath his *talouns* so longe and so large and grete upon his feet, as though thei weren hornes of grete oxen'; and again, in the alliterative *Romance of Alexander*, ed. Stevenson, l. 5454, some griffins are described as taking knights up 'in thaire *talons*.' Palsgrave has, '*Talant* of a byrde, the hynder claw, [in French] *talon*.' There cannot be a moment's doubt as to the etymology; it meant originally the hinder claw of a bird's foot, from Low Lat. acc. *talonem*, a derivative of *talus*. I suspect that the peculiar sense is English or Norman only, and due to the old terms of hawking. It was quite the etiquette of hawking to have a peculiar name for every conceivable part of a hawk's body.

### 180. Talon. II (6 S. vi. 417; 1882).

I am now in a position to explain this word fully. DR. CHANCE has told us that it must have meant, not the hinder claw of a bird merely, but the hinder claw together with the toe, taking 'claw' in the fuller sense. No doubt this is what the word *ought* to have meant; but, as a matter of fact, it is not what it *did* mean. The misuse of the word, that is, its employment in the restricted sense of a mere *claw*, was due to the absurd affectation of the terms used by hawkers. It is an old story that a hawk had no *feathers*, only *plumes*, and so forth, though the word *feathers* was frequently used by hawkers when they were off their guard, or when explaining things to the uninitiated. The authoritative passage on the subject is the following :—

'*Talons*.—Fyrst, the grete Clees [*claws*] behynde, that strenyth the bake of the hande, ye shall call hom [*them*] Talons. *Pownces.*—The Clees, within the fote, ye shall call of right her Pownces' (*Book of St. Albans*, fol. a 8).

Thus we find that it pleased the inventors of the terms of hawking to confine the sense of *talon* to the claw, at the *back* of the foot, whilst the claws of the toes in front were called *pounces*—a use which occurs again in Spenser, *F. Q.*, i. 11. 19, as I have already elsewhere noted. From the latter substantive the verb *pounce* is derived, though the substantive itself is obsolete; and the modern *talon* includes the *pounce*.

### 181. 'Manacus' (6 S. v. 464; 1882).

I have been referred to the curious word *manacus*, given both by Scheller and Forcellini, as being just possibly allied to *almanac*. On investigation there turns out to be no such word in the Latin language; it is a pure fiction, due to a misreading. The only reference is to *Vitruvius*, l. 9, c. 3 (for which read c. 8). The best edition of *Vitruvius*, by Rose and Müller-Strubing, Leipzig, 1867, gives *menaeus*, with the variants *maneus*, *manaeus*. *Menaeus* is merely the Greek μηναῖος in a Latin dress, and is used substantively to signify the ecliptic. This is one more instance of the soundness of the advice to 'verify quotations.'

[I hunted up this reference (with the help of my late dear friend, Mr. Boase, of Exeter College) for Dr. Murray. He gives it in 'Note 3,' at the end of *Almanac*.]

### 182. The Etymology of 'Spawn' (6 S. v. 465; 1882).

The etymology suggested by Mr. Wedgwood, and adopted by me as being most likely right (viz. from O. F. *espandre*), admits of exact proof, as I have just discovered.

The O. F. *espaundre*, a variant of *espandre*, occurs in Thomas Wright's *Vocabularies*, i. 164, and is glossed by *scheden him frome*, as Wright prints it. But Mr. Aldis Wright tells me that the MS. has been misread, and the right reading is 'scheden his *roune*,' i. e. shed his roe. With this correction we now read :—'Soffret le peysoun en ewe espaundre,' with the gloss 'scheden his roune.' Thus *espaundre* is precisely *spawn*, from Latin *expandere*.

### 183. 'Welted' (6 S. vi. 113; 1882).

This word is duly entered in the E. D. S. *List of Surrey Provincialisms*, and is a mere variant of *welked*, used by Sackville in his *Induction*, st. 12, and by Spenser in his *Shep. Kal.*, November, l. 13. The latter uses it as a transitive verb; Chaucer also has it, *Pard. Tale*, l. 738, and it occurs much earlier. See Stratmann's *Old English Dictionary*. It is found, in fact, in Old English, in Old and Modern Dutch, and in Old and Modern High-German. It is discussed by Fick, iii. 298, who connects it with A. S. *wlæc*, O. H. G. *welc*, *welh*, soft, moist, flabby; Russian *vlaga*, moisture; Lithuanian *wilgyti*, to soften, moisten. It properly means 'rendered flabby by moisture,' hence 'spoilt'; but is also used, by an easy tradition, to signify 'dried up by heat.'

### 184. 'Wimbledon' (6 S. vi. 94; 1882).

The quotation from the A. S. *Chronicle* (containing the words *on Wibbandūne*) serves to explain the name at once, if it be rightly interpreted. The supposition that the last syllable 'is the A. S. *dūne*' is incorrect. There is no such word in A. S. in the nominative case, which takes the form *dūn*; but in the dative it becomes *dūn-e*, with final *-e*, being governed by the preposition *on*. The other supposition, that if the former part of the word were a proper name 'it would have the letter *s*,' is also incorrect. A large number of proper names, including all masculines in *-a*, make the genitive in *-an*. The true interpretation is as follows: *Wibbandūne* is the dative of *Wibbandūn*, meaning 'Wibba's down.' Next, *dūn* is not a true A. S. word, but borrowed from Celtic, as explained in my *Dictionary*; the equivalent English word being *tūn*, mod. E. *town*.

### 185. Lytton (6 S. vi. 273; 1882).

*Lytton* for 'churchyard' is the same as *litten*, given by Halliwell with the same sense. The etymological spelling should rather be *litton*; and, of course, this word explains *Lytton*, when occurring as a proper name. It is formed, by assimilation of *tt* from *ct*, from A. S. *līc-tūn*, lit. 'a corpse-town,' compounded of *līc*, body, and *tūn*, town. Compare *lichgate*. The word is not very common, but is used in the Old English translation of Beda, lib. iii. c. 17, where it occurs in the dative case: 'And thær on thæra brōthra *līctūne* bebyriged,' i. e. and there buried in the cemetery of the brethren.

### 186. The Names of Chanticleer's Wives
### (6 S. vi. 304; 1882).

In Gawain Douglas's Prologue to the twelfth book of *Virgil*, l. 159, we have an allusion to Chanticleer's wives. In my *Specimens of English Literature*, p. 132, I printed their names as 'Coppa and Partelot,' because I found them so written in the MS. In Mr. Small's edition the former name appears as Toppa, and he obviously follows the edition printed at Edinburgh in 1839. My belief has always been that this old edition misled him, and that he would not otherwise have imagined the Trinity MS. to have the letter T. I have also always thought his note upon the line to be mistaken. It runs thus:—

'The Rev. Mr. Skeat thinks that this word should be *C*oppa, although written *T*oppa in all the MSS. ... It does not seem difficult to recognize in *T*oppa the old Scottish description of a hen with a good head or tuft—"a weel-tappit hen" being an expression still in use.'

To this my reply would be that the Trinity MS. contains, in my opinion, the reading Coppa, and that I cannot understand how it can be read otherwise; also, that I do not see how 'a weel-tappit hen' opposes my solution. However, as I always avoid discussion till I think I see sufficient evidence in my favour, I have never till now protested against the above criticism. But there is a most conclusive piece of evidence which, to my mind, settles the matter. We have both of us missed the point which we ought not to have missed. The name Coppa was not invented by Douglas, but is simply copied from the old Flemish story known as *Reynard the Fox*. In Mr. Arber's reprint of Caxton's translation of this wonderful epic, the name of Chaunticleer's daughter appears as Coppe and Coppen (see pp. 9 and 11). Similarly the name of Pertelot was borrowed from Chaucer's *Nun's Priest's Tale*. My present contention is that this fact ought to settle the question. Moreover, the name is Dutch. In Hexham's *Dutch Dictionary* I find: ' een *kop*, *koppe*, *kobbe*, *ofte hinne*, a hen, or a pullet'; also, '*kop*, a head, pate, or noddle.' This precisely agrees with the explanation which I gave in 1871.

### 187. Beef-eater (6 S. vi. 432; 1882).

I think DR. C. strains the supposed points in favour of the 'opinion now so commonly entertained,' rather beyond the fair interpretation of the known facts. At the outset he suggests that Steevens ' lived before the time of Johnson,' whereas they were, in fact, contemporaries, Steevens being the younger man of the two, as may be seen by a glance at Hole's *Brief Biographical Dictionary*. It is clear that Steevens was trying to gain a reputation, and that his hint to Johnson was one of his attempts in this direction. The facts are these:—

(1) No English book knows of any spelling but *beef-eater*. In my additional note, at p. 780 of my Dictionary, I gave an example from the play of *Histriomastrix*, which cannot, I suppose, be later than A. D. 1610.

(2) I know of no proof that *beef-eater* ever meant 'a waiter at a sideboard.' It is a pure assertion, made in the interests of forcing upon us the supposed French origin. It merely means servant or yeoman.

(3) I have shown that a servant was familiarly called 'an eater.'

(4) I have also shown (p. 780) that a servant was called 'a loaf-eater' long before the Norman Conquest. Surely this is to the point, and proves that at any rate the English were capable of making such a compound without any borrowing from French. If we had *eater, loaf-eater, wine-bibber,* and the like, why not *beef-eater?* Where is the difficulty?

(5) There is absolutely no link fairly joining *beef-eater* with *buffetier.* As to form, the junction breaks down, the English spelling having always been what it is now. As to sense, it equally breaks down, (1) because it cannot be proved that the English *beef-eater* ever meant specifically a waiter at a sideboard; and (2) because it is admitted that, if the French *buffetier* ever meant a waiter at a sideboard (and even this is only a guess made in the interests of this precious etymology), at any rate it was not the usual sense of the word. If we had borrowed the word, it would have been more sensible to have given it the sense of 'wine-taster.' On the whole, I see no good reason for going out of our way to make a supposition involving all sorts of difficulties, when we have a homely derivation at hand from a pure English source. The word stands on quite a different footing from those of known corruptions. The latter can be accounted for; but the alleged 'corruption' in *beef-eater* rests upon mere paradoxes.

[My explanation of this word is adopted in the *New Eng. Dictionary* and in the *Century Dictionary.* The former cites A. S. *hlāf-ǣta,* a loaf-eater. The latter quotes the passage from Ben Jonson, which I give in my (larger) *Etym. Dictionary*]

### 188. Wrinkle=New Idea (6 S. vi. 456; 1882).

Mr. Terry's quotations are very acceptable. I have already pointed out that A. S. *wrenc* had a meaning not very dissimilar. Perhaps a quotation from King Ælfred may help to show how old the word really is: 'Thā fōr Theodosius thyderweard, and wiste thæt hine man wolde mid tham ilcan wrence bethrīdian,' i.e. Then went Theodosius thither, and knew that they wanted to surround him by (using) the same *wrinkle* (or stratagem). See Ælfred's translation of *Orosius*, bk. vi. chap. xxxvi. § 2.

### 189. Ollands, a Norfolk Word (6 S. vi. 475; 1882).

It is the old story. Men cannot be content with telling us about a word of this sort without insinuating an etymology, while, of course, they never dream of investigating before guessing. The suggested etymology of *olland* from *out-land* is really too much. In 1691, Ray spelt it *old land*, in two words (E. D. S., B. 16, p. 88); and it is always a comfort to crush a bad guess easily.

### 190. Tennis (6 S. vi. 543; 1882).

I am quite ready to bow to Mr. J. Marshall's decision as to the original form of the game itself. What I say is that, if we really wish to discover the etymology, it would be better to consider the old forms *tenise*, *teneys*, and the Latin names *tenisia*, *teniludus*, instead of persistently ignoring these forms. We should also remember that *e* frequently means *æ* in Latin MSS. of this period, the *æ* being seldom written. The word is almost certainly French, as no other language could have given the suffix *-eys* or *-ise*. It does not in the least follow that we got the game from France; for Anglo-French (less correctly called Norman-French) was practically a distinct language from the French of France, with its own peculiar laws, and with a power of throwing out new forms. The collection of Anglo-French words lately made by me for the Philological Society suggests how very little has hitherto been done for the study of forms which, for explaining English, are of the highest value.

[Gower has an older form *tenetz*. The etymology is unknown. Is it from A. F. *tenez*, meaning 'play'?]

### 191. The Dunmow Flitch (6 S. vii. 135; 1883).

The earliest allusion to this is in *Piers the Plowman*, A-text, pass. x. 188. It is also mentioned in Chaucer, *Wyf of Bathes Tale*, and in a poem in MS. Laud 416 (about 1460). There is a note, a page and a half long, on the subject in a book which abounds with illustrations of old words and manners, but seems to be only known to few; viz. my *Notes to Piers the Plowman*, published by the Early English Text Society in 1877. See p. 227 of that work.

### 192. Devonshire Dialect (6 S. vii. 272; 1883).

The explanation of *stain* is as follows. The A. S. for *stone* is *stān*; whence, by the usual vowel-change, was formed the adj. *stǣnen*, pronounced nearly as *stain-en* (but with a more 'open' vowel), and meaning, literally, 'made of stone.' But the sense seems to have been extended to mean 'made of earthenware,' because of the stone-like hardness of such pans, &c. In St. John, ii. 6, we are told that there were set *six stǣnene water-fatu*, i. e. six 'stain-en' water-vats; and in Exodus, vii. 19, there is mention, in the A. S. version, of vats or vessels of tree (i. e. wood) and 'stain-en' vats. In these passages the use of 'stain-en' is, of course, due to the occurrence of the words *lapideæ* and *saxeis* in the Vulgate version, from which the A. S. translation was made; but, independently of this, there is reason to believe that vessels for kitchen use were commonly divided by our ancestors into vessels of metal, tree, and stone. Thus, Lye cites from a glossary the A. S. *stǣna*, sb., Lat. *gillo*, i. e. a stone vessel holding a gill. ... Pegge, in his *Kenticisms* (E. D. S., C. 3, p. 49), tells us that in Derbyshire *a stean pot* means a stone pot, whilst in Kent *to stean a wall* is to build up the sides with stones. This Kentish verb is precisely the A. S. *stǣnan*, to stone, also formed from *stān*. I think it is quite clear that the Devonshire *stain* represents, not the A. S. *stān*, stone, but the modified form *stǣn-* as occurring in the adjective *stǣn-en* and the verb *stǣn-an*. It is highly important in scientific etymology to pay great heed to the vowel-sounds.

[Mr. Elworthy, in his *Dialect of West Somerset*, gives glossic 'stoo·an' for *stone*, and 'wai·t' for A. S. *hwǣte* wheat. Cf. *stǣnen* in Toller's *A. S. Dictionary*.]

### 193. Thel (6 S. vii. 293 ; 1883).

Mr. North has found a good example of a rare and valuable word, illustrating a rather dark place in English etymology. I regret that in [the first edition of] my *Dictionary* the account of *deal*, in the sense of 'deal board,' is utterly wrong ; it has no connexion with Du. *deel*, a deal or part (which is neuter, and answers to A. S. *dǣl*), but is borrowed from Du. *deel*, a deal board, plank, which is feminine. Now *thel* is the true *English* word corresponding to *deal board*, and has the same sense of 'board' or 'plank'; if there was any difference, it is probable that a *thel* was thinner or smaller than a plank. The A. S. *thel*, a plank, occurs in several compounds, all given in Grein's *Dictionary*; and the closely allied word *thill*, the shaft of a cart, is still in use, and is fully treated of in my *Dictionary*. Corresponding to the theoretical Teutonic form \**theliz*, we have A. S. *thel*, Icel. *thili*, a wainscot, plank, O. H. G. *dil*, *dilo*, a plank ; and corresponding to the theoretical Teutonic form \**thiljōn*, a substantive of the weak declension, we have A. S. *thille*, E. *thill*, Icel. *thilja*, planking, a bench for rowers, a deck; Du. [or Low G.] *deel*, a plank, deal board; G. *diele*, a deal, plank. The interesting point is this, and should be noted, that at least three Dutch [or Low German] words have been taken into English in which *d* corresponds to an original *th*, and we have sometimes retained, nevertheless, the allied E words. Examples are seen in *drill* (Dutch), the native E. word being *thrill*; *deal* board (Dutch), the native E. word being *thel*, allied to *thill*; and lastly *deck* (Dutch), the native E. word being *thatch*. One result is that *drill, deal, deck* cannot be found at an early date. For the first, I know of no examples earlier than Cotgrave and Ben Jonson; for the last, none earlier than Lord Surrey; whilst for *deal* I can find nothing earlier than the mention of 'a thousand *deal boards*' in Clarendon's *Civil War*, ii. 675, cited by Richardson. Any earlier quotations for any of these words would be a gain.

[A correspondent in *N. and Q.*, 6 S. viii. 389, cited 'xvj *deles*' as being mentioned in 1600; but Dr. Murray finds that *deles* occurs as early as in 1402, in the records of Hull. And see the article on *Deal* (3) in the Errata and Addenda to my *Etym. Dict.*, p. 799.]

**194. Anglo-Saxon Numerals** (6 S. vii. 365; 1883).

Many persons who have some acquaintance with Anglo-Saxon must have felt puzzled at the curious use of the prefix *hund-* before certain numerals. If we write out the numbers 10, 20, 30, &c., up to 120 in Anglo-Saxon, the series is *tỹn, twentig, thrittig, feowertig*, &c.; or, expressing the same as nearly as possible in modern English spelling, we get the series *ten, twenty, thirty, forty, fifty, sixty, hund-seventy, hund-eighty, hund-ninety, hund* (also *hundred*), *hund-eleventy*, and finally *hund-twelvety* (also called *hund-twenty*). As to the meaning of *hund* there is no dispute; it means *decade* (P. 118), and is merely short for Goth. *taihund*, just as Latin *centum* is short for *decentum*. But the point is, why should the addition of the prefix *hund-* begin with the numeral *seventy* rather than at any other point? The answer is, simply, that this reckoning refers to a time when what is still called 'the great hundred,' meaning thereby 120, was in common use. The half of 120 is 60; and up to 60 all is straightforward. But after passing 60 we come to a reckoning of the latter half of the 120, involving higher numbers, and perhaps regarded as requiring greater effort to secure accuracy. These higher numbers were, of course, in less frequent use than the lower ones, and the prefix served to mark the notion that 60, the half of 120, had been reached, and that the reckoning of the second half had begun. Hence the prefix was continued throughout, with the necessary introduction of the curious words *eleventy* and *twelvety*, which are perfectly legitimate formations, and were once in actual use. The most curious use of the 'great hundred' which I remember to have met with is in Fitzherbert's *Husbandry* (E. D. S., p. 41), where the symbol 'C' is actually used to denote, not 100, but 120.

This consideration of reckoning by the 'great hundred' is the obvious explanation of the French numerals also. The reckoning is regular up to *soixante*, i.e. 60; after that the reckoning proceeds by *scores*, the next resting-place (so to speak) being *quatre-vingt*, or four score, whilst 70 is merely called *soixante-dix*, 60 and 10. So also 90 is 80 and 10, or *quatre-vingt-dix*, and the next score is reached at 100. The last score of the 'great hundred' is reached at 120, formerly called *six vingts*, or six score, as noted by Littré, s. v. 'Vingt.'

### 195. Ever- (6 S. vii. 456; 1883).

I would remark that it is perfectly well known that the prefix *Ever-* [in some place-names] is derived neither from the Latin *aper* nor from the German *Eber*; for neither of these forms could give us *ever-*. The modern *ever-* is merely the modern way of representing the A.S. *eofor*, a boar, which is *cognate* with the Latin and German forms, and not derived from either of them; the same is true of the Russian word *vepre*. It would conduce much to clearness of thought if the difference between cognation and derivation were more clearly apprehended.

**196. Darbies; or 'Darby's Bonds'** (6 S. vii. 498; 1883).

The phrase 'Darby's bonds' occurs in Gascoigne's *Steel Glass*, l. 787, which runs thus

'To binde such babes in father Derbies bands.'

The passage is given in Skeat's *Specimens of English Literature*, p. 316. My note on it is as follows:—

'*Father Derbies bands*, handcuffs. Why so called, *I* know not, but *darbies* is still a slang term for the same.'

We shall not obtain any further light upon the term until we can discover who was 'father Derby.' All we know of him at present is that his name was already proverbial in 1576.

**197. Basque = Gascon = Euskarian** (6 S. vii. 516; 1883).

I am not aware whether any reader knows what this article means, but it is perhaps as well to point out that the writer expects us to accept, as 'familiar examples' of letter-change, that *wood* is the same word as F. *bois*, that *good* and *better* are from the same root, that *boor* and *vir* are likewise one word, that *wet* is the German *nass*, that *nigh* is merely *vicinus*, and so forth. I am quite sure that such statements would not be tolerated in discussing geology and botany; but in matters of 'philology' such crudities are thought worthy of being written [and printed].

**198. The Story of 'The pound of flesh'** (6 S. viii. 105; 1883).

I do not know whether it has been pointed out that the story of 'the pound of flesh,' in the *Merchant of Venice*, occurs in the *Cursor Mundi*, ll. 21413-21496. I suspect this to be the earliest version of the tale in the English language.

**199. Chaucer: 'Canterbury Tales'** (6 S. viii. 125; 1883).

In the *Parson's Prologue*, l. 43, we have the well-known lines :—

'I can nat geste, *rom, ram, ruf*, by lettre,
Ne, god wot, *rym* holde I but litel bettre.'

Compare the curious use of *rim ram* in the Walloon dialect. Sigart gives two examples : '*Ca n'a ni rim ni ram*, it has neither rime nor reason ; *c'est toudi l'même rim ram*, it's always the same song.'

**200. Three-way Leet** (6 S. viii. 217 ; 1883).

MR. TERRY does not give all the latest information. I have since shown, in the *Academy*, that the Essex *three releet* [a place where three ways meet] is not particularly corrupt, but is merely misdivided. It should be *threere leet*, A. S. *thrēora lǣtu*, meetings of three ways. The suffix *-re*, A. S. *-ra*, is the mark of the genitive plural. So also *twegra wega gelǣtu*, meetings of two ways, in a gloss quoted in Bosworth's *Dictionary*.

**201. Skellum** (6 S. viii. 375 ; 1883).

In reply to MR. J., I have to say that *sk* does not always point to a Scandinavian origin for a word. It may point to a Dutch origin, as in *landscape*, the Dutch *sch* being difficult to an Englishman, who likens it to *sk*[1]. *Skellum*, as in Nares, was borrowed immediately, in the Tudor period, from Du. *schelm*, explained by Hexham as 'a rogue, a villaine, or a wicked person.' The etymology is given by Weigand. The *m* is a noun suffix, and the root-verb is the same as that which gives the E. *skill*. The original

---

[1] So also in *skipper*, from Du. *schipper*.

sense was a thing separated or cast away; hence M. H. G. *schelme*, carrion, offal, whence finally it came to mean a worthless fellow. See Weigand, *Etym. G. Dict.*, and the remarks on Dutch words in the preface (p. xiv.) to my *Etymological Dictionary*.

[Most words beginning with *sk* are of Scandinavian origin. The A. S. *sc* became *sh*. Many words beginning with *sc* are French; as *scald*, verb, *scandal*, *scarce*.]

### 202. Modern Letter-writing (6 S. viii. 376; 1883).

I beg leave to endorse the statements made at the above reference. I frequently receive letters which are perfectly legible throughout, except that *neither the name nor the address can be deciphered.* How to reply to them is a most harrowing question. I also observe a growing tendency, chiefly in correspondents of whom one knows nothing, to exact immediate answers, regardless of the trouble they may cause. In particular, I would allude to the subject of place-names. I am often expected to solve the sense of a place-name, though it might cost a week's labour to collect the old spellings and all the available facts. I find the answering of letters of this class is harder task-work than any book-writing. A little mercy would be much appreciated.

[As to place-names, I now always expect my correspondent to tell me the earliest known spelling, in old charters.]

### 203. Foxglove (6 S. viii. 392; 1883).

I beg leave to protest against the etymology (!) from *folk's glove*. I do so on principle; it seems to me most mischievous to suggest how a name *might* have arisen, when all the while the facts are on record. As to the suggestion itself, I have heard it only too often, and it is given in Brewer's *Dictionary of Phrase and Fable*. Any attempt at ascertaining the facts would have disposed of the theory at once; for it is perfectly well known that the A.S.

name was *foxes glōfa*, meaning fox's glove, which occurs in vol. iii. p. 327 of Cockayne's *Anglo-Saxon Leechdoms*. It is obviously impossible that the A. S. *foxes* can be a corruption of a form *folk's*, which is of later date. The Norwegian name *revhandskje*, foxglove, is derived from *rev*, a fox, and *handskje*, a glove; and how are we to explain this away? The fact is that Englishmen are always making 'suggestions' of this character, being apparently of opinion that unaided guess-work is the only method of value; yet we do not thus attempt to explain the ordinary facts of botany and chemistry. Dr. Brewer explains *foxes glōfa* by 'red or fox-coloured glove.' It means nothing of the kind; it means just simply 'glove of the fox.' It is only another example of 'suggestion'; it is far better to take the fact as it stands. A study of such a book as Earle's *Plant-Names* will show that our ancestors delighted in names formed from the names of animals; and this fact cannot be upset by merely modern notions as to their inappropriateness. If we exercise our imagination by making bad guesses, we should not blame our ancestors, who exercised theirs quite harmlessly. [It is now considered 'scientific' to turn the old name *hare-bell* into 'hair-bell,' as being descriptive of its slender stalk! That is not the question. The question is, not what *ought* it to be called, but what *was* it called, as a matter of fact.]

### 204. Vild (6 S. viii. 476; 1883).

*Vild* is merely *vile* with an excrescent *d*, due to stress, like the *d* in *sound*, from F. *son*. It is very common, and occurs in Shakespeare and Spenser. Excrescent *d* after *l* does not seem to have received much attention; yet the old spelling of *hold* of a ship was *hole*; *iron-mould* is for *iron-mole*, i.e. iron-spot; and I believe the old word *cole-prophet* (false prophet) appears as *cold prophet*.

[Such is the case; see *Cole-prophet* in the *New E. Dictionary*.]

**205. Setting the Thames on Fire. I** (6 S. viii. 476; 1883).

I have a profound disbelief in this alleged origin of the saying, which is an old popular etymology, given in Dr. Brewer's *Dictionary of Phrase and Fable*. I should like to ask whether a South Lancashire labourer would understand the *phrase*; who uses it of him; and, in particular, whether it is *possible* to set a sieve [*temse*] on fire by friction? These assertions are easily made, but they commonly turn out upon inquiry to be no better than mares' nests. Where can we find 'Set the *temse* on fire' in an old book? Of course the word *temse* itself is common enough, and occurs in the *Promptorium Parvulorum*. [And how do such gentlemen explain—to set the *Seine* on fire? Probably they think that a *seine* is a fishing-net (and so it is), and that the fishermen pull it on board with such hearty diligence that it is easily set on fire by the friction against the boat's side. See further below.]

**206. Setting the Thames on Fire. II** (6 S. ix. 14; 1884).

We have now got a little further in this question. It appears that this fable (as I suspect it will turn out to be) can be traced as far back as March 25, 1865, when it was first started by a correspondent signing himself P. in *N. and Q.* 3 S. viii. 239. Observe that P. puts forward his solution quite as a mere guess, saying that 'the long misuse of the word *temse* ... *may possibly have tended to* the substitution of sound for sense.' Mr. Hazlitt merely *copies* what is there said. The statement made is that 'an active fellow, who worked hard, *not unfrequently* [the italics are mine] set the rim of the temse on fire by force of friction against the rim of the flour-barrel.' Mr. Hazlitt improves this into the '*iron* rim of the temse,' it being, of course, quite easy to set iron 'on fire.' Now I think we have a right to expect some sort of proof of the statement. If 'an active fellow' could do this once, he can do it now[1]. Well, I should like to see him do it. Who can quote the phrase from a book older than 1865? See *P. Plowman*, C. 7. 335.

**207. The Word 'Gā'** (6 S. ix. 14; 1884).

MR. TAYLOR'S statement that the suffix -*gay* is the same as the German *gau*, and his identification of *gau* with Kemble's explanation of *gā*, cannot be admitted without proof. They are against all phonetic laws. The E. *day* is A. S. *dæg*, so that -*gay* would be -*gæg*; or else, since E. *hay* (in names) is A. S. *hege*, -*gay* would be -*gege*. How E. *ay* = A. S. *ā*, is a mystery. Again, the G. *au* = A. S. *ēa*, as in G. *baum* = A. S. *bēam*. Anything can be said if phonetic laws are not to count.

[In Kemble's *Saxons in England* there is a good deal about the *gā* or *scīr*. I once asked Mr. Freeman his authority for this *gā*; and he referred me to Spelman. It turns out that Spelman evolved the word out of two names, viz. *Ohtgaga* and *Noxgaga*, the authorities for these names being themselves by no means clear. We have no right to conclude from them that *ga* was an independent word, with long *ā*. If it were, it would be *go* in mod. E., and *gehe* (probably) in German. It could not possibly be the G. *Gau*.]

**208. By-and-by** (6 S. ix. 34; 1884).

The statement that *by* was repeated in order to signify 'as near as possible' has no true foundation. Examples show that it means rather 'in due order.' Such phrases are best understood by consulting the right books, viz. Mätzner's and Stratmann's Old English dictionaries. Mätzner is quite clear about it. He says that *bi and bi*

---

[1] This is the old suggestion made in the fable, to the man who had taken an extraordinary leap 'at Ephesus.'

sometimes indicates 'in order, with reference to space.' He cites, 'Two yonge knightes, liggyng *by and by*,' i. e. side by side (Chaucer, *C. T.*, 1013); 'He slouh twenti, Ther hedes quyte and clene he laid tham *bi and bi*' (*Rob. of Brunne*, tr. of Langtoft, ed. Hearne, p. 267); 'His doughter had a bed al by hir-selve, Right in the same chambre *by and by*' (Chaucer, *C. T.*, 4140). Here it means in a parallel direction; not as near as possible. Further, says Mätzner, it is used with reference to the succession of separate circumstances; hence, in due order, successively, gradually, separately, singly. 'These were his wordes *by and by*' (*Rom. of the Rose*, 4581); 'Whan William ... had taken homage of barons *bi and bi*' (*Rob. of Brunne*, as above, p. 73); 'This is the genelogie ... Of kynges *bi and bi*' (*id.* p. 111); '*By and by*, si[n]gillatim' (*Prompt. Parv.*). To these examples may be added those already cited. In later times the phrase came to mean 'in course of time,' and hence either (1) immediately, as in the A. V. of the Bible, or (2) after a while, as usual at present. On this later use see Wright's *Bible Word-book*, new edition. We thus see that the earliest authority for the phrase is *Robert of Brunne*, who is one of the most important authors in the whole of English literature, seeing that Mr. Oliphant has shown that it is *his* form of English rather than Chaucer's which is actually the literary language. It seems a pity, under the circumstances, that he should be 'a source unknown' to any one; but Hearne's edition is out of print and scarce, and we still wait for a new one in an easily accessible form. [Dr. Furnivall's edition has since appeared, in the Record Series. See *By* in the *New E. Dictionary*.]

### 209. Thethorne (6 S. ix. 245; 1884).

In Halliwell's *Dictionary* we find that the *thethorne-tre* is explained in the *Promptorium* by *ramnus*. To this

Halliwell appends the note, '*ramnus* is the medlar-tree.' Certainly not; *ramnus*, or rather *rhamnus*, is the buckthorn.

[*Thethorn* is short for *thefthorn* or *thevethorn*; the latter occurs in Wyclif; see Stratmann. The A. S. forms are —— *þēofeþorn*, a gloss to *ramnus* in the *Corpus Glossary* (eighth century), and *þȳfeþorn* in Ælfric's *Glossary* (tenth century). Hence, probably, the prov. E. forms *thebes*, *thepes*, *thapes*, *febes*, *feabes*, *fepes*, *feapes*, usually applied to the fruit of the gooseberry-tree.]

### 210. Eftures (6 S. ix. 245; 1884).

This word is entered in Halliwell, but it has no true existence. There is no such word in English or French, but it has arisen from one of those blunders which dictionaries often perpetrate. The entry stands thus: '*Eftures*, passages; Malory, ii. 376.' It is due to the following sentence in Caxton's edition of Malory's *Morte Arthure*, bk. xix. ch. vii: 'And sir Meligraunce said to sir Launcelot, "Pleaseth it you to see the *eftures* of this castle?"' I quote from Sir E. Strachey's reprint. But *eftures* is an obvious error for *estures*, or rather *estres*, by that confusion between *f* and long *s* which is so common. The word *estres* occurs in a well-known passage in Chaucer's *Knight's Tale*. Cotgrave has: '*Les estres d'une maison*, the inward conveyances, private windings and turnings within, entries into, issues out of, a house.' This fully explains the above passage. I believe the combination *ft* is almost unknown to Latin and French, so that such a form as *eftures* is hardly possible. In fact, the curious use of *pt* in Icelandic to represent the sound of *ft* is due to following a Latin model; for Latin has *pt* only, and knows nothing of *ft*. It follows that Halliwell's *Dictionary*, like every other dictionary with which I am acquainted, cannot be *always* implicitly relied upon. Such an error as the above should have been corrected, especially as *estres* is duly given and rightly explained.

[A note of this mistake duly appears in the *New English Dictionary*, s. v. *Estres.*]

### 211. Etymology of Sulphur (6 S. ix. 471 ; 1884).

The etymology of the Sanskrit *çulvāri* from *çulva*, copper, is by no means certain, and is more likely to be a popular etymology, of no value. The suffix *-āri* can hardly stand for *vairin* (rather than *vairi*), hostile. It is more likely that *çulvāri* is a word foreign to Sanskrit, having no connexion with *çulva*, copper, beyond an accidental partial resemblance. Benfey gives both words, without any hint of a connexion between them. I do not see the use of giving mere guess-work.

### 212. A few words on ' Anglo-Saxon.' I
### (6 S. ix. 302 ; 1884).

With regard to the language commonly called Anglo-Saxon, I have already pointed out in my *Dictionary* that it means one of the three main dialects of the oldest English, viz. the Southern, or Wessex, dialect. The other two are the Old Northumbrian and the Old Midland.

I now wish to draw particular attention to the fact that there are also two distinct kinds of Anglo-Saxon. The former is the real language, as exhibited in extant manuscripts, in trustworthy editions that are not manipulated, and in the best dictionaries only. The other Anglo-Saxon is a pure fiction, a conglomeration of misleading rubbish, but is to be found only too plentifully. It is cited *ad nauseam* by Bailey, Skinner, Johnson, and the rest, and is extremely familiar to those who learn Anglo-Saxon only from books. It is highly prized by some etymologists, because it provides them with etymologies ready made; and no wonder, seeing that it was expressly invented for the purpose!

I give three specimens of this wonderful language, and perhaps may some day give more; they are plentiful enough.

'*Adastrigan*, to discourage; hence *dastard*, a coward' (Somner).

Clearly invented to account for *dastard*. Bosworth records it in his old edition; from the new one it has, happily, disappeared[1].

'*Piga*, a little maid' (Somner).

The mistake is surprising. In the first place, it should have had a long *i*; secondly, it should have ended in *e*, supposing it feminine; and thirdly, it is clearly suggested by the Dan. *pige*. But what is *pige*? It is the Danish form of Icel. *pika*, a girl, of which Vigfusson says that it is 'a foreign word of uncertain origin, first occurring in Norway about the end of the fourteenth (!) century, and in Iceland about the *fifteenth*.' A pretty word this to make 'Anglo-Saxon' out of! Of course it was 'wanted' to account (wrongly) for *piggesnie* in Chaucer, and it has also been used to derive *Peggy* and 'please the *pigs*' from (*N. and Q.* 6 S. ix. 232). Unluckily, by the ordinary phonetic laws, A.S. '*piga*' would become *pye* in Middle English, and *pie* in Modern English; so the usefulness of it even for *piggesnie*, *Peggy*, and *pigs* is not apparent. Only it must be remembered that those who utilize these curious forms do so because they are unfamiliar with A. S. manuscripts, and do not sufficiently heed phonetic laws, which are very discouraging to working by guess.

'*Rascal*, a lean worthless deer; hence a rascal' (Somner).

Oh! the pity of inserting into an A. S. dictionary a word which is so plainly Anglo-French!

[1] [Somner was quite honest, but he misread the word. I find a note by my old master, the Rev. O. Cockayne—'It is an error for the O. Northumb. *adustriga*, used to gloss Lat. *detestari*; Matt. xxvi. 74.']

I hope it may some day occur to those who get so much store by this singular language that these three specimens, and many more of the same character, are such as should be avoided rather than courted. [Somner always has *some* authority for his statements. He did his best; but we must beware.]

### 213. Pseudo-Saxon Words. II (6 S. ix. 446; 1884).

I make a note of a few more so-called 'Anglo-Saxon' words, all to be found in the old edition of Bosworth's *Dictionary* :—

*Aisil*, vinegar.—Quoted as 'A. S.' by Bailey. It is Old French, and may be found in Godefroy. It is derived from a Low Latin diminutive form of *acetum*.

*Braue*, a letter, brief.—Evidently an error for M. E. *breue*, E. *brief*; a French word.

*Broel*, a park, &c.—It is O. F.; from Low Latin *brogilus*.

*Blendan*, to blend.—The A. S. *blendan* means to blind. The A. S. for *blend* is *blandan*.

*Carited*, charity.—This is an O. F. word occurring in the *A. S. Chronicle*. There is no great harm in inserting such a word in an A S. dictionary; only readers must not imagine it to be 'Saxon.'

*Cite*, a city.—Inserted as an A. S. word without any reference. It is French.

*Pouerte*, poverty.—The same remark applies.

*Pynt*, a pint.—Mere French.

Moreover, the A. S. dictionaries abound in words which are pure Latin, or Latin slightly altered, and are not to be regarded as Teutonic. Thus *cæfester*, a halter, is merely *capistrum*. The citation of A. S. words requires much heed and knowledge; and that is why people generally rush at it blindfold, to save trouble.

**214. Notes on Phrase and Inflection. I** (6 S. ix. 32; 1884).

We ought to be much obliged to Sir J. A. Picton for protesting against the worthless rubbish which is being printed in *Good Words* upon this subject, and which seems to prove that any one who is utterly ignorant of the facts of the formation of the English language has a much better chance of being listened to than those who have studied the subject. I have not been able to find, during twenty years' search, that there is *any other subject*, in which ignorance is commonly regarded as a primary qualification for being chosen to write 'popular' articles on it. At the same time I am rather sorry to see that Sir J. A. Picton's communication contains several inaccuracies; in many cases he has not followed that historical method which he justly advocates. The formation of weak verbs has been, in all details, correctly explained in the introduction to Morris' *Specimens of Early English*, pt. i. p. lxi, which the student should consult. It will thus appear that the original suffix in the verd *send* was *-de*, not *-ed*. This gave *send-de*, written *sende*, once a common form.

This became *sente*, as being more easy to pronounce rapidly, and finally *sent*. *Sende* is the only form which is found in Anglo-Saxon, and the word *sended* never existed, except (perhaps) by misuse. . Another inaccuracy is the fancy that the Middle English suffix *-te* is High German. It has, in English, nothing to do with High German, but depends upon phonetic laws. The suffix appears as *-te* after voiceless consonants, such as *p, t, k* (*h, gh*). Hence the M. E. *slep-te, met-te, brough-te*, mod. E. *slept, met, brought* (never *slepd, metd, broughd*). Some verbs inserted [what has been called] a connecting vowel[1]; hence *lov-e-de, hat-e-de*, whence *lov-ed, hat-ed*. It is quite a mistake to suppose that Landor originated such a form as *slip-t*. As a fact, it is

---
[1] A misleading term; see p. 178.

correct, and occurs, spelt *slip-te* (dissyllabic), in Gower's *Confessio Amantis,* ed. Pauli, vol. ii. p. 72, where it rhymes with *skip-te.* No one who thinks that the putting of *t* for *ed* is 'of late years a fashion in certain quarters' can have examined a certain book known as the first folio of Shakespeare. I open Booth's reprint *at random,* and my eye lights on p. 91, col. 2, of part ii, and I at once find *chanc't* for *chanced;* there are several thousand such examples in that work. It is, in fact, a great misfortune that such pure and correct formations as *skipt* and *slipt* have been absurdly spelt *skipped* and *slipped,* while no one writes *slepped.* Such is the muddle-headedness of modern English spelling, which seems to be almost worshipped for its inconsistencies.

### 215. Notes on Phrase and Inflection. II
### (6 S. ix. 130; 1884).

I must ask for a short space for explanation. I see where I have made myself obscure, viz. by not precisely defining my limits. In saying that the form *sended* (for *sent*) never existed, I meant that it does not occur in any extant written English, which is the natural meaning of my words. Before this prehistoric form came in view, it was *already* cut down to *sende* (short for *send-de*). Now compare this with what Sir J. A. Picton tells us. I quote his words: '*Send* had its original preterite *sended;* but when an attempt was made to reduce it to one syllable, *send'd,* it will be at once seen that *sent* was the inevitable outcome.' I will now prove formally that this is perfectly well known to be incorrect. The attempt to reduce the word to one syllable was never made till long after the Conquest; the written history of the word is totally different. What really happened was, that the *i* of the Gothic *sandida* dropped out, thus giving *sende*[1], which is the *only* form in A. S. poetry

---

[1] *Sende* shows the *i*-mutation of *a* to *e,* and is thus short for a *prehistoric* form *send(i,de,* mutated form of *sandida.*

and is extremely common; see Grein's *Wörterbuch*, ii. 431. The Mid. Eng. *sende* sometimes became *sente*, by a natural phonetic law, as being capable of more rapid utterance; after this the *e* dropped off, and the modern *sent* resulted [1]. This explanation, which is a mere statement of facts easily verified, is quite different from what SIR J. A. PICTON *at first* told us. I may add that I am perfectly acquainted with the *Gothic* forms of the weak verbs, having already printed two accounts of them.

Next take SIR J. A. PICTON's account of *loved*, which is not correct. He tells us: '*Lov-ed* was originally *lov-dyd* or *-ded*. It required little effort to make the euphonic change to *lov-ed*.' Here are three mistakes at once. The original form *lov-ded* is not the right form to take; the change is not 'euphonic' when made suddenly, as here directed; and the effort to make such a change would have been considerable, not 'little.' We must start, rather, from a form *lov-e-de*, precisely parallel (as a Mid. English form) [2] to the Gothic pt. t. *lag-i-da* already cited. This *lov-e-de* lasted down to Chaucer's time. Then the final *e* dropped, and we obtained *lov-ed*, in two syllables, now called *lov'd*, in one.

The fact is, that SIR J. A. PICTON has fallen into the common mistake of supposing that *lov-ed* stands for *lov-d-ed*, by a dropping out of the former *d*. This error has arisen from not understanding the origin of the *e*, which even Dr. Morris somewhere calls 'a connecting vowel.' It is nothing of the kind, but a part of the root. Weak verbs end in Gothic in *-j-an* and in A. S. in *-i-an* or *-ig-an*. Thus the A. S. for 'to hate' was not *hatan*, but *hat-ian* (for *hat-jan*). It just makes all the difference. *Hat-an* would have made a past tense *hat-de*, turning (of course) into *hat-te*. This is not a guess, for there *is* a verb *hātan*, and its past tense is *hāt-te*. But *hat-i-an* made its past tense as

---

[1] This is very nearly what we are *now* told; 6 S. ix. 92.
[2] The A. S. form is *luf-o-de*.

*hat-ja-de*, usually written *hat-o-de*. As late as in Chaucer we still have *love-e-de*, *hat-e-de*, in three syllables. Then the *e* dropped, giving the modern *lov-ed* or *lov'd*, and *hat-ed*, and there we stop, without bringing in any 'euphonic' laws at all. I am not aware that this has been clearly explained before, at any rate in any English grammar; but any German accustomed to such matters will at once see (though he probably knows it already, if a student of Old English) that the -*e*- in *hat-e-d* is a *part of the formative stem of the verb itself* (the A. S. infinitive being *hat-i-an*), and that all that is now left of the pt. t. suffix answering to the third pers. plural -*dedun* in Gothic is the *initial*, not the *third* letter[1]. Thus *send-e* is short for \*sand-i-da; and the plural *send(d)on*=\**sand-i-don*, is short for *sand-i-dedun*.

As to the formation of such words as *skipt*, it is clear that Sir J. A. Picton takes a very different view from mine. I could explain *skipt* if I had the space, and I could show why it is quite 'correct,' and that the unphonetic *skipped* is a modern error. I will add that those who know what *umlaut* means will see that *send-e* really stands for *sand-i-da*, as above.

I must add one more remark. Sir J. A. Picton objects to calling *slipt* and *skipt* 'pure and correct formations.' But he avoids telling us what name he would give to such forms as *slepped* or *kepped*, or why *skipt* should be wrong and *slept* and *kept* right.

### 216. Notes on Phrase and Inflection. III
(6 S. ix. 191; 1884).

I had not intended to write more on this subject, but the note at the last reference leaves the matter in such a tangle that it is necessary to put it somewhat straight. It gives us the clue at last, and shows how Sir J. A. Picton has been

---

[1] Max Müller *has* seen this; see his *Lectures*, eighth ed., i. 270. But we no longer believe that the Goth. pl. suffix -*dedun* meant 'did.'

entirely misled by Bosworth's *Dictionary*. The fact is that this dictionary contains some errors, there being a misprint in the very passage cited; whilst at the same time the very best dictionary is likely to mislead any one who trusts to it without entirely comprehending its full meaning. Bosworth[1] gives the present tense of *wendan*, to go, as *ic wend, thu wentst, he went*. Now, *ic wend* is a pure misprint for *ic wende*, as any grammar will show; or perhaps it is simpler to state that *ic wende* occurs in *Elene*, 348; *Solomon and Saturn*, 19; see Grein. Hence, in form, the present and past tenses were exactly alike in the first person; the reason being that *wende* is the true form for the present, whilst the past *wende* is short for *wend-de*, a contraction of \**wand-i-da*, as explained in my last. But the third person singular indicative is given as *went*. This occurs in Luke xvii. (not xviii.) 31, where *he went* does not mean *precisely* 'let him turn back,' but *literally* 'he shall turn back'; the A. S. always expressing the future by the present form. Now, the tangle arose on this wise. This form *went* is really a mere contraction of *wendeth*; in the very passage cited, the Rushworth MS. has *awendeth*, and the Lindisfarne MS. has *awoendath*. In the metrical Psalms, cxiii. 8, the Latin *convertit petram* is translated by *he wendeth stān* (not *he went stān*). But this *went* (for *wendeth*) is the Mod. E. *wends*, third person singular indicative, and has nothing whatever to do with our Mod. E. *went*. Hence all the trouble.

The Mod. E. *went* is the same as the M. E. and A. S. *wende*, past tense, of which the thirteenth century form was *wente* (with final *e*), occurring in *Genesis and Exodus*, ed. Morris, 321. The final *e* of this *wente* was essential, the word being dissyllabic; but the Northern dialect dropped it; see *went* (for *wente*) in the *Seven Sages*, ed. Wright,

---

[1] I refer to his *older* Dictionary, mainly copied from Lye; but Lye (as to this point) is correct. In the new edition (continued by Toller) no such error will appear.

1485. On the other hand, the A. S. *went*, third person singular indicative, occurs as *went* as late as in the *Ayenbite of Inwyt*, p. 180. We must no more confuse A. S. *went* (Mod. E. *wendeth* or *wends*) with the A. S. past tense *wende*, M. E. *wende*, *wente* (Mod. E. *went*), than we must confuse other similar words which are much more distinct.

The matter is, in fact, somewhat obscure; but no mistake will be made by such as are wholly familiar with Early and Middle English as well as with Anglo-Saxon literature. Much clearer cases occur in the following. We have *rit* for *rideth*, third person singular indicative, quite distinct from *rode*; *hit* for *hideth*, distinct from past tense *hidde*; *ret* for *redeth* (reads), distinct from past tense *redde* (read); *bit* for *biddeth*; *stant* for *standeth*; *sit* for *sitteth*; and many more such, which I have often enumerated. Indeed, I begin to wonder how often these things will have to be explained before they are clearly understood. At any rate, it should be known that dictionaries and grammars alone will not explain Early English. More is wanted, viz., a close familiarity with the literature and the manuscripts; nothing less will help us to avoid the pitfalls. Perhaps it may make the matter clearer if I take a parallel case. The difference between A. S. *went*, he turns, he goes, and A. S. *wende*, M. E. *wende* or *wente*, Mod. E. *went*, is very much like the difference between the Lat. *servit*, he serves, and the Lat. *serviit*, F. *servit*, he served. Surely no French grammarian would for a moment imagine that the F. *servit*, which is a past form, is the *same word* as the Lat. *servit*. I hope the matter is now clear.

### 217. Offal, its Etymology. I (6 S. ix. 155; 1884).

In one of his interesting papers on 'The Orkneys,' Mr. F. challenges the usual derivation of *offal* from *off* and *fall*. To which I reply, ' Ne sutor ultra crepidam'; for had he looked at my *Etymological Dictionary*, I do not think he would have hazarded his conjecture. He tells us that the Norse equivalent is *or-val*, i.e. refuse. What he means by Norse, I do not know. The Icelandic word is properly written *örvöl* (see Vigfusson), and is derived from *ór* (Goth. *us*), out; and *velja*, to choose. But it is quite a different word from the E. *offal*, notwithstanding the similarity in sense. This is just how so many errors in etymology arise. A man sees some sort of likeness between two words, and immediately rushes at the conclusion that they are related. This would not happen if people would only condescend to remember that words have a history. For want of doing this, your correspondent falls into the very error which he condemns. His words are: 'The factitious meaning has been given, as is not unfrequently the case in English dictionaries, to suit a supposed etymology.' That is a common error; but in this case it is the critic who has warped the sense of the word, in order to suit *his* etymology. The old sense of *offal* really was 'what falls off,' and it is rightly explained by Lat. *caducum* in the *Prompt. Parvulorum*. It meant originally 'what falls off trees,' hence bits of stick, refuse. The equivalent words in other languages are Dan. *affald*, Du. *afval*, G. *abfall*, all of which cannot be so lightly set aside. The practice of most etymologists appears to be the same as in matrimony, viz., to act in haste; and the result is, or should be, much the same. I will add, that the alleged use of the word *wailed*, chosen, by Chaucer, is a new discovery; the usual editions do not give the word. I suppose it is due to some mistake.

### 218. Offal, its Etymology. II (6 S. ix. 231 ; 1884).

I think further controversy about this word will only be unprofitable, as I am sure it is unnecessary. Mr. F. calmly puts aside all analogies as if they did not exist; but he must remember that he has to convince not me alone, but every one else. He tells us 'that the distance between what falls off trees and refuse is much too great to be bridged over by anything like bits of stick.' This argument I have already answered by anticipation, by referring him to the Danish *affald*, under the impression that he was acquainted with that language. But if he is not, I must explain that word more particularly, as I think it will suffice, without going into Dutch and German, though those languages have also to be reckoned with, and I have already cited the forms, which can be looked out at leisure. I must first say that the Danish often has *ld* for *ll*; thus our *fall* is in Danish *fald*. The Danish *af* is our *off*; and the Danish *affald* is exactly *off-fall*, so far as the form is concerned. But the senses of the Danish *affald* are very instructive; and, curiously enough, they exactly 'bridge over the distance' in the manner which has been authoritatively declared to be impossible. I take Ferrall and Repp's *Dictionary*, which is good enough for the purpose. The senses of *affald* there given are, 'Fall, inclination, declivity, slope; decline, abatement, refuse, offal; *lövet's Affald*, the fall of the leaf; *at samle Affald i Skoven*, to pick up sticks in the woods; *Affald i en Have*, windfalls; *Affald i en Huusholding*, broken victuals, leavings; *Affald af Metal*, refuse, dross, residue, scum,' &c. If we look out *offal* in the English-Danish part, we shall find *affald* given as one of the equivalents. Observe that the range of meanings is really far wider than what is declared to be impossible. We pass from *declivity* to *dross*, and include *sticks* and *offal* by the way. So, in German, *abfall*, lit. *off-fall*, is the term for *offal* actually used by the butchers. We have practically been told that they cannot use such a term, but the answer is that they *do* use it, which puts the matter past all argument.

I do not wish to go into technicalities, or it would be easy to show that the Norse *v* answers to an English *w*, and not to *f* at all; so that there are great phonetic difficulties about this new and needless proposal. Curiously enough, this is shown by the very word cited; for the Icelandic *velja* was formerly *weljа*, and became *wale* (not *vale*, still less *fale*) in English.

I will just touch upon the other points raised. As for *orts*, it is fully explained in my dictionary as containing the prefix *ór*; but *ór* is not the *root*, only the prefix. The same prefix occurs in *or-deal*. Certainly Webster quotes 'wailed wine and meats' from Chaucer; but that only proves what we knew before, that his quotations from 'Chaucer' are worthless. The above words occur in the twenty-ninth line of the *Complaint of Creseide*, printed in Speght's edition of Chaucer; but this edition includes poems by Gower, Lydgate, Occleve, Henrysoun and others. The author of the line was Henrysoun, who was not born till after Chaucer's death.

### 219. Balloon (6 S. x. 17; 1884).

Of course the derivation of this word from '*Ballon*, a famous dancing master in the seventeenth century,' is an idle fabrication, which the *Times* should not have repeated. It is false on the face of it, because it is no solution of the problem; for it does not tell us how the dancing master came by the name himself. It is well known that the words which are really due to names of men are comparatively few; whilst, on the other hand, the guessing etymologist usually resorts to the suggestion of such a derivation when he knows not what else to say. It is the last poor shift of a man who pretends to explain what he cannot otherwise solve. Of course the word *balloon* is far older than the seventeenth century. In Florio's *Ital. Dict.*, ed. 1598, we already find the entry, '*Ballone*, a great ball, a ballone (to play at with braces), a footeball.' Cotgrave has '*Ballon*, a fardel or small pack,' and in fact it was at first used in French as a diminutive of *bale*, which is after all a mere doublet of *ball*. Godefroy gives a quotation for *ballon*, dated 1485, in this sense of 'small bale.' Littré has a quotation for it in the sense of 'balloon' in the sixteenth century. The sense of 'great ball' was probably borrowed from Italian, for it is a singular fact that the Ital. suffix *-one* is augmentative, whilst the F. *-on* is properly diminutive. I would suggest that an ordinary irresponsible newspaper is a very poor guide in questions of etymology, wherein at least some small degree of accuracy is required.

### 220. Hag (6 S. x. 31; 1884).

I fear we shall not get much more information as to this word. I presume the reason why Mr. Wright took the word *hægtesse* as better suited to the Latin *Tisiphona* than to the Lat. *parcae* was because we find elsewhere the entry 'Erenis, *hægtes*'; and it is certainly correct to say that Tisiphone was one of the Erinyes or Furies. Hence it is at once proved that the supposition, even if unneeded here, is far from baseless.

The best way is to quote all the entries in full. The word occurs in the glossaries not *nine* times, but *eleven* times, and it is best to arrange the statements in order of date. They are as follows.

In the eighth century: *Eumenides*, haehtisse; *Furia*, haehtis; *Erenis*, furia (with *haegtis* added in a later hand); *Striga*, haegtis.

In the tenth: *Pythonissa* hellerune *uel* hægtesse: *Tisiphona*, wælcyrre; *Parcae*, hægtesse.

In the eleventh: *Erenis*, hægtes; *Eumenides*, hægtesse; *Furia*, hægtesse; *Furiarum*, hægtessa; and yet again, *Furiarum*, hægtessa. It would seem from this that the correct nom. sing. is *haehtis*, later *haegtis*, *hægtis*; whilst *hægtesse* represents the plural and occasionally the singular, perhaps in an oblique case. Schade gives the O.H.G. form as *hagazussa*, which was afterwards contracted to *hazissa*, M.H.G. *hecse*, Mod. G. *Hexe*. Mr. Mayhew has cleared the way as to some points. It may now be accepted as certain that the Du. *haagdis*, a lizard, is the same as the G. *Eidechse*; it may be added that the A. S. form is *āthexe*, and that the provincial E. is *ask* or *arsk*, all in the sense of lizard or newt. On the other hand, *hag* is short for *hægtesse* or *hægtis*, and the cognate G. word is *Hexe*. But it does not follow that *hæg-t-is*, if derived from *haga*, would mean 'a female hedge,' because the *-t-* might easily make all the difference, and render the substantive personal. The real difficulty is to explain this *-t-*, and at the same time, the G. *-z-*. The only three opinions worth considering are those given by Schade. These are (1) the notion of Grimm, that there is a connexion with the Icel. *hagr*, wise; (2) the notion of Weigand (adopted by myself), that it is connected with A. S. *haga*, a hedge; and (3) the ingenious suggestion, due to Heyne, that the word means 'spoiler of the haw or enclosure stored with corn,' &c., the suffix being allied to A. S. *teosu*, harm, damage. The suggestion of Grimm cannot well stand, for *hagr* has not at all the sense of 'wise,' it is merely handy, skilful, and the suffix is left without even an attempt at regarding it.

Both the other suggestions agree in referring the word to A. S. *haga*, our *haw*; *hawe* is used in Chaucer to mean a farmyard, a fact worth noting. Perhaps we shall never get any further than this. Meanwhile, the sense suggested by Heyne is just possible. The difficulty clearly resides in the suffix spelt *-tis* in early A. S., and *-zussa* in O. H. G., and the suffix is chiefly difficult because it is found nowhere else. The suffix in G. *Eidechse* is quite a different thing, though that is almost equally obscure. The Gothic spelling of *Eidechse* would have been \**agi-thaiso*; the suggested sense is 'serpent-spindle,' i. e. spindle-shaped snake; see Schade, s. v. 'Egidëhsá.'

It must not be omitted that there is a passage in the A. S. *Leechdoms*, iii. 54, where the word *hægtessan*, gen.

sing., from nom. *hægtesse*, clearly means 'of a witch,' or 'of a hag.' Thus the problem of the etymology of *hag* is definitely narrowed to the question, What is the sense of the suffix *-tesse* or *-tis*?

[Cf. G. *Hexe*, in Kluge's *Etym. G. Dict.*]

221. '**Hoder-moder**' (6 S. x. 51; 1884).

This word is printed *hedermoder*, which is certainly a false form for *hodermoder*, in the *Paston Letters*, ed. Gairdner, ii. 28. The text in Gairdner is said to be taken from Fenn, iv. 20, yet the spelling differs considerably from that given in 'N. and Q.' I will just remark that confusion between *e* and *o* in MSS. of the fifteenth century is common. So also *b* is frequently misread by editors as *v*; and the word *blavered* in the same passage is a ridiculous error for *blabered*, the regular frequentative form of *blab*. The passage in Skelton (where the same word occurs) is in *Colyn Cloute*, ll. 68–70:—

> 'Alas! they make me shoder!
> For in *hoder-moder*
> The church is put in faute.'

The derivation of *hugger-mugger*, never yet correctly given (to my knowledge), is now plain enough. It is a substitution for the older form *hoder-moder*. Neither is there here any difficulty. The latter part of the word is merely due to reduplication; the significant part is *hoder*. And, as to *hoder*, I have shown, in my dictionary, that it is the M. E. equivalent of *huddle*, itself a frequentative form allied to M. E. *huden*, to hide. In fact, *hoder-moder* should have become *hudder-mudder* or *huddle-muddle* rather than *hugger-mugger*, and it is, practically, a mere derivative of *hide*. Cf. Greek κεύθειν.

[The Gk. εύ is equivalent to Germanic *eu* (A. S. *ēo*, *ū*), whence A. S. *hȳdan*, to hide, by 'mutation' of the vowel. The zero-grade of Gk. κευθ- is κυθ-, answering to A. S. and

M. E. *hud-*, whence the frequentative *huderen*, written *hoderen* by French scribes, who frequently use the symbol *o* for short *u*. The Low G. *hudren* is cited by Bradley, in his edition of Stratmann, s. v. *hodren*.]

### 222. A plea for Place-names (6 S. ˝. 109 ; 1884).

I quite agree with W. M. C. that the collection of place-names will be of great value. We shall never know anything certain about the etymology till we condescend to do the drudgery of collection first. All turns upon this; and Englishmen may as well learn the fact by heart at once.

I have by me the second edition of Mr. R. C. Hope's *Dialectal Place-Nomenclature*, which is an attempt in this direction. In his preface he rightly says, at p. xi, that I recommended him to use 'some *exact* mode of representing pronunciations, such as glossic.' But he did not take my advice, because his work would then have been a sealed book to all who do not understand glossic. I have to reply that I do not care what system is adopted of representing sounds, so long as the system is *somewhere explained*. He carefully refrains from *any* explanation of his symbols, so that his work remains a sealed book to all scientific workers. The same will happen in future in the case of all similar collections. They will all alike be useless for scientific purposes, unless some standard system of pronunciation be employed. Glossic, or palæotype, or Mr. Sweet's romic, or the system employed in Mr. Sweet's *History of English Sounds* will do, or anything else that is *definite*. But to take the common Protean spelling as a guide will *not* do; there is no laying hold of what is meant by it. Thus Mr. Hope tells us that Eye, in Suffolk, is pronounced Aye. Does it, then, rhyme with *my* or with *may ?* We are not 'spinxes,' as Mr. Yellowplush says, to guess such conundrums.

One thing that has to be done is to have a new name-index to all the Anglo-Saxon charters. Mr. Birch is now reprinting these, and promises complete indexes. I hope we may get them [!].

Another thing that has to be done is to collect and tabulate every name in Domesday Book, adding the modern name where it is *certainly* known. Guesses are much worse than useless, for they mislead, hinder, discourage, embarrass and perplex. It is desirable that any one who works at this should learn something about Old French and Anglo-Saxon pronunciation, or he will draw such a remarkable conclusion as one that has been already drawn :—that Brighthelmston cannot mean 'the town of Brighthelm' because of the Domesday spelling [1].

### 223. Totemism; or, English Place-names
(6 S. x. 110; 1884).

Certainly it is well known (or rather, well ascertained) that the syllable *-ing* has many meanings. I have heard people deride Kemble's statements about the tribal *-ing* who were in utter ignorance of what he really says. It may as well be said once more that he actually gives a list of the names in *-ing* to which his tribal explanation applies. Neither Tyningham nor Coldingham is alluded to in that list.

Perhaps it may interest some to see the original passage in *Ælfric the Grammarian*, written in the eleventh century, about patronymics. It occurs in Zupitza's edition, p. 14:—

'Sume syndon *patronymica*, thæt synd fæderlīce naman, aefter Grēciscum thēawe, ac sēo lēdenspræc næfth thā naman. Hī synd swā thēah on Engliscre spræce: *Penda*, and of thām *Pending* and *Pendingas*; *Cwichelm*, and of thām *Cwichelmingas*, and fela ōthre.'

Here he expressly tells us that *Pending* means the son of Penda, and *Cwichelmingas* and *Pendingas* are, respectively,

---

[1] [This begins with *Brist-*. How else could a *F*rench scribe represent the sound of the A. S. *Briht*? His *s* is an obvious attempt to express all that he could make out of this (to him) detestable foreign guttural.]

the Cwichelmings and Pendings, i. e. men of the tribe of Cwichelm and Penda; and he observes that there are many others. Certainly there are hundreds. It is not a sure guide to such names that the name should end in *-ton* or *-ham*. A simple exception is Newington, formerly Newenton, from the A. S. *æt thām nīwan tūne*, i. e. at the new town. The *-ing* is here a corruption of the Middle English *-en*, put for A. S. *-an*, the inflexion of the definite adjective in the dative case. In the name Newnham we have precisely the same A. S. dative, but differently treated.

Whoever said that *eng* is Swedish for 'a meadow' must have had a very moderate acquaintance with the Swedish alphabet. *Eng* is the Danish spelling of the word; in Swedish it is written *äng*. The Icelandic is *eng*, and it seems probable that the original sense was a 'narrow space,' a 'corner' or 'bit' of land, from the Icel. *engr*, narrow, cognate with A. S. *enge*, narrow, and the Lat. *angusta*; the Welsh form is *ing*, but need not be specially invoked. I should guess that *ing*, in the sense of 'meadow,' is Scandinavian, and I find mention of the *Ings*, or meadow-land, near Wakefield. We are constantly told that *ing*, a meadow, is 'Anglo-Saxon.' This statement rests on Lye's *Dictionary*; he calmly assumes it, *more suo*, to explain the Northern English, i. e. the Scandinavian use; and adds that it occurs in Basing, Kettering, Reading, Godelming (i. e. Godhelming, now Godalming), Yelling, Exning and Steyning. But all of these, for anything that we know to the contrary, may be of patronymic origin. The question is, simply, is there a single passage in any A. S. writing where *ing*, a meadow, occurs? I think not.

I have only to add that the etymology of place-names is most slippery and difficult, and I have no faith in three-quarters of the explanations which are so lavishly offered. We want something thorough and systematic to guide us, for which we look at present in vain.

**224. The Names of the Seasons. I** (6 S. x. 215; 1884).

[In reply to an argument that, in Old England, there were but *two* seasons; viz. summer and winter.]

The whole of this article I take to be fundamentally wrong, and due to a total ignorance of the facts. The common Teutonic word for *autumn* is *harvest*, originally 'ingathering,' allied to Lat. *carpere*. *On hærfeste* is the translation of *in autumno* in Ælfric's *Colloquy*. In the A. S. metrical version of Boethius (xiv. 1) *haerfest* means 'autumn.' The spelling of *autumn* in Chaucer is not *autumpe* (l) but *autumpne*; I give the quotation and the right reference. *The Complaint of the Black Knight* was not written by Chaucer, but by Lydgate; the word *autumne* occurs in Stanza ix; the remark that '*harvest* is found before *autumne*' in it I cannot understand, not observing *harvest* at all. The word *spring* is purely English, and derived from A. S. *springan*, to spring up; the Flemish form does not much matter, and in fact has a different vowel.

The reason why *spring* was not early used in English was simply that the old word was *lent*, A. S. *lencten*; but when *Lent* was appropriated to ecclesiastical purposes, *spring* came into use. In a supplement to Ælfric's *Vocabulary*, ed. Wülcker, col. 176, we already find:—

'Uer, *lencten* (on which see Wright's note); Æstas, *sumor*; Autumnus, *hærfest*; Hyems, *winter*; Uernalis dies, *lengtenlic dæg*; Uer nouum, *forewærd lencten*, vel *middewærd lencten ;* Uer adultum, *æfterwærd lencten*; Eodem modo et æstas et autumnus uocantur, *on tha ylcan wisan sumor and hærfest bioth gecigede*; Æstiuus dies, *sumorlic dæg*; Autumnalis dies, *hærfestlic dæg*; Hiemalis dies, *winterlic dæg*.'

It is difficult to see how the old glossarist could have been more explicit; he even recognizes three English divisions of each season, each obviously consisting of a month.

The Flemish word *lente* is a mere contraction, the A. S. being the fuller form. The Flemish *lente* has no connexion whatever with '*lint*,' which is only a misspelling of *lind*, and cognate with English *lithe*. The Middle-English actually had yet another term for spring, viz. *ver*, used by Barbour, with the spelling *were*, in *The Bruce*, v. 1. This may have been borrowed from Latin, but there are also cognate (not borrowed) forms in Scandinavian, viz. Icel. *vár*, Swed. *vår*. I have no time to write more; I have given *summer* and *winter* in my *Dictionary*. I may just add, however, that the notion of connecting *hiems* with *imber* would astonish Vaniçek.

**225. The Names of the Seasons. II** (6 S. x. 338; 1884).

As Mr. M. is the more confirmed in his view that there were only two seasons known to our Teutonic ancestors in proportion to the amount of evidence which is produced to the contrary, I notice a few more points. In Schade's excellent *Old (High) German Dictionary* I find the following: '*Herbist, herpist*, M. H. G. *herbest*, Mod. G. *Herbst*, auctumnus: *der érst herbst*, September; *der ander herbst*, October; *der drit herbst*, November.' This shows that the autumn season was divided into three parts in Germany as well as in England. Another curious thing is that yearly accounts were made up from Michaelmas to Michaelmas in the fourteenth century, at any rate; and it would be interesting to know at how early a date this custom arose. I suspect it was due to the time of harvest. The Icelandic *haust* simply means *autumn*; see the numerous derived words in Cleasby and Vigfusson. The following passage in Ælfric's *Colloquy*, in the article about the fowler, is of some interest.

In Latin it runs thus:—

'*I*psi [i.e. the hawks] pascunt se et me in bieme, et in uere dimitto eos avolare ad siluam, et capio mihi pullos in autumno, et domito eos.'

The English is:—

'Hig fēdath hīg sylfe and mē on wintra, and on lencgten ic lǣte hīg ætwindan to wuda, and genyme mē briddas on hærfeste and temige hīg,' i.e. they feed themselves and me in the winter, and in spring I let them go away to the wood, and catch for myself young birds in autumn, and tame them.'

In Kluge's *Etymological German Dictionary*, s. v. *Herbst*, it is shown that Tacitus was wrong in imagining that the Germans had no name for autumn.

### 226. Caterwaul. I (6 S. x. 237; 1884).

I merely give the old etymology found in Bailey and Todd's *Johnson*. The statement that it is unconnected with *cat* is pure assumption, and I do not see how it can be maintained in the face of the extract from Chaucer, which is so carefully ignored, though Pope rightly understood it. Phillips, in 1706, explains *catterwaul* of cats; Sewel, in 1754, translates it by an equivalent Dutch word *kattengelol*. In any case, I shall not admit that *wail* and *waul* are the same word; *ai* and *au* are different sounds. *Wail* is formed, by vowel-change, from the Scandinavian for 'woe'; but *waul* from the M. E. *wawen*, to cry *waw*. The *l* is frequentative; cf. F. *miauler*, 'to mewl or mew like a cat' (Cotgrave); Ital. *miagolare* (Florio). As for (the alleged) *catter*, to chatter, I do not know where to find it in Middle English.

### 227. Caterwaul. II (6 S. x. 356; 1884).

The suggestion made in *N. and Q.* 6 S. x. 317, that the syllable *waul* has something to do with A. S. *wealh*, foreign, is certainly wrong, and could not have been made by any one who had read the article in my dictionary with reasonable care. I have shown that the M. E. verb was not *waul*, but *wawen*, which certainly meant 'to make a disagreeable noise.' Of this verb *waul* is the frequentative form ; the *-l* is the same as in *wai-l, mew-l, squea-l,* and we have very many instances of final *-le* with the same frequentative meaning. Moreover, the most elementary knowledge of English phonetics will show that *au* does not answer to A. S. [short] *ea* ; as a fact, the A. S. *wealh* became *wale*, and is still preserved in *Wales*, i. e. the foreigners, now misused as the name of a country instead of the name of a people. The adjective is *Welsh*, i. e. *Wale-ish*, with the usual *umlaut*, and this is still further from the sound of English *au*.

The real difficulty is in the syllable *-er*, which I regret that I have not hitherto explained. It is, however, an old Scandinavian genitive suffix, not uncommon in Middle English. Readers who know no more of Chaucer than the first hundred lines must have seen the word *night-er-tale*, which is precisely the Icelandic *náttar-tal*, a number or succession of nights; so that *nightertale* really means 'for a succession of nights,' but is vaguely used by Chaucer with the general idea of 'night season.' So in the present case, the M. E. *cater* is the Icel. *kattar*, of a 'cat, gen. case of *köttr*, a cat, and is the form used in composition; hence *kattar-auga*, cat's eye (a plant) ; *kattar-rófa*, cat's tail ; *kattar-skinn*, cat's skin ; *kattar-tunga*, cat's tongue. Hence *cater-waw*, sb., would mean 'cat's cry'; and *cater-wawen*, vb., 'to utter a cat's cry'; whence *cater-waul*, sb., 'a continuous cat's cry,' and the verb *cater-waul*, 'to go on uttering a cat's cry.' Cf. W. *cathderig*, caterwauling, from *cath*, a cat, and *terig*, rutting. I hope I have now made this sufficiently plain, and that we may be spared any further discussion of the matter.

The suggestion that *cater* is equivalent to the G. *Kater* is, of course, out of the question. It actually requires the supposition that the final *-er* is [here] a High German suffix, which is wholly out of place in a Middle English word.

[The *New E. Dict* mentions Icel. *kattar-* as a possible source of *cater-*, without adopting it. But the analogy of *night-er-tale*, here very important, has been missed. On the other hand, the *r* in *byrlaw* is unhesitatingly explained from *bȳ-jar*, gen. case of *bȳ-r*; which is strictly analogous.]

### 228. Caterwaul. III (6 S. xii. 232; 1885).

I think I am entitled to say a last word about *caterwaul*, because the whole of the difficulty arose out of a remark by C. M. I., that his intimate acquaintance with the literature of the sixteenth and seventeenth centuries enabled him to assert that *caterwaul* was originally used of apes and monkeys, not of cats. Now in the *Retrospective Review* for May, 1854, p. 265, the reviewer cites the expression 'heare a dogge howle or a *cat waule*,' from Melton's *Astrologaster*, printed in 1620. This is in addition to the instance given in 6th S. x. 521.

### 229. Scottish Proverb in 'Don Juan' (6 S. x. 315; 1884).

The old form of the proverb was certainly 'Ka mee ka thee' (see Hazlitt's *Collection of Proverbs;* Heywood's *Proverbs*; Skelton, ed. Dyce, vol. i. p. lxv, l. 7). It is explained to mean, 'Swear for me, and I'll do as much for you,' i. e. '*Call* me as a witness, and I'll *call* you.' Thus *ca* would appear to be, as usual, the Scottish form of *call*. I have little doubt that there was a parallel form, 'Claw me, claw thee,' but I suspect it to be a later substitution. I have also somewhere met with it in the plain English form, 'You scratch my back, and I'll scratch your back.' See the illustrations in Hazlitt, which I omit to save space.

• [*Clawe* (scratch) *me, clawe thee*, is used by Tyndale, and subsequently by others; see *Claw*, verb, 5 b., in the *New E. Dictionary*. I fail to find *ka me, ka thee*, s. v. *call*.]

### 230. Phaeton (6 S. x. 476; 1884).

I am obliged to MR. TERRY for pointing out an unlucky misprint in my reference for this word; a misprint which really had its origin in my attempt to give fuller information. I ascertained from Todd's *Johnson* that the word *phaeton* occurs in 'Night 5' of Young's *Night Thoughts*, and at once endeavoured to verify the reference. I found that in my own copy of the work the lines were not numbered, and that 'Night 5' was a canto of considerable length. I thought it would save my readers trouble to count from the end of that canto instead of from the beginning, and accordingly made a note that the required line is 'line 245 from end.' But alas! after ascertaining this, the words 'Night 5' slipped out of the reference, and left it incomplete after all. I now think it probable that (as the new quotations seem to show) we took the word from Latin, but should be very glad of further information as to the date and manner of the introduction of phaetons. I may add that I remember such a carriage nearly forty years ago, which was always called a *faytun*, or in glossic spelling *fai·tn* (romic *fei·tn*). This was in the neighbourhood of London. [At Perry Hill, Sydenham; the *phaeton* was my father's.]

### 231. Colour in Surnames (6 S. x. 520; 1884).

At the last reference J. H. Brady is quoted as asserting, 'A Mr. Red we have never yet met with'; and the writer adds, 'and most people will agree with him.' I am not among the number of 'most people' in this instance. When we notice that Camden refers to the Latin *Rufus* and the O. F. *Rous* we might expect the corresponding English *Red* to be a very common name. And so it is. Only we have to remember that the spelling *red* is modern, like the pronunciation. The *e* was originally long, and in Chaucer MSS. the form is usually *reed*. In later English it was *reede, read, reade*; in Scottish, *reid*. In my experience, the surnames Reed, Read, Reade, Reid, are all extremely common; and I think most people must have heard of Charles Reade. I may add that I have already shown, in my Dictionary, that the A. S. form was *rēad*, answering to a Gothic *raud-s*. Cf. Lat. *ruf-us*, *rub-er*, Gk. ἐ-ρυθ-ρός. [Mr. *Rouse* has helped to translate Brugmann.]

### 232. Reckan (6 S. xi. 65; 1885).

This Northern wórd is duly explained in Atkinson's *Cleveland Glossary* as 'an iron crane, on which are suspended the pot-hooks, and which, being hinged at one end to the masonry of the chimney, will move in any direction over the fire.' Mr. Atkinson gives it under the form *reek-airn*, but observes that it is pronounced *reckon* or *reckan*. His reason for spelling it *reek-airn* is that he supposes this to be the etymological spelling, and that the sense is *reek-iron*, i.e., 'iron in the smoke.' It is rather hard that words should be quoted under an assumed etymological spelling; but it is the old, old way, and the source of endless trouble.

I think it is quite certain that the above etymology is wrong; for I find in a will, 1454, the following entries: 'J. craticula ferrea, j. par tanges de ferro, ij crassetes et j. *rekand* de ferro,' &c., in a list of cooking utensils—*Testamenta Eboracensia*, ii. 194. Obviously the modern *reckan* is the old Yorkshire *rekand*, which cannot stand for *reek-iron*, and has to be described as being 'de ferro,' because the word *rekand* in itself does not already contain the idea of 'iron.'

The etymology is easy and obvious, viz., from the Icel. *rekendr*, a chain, a derivative of the verb *reka*. The A. S. word is *racenta*, a chain, which is sufficiently common; from the same root as *rack* and *reach*. This explains the modern pronunciation, which happens to be quite correct.

This is one more example of the danger of guessing

without sufficient evidence. We learn also that the true sense of *reckan* was 'chain'; it was doubtless at first applied to a simple plan of suspending pot-hooks from the links of a chain, so as to regulate the height; and the name was retained when the apparatus became more complex. This is much more satisfactory than the popular etymology from *reek*.

**233. Bewray** (6 S. xi. 66; 1885).

An earlier example of this word than any given by Mätzner or myself is in Robert of Brunne's *Handlyng Synne*, 3621: 'That y ne wylle telle ne *bewrey*,' i. e. disclose. Mätzner well compares it with the O. Friesic *biwrogja*, which, indeed, I have already cited. This O. Friesic verb preserves the original *o* (long), which passed into *e* (long) in A. S., by the usual vowel-change.

[An earlier example, in this sense, than any that are given in the *New E. Dictionary*.]

**234. Awork** (6 S. xi. 66; 1885).

I have derived this from *on work*, though I have hitherto failed to find such an expression. It occurs, however, in the following: 'As for the wagges that set us *on work*'; Lyly, *Mother Bombie*, V. iii.

[Cf. *Awork* in the *New E. Dictionary*.]

**235. Oil on Troubled Waters** (6 S. xi. 72; 1885).

To the references already given add Pliny, *Nat. Hist.*, lib. ii. c. 103. Holland's translation has, 'All seas are made calme and still with oile.' I gave this quotation some two years ago to a friend, and I believe it found its way into print.

[For some occult reason, the origin of 'pouring oil on troubled waters' is perpetually being inquired after. It is simply a well-known fact, that it is no bad thing to do. Pliny makes this very remark: 'Now, that all Springs are colder[1] in Summer than Winter, *who knoweth not?* . . . And, that all seas are made calme and still with oile.' Why we need worry over it I do not know.]

### 236. Janissary. I (6 S. xi. 138; 1885).

I am surprised to find that I am quoted as giving in my Dictionary the derivation from *yeñi cheri*, new soldiery. I cannot find it there, though I heartily wish I could, as it is certainly right. I most unfortunately quoted the wrong Turkish form for 'soldier,' and it was just because I did so that the subject has been discussed[2]. As I have already been corrected several times, and I accept the correction, I think the subject may be allowed to drop.

At the last reference, however, the old 'popular etymology' from Persian *ján nisári*, one who throws away his life in battle, is trotted out once more. There is not a tittle of evidence for it; but we are, forsooth, to accept it because it is 'obvious' to a layman who is no philologist. We are not even offered any proof that the compound *ján-nisári* was ever used in Turkish to express a 'janissary,' nor any proof that it was ever used at all. The Turkish word is not *ján-nisári*, nor anything like it; it is *yeñicheri*, with the specific meaning of 'janissary,' as may be seen in Zenker's *Turkish Lexicon*. No one says that the English form *janissary* is derived from *yeñi* and *cheri*; but every one says that the Turkish word for janissary is so derived. The English word is merely an English spelling of the Italian *ianizzeri* (Torriano), and the identity of the Italian with the Turkish word is very much closer. The English form is

---

[1] I suppose he means *relatively* colder, in comparison with other things near them. Otherwise, it can hardly be true.

[2] [My larger Etym. Dict. cites the Turk. *yeñi*, new, and *'askari*, a soldier. But the right words are *yeñi*, new, and *cheri*, soldiery. My concise Etym. Dict. gives the right forms.]

a mere travesty of the original, after passing through Italian and French. The Italian preserves the true Turkish *y* at the beginning and the *e* sound in the penultimate. But the English initial letter badly expresses this Italian sound by *j*, thus producing an accidental coincidence with the Persian *j*, which is quite misleading. . I am quite contented with the explanations of such scholars as Devic and Zenker, and I should think others are the same. Meanwhile we have one more example of the uselessness of an 'obvious' etymology to anybody but the inventor of it.

### 237. Janissary. II (6 S. xi. 270; 1885).

As I am asked to explain this word again, I do so, but must decline further discussion. The mistake lies in calling *janissary* a 'Turkish' word; it is not so, but only a word of Turkish origin, which is quite a different matter. It is an *English* word; and, as far as we are concerned, we merely borrowed it from the French *janissaire*, the plural of which is spelt *jannissaires* in Cotgrave's *Dictionary* (1660), where it is explained as 'Janizaries.' The French word, in its turn, was a French misspelling of the Italian plural *janizzeri*, spelt *ianizzeri* in Florio's *Italian Dictionary* (1598), and explained as 'The Turkes gard, Janizers.' So that, in fact, even in English, the earlier form was *janizers*. The peculiar sounds of the Ital. *i* (as *y*) and of the Ital. *zz* (as *ts*) at once show that the Ital. word, in its turn, was borrowed from the Turk. *yeñi-cheri*; and there the matter ends.

The Turk. *yeñi* is a genuine Turkish word, having the peculiar *n* which is unknown to the Persian alphabet; but *cheri* is merely borrowed from the Pers. *charík*, auxiliary forces. It is interesting to notice that the Turkish 'noun of multitude' was ingeniously rendered by an Italian plural, owing to the peculiar luck that *i* is an Ital. plural suffix; and being thus established as a plural, it became *janissaires* in French, and *janizers* (later form *janizaries*) in English.

Out of this false plural *janizaries* the singular form *janizary* (later *janissary*) was at last evolved; and I believe it will be extremely difficult to find any early instances of the 'singular' spelling. In old books the English word is common enough, but *only* (I think) *in the plural*. The same remark applies to the French and Italian forms.

The fact is, accordingly, that there is no evidence whatever for the existence, at any date whatever, of the compound word *ján-nisári*, a thrower away of life, either in Persian or in Turkish, or indeed, anywhere at all, except by imaginary connexion with an English word which sounds somewhat like it, but was really evolved out of a false plural. There is no difficulty about a Turkish word being of Persian origin, as the very word *cheri* shows; but this proves nothing as to the *necessity* of a Persian origin for every word in Turkish. We have borrowed thousands of words from French; it does not follow that *house* is a French word. The existence of the word *jān-bāz*[1], which I take to be purely modern, has nothing to do with the question, as can easily be perceived. But it may nevertheless be true that *jān-bāz* was at first suggested by previous acquaintance with the *English* (not the Persian) word *janizary*, which was entirely misunderstood and misderived; and if so, nothing is more natural than that the supposed connexion of the words should be repeatedly pointed out. There is great confusion constantly at work in every language, owing to the very potent and subtle influence of popular etymology. It is so extremely easy to *see* resemblances, and so extremely arduous a task for a man to render himself sufficiently acquainted with the secret structure of languages to see that such resemblances are merely superficial. If philological truth (like other forms of truth) is ultimately to prevail, it is quite certain that she will have a very hard time of it beforehand, particularly in

[1] I. e. Pers. *jān-bāz*, playing with life, venturesome; hence, a rope-dancer, tumbler.

this country, where the enthusiasm for easy solutions is carried to such a pitch, and where so little pains are taken to learn the rudiments of phonetics.

### 238. Burning of Bait: Bait of Hemp (6 S. xi. 178; 1885).

Perhaps *bait* is connected with Icel. *beit*, pasturage. Cf. Icel. *beiti*, (1) pasturage, (2) heather, ling.

[But it is shown, in the *New E. Dict.*, s. v. *Beat*, sb. (3), that a better spelling seems to be *beat*. If so, the etymology remains unknown.]

### 239. Definition of Genius (6 S. xi. 190; 1885).

I wish to draw attention to the fact that the definition of *genius* as 'the capacity for taking infinite pains,' or, 'an infinite capacity for taking pains,' is not a true one. At best it merely expresses a portion, and that the least important portion, of the truth. To complete the definition we require the addition of the following words, viz. 'combined with the faculty of discerning whether the object is worth the trouble, and in which direction success is the most probable.' These conditions are absolutely necessary. The true genius is he who *sees his way*, and who, seeing it, pursues it with the utmost care, neglecting no circumstance as being too trivial, and concentrating his strength upon the most hopeful point of advance. The mere taking of infinite pains, without any guiding power to render such pains successful, is nothing but dunderheaded stupidity. Whilst the dull plodder wastes his energy upon work that leads to nothing further, the genius concentrates it upon work which to every one else around him may seem trivial enough ; but *he* sees further than others, and knows that a splendid ultimate success is probable. Surely the faculty to know *what work is worth doing* is immeasurably greater than the mere dogged resolution which goes round in a hopeless circle.

**240. Green Baize Road** (6 S. xi. 198; 1885).

There is really no such phrase. Dickens puts together two expressions. One is 'gentlemen of the road,' i. e. highwaymen, robbers. The other is 'green baize,' i. e. whist-table, card-table. Hence 'gentlemen of the green baize road' means 'plunderers at the card-table,' i. e. card-sharpers. I do not see the use of reference to *pages*. The right reference is to '*Bleak House*, ch. xxvi. par. 1.' In prose books readers might count the paragraphs.

N.B.—'Green cloth' means billiards; but 'green baize' is a whist-table. [The passage from Dickens is quoted in the *New E. Dict.*, s. v. *Baize*, sb., § 3.]

**241. Fratry** (6 S. xi. 205; 1885).

I find that Mr. Palmer explains this word quite correctly in his *Folk-Etymology*, and duly cites from my *Notes to Piers Plowman*, p. 97. *Fratry* is from *frater-y*, misspelling (with added -*y*) of M. E. *freitour*, short for O. F. *refreitour*, from Lat. *refectorium*. Littré, s.v. '*Réfectoire*,' gives the O.F. forms *refreitoir*, *refretor*, *refrictur*; Provençal *refeitor* (without the intrusive *r*). The puzzle in this word is really the intrusive *r*; but there are other instances. I have given several examples of intrusive *r* and intrusive *l* in a paper read before the Philological Society, and now in the press. Note, e. g., F. *fronde*, a sling, from Lat. *funda*; E. *treasure*, F. *trésor*, Ital. *tesoro*, from Lat. *thesaurus*. The latter is a most striking example. The E. *fringe* is somewhat similar, but here the *r* was suggested by that in the second syllable of Lat. *fimbria*. The Wallachian for *fringe* is *frimbie*. For other examples see *cartridge, partridge, jasper, roistering*. [Cf. also F. *chanvre, encre*.]

**242. Bishopric of Sodor and Man** (6 S. xi. 216; 1885).

I hope I may be allowed to make a slight addition to the reply by CANON VENABLES at the last reference. The word *sudreyjar* is now written with a stroke through the *d*. It is from Icel. *suðr*, south, and *eyjar*, plural of *ey*, an island, cognate with A. S. *īg* (preserved in M. E. *i-land*, now misspelt *island*); so that Sodor = 'southern islands.' My index to Cleasby and Vigfusson's *Icelandic Dictionary* duly contains the entry, 'Sodor (name), *Suðreyjar.*' *Sodorensis* is a mere Latin derivative.

### 243. 'Wolf,' in Music (6 S. xi. 264; 1885).

This name is applied to a false or harsh fifth. See Webster's *Dictionary*, &c. The following is the story about it as given in Ferne's *Blazon of Gentrie* (1586), as cited in the *Retrospective Review*, February, 1853, p. 129:—

'Nature hath implanted so inveterate a hatred atweene the wolfe and the sheepe, that, being dead, yet, in the secret operation of Nature, appeareth there a sufficient trial of their discording natures, so that the enmity betweene them seemeth not to dye with their bodies: for if there be put upon a harpe, or any such like instrument, strings made of the intralles of a sheep, and amongst them but only one made of the intralles of a wolfe, be the musitian never so cunning in his skil, yet can he not reconcile them to an unity and concord of sounds; so discording alwayes is that string of the wolfe.'

The writer who quotes this adds a curious story of a Hindoo who stole a wolf's skin in order to convert it into the head of a tom-tom. His idea was that the sound of his drum would burst the drums of all his neighbours, since theirs were made of *sheep*-skin.

### 244. 'Cut away' (6 S. xi. 264; 1885).

In Holland's translation of *Pliny*, bk. viii. c. 22, we read as follows:—

'In the case of presages ... this is obserued: That if men see a wolfe abroad *cut his way* and turne to the right hand, it is good.'

This leads me to suggest that the original sense of to 'cut a way' was to cut or force one's way through a wood; for it is clear from the above example that *way* was once a substantive. The change from 'cut a way' to 'cut away' was easy, but rendered the phrase unintelligible, so that it degenerated into mere slang, upon which numerous changes were rung. This I suspect to have been the origin of 'Cut away'; and perhaps even of 'Cut a stick,' and 'Cut one's sticks.'

[The laconic 'Cut' seems to be short for 'cut and run,' i.e. cut *one's cable* and run away; see the *New English Dictionary*.]

**245. 'One Touch of Nature'** (6 S. xi. 396; 1885).

I am afraid it is perfectly useless to hope that this quotation will ever be rightly used, for the simple reason that those who quote it are those who do not read Shakespeare for themselves; and the number of those who really read him is, I fear, not very great after all. But I should like to say that I have already explained this error in print *twice*; once at p. xvi. of my *Questions for Examination in English Literature*, published in 1873, and once in a letter to the *Academy*, which I cannot now find. I have also pointed out that the phrase 'natural touch,' quite in the modern sense, occurs in Shakespeare after all, viz. in *Macbeth*, iv. 2. 9. And I have explained that *touch* in this famous quotation means 'defect' or 'bad trait,' from confusion with the once common word *tache*, sometimes misspelt *touch*[1].

---

[1] [All the trouble arises from taking the line away from its context. Of the hundreds who misunderstand it, probably not one knows what the context is. So I here quote the whole passage:—

'*One* [emphatic] touch [defect] of nature makes the whole world kin,
That all, with one consent, praise new-born gawds,
Though they are made and moulded of things past,
And give to dust that is a little gilt
More laud than gilt o'erdusted.'—*Troil*. iii. 3. 174.

Observe how the author *reprobates* this evil tendency in human nature.]

Another point to be noticed is that Messrs. Clark and Wright had no sooner finished their very valuable edition of *Shakespeare* in a portable form, than the publisher of the volume at once stamped this line (in itself meaningless) on both sides of the cover, in order that 'the whole world' might call the book the 'Globe' edition. It is obvious that the author did not know how he *ought* to have understood his own words either in this, or (according to some commentators) in *any other* passage.

[I have seen it gravely argued that misconceptions of this character become sacred when once popularized, and ought on no account to be exposed, still less discarded.]

### 246. 'Magdalene' as the Name of a Boat
(6 S. xii. 47 ; 1885).

Chaucer's Shipman had a barge named 'The Maudelayne.' There was a ship of that name in 1390, belonging to Robert Titlok de Hornesbek, who left to his brother William 'unam naviculam vocatam *Mawdeleyn.*' The same man had a ship called 'Farcost,' and a third called 'Garland.' See *Testamenta Eboracensia*, i. 139. Robert Ryllyngton of Scarborough had two ships called 'Saintmarybote' and 'Le Katerine' (*id.* i. 157). [See further in my *Notes to Chaucer*; *Works*, vol. v.]

### 247. Early Notices of Zebra : Kangaroo
(6 S. xii. 48 ; 1885).

In Dampier's *Voyages*, 1699, i. 533, we read as follows :—

'There is a very beautiful sort of wild Ass in this Country [Cape of Good Hope], whose body is curiously striped with equal Lists of white and black,' &c.

This is a very early description of the zebra. The name of the animal is not given. In vol. iii. p. 123, there is a description of the kangaroo, which also is unnamed.

**248. Robinson Crusoe anticipated** (6 S. xii. 48; 1885).

We are all familiar with the story of Alexander Selkirk who was rescued from the island of Juan Fernandez in 1709. But W. Dampier, in his *Voyages*, ed. 1699, vol. i. p. 84, already tells us the story of an Indian whom he had left behind at John Fernando's Isle in 1681, when chased by some Spanish ships. This Indian lived on the island for three years. He had his gun, a knife, a small horn of powder, and some shot. When the powder failed, he made his gun-barrel into harpoons, lance-heads, hooks, and a long knife. See the story.

**249. The Lord's Prayer in Verse. I** (6 S. xii. 169; 1885).

The notion of attributing to Nicholas Breakspeare the version of the Lord's Prayer printed in 6 S. xii. 112, is a mournful example of the ignorance prevalent as to the history of the English language. He died in A.D. 1159, quite half a century before the earliest known instance of the metre in which this version is written[1]. Camden's spelling of the old English is abominably bad, and abounds in grammatical errors.

Of course *fonding* or *fanding* does not mean 'confounding' (l), but 'temptation.' The *originals* may, all three of them, have been written in the time of Henry II, but the existing copies exhibit a mixture of Plantagenet-English and Tudor-English spelling. The language of the time of Henry II was far more antiquated than the oldest form of these versions could ever have been; and plainly Pope Adrian IV could not have written in a form of language which was at that time known to no one.

---

[1] The earliest known example of rimed metre with four accents is in *Soul's Ward*, which Dr. Morris dates about A.D. 1210. I should put the prose text rather later; and probably the verses are later still.

However, this version is interesting; and I will venture to restore it to something more like its original spelling and grammar. It is obvious that the fourth line has been lost, and must be supplied. Probably it contained the once common expletive phrase *mid iwisse*, i. e. 'certainly.' *Heuen-riche* is all one word, and means the kingdom of heaven. *Eche other mon* means 'each (of us) another man.' *Fonding* is temptation, A. S. *fandung*. The final *e* is a separate syllable. *Euer yliche* means 'ever alike,' or 'continually':—

> '*F*ader vre, in heuen-richĕ,
> Thy name[1] be haliyed euer ylichĕ.
> *T*hou bring vs [to] Thy michel blissĕ.
> [*T*hy willĕ, Louerd[2], mid iwissĕ,]
> Als hit is in heuen y-do,
> Euer in erthe[1] be hit also.
> *T*hat holi breed that lasteth ay,
> *T*hou send hit vs this ilkĕ day.
> Forgif vs al that we han don,
> As we forgiue eche other mon.
> Ne let vs falle in no fonding,
> Ac shelde vs fro the foulĕ thing.'

Even this remains unsatisfactory. The rhyming of *don* (with long *o*) with *mon* (with short *o*) is against the rule, and is quite unexampled.

**250. The Lord's Prayer in Verse. II** (6 S. xii. 258; 1885).

I have just come across a most remarkable confirmation of all that I have said about the version which Camden gave, and which I attempted to restore. I said it was of the thirteenth century; that the fourth line was lost, and should be restored as 'Thy wille, Louerd, mid iwisse,' or something of that kind; and that Camden's version was

---

[1] Something wrong; the final *e* is suppressed, which it should not be. Read *hit be* in line 6, and the line will then scan.

[2] *Louerd*, Lord, was then dissyllabic.

corrupt. I now find that there is still extant a copy in a hand of the thirteenth century; that the fourth line is there given as 'Thi wille to wirchë thu us wisse¹'; and that my restoration of the spelling brings it very close to the spelling of the manuscript, and would have agreed with it even more closely if the old scribe had been a little more careful. This MS. copy is extant, is the Harleian MS. 3724, leaf 44, and has been printed in *Reliquiæ Antiquæ*, vol. i. p. 57. This leaves no more to be said as to this version.

**251. English compared with German** (6 S. xii. 183; 1885).

Much experience of the difficulties encountered by the students of English etymologies has led me to see that, in many cases, a knowledge of German, generally advantageous, is turned into quite a curse by the failure of the student to understand the *essential difference* between English and German as to their treatment of consonants and vowels. The current, but most ignorant and pernicious doctrine is, that English is *derived from* modern German, the latter being looked upon as the standard and correct Teutonic or Germanic form! The right doctrine is that, of all modern Teutonic languages, the German is, for all practical purposes, the most corrupt and the furthest removed from the original Germanic form; and the corollary is, that it would be far better to take English as near to *the standard* form, and to deduce modern German from it. This is a point to which I have drawn attention over and over again; but it has to be constantly repeated, owing to the extraordinary persistence of the old erroneous notions on the subject.

The idea of dispraising themselves seems to be inherent in some Englishmen; they are never tired of comparing

[1] I.e., 'Do thou instruct us how to work thy will.' *Wissen* is to cause *to wit*, to instruct, teach.

themselves with other nations, to their own disadvantage. This class of men has seized upon the notion that all English is derived from German, and they will hear of nothing else. It is nothing to them that even the Germans take Gothic as the standard spelling for etymological purposes, and next to that regard the Old English and Icelandic forms. It is nothing to them that many of our Anglo-Saxon MSS. were written down before any but the very scantiest scraps of Old High German. It is nothing to them that one system of spelling, at any rate as regards the consonants, is common (with trivial exceptions) to English, Friesic, Gothic, Dutch, Icelandic, Swedish, Danish, and the Low German specially so called; whereas the German is in a minority of one, and differs remarkably from all the rest. They happen to have a fair knowledge of German, and therefore idolize it; and they know nothing of Old English, Friesic, Gothic, Dutch, Icelandic, Swedish, or Danish, and do not care to know anything. It is to their interest to disregard all these; for why should not their German suffice? So it would, if they would but study it historically, and condescend to learn the Old High German original forms. But they will not do that either. Hence comes that painful, that disgraceful blundering over many perfectly simple etymologies which renders us the laughing-stock of Germany and America.

Surely this is a painful subject! Unfortunately it is made all the worse by the singular fact that false doctrine as regards all that is Teutonic is taught most often by men who are thorough and brilliant Greek and Latin scholars in all respects except as regards phonetics and the physiological principles of philology. Yet these are men whom we naturally respect; these are the men who often know German (except from a philological point of view) well. Their influence is great; and they know no better than to exercise it even where they are wrong.

Such an extraordinary perversion as the German *zahn*, as compared with the Gothic *tunthus*, and modern English *tooth* (for \*tonth) ought to make any sensible person *think*. How can we possibly *derive* the English *am* from German *bin*, or the English *are* from the German *sind*? It is true that *are* and *sind* are mere variants, but the English *are* actually preserves the *a* (for *e*) due to the original root, which in German is lost; but *am* and *bin* are not even from the same root!

If these few lines of remonstrance will only lead some of our great scholars to reconsider one of their favourite doctrines, a great deal of good will result. Nothing keeps us back so much as persistence in old exploded fancies.

### 252. Caucus (6 S. xii. 194; 1885).

I suspect that MR. TRUMBULL is quite right. I can point out the source of his information, viz. Captain John Smith's *Works*. At p. 347 of Arber's edition we find a notice of 'their Elders called *Cawcawwassoughes*,' where he is speaking of the Indians of Virginia. At p. 377 he says that *caucorouse* (not *cockarouse*) means 'captain.' The date is 1607-9.

[Given in the *New E. Dict.* as a *possible* explanation of this difficult word.]

### 253. Knout (6 S. xii. 226; 1885).

I have not (in my *Etymological Dictionary*) given any early example of the use of this word. It occurs so early as 1716, in a book on the *State of Russia*, by Capt. J. Perry, quoted in the *Retrospective Review* for February, 1824, p. 159.

### 254. Lammas Monday (6 S. xii. 275; 1885).

*Lammas* is explained in both the larger and smaller editions of my *Dictionary*. It merely means *loaf-mass*, or day of first-fruits (see *Chambers's Book of Days*, p. 154). The equivalence of *lammas* to *loaf-mass* is an historical fact, easily ascertainable by every one who will look up the references. But in the last century, when guess-work was idolized, a common derivation was *lamb-mass*, the form *lamb-mass* being forged for the purpose of deceiving the unwary. This was outdone by Vallancey, who says it is *la-ith-mas*, where *ith* is Irish for 'grain,' and *mas* for 'acorns' or 'mast.' What *la* is he does not say; perhaps he meant it to be the French definite article. See Brand, *Popular Antiquities*, vol. i. As to the time when the word first appeared in our calendar, all that is known is that it was *before* King Ælfred's time, for in his translation of *Orosius*, bk. v. c. 13, he says:—'Thæt was on thǣre tīde calendas Agustus and on thǣm dæge the wē hātath hlāf-mæsse,' i. e. 'It was at the time of the calends of August, and on the day that we call Loaf-mass.' Surely this is sufficient for us to know with certainty. Our good king's writings deserve to be better known. [I know of a clergyman who, with King Alfred's words before him, persists in saying that the derivation of *Lammas* from *lamb-mass* is the only one possible. Such is English reasoning, though it is sane on other points. See above, p. 71.]

### 255. Punt (6 S. xii. 306; 1885).

I have never seen a quotation showing the use of this word in Tudor-English. Here is one:—

'As for *Pamphilus*, ... of his making is the picture of *Vlysses* in a *punt* or small bottom' (Holland, tr. of Pliny, bk. xxxv. c. x; ii. 537).

A small 'bottom' is a small boat. [So used by Canning.]

### 256. En pronounced as In (6 S. xii. 463; 1885).

I do not remember to have seen it noticed that the M. E. *en* has frequently become *in* in modern English, though I dare say this note will soon elicit contradiction.

It is sufficient for me if I contribute something towards the recovery of a note by a former discoverer.

In the words *England, English*, we have a clear example of the tendency to pronounce *en* as *in*. In many instances an actual change of spelling has taken place. Thus our verb to *singe* was in M. E. *sengen*; similarly we find M. E. *henge*, a hinge; M. E. *hengil*, Mod. Prov. E. *hingle*, a small hinge; M. E. *frenge*, Mod. E. fringe; M. E. *swengen*, to swinge; M. E. *twengen*, to twinge; M. E. *grennen*, to grin; M. E. *wenge*, a wing; M. E. *preinte*, *prente*, Mod. E. a print; M. E. *splent*, now often called splint; M. E. *pennen*, to pen up, is spelt *pinnen* in *P. Plowman*; M. E. *lenge*, a ling. Here are already twelve examples. We may notice also the Irish *rint*, *sinse*, for rent, sense; Prov. E. *rench*, to rinse; *agin* for 'agen,' i. e. again; *bin* for 'ben,' i.e. been; *ingine* for engine; *wimmin* for 'wimmen,' i.e. women; *sevin* (not uncommon) for seven, &c. *Dent* is also spelt *dint*.

The use of the above note consists in its application to other cases. For example, it shows that our *link*, a chain, is a regular formation from the stem of the A. S. *hlence*; and *ink*, from M. E. *enke*, may be compared with F. *encre*.

It also follows that a like change from *em* to *im* is to be expected. Accordingly, we find that *alembic* became *limbeck*; and our *limp* is certainly connected with the A. S. *lemp-halt*, as seen in the following glosses:—' Lurdus, *lemp-halt*,' Wright's *Vocab.*, ed. Wülcker, 31, 6. ' Lurdus, *lemp-healt*,' ib., 433, 17; 476, 24. ' Lympe hault, *boiteux*,' Palsgrave.

### 257. Carminative (7 S. i. 276; 1886).

Mr. Terry points out that this word occurs in Swift, ' 'Strephon and Chloe,' 1731, l. 133, as well as in Arbuthnot. He quotes the etymologies given in Johnson, Ogilvie, and Littré. I find that the word is already in Coles's *Dictionary*,

1684. It is obviously borrowed from the F. *carminatif*, explained by Cotgrave as 'wind-voiding . . . also flesh-taming, lust-abating.' Ogilvie derives it from Low Lat. *carminare*, 'to use incantations, to charm . . . *because it acts suddenly, as a charm is supposed to do*.' This seems to be an invention; and indeed we may always suspect invention when the fatal word 'because' is introduced. The Low Lat, *carminare* means properly 'to make verses' (see Lewis and Short); and though it also means to charm, and even to cure wounds by charms (Ducange, s. v. 'Carmen'), this proves nothing as to *carminative*. Littré is clearly right in deducing it from the *other* Lat. *carminare*, to card wool or flax, from *carmen*, a card for wool, from *carere*, to card. [See *Carminate* in the *New E. Dictionary*.]

The idea is extended from the carding of wool to the taming of the flesh (as Cotgrave puts it), or to the expelling of wind. Indeed, we actually find in Blount's *Glossographia*, 1681, the verb *carminate*, 'to card wool, to hatchel flax, to sever the good from the bad.' Coles (1684) gives '*Carminate*, to card wool,' and '*Carminative* medicines, breaking wind.' In Ducange, we have the following: *Carminativum, dissipativum, discussivum*, in *Amalthea, Medicina Salern*, p. 59, edit. 1622; 'Innoxia sunt (pyra) si una cum Carminativis vulgo dictis, hoc est, calefacientibus tenuantibus et flatum expellentibus comediantur, vel super his vinum vetus et odoratum bibatur.' I suppose the word is not found at all before the seventeenth century.

Let me strongly recommend the new and concise *Dictionnaire Synoptique d'Étymologie Française*, by H. Stappers, published at Brussels last year. Stappers gives the etymology from '*carminare*, carder, et par extension, dissiper.' Those who are curious to know how extremely bad a modern book upon etymology can be, may consult the *Glossaire Etymologique Anglo-Normand*, by E. le Héricher, Avranches, 1884.

**258. Dryden's use of Instinct** (7 S. i. 306 ; 1886).

In *Absalom and Achitophel,* pt. i, we find the line:—

'By natural instinct they change their lord.'

A note in Bell's edition says : 'A slight alteration would redeem the metre: "How they, by natural instinct, change their lord." ... This is the only line in which the melody is flattened into prose.' The silliness of this note is only equalled by its impertinence. Of course the line is quite right as it stands. The word *natural* has its three full syllables, and the word *instinct* is accented *on the second syllable,* which the annotator never thought of! Yet he might have found it in Shakespeare, if he ever read that author ; see *Cor.* v. 3. 35 ; *Cymb.* iv. 2. 177 ; v. 5. 381 ; *Rich. III.,* ii. 3. 42, &c. It is rather hard that ignorance should be made the ground for condemning a good writer.

**259. Meresmen** (7 S. i. 312 ; 1886).

It simply (I had almost said merely) means 'boundary-men.' *Meer-stone,* i.e. boundary stone, occurs in Bacon's *Essays.* From A. S. *gemære,* a boundary.

**260. Yorkshire Words: Lathe, a barn** (7 S. i. 355 ; 1886).

It does not seem to be known that the derivations of a large number of provincial English words are given in my Appendix to Cleasby and Vigfusson's *Icelandic Dictionary,* published at Oxford in 1876. By merely referring to it, I find at once the following entries: '*Ket (carrion),* Icel. *kjöt.*' '*Lathe* (barn), Icel. *hlað, hlaða,* and *hlaði.*' '*Lea* (scythe), Icel *lé, ljár.*' The Icel. words are further explained in the *Dictionary* itself. Surely the true Northern name for *barn* is *lathe,* a word actually used by Chaucer when imitating the Northern dialect ; *Cant. Tales,* 4086 (A. 4088).

### 261. Knave of Clubs = Pam (7 S. i. 358; 1886).

It is surprising that Johnson's *Dictionary* should still be seriously consulted for etymologies. His derivation of *Pam* from *palm*, because *Pam* triumphs over other cards, is extremely comic. Of course, *Pam* is short for *Pamphile*, the French name for the knave of clubs; for which see Littré's *French Dictionary*. Cf. p. 135.

### 262. Pronunciation in the Time of Chaucer
### (7 S. ı. 497; 1886).

Questions concerning the pronunciation of Middle English are often asked, but it is quite impossible to deal with them within a reasonable space. It is difficult even to give so much as a notion of the vast and extraordinary changes through which English pronunciation has passed. The mere statement that the Anglo-Saxon long $i$ was pronounced as modern English *ee* in *beet*, and so continued down to at least A.D. 1400, and probably later, when it gradually gave place to the sound of *ei* in *rein*, and after that again to the modern *i* in *pride*, is quite sufficient to arouse the disbelief, perhaps the derision, of those who have never even attempted to look at the evidence, and would rather disbelieve than do so. Those who know less of the subject than Mr. Ellis does will do wisely to believe what he says. It strikes me that one easy example, familiar to many, may perhaps arouse the attention of the incredulous. I take the case of the common name *Price*, which undoubtedy now rhymes to *rice*. The etymology is well known to be from the Welsh *ap Rhys*, pronounced *ap Reece*. The Welsh name is represented in modern English by two forms, viz., *Reece* or *Rees*, preserving the old pronunciation, and *Rice*, in which the pronunciation has changed according to the regular English laws. Similarly, the derivative *ap 'Rhys* is likewise represented both by *Preece* and *Price*. Here we have an example of the change from long *ee* to long *ī*, which can readily be seen to be real.

The intermediate change is best seen in German. The Old High German *wîn*, pronounced as E. *ween*, gave way to the Middle High German *wein*, rhyming with the English *rein*. This spelling is still retained in the modern form of the language to such an extent that the spelling *ei* (really due to the sound in the French *reine*, E. *reign* or *rein*) is used almost universally to denote the sound of the modern English long *i* in *wine*. The modern German word ought, from a phonetic point of view, to be spelt *vain*, but we all know that it is not.

### 263. Slare. (7 S. ii. 12 ; 1886).

The statement that this word cannot be found in a dictionary is a little odd. A good deal depends on knowing where to look, and what to look for. I found it in the first book I opened, and found some light upon it in each of the next six books which I consulted. Peacock's *Dictionary of Manley Words* (E. D. S.) gives:—

'*Slare*, to make a noise by rubbing the boot-soles on an uncarpeted floor. Crockery-ware, when washed in dirty water, or dried badly so as to leave marks thereupon, is said to be *slared*.'

It is even in Halliwell's *Dictionary*, the best-known and most accessible of all dialect dictionaries. My larger *Etymological Dictionary* gives such an account of *slur* as to throw much light on the word. (In the smaller one, I find, to my surprise, *slur* has been omitted, purely by accident.) The *Icelandic Dictionary* gives *slōra*, to trail, contraction of *slōðra*, from *slōð*, a trail, slot. Rietz's *Provincial Swed. Dict.* gives *slöra*, to be negligent. Aasen's *Norweg. Dict.* gives *slöe*, to sully ; *slöe*, short for *slöde*, to trail, and so on. Still closer in form is the Icel. *slæður*, a gown that trails on the ground, which would give *slæur* by the loss of (crossed) *d*. I have already said that 'the key to *slur* is that a *th* or *d* has been dropped; it stands for *slother* or *sloder*; cf. prov. E. *slither*, to slide; *slodder*, slush.' Similarly *slare* is for *sladder* or *slather*. Halliwell gives '*Slather*, to *slip* or slide (Cheshire); *sladdery*, wet and dirty.' Also '*Slair*, to walk slovenly; *slairg*, mud; *slare*, to smear; *slary*, bedaubed.' Also '*Slidder*, to slide,' with its contracted form '*Slir*, to slide.' [I am not quite happy as to all these points.]

264. Henchman I. (7 S. ii. 246; 1886)

I find that in Annandale's *Dictionary* the old bad guess, that this means *haunch-man*, one who stands at one's haunch, is once more offered. How often must I protest against this utter neglect of vowels? How can *aun* pass into *en*? The converse is possible, since *en* may become *an*, and *an* may become *aun* (see below). My own guess, that it stands for *hengst-man*, i. e. horse-boy, is surely far better. I now write to say that I look upon my guess as being fairly proved. For, firstly, the A. S. *hengest* was cut down to *hengst*; see Wright's *Vocab.*, ed. Wülcker, 119, 37. Secondly, we find *Hinxman* as a proper name in the *Clergy List*, where *Hinx-* is certainly for *Hengst*. So much we know from the Index to Kemble's *Charters*, which gives *Hengestes-brōc*, Hinxbrook; *Hengestes-geat*, Hinxgate; *Hengestes-hēafod*, Hinxhead; *Hengestes-īge*, Hinxey. Cf. also Dan. and O. Friesic *hingst*, by-form of *hengst*. Thirdly, *hengst-man* is the exact equivalent of the Icelandic *hesta-maðr*, a horse-boy, groom; cf. O. Swed. *hæsta-swen*, a horse-swain, groom. Rietz gives Swed. dial. *hæsta-man*, which he translates as *häst-man*, i. e. horse-boy. Aasen gives *hest*, a horse; *heste-dreng*, *heste-svein*, as Norwegian words for horse-boy. The Middle Low German dictionary by Schiller gives *hengest*, *hingest*, *hinxt*, a horse; and *hengestrider*, a groom, lit. horse-rider; and I suspect that the word was borrowed from the Continent shortly before 1400. Fourthly, Blount explained *henchman* as I do, in 1691, and cites the spelling *henxman*.

Spelman says the same. The *Prompt. Parv.* has *heyncemann, hench-manne.* The wretched guess about *haunch* began with Bishop Percy, who may have been misled by the spellings *haunsmen, hanshmen* (but not *haunchmen*), in a household book of 1511, which can hardly be depended on. Fifthly, it should be remembered that in *The Flower and the Leaf*, the *henchmen* are described as *riding behind* the knights, their masters. I confess I cannot see where this breaks down; but if there is any flaw in the argument, perhaps some of your readers can find it out. I ought, however, to explain the *ch*. It arose from turning a sharp *s* into *sh*, after *n*; so that *hensman* became *henshman*, also written *henchman*. The spelling *heyncemann* in the *Promptorium* shows this spelling with ȝ, there written *ce*. The process is precisely the same as in *linchpin* for *linspin*, and in *pinch* from F. *pincer*.

[For a great deal more upon this difficult word, see p. 220 below.]

### 265. Limehouse (7 S. ii. 437; 1886).

*Lymoste* (the old spelling of *Limehouse*) is the correct Tudor spelling of *lime-oast*, i.e. lime-kiln. The whole matter is explained in Mr. Scott Robertson's note to Pegge's *Kenticisms*, published by the English Dialect Society, s. v. 'Oast.' See also 'Oast' in my *Dictionary*.

### 266. Shakesperian Words (7 S. ii. 491; 1886).

In this article [viz. in one printed at p. 424 of the same volume] we are informed of the following 'facts': (1) the Eng. *bale* is the same word as the Lat. *malus*; (2) *dirimeo* (which does not exist) is the same as the Lat. *diribeo* (*dirimo* is probably meant); (3) the Lat. *magnus* is the same as the Turkish *beg*; (4) *lief* is the same word as *love, life,* &c., but differs in meaning conventionally. Comment is needless.

### 267. Bandalore (7 S. iii. 66; 1887).

The earliest quotation given by Dr. Murray is dated 1824; but the date of the toy is about 1790. It is also defined by him as 'containing a coiled spring,' which must be a mistake for 'string,' as 'string' occurs below, in the next line but one.

Besides, we know it had a string, not a 'spring.'

In *N. and Q.*, 5 S. i. 452, there is an extract from Moore's *Life*, i. 11, in which Moore says that his earliest verses were composed on the use of the toy 'called in French a *bandalore*, and in English a *quiz*.' Hence the verb to *quiz*, in the sense to play with a bandalore, and *quiz* in this sense is plainly nothing but *whizz*. As no one guesses at the etymology of *bandalore*, I suggest that it is a mere made-up phrase.—French *bande de l'aure*, string of the breeze, or whizz. See *aure* in Cotgrave; who has: '*Aure*, a soft, gentle, coole wind or aire.' [A guess.]

### 268. 'The Sele of the Morning' (7 S. iii. 75; 1887).

*Sele*, better *seel*, was once a very common word. It is the A.S. *sǣl*, M.E. *seel*, time, season. 'The *sele* of the morning' is simply 'the time of day.' The mod. E. *silly* is the derived adjective. *Haysele*, haytime, is common in East Anglia. All this has been explained over and over again. See 'Silly' in my *Dictionary*.

### 269. Atone (7 S. iii. 86; 1887).

Dr. Murray shows that this verb arose from the use of such phrases as 'to be at one,' or 'to bring, make or set at one.' I wish to point out that I believe I have discovered that such phrases arose out of a translation from similar French phrases, so that it is really of French origin, as doubtless many of our English phrases are. In *Le Livere de Reis de Engleterre*, ed. Glover, p. 220, we find that a reconciliation was attempted between Henry II and the Archbishop

Saint Thomas, but they could not be at one; or, in the Anglo-French original, 'il ne peusent mie *estre a un*,' i.e. they could not be reconciled; or, as Shakespeare would have said, 'they could not "atone together."'

### 270. Darkling ( S. iii. 191 ; 1887).

Please note that *darkling* is an adverb. Keats is quite wrong in using it as an adjective; perhaps it was a beautiful word to him, because he did not clearly understand it.

It occurs in Shakespeare not once, but thrice.

Dr. Schmidt explains it quite correctly : '*Darkling*, adv., in the dark; *Mids. N. Dr.*, ii. 2. 86 ; *King Lear*, i. 4. 237 ; *Antony*, iv. 15. 10.'

The adverbial suffix *-ling* is explained in Morris, *Hist. Outlines of Eng. Accidence*, p. 220. It is of A. S. origin, and there is no mystery about it. Examples: *darkling, hedling* (Mod. E. *headlong*), *sideling, flatling, backling. Darkelyng* occurs in *The Knight of La Tour-Landry* (*temp.* Henry VI), ed. Wright, p. 21.

### 271. Cards (7 S. iii. 206 ; 1887).

The following is a very early mention of card-playing in England :—

'*I*tem to the Quenes grace upon the Feest of Saint Stephen for hur disporte at *cardes* this Christmas : c. s. (i. e. 100 shillings).'—*Privy Purse Expenses of Elizabeth of York*, ed. N. H. Nicolas, 1830.

The date is December, 1502 ; and the queen is Elizabeth, wife of Henry VII. Strutt's earliest date for a mention of cards in England is 1495. [Cards are mentioned in the Chester Plays soon after 1400; see the *New E. Dict.*]

### 272. Henchman II. (7 S. iii. 212 ; 1887). Cf. p. 217.

I venture to say something more on this subject, because I have a new piece of evidence to adduce. In the *Privy Purse Expenses of Elizabeth of York*, ed. N. Harris Nicolas,

1830, p. 90, we have the entry, 'Item, to the KInges Hexmen, xiij*s*. iiij*d*.' Here 'hexmen' is obviously miswritten for 'hēxmen,' i. e. 'he*n*xmen.' The date is 1503. A note at p. 200 says :—

'Pages of honour. They were sons of gentlemen, and in public processions walked by the side of the monarch's horse. See a note on this word in the *Privy Purse Expenses of Henry VIII*, 1532, p. 327.'

The same volume contains the Wardrobe Accounts of Edward IV, mostly for the year 1480. At p. 167 we find an account 'for th' apparaile off the sayde maister[1] and vij *henxmen*,' which begins :

'To John Cheyne, Squier for the Body of oure said Souverain Lorde the King and Maister of his *Henxmen* for th' apparaile of the saide Maister and vij of the Kinges *Henxemen* ayenst the feste of Midsomer in the xxti yere of the mooste noble reigne,' &c.

Accordingly these men had eight long gowns of camlet eight of woollen cloth, and sixteen doublets.

On the next page is an account 'for th' apparaile off the kynges fotemen.' We thus get a distinction drawn between *henchmen* and *footmen*. We should also notice the statement that the henchmen were 'sons of gentlemen,' and 'walked by the side of the monarch's horse.'

In the *Princess Mary's Privy Purse Expenses*, ed. Madden, 1831, there are New Year's gifts mentioned. These were given, in 1543, to the king's gentlemen ushers, the yeomen ushers, yeomen of the chamber, pages, heralds, 'trompettes' (i. e. trumpeters), 'henchemen,' players, &c. So again, in 1544, to the gentlemen ushers, grooms of the chamber, guards of the king's bed, footmen, heralds, trumpeters, 'henchemen,' king's players, minstrels, &c. See pp. 104, 140. A note at p. 238 says :—'See *Archaelogia*, i. 369; Strype's *Eccl. Mem.* iii. 2, p. 506.'

[See further at pp. 342–344 below.]

[1] The 'said master' is the 'master of the henxmen.' This 'heading' of the account was probably added afterwards.

### 273. Egle = Icicle (7 S. iii. 234; 1887).

The remarkable article on this word is of great interest, as showing the determined way in which Englishmen prefer guess-work to investigation when they have to do with a word belonging to their own language. They never treat Latin and Greek after this fashion. But when it comes to English, then speculation becomes a pleasure and delight to the writer. I can only say that some readers at least feel a humiliating sense of shame and indignation at seeing such speculations in all the 'glory' of print.

On the writer's own confession, he first guessed the word *egle* to be the French *aiguille*, which it is not. Then he guessed it to be a diminutive of *ice* (which still ends in *s* to the ear, as it did in our old spelling), because 'pickle [pikle?] is a diminutive of *pike*'; whereas his logic requires that *pickle* should be a diminutive of *pice*! Then he guessed it to be a diminutive Latin suffix; but rejected this third guess. Then *at last* he found that *aigle* is a Leicestershire word; and that *ickle* is in the dictionaries (it is in Webster!). Why are we to be treated to all these guesses, which are admittedly wrong? Obviously, because it amuses the writer. But it does not amuse the philologist; it saddens him.

By way of finish, the worthless suggestion is quoted that the Icel. *jökull*, carefully misprinted *jokul*, is 'even the proper name Heckla!' Is it, indeed? Then Dr. Vigfusson has made a very great mistake about Hecla in his *Icelandic Dictionary*!

And all this half-page of speculation is about a perfectly well-known word, merely the A. S. *gicel*, and the familiar latter half of the well-known *ic-icle*, explained in full in •Ogilvie's *Dictionary* (new edition), and in my *Etymological Dictionary*.

Of course it is in Halliwell, s. v. 'Iccles.' The spelling

*aigles* occurs in Marshall's *Rural Economy of the Midland Counties*, 1796.

**274. Phenomenon versus Phænomenon. I** (7 S. iii. 235, 370; 1887).

This note opens up the whole question of so-called 'etymological' spelling. Those who know the whole history of our spelling from the eighth century till the present time best understand the harm done by the pernicious system of trying to transplant Latin and Greek symbols into the English language. The symbols *æ* and *œ* are not English, and are best avoided. Indeed, this is done in practice, when once a word becomes common. *Æther* and *ætherial* have been sensibly replaced by *ether* and *etherial*. No one now writes *æternal*. *Solœcism* is now *solecism*; and I trust that *primeval* and *medieval* will soon prevail over *primæval* and *mediæval*. Pedantic spellings are most objectionable, because they are useless and unphonetic. It is singular that so much zeal is displayed with regard to words of *Greek* origin, whilst none at all is displayed with regard to the far more important words of *native* origin. Such spellings as *sithe* for *scythe*, *siv* for *sieve*, *coud* for *could*, *rime* for *rhyme*, and the like (all of them being at once phonetic, historical, and etymological) find no supporters. This is a bitter satire on our ignorance of our own language. The French spelling is bad enough, but is, at any rate, sufficiently independent to prefer *phénomène* to *phænomenon*. Portuguese, Spanish, and Italian all have *fenomeno*. The reason why we write *Egypt* is because the word is thoroughly naturalized, and was already so spelt in the fourteenth century; i.e. we do not spell it in the *Greek*, but in the *English* fashion. We write *Æschylus* because we wish to show that it is a Greek name, and not English at all; curiously enough, even this is wrong, as it ought rather to be *Aischulos*, if spelt pedantically. Our interest in Egypt is of a very different character; at any rate, I am thankful that the spellings *Egypt* and *Egyptian* cannot now be displaced by any number of 'scholars.' Perhaps 'scholarship' may one day include a knowledge of the native source of English; it will make a great difference. (See further below.)

### 275. Phenomenon versus Phænomenon. II (7 S. iii. 370; 1887).

I think I am entitled to reply that my note was meant for the guidance of the general public. I did not suppose it would convince MR. T. When he asserts that the word *archæology* has never been spelt with *e* for *æ*, he is careful to ignore Dr. Murray's *Dictionary*. The word was spelt *archeologie* by Gale in 1669; and it was spelt *archaiology* by Bishop Hall. The only good reason for retaining the *æ* is phonetic, viz. because a vowel follows.

The retention of original spellings in borrowed words is not only absurd, but is frequently (I am thankful to say) impossible. We cannot *make* people write *pankhá*; they will be sure to write *punkah*. Written language does not go by logic at all; it goes by convenience. It is a mere servant-of-all-work, not a schoolmaster. This is the very point which many fail to understand.

As to the derivation of 'rhyme,' MR. T.'s statement is delicious, viz. that it is a derivative of *rhythmus*, 'say what I will.' The question is not what *I* say, but what every other philologist of any note says throughout Europe. Kluge, for example, in giving the etymology of the G. *Reim*, neatly observes that the Lat. *rhythmus* never had the sense of the G. *Reim*, and naturally enough denies the connexion. Besides, it is useless to deny all the facts in the well-known history of the word.

The best of it is, that it is the word for 'hoar-frost,' which has the true right to the *h*. The A. S. word is *hrīm*, and the Icelandic word is spelt so still.

### 276. Brewery (7 S. iii. 278; 1887).

Hexham's *Dutch Dictionary*, 1658, has 'Een *Brouwerye*, a Brewerie, or a brewing-house.' This carries us back more than a century for the name of the place. The Unton Inventories have only *brew-house*.

### 277. Watchet Plates (7 S. iii. 296; 1887).

The word *watchet*, light blue, has been fully discussed by me in a late number of the Philological Society's *Transactions*. I need only say here that it occurs in Chaucer, and is borrowed from Old French; see *vaciet* in Roquefort's *Old French Dictionary*. He says, '*Vaciet*, mégaleb, arbrisseau qui porte une graine noirâtre propre à teindre en violet; c'est le fruit et la teinture; *vaccinium hysginum*.' Old French is not derived from a town in Somersetshire; the suggestion is a mere flourish of assumed knowledge, appropriate for a (very splendid) work of fiction. [This last remark refers to a quotation from *Lorna Doone*, ch. xiii: 'plates from Watchet, ... with the Watchet blue upon them.']

### 278. Blazer (7 S. iii. 436; 1887).

Dr. Murray rightly explains the word as 'a light jacket of bright colour,' &c. We should always go by history, not guess. The emblazoning of arms on *blazers* can hardly have been the original fact. I have seen such arms on *blazers*, but I remember *blazers* at Cambridge without them; and to this day the arms are much less common at Cambridge than at Oxford—in fact, *quite exceptional*. The term has gradually come into use during my residence here [in Cambridge], and I remember its being especially used in the phrase 'Johnian *blazer*.' This *blazer* always was, and is still, of the brightest possible scarlet; and I think it not improbable that this fact suggested the name, which became general, and (as applied to many *blazers*) utterly devoid of meaning. All this is instructive.

### 279. Dulcarnon (7 S. iv. 76; 1887).

This is a long story, and a great deal has been said about it. I merely summarize the results.

1. *Dulcarnon* is Chaucer's spelling of the Eastern word, meaning 'two-horned,' which was a common medieval epithet of Alexander the Great; for he claimed descent from Ammon.

2. It was applied, in joke, to Euclid I. 47; because the two upper squares stick up like two horns.

3. Chaucer goes on to call it 'the fleming of wrecches,' i. e. flight of the miserable. This is his translation of Lat. *fuga miserorum*, a jocular name for Euclid, I. 5. That is, he mixes up the two propositions; both being puzzling.

4. I do not think any one but Chaucer (or some one quoting or referring to Chaucer) ever employs the word.

### 280. Slughorn (7 S. iv. 276; 1887).

Borrowed by Browning from Chatterton, who took it from Kersey, who took it from Gawain Douglas. Not a horn at all, but a mistake for *slogan*. See the whole story in the second edition of my *Etym. Dict.* (or in the Supplement to the first edition), p. 828.

### 281. Wag (7 S. v. 4; 1888).

It was suggested by Wedgwood that the sb. *wag* is short for *wag-halter*; and those who know our old plays will accept this. In Saintsbury's *Elizabethan Literature*, p. 126, there is a striking proof of it in a poem by Sir Walter Raleigh. Sir Walter explains the meaning of the words *wood*, *weed*, and *wag* very clearly, the *weed* being hemp, and the *wag* being the wag-halter, or man to be hung. Your readers will no doubt see the application.

> 'Three things there be that prosper all apace,
>   And flourish while they are asunder far;
> But on a day they meet all in a place,
>   And when they meet, they one another mar.

And they be these—the Wood, the Weed, the Wag;—
  The Wood is that that makes the gallows-tree;
The Weed is that that strings the hangman's bag;
  The Wag, my pretty knave, betokens *thee*.

Now mark, dear boy—while these assemble not,
  Green springs the tree, hemp grows, the wag is wild;
But when they meet, it makes the timber rot,
  It frets the halter, and it chokes the child.'

### 282. Sparable (7 S. v. 5; 1888).

A *sparable*, i. e. a small nail used by shoemakers, is said to be a contraction of *sparrow-bill*. The following quotation helps to prove it:—

' Hob-nailes to serve the man i' the moone,
And *sparrowbils* to clout Pan's shoone.'
    1629, T. DEKKER, *London's Tempe* (The Song).

### 283. Alwyne (7 S. v. 32; 1888).

In *N. and Q.* 7 S. iv. 534, we are told that the original form was *Æthelwine*; but no reason is given for this singular notion, nor is any reference given either. In the translation of the *A. S. Chronicle*, in Bohn's Library, we find Alwyne mentioned three times. In each case the original has *Ælfwine*, i. e. 'elf-friend'; the transition from which to *Alwyne* is easy enough, by mere loss of the *f*.

We are also told that *ealh* means a hall; but the connexion of *ealh* with either *healh* or *heall* may be doubted, whatever the dictionaries may say. It is much more likely that *ealh* means 'a protected place' or 'asylum,' as Ettmüller suggests; cf. *ealgian*, to protect.

### 284. Additions to Halliwell's 'Dictionary.' I
(7 S. v. 82, 164; 1888).

Now that Dr. Murray is at work upon the letter C, the following MS. notes from my interleaved copy of Halliwell's *Dictionary* may be of interest. I have been too busy to copy them out earlier. I send the list unweeded. Many of the words are common enough, but references are always useful.

*Caddle*, to worry. See 'Scouring of the White Horse,' p. 71.

*Cadowe*. 'A *Cadowe* is the name of her'; Golding's 'Ovid,' fol. 85 b It translates *monedula* in Ovid, 'Met.,' vii. 468.

*Calk*, to calculate, reckon, Bale, 443; *calked*, Tyndale, ii. 308 (Parker Soc. *Index*).

*Caltrop.* See Bradford, ii. 214 (ditto).

*Cambril.* 'His crooked *cambrils* armed with hoof and hair'; Drayton, 'Muses Elysium,' Nymphal 10.

*Camelion.* In Coverdale's Bible, Deut. xiv. 5, where the A.V. has *chamois*. This does not mean *Chameleon*, as in Levit. xi. 30. Coverdale renders that by *stellio*.

*Camisado*, a night-attack. Jewel, i. 110 (Parker Soc.).

*Carle*, one of low birth. Pilkington, 125 (ditto).

*Carling-groat.* See Brand, 'Pop. Antiq.,' ed. Ellis, i. 114.

*Cast.* (See 'Cast' (3) in Halliwell), a calculated contrivance; Becon, ii. 575; Tyndale ii. 335 (Parker Soc.).

*Casure*, cadence, Calfhill, 298 (ditto).

*Caterpillars to the Commonwealth.* So in Dekker, 'Olde Fortunatus,' in his 'Plays,' ed. 1873, i. 140; (with *of* for *to*) Hazlitt, 'O. Eng. Plays,' vi. 510.

*Cat-in-pan.* See Wyclif's 'Works,' ed. Arnold, iii. 332.

*Causeys.* See Somner, 'Antiq. of Canterbury,' ed. 1640, p. 3.

*Cawthernes*, cauldrons. Parish documents at Whitchurch, near Reading, about A.D. 1574. The singular is *cawtron* in 1584 (so I am told).

*Chafts*, chops (Aberdeenshire). I probably found this in John Gibbie.

*Cham*, to chew. Tyndale, iii. 163 (Parker Soc.).

*Chap*, a fellow. Cf. the use of *merchant*.

*Chavel, Chavvle, Chevvle*; to keep on chewing (Tadcaster, Yorkshire). So I am told.

*Chaws*, jaws. Bullinger, i. 4 (Parker Soc.).

*Cherry-fair.* See Brand, 'Pop. Antiq.,' ii. 457; my 'Notes to Piers Plowman,' p. 114.

*Cholder in* (see 'Chalder' in Hall.), to fall in, as the sides of a pit (Brandon, Suffolk).

*Chopine.* See Puttenham, ed. Arber, p. 49.

*Chopological.* Tyndale, i. 304, 308 (Parker Soc.).

*Chowder*, a kind of stew, a fish (Boston, U.S.). See 'N. and Q.,' 4 S. iv. 244, 306.

*Clamb*, climbed. Tyndale, ii. 256 (Parker Soc.). *Clomb*, Byron, 'Siege of Corinth,' l. 6.
*Clam-bake*, a picnic with clams (U. S.). 'N. and Q.,' 4 S. v. 227.
*Clang-banger*, a gossiping mischief-maker. 'N. and Q.,' 4 S. v. 487.
*Clawbacks*, flatterers. Latimer, i. 133 (Parker Soc.).
*Clayen cup*, an earthenware cup full of liquor, used on the eve of Twelfth Day (Devon). See Brand, ' Pop. Antiq.,' i. 29.
*Cleck*, to hatch (Hall.). Precisely Swed. *klächa*.
*Clene Lente*. 'The ij Munday of *clene Lente*'; ' Paston Letters,' ed. Gairdner, ii. 149
*Click*, to catch hold of (Newcastle). '*Gent. Mag.*' 1794. pt. i. p. 13.
*Cloud-berries*. Some were seen by me growing on Pen-y-ghent Yorkshire, in 1873. I was informed that they were locally called *nout-berries* (with *ou* as in *cloud*).
*Clowres*, (apparently) turves. Golding's 'Ovid,' fol. 47. I suppose it corresponds to Ovid's ' *cespite*,' ' Met.,' iv. 301.
*Coals, fetched over the*. In Fuller, 'Holy War,' bk. v. c. 2. See ' N. and Q.,' 4 S. iv. 57.
*Cobloaf-stealing*. See Aubrey's 'Wilts,' Introduction.
*Cock, to whip the*, a sport at fairs (Leic.). Quoted by Brand, ' Pop. Antiq.,' ii. 469 (ed. Ellis), from Grose.
*Cock-a-hoop*. Compare ' John at Cok on the Hop,' i.e. John, living at the sign of the Cock on the Hoop; Riley's 'Memorials of London,' p. 489. A *hoop* is the old combination of three hoops, also called a *garland*, common as a sign of an inn, like the *ivy-bush* or *bush*.
*Cock-on-hoop*, an exclamation of rejoicing; hurrah ! 'Then, faith, *cock-on-hoop*, all is ours,' ' Jacob and Esau,' in ' Old Plays,' ed. Hazlitt, ii. 246.
*Cock-sure*. See references in Parker Soc. Index.
*Cocket*. Explained in Hutchinson, p. 343 (Parker Soc ).
*Codlings-and-Cream*, great willow-herb, *Epilobium hirsutum*. ' N. and Q.,' 4 S. iv. 467.
*Cods*, husks. Ditto.
*Coil*, a noise. Ditto.
*Coke-stole*, a *cucking-stool*. Skelton's 'Works,' ed. Dyce, i. 119.
*Cokes*, v. to coax. Puttenham, ed. Arber, p. 36.
*Coket*, a seal; also a custom paid when cloths, &c. were sealed with a seal; ' Rot. Parl.' iii. 437 (2 Henry IV).
*Cole*, deceit; *cole under candlestick*, deceitful secrecy. Ditto.
*Coll*, to embrace about the neck. Parker Soc.
*Collop-Monday*, Shrove Monday (North). Brand's ' Pop. Antiq.,' ed. Ellis, i. 62.

*Comber*, trouble. Parker Soc.
*Commerouse*, troublesome. Ditto.
*Connach*, to spoil, destroy (Aberdeensh.).
*Copy*, copiousness. Parker Soc.
*Coram*, quorum. 'Οὐ συντέταγμαι, that is, I am none of those which are brought under *coram*'; Udall, tr. of 'Apophthegmes' of Erasmus, ed. 1877, p. 380.
*Cornlaiters* (Halliwell; no ref.). *F*rom Hutchinson, 'Hist. Cumb' i. 553. See Brand's 'Pop. Antiq.,' ed. Ellis, ii. 145.
*Cosy*, a husk, shell, or pod (Beds.). So in Halliwell; but a ridiculous error. *Cosy* is Batchelor's 'phonetic' spelling of *cosh* which is the word meant. See Batchelor's 'Bedfordshire Words.'
*Cour*, to recover health (Aberdeensh.).
*Couring*, crouching down. Puttenham, ed. Arber, p. 292.
*Coye*, v. to stroke. Golding's tr. of 'Ovid,' fol. 79, back.
*Cracker*, a small baking-dish (Newcastle). 'Gent. Mag.,' 1794, pt. i. p. 13.
*Craft*, a croft (Aberdeensh.).
*Crake*, to boast. 'Fellows, keep my counsel; by the mass I do but *crake*'; *T*hersites, in 'Old Plays,' ed. Hazlitt, i. 410. 'All the day long is he facing and *craking*'; 'Roister Doister,' i. 1.
*Cranks*, two or more rows of iron crooks in a frame, used as a toaster (Newcastle). See 'Gent. Mag.' 1794, pt. i. p. 13.
*Cras*, to-morrow (Latin), compared to the cry of the crow. 'He that *cras*, *cras* syngeth with the crowe'; Barclay's 'Ship of Fools,' ed. Jamieson, i. 162.
*Crassetes*, cressets, A.D. 1454. '*T*estamenta Eboracensia,' ii. 194.
*Craumpish*, v.—
  'By pouert spoiled, which made hem sore smert,
  Which, as they thouhte, *craumpysshed* at here herte.'
  Quoted (in a MS. note sent to me) as from Lydgate's 'St. Edmund,' MS. Harl. 2278. fol. 101.
*Cray*, a small ship. 'For skiffs, *crays*, shallops, and the like'; Drayton, 'Battle of Agincourt.'
*Creak*, *Creek*, (Glossic, kree·k), an iron plate at the end of a plough-beam, furnished with holes and a pin, for adjusting the horse's draught-power. Heard at Ely by Miss *G*eorgina Jackson.
*Cresset*. In Golding's tr. of 'Ovid,' fol. 50.
*Cribble*, coarse flour. Parker Soc.
*Crink*, a winding turn. Golding's 'Ovid,' fol. 95.
*Cromes*, hooks. Parker Soc.; and 'Paston Letters,' i. 106.
*Crones*, old ewes. Ditto.
*Cross-bitten*, thwarted. Ditto.

*Crow, to pull.* 'He that hir weddyth, hath a *crowe to pull*'; Barclay's 'Ship of *F*ools,' ed. Jamieson, ii. 8.

*Crowdie,* a mess of oatmeal (Scotch). See Brand's 'Pop. Ant.,' ed. Ellis, i. 87.

*Cucquean* (i. e., *C*uck-quean in Halliwell). In *G*olding's 'Ovid,' fol. 74, back.

*Cue,* humour. Spelt *kew* in *G*olding's 'Ovid,' fol. 116, back.

*Culme,* smoke. In *G*olding's 'Ovid,' fol. 18, back.

*Curry favel.* In Puttenham, ed. Arber, p. 195.

*Curtelasse,* a cutlass. *F*igured in Guillim's 'Display of Heraldry,' ed. 1664, p. 316. Like a stumpy scimetar.

*Cut,* voyage. Golding's 'Ovid,' fol. 179.

*Cut over,* sailed over. Ditto, fol. 179, back.

## 285. Additions to Halliwell's 'Dictionary.' II (7 S. v. 301; 1888).

*Daintrel,* a delicacy (Halliwell; no ref.). It occurs in the Parker Soc. *I*ndex.

*Daker,* a set of skins, usually ten. See Webster's 'Dict.' 'Lego ... fratri meo unum *daykyr* de overledder, et unum *daykyr* de soleledder'; 'Test. Eboracensia,' ii. 218 (A. D. 1458).

*Dalk.* The ref. to 'Rel. Ant.,' ii. 78, merely gives—'Dalke, un fossolet.'

*Damp,* astonishment. Becon, i. 276 (Parker Soc.).

*Dandyprat,* a small coin. Tyndale, ii. 306 (Parker Soc.).

*Dangerous,* arrogant. Puttenham, ed. Arber, p. 301.

*Daubing,* erection of a clay hut (Cumb.). Brand, 'Pop. Antiq.,' ed. Ellis, ii. 150.

*Debelleth,* wars against. Becon, i. 201 (Parker Soc.).

*Debile,* weak. Becon, i. 128 (Parker Soc.).

*Deck,* a pack of cards. Still in use in America; see 'N. and Q.,' 4 S. v. 198.

*Devoterer.* See Becon, i. 450 (Parker Soc.).

*Dight,* pt. t. prepared. 'Jacob *dight* a mease of meete'; Coverdale's Bible, Gen. xxv.

*Dingly,* forcibly. Philpot, 370 (Parker Soc.).

*Dingy,* the word explained. Bradford, i. 111; note (ditto).

*Dite,* a saying. Parker Soc. *I*ndex.

*Ditty,* a song. Ditto.

*Dive-doppil,* dab-chick; Becon, iii. 276 (Parker Soc.).

*Dizzard,* a blockhead. Parker Soc. *I*ndex.

*Do*, if you do (Cambs., common). 'Don't go a-nigh that ditch; *do*, you'll fall in.'

*Dockey*, a light dough-cake, quickly baked in the mouth of the oven, and eaten hot. Ref. lost; prob. E. Anglian.

*Dodkin*, a small coin. See Parker Soc. Index.

*Dodypole*. Ditto.

*Dog-hanging*, a money-gathering for a bride (Essex). See Brand 'Pop. Antiq.,' ed. Ellis, ii. 150.

*Doll*, a child's hand; Golding's 'Ovid,' fol. 71, back.

*Domifying*, housing; a term in astrology.

'Nother in the stars search out no difference,
By *domifying* or calculation.'

Lydgate, '*Dance of Machabre* (the Astronomer),' in a miserable modernized edition.

' By *domifying* of sundry mancions.'

Lydgate, 'Fall of Princes,' Prol. st. 43.

*Dor*, a drone; Bullinger, i. 332 (Parker Soc.).

*Dories*, drone-bees; Philpot, 308 (Parker Soc.).

*Doted* (foolish); Becon, ii. 646 (Parker Soc.).

*Dotel*, a dotard; Pilkington, 586 (Parker Soc.).

*Dottrel*, bird; Bale, 363 (Parker Soc.).

*Dough*, a little cake (North); Brand, 'Pop. Ant.,' ed. Ellis, i. 526.

*Dough-nut-day*, Shrove Tuesday (Baldock, Herts). 'It being usual to make a good store of small cakes fried in hog's lard, placed over the fire in a brass skillet, called *dough-nuts*, wherewith the youngsters are plentifully regaled.' Brand, 'Pop. Ant.,' ed. Ellis, i. 83.

*Dover's meetings*, apparently the same as *Dover's games*. Brand, as above, i. 277.

*Dowsepers*, grandees; Bale, 155, 317 (Parker Soc.).

*Draffe*, hog-wash. Either the coarse liquor or brewer's grains; Skelton, ed. Dyce, i. 100, ii. 164. Food for swine; Bale, 285 (Parker Soc.).

*Drafflesacked*, filled with draff; Becon, ii. 591 (Parker Soc.).

*Dragges*, dregs, or drugs [*sic*, it makes a difference!]; Pilkington, 121 (Parker Soc.).

*Drift*, a green lane. Also used in Cambs.

*Drum*, an entertainment (A.D. 1751). See 'N. and Q.' 4 S. ii. 157.

*Drumslet*, a drum; Golding's 'Ovid,' fol. 149, back.

*Drunkard's cloak*. See Brand, 'Pop. Ant.,' ed. Ellis, iii. 109.

*Dryth*, dryness; Tyndale, ii. 14 (Parker Soc.).

*Dudgeon-dagger*. See Hazlitt's Dodsley's 'Old Plays,' v. 271.

*Dummel*, stupid, slow to move; said of wild animals (prov. Eng.; ref. lost).

*During*, enduring. Tyndale, iii. 264 (Parker Soc.).
*Dyssour*, tale-teller, boaster. 'He shal become a *dyssour*'; Rob. of Brunne, 'Handlyng Synne,' 8302.

### 286. Additions to Halliwell's 'Dictionary.' III (7 S. v. 503; 1888).

*Eargh*, adj., frightened, superstitiously afraid (Aberdeenshire). This is the word of which *eerie* is a later form. The A. S. form is *earh*.
*Earn*, s., eagle; Golding's 'Ovid,' fol. 184, back.
*Earshrift*, s., auricular confession. Parker Soc. Index.
*Eftsoons*, adv., soon afterwards. Parker Soc.
*Egal*, adj., equal. Same.
*Egally*, adv., equally. Same.
*Egalness*, s., equality. Same.
*Eisel*, s., vinegar. Also *esel*, *eysil*. Same. Old Fr. *aisil*, extended from Old Fr. *aisi*, answering to Low Lat. *acitum*, variant of Lat. *acetum*.
*Embossed*. See Dodsley's 'Old Plays,' ed. Hazlitt, xi. 406, and note.
*Endote*, v., to endow. Parker Soc.
*Enforming*, pr. pt., forming. Same.
*Esters*. See also 'King Alisaunder,' ed. Weber, 7657. The entry *eftures* in Halliwell is a ridiculous blunder, due to misreading a long *s* as an *f*. The word meant is *estures*, bad spelling of *estres*; and *eftures* is a ghost-word. [See above, p. 171.]
*Evelong*, adj., oblong; Golding's 'Ovid,' fol. 101. [*Avelonge* in N.E.D.]
*Ewrous, Eurous*, adj., successful. 'Lothbrok was more *eurous* and gracious unto game,' Lydgate, St. Edmund, MS. Harl. 2278, fol. 44. From O. F. *eur*, Lat. *augurium*.
*Eye, at*, at a glance. Parker Soc. Also, to the sight; Chaucer, C. T., Group E, 1168.

### 287. Buffetier; the supposed original of Beef-eater (7 S. v. 216; 1888).

I wish those who write about this word would read the article in my *Dictionary*; they might then come to know *what they are talking about*. *Buffetier* is *not* the word from which Mr. Steevens evolved his famous, much admired and wholly ridiculous etymology. The form he gave was: *Beaufetier*, one who waits at a side-board, which was anciently placed in a *beaufet*.' See Todd's *Johnson*. The *real* question is this, What was a *beaufet*, and how could a side-board be placed *in* it? But to *this* question no one will address himself.

### 288. Legerdemain (7 S. v. 246 ; 1888).

Examples of this word have been quoted from Spenser and Sir T. More. But it was used much earlier, by Lydgate, in his *Dance of Machabre*, where the Tregetour is represented as saying:—

'*Legerdemain* now helpeth me right nought.'

### 289. 'Familiarity breeds contempt' (7 S. v. 247 ; 1888).

This proverb was already current in the twelfth century, as the following extract shows: 'Ut enim vulgare testatur proverbium, Familiaris rei communicatio contemptus mater existit'; Alanus de Insulis, 'Liber de Planctu Naturae,' as printed in *Minor Anglo-Latin Satirists*, edited by T. Wright (Record Series), vol. ii. p. 454. Perhaps it can be traced still further back.

### 290. Robin (7 S. v. 345 ; 1888).

I quote in my *Dictionary* the phrase 'Robin redbreast' from Skelton's *Philip Sparowe*, l. 399. In a MS. of the fourteenth century, Camb. Univ. Library, Gg. 4, 27, fol. 9 b, the first line is—

'*Robert* redbrest and the wrenne.'

### 291. Ghost-word (7 S. v. 465 ; 1888).

This useful word was first employed by myself in 1886; and its first appearance in print is at p. 352 of the Philological Society's *Transactions* for that year. A good example is <u>abacot</u>, which is in many dictionaries, but was rightly omitted by Dr. Murray. It is a mistaken form, put for *a bycocket*, the *a* being the indefinite article. With reference to words of this class, I say:

> 'As it is convenient to have a short name for words of this character, I shall take leave to call them <u>ghost-words</u>. Like ghosts, we may seem to see them, or may fancy that they exist; but they have no real entity. We cannot grasp them. When we would do so, they disappear.'

At p. 373 of the same, I give a list of one hundred and three ghost-words, <u>due, for the most part, to the ignorance of editors of Middle English works</u>. Formerly it was not at all expected of an editor that he should have any real knowledge of the language of his MSS. Even now editors are more adventurous than is quite honest.

### 292. To make Orders (7 S. v. 484; 1888).

I give the explanation of this phrase for the benefit of the sub-editor of O in the *New English Dictionary*. It is past all guessing, but I happen to know the answer from having met with similar expressions. It occurs in the *Sowdone of Babylone*, ed. Hausknecht, l. 2036. The editor confesses that he can make nothing of it, and his suggestion is beside the mark. When the twelve peers attacked the Sultan and his men, we are told that they

> '*maden orders* wondir fast;
> Thai slowe doun alle, that were in the halle,
> And made hem wondirly sore agast.'

It is a grim medieval joke. A clerk in holy orders was known by wearing the tonsure, that is, he had a shaven crown. A medieval hero sometimes made his foe resemble a clerk by the summary process of shaving off a large portion of his hair by a dexterous sweep of his sword.

To accomplish this feat was called 'to make orders'; and the line implies that they 'sliced pieces off their adversaries' heads at an amazing rate.' To do this was a frequent amusement with the famous twelve peers.

### 293. Catsup : Ketchup (7 S. vi. 12 ; 1888).

It will be observed that the answers hitherto given to the question as to the derivation of *ketchup* are all useless. To derive it from the 'Eastern word *kitjap*' is ridiculous, for there is no such language as 'Eastern.' Dr. Charnock tells us it is Hindustani, to which I have only to say that I wish he would prove his point by telling us in what Hindustani dictionary it can be found. I have been looking for this word these six years, and am as far off as ever from finding it; simply because no one condescends to mention the dictionary that contains it.

I would earnestly commend to the consideration of all contributors to *N. and Q.* that they should give their references. In philology, especially, it is worse than useless to quote words as belonging to 'an Eastern language'; we want to know the precise name of the language. Again, it is useless to say that a word is French, or Spanish, or what else, unless it can be found in any common dictionary. Unfortunately, it is precisely when a word is rare, and only to be found in works of great research, that the language to which it belongs is most airily cited. All inexact knowledge is distressing rather than helpful.

### 294. Ohthere's Voyage (7 S. vi. 44; 1888).

There is a passage about Ohthere's voyage in Ælfred's translation of *Orosius* which has been curiously misunderstood. Dr. Bosworth's translation, p. 41, gives it thus :—

'He chiefly went thither, in addition to the seeing of the country, on account of the horse-whales [walruses], because they have very good bone in their teeth; of these teeth they brought some to the king; and their hides are very good for ship-ropes. This whale is much less than other whales; it is not longer than seven ells; but in his own country is the best whale-hunting; they are eight and forty ells long, and the largest fifty ells long; of these, he said, that he was one of six who killed sixty in two days [i. e. he with five others killed sixty in two days '].

Dr. Bosworth's note is:—

'Every translator has found a difficulty in this passage, as it appeared impossible for six men to kill sixty whales in two days.'

After which follows a long discussion, showing the impossibility of the feat.

The passage is printed in Sweet's *Anglo-Saxon Reader;* but no notice is taken of the difficulty, nor is any solution offered. The true answer is extremely simple—when you know it. Any one acquainted with the colloquial character of Anglo-Saxon narrative will, of course, easily see that the words 'of these' in the last paragraph refer to the *walruses.* The preceding sentence is a mere parenthesis. Ohthere was a practical man, and an honest, and knew what he was talking about. He tells us that the horse-whale is but seven ells, or fourteen feet long. Then he adds, parenthetically, 'but in my country, the real whales are ninety-six or one hundred feet long;' and then, continuing his narrative, '*he said*, that he with five others killed sixty of them in two days.' The A.S. *thæra* is best translated by 'of them,' as usual.

Thus the whole difficulty utterly vanishes. I have no doubt whatever that six men could kill five walruses apiece in the course of the day, at a time when they could be found plentifully. Perhaps it could even be done now. A little pamphlet on *Orosian Geography* has just been published by W. & A. K. Johnston. It is written by J. Mc.Cubbin and T. D. Holmes, and gives a translation of the *Voyages of Ohthere and Wulfstan,* with three illustrative maps.

**295. Knowledge for the People** (7 S. vi. 63; 1888).

In the number of the paper called *Knowledge* for July 2, p. 196, there is an article on 'English Pronunciation,' containing some extraordinary mis-statements, which it is worth while to set right.

The writer first gives us a specimen of the Lord's Prayer in English, which he attributes to Bishop Edfrid, about 700. It begins: 'Uren fader thie arth in heofnas,' &c. The mis-spellings throughout are of the most startling description; such a wonderful form as *thic* for *thu* (i.e. thou) is enough to make the dullest reader suspicious. But what does it all mean?

The fact is, that the well-known Lindisfarne MS. in the British Museum was written out by Bishop Eadfrith [not Edfrith], who was Bishop of Durham from 698 to 721. This is clearly the MS. referred to. However, the text of the MS. as written by Eadfrith happens to be not in English at all, but wholly and solely *in Latin!*

At a much later date, variously given as about 950, or about 970, or even (as some contend) much later, a Northern-English gloss was supplied above the Latin text by a certain Aldred. The gloss to S. Matthew, vi. 9, begins the Lord's Prayer with the words: 'fader urer thu arth . . . in heofnas'; and this is sufficiently near to show us that *uren* and *thic* are mere blunders for *urer* and *thu*. Thus the error in chronology amounts to nearly three centuries, which is a good deal in the history of a language.

The writer next gives us another specimen, dated by him about 900. It is difficult to guess what is meant, but the reference is probably to the Mercian Gloss in the Rushworth MS., which can hardly be earlier than the latter half of the tenth century, though the Latin text dates from about 800.

Probably the information was taken from Camden's *Remains*; if so, he is a very unsafe guide.

Next we find quoted a *rimed version* of the Lord's Prayer, attributed to Pope Adrian, who died in 1159; i.e. about half a century before rimes of this character appear in

English for the first time. This is an old fable, which ought to be considered as exploded. (See above, p. 206.)

Next, leaving these specimens, the writer quotes the well-known passage from Trevisa about the English dialects. This also contains several errors, and we are referred to Dr. Hicks (mis-spelling of Hickes) for the information that the author of this passage is unknown. However, Dr. Hickes expressly assigns it to Trevisa, at p. xvii. of his well-known *Thesaurus*.

Would it not be much better for a writer who is so imperfectly acquainted with his subject to *let it alone?* It is not the first time that I have called attention to the fact that the English language is the *sole* subject which is treated of by those who have never properly studied it. If botany or chemistry were so treated it would be considered very strange; but when the subject happens to be the English language, a want of scientific knowledge seems to be considered as being absolutely meritorious.

**296. Herewards: Howard: Leofwine** (7 S. vi. 93; 1888).

I cannot agree with any of the startling propositions in this article. Heward is treated of by Mr. Bardsley as being a variant spelling of Heyward; and I believe he is quite right. There is no phonetic law against it. But how Hereward can be twisted into Heward is quite beyond me.

We are further told that Howard is a contraction of 'the Anglo-Saxon *Holdward*, the governor of a hold or keep.' The objections to this are overwhelming.

Howard is a mere variant of Haward, another form of Hayward; this has been shown in *N. and Q.*, 3 S. x. 29, 60, 74, and still more conclusively from registers, also in *N. and Q.*; but I forget the reference, and cannot just now recover it.

The derivations from *hogward* and *hallward* are both bad

guesses and unsupported. However this may be, I, at any rate, should like to ask where we can find 'the A. S. Holdward'; and, for the matter of that, where we can find the A. S. *hold* in the sense of stronghold or 'keep.' I do not think it at all right that we should be perpetually troubled with 'bogus' Anglo-Saxon words that seem to have originated merely in imaginative brains. Every one who knows Anglo-Saxon at all knows that *hold* is an adjective meaning 'faithful' or 'true.' When (very rarely) it is used as a substantive, it means 'a carcase.' The A. S. form of *hold*, a fortress, is not *hold* but *heald!*

Next, we are told that 'Leofwin' means 'a lover of war.' It is really too much that such an astonishing mistake should be inflicted on us. It is a quadruple blunder. For first, it is mis-spelt; the word meant is Leofwine, and the final *e*, being agential, makes all the difference.

Secondly, *leaf* (rather *lēaf*) does not mean 'lover,' nor is it a substantive; it is an adjective, meaning 'dear,' Modern English *lief.* Thirdly, *win* does not mean '*war*'; the proper spelling of the word is *winn* with a double *n*, and it makes a difference in Anglo-Saxon etymology whether an *n* is really double or not. And fourthly, the word meant is *wine*, a friend. *Leofwine* is simply 'dear friend.' What then becomes of 'lover of war'?

### 297. The letter H (7 S. vi. 110; 1888).

Some guesses of mine (they are no better) on this subject will be found in my *Principles of English Etymology*, p. 359. The mis-pronunciation of initial *h* is not 'a comparatively late phenomenon,' for some remarkably early examples may be found. It is common in the romance of *Havelok*, about A.D. 1280. I enumerate several instances in my preface to that poem, at p. xxxvii, such as *holde* for *old*, *hevere* for *ever*, *Henglishe* for *English*, &c.; whilst, on the other hand, we find *Avelok* for *Havelok*, *aveden* for *haveden* (had), &c. I believe a few sporadic examples may be found in Anglo-Saxon. Only last week I found *ors* for *hors* (horse) in an inedited A. S. manuscript.

**298. English Grammars** (7 S. vi. 121, 243, 302 ; 1888).

A collection of the names of some of the older English grammars, and of books more or less interesting to the student of English grammar, was made many years ago by Sir F. Madden, and is now in my possession. It is doubtless imperfect, but it may prove of some interest [1]. I therefore give it nearly as it was made. It was collected by the simple process of making cuttings from booksellers' catalognes. Few of the books mentioned are of very recent date. I have compared the list with Lowndes's *Bibliographer's Manual*, which fails to mention several of them. The abbreviations 'E.' and 'G.' mean English and 'Grammar' ·

> Adams, Rev. James. Euphonologia Linguae Anglicanae. 1794. 8vo.
> —— The Pronunciation of the E. Language Vindicated from imputed Anomaly and Caprice. Edinburgh. 1799. 8vo.
> Adelung's Three Philological Essays. Translated from the German by A. F. M. Willich. 1798. 8vo.
> Anchoran, J. The Gate of Tongues Unlocked and Opened. 1637. 8vo. Given by Mr. Wheatley in his list of 'Dictionaries,' but not with this date.
> Andrew, Dr. Institutes of Grammar. 1817. 8vo.
> Ascham, R. The Scholemaster. 1571. 4to. A well-known book; the editions are numerous.
> Ash, Dr. Introduction to Dr. Louth's E. G. 1807. 12mo.
> —— A Comprehensive G. of the E. Tongue. Prefixed to his 'Dictionary.' 1775. 8vo.
> B.— I. B. Heroick Education; or, Choice Maximes for the Facile Training up of Youth. 1657. 12mo.
> Also, Of Education, &c. 1699. 12mo.

[1] One addition was supplied by a correspondent of *N. and Q.* In *N. and Q.* 7 S. vii. 54, we read :—' Prof. Skeat can find a very full list of English grammars, giving several scores that he has not on his roll, in the Catalogue of the New York State Library at Albany. I should think there must be three hundred in all.'

Baker, R. Remarks on the E. Language. 1779 and 1799. 8vo.
Bales, P. Writing Schoolemaster, teaching Brachygraphie, Orthographie, and Calligraphie. 1590. 4to.
Barbour, J. An Epitome of G. Principles. Oxon. 1668. 12mo.
Barnes, Rev. W. A Philological G. grounded upon E. London. 1854. 8vo.
—— Early England and the Saxon English. London. fcap. 8vo.
Batchelor, T. Orthoepical Analysis of the E. Language. 1809. 8vo.
Bayly, Anselm. E. G. 1772. 8vo.
Beattie, J. Theory of Language. 1788. 8vo
Bell, J. System of E. G. Glasgow. 1769. 2 vols. 12mo.
Bellum Grammaticale; or the Grammatical Battel Royal, in reflection on the three E. Grammars, published in about a year last past. 1712. 8vo.
Bertram, Charles. English-Danish Grammar. 1750.
—— Essay on the Style of the E. Tongue. Copenhagen. 1749. 12mo.
Blair, D. Practical G. of the E. Language. 1809. 12mo. Also 1816. 18mo.
Bobbit, A. Elements of E. G. 1833. 12mo.
Bosworth, Rev. J. Elements of Anglo-Saxon G. 1823. Royal 8vo.
—— Compendious Grammar of the Anglo-Saxon Language.
Brightland, J. E. G. 1712. 12mo.
Brinsley, John. Ludus Literarius; or, the G. Schoole. London, 1612; reprinted 1627. 4to.
Brittain, Lewis. Rudiments of E. G. Louvain. 1778. 12mo.
Buchanan, Dr. On the Elegant and Uniform Pronunciation of the E. Language. 1766. 8vo. Later ed., 1827 (?).
Bucke. Classical E. G. 1829. 12mo.
Butler, Charles. E. G. Oxford, 1633. See preface to Johnson's 'Dict.' His system of orthography is exemplified in his 'Principles of Musick' (1636) and his 'Feminin Monarchi, or, the Histori of Bees' (1634).
Callander (John?). Deformities of Dr. S. Johnson. 1782. 8vo.
Campbell, A. Lexiphanes [against Dr. Johnson's style]. London, 1767. 12mo. Later, 1783.
Care, H. Tutor to True English. 1687. 8vo.
Carew, Richard. Survey of Cornwall; with an Epistle concerning the excellencies of the E. Tongue. London, 1769. 4to.
Casaubon, Meric. De Lingua Hebraica et de Lingua Saxonica. London, 1650. 12mo.
Cassander, I. Criticisms on Tooke's Diversions of Purley. 1790. 8vo.

## ENGLISH GRAMMARS.

Chapman, Rev. J. Rhythmical G. of the E. Language. 1821. 12mo.

Churchill, O. New G. of the E. Language. 1823. 12mo.

Cleland, John. Way to Things by Words: an Attempt at the Retrieval of the Ancient Celtic. London, 1766. 8vo. Also 1768-9.

Cobbett, Wm. E. G. 1819 and 1826, &c. 12mo.

Conjectural Observations on the Origin and Progress of Alphabetic Writing. 1772. 8vo.

Cook's (Coote's ?). E. Schoolmaster. 1652.

Cooperi Grammatica Linguae Anglicanae. 1685. 12mo.

Coote, Charles. Elements of E. G. 1778 [1788 ?] 8vo.

Coote, Edw. The E. School-master. 1636, 1658, 1665, 1692, 1704. 4to.

Croft, Herbert. Letter to the Princess Royal of England, on the E. and German Languages. Hamburg, 1797. 4to.

Crombie, Alex. The Etymology and Syntax of the E. Language. 1802, 1809, 1830, 1838. 8vo.

—— Reply to Dr. Gilchrist on E. G. 1817. 8vo.

Davies, Rev. Edw. Celtic Researches. London, 1804. Royal 8vo.

Delamothe, G. The French Alphabet, &c. London, 1595. 8vo. 1631. 18mo.

Devis, Ellin. Accidence; or, First Rudiments of E. G. 1786. 12mo.

Dictionnaire de la Prononciation Angloise. London, 1781. 8vo.

Dissertation on the Beauties and Defects of the E. Language. Paris, 1805. 12mo.

Dutch and E. Grammar. 1775. 12mo.

Du Wes, Giles. An Introductorie for to Lerne to Rede, to Pronounce, and to Speak French Trewly. London, by Nic. Bourman, n. d. [about 1540]. Also by J. Waley; also by T. Godfray. Reprinted, together with Palsgrave's 'Dictionary,' at Paris, 1852.

Elphinston, James. Analysis of the French and E. Languages. 1756. 2 vols. 12mo.

—— Principles of the E. Language. London, 1765. 2 vols. 12mo.

—— Propriety ascertained in her Picture; or, E. Speech and Spelling, &c. 1787. 2 vols. 4to.

—— E. Orthography Epitomized. London, 1790. 8vo.

—— Fifty Years' Correspondence between Geniuses of both Sexes. [In reformed Spelling.] London, 1791-4. 8 vols. 12mo.

—— Miniature of Inglish Orthography. 1795. 8vo.

Elstob, Elizabeth. Rudiments of G. for the E. Saxon Tongue. London, 1715. 4to.

English, J. Observations on Mr. Sheridan's Dissertation concerning the E. Tongue. 1762. 8vo.

E. G., Royal ; Reformed into a more easie Method. 169;. 12mo.

E. Language, Observations upon the. N. d. [about 1715]. 8vo.

—— Reflections on the ; being a Detection of many Improper Expressions, &c. 1770. 8vo.

—— Vulgarisms and Improprieties of. 1833. 12mo.

E. Orthographie. Oxford, 1668. 4to. Said to be by Owen Price (Wood, 'Ath. Ox.' ii. 490).

E. Tongue, G. of the ; With the approbation of Bickerstaff. 1711. 12mo.

E. Words, Vocabulary of ; of dubious Accentuation. 1797. 8vo.

Errors of Pronunciation ... by the Inhabitants of London and Paris. 1817. 8vo.

Essay upon Literature ; an Enquiry into the Antiquity and Original of Letters. 1726. 8vo.

Essay upon the Harmony of Language ... to Illustrate that of the E. Language. 1774. 8vo.

Explanatory Treatise on the Subjunctive Mode. 1834. 8vo.

Familiar E. Synonymes, Critically and Etymologically Illustrated. 1822. 12mo.

Fearn, Jo. Anti-Tooke: an Analysis of Language. London 1824. 8vo.

Fenner, Dudley. The Artes of Logike and Rhetorike. Middleburgh, 1584. 4to.

Fisher and Tryon's New Spelling-Book. 1700. 12mo.

Forneworth, R. The Pure Language of the Spirit of Truth ; or Thee and Thou, &c. [Defence of Quaker Idiom.] 1656. 8vo.

Free, Dr. John. Essay towards a History of the E. Tongue. London, 1749, 1773, 1788. 8vo.

French Alphabet (a Quaint Assemblage of Grammatical Dialogues, in French and E.). 1639. 18mo.

Gardiner's E. G. Adapted to Different Classes of Learners. 1809. 12mo.

Grammar. Some New Essays of a Natural and Artificial Grammar .. for the Benefit of a Noble Youth (W. Godolphin, Esq ' 1707. folio.

—— Short Introduction of G., generally to be used. Cambridge, 1668.

—— G. of the E. Tongue, With Notes, &c. 1711. 8vo. Also n. d. 12mo.

—— G. of the E. Verb. 1815. 12mo.

—— Two Grammatical Essays on a Barbarism in the E. Language. 1768. 8vo.

## ENGLISH GRAMMARS.

Greenwood, James. Essay towards a Practical E. G. 1729, 1753. 12mo.
Grimm, Jacob. Deutsche Grammatik. Göttingen, 1822-37. 4 vols. 8vo.
Groombridge, H. The Rudiments of the E. Tongue. Bath, 1797. 8vo.
Gwilt, Joseph. Rudiments of a G. of the Anglo-Saxon Tongue. London, 1829. 8vo.
Hall's Lessons on the Analogy and Syntax of the E. Language. 1833. 12mo.
Haltrop (Jo.). E. and Dutch Grammar. Dort, 1791. 8vo.
Hampton, Barnaby. Prosodia construed. 1657. 12mo.
Harris, J. Hermes; or, Inquiry concerning Language. London, 1751. 8vo. Also 1765, 1771, 1777, 1781, 1786.
—— Verbs of the E. Language Explained. 1830. 8vo.
Hart, John, Chester Herault. An Orthographie. London 1569. 16mo.
Hazlitt, Wm. G. of the E. Tongue. 1810. 12mo
Head, Sir E. 'Shall' and 'Will.' 1858. 12mo.
H[eath], W[m.]. Grammatical Drollery. [An accidence in rhyme.] 1682. 8vo.
Henley, J. The Compleat Linguist. London, 1719-21. 8vo.
—— Anglo-Saxon Grammar. 1726. 8vo.
Henshall, S. The Anglo-Saxon and E. Languages reciprocally illustrative of each other. London, 1798. 4to.
—— Etymological Organic Reasoner. London, 1807. 8vo.
Hickes, Dr. Geo. Institutiones Grammaticae Anglo-Saxonicae, &c. Oxford, 1689. 4to.
—— Linguarum Veterum Septentrionalium Thesaurus. Oxford, 1705. 3 vols., folio.
—— Grammatica Anglo-Saxonica. Oxford, 1711. 8vo.
Hill, W. Fifteen Lessons on the ... E. Language. Huddersfield, 1833. 8vo.
Hodges, Rich. A Special Help to Orthographie. London, 1683. Small 4to.
—— The Plainest Directions for True Writing of English. London, 1649. 12mo.
Holder, W. Elements of Speech. London, 1669. 8vo.
Hollyband, Claudius. The French Schoolemaster. London, 1573. 12mo. Also 1631.
—— The Italian Schoolemaster. London, 1575. 12mo. Also 1583, 1591, 1597, 1608.
—— The French Littleton. London, 1625. 18mo.
—— Treatise for Declining of (French) Verbs. London, 1641. 8vo.

Hunter, W. Anglo-Saxon Grammar. 1832. 8vo.
Hutchinson, F. Many Advantages of a Good Language, with the Present State of our Own. 1724. 8vo.
Irving, David. Elements of E. Composition. London, 1801 and 1820. 12mo.
Jamieson, John. Hermes Scythicus. Edinburgh, 1814. 8vo.
Jodrell, Rich. Paul. Philology of the E. Language. [Really a Dictionary of quotations.] London, 1820. 4to.
Johnson, R. The Scholar's Guide from the Accidence to the University. 1665.
Johnson, Rich. Grammatical Commentaries. London, 1706. 8vo. Also 1718. 8vo. 1818. 8vo.
—— Noctes Nottinghamicae. Nottingham, 1718. 8vo. Also 1814. 8vo.
Jones, J. Practical Phonography. London, 1701, 4to.
—— New Art of Spelling. [The Same?]. London, 1704. 4to.
Jones, Rowland. The Origins of Languages and Nations. London, 1764. 8vo.
—— The Circles of Gomer. London, 1771. 8vo.
—— The Philosophy of Words. London, 1769. 8vo.
—— Io-Triads, or the Tenth Muse. London, 1773. 8vo.
—— English, as a Universal Language. London, 1771. 8vo.
Jonson, Ben (the Dramatist). An E. G. 1640. Folio.
Junius, F. Etymologicum Anglicanum. (With A. S. Grammar.) Oxford, 1743. Folio.
Lane, A. Key to the Art of Letters; or E. a Learned Language. 1700, 1705, 1706. 12mo.
Language, a Dissertation on; more particularly ... the E. Language. Paris, 1805. 12mo.
Latham, Dr. R. G. E. G. (several editions).
Leibnitz, G. W. Collectanea Etymologia. Hanover, 1717. 8vo.
Leigh, Edw. A Philologicall Commentary ... of Law Words. London, 1652. 8vo. Also 1658 and 1671.
Lewis, M. Essay to facilitate ... the Rudiments of Grammar. 1674. 8vo.
Lexiphanes. See Campbell, A.
Lhuyd, Edw. Archæologia Britannica. Oxford, 1707. Vol. I. Folio. [No second volume].
Lilly, Wm. Short Introduction of Grammar. London, 1574. 4to. [several editions].
—— E. G. with Preface by John Ward. London, 1732. 8vo.
Loughton, W. Practical G. of the E. Tongue. 1739. 12mo.
Lowth, Bp. Rob. A Short Introduction to E. G. London, 1762,

8vo. Later editions, 1764, 1767, 1769, 1772, 1775, 1778, 1787, 1789, 1791, 1795.

Ludus Literarius ; or, the Grammar Schoole. Kingston, 1627. 4to.

Mackintosh's Essay on E. G. 1808. 8vo.

Maittaire, Michael. Essay on the Art of E. G. 1712. 8vo.

Martin's Lingua Britannica Reformata. 1748. 8vo.

Martin, B. Institutions of Language. 1748. 8vo.

—— Introduction to the E. Language. 1754. 12mo. Also 1766.

Martin, T. Philological E. G. 1824.

Mitford, W. Essay upon the Harmony of Language. London, 1774. 8vo.

Monboddo, Lord. Of the Origin and Progress of Language. Edinburgh, 1774. 6 vols. 8vo.

Murray, Dr. Alex. History of the European Languages. Edinburgh, 1823. 2 vols. 8vo.

Murray, Lindley. E. G. First edition. York, 1795. 12mo. (See the long list in Lowndes).

—— Examined by an Oxonian. 1809.

Nares, Rob. (Archdeacon). Elements of Orthoëpy. London, 1784. 8vo. Reprinted 1792.

Nelme, L. D. An Essay on the Origin and Elements of Languages, &c. London, 1772. 4to.

Odell, J. An Essay on the Element, &c. of the E. Language. London, 1806. 12mo.

Oliver, S. General Critical G. of the E. Language. London, 1825. 8vo. Also 1826.

Palsgrave, J. Lesclaircissement de la Langue Francaise. London, J. Haukyns, 1530. Fol. Reprinted at Paris, 1852. 4to.

Parsons, J. Remains of Japhet, being Historical Enquiries into the Origin of the European Languages. 1767. 4to.

Parvulorum Institutio. [Latin and E. G.] London in Southwarke, by P. Treveris. N. d. 4to.

Pegge, S. Anecdotes of the E. Language. London, 1803. 8vo.

—— The Same ; with Supplement to Grose's Glossary. London, 1814. 8vo.

—— Third edition, ed. by H. Christmas. London, 1844. 8vo.

Perry. The only sure Guide to the E. Tongue. Edinb., 1776. 12mo.

Phillips, J. T. Compendious Way of Teaching Antient and Modern Languages. 1727. 8vo.

Pickbourn, Jas. A Dissertation on the E. Verb. London, 1789. 8vo.

Priestley, Dr. Jos. A Course of Lectures on the Theory of Language and Universal G. Warrington, 1762. 12mo.

Priestley, Dr. Jos.  Rudiments of E. G.  London, 1768, 1769, 1771. 12mo.  Reprinted 1826, &c.
R., A. M.  An E. G.  1641. 8vo.
Raine, Rev. Mat.  E. Rudiments; or, an Easy Introduction to E. Grammar.  Darlington, 1771. 12mo.
Rask's Anglo-Saxon G.  Translated by Thorpe.  Copenhagen, 1830. 8vo.
Richardson, C.  Illustrations of E. Philology.  1815. 4to.
Robinson, J.  Art of teaching the E. Language by Imitation.  1800. 12mo.
Rudd, S.  Prodomos; or, Observations on the E. Language.  1755.
Rudiments of E. G. for the Use of Beginners.  Falmouth, 1788.
Rudiments of the E. Tongue.  Newcastle, 1769. 12mo.
Rylance, R.  Vocabulary of E. Words derived from the Saxon, with their Signification in Spanish.  1813.
S., M.  E., Latine, French, and Dutch Scholemaster.  By M. S. 1637 12mo.
Sharp, G.  Short Treatise on the E. Tongue.  1767. 8vo.
Sharpe.  Essay towards an E. G.  1784. 12mo.
Shaw, Rev. John.  A Methodical E. G.  1778, and four later editions.
Sheridan, T.  Discourse delivered at the Theatre in Oxford on Elocution and the E. Language.  1759. 8vo.
——  On the Causes of the Difficulties in Learning the E. Tongue, with Scheme for a G.  1762. 4to.
Sinclair [Sir] Jo.  Observations on the Scottish Dialect.  London, 1772. 8vo.  Also 1782.
Smart, Benj. H.  Practical G. of E. Pronunciation.  London, 1810. 8vo.
——  G. of E. Sounds   London, 1813. 12mo.
——  Rudiments of E. G. Elucidated.  London, 1811. 12mo.
——  Guide to Parsing.  London, 1825. 12mo.
——  Accidence and Principles of E. G.  London, 1841 and 1847. 12mo.
Smith, Jo.  G. of the E. Language.  Norwich. 12mo.
Smith, J.  G. for the French, Italian, Spanish, and E. Tongues, with Proverbs.  1674. 8vo.
Smith, Peter.  Practical Guide to the Composition and Application of the E. Language.  1824. 8vo.
Stackhouse, T.  Reflections on Languages, and on the Manner of Improving the E. Tongue.  1731. 8vo.
Stanbridge, John.  His Accidence.  N. d. [See Lowndes.]
Stirling, J.  Short View of E. G.  1740. 8vo.
——  Short System of E. G.  8vo.  Same as above (?).

## ENGLISH GRAMMARS.

Stockwood, Jo. A Plaine and Easie Laying Open of the Meaning . . . of the Rules . . . in the E. Accidence. (Black letter.) London, 1590. 4to.
Strong, Nathaniel. England's Perfect Schoolmaster. London, 1692. 12mo. And 1699. 12mo.
Swift, J. Proposal for Improving the E. Tongue. 1712. 8vo.
Taylor, Bp. Jeremy. A New and Easie Institution of G. London 1647. 12mo. On Latin G.
Thelwall, Jo. Essay on Rhythmus, and the utterance of the E. Language. London, 1812. 8vo.
Thomas, E. Traité Complet de Prononciation Angloise. 1796. 8vo.
Thomas, L. Milke for Children; or, a Plain and Easie Method teaching to Read and Write. 1654. 12mo.
Thomas, Wm. Principal Rules of the Italian G., with a Dictionarie (Black letter.) London, 1542. 4to. And 1550.
Thomson, J. Observations Introductory to a Work on E. Etymology. 1818. 8vo. Also 1819. 4to.
Thornton, W. Cadmus; or, a Treatise on the Elements of the Written Language. Philadelphia, 1796. 8vo. On Orthography.
Tooke, John Horne. Diversions of Purley. Vol. i (all published). First edition. London, 1786. 8vo.
—— London, 1798-1805. 2 vols. 4to.
—— New edition, revised by Rich. Taylor (with the letter to J. Dunning). London, 1829. 2 vols. 8vo. Reprinted, London, 1840 One vol. 8vo. Reprinted, 1857.
—— Letter to Jo. Dunning on the E. Language. 1788. 8vo.
Towgood, M. Remarks on the Profane and Absurd Use of the Monosyllable ' Damn.' 1746. 8vo.
Townsend, J. Etymological Researches. 1824. 4to.
Tremblay's Treatise of Languages. 1725. 8vo.
—— Many Advantages of a good Language to a Nation. 1724. 8vo.
Trusler, Dr. Jo. Synonymous Words of the E. Language. London, 1766. 2 vols. 12mo. Also 1781. One vol. 12mo.
Turner, D. Abstract of E. G. and Rhetoric. 1739.
Udall, Nich. Floures for Latine Spekynge . oute of Terence . tr. into E. (Black letter.) London, 1533. 8vo.
Vindex Anglicus; or, the . . . E. Language Defended. 1644. 4to.
Vocabulary of such Words in the E. Language as are of Dubious Accentuation. 1797. 8vo.
Vulgarisms and Improprieties of the E. Language. 1833. 12mo.
Vulgarities of Speech Corrected, with Elegant Expressions for Provincial and Vulgar E., Scots, and Irish. 1826. 12mo. Also 1830. 12mo.

Walker, Jo. Rhetorical G. London, 1801. 8vo. Fourth edition. 1807. 8vo. Sixth edition, 1816. 8vo. And 1823. 8vo.
—— Outlines of E. G. London, 1805. 12mo. And 1810. 12mo.
Walker, Wm. Treatise of E. Particles. London, 1655. 8vo.
—— Phraseologia Anglo-Latina. London, 1672. 8vo. With E. and Latin Proverbs.
Wallis, Jo. Grammatica Linguae Anglicanae. First ed., Oxford, 1653. 12mo. Also 1674. 8vo. Sixth ed., London, 1765. 8vo. (Valuable.)
Ward, Dr. Jo. Four Essays on the E. Language. London, 1758. 8vo.
Ward, Wm. Essay on G., as it may be applied to the E. Language. London, 1765. 4to.
—— Short Questions upon the Eight Parts of Speech. 1629. 4to.
Webster, Noah. Dissertation on the E. Language. Boston (America), 1789. 8vo.
Weston, Stephen. Specimen of the Conformity of the European Languages, particularly the E., with the Oriental Languages, especially the Persian. London, 1802. 8vo. (or 12mo.?)
White's Grammatical Essay on the E. Verb. 1761. 8vo.
White, T. Holt. Review of Johnson's 'Criticism on the Style of Milton's Prose.' 1818. 8vo.
Wild, Jo. Twopenny Accidence. Corn without Chaff. Showing how to form Verbs without Mood and Tense. Nottingham [1720]. 12mo.
Whittinton, Rob. Grammatical Works. See the list in Lowndes.
Williams, J. Thoughts on the Origin of Language. 1783. 8vo.
Willymott, W. English Particles. 1794.
Wilson, J. P. Essay on Grammar, exemplified in an E. G. Philadelphia, 1817. 8vo.
Wilson, Sir Thos. Arte of Rhetorike. London, 1553. 4to. For other editions see Lowndes.
Winning, Rev. W. B. Manual of Comparative Philology. 1838. 8vo.
Withers, E. Observations upon the E. Language. N. d. 8vo.
Withers, Dr. Philip. Aristarchus; or, the Principles of Composition. 1789. 8vo. Also 1790. 8vo. Reprinted, 1822. 8vo. (Praised.)
Wodroephe, Jo. The Spared Hours of a Soldier . . . or the True Marrow of the French Tongue. Dort, 1623. Fol. And 1625. Fol.
Wotton, H. Essay on the Education of Children in the First Rudiments of Learning. 1753. 8vo.

Wotton's Short View of Hickes's Treasure of the Northern Languages. By M. Shelton. 1735. 4to.
Wynne's Universal G. for the E. Language. 1775. 12mo.
Young, E. Compleat E. Scholar in Spelling, Reading, and Writing. 1722. 8vo.
Zankner's German and E. G. Strasbourg. 1806. 12mo.

The above list is extremely imperfect, and only comes down, in the main, to about 1840. But it will suffice for pointing out the names of some of the older works on the subject of English philology, many of which, I believe, might advantageously be read for Dr. Murray's *Dictionary*.

Any one who wishes to do the English nation a service may easily do so. We want to know which, among the above, are the best dozen books for such a purpose, especially amongst the older ones. None of them, I am told, has been read hitherto. The works by Coote, Lowth, Priestley, Walker, Wallis, and Whittinton should certainly be examined.

### 299. The Man with the Muck-rake (7 S. vi. 366; 1888).

This well-known figure in Bunyan's *Pilgrim's Progress* was doubtless described from a scene depicted on tapestry and hung on walls. There is an early mention of it in W. Bullein's *Dialogue,* first printed in 1578. (See E.E.T.S. reprint, p. 82.) We there find three pictures on tapestry described together :—

'The first of them with a Rake in his hand with teeth of golde, doe stoup verie lowe, groping belike in the Lake after some-thyng that he would finde; and out of this deepe water, above the Rake, a little steeple.'

See the context, which gives a full explanation, showing the reference to simony.

### 300. Does Mr. Gladstone speak with a Provincial Accent? (7 S. vi. 178; 1888).

The answer is that much depends on the listener. I can tell a story to the point. I never heard Mr. Gladstone speak but once, and that was in Cambridge, more than a quarter of a century ago.

I had at the time no idea that he came from Lancashire.

But, after the speech, I made careful inquiries as to where he came from, and soon obtained the information. I was not then at all accustomed to 'take notice,' and the traces which I observed were very slight. In a large portion of the speech, even after I had noticed some peculiarities, I could detect nothing unusual. At this distance of time I only remember one test word. He undoubtedly at that time said *strenth* for *strength*; and I said to myself, 'North.'

### 301. Wipple-Tree, otherwise Whipultre: Gaytre
(7 S. vi. 434; 1888).

Many guesses have been made as to the sense of '*Whipultre*' in Chaucer's *Knight's Tale*. At last Mr. Mayhew has got it right. It is the cornel-tree or dogwood (*Cornus Sanguinea*), also called dog-tree, &c. See Britten's *Plant Names*, p. 577. He points out that it is clearly the Middle Low German *wipel-bom*, the cornel (Pritzel, later edition). This is verified by the entry in Hexham's *Dutch Dictionary*; '*Wepe* or *weype*, the dog-tree.' It is so named from the waving of its branches. Cf. M. Dutch *wepelen*, to totter, waver (Hexham); E. Fries. *wepeln*, also *wippen*, to waver, jump. Cf. E. *whip about* (properly *wip about*), whence probably *whipp-et*, for *wipp-et*, a kind of dog; G. *wippen*, to see-saw.

The *gay-tre* in Chaucer's *Nun's Priest's Tale* is said to be the same tree, the reason being simply this, that whilst *wippel-tre* was the Southern or Midland name, *gaytre* was the Northern name; and Chaucer borrowed it from the Northern dialect.

It is also called *gaiter-tree*, and the etymology is easy.

A goat was called *goot* in Middle English in the Midland

and Southern dialects; but *gait* in the North. The one is A. S. *gāt*, the other is Icel. *geitr*. As for *gaiter*, it is simply the Icel. gen. *geitar*, also used in forming compounds. Hence the *gaytre* is really the *gait-tree* or *goat-tree*. It is also called *dog-tree* and *cat-tree*; so there is no great difficulty about *goat-tree*.

I have, however, a further suggestion to make, in opposition to the authorities. Seeing the particular purposes for which the cock wanted the berries, it would fit admirably to suppose that for this occasion the *gait-tree* was the *Rhamnus catharticus*, which, according to Johns, 'bears black, powerfully cathartic berries.' Now it is not a little remarkable that, according to Rietz, the name in Swedish dialects for this *Rhamnus* is precisely *getbärs-trä*, i. e. 'goat-berry tree,' or the tree bearing goat-berries (Chaucer's *gaytre-beries*).

### 302. A Curious Etymology (7 S. vii. 5; 1889).

If ever an 'etymology' deserved to be 'gibbeted,' certainly the following deserves it richly. It is from the *Gentleman's Magazine*, Dec., 1888, p. 605:—

'One word in conclusion on the word *gallows*. The old word for the gibbet is *galg*, and *gal-low* is the *low*, or place for the gibbet.'

It follows that *gallows* are 'the *places* for the "gibbet,"' which is highly satisfactory. In what language the 'old word' *galg* occurs in a monosyllabic form we are not told. Such is 'etymology' in the nineteenth century.

### 303. Hampole's Version of the Psalms (7 S. vii. 5; 1889).

I have said in *Specimens of English*, part ii. p. 107, that Hampole was 'the author of a metrical version of the Psalms,' &c. I took this statement from Prof. Morley's *English Writers* without suspicion. Since then Mr. Bramley has edited Hampole's version, and lo! it is in prose! How, then, did the error arise? Perhaps thus. The copy of the work in MS. Laud. 286, begins with sixty lines of verse, which may easily have induced the consulter of the MS. to suppose it was wholly in verse. However, these sixty lines are a mere prologue; they are not by Hampole, but by another hand; and they do not appear in any other of the rather numerous copies. I conclude that a verse translation of the Psalms by Hampole does not exist.

**304. 'The Morians' Land'** (7 S. vii. 66; 1889).

For 'the Morians' land' in the Prayer Book Version of the Psalms, the A. V. has 'Ethiopia.' Wright's *Bible Wordbook* tells us that 'Morian' is used by old writers for 'moor, blackamoor.' Cotgrave explains *More* by 'a Moore, Morian, Blackamoore.' But I do not know that any one has explained the etymology.

At first it might be thought to be Dutch, since Sewel gives *Moriaan*, and Hexham *Morjaen*, with the same sense. But the Dutch suffix *-aan* is from Latin *-anus*, and is non-Teutonic. Both the English and Dutch forms are doubtless of Romance origin. Godefroy quotes, from a MS. of the fifteenth century, the O. F. form *Moriaine*, meaning a Moor. This I take to represent Latin *Mauritanicus* (or perhaps *Mauritanius*), the *t* being dropped as usual between two vowels in the middle of the word. We also find O. F. *Moriant* for 'the land of the Moors,' which represents the Latin *Mauritania*. Thus we see that *Morian* is simply another form of *Mauritanian*.

**305. Kittering** (7 S. vii. 76; 1889).

This word presents no difficulty. It is a disguised form of the Provincial English *catering*, which the witness probably pronounced better than it was taken down, and which the judge explained with perfect correctness[1]. *Cater*, to cut

[1] In the examination of a witness lately, he was asked how the boy crossed the street; to which he replied, 'A little bit *kittering,*

diagonally, is duly given in Halliwell; and it is used in Kent and Surrey. In the list of Surrey provincialisms (E. D. S., Gloss., c. 4) we find '*Caterways, Catering,* adv. used of crossing diagonally.' It would be of much assistance to me if those who inquire after words, and who by so doing confess that they do not quite understand them, would refrain in every case from suggesting an etymology. In the present case the suggestion that *kittering* represents 'quartering' is just the very thing to throw an investigator off the track, precisely because there is a real ultimate connexion between the words. *Quartering* is ultimately due to the Lat. *quartus,* an ordinal numeral. *Cater,* on the other hand, is due to the Lat. *quatuor,* a cardinal number. It makes all the difference, because the former *r* in *quarter* would not have disappeared after that fashion. *Cater* is the correct Old English word, the number 'four' on a die being so called. It is the correct descendant of the Old French *katre,* four. The names of the marks upon dice were formerly (and even now) the following:—*ace, deuce, tray, cater, sink, size* (or *six*). *Cater* gave the notion of four corners; and to *cater* a field is to cross it corner-wise, i. e. diagonally. It obviously gives double trouble when one has to explain both a word and its mistaken origin.

### 306. Sloyd (7 S. vii. 105; 1889).

The following deliciously inaccurate statement appeared in *Chambers's Journal,* Dec. 22, 1888, p. 815:—

'*Slöjd,* the Scandinavian word which is termed *sloyd* in English for convenience, means originally *cunning, clever, handy.*'

Here 'Scandinavian' is slipshod English for *Swedish.* Scandinavian is the name of a group of languages, not of any one language. For 'termed' read 'spelt'; and why it

I should say.' The presiding judge explained to the jury, 'He means obliquely.'

cannot be spelt 'sloid' it is hard to see. We do not write *boyl*, *toyl*, *voyd*, in modern English. Thirdly, 'means' is false grammar for 'meant.' Lastly, the assigned sense is all wrong, for the word is not an adjective, but a substantive. Let us put it right. The Swedish word is *slöjd*. English people pronounce it *sloid*, as if it rimed with *void*, because they cannot give the true sound. Silly people will persist in writing *sloyd* with a *y*, merely to cause more confusion in our confused system. Lastly, the word is merely the same as our word *sleight*, the substantive formed from the adjective *sly*; it originally meant *sleight* or dexterity, but is now applied to wood-carving in particular. But for this it should have been called *sleight* in English.

**307. English** (7 S. vii. 189; 1889).

[In reply to the suggestion that the name *English* is not derived from *Angle*, but from *ing*, a field!]

I am not concerned with the etymology of this word except so far as relates to the following statement: 'The guess that England is named after the Angles, started by Bede, is not supported by history.' The coolness of this assertion is amazing; and it seems to me altogether too bad that no attempt whatever has been made to inquire into the matter. A man who deliberately shuts his eyes to all evidence is not entitled to ask us to follow his leading; at any rate, we shall be very foolish to take him for a guide.

Perhaps no fact is better supported by history in the true sense, i. e. by ancient records. If we are bound to ignore Beda, we are not bound to ignore the Old English translation of him. In *Hist.* iii. 2, where the original has 'in lingua Anglorum,' the translation has 'on Englisc.' Here the *E* in *Englisc* is the regular mutation of *A*; and we can no more dissociate *English* from *Angle* than we can dissociate *French* from *France*. We find 'Frencisce menn' and

'Densce' in the *A. S. Chronicle*, Laud MS. an. 1700; and, of course, we see that the *e* is the mutation of the *a* in *Frank* and *Dane*. *French* means *Frankish*, and has nothing to do with *frink* (whatever that may mean); and similarly *English* means *Angle-ish*, and has nothing to do with *ing*.

It is impossible to ignore the known connexion of *English* with *Angle*. It is indelibly recorded in such forms as *Anglia*, *Anglicus*, *Anglicanus*, as well as in the common Old English terms *Angelthēod*, *Angel-cynn*, meaning English or Angle-people, English or Angle-race, and so on. For these words see the Bosworth-Toller *Dictionary*, the referenees in which might be multiplied largely. Thus *Angoltheod* (*sic*) is in Ælfred's translation of Beda, ed. Smith, iii. 5; and *Angel-cynn* is in the same chapter. In the next chapter is the gen. pl. *Angla*, and the dat. *Angel-thēode*. It is tedious to hunt up all the passages, and I do not see what is to be gained by repeating what every one ought to know, and what no one who knows the phonetic laws of Anglo-Saxon can possibly call in question.

That the *E* in *Engla* is really a mutation of the *A* in *Angle* appears also from the purely philological consideration that we sometimes find the alternative spelling with *Æ*. It is scarce, of course; but here are references: *Ængla-land*, *A. S. Chronicle*, Parker MS. an. 1070; other MSS. *Engla-land*; *Ængla-landes*, *A. S. Chronicle*, Laud MS. an. 1100. So also *Ænglisc*, *A. S. Chron.*, Laud MS. an. 1016; *A. S. Chron.*, introduction in MS. Cotton, Tib. B. 4, ed. Thorpe, p. 3. If any one wants to realize the difficulty of finding such spellings, let him hunt for the form *Frænscisc*.

In the introduction to Gregory's *Pastoral Care*, as translated by Ælfred, he calls the English people *Angelcynn*, and their language *Englisc* in the same sentence. It is absurd to expect the whole English nation to give up such facts at a moment's bidding, and for a whim.

It seems to me that the whole trouble has arisen from not understanding that the change from M. E. *en* to modern *in*, in pronunciation, is sufficiently regular. Many common people talk of the *Frinch* and *Frinchmen*. I have explained all this in my *Principles of English Etymology*, p. 402 ; but I suppose I must repeat some of the instances. *Inglish* is the pronunciation of *English*, and is derived from *Angle* ; *mint* is from Lat. *mentha* ; *grin* is from A.S. *grennian*, M. E. *grennen* ; *blink*, from M. E. *blenken* ; *link* (of a chain), from A. S. *hlence*; *skink*, from A. S. *scencan*; *think*, from A. S. *thencan* ; *wing* is M. E. *wenge*, &c. We get back to original *a* sometimes. Thus *think* is allied to *thank*; *ling* to A. S. *lang* (long) ; *mingle* is allied to A. S. *on-mang* (among) ; *hinge*, M. E. *henge*, is derived from *hang*; *singe*, M. E. *sengen*, is allied to A. S. *sang*, pt. t. of *singan* ; *swinge*, A. S. *swengan*, to *swang*, pt. t. of *swing*; *string*, A. S. *streng*, is from *strang* (strong).

We even find similar changes in words of French and Latin origin. Thus *pin* is allied to Lat. *penna* ; *ink*, M. E. *enke*, to Lat. *encaustum*; *print* is from *premere*, and was often spelt *prente*. Dr. Murray records *bink* for *bench*, and of course *stink* is allied both to *stench* and to the pt. t. *stank*. *Strinth* for *strength* is not uncommon. But we do not find *en* coming out of *in*, nor *eng* out of *ing*.

It is not at all the case that Dr. Sweet knows nothing at all of this. He marks the old vowels of *stench, wrench, French, quench, drench, bench,* &c., also of *England, English,* also of *singe, string, wring, mingle,* all alike, to show that they all go back to an original *a*. See his *Hist. of English Sounds*, p. 313. If the appeal is to phonetics, the answer is decisive.

♦ **308. Latten and Pinchbeck** (7 S. vii. 206 ; 1889).

In *N. and Q.*, 3 S. xiv. 396, the analysis of the metal called *latten* is given as being composed of copper, 64 per cent. ; zinc, 29½ per cent. ; lead, 3½ per cent. ; and tin, 3 per cent. In the same, 6 S. i. 213, *pinchbeck* is said to be composed of copper, 75 per cent., and zinc, 25 per cent. It is worth while to notice the close resemblance of these compounds. Pinchbeck is a simplified latten, with a little more copper and a little less zinc.

**309. 'Sweetness and Light'** (7 S. vii. 285 ; 1889).

This is a meaningless expression unless we know the context. It may, therefore, be useful to give it. In Swift's *Battle of the Books* there is a dispute between a spider and a bee. Afterwards Aesop takes up the cause of ancient authors, whom he likens to bees, and says that 'instead of dirt and poison [such as are collected by modern authors or spiders] we have rather chose [*sic*] to fill our hives with *honey* and *wax*, thus furnishing mankind with the two noblest of things, which are *sweetness* and *light*.'

**310. The Anglo-Saxon Names of the Months**
(7 S. vii. 301 ; 1889).

In Verstegan's *Restitution of Decayed Intelligence* the author gives what he is pleased to call 'the Anglo-Saxon names of the months' after the following fashion, beginning with January. They were, he says, *Wolf-moneth, Sprout-kele, Lenct-monat, Oster-monat, Tri-milki, Weyd-monat, Heu-monat, Arn-monat, Gerst-monat, Wyn-monat, Wint-monat, Winter-monat.* This is in the true old spirit of hardy guess-work, and is wrong on the face of it, because such forms as *monat, Oster, heu*, and others, are plainly German, and cannot possibly be Anglo-Saxon. It will suffice to show how he came by the name of *Sprout-kele* for February, as we can then tell how worthy he is of trust. His own account is :—

'They called February *Sprout-kele*, by *kele* meaning the *kele-wurt*, which we now call the cole-wurt. . . . It was the first herb that in this moneth began to yeeld out wholesome young sprouts, and consequently gave thereunto the name of *sprout-kele.*'

This is a specimen of the daring imagination with which the whole book teems. It is all rubbish, of course, and crumbles to pieces on investigation. It will suffice to mention two points.

The A. S. for *cole* is not *kele* at all, but *cāwl*, being merely the Latin *caulis* in a slightly disguised form. Secondly, the native Dutch name for February is *Sprokkel-maand*, where *Sprokkel*, according to Koolman, means 'thaw' or 'thawed earth,' whence the adj. *sprokkelig*, crumbling, friable. It is clear that Verstegan's *Sprout-kele* is due to a desperate attempt to find an etymology for *Sprokkel*, a word which he did not understand.

Not to waste more words upon the above farrago, which is not even correct for the Dutch language, whence several of the examples are drawn, it may suffice to say that not one of the names is correctly given, and most of them are entirely wrong.

By good fortune the A. S. names of the months are all of them found in a manuscript printed in Cockayne's *Shrine*, p. 47. Some of them occur in the *Menologium*, printed by Fox, and reprinted by Grein, and some in a manuscript in Corpus Christi College, Cambridge, described in Wanley's *Catalogue*, p. 106, and elsewhere. Beginning with January, the names are as follows: (1) Se æftera Geōla (the latter Yule); (2) Sol-mōnath; (3) Hrēth-mōnath; (4) Eāster-mōnath; (5) Thrīmylce; (6) Se ærra Līþa (the former Līþa); (7) Se æftera Līþa (the latter Līþa); (8) Wēod-mōnath; (9) Hālig-mōnath; (10) Winter-fylleth; (11) Blōt-mōnath; (12) Se ǣrra Geōla (the former Yule).

A few notes may be added. The old notion that in the name of February the *o* should be long, and that the word *sol* would then mean 'sun,' is absurd. February is not usually a 'sun-month.' *Sol* means simply *mire* or *mud*, whence E. *sully*. I regret to say that 'mud-month' is sadly appropriate, and answers to the Old Dutch name *Sprokkel-maand*, discussed above. The name for March is said to be from a certain goddess Hreda (see the note in Bosworth and Toller's *Dictionary*). I do not quite see why it may not mean simply 'fierce-month.' April is 'Easter-month.' May is 'three-milkings-month,' i.e. the cows might then be milked thrice a day. The name Litha is merely the definite form of *līthe*, mild, so that June and July are the mild, or warm months. August is 'weed-month.' September is 'holy month,' and it is on record that it was so called as being a great time for sacrifices to idols in the heathen days. Compare the offering of first-fruits. The reason for the name of October is left unexplained [1]. November is 'sacrifice-month,' and is also explained to refer to heathen sacrifices.

It appears that out of Verstegan's twelve names only two are even approximately correct; and these two, *Oster-monat* and *Tri-milki*, are given in foreign spelling.

### 311. Vowel-shortening in English Place-names
(7 S. vii. 321 ; 1889).

In my *Principles of English Etymology*, chap. xxv, I have given examples of vowel-shortening in the former syllable of dissyllabic words, and at p. 494 I instance Whitby, Whit-church, from the adjective *white*. A few more examples may be interesting by way of making the principle clearer.

The A. S. *āc*, oak, with loss of accent, becomes *ac*; hence Acton, Ackland. I remember once being at Acle, in Norfolk, and remarking that it ought to be called *Ack-ley*, and

---

[1] As a guess, I should refer *fylleth* to the verb *fyllan*, to fell, to cause to fall, and so explain *Winter-fylleth* by 'storm-felling,' i.e. the time of year when a storm or colder weather causes the leaves to fall from the trees. Compare the old name *fall*, the equivalent of *autumn*.

not *Aikl*, as is now usual. I was at once informed that 'that was just what the old people did call it.' This piece of information may as well be put on record. It is fair to conclude that it meant *oak-lea*.

Perhaps Benacre (Suffolk) means *bean-acre*. We have Benefield (Northampton). But this is a guess, and guesses are not at all advisable in the present disgracefully backward state of the etymology of place-names. Most books on the subject are ludicrously wrong.

A word like Black-more presents great difficulty. I do not see how to decide whether it is from A. S. *blāc*, bleak, or from A. S. *blæc*, black. Let us wait for evidence.

The A. S. *brād*, broad, becomes *brăd*; hence Bradford.

The A. S. *brōm*, broom, becomes *broom*, and then *brum*; hence Bromyard, Bromley, Brompton.

The A. S. *dīc*, dyke, becomes *dic*; hence *dicton*, and by assimilation, Ditton.

The A. S. *dūn*, a down, becomes *dun*; hence Dunton, Dunwich, Dunmow. We also have Downton. In such cases we may expect Downton to be a later form—i. e. that the place is of less antiquity than Dunton.

The A. S. *fūl*, foul, becomes *ful*; hence Fulbourne, in which the vowel was formerly long. It is spelt Fuulburne in a charter.

The A. S. *gōs*, goose, becomes *gos*; hence *gosling*, and Gosfield (Essex).

The A. S. *hām*, home, becomes *ham*; hence Hampstead, parallel to E. *homestead*. But there is also A. S. *hamm*, gen. *hammes*, an enclosure, quite distinct from *hām*. So we cannot always be sure as to this prefix.

The A. S. *hǣth*, a heath, becomes *hæth*, pronounced as E. *hath*. Slightly altered, this occurs in Hadley and Hatfield, spelt in the charters with the form for *heath*.

The A. S. *mōr* becomes *mor*; hence Morton and Morland and Westmorland.

The A. S. *rēad*, red, is now *red*; and the A. S. *hrēod*, a reed, also becomes *red*. In Red Hill we probably have the former. In Redbourne (Hants), the A. S. form *Hrēodburne* shows that we have the latter.

The A. S. *scēp*, a sheep, gives a form *shep*. In Shropshire, sheep are called *ships*. Hence Shepton, Shipton, Shipley.

The A. S. *stān*, a stone, becomes *stan*; hence Stanton, Stanford, and perhaps Stamford. We also find Stainton and Stonton, where *stain* is the Norse form, and *ston* is from M. E. *stoon*.

The A. S. form of Sherborne is *Scīre-burne*; from *scīre*, pure, clear, Mod. E. *sheer*.

The A. S. *strǣt* becomes *stræt*, pronounced *strat*; hence Stratford. The Mercian form was *strēt*, which becomes *stret*; hence Stretton, Streatham.

The A. S. *Stūr*, the river Stour, becomes *stur*; hence Sturminster.

The A. S. *sūth*, south, becomes *suth*; hence Sutton (for *suth-ton*), Sudbury (for *suth-bury*), Sussex (for *suth-sex*), and Surrey (A. S. *Sūthrige*).

The word *swain* is of Norse origin. The A. S. form is *swān*. This, shortened to *swan*, appears in Swanswick, as Prof. Earle[1] can tell us.

The A. S. *swīn*, swine, becomes *swin*; hence Swinden, Swinford, Swindon.

The A. S. for Tadley is *Tādan-lēah*, i. e. Toadfield. We find the same vowel-shortening in the common *tadpole*.

The river Teme gave its name to Teembury, now spelt Tenbury,—at least, so I have been told, and it seems quite reasonable.

The A. S. *tūn*, town, becomes *tun*; hence Tunbridge, Tunstead.

The A. S. *hwǣte*, wheat, becomes *hwæt*; hence Whatfield

[1] Rawlinsonian Professor of A. S., and rector of Swanswick (also spelt Swainswick), near Bath

(Suffolk), and Wheathampstead. There is an A. S. place-name Hwǣte-dūn, lit. wheat-down. This became Whatdon; then Whotton, by influence of *wh* on the vowel, and by assimilation; and it is now Wotton (in Surrey). This is an excellent example of the futility of guessing and of the exact operation of phonetic laws.

The A. S. *hwīt*, white, became *hwit*; hence Whitchurch, Whitfield (A. S. *hwītfeld*), Whitcliff (near Ludlow).

We must remember, on the other hand, that modern English sometimes *lengthens* the A. S. vowel. In this case the place-name may keep the original short vowel. Such is the case with Cranbourne, Cranfield, Cranford, from A. S. *cran*. The modern word is *crane*. Dalby is from A. S. *dæl*, Mod. E. *dale*.

Denton is from A. S. *děnu*, a valley, a dene, with long *e* in Rottingdean, Ovingdean, though short in Tenterden.

Compton is for Combe-town, from W. *cwm*. The name Quinton illustrates the common English change from *en* to *in*. We also find Quendon, so that Quinton stands for Quenton. *Quen* is the A. S. *cwēn*, a queen, with loss of vowel-length, and substitution of the Anglo-French *qu* for A. S. *cw*.

Of course many of these examples are old; but I have grouped them together so as to illustrate a principle. We shall have to accept principles to guide us if ever any advance is to be made.

**312. East Sheen; 'Sheen' and 'Shine'** (7 S. vii. 337; 1889).

At the latter reference two correspondents drop into an etymological trap, and say, probably for the thousandth time, that *sheen* is allied to the verb *to shine*. One of them compares the G. *schön*, which has certainly nothing to do with G. *scheinen*. *Sheen* is properly an adjective, meaning 'showy,' or splendid, allied to the verb *to show*. The

G. *schön* is exactly parallel to it, and is allied to G. *schauen*. The account of the former may be found in my *Etymological Dictionary*, and that of the latter in Kluge. I know of no example in which a Modern English *ee* is allied to a long *i*, and shall be obliged to any one who will give me one.

[When Lord Byron wrote 'the *sheen* of their spears,' he doubtless thought that *sheen* was a sb., and allied to *shine*.]

### 313. English Long Vowels as compared with German (7 S. vii. 342, 463; 1889).

Mistakes are constantly being made in etymology, especially by those who have not made any study of phonetics, of the most elementary character. I here throw together a few remarks to remind your readers that laws regulate vowel-sounds, and should be regarded. The student who wishes to compare English with German for the purposes of etymology should consult Sievers' *Anglo-Saxon Grammar* on the one hand and Wright's *Old High German Primer* (Clarendon Press) on the other. He will then not go far wrong.

Even in my *Principles of English Etymology*, I mention most of the facts concerning the long vowels. I selected these for the greater clearness; because, if any one can be brought to see that the long vowels follow regular laws, he may then be led to believe that short vowels do the same. A half-knowledge is better than none at all, as it may induce caution.

I here give a few elementary facts, selecting only the more remarkable results. Many details are purposely suppressed.

Teutonic long *a*. There is practically none; the pre-Teutonic long *a* had already become long *o* in primitive Teutonic. Compare Lat. *māter* with A. S. *mōdor*, and Lat. *frāter* with Goth. *brōthar*. See, therefore, under 'long *o*.'

Teutonic long *e*. Original examples are scarce. But we have a few cases in which A. S. *ē* is written *ie* in Modern German. Thus A. S. *hēr*, E. *here*, is G. *hier*. A. S. *mēd*, E. *meed*, is G. *Miethe*. In most cases the A. S. *ē* arose from a mutation of long *o*. See, therefore, under 'long *o*.'

Teutonic long *i*. This is, usually, A. S. *ī*, Modern English long *i*. In Old German it was also *ī*, pronounced as Mod. E. *ee*, but is now written *ei*, and pronounced as *i* in Mod. English. Thus A. S. *bītan*, E. *bite*, is G. *beissen*. This is a very interesting case. The old sound is still kept up in Scandinavian; the Swed. *bita* is pronounced as Eng. *beetăh*. In the Middle Ages it was pronounced, both in English and in German, like the *ei* in E. *vein*; at which time the G. spelling was altered to *ei*, but the English was let alone. Since then, both languages have further developed the sound to the diphthongal *ai*, as it is written in romic. The English and German spellings remain as in medieval times. Hence the English represents its diphthong by means of the A. S. *ī*, which was once pronounced as *ee*; whilst the German represents it by the medieval *ei*, once pronounced as in French. Both are misleading; but the English is the worse. Dutch follows the English system, but represents the old long *i* (*ee*) by the symbol *ij*, now pronounced as E. *i* in *bite*.

Teutonic long *o*. This was of two sorts, viz. from pre-Teutonic long *a* (cf. Lat. *māter*, *frāter*), and (rarely) from pre-Teutonic long *o* (cf. Doric Greek πώς). The usual Mod. E. symbol is double *o* or *oo*, but the sound is that of Ital. *u*, as in E. *cool*, from A. S. *cōl*. The German developed this *u*-sound at a very early period; hence G. *Mutter*, *Bruder*, *Fuss*; also the O. H. G. *kuole*, adv., coolly, though the G. adj. has the mutated form *kühl*.

• In the last word the *u* is written as *uh*, to make sure of the length; so also A. S. *fōr*, he went, is G. *fuhr*. English has shortened the sounds of *moother*, *broother*, *foot* (once rhyming with *boot*), in ways with which we are all familiar. Cf. A. S. *blōd*, E. *blood*, G. *Blut*. The mutated form of this vowel gave us the A. S. *ē*, as in *fēt*, feet. The vowel is also mutated in German, as in *Füsse*, feet. Hence E. *?feel*, G. *?fühlen*, is derived from a stem *fōl*; see Kluge.

Teutonic long *u*. This has developed just like long *i*. Just as long *i* became *ai* (romic), so long *u* has become *au*. In English this is written *ou*, but German correctly writes *au*. Thus A. S. *hūs*, E. *house*, G. *Haus*. The English spelling *ou* is of French origin; the French scribes naturally represented A. S. *ū* by the F. *ou* in *soup*. *Soup* retains the French sound only because it was borrowed in modern times.

For another G. *au*, see under *au* below.

Teutonic long *æ*. This most commonly becomes Mod. E. *ee*; but the G. has long *a*. Ex.: A. S. *slǣpan*, E. *sleep*, G. *Schläfen*. Another A. S. long *æ*, which is much commoner, is the mutated form of A. S. *ā*; for this see below, under *ai*.

Teutonic *ai*. This is commonly A. S. *ā*, E. long *o*, G. *ei*. Ex.: Goth. *haims*, A. S. *hām*, E. *home*, G. *Heim*. Thus it will be seen that German has two distinct *ei*'s; the other is given under long *i*. The mutated form of A. S. *ā* is long *æ*; this commonly gives E. *ea*. Hence from A. S. *hāl*, E. *whole*, comes A. S. *hǣlan*, E. *heal*. Here the German has no mutation, but derives *heilen* from *heil* at once.

Teutonic *au*. This is commonly A. S. *ēa*, E. *ea* (*ee*, *e*), G. *au* or long *o*. Exx.: A. S. *hēafod*, E. *head* (M. E. *heed*), Goth. *haubith*, G. *Haupt*; A. S. *strēam*, E. *stream*, O. H. G. *straum*, G. *Strom*. This diphthong can suffer mutation, giving A. S. long *ie* (or *y*), G. *ö*. Ex.: Goth. *hausjan*, A. S. *hīeran*, E. *hear*, G. *hören*.

Teutonic *eu*. This is Gothic *iu*, A. S. *ēo*, E. *ee*, G. *ie*. Ex.: Goth. *diups*, A. S. *dēop*, E. *deep*, G. *tief*. Examples of its mutation are rare in English, and the G. *ie* is not mutated.

Teut. long *e*. I now give additional examples. Besides E. *here*, G. *hier*, we find A. S. *cēn*, a torch, G. *Kienfackel*, a pine-torch, *Kien*, resinous wood.

Teut. long *i*. E. *dike*, G. *Teich*; so also drive, *treiben*; idle, *eitel*; ride, *reiten*; tide, *Zeit*; bite, *beissen*; smite, *schmeissen*; white, *weiss*; write, *reissen*; thy, *dein*; shive, *Scheibe*; pipe, *Pfeifen*; gripe, *greifen*; ripe, *reif*; glide, *gleiten*; while, *weil*. These are all taken in order from Appendix A to my *English Etymology*, where the correspondence of the consonants is explained.

Teut. long *o*. E. *blood*, G. *Blut*; so also brood, *Brut*; good, *gut*; hood, *Hut*; mood, *Muth*; rood, *Ruthe*; to, *zu*; brother (A. S. *brōthor*), *Bruder* fother (A. S. *fōthur*), *Fuder*· mother (A. S. *mōdor*), *Mutter*; flood, *Fluth*; foot, *Fuss*. All from the same original *ō* (Indo-Germanic *ā* or *ō*).

Under 'Teut. long *o*,' I have already mentioned G. *kühl* as answering to E. *cool*. The fact is that the English *cool* answers to the old G. adverb *kuole*, coolly; whilst the G. adjective has the mutated *ü*, answering (as I have shown) to the E. *ee*. We actually have this mutation in the famous Shakespearian phrase 'to *keel* the pot,' i. e. to keep it cool by stirring it.

The mutated forms of long *ō* appear in E. *feet*, G. *Füsse*; so also breed, *brüten*; brethren (Old North E. *brēther*), *Brüder*; feel, *fühlen*; heed, *hüten*; greet, *grüssen*; sweet, *süss* (for *swüss*); green, *grün*; keen, *kühn*. In the verb *bleed*, the German does not mutate, but has *bluten*; cf. also seek, G. *suchen*; beech, G. *Buche*. On the other hand, where we have *bloom* without mutation, the related G. word is *Blüthe*.

Teut. long *u*. E. *house*, G. *Haus*; so also snout, *Schnauze*; loud, *laut*; mouse, *Maus*; louse, *Laus*; foul, *faul*; sour, *sauer*; sow, *Sau*; thousand, *tausend*. In the word *hide*, A. S. *hȳd*, as compared with G. *Haut*, the E. vowel is mutated; so also mice, *Mäuse*; lice, *Läuse*.

Teut. long *æ*. E. *sleep*, G. *Schlafen*. Examples are rare. E. *deed*, as compared with G. *That*, is similar.

Teut. *ai*. E. *home*, G. *Heim*; so also dough (older form *dogh*), *Teig*; dole, *Theil*; broad (with the old sound of *oa*), *breit*; token, *Zeichen*; goat, *Geiss*; both, *beide*; cloth (long *o* in plural *clothes*), *Kleid*; oath, *Eid*; soap, *Seife*; oak, *Eiche*; stroke, *Streich*; spoke, *Speiche*; stone, *Stein*.

The mutated form usually appears in English only; thus E. *heal*, G. *heilen*; so also breadth, *Breite*; heath, *Heide*; heat, v., *heizen*; lead, v., *leiten*; leave, *bleiben* (for *be-leiben*); sweat, *Schweiss*. On comparing E. *lore* (A. S. *lār*) with the A. S. *lǣran*, to teach, we see that the G. *lehren*, O. H. G. *lēren*, is mutated.

Teutonic *au*. E. *stream*, G. *Strom* (formerly *Straum*); so also heap, *Haufe*; cheap, *Kauf*, s.; East, *Ost*; leaf *Laub*; leek, *Lauch*; dream, *Traum*; leap, *laufen*; be-reave, *rauben*; lead, s., *Loth*; seam, *Saum*; deaf (M. E. *deef*), *taub*.

Teutonic *eu*. E. *deep*, G. *tief*; so also lief, *lieb*; freeze, *frieren*; deer, *Thier*; sick (M. E. *seek*), *siech*; thief, *Dieb*; seethe, *sieden*.

The real value of these equations is best tested and perceived when the correspondences are at first sight anomalous. Thus G. *Stief-mutter* answers to E. *steep-mother*, A. S. *stēopmōdor*; and such, in fact, is the A. S. form. The Mod. E. *e* in *stepmother* has been shortened from an older *ee* by the stress on the closed syllable.

### 314. Theory and Practice (7 S. viii. 26; 1889).

Not long ago I read the story of a boy who summed up the duties of life by saying that 'you first know your work, and then you go and do it.' There is in this a reminiscence of Mr. Squeers, who first of all instructed a boy how to spell '*winder*,' and then made him go and clean one. Nevertheless, the saying, as old Skelton would say, 'hath some pith' in it. A little alteration will produce quite a Miltonic precept:—

'First know thy work, then do it, praising God.'

Perhaps in a few years some querist, with that curious thirst for which the genus is so remarkable, will 'want to know' from what poem this line is taken. I can, alas! only assure a discriminating posterity that there is no more of it.

**315. 'To Ride Bodkin'** (7 S. viii. 76; 1889).

This phrase is fully explained and illustrated in a recent work by Dr. Murray, entitled *A New English Dictionary on Historical Principles*, and printed at Oxford; s. v. *Bodkin*.

**316. Runnel** (7 S. viii. 76; 1889).

The A. S. form is *rynel*; the pl. *rynelas* is in Spelman's *A. S. Psalter*, lxiv. 11, as a gloss to *rivos*. The A. S. *y* becomes *i*; hence the M. E. form was *rinel*. It occurs, spelt *rynel*, in the *Troy-Book*, ed. Panton and Donaldson, l. 5709. *Runnel* is formed, analogically, from the verb *to run*. I mention *runnel* in my *Dictionary*, s. v. *Run*; and refer to Collins, *Ode to the Passions*. I offer my thanks for the new quotations.

[The quotations, furnished by Mr. E. Peacock, are these:—

'Now let me trace the stream up to its source
Among the hills; its *runnel* by degrees
Diminishing, the murmur turns a tinkle.'
Jas. Grahame, *The Sabbath, &c.*, 6th ed. 1808, p. 66.

'There is a *runnel* creeps across a fell,
Far, noteless, poor.'
Sonnet by T. D., in *Blackwood's Maga.*, Mar. 1824, vol. xv. p. 268.

'The little *runnels* leading to our tarn.'
J. E. Taylor, *Half-hours in Green Lanes*, 4th ed. 1877, p. 35.]

**317. Moxon's 'Chaucer'** (7 S. viii. 133; 1889).

With reference to the remark by F. N. that it is strange that any one pretending to know anything about Chaucer should ever have been deceived by the dishonest title-page of Moxon's *Chaucer*, I have to confess, with shame and confusion, that it was really some time before the truth about this title-page dawned upon me; and hence I have not shrunk from saying, in a note to p. xviii of my edition of Chaucer's *Minor Poems*, that 'I cannot but think that this title-page may have misled others, as it for a long time misled myself.' I beg leave to say that I have probably instructed more pupils in Chaucer than any one else; and I never yet met with any one who had *not*, at the outset, been deceived. To every young student the revelation has been a surprise.

The reason is simple, viz. that the unsophisticated reader is quite ready to believe that what a respectable publisher says is really true; though I can quite understand that booksellers and publishers may know better. I think this title-page cannot but mislead; and I would fain hope that cases of equal enormity are uncommon.

The extremely artful way in which the *Minor Poems* are introduced between portions of Tyrwhitt's genuine work is extremely baffling to the uninitiated. There is not the faintest hint anywhere that any one but Tyrwhitt ever touched the preparation of the book. F. N. is mistaken in saying that there are no notes by Tyrwhitt on the *Minor Poems*. The fact is that the 'Remarks on the Minor Poems,' printed in Moxon's edition at pp. 445-452, are palpably Tyrwhitt's own; and I may add that many of them are valuable.

The advertisement at pp. 443, 444, is Tyrwhitt's, and his name is printed on p. 444. The glossary is Tyrwhitt's, bodily.

And it is precisely because the book is all Tyrwhitt's down to p. 209, and again all Tyrwhitt's from p. 443 to the end, that the deception is so clever and so complete.

### 318. Thomas a Kempis (7 S. viii. 171; 1889).

The explanation, that Thomas *a* Kempis is probably nothing more than a corruption or contraction of 'Thomas *at* Kempen,' is wrong. And it is unnecessary to use the word 'probably' when we know all about it for certain. Mr. Bardsley made the same mistake years ago, when he told us that George a Green meant George at Green (*Eng. Surnames*, third edition, p. 111), and went on to tell us that Thomas a Becket is for Thomas atte Becket, i. e. the streamlet. It is almost too absurd; for no one calls a *cat* a *ca*, or a *hat* a *ha*; then why should *at* become *a*? And why do not people reason?

Of course *a* is short for *of*, as in 'what's o'clock,' 'man o' war,' 'John a Gaunt.' And the whole matter is worked out in the *New English Dictionary*, p. 3, col. 3, admirably and fully. It makes me ashamed of my countrymen to observe how frequently this work is snubbed by being left unconsulted; and it seems altogether too bad that writers should take such pains to set wrong, for the hundredth time, what Dr. Murray (it ought to be once for all) has set right.

### 319. Baldacchino (7 S. viii. 172; 1889).

I suppose this word is related to Arab. *baldat*, a city, and the Arabic name could be applied to various cities.

It sometimes means Mecca, and sometimes Constantinople, according to Richardson. Florio's *Ital. Dictionary* has the curious entry, 'Baldacca, Baldacco, an ale-house, a tap-house, a tipling-house, a taverne; it was woont to be the name of an Inne in Florence. It is taken in an ill sense for Babylon, or the whore of Babylon.' This mention of Babylon is probably the origin of Dr. T.'s mistake [i. e. the mistake of supposing that the stuff called *baldacco* was named from Babylon.] The place really meant in connexion with the stuff for canopies was, however, Bagdad.

We can hardly have a better authority for this than Devic. See his *Supplement* to Littré's *French Dictionary*, which is certainly one of the most valuable works on the etymologies of Oriental words.

### 320. The Etymology of 'Town' (7 S. viii. 183; 1889).

The other day I came across the amazing statement that the etymology of *town* depends upon the Gothic *tains*, a twig. And, sure enough, it is all in an old edition of Taylor's *Words and Places* :—

'The primary meaning of the suffix *-ton* is to be sought in the Goth. *tains*, the Old Norse *teinn*, and the Friesic *tene*, all of which mean a twig—a radical signification which survives in the phrase "the *tine* of a fork." '—Ed. 1873, p. 79.

This was all very well in 1873, when the idea still survived that vowels went for nothing, and that the chief qualification for meddling with Gothic, &c., was, *not* to understand the pronunciation or the phonetic laws of the Teutonic languages. But what complex confusion it is!

The Goth. *tains* is quite as remote from 'the *tine* of a fork' as it is from *town*. The *tine* of a fork is a slovenly form of *tind*, just as literary English has turned the beautiful word *wood-bind* into the unmeaning *wood-bine*. All the words should be kept distinct, as in Anglo-Saxon. The A.S. for *tine* is *tind*. The A.S. for *twig* is *tān*; and the A.S. for *town* is *tūn*. They are all quite different words, and all from different roots; and they all survive in English.

From *tind* we have *tine*; from *tān* we have A.S. *misteltān*, Mod. E. *mistletoe*, with the *n* cut off by confusion with A.S. *tān*, Mid. E. *toon*, the old plural of *toe* ; and from *tūn* we have *town*. To connect E. *-toe* in *mistletoe* with E. *town* is like connecting the E. *doe* with E. *down*.

What, then, is *town*? It is A.S. *tūn*, cognate with G. *Zaun*, a hedge, and with the O. Irish and Celtic *dūn*, a fort, which so often appears in the Latinized suffix *-dunum*. The original Teutonic form is *tū-no*, where *-no* is the suffix, and *tū*, equivalent to Aryan *deu*, is the form of the root, though its meaning is unknown. The A. S. *tūn* became *-tun*, Mod. E. *-ton*, in unaccented positions, as in Mod. E. Bar-ton.

*Bar-ton* is the A. S. *bere-tūn*, a barley enclosure, from A.S. *bere*, barley. The former *e* in A. S. *bere* is a mutated form of *a*, as shown by Goth. *baris*, barley. It is therefore quite distinct from the *e* in A. S. *ber-an*, Lat. *fer-re*, Greek φέρ-ειν. Yet here again we are told—

'In many parts of England the rickyard is called the *barton*, i.e. the enclosure for the *bear* or crop which the land *bears*.'

But *bear* simply means 'barley,' and the connexion with *bear* is problematical. Note, too, that the A. S. *týnan*, to hedge (with long *y*), is merely a derivative of *tūn*, not the original of it, and is quite distinct from the *tines* of a fork.

I make these notes just to show the sad confusion of errors which pervade the whole account, and I now enumerate these errors for the reader's convenience:—

1. The suffix *-ton* is here referred to Got. *tains*, a twig.
2. The sense of Goth. *tains* survives in the *tines* of a fork.
3. It is insinuated that *tine*, to hedge, is allied to the *tine* of a fork, i.e. that A. S. *tind* is all one with the secondary verb *týnan* (with long *y*).
4. In Iceland the homestead is called a *tun*. No; it is a *tūn*, with a long *u*.
5. A *barton* means an enclosure for what the land *bears*.
6. Besides this, the connexion between *town* and *tains* is emphasized on the next page by comparing the totally different words *yard*, a stick, and *yard*, a court, though these also are from different roots.

**321. The Name Shakespeare** (7 S. viii. 246; 1889).

As to the etymology of this name no reasonable man has any doubt. The analogies of Feuterspear and Wagstaff are sufficient. But as many unreasonable people, delighting more in paradox than in plain sense, have tried to derive the name (why this name only?) from all kinds of extraneous and impossible sources, I think it is worth while to add to the analogies the following. Being lately in Lichfield, I saw over a shop-door the name of Shakeshaft.

**322. Oandurth; the Lancashire form of Undern** (7 S. viii. 278; 1889).

My respect for A. J. M.'s. contributions is much tried by his astonishing suggestion about this word[1]. I have been accused of caricature in asserting that Englishmen still exist who derive English words, of all languages, from German. The critics say that no one now seriously does so. But alas! I am right. Is it possible that A. J. M. is unaware that the German *th* is a mere *t*, and was formerly so written? The German *roth* was formerly *rōt*, and is merely the peculiar High German form of the English *red*; and the German *Abend* is merely the peculiar High German form of our *even*, in the sense of *evening*. The English form of *Abend-roth* is *evening-red*, a compound which I do not think was ever used by us. And even if the M.E. *euen-reed* or A.S. *ǣfen-rēad* had ever been in use, no force known to me could have twisted either of these phrases into *oandurth*. So I am obliged to add this guess to my collection of 'awful examples'; and I feel sure that the suggestion would never have been made if its author had even the ghost of a glimpse of a notion of its unparalleled comicality.

The fact that many of our words, such as *yea* (A. S. *gēa*),

---

[1] The proposition was this; the Lanc. *oandurth* represents the G. *Abendroth*.

resemble German more or less, is practically accidental, i. e. due to the accident that German is a cognate language. The same is true of Moeso-Gothic, which has perished. And if German had either perished or had never been developed, it would not have made the faintest difference to a single one of any of our dialect words. The case of Old Norse (better called Icelandic) is different. The hardy Norsemen *did* come to England, and are here still; so that if any one proposed to derive the Lancashire *yah* from Icel. *jā*, perhaps there is not much to be said against it, though it is more likely that *yah* is really Old Northumbrian, from which Icelandic differed in most respects very slightly.

I am not able to say what *oandurth* is precisely, the difficulty lying in the *th*. But the *th* is suspiciously like a suffix or an addition. The Shropshire form is *oander*, and so is the Cheshire. Cheshire also has *oanders* for the afternoon-meal. Ray, in his *Glossary*, gives *aandorn*, *orndorn*, *doundrins*, all with a like sense; and the last form shows a prefixed *d*, which is a mere ignorant addition, and raises a suspicion that the Lanc. suffixed *th* is no more. I really cannot go into the whole history of the A. S. *undern* and all its various uses and derivatives, with all the numerous examples that show how precisely it answers to *oander*.

As to the pronunciation, the regular development of A. S. *undern* would naturally be such as to give a Mod. E. *ounder*, just as A. S. *bunden* gives *bound*, whilst the *n* is lost as in the adj. *silvern*. That *ounder* should become *oander* dialectically can cause no difficulty.

See further in Ray, Miss Jackson's *Shropshire Glossary*, Darlington's *South Cheshire Glossary*, &c.

### 323. Bole : Pig (7 S. viii. 396 ; 1889).

Under the heading 'Bole,' I remarked that I did not see any reason for supposing that *pig* is 'the old name for a small bowl or cup.' In reply to this I am told that it is fifty years old, and, again, that Jamieson gives examples of it.

Well, the earliest example I can find is that in Douglas's *Virgil*, bk. vii. chap. xiv. l. 25 (*Aen.* vii. 792), where 'cælata urna' is translated by 'ane payntit *pyg.*' But this does not take us back even to the Middle English period. In questions of etymology, my idea of 'old,' as applied to English words, extends to that period *at least.*

What I desire is some further light upon *pig* and *piggin.* The latter occurs in Cotgrave, as I have shown in my *Dictionary*. I quote [alas!] as the supposed original of the word, the Gaelic *pigean*, and suppose the word to be Celtic. Other etymologists have done the same.

But the chances are that the Gaelic *pigean* and *pigeath*, both beginning with the suspicious non-Celtic *p*, are mere borrowings from English, and do not help us. And my present notion is that *pig, piggin*, and the rest, are all various broken-down forms of M. E. *biker*, a drinking-cup, also spelt *bicker* and *beaker*; see these forms in the *New English Dictionary*, and compare the form *pitcher*

*Biker* occurs in 1348, more than a century before Douglas was born. I should be very glad of further illustrative quotations. A new quotation that tells us something as yet unrecorded will be more helpful than a ton of argumentation. [I do not find that any new quotation was adduced. My experience is, that to ask for a quotation is a sure way of bringing a ridiculous criticism to a sudden stop.]

### 324. Reckling=Wreckling (7 S. ix. 490; 1889).

The word *reckling* is a misprint for, or rather a phonetic spelling of *wreckling*, the old form, as pointed out by Wedgwood. See E. Friesic *wrak*, as explained by Koolman; and compare Swedish *vrak*, refuse. It is closely allied to *wreck* and *wretch*. *Wreckling* simply means a wretched or poor creature; cf. Prov. Eng. *wretchock*, the smallest of a brood of domestic fowls (Halliwell). As for the suffix, compare *weakling*.

It would be easy to write a long article on this word, with crowds of examples.

### 325. Grift, a slate-pencil (7 S. ix. 67; 1890).

I have frequently had occasion to notice that many of our provincial words (contrary to the received opinion) are of French origin. *Grift* is formed by adding *t* to O. F. *grefe*, a style to write with, which is a variant of O. F. *grafe*, whence E. *graft*, also formed with added *t*. Hence were borrowed also Du., Dan., Swed., G. *Griffel*, and all are from Low Lat. *graphium*, from Gk. *graphein*, to write. Thus a *grift* means a pencil, and was originally independent of slate. See Franck, *Etym. Du. Dict.*, s. v. 'Griffel.' It is curious to see that Kluge, who inclines to Teutonism overmuch, can see no origin for *Griffel* but the G. *greifen*.

### 326. The Superlative suffix -erst (7 S. ix. 146; 1890).

I make a note that the form *-erst* is sometimes found as a superlative suffix. It is formed by adding *-st* (for *-est*) to the comparative suffix *-er*. Thus *deep* would have *deep-er* for its comparative, whence the superlative *deep-er-st* might be formed.

Examples occur in Wyclif's *Works*, ed. Arnold, vol. iii.

I note *hei-er-ste*, highest, p. 363; *lewid-er-st*, most ignorant (lit. lewdest), p. 355; *blessid-er-ste*, most blessed, p. 344; and on the same page, both *depp-er-ste*, adj. and *depp-er-st*, adv. Perhaps some one can give us a few more examples.

(POSTSCRIPT; 7 S. ix. 237; 1890.)

I can now add that the superlative suffix *-er-st* probably arose with such words as *hind-er-est*, which occurs in

Chaucer's *Prologue*, l. 622. The Modern E. *nearest* also turns out, on analysis, to contain both a comparative and a superlative suffix. [It is equivalent to *nigh-er-est*.]

### 327. Hedges (7 S. ix. 272; 1890).

It is difficult to see why the etymology of this name is asked for, unless the question is meant as a trap. It is obvious to a plain man that *hedges* is the plural of a well-known English word which must be familiar to all in the form *hedge*.

We have a collection of farm-buildings near Cambridge at a place called the King's Hedges; on which I may remark that King is a very common surname in these parts.

At the same time, it is worth noting that the A. S. dictionaries do not give us the origin of *hedge*; they only give *haga*, the origin of the *haw-* in *hawthorn*, and *heg*, the origin of the *hey-* in *heybote* and of the *hay-* in *hayward*. But there is yet a *third* form, viz. A. S. *hecg*, a feminine sb. representing a Teutonic form *hag-jā*, with the genitive and dative *hecge*; and the Modern English *hedge* is derived, as hundreds of English words are, from the dative case rather than from the nominative. Examples of *hecg* are very rare, but the genitive occurs, with the late spelling *hegge*, in a late copy of a charter of King Offa, originally made in 785. See *Cartularium Saxonicum*, ed. Birch, i. 339. [And the dative occurs, spelt *hegge*, in the *A. S. Chronicle*, an. 547 (Laud MS.). There is even a dative *hecgan* in an early genuine charter of Æthelstan, A.D. 931; see Earle's *Land Charters*, p. 167, l. 1.]

### 328. Ted, Ned (7 S. ix. 305; 1890).

I have often wondered whence came the initial *T* in *Ted*; but I think it is clearly due to the final letter in *Saint*. Similarly we have *Tooley* from St. Olave; *tawdry* from St. Audrey; *Tantony* from *St. Anthony* (see *Tantony-pig* in Halliwell). St. Edward is Edward the Confessor. I am reminded of this by finding 'Sen Tan Welle' in the *Records of the Borough of Nottingham*, iv. 91. It simply means 'Saint Ann's Well.' [And I have met with 'St. Tosting' for 'Saint Austin.'] The N in *Ned,. Noll*, &c., is the final *n* of *mine*; cf. the phrases 'my nuncle,' 'my naunt,' and the like.

### 329. Touter (7 S. ix. 315; 1890).

It is odd that simple common sense, used in all other transactions, cannot be applied to etymology. The derivation of *touter* from *Tooting* (!) is obviously impossible, because such a man would then have been called a *Tootinger*; just as an inhabitant of London is not called a *Londer*, but a *Londoner*. The origin of *touter*, formerly *tooter* (as the quotation given correctly says), is from A. S. *tōtian*, to peep or spy about. It was correctly given by Wedgwood years ago; and why it is pretended that there is any difficulty about it, I do not know.

### 330. To send to Jericho (7 S. ix. 343; 1890).

I have never seen a really satisfactory explanation of this phrase, though Nares seems to have understood it rightly, judging from his *Glossary*, s. v. 'Jericho.' The allusion is, as might be expected, scriptural. The particular story intended will be found twice over, viz. in 2 Sam. x. 5 and 1 Chron. x. 5.

When David's servants had half their beards cut off, and were not presentable at court, the king advised them to 'tarry at Jericho till their beards were grown.' Hence it will be seen that to 'tarry at Jericho' meant, jocularly, to live in retirement, as being not presentable. The phrase could be used, with particular sarcasm, with reference to such young men as had not yet been endowed naturally with such ornaments; and, in their case, they would have to wait some time before their beards could suggest their wisdom.

That this joke was really current is clear from the example which Nares cites from Heywood's *Hierarchie*, bk. iv. p. 208 :—

> 'Who would to curbe such insolence, I know,
> Bid such young boys to stay in Jericho
> Until their beards were growne, their wits more staid.'

But it is remarkable that Nares does not seem to have noticed the above text as being the obvious source of the phrase. We have thus clear evidence that the original phrase was used of bidding young men to 'tarry in Jericho' or to 'stay in Jericho.' The transition from this to 'sending to Jericho' was easy enough. We also see that the original phrase really meant, 'Wait till your beard is grown,' i. e. 'Wait till your wits are more staid or stronger'; and this was satirically equivalent to saying that the party addressed was too young or too inexperienced to give advice. Thus the original saying insinuated a charge of inexperience; and a sending to Jericho was equivalent to making such a charge. The person sent was deemed not good enough for the rest of the company. And this explains the whole matter.

There are other current suggestions, but none of them rests on any evidence. I hope that, now that I have pointed out the allusion quite clearly, we need not be further troubled with their ingenuity. I quite endorse the observation in Nares, that his quotation 'explains the common phrase of wishing a person at Jericho.' All that I have added is a note of the source of that quotation.

### 331. The Sense of 'Chair' in 'Coriolanus'
(7 S. ix. 345 ; 1890).

In the well-known passage in *Coriolanus*, iv. 7. 52, over which many have stumbled, the whole sense comes out at once by simply calling to mind that *chair*, in Tudor English, was sometimes used in the sense of 'pulpit.' Milton has it so; see 'Chair' in the *New English Dictionary*, sect. 5. Cotgrave has, '*Chaire*, f. a chair; also a pulpit for a Preacher.' And in Modern French it still has this sense, as distinct from its doublet *chaise*. And this is the solution of the whole matter.

The idea might have been picked up in any church, for, indeed, the pulpit is commonly more 'evident,' i. e. conspicuous, than any of the fine tombs in the choir. The general sense is just this: 'Power, however commendable it may seem to itself, can find no tomb so conspicuous, no tomb so obvious, as when it chooses for itself a pulpit whence to declaim its own praises.' This agrees very nearly with the explanation in the note to the Clarendon Press edition; but it seems to me to be more emphatic and picturesque to explain the word as 'pulpit' than merely as 'orator's chair.'

## 332. The Occurrence of 'th' in Anglo-French and Anglo-Saxon (7 S. ix. 445; 1890).

There is an interesting note on the occurrence of *th* (= Lat. *d*, *t*) in Anglo-French and Anglo-Saxon in Gröber, *Grundriss der Romanischen Philologie*, i. 397.

The sole English word in which the A. F. *th* is still preserved is the English *ƥaith*, M. E. *ƥeith*, from the A. F. *feith* (*ƥeid*), which again is from the Latin accusative *fidem*. The same change from the Lat. *d* (or *t*) to E. *th* is found in A. S. and in Early English of the twelfth century; in a few cases the words survived till about the fourteenth century, but are all now obsolete, or have lost the *th*.

Examples in A. S. are: A. S. *fithele* (fiddle), from Low Lat. *fidula*, *vidula*; A. S. *sinoth*, also *synoth*, *seonod*, a synod, from Lat. acc. *synodum*; A. S. *Cathum*, from Lat. *Cadomum*, Caen, in the *A. S. Chron.*, under the date 1105; A. S.

*Rothem*, from Lat. *Rotomagum*, Rouen, in the same, under the date 1124.

So also the place now called *Gerberoi* or *Gerbroi*, near Beauvais, appears in the *A. S. Chronicle* as *Gerborneth*, A. D. 1079; and *Condé* appears as A. S. *Cundoth*, A. D. 883.

So also A. S. *nativiteth*, Lat. acc. *natiuitatem* ; *A. S. Chron.* 1106. M. E. *plenteth* (= A. F. *plenteth*), Lat. acc. *plenitatem* ; Genesis and Exodus, 3709. M. E. *daynteth* (= A. F. *deinteth*), Lat. acc. *dignitatem* ; 'Anturs of Arthur,' st. xiv., *Towneley Myst.*, p. 245. M. E. *kariteth*, from Lat. acc. *caritatem* ; Ormulum, l. 2998. And the Lowland Scotch *poortith* must be of F. origin ; from *paupertatem*.

The change from *t* to *th* took place in Gaulish Latin and very early French, when the *t* was *final*. Final *d* was probably sounded as the voiced *th* first of all, and then unvoiced, in accordance with the known habit of French, which delights in voiceless letters at the end of a word.

### 333. Anglo-Saxon Translations of the New Testament (7 S. ix. 475 ; 1890).

Of course Dr. Scrivener's reference to Anglo-Saxon versions of the New Testament is due to some mistake. Except the four Gospels, there is no trace of a translation into Anglo-Saxon of any part of the New Testament. The passage must have been written from imagination. The only thing of the kind is a translation of the apocryphal Gospel of Nicodemus. This was printed by Thwaites in 1698, at the end of his *Heptateuchus*. Many years ago, I pointed out the existence of a *lacuna* in the Cambridge MS. whence his text is taken. In the first volume of Grein's *Bibliothek der angelsächsischen Prosa* we find the A. S. version of the Pentateuch, Joshua, Judges, and Job. There are many A. S. MSS. of the Psalms, and there is an edition by Spelman. I suppose that the only unprinted Biblical specimen is Ælfric's translation of the Book of Esther.

For further information, see Wülker's *Grundriss zur Geschichte der angelsächsischen Litteratur.*

### 334. Peruse (7 S. ix. 506; 1890).

The great difficulty of this word is well known. There are good illustrations of it in Croft's edition of Elyot's *Governour*; and he concludes that it cannot be derived from *per* and *use*. I have shown, in my *Dictionary*, the great probability that it really was from that source; and in the Addenda to the second edition I show that it was really once used in the sense of 'using up.' I now find from Godefroy's *O. French Dictionary*, that there really was an O. F. verb *peruser*, in the very same sense. He explains it by 'user entièrement, achever, consommer.' This goes far to settle the question.

### 335. Prepense (7 S. x. 6; 1890).

In the phrase 'malice *prepense*,' the etymology of *prepense* is not very easy. I give it from Lat. *prae*, beforehand, and the French *penser*. Godefroy's *O. F. Dictionary* gives an example (s. v. 'Porpenser') of the phrase 'de malice *pourpensee*.' This may seem decisive, but it is not so. Scheler (s. v. 'Pour') points out the extraordinary confusion, in French, between *pour*, O. F. *por* (properly Lat. *pro*), and *par* (Lat. *per*); and he might have included French *pré-* as well. The confusion seems to be one of long standing, for in the second section of the *Laws of William the Conqueror*, Thorpe's edition speaks of 'agweit *purpense*,' i. e. premeditated lying in wait. But another reading is *prepensed* (see Littré, s. v. 'Pourpenser,' and Schmid's *Die Gesetze der Angelsachsen*, p. 322). This makes it tolerably clear that the above-mentioned confusion existed. At the same time it is certain that the usual Anglo-French verb for *premeditate* was *purpenser*. Cf. the phrase 'felonie *purpense*' in Britton, vol. i. p. 15, and the long note in Elyot's *Governour*, ed. Croft, vol. ii. p. 375.

### 336. Hone : Hoe (7 S. x. 35 ; 1890).

It is certainly clear that *hone* in Tusser (*Husbandry*, § 46, st. 9) is a misprint for *houe*, i. e. hoe. 'How or Hoe' is the spelling in Phillips, ed. 1706. It is spelt *hough* by Ellis (1750), and *how* by Worlidge (1681); see *Old Country Words*, ed. J. Britten (E. D. S.). The spelling *houe* is the correct French spelling; even Cotgrave, s. v. *Houé*, has, 'opened at the root as a tree with a Houë.' No doubt the spelling *houe* will turn up elsewhere, to countenance Tusser's spelling. Ray has *how* (1691).

### 337. 'Ictibus Agrestis' (7 S. x. 48 ; 1890).

How can I trace this quotation, which I find referred to by Chaucer? In the *Miller's Tale* (Group A. l. 3381), the Ellesmere MS. has—

'For som folk wol ben wonnen for richesse,
  And somme for strokes, and some for gentilesse';

and the side-note is, 'Unde Ovidius: Ictibus Agrestis.' I fear Chaucer's memory was at fault, as I cannot find it in Ovid. I have also tried Virgil, Statius, and Claudian without success. [The problem remains unsolved.]

### 338. The Etymology of 'Anlas' (7 S. x. 65 ; 1890).

The interesting word *anlas*, a kind of dagger or knife, occurring in Chaucer's *Prologue*, is fully explained by Dr. Murray in the *New English Dictionary*. All that is known about the etymology is that it first occurs in the thirteenth century, and is said by Matthew Paris to be a native English word.

It is, therefore, compounded of two Middle English words; and these I take to be simply *an* and *laas*, i.e. 'on' and 'lace'; and that the knife was so called because hung *on* a *lace*, and thus suspended from the neck.

There is a precedent for this in the A. S. name for a kind of pouch. It was called a *bī-gyrdel*, i.e. a 'by-girdle,' because hung at the girdle. Note that in this word the accent was *on the prefix*. This is clear from the alliterated line in *Piers the Plowman*, A. ix. 79; and Dr. Murray clearly explains that such was the fact.

With *on* we have *ón-set*, *ón-slaught*, with the accent on the prefix. The spelling *an* for *on* occurs in M. E. *an-lich*, alike, and in several compounds noted by Stratmann, s. v. 'an.'

That *laas* or *las*, a lace, was the precise word to use, we know from Chaucer, *Prol.* 392 :

'A dagger hanging *on* a *laas* badde he.'

Perhaps we may yet find the variant *onlas*.

### 339. Mustredevilliars (7 S. x. 84; 1890).

This is given by Halliwell as the name of a kind of mixed grey woollen cloth, which continued in use up to Elizabeth's reign; also spelt *mustard-willars*. In the *Records of Nottingham*, iii. 296, is mention of 'ij. yardes and halfe a quarter *mosterdevyllers*,' under the date May 17, 1496. At p. 495 of the same, the editor explains that it was made at the town of Montivilliers (Mouster Villers in Froissart, ix. 164) on the Lézarde (Seine Inférieure). See Kervyn de Lettenhove's edition of Froissart, vol. xxv., 'Table Analytique des Noms Géographiques.' It seems that, by a silly popular etymology and by the shameless guesswork for which English editors are so remarkable, it has been often said that the cloth was of a *mustard* colour! But it was grey. *Moster, mouster, mustre*, &c., are the Old French spellings of Lat. *monasterium*; see '*moustier*' in Godefroy. Hence the etymology is from *moster de Villars*, 'monastery of Villiers, or Villars.'

**340. Archæology or Archaiology** (7 S. x. 170; 1890).

I observe that Canon Taylor, on the assumption that we use the Latin, not the Greek, alphabet, has no difficulty in showing that we should write *archæology* rather than *archaiology*; and certainly it is far better.

But the assumption is not wholly correct. As a fact we do *not* use the Latin alphabet precisely, but the Anglo-French modification of it; and if we were only to use our common sense we should adhere to this throughout, instead of occasionally recurring to the Latin type.

Unfortunately, at the time of the Renaissance the pedants tried to introduce pure Latin spellings, and even wrote *ædify* for *edify*; but in a large number of instances the Anglo-French habit has held its own. Still the pedants have succeeded in introducing confusion and doubt, under the impression that they were 'classical.' The whole matter is explained in my *Principles of Etymology*.

It were much to be wished that 'scholarship' could be taken for granted, instead of being constantly exhibited in Latin and Greek spellings. We do not accuse a man of ignorance of Latin because he writes *edify*; and for the same reason it would be well if we could be content with primeval, medieval, pedagogue, orthopedic, and archeology, all with the French *e*, and not with the Latin *æ* at all. I have been for many years trying to explain to scholars at Cambridge that *medieval* is a better (i.e. a more practical) spelling than *mediæval*. But no one seems to grasp the argument. They will admit *primeval*, because it is in dictionaries; but they will have none of *medieval*, because it looks 'unclassical.' This is a complete answer to the eminently foolish suggestion, frequently made, that we ought to have an 'academy' for settling questions such as these. They will never be settled on any principle except popular caprice. In spelling English words it has long ago been agreed, that no rule or habit shall be carried out *consistently*. There is, in English, nothing 'correct' unless it be confused, inconsistent, and capricious.

### 341. Girl pronounced Gurl. I (7 S. x. 176; 1890).

I beg leave to suggest that spellings convey no true notion of sound to any one, unless they are given according to some phonetic system. I have been wondering, for example, what in the world the above title means. In Southern English we pronounce China, America, &c., in such a way that the final sound is 'the obscure vowel,' represented, in romic notation, by a turned *e* or (ə). The same sound, prolonged and accented, is heard in a large number of words in the neighbourhood of London, in the mouths of people who do not trill the *r*. I was born in London, and have lived in it, and also at Sydenham, Highgate, Woolwich, &c.; and I have always heard and used this sound in *girl* (gəəl), *burn* (bəən), *churl* (chəəl), *heard* (həəd), *bird* (bəəd), &c.

Mr. Sweet's experience is the same. I should be glad to learn how, and where, any difference is made, even by those who trill the *r*, between the vowels in *girl*, and *churl*, and *pearl*. But the information will be useless unless conveyed in some phonetic spelling, such as romic, or palæotype, or the system in the *New English Dictionary*.

### 342. Girl pronounced Gurl. II (7 S. x. 515; 1890).

I recognize the pronunciation to which Dr. C. alludes, now that it is properly explained. Pronunciations can be explained by the ordinary English notation well enough, *when test-words are added for the purpose*. The reason why the ordinary notation is usually a very bad one is, that writers often give a spelling of their own without any hint as to what they mean by it. I should spell the sound of *gairl*, with *ai* as in *air*, as (gaeəl). And now comes in the trouble. It so happens that whilst Dr. C. was taught to look upon *gurl* (gəəl) as vulgar, wherefore he never uses it, I was taught the exact contrary, so that I never use *gairl* (*gaeəl*).

This is what all disputes about pronunciation of English words generally come to. Each man thinks that what he was taught is right; and there is *no* real authority. We have to get along the best we can, and if we can pronounce words as they seem to us to be usually pronounced in London, Oxford, and Cambridge, we shall be understood. But we shall not always satisfy all hearers.

343. **James : Jacob** (7 S. x. 212; 1890).

Dr. C.'s remarks at the last reference are very helpful. I think we may safely say that the *s* in *James* is the Anglo-F. and F. nom. suffix, added to the form *Jame* by analogy with *Charles*, *Jacques*, &c.

Also, that *Jame* was certainly derived from Lat. acc. *Jacobum*. The only difficulty is to ascertain the precise historical order of the facts.

Surely the Mid. Eng. *Jame* (also *James*) must be closely connected with the Span. *Jaime*, in which the initial *J* (though at present sounded like the G. *ch*) was originally sounded like the Mod. and Mid. E. *J* in *James*.

I do not remember any early reference to *James* in Mid. Eng. in which the reference is to any other than the St. James whose shrine was at Compostella. English people (including the Wife of Bath) became familiar with the name by actually resorting to that place. This historical fact seems to me to be of great importance.

I have given several references in my notes to *P. Plowman*, B. prol. 47.

344. **Wayzgoose** (7 S. x. 233; 1890).

Nothing can be sillier than the derivation of this word from German. Surely *goose* is not a German, but an

English word, as a moment's reflexion will show. The guess is plainly due to the notion, which I have so often denounced, viz., that all native English words are falsely imagined to be of 'German' origin. I would rather suppose that *wayz* is a phonetic spelling of *wase*, in the sense of 'stubble'; so that *wayzgoose* is simply 'stubble-goose.' This is the explanation which I have repeatedly offered to correspondents; and oh! the number of times I have been asked! *Wase* is used provincially to mean a 'straw-pad'; see Halliwell. Cf. Icel. *vasi*; Swed. *vase*, a sheaf; Mid. Du. *wase*, a torch (i. e. twist of straw), as in the M. E. *Tale of Beryn*, 2351.

### 345. Grange (7 S. x. 253; 1890).

It is clear, I think, that the assertion that granges necessarily belonged to religious houses must have been derived from two passages in Chaucer (ed. Tyrwhitt, ll. 3668, 12996), i. e. *Cant. Tales*, A. 3668, B. 1256, which seem to favour that supposition. But, of course, as the word simply meant 'a place for grain,' or 'barn,' there was no reason for its use in a restricted sense, and it is constantly used in the general one. It occurs again in *P. Plowman*, C. xx. 71, where I explain it duly in the note. Dr. N. did not find it in the *Promptorium* because he did not look for it under the usual M. E. spellings, viz. *graunge*, or *grawnge*, or *gronge*. Oddly enough it occurs twice there, viz., under 'Grawnge,' and under 'Gronge'; and Mr. Way gives a note on it, which has been quoted. It also occurs, under 'Grawnge,' in the *Catholicon Anglicum*, and here again the editor has a note on it. He quotes the note on the passage in the 'Miller's Tale' in Bell's *Chaucer*; and this is where we come to the information about *grange* being 'applied to outlying farms belonging to the abbeys.' No doubt it was, but not exclusively, nor does Mr. Jephson say so. The earliest quotation I have yet found for it is in the romance of *Havelok*, l. 764, about A. D. 1290. The original Latin form is *granea*. The forms *grangia*, &c. are mere Latin travesties of the French form.

Why the whole of the discussion might not have been saved by simply looking out the word in my *Dictionary*, where I give the etymology, the sense, and two early references, I am at a loss to understand. But the dictionary-maker must expect, on the one hand, to be snubbed when he makes a mistake, and, on the other, to be neglected when he is right.

### 346. 'Write you' (7 S. x. 273; 1890).

Of course 'I will write *you*' is an old formula. Even now we should hesitate to insert *to* in such a phrase as 'I gave *to* you the book'; the *you* alone is sufficient.

*You* is dative as well as accusative. The use of *to* before *you* to indicate the former was once needless. It is amazing that such elementary facts remain unknown. No one would like to confess ignorance of the forms of Latin pronouns; but when the language to be learnt is merely English, ignorance at once becomes pardonable. But why?

### 347. German and English Head-letters (i.e. the use of Capitals in English and German (7 S. x. 311; 1890).

This is an extremely difficult and complex problem. I think it clear that there is no proved connexion between English and German habits in this matter; or, at any rate, they should be considered independently.

As to the use of capitals in English, I do not see that the date 1680 has anything to do with it. Any one who wants to see a good deal of testimony in a small space may turn to my 'uncooked' editions of printed passages, as given in my *Specimens of English Literature*, part III;

from 1394 to 1579. Already, in 1552, John Skott's print of Sir David Lyndesay's *Monarchè* abounds with capitals, especially for substantives; and there are several in Ascham's *Scholemaster*, ed. 1570.

I suppose the practice arose in the case of certain letters. Many MSS. use capitals for initial *a̖*, *c*, and *r*, for no apparent reason. Thus the *Tale of Melusine, or Romance of Partenay*, edited by me in 1866, abounds with *A* for *a* (in such a word as *And*), *C* for *c*, and other curiosities. Chaucer MSS. abound with examples of capitals for such words as *I-wis* and *Iay* (a jay). I open the *Tale of Gamelyn* at a hazard, and find in line 283 in MS. Harl. 7334 the line—

'Thus wan Gamelyn the Ram and the Ryng.'

The whole subject is far more complex, and runs back to a much remoter antiquity, than your correspondents seem to suppose.

### 348. Oubit (7 S. x. 324; 1890).

Most people are familiar with this word in connexion with Kingsley's poem; but the etymology has never been given. Other spellings (see Jamieson) are *vowbet* (for *woubet*), *woubit*, *wobat*, and it is generally explained as 'a hairy caterpillar.' Very likely the M. E. *warbot* (*Prompt. Parv.*) and the prov. E. *warble*, are mere variants. Jamieson feebly suggests A. S. *wibba*, a worm, as the origin, which will not satisfy any student of phonetics. The real origin is suggested by the older spelling *welbode*, which occurs in two glosses, 'hic multipes, a *welbode*,' and 'hec concipita, idem est' (Wright-Wülker, *Vocab.*, 706, 15). Compare 'hic multipes, a tuenti-fot wurme' (id., 766, 28). It is easy to see that here, as in a thousand other cases, *e* is miswritten for *o*, and the right form is *wolbode*. This is curiously illustrated from an unprinted MS. of the *Ortus Vocabulorum*, which has (at p. 28) the entry, 'Multipes, a wolbede,' in which the second *o*, not the first, has gone wrong.

The component parts of the word are clear enough. *Wol-* represents A. S. *wul*, Mod. E. *wool*; and *bode* represents an A. S. form *buda* or *boda*, closely related to A. S. *budda*, a scarabæus or beetle (see Wright-Wülker, *Vocab.*, 543, 10). I take the E. words *bowd*, a weevil, and *bot*, a worm or maggot, to be closely allied. Thus the sense is 'woolly worm,' i.e. hairy caterpillar. Of course *wool* becomes '*oo*' in Scotch.

### 349. Etymology of Hibiscus (7 S. x. 350; 1890).

I do not suppose it is possible to discover the etymology of this word, which seems to have no root in Greek. Liddell and Scott give an unsatisfactory account. Under ἐβίσκος they say it is the same as ἰβίσκος, with a smooth breathing, and that it is feminine. But no such word appears; only ἱβίσκος is given, with a rough breathing, and it is masculine. Of course there is not a tittle of evidence or probability for connecting it with the Egyptian *ibis*. And I should like to remark in passing that nowhere can more ignorant etymologies be found than in works on botany and 'scientific' subjects. Too often, all the science is reserved for the subject, so that there is none to spare for explaining the names.

### 350. Banshee (7 S. x. 370; 1890).

I suppose that Melusine was a kind of *banshee*; at any rate, she 'behaved as such.' See my edition of the *Romance of Partenay*, and the chapter on 'Melusine' in Baring-Gould's *Curious Myths of the Middle Ages*. The Irish spelling *bean-sighe* represents a form in which the *gh* corresponds to an Old Irish *d*, as the Old Irish form for *sighe* is *síde* (Windisch).

### 351. The Utas of Easter (7 S. x. 373; 1890).

The amusing derivation of *utas* from the Latin *ut* (which forms a part of the word *gamut*) is a fine specimen of 'partial' etymology [1]. I define 'partial' etymology as that which only takes account of a part of a word, as if one were to derive *yellow* from the verb to *yell*, without any attempt to account for the *-ow*. But, of course, we must account for the *-as* just as much as the *ut-*. May I repeat that *utas* is merely a variant form of the very word *octaves* itself, as explained in my *Dictionary*?

I have given further references at p. 832 of the second edition of my larger *Dictionary*. The Lat. acc. *octavas* is spelt *utaves* in Anglo-French, in the *Year-books* of Edward I, ii. 407; and *utavs* in the same, i. 75. *Utas* resulted from the loss of *v* in the awkward form *utavs*.

### 352. Curiosities of Derivation: Inkpen (7 S. x. 374; 1890).

The notion of deriving *Inkpen*[2] from *ing*, meadow, and the Celtic *pen*, inverts the order of combination. Surely every one should know that when English and Celtic are combined, the Celtic portion of the word comes first, not second. It is an easy guess that *Inkpen* is from *ing* and *pen*, and, fortunately, it is capable of proof; for the spelling *Inge-penne* occurs in Kemble's *Codex Diplomaticus*, which is the first book to be consulted, and is, therefore, seldom consulted at all. Perhaps it may now dawn upon some

---

[1] [It was actually put thus :—'The octave had the same name as the key-note *ut*. Hence (!) the Utas of Easter are the octaves of Easter.']

[2] [Inkpen is in Berkshire. In *N. and Q.* x. 106, a comic sentence was quoted from Cobbett's *Rural Rides*, 1853, p. 36 :—'At a village, certainly named by some author (!), called Inkpen.' But let us hope that Cobbett was in jest. This was followed up by a serious attempt to derive *Inkpen* from Saxon and Celtic.]

minds that *pen* is an English word altogether, and that *ingpen* is merely a pen (for sheep, &c.) in a meadow.

**353. 'To' as a sign of the Infinitive** (7 S. x. 425; 1890).

This is well treated in Mätzner's *Grammar*; but I do not find any clear example there of the earliest use of *to* with the *simple* infinitive, as distinguished from the *gerundial*. I doubt if it can be found before 1066. I here make a note of its occurrence in the latest copy of the A. S. Gospels, after 1150. We there find, in Matt. xi., the gerundial infinitive *to cumene* in v. 3; the simple infinitive *geseon* in vv. 7, 8; but in v. 9 we actually have *to geseon*, though all the earlier copies omit the *to*.

**354. 'For to'** (7 S. x. 472; 1890).

*For to*, usually expressive of 'purpose,' occurs centuries before Chaucer, as, e. g., in Layamon's *Brut*. Mätzner's *English Grammar*, as translated by Grece, vol. iii. pp. 53-57, gives four pages of explanation and examples. It occurs even in late Anglo-Saxon, as e. g. in the A. S. *Chronicle*, anno 1127, but was probably suggested by the use of *por* (*pour*) with the infinitive in Anglo-French, so that this usage is due to the Norman Conquest. The A. S. infinitive was simple, without *to*; the prefixing of *to* made it gerundial; as in Matthew xi. 3, xiii. 3.

**355. Rimer: the name of a tool** (7 S. x. 456; 1890).

The meaning and etymology of this word are duly given in my *Principles of Eng. Etymology*, first series, sect. 197, p. 209. It merely means 'roomer,' or 'enlarger,' being regularly derived, by vowel-change, from A. S. *rūm*, room; just as *mice* is the plural of *mouse*, A. S. *mūs*. The pronunciations *reamer* and *rimmer* are interesting and regular. The former is the archaic pronunciation of the Middle English period, the latter is the regular shortening of the old long *i* (pronounced *ee*) caused by accentual stress.

**356. 'Nineted' or 'Nighnted' Boys** (7 S. xi. 37; 1891).

Merely bad spellings of *'ninted*, a provincial pronunciation of *anointed*. It has been discussed long ago; see *N. and Q.*, 3rd S. viii. 452, 547; ix. 359, 422. Halliwell gives :—

'*Anointed*, chief, roguish; " an *anointed* scamp; *West*." '

The spelling with *ghn* is not justifiable in English. Those who can believe that *'ninted* is short for 'nigh-unto'd' must be strangely credulous. [See above, p. 4.]

**357. Kilter. I** (7 S. xi. 38; 1891).

[In answer to the question as to the meaning of *kilter*, as used by Howells, in his novel *The Shadow of a Dream* (p 17, and a little further on). 'He was rather expecting the doctor himself in the afternoon; he had been out of *kilter* for two or three years, but he was getting all right now.' Again—'I left him to infer that everybody was out of *kilter*.']

*Kilter* or *kelter* was an 'Anglicism' long before it was an 'Americanism.' Skinner, in 1671, has '*kelter*; he is not yet in kelter, nondum est paratus.' It is also given in my reprint of Ray's Collection of 1691. The *k* before *i* points to a Scandinavian origin. Cf. Dan. *kilte*, to truss, tuck up, whence E. *kilt*. Rietz gives Swed. dial., *kilter-band*, a band for holding up tucked-up clothes; *kiltra sig*, to gird up, tuck up and fasten. The metaphor is obvious enough.

**358. Kilter. II** (7 S. xi. 96; 1891).

At the last reference (xi 38) we are correctly told that in Johnson's *Dictionary* this word is derived from 'Dan. *kelter*, to gird.' I merely wish to warn all who care for facts not to trust Johnson's *Dictionary* for etymologies. The Danish verb is not *kelter*, but *kilte*.

The final *r* in *kelter*, as here quoted, really means that Johnson gives Danish verbs under the form of the present singular indicative, first person. Thus Dan. *kilter* (not *kelter*, after all), means 'I gird.' This peculiarity pervades Johnson's *Dictionary*; he probably never realized the difference between this part of the verb and the infinitive mood.

It is a curious fact that our Latin-Dictionary writers are just as bad. They tell us that *amo* means 'to love.' Does it, indeed? Then what is Latin for 'I love'?

### 359. Leezing or Leesing = Gleaning (7 S. xi. 156; 1891).

The usual spelling is *leasing*, and it is duly explained in Miss Jackson's *Shropshire Word-Book*. Why the propounder of the query, whilst deprecating the scorn of etymologists (which means, I suppose, that he is ignorant of the etymology), should nevertheless feel himself constrained to give a fatuous guess, is one of those things that I never could understand. Guessing is not so meritorious or glorious after all, though it has long been adored as if it were. *Lease* is simply the A. S. *lesan*, to glean, which became *lease* in Tudor English, because the A. S. short *e* passed into the open *ē* (denoted by *ea*), in an open syllable. Cf. *brecan*, to break.

### 360. Mattins (7 S. xi. 196; 1891).

This spelling is nothing new; it has been discussed over and over again (see e. g. *N. and Q.*, 3 S. x.). To call the spelling 'trying' is to judge by the eye, whereas spelling should be judged by the ear. *Matins* is the usual spelling, certainly; only the word was once *matínes*, with short *a* and long accented *i* (*ee*). When the accent was thrown back, it would have been just as well to double the *t*, as in *matter*, from M. E. *matére*. But it was stupidly left unmended. This is just why our spelling is all in confusion. There is never anything right in spelling, except when (as is often the case) it has the luck to be phonetic.

### 361. The Surname Egerton (7 S. xi. 233; 1891).

The derivation of this name from Lat. *agger* (!) suggested at the last reference, is wholly out of the question. There is no mystery about it. *Eger-* is merely a worn-down form of A. S. *Ecgheard* (lit., edge-hard, i. e. with keen sword), a name which appears in the *Liber Vitae* and in the A. S. charters. An intermediate form is *Ecgerd,* appearing in *Ecgerdeshel,* which Kemble identifies with Eggershall, Hants. *Ecgeard* regularly became *Edgerd* or *Egerd,* whence *Eger,* by the loss of final *d* before the *t* in *-ton.*

### 362. Swastika: Fylfot (7 S. xi. 278; 1891).

Before this subject is dropped I should like to ask for a reference for the word *fylfot* in any old book. I really cannot find it, except in books of quite modern date. No one has thrown the faintest light as yet on the history and chronology of the first appearance of this word in English. Even a quotation as old as 1800 would be better than nothing. Where in any reasonable book, not written by an 'etymologist,' can I find it spelt *fugelfot,* or *felafote,* or *fuelfot,* or, in fact, in any form at all? I have no belief in these spellings, except as representing guesses.

*Svastika* is duly explained in Benfey's *Sanskrit Dictionary,* with a reference to the ' Mālatīmādhava,' ed. Calc, 73, 15.

[No one was able to give an old quotation for *?fylfot.*]

### 363. Anglo-Saxon Personal Names: the 'Liber Vitæ' (7 S. xi. 376; 1891).

I am glad to see that Canon Taylor calls attention to the *Liber Vitae,* and to the shortcomings of Stevenson's edition. But I do not know that a photographic reproduction of the MS. is a necessity. There is an edition of it by Dr. Sweet, published only six years ago, which may fairly serve the purpose for a while. The name of the book is *The Oldest English Texts*, and it was published for the Early English Text Society in 1885. The *Liber Vitae* occupies pp. 153-166.

The names are all indexed, I believe; but the way of working the index is peculiar. Thus, I want, let us say, the name 'Eatthegn.' I look out 'Eat' in the index, and get a reference to p. 615; but the word is not under 'Eata.' Then I look out 'thegn,' and get a reference to p. 524, and there I find 'Eadthegn,' with its variants. Now that I know that 'Eadthegn' is a more correct spelling, I can look out 'Ead' in the index, and get a reference to p. 615 again. There, at last, I find it, under 'Ead.' The system is peculiar, but it will serve—when you have learnt the trick of it. [The diphthong in *ēad* is long.]

### 364. 'Out and Out' (7 S. xii. 5, 95; 1891).

It might be supposed that this is a modern phrase; but it is at least as old as the fifteenth century. 'Telle us now thi qwestyon alle *out and oute*' (i. e. entirely, fully) occurs in the *Coventry Mysteries*, ed. Halliwell, p. 205.

Further, Richardson quotes it from Chaucer, but gives an inexact reference. It occurs in *Troilus*, bk. ii. l. 739.

Before that, it occurs in the *Lives of the Saints*, formerly attributed to Robert of Gloucester. This I gather from the new edition of Kington Oliphant's *Old and Middle-English*, a book never to be neglected. [This *Lives of the Saints* is the same as the *Southern English Legendary*, edited by Dr. Horstmann for the Early English Text Society. But the reference for *out and out* was unluckily omitted by Mr. Oliphant, and I cannot find the phrase there.]

### 365. Sindbad's Voyages (7 S. xii. 30; 1891).

Surely students of Old English know the mention of the whale in *St. Brandan*. In Wright's edition of *St. Brandan*, published for the Camden Society in 1844 (forty-seven years ago), the editor says, in the very first page :—

'There are several remarkable points of similarity between St. Brandan and the Sindbad of the *Arabian Nights*, and at least one incident in the two narratives is identical—that of the disaster on the back of the great fish.'

I have my doubts about the story being brought from the East 'by Crusaders and palmers,' as Mr. Clouston suggests.

I suggest that it was 'brought from the East' before either Crusaders or palmers were invented; for it is a certain fact that the same story is familiar to students of our oldest English, from its occurrence in the Anglo-Saxon poem of 'The Whale,' printed at p. 360 of Thorpe's edition of the *Codex Exoniensis*, or Exeter Book. Thorpe's translation is so extremely bald that perhaps some of your readers may thank me for a less literal, yet sufficiently exact translation of a few lines of it. Speaking of the whale, the poet says :—

'Its appearance is like that of a rough rock; [it seems] as if it extended [lit. wandered] beside the shore of the channel, like the greatest of reedy islands surrounded by sand-dunes. Whence it happens that seafarers imagine that they are gazing with their eyes on some island, and so they fasten their high-stemmed ships with anchor-ropes to this false land; they make fast their sea-horses as if they were at the sea's brink, and up they climb on the island, bold of heart; the vessels stand, fast by the shore, surrounded by the stream. And then the voyagers, weary in mind, and without a thought of danger, encamp on the isle. They produce a flame, they kindle a vast fire. Full of joy are the heroes, late so sad of spirit; they are longing for repose. But when the creature, long skilled in guile, feels that the sailors are securely resting upon him, and are keeping their abode there, in enjoyment of the weather, suddenly into the salt wave, together with his prey, down dives the ocean-dweller and seeks the abyss; and thus, by drowning them, imprisons the ships, with all their men, in the hall of death.'

Nor is this the only reference earlier than *St. Brandan*. The story occurs in the Old English Bestiary, printed in

*An Old English Miscellany*, ed. Morris (E. E. T. S.), p. 17, and this poem can hardly be later than 1250. We know, too, the source of it, since it is translated from the Latin *Physiologus*, by Thetbaldus. Compare, too, the 'Livres des Creatures,' by Philip de Thaun, as printed in Wright's *Popular Treatises on Science*, pp. xiii, 108.

It is clear that the stories of the whale, the panther, the sirens, &c., found their way into English at an early period from Latin bestiaries, and the latter contain some embellishments of Eastern origin. This is the true history of the matter.

### 366. Words in Worcestershire Wills: 'Trow, a barge.' I (7 S. xii. 35; 1891).

The derivation of the name *Trowman* from *trow*, a Severn barge, is clear enough. But at the last reference (xi. 474) we are told that '*trow* is simply the O. E. *treo*,' a tree. This is not at all 'simple,' but decidedly difficult. The O. E. word was not *treo*, but *trēo*, and the O. E. *ēo* usually (simply) becomes Mod. E. *ee*; so that the result would be *tree*, as it is. It is true that the O. E. dat. case *trēowe* produced an occasional by-form *trou* in the Kentish dialect; but it would be better to suppose that *trow* represents the Mod. E. *trough*, which frequently appears as *trow* in Mid. Eng.; from O. E. *trog*.

### 367. Words in Worcestershire Wills: 'Trow a barge.' II (7 S. xii. 177; 1891).

I now find more evidence about the word *trow*. Before, I only suggested that *trow* represents the A. S. *trog* (sometimes spelt *troh*), a trough; but now I am sure of it. My new witness is our beloved king Alfred.

In his translation of *Orosius*, bk. ii. c. 5, we are told how Xerxes was fain to flee homewards in a fisher's boat. 'Hē eft wæs biddende ānes lytles *troges* æt ānum earmum men'; he was begging from a poor man the use of a little *trow*.

It turns out that the word *trog*, a trough, was also commonly used (as I expected) in the sense of a small boat. The glossaries published by Wülker give several examples; *e. g.*, in a list of boats, at col. 166, we find : 'Littoraria, *troh-scip*,' lit. trough-ship. *Littoraria* means a small boat that hugs the shore. And again, in another list of boats, at col. 289 : 'Littoraria, *troch-scip*.'

I conclude that it is better to work by phonetic laws than to guess.

### 368. Mute (7 S. xii. 46 ; 1891).

I find that the account of the word *mute* in my *Dictionary* is incorrect. It is not of French origin, but borrowed immediately from Latin. The M. E. *muet* is not the same word, but is borrowed from the O. F. *muet*, which represents a diminutive form *mutettus*, and not the primary form *mutus*. *Mute* is common in Shakespeare, but I presume that it was not in use at a much earlier date.

### 369. Drawing, Hanging, and Quartering (7 S. xii. 131 ; 1891).

Surely it is too late in the day to pretend that there is any ambiguity about the meaning of 'drawing' in the above phrase. Any one who has really read our Middle English writers with decent attention must know perfectly well that drawing *preceded* hanging. It ought not to be difficult to produce a vast number of quotations to prove this, but I do not mean to be at the trouble of looking for them. I will merely adduce the first instance that turns up :—

> 'Edrik was *hanged* on the toure, for his trespas.
> Than said the quene, that Edrik the giloure
> Had not fully dome, that fell to traytoure.
> Traytours with runcies [horses] suld men *first drawe*,' &c.
> Rob. *of Brunne*, tr. of Langtoft, ed. Hearne, p. 50.

### 370. Rake, a track (7 S. xii. 135; 1891).

*Rake*, in *Gawain and the Grene Knight*, l. 2144, clearly means horse-track, or road :—

'Ryde me doun this ilk *rake*, bi yon rokke-syde.'

In 1886 I published, for the Early English Text Society, the *Wars of Alexander*. The large glossary to that work is very helpful for Northern words. In l. 3383, the path of righteousness is called 'the *rake* of rightwysnes'; and, in l. 5070, a man is advised, of two roads, to choose 'the *rake* on the right hand.' Cf. Swed. *rak*, straight; *raka*, to run.

### 371. 'The Crow, with Voice of Care' (7 S. xii. 145; 1891).

In Chaucer's *Parl. of Foules*, l. 363, we have the fine expression: 'The crow with vois of care.' It is curious that this phrase is really due to a mistranslation.

The original line is in Vergil, *Georg.* i. 388 :

'Tum cornix plena pluuiam uocat *improba uoce*.'

The same mistake recurs in Batman's translation of *Bartholomè*, lib. xii. c. 9. Batman quotes the above line, and adds :—

'That is to understande, Now the Crowe calleth rayne *with an eleinge* [sad] *voyce*.'

### 372. Flaskisable (7 S. xii. 146; 1891).

This curious word is given neither in Stratmann nor in Halliwell. It occurs at least twice in Lydgate's *Siege of Troye*. Speaking of the inconstancy of women, he says that they afford the true 'patron,' i. e. pattern,

'Of inconstaunce, whose *flaskysable* kynde
Is to and fro meuynge as a wynde.'
Book I. ch. v. ed. 1555, fol. C 6, back.

Again, in speaking of the common herd of men, he says :—

'The comon people chaungeth as a phane [vane].
To-day they wexe, to-morrow do they wane
As doth the mone, they be so *flaskesable.*'
Book I. ch. vi. ed. 1555, fol. E 3.

It is clear that the sense is 'variable, changeable or inconstant.'

As to the etymology, I suppose it to be a mere variant of O. F. *flechisable*, the O. F. equivalent of our *flexible*, from *flechir*, to bend. *Flechisable* is sometimes spelt *flacisable*, and *flechir* is also *fleschir*, and even *flanchir*. Moreover, *flechisable* occurs in the very sense of 'variable,' and is applied, as in Lydgate, to the nature of women (see examples in Godefroy). Perhaps Lydgate confused it with O. F. *flasquir* or *flachir*, which means to soften or render flaccid, from *flaccidus*.

### 373. Kilt (7 S. xii. 156; 1891).

With regard to the quotation cited at this reference, showing that *kelt*, sb., was in use in 1786[1], and the request for an earlier instance, I can give one that is earlier by more than two centuries. In Douglas's translation of Vergil we are told that the goddess Venus wore 'hir skirt *kiltit* till hir bair kne.' Cf. *Nuda genu*, *Aen.* i. 320. Probably she set the fashion. [See *Kilter*, p. 296.]

### 374. Ceriously, or Seriously (7 S. xii. 183; 1891).

*Ceriously* occurs in Chaucer's *Man of Lawes Tale*, l. 185, and is merely another spelling of *seriously*; but is used in the peculiar sense of Lat. *seriatim*, in due order, in detail, minutely. In my note on the passage I give a quotation for it from Fabyan's *Chronicle*. The *New*

---

[1] 'A volunteer of the 73rd Regiment lost his *kelt* in the attack.' Capt. Drinkwater, *History of the Siege of Gibraltar*, 1786 (fourth ed.), p. 202.

*English Dictionary*, quite rightly, s. v. 'Ceryows,' refers us to 'Serious.' Meanwhile, some further illustrations of this word will be acceptable to many readers of Chaucer.

In Skelton's *Garland of Laurell*, l. 581, we have:—

'And *seryously* she shewyd me ther denomynacyons.'

Dyce's note (vol. ii. p 452) has:—

'I. e. *seriatim*. So in a letter from Tuke to Wolsey·—"Thus proceding to the letters, to shewe your Grace *summarily*; for rehersing every thing *seriously*, I shal over long moleste your Grace."' (*State Papers*, 1830, i. 299.)

But the most interesting point is that Lydgate caught up this word from his master, and in his *Siege of Troye* has used it over and over again. I give only a few examples:—

'And whan the kyng had herd *ceriously*
Thentent of Jason sayd so manfully.'
Book I. ch. v, ed. 1555, fol. C 4, back.

'As in this boke ye may hereafter rede
*Ceryously*, if that ye list take hede.'
Book II. ch. x, fol. F 2, back.

'How *seryously* Guido doth expresse.'
Book II. ch. xv, fol. K 1.

(The context is too long to quote.)

'I must the trouthe leue
Of Troye booke, and my mater breue,
And ower passe, and not go by and by,
As doth Guydo in ordre, *ceryously*.'
Book II. ch. xv, fol. K 2.

'And fyrste in Messa he telleth of the fyght
Whan they entred, and of their welcomyng,
And *ceryously* he tolde eke of the kynge.'
Book II. ch. xx, fol. M 5.

'And she him tolde the aunswere of the kynge,
*Ceryously*, gynnynge, and endinge.'
Book IV. ch. xxx, fol. T 3, back.

Other references are book IV. ch. xxx, fol. T 5, col. 2; id., fol. U 4, col. 1; book IV. ch. xxxii, fol. X 3, l. 1; id., fol. X 3, back, col. 2, &c.

We thus have the clearest proof of the sense attached by Lydgate to Chaucer's word; and Lydgate is the best commentator we have upon Chaucer's language.

In Shakespeare, *seriously* has its usual sense; but in Chaucer its equivalent *ceriously* has a sense which has long been obsolete.

### 375. Old (7 S. xii. 186; 1891).

Those who are interested in Shakespeare's familiar use of this word in such phrases as '*old* swearing,' '*old* coil,' and the like, may be pleased to see a fifteenth-century example of the same :—

'With sharpe swyrdys faght they then,
They had be two full doghty men,
Gode *old* fyghtyng was there.'
'Le Bone Florence,' l. 679, in Ritson's *Metrical Romances*, iii. 29.

### 376. Styed=Advanced (7 S. xii. 231; 1891).

Certainly 'advanced' is a very misleading explanation of *styed*. *Styed* simply means 'climbed,' and hence 'ascended,' as in the illustration given. *Sty*, a ladder, something to climb by, is one of its derivatives, as has been explained over and over again. *Stirrup*, 'a rope to climb by,' is another derivative.

It is inconceivable to me how any one can confuse this with 'stricken in years,' as it has nothing whatever to do with it. However, both words begin with *st*, and that seems to be enough to send people all astray.

The Swedish word *ålderstigen* (the first letter is not *a*, as printed) means 'advanced in years,' and may, if you please, be translated by 'styed in years'; but it is misleading, because, though the Swedish verb *stiga* came to be used in this way, there is nothing (that I can find) to show that the English *sty* was ever so used. Any one who thinks otherwise can convince me by producing a quotation.

But what has *styed* to do with *stricken*? By what process can human ingenuity torture one word into the other?

It is true that the A. S. *stīgan* (not *stigan*, for the *i* was long) was a strong verb, and should rather have produced the pp. *styen*, and might conceivably do so in dialects.

And we may admit that the A. S. pp. form was *stigen*.

Then, I suppose, the (imaginary) steps are these: *stigen* became *stiken*, on the principle that water runs uphill; and *stiken* became *striken*, and *striken* came to be written *stricken*.

If your correspondent can produce a quotation for '*stiken* in years' or '*sticken* in years,' I do not care which, I am convinced at once. No one ever saw it yet.

It is clear that your correspondent knows nothing about the A. S. *g*. He probably thinks that *stīgan* was pronounced with a *g* like that in *go*. So it was, just at first, but it soon passed into the sound of *y*, and practically disappeared. This is why there is no *g* in *sty*, to climb; nor in *sty*, a ladder; nor in *pig-sty*; nor in *stirrup*.

All this is familiar to any student of English philology and it is all in my book on *English Etymology*, vol. i.

Perhaps the insinuation is that we borrowed the term bodily from Scandinavian. But that will not do either, because we should then have borrowed the whole word, and if it had been borrowed at all early, the *g* in *stigen*, being between two vowels, would have passed into *y* and disappeared, like all others in the same condition throughout the language. It certainly could never have become a *k*, because the tendency is exactly the other way, viz., from *k* to *g*; as in *flagon* for the older *flacon*.

And all this impossible theory is put forward to account for *stricken*, which (it is calmly assumed) cannot (why not?) be derived from A. S. *strīcan*, to advance!

And the argument is, that *strīcan* did not exist in A. S., because none of the other Teutonic tongues has this verb!

At this rate we are obliged to ask leave of all other nations before we may have a verb of our own—a thing which no other nation would dream of doing. I protest strongly against this extraordinary method of limiting English, which is one of the most original of all Teutonic tongues, and abounds with archaisms unknown to them. And the last argument is—'*if* the quoted *strican* goes so far back.'

Well, the phrase, 'strīceth ymbūtan,' i.e. goes about, occurs in Rawlinson's edition of Alfred's *Boethius*, p. 177. What other 'Teutonic tongue' can show a quotation for it as old as Alfred's time? So that is soon settled.

However, it is common also in Old German. Schade's *Dictionary* explains how the O. H. G. *strīhhan* not only meant to 'stroke' and to 'strike,' but also, intransitively, to 'hasten,' to 'go about,' &c. ('sich rasch bewegen, ziehen, wandern, streifen, herumstreifen, eilen').

As for the Mid. Eng. use, see Stratmann; I really cannot quote about the 'streem that *striketh* (flows) stille' all over again. The pp. is *striken*. It never has any other form, but its senses vary wonderfully. A similar phrase is 'he *strek* into a studie,' he fell into a revery; *William of Palerne*, 4038.

I am sorry this is so long; but it takes up much room to unravel a tangle of this description.

377. **Welsh, adj. 'nauseous'** (7 S. xii. 236; 1891).

*Welsh* means nauseous, insipid, mawkish; it implies something that *turns* the stomach. It is another form (but with mutation of *a* to *e*, as in *Welsh* from *Wales*) of *wallowish*. Halliwell has '*Wallow*, flat, insipid'; also '*Wallowish*, nauseous. Hereford.' In the *Promptorium Parvulorum*, p. 515, we have '*walhwe-swete*, or *walow-swete*,' i.e. so sweet as to make one bilious. It is allied to the Eng. *walk* and *wallow*, and to Lat. *uoluere*, all with the notion of rolling about.

Still more closely allied are the Low German *walgig* and *walghaftig*, adjectives signifying 'productive of nausea'; and the Low German *walgen*, to feel nausea. The root-verb occurs in the Mid. High German *welgen*, to roll about, pt. t. *walg*; see Schade. Schade gives a large number of related words, such as *walg*, rounded; *walgern*, to roll; *walagōn*, to roll oneself about, also to walk; *wulgerung*, nausea, &c. It is, therefore, quite free from all connexion with *Wales*.

### 378. Whitsun Day I (7 S. xii. 277; 1891).

At the last reference (7 S. xii. 233) Mr. W. says that 'we have the word *whitsul*.' Where, pray, does it occur? Let us have the reference for it. And, after that, let us have the reference for *Whitsulday*. I believe both forms to be wholly unauthorized; and I do not see how the process of inventing forms can be justified.

[It turned out that the word intended was certainly *whitsul* in form, but the sense of it was so entirely remote from any connexion with *Whitsunday*, that it is hardly wonderful that I did not, at the moment, recognize it. The argument was this: '*Whitsul* is given as a provincial word in Todd's *Johnson*, with a passage from Carew explaining it. *Sool* is anything eaten with bread to flavour it, as butter, cheese, milk. With milk it would be *whitsul*. The white meat given to the poor at Whitsuntide brings the whole into connexion' (!) The last sentence is delicious. See further in my reply below.]

### 379. Whitsun Day. II (7 S. xii. 449; 1891).

The etymology of *whitsul* at the last reference is quite correct, viz., from *white* and *sool*. *Sool* is explained in my notes to *Piers Plowman*, and again in my glossary to *Havelok*. It not only occurs at line 767 of that poem, but again at ll. 1143, 2905.

Further information about it is given in **Herrtage's** notes to the *Catholicon Anglicum*, p. 349, and the etymology is from the A. S. *sufol*, which occurs in my edition of the *A. S. Gospels* (John xxi. 5), to translate the Latin *pulmentarium*.

But all this has nothing whatever to do with *Whitsunday*, which certainly never was called *Whitsulday*; neither is there the slightest evidence that such a compound as *Whitsulday* was ever dreamt of. On the other hand, not only is 'Whitsun-week' a legitimate expression, but I have already given a reference for it in a dictionary which seems to have been neglected. It occurs in Wycliffe's *Works*, ed. Arnold, ii. 161. It is a mere contraction for *Whitsunday week*, which is called *hvítasunnudagsvika* in Icelandic. In the *Ancient Laws of Norway*, previous to A.D. 1263, as published by Munch and Keyser, Christiania, 1846–47, we already find the expression 'Paskaviku, ok *Hvítasunnudagsviku*,' vol. i. p. 150. Curiously enough, it was sometimes the syllable *sun* that was dropped, and then we find mention of *Hvitadagavika*, lit. 'Whiteday-week,' or 'Whitday-week.' There is nothing remarkable about such dropping of a syllable; every one says *?fo'c'sle* for *?forecastle*. It would be comic enough if we were to pretend on that account that *?fo'c'sle* is 'derived' from *fox-hole*; although phonetic laws would certainly admit of such a derivation.

I showed once, in the *Academy*, that *Palm Sunday* is abbreviated to *Palmsun*, and that even such a phrase as *Palmsun Tuesday* has been in use. The note at the end of my Supplement to the second edition of my *Dictionary* seems as applicable now as ever. 'The Welsh name *Sulgwyn*, Whitsuntide, is literally *white sun*, from *sul*, sun, and *gwyn*, white. This name is old, and is a mere translation from the English name at a time when it was rightly understood. But experience shows that no arguments will convince those who prefer guesswork to evidence. The wrong ideas about this word are still persistently cherished.'

For those who wish to come at the truth I have one more word, which will, I believe, interest them. In Westwood's beautiful book called *Palæographia Sacra Pictoria*, the last facsimile but one gives a specimen from MS. Addit. 503 in the British Museum, an Icelandic MS. which he attributes to the twelfth century. This quotation, accidentally chosen, actually refers to the services for Whitsunday, and the editor has failed to read it correctly. His version is: 'A Himta Sunnu Dag skal fyrst syngia Veni, Creator Spiritus.' There is no such word as 'Himta,' and when we turn to the facsimile, we see that the real word is 'Huyta,' where *u*, as usual, is used for *v* before a following vowel, and *y* is miswritten for *i*, as is so common, not only in Icelandic, but in Anglo-Saxon MSS., owing to the confusion between the sounds which they denoted, viz., the sound of the G. *ü* in *übel*, and the sound of the E. *ee* in *deep*.

The real reading of this beautifully written and early MS. is as follows: 'A Huyta Sunnu Dag skal fyrst syngia Veni, Creator Spiritus: Kom thu göde heilage ande,' &c. That is, 'On White Sunday shall (one) first sing *Veni, Creator Spiritus*: come, thou good holy Spirit,' &c.

What can be more satisfactory to those who care for evidence?

### 380. Commence to (said to be not an English Idiom) (7 S. xii. 294; 1891).

Surely this was an English idiom from the outset! Thus in *P. Plowman*, C. xv. 203, we are told that Imaginative 'comsed to loure,' i.e. commenced to frown. Many more examples might be given.

**381. The Treatment of Triple Consonants** (7 S. xii. 322; 1891).

The occurrence of three consonants together in the middle of a word necessarily gives rise, in many instances, to a difficulty of pronunciation. The simplest way of getting over this is to drop one of them, and the one usually dropped is the middle one. If the middle one be *s*, it remains; as in *bust* for *burst*, *gorse* for A. S. *gorst*.

We have several examples in English in which, though all three consonants are retained in spelling, the middle one is either not pronounced at all or else is very lightly touched.

Examples are: castle, nestle, wrestle, thistle, whistle, epistle, bristle, gristle, apostle, jostle, bustle, rustle, and, generally, words ending in *-stle*. Even for *ghastly* speakers of dialect are apt to say *gashly*; see Tregellas on the Cornish dialect.

Again, it is quite common to hear people (even those who protest that they certainly do not) drop the *p* in *redemption, exemption, assumption, consumption, presumption*, so also in *Campbell, Hampden, Hampton*. Most people confuse *handsome* and *Hansom*, and it is probable that, etymologically, the words are identical. The *t* is dropped in *waistcoat*.

In place-names the same principle is still more strongly at work. Hence the common pronunciation of Windsor, Guildford, Hertford, Lindsey, Landguard, and many others.

The cases most interesting to the etymologist are those in which the middle consonant has actually disappeared from the spelling. I have noted the following: *garment* for *garn(e)ment*, allied to *garn-ish*; *worship* for *worth-ship*; *worsted* for *Worthstead*; *wilderness* for *wild-deer-ness*; *blossom* from A. S. *blōstma*, with loss of *t*; *Norman* for *Northman*.

In place-names this result is common; as in Norfolk for Northfolk, Norton for Northton, Weston for West-ton, Easton for East-ton, Kirby for Kirkby; Kirton for Kirkton, Sanford for Sandford, Burford for Burghford; Burley for Burghley; Burstead for Burghstead, Burton for Burghton.

In some cases especial care must be taken in order to prevent mistakes. Still, when we find that *Preston* is short for *Prest-ton* (Priest-town), we shall hardly be wrong in assuming that *Prescott* is for *Prest-cott* (Priest-cot). But, in order to be sure, we must always rely, as has been usual, upon the older spellings found in the charters.

### 382. Leighton (7 S. xii. 345; 1891).

The explanation of this name is an interesting example of the operation of phonetic laws. The A. S. *lĕac-tūn*, lit. 'leek-town,' i.e. vegetable enclosure, garden, became *lĕactun*, with shortening of *u*. But the combination *ct* becomes *ht* in Anglo-Saxon (see Mayhew, *O. E. Phonology*, p. 140). Hence we also find the forms *lĕahtun*, *lĕhtun*. The Latin *hortus* is glossed by *lehtun* in the Lindisfarne MS., John xviii. 1. The A. S. *ht* became M. E. *ght*, and so we should get a Mod. E. *Leghton* or *Leighton* (with *ei* as in *vein*) quite regularly.

I believe the derivation of M. E. *leih-tun*, a garden, from A. S. *lēah*, fallow land, given in Stratmann, to be a pure oversight. It is needless, and gives no sense. A garden and fallow-land are very different things. Of course, some of the place-names of this form may be due to a combination of *lēah*, lea, and *tūn*, town; but the derivation from A. S. *lēhtun*, a garden, a compound already existing in A. S., really seems more probable. The change from the *k* in *leek* to the guttural *h* (*gh*) presents, in this case, no difficulty at all, being quite regular.

It is possible that the spelling Leyton is from a different source,—viz. *lēah*; but I think that our rather numerous Leightons are due to the fact that gardens were not uncommon; and I think they should be dissociated from the form Leigh, a lea.

### 383. Stalled (i.e. sated, tired) of walking: Stalled Ox (7 S. xii. 357; 1891).

These phrases are connected. The word is practically explained in my *Dictionary*, though I do not give all the senses.

The first occurrence of *stall* in English is in the *Corpus Glossary* of the eighth century, written in the true Mercian dialect. We there find 'Stabulum, *stal*'; see Hessels's ed., under 'S. 512.' Thus the earliest recorded sense is 'stable' or 'stall for cattle,' still in common use.

The corresponding Icelandic sb. is *stallr*, stall, a crib for cattle, whence was made the verb *stalla*, to put in a stall. The Swedish use is particularly clear; Widegren's *Dictionary* gives:—

'*Stall*, a stable for horses; *stalla*, to stall-feed, to stall; *stallad boskap*, stall-fed cattle; *stalla oxer*, to stall-feed bullocks.'

In Prov. xv. 17, I have already said that *stalled* means 'stall-fed.' In fact the Vulgate has *saginatum*, and Wyclif has 'maad fat.' Thus *stalled* meant *stall-fed* (for which I refer to Chapman's *Homer*, *Od.*, xv. 161) i.e. fatted, as in 'fatted calf.' Hence the notion of full-fed, satiated, sated; and to be *stalled* of walking is to be sated with walking, hence tired, &c. See Peacock's *Manley and Corringham Words* (E.D.S.); other publications of the E.D.S.; Kluge's *Germ. Dict.*; Skinner's *Dict.* 1671; Richardson's *Dictionary*; Johnson's *Dictionary*; Webster's *Dictionary*; the Century *Dictionary*, &c.

### 384. Godiva (7 S. xii. 404; 1891).

Tennyson has the line:—

'Godiva, wife to that grim earl, who ruled,' &c.

We are all agreed to accent *Godiva* on the *i*, and to call it a long vowel (strictly a diphthong). Still, as a matter of curiosity, there is no harm in knowing that the accent was on the *o*, and that the *i* was short, i.e. it was 'Gódĭva.' For it is a Latinized spelling of A. S. *God-gifu*, lit. 'God-gift'; see Freeman's *Old Eng. History*. And we do not pronounce *give* so as to rhyme with *strive*.

### 385. Paragon (7 S. xii. 412; 1891).

Two correspondents kindly suggest a reference to my *Dictionary*, where I give the etymology from the Span. prepositions *para con* (for Lat. *pro*, *ad*, and *cum*). This is the etymology given by Diez, and long accepted without dispute. But an article which has appeared in the *Zeitschrift für Roman. Philol.*, iv. 374, makes out a better case for a derivation from the Greek, viz. from Greek παρακόνη, a touch-stone. Despite the great authority of Diez, the derivation from three prepositions presents much difficulty.

### 386. 'Bravo': sometimes (wrongly) applied to a woman (7 S. xii. 432; 1891).

Alas! is the glory of Charles James Yellowplush indeed departed? Does no one recall his weighty words? I, for one, do not forget what he once wrote in his *Diary*:—

'Been to the Hopra. Music tol lol. That Lablash is a wopper at singing. I coodn make out why some people called out *Bravo*, some *Bravar*, and some *Bravee*.

"*Bravee*, Lablash," says I, at which hevery body laft.'

I withhold the reference. Let your readers discover how great a master they have neglected.

### 387. A Woodcut; with the legend 'Strike here' (7 S. xii. 478; 1891).

The words 'Strike here' translate *Percute hic*, a saying on which turns the story of Gerbertus, in the *Gesta Romanorum*; Tale 107, in Swan's translation. The story is retold in my poem entitled *The Dyer's Tale*, written in imitation of Chaucer, and printed in the *Universal Review* for December 16, 1889.

I have since observed that it is also given in William Morris's *Earthly Paradise*.

### 388. Wicket (7 S. xii. 506; 1891).

In my *Dictionary*, I derive this form from an *assumed* Anglo-French form *wiket*, which, as I have shown, must have been the right form, though no quotation occurs for it. And now I have found it!

'Li fol entre enz par le *wiket*';

i. e. the fool enters in by the wicket. It occurs in *Le Roman de Tristan*, ed. Michel, vol. ii. p. 101, l. 245. It is always a comfort to find a predicted form.

### 389. St. Parnell (8 S. i. 10; 1892).

I thought every one knew that *Pernel* was a medieval saint. My note to *Piers Plowman*, C. v. 111 (B. iv. 116) is clear enough:—

'*Purnele*, or *Peronelle*, from Petronilla, was a proverbial name for a gaily-dressed, bold-faced woman. . . . May 31 was dedicated to St. Petronilla the virgin. She was supposed to be able to cure the quartan ague; Chambers, *Book of Days*, ii. 389. The name, once common, now scarcely survives except as a surname, in the form Parnell; see Bardsley's *Eng. Surnames*, p. 56.'

• Any book of saints' lives will explain the matter, under the date May 31. That the same person is called *Petronilla* in Latin, and *Peronelle*, *Pernell*, or *Purnel* in English, is obvious from a comparison of the various accounts. Cf. Brand's *Popular Antiquities*, ed. Ellis, pp. 359, 363.

The inquiry 'by what stages Petronilla became Parnell,' is one that fills me with delight. For if once scientific explanation comes to be demanded, the day of the etymological guess-mongers will be gone for ever.

The answer is: by regular and recognized phonetic changes, which have all been duly tabulated by scientific workers. *Petronilla* became *Parnell* for the simple reason that it could not, under the circumstances, become anything else. Cf. F. *père* from *patrem*, F. *errer* from Lat. *iterare*, folk-Latin *eterare* or *etrare*. Also F. *?fermer* from Lat. *firmare*, illustrating the change from *i* to *e*. The Anglo-French was properly *Pernel*, which is the usual form in Middle-English; and this became *Parnell*, just as *person* became *parson*, viz. by the usual change of the M.E. *er* to the modern English *ar*.

### 390. The Genders of English Substantives
(8 S. i. 43; 1892).

Modern English gender is mainly logical, depending upon the thing signified. But Old English gender was purely grammatical, depending, in a great measure, upon the form of the word.

One of the greatest gains of modern English is the abandonment of grammatical gender, so that we no longer have to burden our memories with the differences of usage due to this source. Grammatical gender has thus become a mere matter of history, and is now only a curiosity. I think many of your readers may be pleased to learn from how much they have thus been delivered. To this end, I here give a brief list, by way of specimen, of a few of our principal substantives, with their original genders. I purposely avoid the mention of things having life. With respect to these, it may suffice to notice that a *bear*, a *fish*, a *ghost*, a *hound*, and a *wolf*, were all masculine; a *crow* and a *fly* were feminine; and a *child*, a *maiden* and *wife* (being things, apparently, of small significance) were all neuter.

The following nouns in Anglo-Saxon were all masculine:—
Ache, acre, apple, arm, ash (tree); beam, broom; cove (i.e. creek); day, deal, death, dew, dint, doom, dough, drop.

Ebb (of the tide), end; field, finger, flight, flood, foot, furze; gall, gleam, gloom; hate, helm (i.e. helmet), hip, holm, horn, hunger; loaf.

Meat, moon, mouth; neck; oath; path; rain, ridge, ring.

Shank, shield, shoe, sleep, smoke, snow, spark, staff, stake, stone, storm, stream, summer; tear (from the eye), thirst, thorn, thunder, tooth; way, wedge, well, will.

The following nouns were all feminine:—

Ashes (of wood), ax; bench, bliss, book, borough, bridge; cap, care, chin, chine (i.e. fissure, ravine), claw, crib (for cattle); deed.

Earth, edge; feather, furrow; glove; half, hall, hand, heart, heat, hell, hide, hose; liver, lore.

Mead or meadow, might; need, needle, night; oak; rung (of a ladder).

Sheath, sedge, shell, sill (of a door), sin, sinew, spade, speed, sun; thought, throat, tongue, toe, turf; week, weird (fate), womb, wort.

The following nouns were all neuter:—

Bale (evil), bath, bed, blood, bone, brim; cliff, coal, cud; dole, deer.

Ear, errand, eye; fire, flesh, foam; glee, gold, grass; head, hilt, holt; iron; kin; lair, land, leather, lid, light.

Main (i.e. force), meal (of corn), mood; net; seed, ship, shroud, sore; thigh, token, tree; water, web, wed (pledge), wonder, work; year, yoke.

Almost the only discoverable principle is that substantives denoting abstract qualities have a tendency to be feminine.

Examples are: bliss, care, heat, might, speed, thought, in the above list. Deed and lore are the same, as denoting doing and teaching. And we may add to this list an enormous number of substantives now ending in *-ing* and *-ness*.

It is very striking to observe with what impartiality the parts of the body are distributed. Thus—*arm, finger, foot, gall, hip, mouth, neck, shank, tooth,* are masculine · *chin, claw, hand, heart, hide, liver, sinew, throat, tongue, womb* (belly), are feminine; whilst *blood, bone, ear, eye, flesh, head, lid, thigh,* are neuter.

### 391. Saxon : derived from 'Sike,' a water-course (8 S. i. 51 ; 1892).

Whatever be the etymology of this word, it cannot be derived from *sike*! There is nothing in common but the letter *s*, so that Saxon is quite as nearly allied to *sag*, or *sack*, or *sick*, or *sock*, or *suck*, or half a score words more. Neither is *sike* an 'overlooked word'; it is familiar in the North. Any Northerner will tell you that it is far removed from the sense of 'marsh'; it means a 'channel' or 'water-course,' being the Icel. *sīk*, a ditch. There is a fine specimen between Caldron Snout and High Cup Nick.

It is certainly the origin of the name Sykes; but *Sykes* is not remarkably like *Saxon*. The usual old guess that connects Saxon with *seax*, a knife, short sword, is far more plausible, for it is possible; see *Sahso* in Schade. It is more sensible to wear a short sword than to squat in a water-course.

### 392. Cœlum : Cœlestis (8 S. i. 74 ; 1892).

The correct spellings are *cælum, cælestis* (with *æ*); or *caelum, caelestis* (with *ae*). See Lewis and Short's *Latin*

*Dictionary.* No authority now admits the derivation of these words from Greek. See Vaniček's *Griechish-Lateinisches Etymologisches Wörterbuch*, and Bréal's *Dictionnaire Étymologique Latin*. *Cælum* (with *æ*) is a mere dream of meddling editors: all MSS. spell it either *caelum* or *celum*. The word is, of course, very common even in English MSS.; it occurs in the *Lindisfarne MS.* as *caelum*, Matt. v. 18; and as *celis* (abl. pl.) in *Piers Plowman*, B. vii. 175.

### 393. Bayonet (8 S. i. 95; 1892).

Why not look up *bayonet* in the Oxford *Dictionary*? The word is there; and it is rather hard to ignore a book which, with all its faults, is by far the best dictionary we possess. I do not agree with the attacks that are made upon it.

The word meant 'a dagger' long before it meant a bayonet. Even the Supplement to my own *Etymological Dictionary* gives the usual quotation from Cotgrave (1611) and refers us to a publication named *N. & Q.* (3 S. xii. 287). The O. F. *baïon* is said by Roquefort to have meant an arrow or bolt of a crossbow. The earliest trace of this that I can find is in Godefroy, who says, 'Les arquebusiers sont appelés *bayonniers* dans la vielle *Chronique de France*, ch. xiv. citée par Dedaurière.' We are in great want, not of talk, but of early quotations.

### 394. Velvet (8 S. i. 177; 1892).

The list, *with references*, given at the last reference (8 S. i. 128) is most valuable[1]. We should be glad of

---

[1] The list contains early references for many fabrics. For *velvet* we have these:—'Velvet, 1319 (Wardr. Acct., 13 Edw. II, 22/14); velvet on satin, 1497 (Ib. 8-9 Hen. IV, 46/14, Q. R.); velvet on velvet, 1444 (Ib. 22-3 Hen. VI, 48/18, Q. R.); velvet plunket, 1337 (Ib. 10-12 Edw. III, 94/1, Q. R.); velvet bastard, 1420 (Ib. 8-9 Hen. V, 46/14, Q. R.); velvet figure, 1465 (Close Roll, 5 Edw. IV).

more contributions of this kind. I wish there were a law that we must all give our references. I should be glad to know how *velvet* is spelt in the documents referred to, i. e. if the MS. spellings are accessible. There is a special reason in this case, for it is tolerably certain that the form *velvet* is really due to a mistake.

The second *v* was once the vowel *u*, not the consonantal *v* (written as *u*); see my *Principles of English Etymology*, Second Series, p. 296, note. The old form *velu-èt* (=*velou-et*) was a trisyllable, in my belief.

Mr. Planché's earliest reference for the word is 1403, but we are now told that it occurs in 1319 (Wardr. Acct., 13 Edw. II, 22/14). In my list of *English Words in Anglo-French*, Second Series, I show that it occurs in 1361, in 1376, and in 1392 (see *Royal Wills*, ed. J. Nichols, 1780, pp. 48, 69, 130). In 1392 it is spelt *velwet*, as in the *Promptorium Parvulorum*, and this is practically a more original spelling than that with two *v*'s. The M. E. *u* is of so doubtful a value that it is difficult to tell whether it is a vowel or a consonant.

The trisyllabic form occurs in l. 1420 of the *Romaunt of the Rose*, where we have :—

'As softe as any velu-ët.'

And in Lydgate, *Complaint of the Black Knight*, l. 80—

'And softe as velu-ët the yong-ë gras.'

### 395. Suent : Suant ; a Devonshire word (8 S. i. 212 ; 1892).

The etymological spelling is *suant*, the pres. part. of *sue*, to follow, as *trenchant* is of the vb. *to trench*. So also *pur-suant*, from the verb *to pursue*. *Suant* means following, hence keeping on, continuous, regular, even, unremitting, and the like. I have explained it twice before. See my *Notes to P. Plowman*, p. 375 ; and Elworthy's *Glossary of W. Somersetshire Words*, s. v. 'Suant.'

### 396. Leary, 'knowing' (8 S. i. 244; 1892).

I believe this slang word, often used in the sense of 'knowing,' to be a word of quite respectable origin. It has been derived from M. E. *leren*, to teach; but that is not the way to form an adjective, and the substantival form is *lore*. I have no doubt that, like several other slang terms, it is of Dutch origin.

If we start, not from the E. sb. *lore*, but from the cognate Du. sb. *leer*, all comes right. Kilian gives '*Leerigh*, docilis'; so that the original sense was 'apt to learn.'

I think it very likely that we borrowed the substantive at the same time, as I find it in the last line but one of 'The Wife Lapped in Morrelles Skin,' printed in Hazlitt's *Early Popular Poetry*, iv. 226 :—

'Because she was of a shrewde *leere*,
Thus was she served in this manner[e].'

The date of this piece is a little before 1575. Words came in from the Dutch in the reign of Elizabeth.

### 397. On the Loss of v in English (8 S. i. 245; 1892).

There is still a good deal to be done in the way of tabulating phonetic changes in English, and I hope that the faithful drudges who attempt to register examples contribute somewhat to the clearer understanding of the subject. It occurs to me that the loss of *v* in English words seems to take place most commonly before *r*, *n*, and *l*.

Before *r*. We are accustomed, in poetry, to *e'er* for *ever*, *ne'er* for *never*, *o'er* for *over*. A similar effect is observable in Middle-English, where we find *discure* used for *discover*, and *recure* for *recover*; whilst the simple word *cover* sometimes became *cure*, as is attested at the present day by the word *curfew*. Two striking instances occur in *poor*, for the Middle-English and Anglo-French *povre*; and in *lark*, short for M. E. *laverk*, from A. S. *lāwerce*, later *lāferce* (=*lāverke*). In this connexion, we may compare the E. *surplus* with the Ital. *sovrappiù*. I explain the Scotch *orra*, 'superfluous,' as standing for *ovra*, as if it meant (so to speak) *over-y*; cf. G. *übrig*.

Before *n*. In poetry we often use *e'en* for *even*, cf. also *Hallowe'en*. Prov. E. has *gin* for *given*, and *aboon* for *aboven*. M. E. has the infin. *han* for *haven*. The most remarkable example is that of *laundress* for *lavandress*, from F. *laver*, to wash.

Before *l*. We often see *de'il* for *devil*, and the word *shovel* becomes *shool* or *showl* in Prov. E.

> 'I, said the Owl,
> With my spade and *showl*,
> I'll bury Cock Robin.'

There is a slight tendency to drop final *ve*, as in *gi'* for *give*. In M. E. the word *corsive*, sb., meaning something corrosive, also occurs as *corsy*; and the O. F. *pourcif*, short-winded, is now *pursy*. The commonest example is *jolly*, which even in Chaucer was spelt *iolif*. The final *f* in these words was voiced to *v*, owing to lack of stress, and then dropped. Cf. also *braw* for *brave*, and *doo* for *dove*; also *fi'-pun'-note*, and *twel'-pun'-ten*.

I have noted (*Eng. Etym.* I. 374) the loss of A. S. *ȝf* in *head, lord, lady, women, leman, Lammas*, and *stem* (of a tree); in all these cases the *ȝf* was voiced to *v* before disappearance.

**398. Curiosities of Interpretation. I** (8 S. i. 309; 1892).

Perhaps nothing strikes the student of English literature more than the curious helplessness of our editors, especially in former years, whenever they had to deal with somewhat difficult words. No doubt their books of reference were far inferior to what we have now; but in some cases they really do not seem to have used their common sense. The opinion was no doubt current, and still obtains in some quarters, that there is no such thing as skill or scholarship in relation to the English language; for these should be wholly reserved for the 'classical' languages, wherein 'accurate' knowledge is of course indispensable; although curiously enough, it does not usually extend to any care about correct pronunciation.

Almost any book of some slight antiquity yields some amusing specimens. I happen to take up *Early Ballads*, edited by Robert Bell. It is not worse than other books; indeed, it is better than many. But it will serve. Page 30: 'Now lith and listen, gentlemen.' The note is, '*Lith* or *lithe*, to tell or narrate.' This is all pure invention. If we apply it, we obtain as the sense, 'Now narrate and listen,' i.e. the auditors are requested to tell the story themselves. Of course, *lithe* means 'hearken,' and is synonymous with 'listen.'

 p. 44. 'Each of them slew a hart of greece.'

The note is, 'Also spelt *grize*, *greese*, &c. Literally a step or degree.' It therefore means 'a hart of steps.' But surely a hart is not usually so made as to resemble a staircase! The *greece* here meant is *grease*, in the sense of fatness, not the *greece* or *grees* which is the plural of *gree*, a step.

 p. 58. 'Forth they went, these yeomen two,
    Little John and Moche infere,
    And looked on moch emys house;
    The highway lay full near.'

The note says that *emys* means '*enemies*.' What *moch* means we are not informed. But *moch* should be *Moch*, with a capital, and 'Moch emys house' means 'the house of the uncle of Moch.' If they had resorted for repose to a house of their enemies, they must have been very stupid fellows.

p. 61. 'They slew our men upon our walls,
And sawtene us every day.'

The note says, '*Sawtene*, assaulted.' But it means 'assault'; the form for 'assaulted' would be *sawteden*. However, to have set this right would have required an elementary knowledge of English grammar.

p. 64. 'I gave him grithe, said our king.'

The note is '*Grithe*, grace.' But it means 'protection.'

p. 97. 'The Earl of Huntley, cawte and keen.'

The note is '*Cawte*, cautious.' This is obviously a guess, and of course no authority is either given or supposed to be necessary. The right solution is that *cawte* is written for *caute*, and *caute* is an error for '*cante*,' i.e. 'brisk,' by the usual confusion of *u* with *n*. As for '*cant* and *keen*,' it is the old, old phrase; as noted by Halliwell.

### 399. Curiosities of Interpretation. II (8 S. i. 349; 1892).

A famous book is Percy's *Reliques of Ancient Poetry*. I happen to possess a popular edition, edited by R. A. Willmott, a favourite book of mine, and convenient enough. Whether the interpretations of the hard words are Willmott's or Percy's, I do not stop to inquire. On the whole they are fairly correct, but the curious critic will find some strange examples in it.

One striking feature is the minute care with which, in some passages, words are explained which could hardly puzzle a small child, whilst in other cases words of some difficulty are carefully let alone, lest the editor should commit himself. At p. 76, for example, is this terribly tough line:—

'When we se tyme and nede.'

A note informs us that 'se tyme and nede' means 'see

time and need.' And now at last we make it out; but what a headache it must have cost the editor!

At p. 92, we are informed that *pyrats* means 'pirates,' and, again, that *thow* means 'thou.' It is clear that the editor found some difficulty here, and we can but wonder at his want of familiarity with old spelling.

In the poem of *Adam Bell*, on the other hand, at p. 87, we have the lines:—

> 'Over Gods forbode, sayde the kinge,
> That thou shold shote at me!'

The phrase 'Over Gods forbode' is left unexplained, probably because it is really difficult. It is, in fact, a false expression, due to a confusion of ideas.

The *literal* sense is '(may it be) against God's prohibition,' involving the confusion of two distinct phrases, such as 'God be *against* it,' and 'may God's prohibition prevent it'; in other words, 'God's forbode (be) over (it)' is turned precisely upside down, as if it were all one with '(be it) over God's forbode.' See *ofer* in Bosworth's *A. S. Dictionary*, and *forbod* in Mätzner. As this would have required rather a long note, and involves some investigation, the obvious plan was to say nothing.

In *Robin Hood and Guy of Gisborne* (p. 45), we have:—

> 'A sword and a dagger he wore by his side,
> Of manye a man the bane.'

And *bane* rhymes with *mayne*. The note tells us that *bane* means 'the curse';—that is to say, the words *ban*, a curse, and *bane*, the death, or the slayer, are actually confused together.

In *Henry, Fourth Erle of Northumberland* (p. 54) we have the lines:—

> 'Moste noble erle! O fowle mysuryd grounde
> Whereon he gat his fynal dedely wounde.'

The only interpretation of *mysuryd* here given is quoted

as Percy's own; and here it is: 'Misused, applied to a bad purpose.' And perhaps we may allow that a man puts a place to a very bad purpose if he employs it for the sake of getting a final wound on it. But the *ure* here meant has no connexion with *use*; it is merely the O. F. *eur* (F. *heur* in *bon-heur, mal-heur*) which popular etymology usually 'derives' from the Latin *hora*, though it really represents *augurium*. When we know this, it is easy to see that *mysuryd* means 'of ill augury,' i.e. fatal, unfortunate, unlucky, which is much more to the 'purpose.'

In the *Tournament of Tottenham*, st. xii, one of the combatants thus describes his crest:—

'I bere a reddyl and a rake,
Poudred wyth a brenand drake.'

*Reddyl* is not explained; it means 'a riddle,' i.e. a sieve. *Poudred* is not explained, nor is it easy. It is equivalent, in heraldry, to *semée*, i.e. strewn over, and is here incorrectly used, probably of set purpose. Strictly, it is only used of small objects, such as roses or fleur-de-lis, strewn over the field of the shield; but the poem is a burlesque, and the expression is put in the mouth of an ignorant clown. But when we come to 'a brenand drake' the explanation is given pat: 'Perhaps a firework so called, but here it seems to signify burning embers, or firebrands.' However, a *drake* is neither a firework, nor embers, nor firebrands, but simply a dragon, and 'a brenand drake' is our old friend 'a fiery dragon.' The joke of 'strewing the shield with a fiery dragon' has, I fear, been entirely lost upon the editors, and perhaps upon the readers, of Percy's *Reliques*.

**400. Curiosities of Interpretation. III** (8 S. i. 410; 1892).

I happen to take up a nice copy of the *Poetical Works* of Surrey and others, edited by Robert Bell. When it appeared I do not know, for it is undated. I find that the explanations of words in it are just of the usual sort; and that, whilst it is doubtless as good as other books of its kind, some of the statements display precisely such recklessness as we should expect to find. It is clear that it never used to be considered the duty of an editor to have any special knowledge of the older forms of English. But it should be known that it will not do to trust, in such a case, to the 'light of nature.'

I begin with the poems of Surrey. He says that, on reviewing his course :—

'I looked back to mete the place
From whence my weary course begun.'—p. 41.

As *mete* here means 'measure,' it would hardly seem to need a note; but we find this :—

'To dream; from *meteles*, dreams, Anglo-Saxon; also to measure. Drayton has *meterer*, a poet, which may be taken in either sense, a dreamer, or measurer of lines.'

Here are four mistakes at once. For (1) *mete* does not here mean to dream; (2) it is not derived from *meteles*, the derivation being the other way; (3) *meteles* is not the correct form at any date, neither is it a plural, the word meant being the M. E. *metels*, a dream; and (4) *meterer* means one who makes metres, and has nothing to do with it. Here is a fine bundle of blunders.

P. 85: *Reaveth* means 'bereaves'; but the note says: 'To *reave*, literally meant to unroof a house.' This is delicious. There was, indeed, a very rare word with this sense; but it is from another root.

P. 91, note 1: '*Wend* is the past participle of the verb *wene*, or *ween*, to suppose.' The context proves that it is the past tense.

P. 177, note 3: Surrey translates Virgil's *manes sepultos* (*Aen.* iv. 34) by 'graved ghosts.' The note says that *graved*

## CURIOSITIES OF INTERPRETATION.    329

is 'the preterite of the verb *grave*, to bury.' I put this note next the former to show that it is no part of an editor's duty to know a past tense from a past participle in English. But he ought to have known better as regards *sepultos*; for Latin grammar is taught in our schools.

P. 115: Surrey uses *vade* for 'to fade,' which is common enough. The note says it is 'from *vado*.' The spelling with *f* should have warned the editor against so bad a shot.

P. 166, note 3: Surrey has the form *lopen*, with the sense 'leapt.' The note says: 'Leapt; from the verb *lope*, to leap.' Where the editor found the form *lope* in MS., he does not tell us. *Loopen* is mere Dutch; the M. E. verb is *lepen*. The Mod. E. *leap* would make the pp. *lopen* still, if it had not been changed from a strong verb to a weak one. I am not surprised that our editors do not know English grammar; but I am surprised at their supposing that every one is bound to swallow any conjectures about it that it amuses them to make.

P. 173: Surrey has 'I wot not how.' The note says: 'Knew, from the Saxon verb *wote*, to know.' Here again the grammar is nowhere. I *wot* means I know, and the Saxon verb, in the infinitive mood, is *witan*, pres. t. *wāt*, pt. t. *wiste*. No one should edit an old English author till he knows the difference between *wit*, *wot*, *wist*, *wissen*, and *y-wis*. This is a fair test, and does not require too much. *I-wis* (the same as *y-wis*) is accordingly misinterpreted at p. 106. In the very next note the editor complains that Dr. Nott was 'misled by the orthography of *betook*' (which is perfectly correct). He explains that it is 'the Saxon *betoke*,' which is curious, as the word is of Norse origin. He clearly considers that you can manufacture 'Anglo-Saxon' forms by spelling words badly. And, in this particular, there are many who are of the same mind.

P. 179: Surrey translates *Aen.* iv. 92, thus:—

'Saturne's daughter thus *burdes* Venus then.'

The note is:—

'Beards. The word is frequently used by the Elizabethan dramatists, signifying to oppose face to face, to threaten to the beard, and hence to imply an open menace.'

Unfortunately this only explains *beards*, with which *burdes* has nothing whatever to do. For it is another form of *bordes* or *boards*. See the *New Eng. Dict.* s. v. 'Board,' verb, sense 4, where another quotation, from the same poem by Surrey, shows that *burdes* means 'accosts.'

In the same volume are some poems by Grimoald.

At p. 212 Grimoald uses the common phrase 'and pincheth all to nye,' i. e. too nigh. But, oh! the note! It says, '*Nye*, annoyance, trouble.' I admit the annoyance —to the reader.

At p. 215, in the fine poem of *The Death of Zoroas*, Grimoald says:—

> 'Whether our tunes heav'n's harmony can yield;
> Of four begyns, among themselves how great
> Proportion is.'

As the whole context is about the learning of Zoroas in astronomy and philosophy, we might fairly guess *begyn* to be a somewhat licentious form for *beginning*; and we might fairly suppose that this is the very passage which induced Spenser to use the same form in his *Faery Queen*, iii. 3. 21. Moreover, the 'four beginnings' may fairly be considered to mean the four elements; but the note knows better. It simply and oracularly says that the sense is 'biggins.' It must therefore mean four child's caps, or four night-caps, or four coifs, or four coffee-pots. To such a choice are we thus reduced. And why, in that case does Grimoald seem to accent the latter syllable?

**401. Curiosities of Interpretation. IV** (8 S. ii. 3; 1892).

A famous antiquary and editor was Joseph Ritson. We all remember the acrimony with which he attacked Warton.

Frequently, but not always, he had good reasons to show for his strictures. If, however, we were to draw the conclusion that he was himself accurate, we should be very much mistaken. His throwing of stones was doubtless intended to let us know that he did not himself live in a glass house. Nevertheless that house had an over large proportion of windows in it, as may easily be seen.

Ritson's *Metrical Romanceës* (to adopt his own peculiar spelling) is a valuable book in its way, but we must not trust it too much. I give a few samples of some of its peculiarities, for which purpose it is simplest to examine the glossary.

In *King Horn*, 1120, we read how Horn craved some drink, because he and his companions 'bueth afurste,' i. e. are athirst. The glossary says that *afurste* here means 'at first,' which makes nonsense of the whole passage.

In the *King of Tars*, 605, it is said of a man that he is 'in his herte sore attrayed,' i. e. sorely vexed at heart.

See *Atray* in the *N. E. D.* The glossary has '*Attrayed*, poison'd.' This is a very bad shot, for the A. S. *āttor*, poison, could not possibly produce such a verb as *attrayen*.

*Blyve*, we are told, sometimes means *blithe*, and is corrupted from it. It never has that sense, and the assumed 'corruption,' like most others, is unwarranted. [It is for *bi live*, with life; hence, quickly.]

'*Borken*, barking,' is entered without a reference. It occurs in the *King of Tars*, p. 400, and is the past tense plural, meaning 'barked.' Mr. Ritson should have known that *-en* is not the suffix of a present participle. If the hapless Warton had been caught in such an error, Ritson would have called the statement 'a lye.'

The glossary gives us *cronde*, unexplained. This is an error for *croude*, as shown by Price.

*Dang*, we are told, is the 'plural' of *Ding*; but it is charitable to suppose that 'plural' is a misprint for 'preterite.

'*Denketh roun*, thinks to run,' is surely comic. The text has *roune*, i. e. to whisper.

*Druye* is unexplained, yet it is merely our 'dry.'

'*Ernde*, yearn, desired.' But it means 'he ran,' as the context requires. See *rennen* in Stratmann.

'Glyste up,' not explained. The *s* is printed as a 'long *s*'; in fact, it is an error for *glyfte up*. To *gliff* is to glance quickly, to look, gaze. It is duly explained in Stratmann.

*Hone* is explained by 'shame; Fr. *honte*.' But 'withouten hone' means 'without delay,' and is a fairly common phrase.

'Pende, hond,' must be a misprint of *hond* for *pond*. *Pende* is explained by Stratmann as a pound, or (perhaps) a pond.

'*Ryne*, rine [sic], the white covering of a nocturnal frost.' This is a complex error, and refers to *King Horn*, p. 11: 'For reyn ne myhte by ryne.' The answer is simple; read *by-ryne*, i. e. be-rain, rain upon.

In the *Erle of Tolous*, p. 337, we have, 'He behelde ynly hur face,' where *ynly* (for in-ly) means inwardly, hence, intently. But Ritson was entirely puzzled by it, and misprints it *yuly*. Hence the curious entry in the glossary, '*Yuly*, handsome, beautiful[1].' This he supports by a quotation about 'a captain's wife most *yewly*,' adding, 'though it must be confess'd that the original has not *yewly*, but *vewlie*, unless the tail of the *y* have been broken off at the press'; that is, his imaginary word is to be explained by manipulating another passage to suit it.

In *Ywaine and Gawaine*, p. 677, is a curious passage about Sir Ywaine riding under a portcullis.

'Under that than was a *swyke*.'

The knight's horse's foot touched the *swyke*, i. e. the trap or contrivance for letting the portcullis go, and down it came. But Ritson coolly identifies *swyke* with *syke*, and explains it by 'sike, hole, or ditch.'

[1] Carefully preserved in Halliwell's *Dictionary*.

Under the word *thoghte*, however, he succeeds in gibbeting a mistake of 'mister Ellises' very neatly, as follows · 'In mister Ellises edition, the text has *hym poghte*; the comment [is], "*In posté*, Fr. in power"; than which nothing can be more ridiculous.'

### 402. Gruesome (8 S. i. 420; 1892).

A reference to my *Dictionary* will show that Burns speaks of death as 'a *grusome* carl,' and that '*grousome*, horrid,' occurs in Levins, *Manip. Vocabulorum*, printed in 1570; so it is nothing new. Not only have we the G. *grausam* and the Du. *gruwzaam*, but the Middle-Danish *grusom*, which is probably the real source of our English word. According to Kalkar, the derivative adj. *grusommelig* occurs in Danish in 1580. The A. S. *gryre*, horror, is from the same root. See *Gräuel* in Kluge. The E. Friesic form is *grausam*, so the word must have been rather widely known.

### 403. Groundsel (8 S. i. 441; 1892).

I shall be much obliged if I may be allowed to explain the history of this word fully. We must never try to twist etymologies to suit ideas of our own, but must go strictly by evidence. We must be careful as to plant-names, which are peculiarly liable to be recast by popular etymologists. There is no doubt at all as to the fact that in the tenth century the plant was named *grunde-swelge*, with variations in the latter half of the word. The variations are *swelige*, *swilige*, *swylige*, *swulie*, all given, with refercnees, in Bosworth's *Dictionary*. Any one who understands A. S. phonetics will easily see that all these variants have the same sense; and that sense is 'swallower.' Hence, in the tenth century, the popular etymology of the word was that it meant 'ground-swallower'; and the only way we can make sense of  is by giving it the sense of 'abundant occupier of the ground.' This is the only result possible as to the meaning of the word at that date.

With this we should have to remain content but for new evidence, which has not long been known, and has not been explained till recently. To the best of my belief it was explained by me in a review of Mr. Sweet's edition of the *Epinal Glossary*, which appeared in 1883. My explanation at once became common property, and is reproduced both in the *Century Dictionary*, and in the new edition of Webster.

The fault is not in the latter half of the word, but in the former. The A. S. scholar at once observes that *grunde* is a false form; the A. S. for 'ground' is not *grund-e*, in two syllables, but *grund,* in one. Hence *grunde* is probably a substitution for something else. That 'something else' first sprang to light on the publication of the *Epinal Glossary*, and the other early glossaries known as the Erfurt and Corpus *Glossaries*. These take us back to the eighth century, when the form in use was *gunde-swilge* or *gunde-swelge*. This alters the sense altogether, and shows that the original name was 'matter-swallower,' or remedy against a certain disease called the *gund*, M. E. *gound*. This was a disease of the eyes, in which matter exudes consequent on inflammation or ailment. It is fully explained in my note to *Piers Plowman* on the word *rade gounde*. The disease is still called *red-gum*, a corruption of *red-gund*. The intense belief of our ancestors in the virtues of plants is well known; see all about the virtues of groundsel in Cockayne's *Leechdoms*. In East Anglia we call it *simpson*. This is from O. F. *seneçon*, Lat. acc. *senecionem*.

**404. Verses by the Pope** (8 S. i. 452; 1892).

\* The following paragraph appeared in the *Standard*, May 3, 1892:—

'Princess Isabella of Bavaria, having had the idea of preparing for a sale for charitable purposes an album of royal photographs and autographs, begged of Pope Leo XIII the favour of being allowed to inscribe his name among the patrons of the work. His Highness replied by sending the following verses, celebrating the art of photography :—

*Ars Photographica.*

Expressa solis spiculo,
Nitens imago, quam bene
Frontis decus, vim luminum,
Refers, et oris gratiam.

O mira virtus ingeni
Novumque monstrum! imaginem
Naturae Apelles aemulus
Non pulchriorem pingeret.
                    Leo P.P. XIII.'

A friend, who sent me this information, asked me for a translation; and I ventured to return him the following :—

'Bright picture, drawn by Phoebus' beam
    How faithfully dost thou retrace
The forehead's breadth, the eye's bright gleam,
    The smiling lip's enchanting grace!

'O wondrous art, invention new!
    Earth's latest marvel! Surely ne'er
Apelles, Nature's rival, drew
    A portrait with minuter care!'

**405. First Editions** (8 S. i. 480; 1892).

I think that in considering the comparative value of various editions, we must draw a sharp line between real second editions and mere reprints.

In the sixteenth century, the first edition of a book is, as a rule, much the best. Later editions are mere reprints, each less correct than its predecessor. Take the case of *Piers the Plowman*, printed thrice in one year by Crowley, and afterwards reprinted by Rogers. Crowley's first edition, dated (by a misprint) 1505 instead of 1550, is worth having.

But the later ones grow steadily worse; and Rogers's edition is highly incorrect. Yet I have seen the worthless fourth edition highly priced, on the speculation that the purchaser would give about thrice its real value. In the present century all depends on the amount of revision. The general rule is that the first edition is by far the worst, especially in cases where much revision is possible. But to take the case of *Piers Plowman* once more. Mr. Thos. Wright issued a capital edition in 1842; but his second edition, in 1856, though it seems to have been revised, contains eighteen errors in the text, from which the first edition is free.

I have myself issued various editions of a portion of the text, with notes. As a rule, each of these is better than its predecessor, yet only the other day I discovered a misprint in the text in the later editions which does not appear in the earlier ones. This is one of the dangers of reprinting; a letter is dropped, and its loss is not perceived in the revision unless the false form happens to catch the eye.

I conclude that the general rule is this—to seek after the first editions of early books, and the last editions of modern ones. But there will always remain special cases to which this rule does not apply. In particular, unrevised reprints are not likely to improve; they will rather be found to deteriorate. There seems to be, moreover, a considerable difference between one text and another. In the case of a novel I should prefer an early copy, but in the case of a scientific treatise a late one. Yet the reprinting of novels is, as a rule, so easy that even the latest copies may be quite correct, or at least free from material errors. This is where the question of sentiment arises; the relative value of the various editions must be left to the fancy of the purchasers, and the seller must select his purchaser as well as he can.

**406. Swedish and English** (8 S. i. 488; 1892).

Every now and then a deliciously innocent article on language escapes editorial supervision, and finds its way into print. An amusing instance may be found in the June number of the *Journal of Education* (1892), entitled 'Gleanings amongst Swedes.'

The author was led to his knowledge of Swedish, he tells us, by observing the word *Tandsticker* on a box of matches. This, he kindly informs us, is derived from *tand*, a tooth, and *sticker*, a splinter. Here there are only *four* errors. The word is *Tändstickor*, with *ä* and *o* (not *a* and *e*). *Tänd* has nothing to do with *tooth*, but is from *tända*, to kindle, akin to *tinder*. And lastly, *stickor* is not singular, but plural.

After this somewhat inaccurate introduction to the language, many curious discoveries followed. The following are specimens.

*Gammer* (which really means grandmother, as *gaffer* does grandfather) is from Swed. *gammel*, old. (The right spelling is *gammal*, but we must not be particular.)

The Swed. *basun*, must be a relative of *bassoon*. Unluckily, there is no kinship at all; see *Posaune* in Kluge. *Basun* is merely a borrowed word in Swedish, having no original value in that language; and it means a trumpet. The Swedish for *bassoon* is *Bassong*.

*Lin* (we are told) means flax, as *linum* does in Latin. Considering that *lin* is nothing but the Lat. *linum* done into Swedish, the coincidence, after all, is hardly to be considered as wonderful.

Next comes a new notion of borrowing native English words from Swedish. Thus, we are told that our *acre* is either borrowed from the Lat. *ager* or from Swed. *åker*. Well, it so happens that our *acre* is the A. S. *æcer*, not borrowed from either one or the other, but cognate with both.

At any rate, we are told, if we do not admit that *acre* is borrowed from Swed. *åker*, we must at least admit that *ochre* is derived therefrom. This is curious, for *ochre* is Greek! Funniest of all is the notion of deriving an English word from a combination of Swedish words. Thus, our *hide* is not derived merely from Swed. *hud*, a hide, but at the same time from *hy*, skin. The forms *hud* and *hy*, neatly fused together, give *hide*. This is our old friend the 'portmanteau' word, familiar to *Alice in Wonderland*. But the truth is that *hy* does not primarily mean 'skin,' but 'colour.' It is cognate with A. S. *hiw*, our *hue*, and has nothing whatever to do with *hide*. As to *hud*, it is merely a cognate form.

Like Oliver Twist, we can but 'ask for more.'

**407. Julius Caesar, iv. 3. 218** (8 S. ii. 63; 1892).

The famous passage, 'There is a tide in the affairs of men,' &c., may be compared with the following stanza in Chaucer's *Troilus*, ii. 281 :—

>'For to every wight som goodly aventure
>Som tyme is shape, if he can it receyven;
>And if that he wol take of it no cure,
>Whan that it comth, but wilfully it weyven,
>Lo! neither cas nor fortune him deceyven,
>But right his verray slouthe and wrecchednesse;
>And swich a wight is for to blame, I gesse.'

Chaucer's stanza is to some extent borrowed from Boccaccio's *Filostrato*, book ii. Mr. Rossetti thus translates the Italian passage: 'Every one has a chance in life, but not a second chance.'

**408. Racoon** (8 S. ii. 111; 1892).

I regret that I gave the wrong account of this word in the first edition of my *Dictionary*. But I corrected it in the second. It is clearly a corruption of the Indian name.

The earliest quotation I have found is the following,

dated 1607-9: 'There is a beast they call *Aroughcon*, much like a badger, but vseth to liue on trees as Squirrels doe.' Capt. John Smith, *Works*, ed. Arber, p. 59. [At p. 355 of the same, it is spelt *aroughcun*; and in a glossary of Indian words subjoined to *A Historie of Travaile into Virginia*, by W. Strachey (published by the Hackluyt Society in 1849) we find '*Arathkone*, a beast like a fox.']

### 409. Windmills (8 S. ii. 138 ; 1892).

An early instance of an English windmill is that in which Richard, earl of Cornwall and 'King of Almaigne,' took refuge after the battle of Lewes in 1264. In the famous song against the King of Almaigne, the 'sayles' of the 'mulne' are mentioned, showing that it really was a windmill.

So also *Rob. of Gloucester*, l. 547, has: 'The king of Alemaine was in a windmulle nome.'

### 410. 'Buffetier' as an English word (8 S. ii. 194; 1892).

The reasoning in the last article seems to me quite beside the mark [1]. Before the word *buffeteer* (which has not been shown to exist) could have been coined in England, we must have had *buffet* to coin it out of. Now the earliest known quotation for *buffet* in English is dated 1718. These are precisely the wild suggestions that 'require to be narrowly watched.'

### 411. Edwards's 'Words, Facts, and Phrases' (8 S. ii. 246; 1892).

I am of opinion that this book ought not to be seriously quoted by any scholar. It is a mere compilation, and

---

[1] Argued—'that *buffeteer* (*sic*) is not to be found in the English sense in any French author proves nothing.' And, 'that historical etymology is valuable, but requires to be narrowly watched.' [It never occurred to the writer that *buffeteer* has no more existence in English than *buffetier* has in French.]

abounds with errors. Yet it is quoted twice in *N. and Q.*, *ante*, pp. 211, 214. In both instances it contains a blunder.

At p. 211 we are told that 'a small figure of the devil *stands* on the top of Lincoln College'; whereas a few lines below we read that it was taken down in 1731. At p. 214 the origin of the well-known word *maundy* is said to be from *manducate*! I advise correspondents not to put any trust in this very poor book.

**412. Luce; a quadruped. I** (8 S. ii. 353; 1892).

*Luce*, as a fish, is a pike. But *luce*, as a quadruped, is a lynx. Cf. A.S. *lox*, Du. *los*, O.H.G. *luhs*, G. *Luchs*, a lynx. *Flower de luce* is simply a comic blunder of some one who wished to show off, and was made by prefixing *flower-de-* to *luce* in the sense of *lynx*[1]. See '*Lucern*, a lynx,' in Halliwell. In a pageant by Dekker, called *Britannia's Honour* (1628), the supporters of the Skinners' arms are said to be 'two *luzernes*.'

**413. Luce; a quadruped. II** (8 S. ii. 435; 1892).

Surely your correspondent at the last reference (ii. 391) cannot have read the articles to which he refers with due care.

In *N. and Q.* 8 S. ii. 328, the statement really made is this: 'In Harl. MS. 2125 is recorded the cost of making anew the four beasts called the unicorne, the antelop, the flower-de-luce, and the camell.' *My* statement was that 'the *flower-de-luce* is a comic blunder.' However, your correspondent is entitled to the opinion that it is correct!

My suggestion, of course, was that the *flower-de-luce* was a blunder for *luce*, and that the *luce*, which is also *a beast*, was probably a lynx. No one need adopt this suggestion if he can find a better one. But he must find us a quadruped of some sort.

[1] For *flower-de-luce*, see the next article.

Again, in the catalogue, 'one unicorn, one dromedary, one *luce*, one camel,' it is also probable that the *luce* here meant is a quadruped, and not a pike.

I cannot produce further authority for *luce* in the sense of 'lynx,' because it is extremely difficult to find, but I believe it can be found, and that I have met with other instances. And, surely, if *luce* ever did mean a quadruped, etymology tells us that it is the lynx, and nothing else. I do not for a moment believe that the existing heraldic authorities are exhaustive, or that the compilers of them necessarily understood every old English term they ever met with. There is a large number of words in Randell Holme of which modern heralds have probably never heard. Very likely he explains *luce*, but I have not the book at hand. Few glossaries of heraldry are more complete than Elvin's, but he does not give *luzern* at all.

I do not understand what is meant by saying, 'Part of the charges on the arms of the Skinners' Company, London, is fleurs-de-lys or.' For it so happens that a large, well-painted copy of these arms was kindly given me but a short time ago by the Master of the Company, and I believe it accordingly to be authentic. These arms contain three coronets proper on a chief gules, and the rest of the field is ermine. I cannot find a single 'fleur-de-lys' anywhere, and the ermine is not 'or,' but 'sable on argent,' as usual.

As to *lucern*, see seven quotations in Nares's *Glossary*; he does not explain it properly, as he failed to see that it meant a lynx.

### 414. 'Strachy' in Twelfth-Night, ii. 5. 45
(8 S. iii. 14; 1893).

I should think that too much has already been said about the hopeless crux of *Strachy* in *Twelfth-Night*, ii. 5. 45; and I suppose that all that has been said is worthless.

Yet I beg leave to offer one more guess, probably also worthless. The O. F. *estrache* (see Godefroy) occurs as a variation of *estrace* (meaning extraction, race, rank, family), from Lat. *extrahere*. So perhaps 'the lady of the strachey' (small *s*) was 'a lady of rank or good extraction.'

### 415. Henchman. I (8 S. iii. 194; 1893).

This word has been several times discussed. I write further about it solely because I have found more evidence. In *A Collection of Ordinances and Regulations for the Government of the Royal Household*, London, 1790, I find several facts. The oldest spelling [there] is *henxmen*. In the thirty-third year of Henry VI we find ' Henxmen 3.' This means that their number was then limited to three · see p. 17* of the above-named work.

In the time of Edward IV, their number was really five (p. 99), though the Ordinances say that their number was to be 'six or more' (p. 44)[1]. But it is more important to observe that they were not mere servants, as is usually believed, but something very different. It is clear that their office was purely honorary, for nowhere are any wages assigned them. Doubtless they were a kind of pages, all quite young men or growing boys, who had a paid master assigned to teach them, and who had, moreover, servants of their own. Their place was one of some honour, and they served the king himself, and him only. They were specially assigned 'to the riding household' on p. 99; and everything points to the fact that they were far removed from being mere servants. I find the latest mention of them in the time of Henry VIII (p. 198). I think all this affects the etymology, and renders all connexion with the word *Hans* (Jack) unlikely; [but see later articles by DR. CHANCE.]

[1] *Note in* 1895. *Six;* because the Master of the Horse counted along with them. See p. 345 below.

The passages are too long for quotation, I only give a few extracts :—

'Maistyr of Gramer . . . [is to teach] the kings *Henxmen*, the children of chapell . . the clerkes of the awmery, and other men and children of courte; which mayster . . . if he be a preeste,' &c. (p. 51).

'*Henxmen*, vj enfauntes, or more, as it shall please the kinge; all these etyng in the halle, and sitting at bourde togyder . . . and if these *gentlemen*, or any of them, be *wardes*, then after *theyre byrthes and degrees* . and everyche of theym an honest servaunt to kepe theyre chambre and *harneys* [i. e. armour], and to array him in this courte' (p. 44).

'Maistyr of *Henxmen*, to shew the schooles of urbanitie and norture of England, to lerne them *to ryde* clenely and surelye; to draw hem also to *justes*; to lerne them were theyre harneys; to have all curtesy, in wordes, dedes, and *degrees*, diligently to kepe them in rules of goynges and sittings [i. e. in rules of precedence] after they be of honour [i. e. according to their rank]. Moreover, to teche them *sondry languages*, and other lernynges vertuous, to harping, to pype, sing, daunce . . . and to kepe . . . with these *children* dew covenitz [sic], with corrections in theyr chambres, according to *such gentlemen*. This maistyr sitteth in the halle, next unto these Henxmen, at the same borde, to have his respect unto theyre demeanynges . . . and for the *fees* that he claymyth amonges the Henxmen of all theyre apparayle, the chamberlayn is juge' (p. 45).

This shows that they were not menials at all, but young men of high rank, who rode in tournaments.

'The officers of the *ridinge* houshold Item, five Henxmen, and one of the said xij squiers to be maister of them . . . Item, a hackney for the henxmen's man' (p. 99).

'Item, the king [Henry VII, A.D. 1494] would . . . suffer noe lord's servaunt to awaite there, but only the *henchmen*' (p. 109).

'Master of the Henxmen, stabling for *six* horses' (p. 198).

### 416. Henchman. II (8 S. iv. 16 ; 1893).

The quotation of the spelling *Henxtmen* in the earliest known use of the word, viz. in 1400[1], surely settles, at

---

[1] 'The word is older than 1415. It occurs in 1400—"Henxtmen Dominae" (Wardrobe Account, 2 Hen. IV, 95/30, Q. R.')—*N. and Q.* S. iii. 478.

last, the etymology of the word. I have always contended that it represents the Dutch *hengst* compounded with *man*; the compounds *hengst-loon* and *hengst-geld* are given in Kilian, ed. 1777. The difficulty, for me, was to find the *t*, as the more usual spelling is *henxman*. But here is the *t* in the oldest form; and my present contention is, that my opponents will now have to explain away this *t* instead of asking me to produce it; and till this is done I do not see what more can be said. The easiest course, for those who can bring themselves to do it, will be to admit that appearances are now very much in my favour.

### 417. Henchman. III (8 S. vi. 245; 1894).

This word has been often discussed in *N. and Q.* I have to note a very early use of it.

*The Treasurer's Accounts for the Earl of Derby's Expeditions in* 1390-3, have just been edited by Miss L. Toulmin Smith for the Camden Society. The index gives several references for *henksman*; so spelt.

The Earl of Derby had two *henksmen*, and they certainly rode on horseback at times. The first entry is: 'Diversis hominibus pro tribus equis ab ipsis conductis pro equitacione domini et ij henksmen apud Dansk decimo die mensis Augusti, xv. s. pr.' The date is August 20, 1392. The *henksmen* were named Bernard and Henry Tylman.

On another occasion a horse was hired for one of them to take a journey, and an ass for his return, whilst travelling in Judea.

### 418. Henchman. IV (8 S. viii. 335; 1895).

This word has been so frequently discussed that I should not have written again about it, were it not that I have obtained quite a flood of new light upon it.

I have always contended that henchmen were horsemen,

few in number, personally attendant on the king, and sometimes men of rank. All this is entirely verified by the account given in the *Antiquarian Repository*, ii. 241-277, of the coronation of Richard III, in 1483. The word is there spelt 'henxemen.' The king's henchmen were the Master of the Horse (who counted as one) and seven others, one of them being Lord Morley. Moreover, the queen had her henchmen, viz. five ladies, riding upon 'women's sadelles.'

In the account of the expenses we first have mention of the king, and then of his henchmen; next of the queen, and then of her lady-henchmen (to coin a queer word). Next to them in importance comes the Archbishop of Canterbury. It is, therefore, quite idle to pretend that a henchman was a mere page of inferior rank.

Unless it be remembered that the Master of the Horse was one of them, it will not be understood how it was that the seven henchmen required eight doublets, eight black bonnets, and so on (pp. 255, 256). Note, for instance, p. 248: 'And to the Maister and to each of the same henxemen a paire of blac spurres, and for ledyng-rayns xxij yerds of broode riban silk.'

### 419. Fod (8 S. iii. 266; 1893).

I have no doubt that this is a 'ghost-word.' Halliwell's edition of Nares gives it, on the strength of a quotation from the *Paradyse of Dayntie Devices*, 1576: 'As we for Saunders death have cause in *fods* of teares to saile.' It is the old story; a letter has 'dropped out.' Read *flods*, i. e. floods.

### 420. Julius Caesar, iii. 1. 58-70 (8 S. iii. 284; 1893).

Compare the following lines from the second chapter of the *Parabolae* of Alanus de Insulis :—

'Aethereus motus mouet omnia sidera praeter
Unum, sed semper permanet illud idem;
Sic constans et fidus homo sine fine tenebit
Hunc in more modum, quem tenet ipse polus.

### 421. Chaucer's 'Stilbon' (8 S. iii. 293; 1893).

As to Stilbo [*Pard. Tale*, C. 603], I am behind the age. Dr. Köppel showed, in *Anglia*, xiii. 183 (1890), that he was Stilpo, of Megara, mentioned by Seneca; also, that Chaucer got the name from Walter Map's *Valerius*, cap. 27. Stilbon, for Mercury, occurs in Alanus, *Anticlaudian*, iv. 6.

### 422. Chaucer's Legend of Good Women, line 16
(8 S. iii. 293; 1893; same article as above).

It is of no consequence what new opinion may be offered as to the person meant by 'Bernard the Monk.' He is certainly Bernard of Clairvaux, as was expressly explained, more than 200 years ago, in J. J. Hofmann's *Lexicon Universale* (Basileae, 1677), s. v. BERNARDUS. The passage concludes with the words: 'Nullos habuit praeceptores praeter quercus et fagos. Hinc proverb. Neque enim Bernardus vidit omnia.' I admit that I failed to give this reference in 1889; but that, to a student who is always learning, is a long while ago.

### 423. Merestones (8 S. iii. 329; 1893).

*Mere* is a pure English word, independent of the Gk. μείρομαι, 'I receive as a portion.' *Merestone* is not 'a misprint for *milestone*,' but is quite right. The 'old verb *to mere*,' spelt *mear* by Spenser [*Ruines of Rome*, st. 22], is not an old verb, but a 'mere' invention of Spenser himself, coined out of the substantive; and the substantive is also used by Spenser, in a quotation duly given in Johnson's *Dictionary*.

*Mere-stone* is not given in my *Etymological Dictionary*; nevertheless, it occurs in a dictionary in which I had a hand; and I here quote the article.

'MERE, sb. limit, boundary, S 2; *meer*, Prompt. Comb. : *mere-stane*, boundary stone, Cath.—A. S. (*ge*)*mǣre*.'—Mayhew and Skeat, *Concise M. E. Dictionary*, Oxford, 1888, p. 146.

Here 'S. 2'=*Specimens of English*, ed. Morris and Skeat; 'Prompt.' = *Promptorium Parvulorum* (Camden Society). 'Cath.' means that *mere-stane* is a compound given in the *Catholicon Anglicum*. A reference to Stratmann's *Mid. Eng. Dict.* will furnish quotations from *Layamon*, the *Coventry Plays*, the *Alliterative Poems*, *Trevisa*, &c. And see the *A. S. Dictionary*.

The best example is in St. Mark, v. 17. Here the Vulgate has: 'A finibus eorum.' The Old Northumbrian version has: 'from gemærum hiora.' The older A. S. version has: 'Of hyra gemærum'; and the later one: 'of hire mæren.' The *æ* is long, though not so marked.

**424. The Metre of 'In Memoriam'** (8 S. iii. 337; 1893).

I have always thought that it was derived from Geo. Sandys's 'Paraphrase upon the Psalms of David,' 1636. Thus, in Ps. cxxx, we have the remarkably fine stanza :—

> 'What profit can my blood afford
> When I shall to the grave descend?
> ·Can senseless dust thy praise extend?
> Can death thy living truth record?'

It is a question of chronology for one thing. Who can give us dates or facts?

[In *N. and Q.* 8 S. iii. p. 430, Mr. Adams quoted from F. Davison, who died about 1619; his translation of Ps. cxxv (in this metre) is given in Farr's *Select Poetry*, p. 325. But this does not strike one as being very accessible; whilst the *tone* of Geo. Sandys is strikingly like that of

Tennyson's poem. Others pointed to Lord Herbert of Cherbury's Ode, which is of later date (1665); also a Luttrell broadside (about 1660). And Mr. Thomas Bayne referred to an Elegy in Ben Jonson's *Underwoods*, which appeared in 1641. I still think that Tennyson imitated Sandys; or, if not, then certainly Ben Jonson.]

**425. Yetminster and Ockford (spellings in Domesday)** (8 S. iii. 409; 1893).

[I only quote a part of the article, which was occasioned by Canon Taylor's references to Domesday Book.]

It cannot be too clearly understood that Domesday abounds with the most ludicrous mistakes, and is only of value when properly collated with and controlled by other authorities. It could not be otherwise. The Anglo-French scribes had to spell, how they could, words which had no meaning for them, and which frequently they could not pronounce. We may illustrate this by considering what value we should attach to the spellings of an Englishman ignorant of Arabic when he tries to write down Arabic words.

For this reason, even modern English pronunciation is often of superior value to the Domesday spellings. It is, at any rate, English, and not a mere travesty of it. And it is easily seen that in the case of Ockford [Domesday, *Adford*], it is an excellent witness.

The word 'corruption' is continually misused. When we are told that the Domesday names Everslage, &c. *have become* Yearsley, &c., we naturally ask—how? There is, properly speaking, no such thing as 'corruption.' It is a term due to the old and vicious habit of ignoring all phonetic laws. These laws act with surprising regularity, and when exceptions occur, they are not due to 'corruption,' but to downright and intentional substitution of an apparently intelligible syllable or word for one of which the meaning has been lost. Till this is better understood, no progress is possible.

The Domesday spelling *Adford* is, on the face of it, absurd. If *Ad-* was written for *At-* [as was suggested], it is at once conceded that the scribe was writing down what he could not pronounce, and did not understand. If, in another instance, he (or another scribe) wrote *Acford* for *Oakford* [as was also alleged], he was clearly trying to reproduce the A. S. *Acford*, originally *āc-ford*, i. e. oakford. Cf. *Ashford*. The A. S. *Acford* is correct, because written by an Englishman; see Kemble for the reference. The A. S. *āc-ford* can appear in modern English in the forms *Acford*, *Ockford*, or *Oakford*, all regular developements, petrified at varying dates; and when we collate Ockford with the A. S. form, we see at once that the Anglo-French scribe has miswritten *Adford* for *Acford* because he did not understand it. These spellings are easily understood when we have the clue to them; when we have not, it would be quite a mistake to trust them overmuch.

Next, to take the Domesday *Etiminstre* for Yetminster. It is obvious that *eti-* can hardly mean *at* [as was alleged], because *eti* for *at* is unknown. It is equally obvious that it cannot mean *atte* (for *at the*), because the scribe had not the gift of prophecy, and could not tell that that form would be invented after his death. But when we collate this *Eti-* with the Mod. Eng. *Yet-*, very common for 'gate,' and the direct descendant of A. S. *geat* (with $ge=y$), we can see that the scribe simply dropped the initial *y* for the reason that he could not pronounce it, as it was not in his (pronounced) alphabet ... My point is, that we must control the Domesday forms by our knowledge of the actual changes that have taken place in English.

I deny the fact of 'corruption' in language, except by the way of forcible and intentional substitution, which only takes place when an attempt is made to give a thing a new sense. Thus *crayfish* from *écrevisse* gives an apparent sense to half the word. I think it also likely that the A. S. *Eofor-wīc*, i.e. Boar-town, whence Mod. E. *York* (where again *y* is due to *eo*), was a deliberate substitution for a Celtic name which the English voted to be unintelligible. This is not corruption, but intention. It just makes all the difference.

### 426. Dimanche de Quasimodo (8 S. iii. 437; 1893).

The phrase *quasi modo geniti* occurs in *Piers Plowman*, B. xi. 196, C. xiii. 110. My note on the passage explains that the reference is to the First Sunday after Easter, 'because, in the *Sarum Missal*, the office for that day begins with the text, 1 Pet. ii. 2: Quasi modo geniti infantes, rationabile sine dolo lac concupiscite.'

### 427. 'Stoat,' its derivation (8 S. iii. 455; 1893).

[In reply to the assertion that *clubstart* is a name for the stoat, which shows that *stoat* is from A. S. *steort*.]

*Clubstart*, from A. S. *steort*, a tail, is quite another name from *stoat*. A moment's reflexion will show that *stoat* and *start* are different words, just as *coat* and *cart*, or *moat* and *mart*. That any one should for a moment deem it possible to derive *stoat* from A. S. *steort*, is a clear proof of the inability of the English mind to conceive that etymology obeys fixed laws.

### 428. Trouts (8 S. iii. 474; 1893).

[It was first said that the pl. form *trouts* occurred in Sir W. Scott's *Diary*. Next, that it was older, occurring in Beaumont and Fletcher's *The Scornful Lady*, Act iii. sc. 2. Next, that it is in Shakespeare, *Measure for Measure*, i. 2. 91.]

The plural *trowtis* occurs in Barbour's *Bruce*, ii. 577. The date of the *Bruce* is 1375, i.e. 241 years earlier than

Beaumont and Fletcher's *Scornful Lady*, and nearly 400 years earlier than the birth of Sir Walter Scott. This shows how easy it is to 'go one better' in questions as to English usage.

[Nor is this the oldest example; for on the same page of *N. and Q.*, a mention of '3 Troghtes' was cited from the *Wardrobe Account*, 62/7; A.D. 1344-7. The A. S. *truht* only occurs in the singular.]

### 429. 'Cavalry Curates' and Preaching Ponies (8 S. iv. 25; 1893).

The following remarkable announcement occurred in the *Daily Telegraph*, June 10, at p. 7 :—

'The latest development of the mounted brigade is an ecclesiastical corps called "Cavalry Curates," in connexion with the Church of England. . . . In out of the way districts, where the population is scant and sparse, small chapels of iron or other material will be constructed, in which the services will be conducted by "Cavalry Curates," supplied with lithe and strong ponies for the purpose, who will not only preach in half a dozen places on Sunday, but will arrange to hold galloping ministrations during the week.'

The suggestion that litheness and strength are requisite for enabling ponies to preach in half a dozen places at once, deserves attention. What is meant by 'galloping ministrations' I do not quite understand; it seems to refer to some form of spiritual polo.

### 430. Mrs. Cowden Clarke's 'Concordance to Shakespeare' (8 S. iv. 135; 1893).

It is startling to find that Astarte still clings to this once useful, but now obsolescent work, and recommends utilization of the numbered lines in the *Globe Shakespeare*.

Let her at once order a copy of Schmidt's *Shakespeare Lexicon*, first printed in 1874-5, and now (for all I know) in some later edition. It gives all the references, noting acts and scenes and lines; and it includes the poems.

That any student of Shakespeare should never have heard of Dr. Schmidt is quite sensational. Most sincerely do I trust that the 'labour has paid its expenses.' It is the most meritorious work of its kind in the whole range of our literature.

The Concordance to the sonnets and poems, to which allusion is made, is that by Mrs. H. H. Furness, printed at Philadelphia in 1874. I am the proud possessor of a copy sent to me by her husband, the editor of several of Shakespeare's plays, the completeness and excellence of whose work leave but little to be further desired. I remember that it was simply addressed to 'Mr. Skeat, London,' and it says something for the intelligence of St. Martin's-le-Grand that it reached me without delay.

### 431. 'Runawayes Eyes' (8 S. iv. 84; 1893).

I cannot for a moment accept the ridiculous guess that we have here a misprint for *unawayrs*. It is founded on the cool statement that 'the old mode of spelling *unawares* was *unawayrs*.' Was it, indeed? Then will any one kindly submit some quotations to prove it? It was certainly not the normal spelling, and I can see no reason for the insertion of the diphthong *ay* instead of the usual and correct *a*. This is how Shakespearian 'emendations' are produced; they are frequently founded on unsupported assumptions.

### 432. English Words ending in '-ther' (8 S. iv. 162; 1893).

I wish to draw attention to a remarkable phenomenon, on which much more light is desirable.

The English words ending in *-ther* fall into two distinct sets.

1. The following words are spelt with *th* in Anglo-Saxon and Middle English, and give no trouble to the etymologist.

## ENGLISH WORDS ENDING IN '-THER.'

*Brother, either, ?feather, lather, leather, neither, nether, other, rather, whether, wether.* With them we may class *heather,* as being formed from *heath; smother,* of which the M. E. form is *smorther;* and even ?*fathom* as compared with A. S. *faeðm,* though ending in *-thom* instead of *-ther.* Related words in German end in *-der.* Compare *Bruder, Feder, Leder, nieder, ander, entweder, Widder;* also *Faden.*

2. But the following words are spelt with *d,* not only in Anglo-Saxon, but even in Middle-English: ?*father, gather, hither, mother, tether, thither, together, weather, whither, wither.* Related German words end in *-ter;* compare *Vater, Gatter, Mutter, Wetter.* Of course *hither, thither,* and *whither* all changed together, and the words *together,* and *gather* (being closely related) did the same. Moreover, *wither* is a mere derivative of *weather.* Hence the list of independent words is reduced to *Father, gather, hither, mother, tether, weather;* but we may add to the list the provincial word *ether,* A. S. *edor,* O. H. G. *ëtar,* a pliant rod. The remarkable point is this: that the change in these words from *d* to *th* is quite late. Stratmann's *Dictionary of Middle English* gives *only* forms with *d*; there is (with one exception, for which see p. 354) not a single form with *th,* so far as I can discover. That is to say, the change was later than 1400, and not long, perhaps, before 1500. What was the cause of it?

I believe it was due to the Wars of the Roses, when the dialects seem to have been mixed up. I have little doubt that the forms in *-ther* were Northern; and perhaps ultimately due to Scandinavian influence.

The most remarkable case is that of the verb to *wither.* The A. S. verb is *wedrian,* to weather; but the Icel. verb is *vithra,* with an *i,* as in modern English. I think this goes far to prove my point.

I would appeal to correspondents to produce, if they can, any dated example in which any of the words in my second list is spelt with *th*, at an earlier date than 1500. It is no easy task—I have, for years, been hunting for the form *yfather*, and can find nothing earlier than a quotation from Skelton; see Dyce's edition, i. 139. A collection of quotations, for spellings with *th*, older than 1500, may help us greatly. I repeat the list of words for which they are desired. They are; *ether* (a rod), *yfather, gather, hither, mother, tether, thither, together, weather, whither, wither*.

[In the Cambridge MS. of *Thomas of Erceldoune*, ed. Murray, l. 437, we find *teyryt*, probably meant for *teþryt* (tethered). The MS. is Northern, and of the middle of the fifteenth century. Cf. Icel. *tjöðra*, to tether.]

433. Spenser; F. Q., i. 1. 8 (8 S. iv. 215; 1893).

The fact that Spenser's 'tree-list' is imitated from Tasso, *Gier. Lib.* iii. 75, is perfectly well known. It is printed, for example, in my edition of Chaucer's *Minor Poems*, 1888, p. 292. Warton says: 'Ovid, Seneca, Lucan, Statius, and Claudian, have all left us descriptions of trees,' and gives the references.

The fact is, that this 'tree-list' has been trotted out by the poets over and over again. I give a rather long list in my note, but it is easy to make it longer. Some of the poets who have made use of a similar list, are these in chronological order: Ovid, Seneca, Lucan, Statius, Claudian, Guil. de Lorris, Boccaccio, Chaucer, Tasso, Spenser. I daresay there are more of them. The hint for it perhaps came from Vergil, *Aen.* vi. 179; see Ovid, *Met.* x. 90; Seneca, *Oedip.* 532; Lucan, *Phars.* iii. 440; Statius, *Theb.* vi. 98; Claudian, *De Raptu Pros.* ii. 107; Guil. de Lorris, *Rom. Rose*, 1338-1368; Boccaccio, *Teseide*, xi. 22-24; Chaucer, *Parl. Foules*, 176, and *Kn. Tale*, 2063; Tasso, *Gier. Lib.* iii. 75; Spenser, *F. Q.* i. 1. 8. As to Spenser, it is quite certain that one of his authorities here was Chaucer's *Parlement of Foules*.

## 434. 'To Launder' (8 S. iv. 216; 1893).

Schmidt's *Shakespeare Lexicon* duly records *laundering*; with a reference to *A Lover's Complaint*, l. 17. It is never safe to omit consulting him. The pp. *landered* occurs in *Hudibras*, ii. 1. 171, as the *Century Dictionary* correctly observes.

## 435. A Comic Etymology of 'Beadle' (8 S. iv. 306; 1893).

The following appeared in the *Saturday Review*, September 9, p. 306, in a review of Professor Bright's edition of the *A. S. Gospel of Luke* :—

'The officer ... to whom the judge delivers the criminal becomes the *beadle*, or *by-del*, who, we need hardly say, is not the modern Bumble, but the officer of the *by*, or township.'

This is delicious. If *by-* in *by-del* means a township, what is *-del*? If it is our *deal* or part, we gain the information that a beadle is 'a part of a town.' Perhaps he is the parish-pump. Unluckily, the word *by*, for township, is not Anglo-Saxon, but Norse. It occurs once, in the Northumbrian version of Mark v. 3, as a gloss upon *hūs*, a house, but only as a borrowed word from Norse.

Again, the *y* in *bydel* was short, as the cognate German word *büttel* shows. It is true that the *y* was marked long in Bosworth's *Dictionary*, and I find (somewhat to my surprise) that I inadvertently copied this mark of length in the first edition of my *Dictionary*; but it was corrected in the Supplement, at p. 784. However, I gave the right etymology, from *bēodan*, to command; and the whole account of the word is now given in full in the *New English Dictionary*. The etymological division of the word is *byd-el*; where *byd-* is derived, by mutation, from the zero-grade of the strong verb *bēodan*.

**436. May-Day: Marigold** (8 S. iv. 311; 1893).

At the last reference (iv. 272) we are told *marigold* has been referred to an A. S. form *meregold*, gold of the mere. If the A. S. *mere* is now *mere* (as is the case), then it cannot also be *mary*! Else we should have to admit that a *deer* is all one with a *dairy*, and ?*fear* is but another form of ?*fairy*. The A. S. *mere-gold* is a pure fiction, invented by some 'etymologist,' in the hope that he would not be detected. A large number of 'Anglo-Saxon' words were composed in the last century, from a prevalent idea that to invent forms as required was a pious thing to do, as being likely to forward the cause of truth.

I suspect that this A. S. *meregold* is due to the amusing suggestion in Dr. Prior's *Plant Names*, that *marsh-marigold* is the A. S. *mersc mear-gealla*, a suggestion which may serve to measure Dr. Prior's knowledge of English phonology. As a fact, *mersc* means marsh (right so far); *mear* (for *mearh*) is a horse; and *gealla* is the Mod. E. *gall*, which is quite a different thing from *gold*. Moreover, this 'marsh horse-gall' is not a marigold at all, but a gentian,—the *Gentiana pneumonanthe*, also called *bitter-wort*, for gall is bitter.

Surely *marigold* is just *Mary-gold*, precisely as *beefeater* is *beaf eater*. The Irish name *lus mairi*, leek of Mary, clinches the matter.

**437. Second Sight** (8 S. iv. 315; 1893).

The incident here given from the *Scotsman* is one of those stupid fabrications which carry with them their own refutation. The story amounts to this. A certain incident at Sierra Leone was seen in England at the same moment, as shown by clocks or watches.

But Sierra Leone is in 13° 50′ of West longitude, which makes a difference in time of about fifty-three minutes.

Hence the lady in England saw the incident nearly an hour after it occurred. Clumsy forgers are requested, for the future, to remember that a difference in longitude makes a difference in time.

### 438. Tarring-iron (8 S. iv. 317; 1893).

This well-known puzzle is fully described at p. 837 of Cassels' *Book of Sports and Pastimes*, n. d. It is there called 'The Puzzling Rings,' to which is added, 'but it has been so many times christened, that no list of names could claim to be a complete list.' Even when you know how to do the puzzle, it takes some time to accomplish. It is, or was, extremely common.

*Tarre* is another form of *tarry*. Usually, *tarre* meant to vex; to *tarre on* is to set on a dog; but it is, etymologically, the same word as *tarry*. See *teryen* in Stratmann.

### 439. Sith: Sithence: Since (8 S. iv. 358; 1893).

*Sith* is not 'shortened from an older form *sithen*,' but is an independent word. *Sith-en* is a compound word; from *sith* and *then*. So, also, the German *seit* is not shortened from an older form *seitdem*, but is an independent word. *Seit-dem* is compounded of *seit* and *dem*. Explained in my *Dictionary*, s. v. 'Since.'

### 440. 'Gingham' (8 S. iv. 386; 1893).

According to Littré, s. v. *guingam*, this stuff is named from Guingamp, in Brittany.

The *Century Dictionary* also mentions an unlikely etymology from a Javanese word *ginggang*, perishable! No one explains the spelling. I think the right explanation is, simply, that *gingham* is an old English spelling of *Guingamp*. See the account of 'the towne of Gyngham,' i. e. Guingamp, in the *Paston Letters*, ed. Gairdner, iii. 357.

**441. Holt=Hill!** (8 S. iv. 392; 1893).

The interpretation of *holt* as 'hill' is somewhat modern, and may have arisen from popular misuse. The fact that both words have an *h* and an *l* in them is quite enough to 'establish a connexion' in the minds of those who do not care to investigate the meanings of words historically. The original sense of *holt* is 'wood'; and this is verified by observing the senses of cognate words; such are G. *Holz*, wood; Du. *hout*, wood, timber, fuel (you cannot burn hills!); Russ. *koloda*, trunk, log; Polish *kloda*; Gk. κλάδος, branch; Irish *coill*, a wood.

**442. Sunset** (8 S. iv. 521; 1893).

I observe in *N. and Q.*, 8 S. iv. 455, the following question: 'Is the phrase "the sun sets in the west" good grammar? Ought it not to be—"*sits* in the west?"'

This shows a very common confusion of thought as to what constitutes grammar. Grammar is wholly concerned with prevalent usage, and is distinct from logic. No one ever said, ever has said, or ever will say, that the sun *sits* in the west; which is quite enough to show that *sits* is here ungrammatical.

Of course the question means, Is the phrase involving *sets* good logic? This is a totally different question, and is worth considering. But it is really high time to begin to understand that logic and grammar cover different ground, and should be kept apart. Nearly all the disputed questions about grammar involve this fundamental confusion of ideas; and this is why such discussions are often so wearisome, so full of useless wrangling, and so unsatisfactory.

The right way to investigate grammar is to do so historically. Never mind whether 'sets' is 'right' or 'wrong,' whatever those terms may seem to imply. We have, first of all, to inquire into the history of the phrase.

The history shows that there were really two distinct

uses of *set*. The usual A. S. *settan*, the causal of *sittan*, is regularly transitive. But there was a single instance in which *settan* was intransitive, viz. when it was used of a swelling that subsided; in this instance it is probable that the reference was not to the verb to *sit*, but to the derived substantives *set*, a seat, *setl*, a seat; and to the verb *settan*, to take a seat, to settle down. To say that a swelling *sits* would have been absurd; subsidence expresses a sort of movement, or alteration of position, which the mere verb to *sit* entirely fails to suggest. Hence the A. S. verb was, in this case, *settan*. The A. S. *settan*, however, is never used of the sun; this usage is somewhat later, being found, at any rate, in the thirteenth century; but the history of *sunset* runs upon a line parallel with that already indicated. The sun never sits in the west, as it is always (apparently) in motion; it subsides there. And these two things, being logically distinct, may well be distinguished in grammar also; although grammar (as already said) is not pledged to be always logically correct. A ship is feminine in English grammar, and a wife is neuter in German grammar. It may be 'logic' to refuse to conform to such usage; but it is not 'grammar.'

The oldest English expressed *sunset* by various phrases; they are all well illustrated in Bosworth and Toller's *A. S. Dictionary*. Thus the A. S. *set* meant a seat; hence, 'to sete ēode sunne,' the sun went to its seat, the sun set. Another word was *set-gang*, i.e. a going to one's seat; as in 'ofer set-gang,' after the seat-going of the sun, after sunset. Much commoner was the sb. *setlgang*, with a similar sense and use; as in 'æt sunne setlgang,' at the sun's seat-going, at sunset. Sometimes it was *setlung*; as in 'æfter sunnan setlunge,' after sunset.

Out of these usages arose the M. E. use of the verb *setten*, with reference to the subsidence of the sun. This occurs in *Havelok*, l. 2671: 'til that to sette bigan the sunne,' till the sun began to set. It clearly arose from a desire for abbreviation.

It is hardly necessary to go on. History shows that *set*, to subside, is properly intransitive, and arose in a somewhat different manner from the ordinary transitive *set*, the causal of *sit*.

The moral is, that we should never call grammatical usages in question till we have first looked at their history. It is just as unfair as it would be to brand a man as wicked of whose conduct we know nothing whatever.

### 443. 'Tooth-saw' (8 S. iv. 525; 1893).

We are all fallible; and even *N. and Q.* can err. I have just observed a curious misprint, which has produced a word such as Dr. Murray will carefully avoid; at any rate, in such a context.

In *N. and Q.*, 6 S. x. 422, col. 2, is a notice of a book called *Chaucer's Beads*, which is said to contain 'a concordance of Chaucer's proverbs and *tooth-saws.*'

However, Chaucer was no dentist; he only originated 'sooth saws,' i. e. true sayings. The expression 'sooth sawe' occurs in his *House of Fame*, l. 2089.

### 444. To 'hang out' (8 S. v. 366; 1894).

The phrase 'to hang out,' in the sense 'to lodge, reside,' is well known. See *Pickwick*, chap. xxx; *Daniel Deronda*, chap. xxxvii, in the *Century Dictionary*, which adds—'in allusion to the custom of hanging out a sign or "shingle" to indicate one's shop and business.'

No early instance of this is given; but I can supply it. In Middleton's play of *The Widow*, iv. 1, there is reference to a quack doctor who has lately come to reside in a certain town, and has taken up his quarters at the 'Cross Inn.'

'His flag *hangs out* in town here i' the Cross Inn,
  With admirable cures of all conditions.'

The editor's note says, 'It was usual for quacks to hang out a flag when they took up their quarters in a town.'

I presume the custom was not at all confined to quacks; they would hardly care to proclaim themselves *as such*. Of course they only did what other tradesmen did; the practice of hanging out 'signs' was common amongst tradesmen of all descriptions. In *The Alchemist* it is Abel Drugger, 'a seller of tobacco,' who asks the expert to invent a sign for him.

The *Century Dictionary* further explains that in the United States a 'shingle' means 'a small sign-board, especially that of a professional man,' whence the colloquial phrase 'to hang out one's shingle.' This shows that the custom found its way to America, where it is still practised; and that the phrase 'to hang out' is still known there in its original sense.

**445. Flotsam and Jetsam** (8 S. v. 475; 1894).

The explanations of these words in my *Dictionary* are incorrect. The correct explanations were, however, first given by myself in *Notes* printed for the Philological Society in 1888–90. My paper on the words was read on November 4, 1887.

*Flotsam* is an adaptation of the Anglo-French *floteson*, for which see p. 82 of the *Black Book of the Admiralty*, ed. Sir Travers Twiss, 1871, vol. i. It occurs, with various spellings, in Cotgrave (s. v. *flo*), Minsheu (1627) and Blount (1691). I further prove that *floteson* answers precisely to a Low Latin form \**fluctationem*, a barbarous variant of the accusative of *fluctuatio*.

*Jetsam*, better spelt *jetsom* or *jetson* (as in Minsheu), is an adaptation of the Anglo-French *getteson*, occurring in the same volume of the *Black Book*, pp. 96, 170. It presents no difficulty, being precisely the Lat. *iactationem*; from *iactare*, to cast.

My supposition that the words were partly of Scandinavian origin is wrong. They are both of Latin origin; from the root-verbs *fluere* and *iacere* respectively.

### 446. St. Swithun, Swithin, or Swith-hun (8 S. vi. 46 ; 1894).

The A. S. spelling was Swith-hun, as in Ælfric; for it is compounded of *swīth*, strong, and *hūn*, savage. One *h* was dropped (like the one *t* in *eight-th*) because *Swithhun* looked odd. The spelling *Swithin* arose from loss of the etymology and indistinctness of speech; it has nothing to recommend it except that it is much in vogue.

### 447. Edinburghean Grammar; as, 'He told you and I' (8 S. vi. 53; 1894).

We make, in English, no distinction of form between the nominative and accusative in the case of nouns. This has led to occasional confusion between the cases of pronouns; and that is all

The matter is discussed in Mätzner's *English Grammar*, tr. by Grice, vol. i. p. 294. The confusion spoken of is there said to be common in Yorkshire, Hampshire, Gloucestershire, Warwickshire, Worcestershire, and Herefordshire. In fact, it is common everywhere, and is nothing new, being found in many authors, from the fourteenth century to the present day; only, of course, meddling editors usually try to suppress the evidence. Mätzner gives numerous references. It is sufficient to give one of them:—'Yes, you have seen Cassio and *she* together'; *Othello*, iv. 2. 3.

### 448. 'Boneshaw' (8 S. vi. 65; 1892).

For this word, see the *New English Dictionary*. Dr. Murray does not give the etymology of the latter syllable.

*Shaw* corresponds to a Norse *skag-*. The Icel. *skaga* is

to project, stick out; and *skagi* is a projection of almost any kind; see Norweg. *skage*, sb., anything that sticks out; and see Rietz' *Swedish Dialect Dictionary*.

Hence *boneshaw*, or 'sciatica,' was supposed, originally, to be caused by some sort of lump on the bone. This is not true, so far as I know, but was a natural idea. In modern times, the sense of *shaw* being lost, it has been altered to *shave*, as if the disease were due to a scraping of the bone; hence *boneshave*. But in Somersetshire, *boneshave* meant (in 1790) 'a bony or horny excrescence or tumor growing out of horses' heels' (Grose). Precisely so.

### 449. Thackerayana (8 S. vi. 85; 1894).

The following nonsense verses by Thackeray, quoted in the *Daily Telegraph* of July 18, 1894, are too good to be lost:—

'When the bee is in the bonnet, and the heather on the brae,
And the lilting bubbly-jockey calls forth on every spray;
When the haggis in the muirland, and the estrich at the tree
Sing their matins at the sunset, dost thou think, my Jean, of me?'

*Bubbly-jockey* is, of course, a turkey. 'The haggis in the muirland' is a fine image.

### 450. Indian Magic: the Mango-growing trick (8 S. vi. 94; 1894).

The explanation of this trick is well known. It is given in detail in a book on conjuring by Hofmann. Practically, it is done by sleight of hand.

On each occasion the plant is covered up and again uncovered, so as to show its stages of growth; and on each occasion you see a different plant; so that it is done by repeated substitution.

Crude and unlikely as this explanation seems, it gives the right answer; for details, see a printed account. It can be done in any country, and is not peculiar to India.

**451. The Pronunciation of 'Iron'** (8 S. vi. 96; 1894).

Some say the *r* is mute; and some say it is not so, because we say 'iern.' All turns on the difference between sound and symbol. When a Southerner says 'iern,' he does not really sound the *r* at all. Neither is the *r* 'mute.' What really happens is, that the supposed non-mute *r* is really pronounced, as Mr. Sweet says, as 'a vocal murmur.' Instead of the trilled consonant, we hear the 'obscure vowel,' hardly differing (if at all) from the sound of *a* in *China*. This is why it rimes to 'thy urn,' as Mr. T. says; only let it be noted that the *ur* is really vocalic.

The obscure vowel is commonly denoted by a 'turned' *e*. Hence *iron* is pronounced as 'aiən'; *urn*, as 'əən'; and *Byron* as 'bairən' or 'baiərən,' the *r* being in this case trilled. In some districts the *r* is trilled, and *iron* then rimes with *Byron*. I have heard it, but I forget where. The phonetic symbol for our 'long *i*' is (ai), more strictly (əi).

**452. A Queer Etymology: 'gnoffe'** (8 S. vi. 143; 1894).

I have seen some strange etymologies in my time, but I think the following is the worst case.

In *A Dictionary of Slang*, by Barrère and Leland, p. xxi, we are offered the etymology of *gnoffe*, meaning a churl or miser.

'Its true root is probably the A. S. *cneov, cnuf*, or *cnūvan* (also *cneav*, knave), to bend, yield to, *cneovjan* (genuflectere).'

For whom is this written? Certainly not for such as know the A. S. alphabet. The following are the errors.

1. There is no A. S. *cneov*. Some Germans write *v* for *w*; but the sound of *v* is not intended by it. Probably *cnēow* is meant.

2. But *cnēow* is a sb., and means a knee. It is merely

the old form of *knee*. But what has *knee* to do with *gnoffe*?

3. There is no A. S. *cnuf* nor anything like it.

4. There is no A. S. *cnūvan*. If *cnāwan* is intended, it is the old spelling of *know*; which has nothing to do with *knee*, nor yet with *gnoffe*.

5. There is no A. S. *cneav*, nor yet *cneaw*. The A. S. for 'knave' is *cnafa*, or *cnapa*.

6. *Knave* has nothing to do with *gnoffe*, nor yet with *knee*, nor yet with *know*.

7. By *cneovjan* is meant *cnēowian*, to kneel. But what has this to do with *gnoffe*?

Surely it is mere charlatanry to cite non-existent words, and to pretend to have a knowledge of Anglo-Saxon when not even the sense of the symbols has been ascertained. It would have been better to say, in plain English, that *gnoffe* is derived from *knee*, or from *knave*, or from *know*, or from *kneel*. Then any plain man could have seen at once the absurdity of the suggestions. Of course *knee*, *knave*, and *know* are unrelated words, so we have no clue as to which of them is really meant. *Knave* comes, perhaps, the nearest, but it does not much matter; for, even in this case, there is no connexion whatever.

The days are past when sham Anglo-Saxon can be seriously quoted without discovery. There must be several hundred students by this time in England, Germany, and America, who have learnt the simplest rudiments of the language; and all such will regard the above performance with more amusement than respect.

[*Gnoffe* occurs in Chaucer (see my notes); and is derived from Heb. *ganāv*, a thief.]

### 453. The Etymology of Jingo (8 S. vi. 149; 1894).

It is an old superstition that *Jingo* is derived from the Basque word for God; but I know of no reason why we should believe it. This strange notion is, however, put forward for acceptance in the *Century Dictionary*, which has no evidence to offer, but the following vague and unlikely guess that it is 'probably[!] a form, introduced perhaps[!] by gipsies or soldiers, of the Basque *Jinkoa, Jainkoa*, contracted forms of *Jaungoicoa, Jangoikoa*, God, lit. the lord of the high.' So that the true Basque form has first to be contracted; then it must be used by gipsies, who notoriously come from Biscay, or else by soldiers, who must have come over the Pyrenees, and then across the whole of France to get here; and then these gipsies or soldiers further mauled the word till they reduced it to a form comfortable to swear by, and so on. And all this is so extremely probable! It all tallies with the old-world style of etymology—viz. that we must always have a make-up story, which is to be accepted without proof, and handed on as an article of faith, to disbelieve which is to be 'ill-informed!'

If we must have a guess, let it at least be a probable one. And this is why the rival theory, given in Webster's *Dictionary*, is worth notice: 'Said to be a corruption of St. Gingoulf.' Who this was we are not told; but, of course, it means St. Gengulfus.

The statement that it is 'a corruption' is erroneous. *Jingo* comes from *Gengulphus* or *Gengulfus* not by corruption, but by the strictest phonetic laws. It was not possible for it to become anything else, as any one who knows the phonetic laws of Anglo-French and of English can easily see for himself.

*Gengulfus* must, in French, become *Gengoulf, Gengoul, Gengou*, and, in English, can only be *Jingoo* or *Jingo*. We can test the ending *-ulfus* by the word *werwolf*; in the French *loup-garou*, the *ou* represents the Latinized *-ulfus*, corresponding to the Teutonic *wulf*. The change of *en* to *in* is a fixed law in English; the very word 'English' itself is pronounced *Inglish*, and I have given a list of words showing the same sound-change. See p. 258.

Who was St. Gengulphus? Alban Butler strangely omits him; yet most of us must have met with him in the *Ingoldsby Legends*. His day was May 11, and his life is given at length in the *Acta Sanctorum*. He was a Burgundian in the reign of King Pepin (752–768), and was martyred on May 11, 760. It is especially noted in the *Acta* that Belgians called him *Gengoal*:—'Gengulphum Belgae *Gengoal* vocant'; though the right phonetic form is rather *Gengoul*.

Sir H. Nicolas quotes him as 'Gengoul, Gengoux, and Gengou, in the Low Countries, or Gengulph.' Note that a place named St. Gingoulph lies on the lake of Geneva, opposite Vevey.

That we should love to swear by French saints needs no proof. Even Chaucer's Prioress swore by St. Loy, who was the Eligius of Limoges and Paris, just a century earlier than St. Jingo. Our ancestors swore by St. Martin of Tours, by St. Loy, by St. Denis, and many more. But we shall long wait for evidence that they swore in Basque! It is a pity that they did not.

### 454. Golf (8 S. vi. 158; 1894).

At the last reference, Webster's *Dictionary* is misquoted. Webster refers us, not to 'the Danish *kolf*,' but to the 'D. *kolf*'; and D. means 'Dutch.' He is, of course, quite right; the Danish form is *kolv*, the proper sense of which is 'shaft' or 'arrow,' originally, a cross-bow bolt. In my *Dictionary*, I refer to the account in Jamieson's *Dictionary*, and I quote the Dutch *kolf*, 'a club to strike little bouls or balls with,' from Sewel's *Dutch Dictionary*, 1754. I ought to have cited Hexham's *Dutch Dictionary*, 1658 (ninety-six years earlier). He gives: '*Een kolve*, a Banding-staff to strike a ball.' Koolman and Kluge show that *kolf* is related to Eng. *club* and *clump*, and even to the Lat. *globus*.

### 455. A Handful of Queer Etymologies (8 S. vi. 204; 1894).

To find startling etymologies we have only to consult books upon English antiquities written in the eighteenth century, or in the early part of the present century. The fashion at that time was to favour such as were most outrageous, or, at any rate, to quote them with admiration and respect.

Hampson's *Medii Ævi Kalendaria* (1841) is a capital book with an awkward title. It contains several etymologies which are highly ingenious. I quote a few.

'*Perseus*, from *P'Eres Zeus*, the sun' (sic); p. 53.

*Zeus* is, I suppose, Greek; to what language *P'Eres* belongs no clue is offered, nor are we informed how it comes to mean 'the sun.'

'*Charing Cross*, as it was erected by Edward *pour sa chere reine*, has been plausibly derived from the French'; p. 190.

I believe this delicious piece of humbug is still admired.

'*Gauch*, whence *jocus*'; p. 212. *Gauch*, here quoted, is the German for a simpleton. Germanic words are so often derived from Latin that it is quite refreshing to find a Latin word derived from German, for a change.

'In Yorkshire a third part of the county is of vast extent, and shires, hundreds, and wapentakes being formerly set out *per ambulationem*, by processions on foot, this was performed by processions made on horseback; and hence the name of "Ryding";' p. 228.

This is not Hampson's own; it was invented by Dr. Kuerden, 'a learned antiquary of the seventeenth century.' Hardy guess-work was evidently regarded as 'learning,' not by any means as presumptuous ignorance.

'The word *goblin* has been derived from *God Belin*, who is the same as Bel or Belus'; p. 249.

Certainly *God Belin* is excellent French.

'*Pales*, the tutelary deity of husbandry and grazing, whose name bears a great affinity to *Baal, Belus*, the sun'; p. 249.

All our old antiquaries had 'Baal' on the brain; it was a blessed name to them.

'Hills in England which have been the site of heliacal idolatry [how is this ascertained?] are commonly called *Toot Hills*, from the Egyptian *Thoth, Taut, Teut, Tet*, or *Taautres*, who is the same as Mercury, or Buddha, Osiris, and Maha Deva. He was known to the Irish as *Tuth*, and gave rise to the English letter *Te*, the Greek *Tau*, and the Hebrew *Thau* and *Teth*'; p. 254.

This is all a revelry of delight. It follows that the Hebrew *Thau* and *Teth* are the same letter, and that Egyptian was freely spoken all over England.

'I suspect that we owe the word *aroynt* to the *rowan-tree* ... quasi, a roant thee, or a roan to thee, witch'; p. 272.

'*La-ith-mas*, the day of the obligation of grain, is pronounced *La-ee-mas*, a word readily corrupted to *Lammas*; *ith* signifies all kinds of grain, particularly wheat; and *mas* signifies all kinds of fruit, especially the acorn, whence the word *mast*'; p. 334.

*La-ith-mas* is meant to be Irish. It follows that *Candle-mas* is 'candle-mast.'

### 456. Geason or Geson (8 S. vi. 232; 1894).

The more correct spelling is with *ea*, as the Middle-English was *gēsen*, with open *e*. It means 'rare' rather than 'wonderful,' and a still better translation is 'scarce.' It was fairly common in the sixteenth century, and previously; but I should say that it was not *much* used after 1660. The A. S. form was not *goesne*, because there is no *oe* in Anglo-Saxon, though the symbol occurs in Northumbrian. The A. S. word was *gæsne*, with long *æ*, which produced long open *e* in Mid. English; and such words were spelt with *ea* in Tudor times. It is allied to A.S. *gād*, Goth. *gaidw*, lack.

For examples, see four in Stratmann's *Mid. Eng. Dictionary*; five in Halliwell's *Dictionary*, under 'Geason' and 'Geson'; and further, in my *Notes to P. Plowman*, p. 318, where I observe that Ray notes '*Geazon*, scarce, hard to come by,' as being an Essex word. As Ray wrote in 1691, he gives a later instance than that in 1660; but he considered the word provincial, and I dare say it is still in use. Nall includes it in his *East-Anglian Glossary* printed in 1866.

### 457. St. Parnell (8 S. vi. 256; 1894).

The answer to this question (as to many others, e. g. that about *geason* on the same page) is given in my *Notes to Piers Plowman*. These notes have been plentifully pillaged by exactly one writer[1], but are wholly unknown to the general, who have no conception of their extent and usefulness. On this occasion I shall quote from p. 80:—

'"May 31 was dedicated to St. Petronilla the Virgin. She was supposed to be able to cure the quartan ague."—Chambers, *Book of Days*, ii. 389. The name, once common, scarcely survives, except as a surname in the form Parnell; see Bardsley's *English Surnames*, p. 56.'

### 458. Lagan (8 S. vi. 265; 1894).

I suspect that lawyers are quite as much given to bad etymology as other people; and certainly the word *lagan* has been queerly defined.

In Cowel's *Interpreter*, as reprinted in 1701, we find, s. v. 'Flotson,' that 'Lagon, alias Lagan or Ligan, is that which lieth in the bottom of the sea.' Cowel here agrees with Blount's *Nomolexicon*, which has the same, and gives the derivation from A. S. *licgan*, to lie.

The very same work, s.v. 'Lagan,' declares that *lagan*

---

[1] [The editor of the *Catholicon Anglicum*.]

are goods cast out of a ship, and that the sailors fastened a buoy to them. 'If the ship be drowned, or otherwise perish, these goods are called *ligan*, a *ligando*; and so long as they continued upon the sea, they belong to the admiral; but if they are cast upon the land, they are then called a wreck, and belong to him that hath the wreck.'

We thus gather that the goods were both at the bottom of the sea, and upon it; that they were stationary and marked with a buoy, and that they also floated about, and could be cast ashore. A very remarkable story.

Of course the false spelling *ligan* was invented to get hold of a Latin etymology, from *ligare*. It is impossible that it can come from *ligare*, because the Lat. *ligamen* became *lien* in French and English; and the attempt to derive it straight from Lat. *ligamen* is hardly satisfactory. The whole story is knocked on the head by the fact that the original Old French word was also *lagan*.

It is given in Godefroy, who has: '*Lagan, lagand, lagant, laguen*, s. m., débris d'un vaisseau que la mer jette sur le rivage, les épaves.' Godefroy gives several quotations. One valuable one is from a letter of Edward II of England, dated July 22, 1315, in which our king says: 'Tous les *lagans* qui eskieent ou pueent eskier en toute le coste de le mer.' All the quotations refer to wreckage thrown ashore; there is no word about buoys.

The problem is thus narrowed to this, viz. to find the origin of the O. French *lagan* or *lagand*.

I have solved many such problems, and have incurred some obloquy, in consequence, from such as had pet theories of their own. Let some one else try his hand this time. [Ducange, s. v. *Lagan*, is mistaken.]

### 459. 'Huckshins' (8 S. vi. 326; 1894).

This is explained in Elworthy's *Somersetshire Wordbook* as the 'hock-shins; under side of the thighs, just above the bend of the knee'; with a quotation from the *Exmoor Scolding*. Halliwell also gives *hucksheens*, from the same. Please note that this is 'folk-etymology.' The real sense is not 'hock-shins,' but 'hock-sinews,' as any one may see by consulting Stratmann, s. v. '*hoh*.' The verb *to hox* (Halliwell) is merely a truncated form of *to hock-sinew*.

### 460. 'Horkey' (8 S. vi. 334; 1894).

At the last reference we are told that *hawkey* is a mispronunciation of *horkey*. It is quite clear, however, that *horkey* is a misspelling of *hawkey*.

We must not follow the late spelling of Bloomfield, but the spelling in older books.

The information in Brand really helps us. It is clear that *hawky*, or *hoky*, or *hocky* is an adjectival form, from the substantive *hawk*, *hoke*, *hock*, whatever that may mean. The substantive appears in the compound *hock-cart*, in Herrick's *Hesperides*, and in *Otia Sacra*, 1648 (Brand). Hence *hockey-cart*, in Salmon's *Survey*; *hoky* or seed-cake, in Sir Thos. Overbury; and in *Poor Robin's Almanack* for August 1676:—

> '*Hoacky* is brought home with hollowing,
> Boys with plumb-cake the *cart* following.'

The real difficulty in this word is to know whether the vowel was originally long or short. If short, which is quite possible, then there may be a connexion with the E. Friesic *hokke*, a set-up heap of corn or turves; Low German (Bremen) *hokke*, a set of four sheaves set up in a small shock; Ger. *hocke*, a heap of corn or hay (Kluge).

* The etymological difficulty is very great, so that there is a wide field for talk that cannot easily be shown to be irrelevant. [No such talk ensued.]

### 461. So-ho (8 S. vi. 365; 1894).

The origin of *so-ho* was discussed in *N. and Q.* some years ago, but the right result was not given.

I find that the *Century Dictionary* is also incorrect as regards this matter. It gives the etymology as from the Eng. *so*, adverb, and *ho*! an interjection.

This, however, is only the popular etymology, due to substitution of the Eng. *so* (which makes no sense) for an Anglo-French word which was less generally understood.

By good fortune, the exact origin of the expression is precisely recorded, on high authority. It is given in the *Venery de Twety*, originally written in the time of Edward II, printed in the *Reliquiae Antiquae*, by Halliwell and Wright, vol. i. pp. 149-154. On the last of these pages we read: '*Sohow* is [as] moche to say as *sa-how*, for because that it is short to say, we say alway *so-how*.' This means that *so-how* was the English adaptation of the original Anglo-French *saho*, in which the sense of *sa* had been lost.

The sense of *sa* is, practically, given more than once. One of the hunting cries is given in full as ' Ho, so [*for* sa], amy, so, venez a couplere, sa, arere, sohow'; and the like. *Sa* is merely the Norman form of the Mod. French *ça*, which Cotgrave explains by 'hither, approach, come neer.' Similarly *cy* is for *ici*, here. Hence the cry means 'Come hither, ho!' which makes good sense. [Compare '*Sa, sa, sa, sa*,' in *King Lear*, iv. 6. 207.]

### 462. Chaucer's 'Anelida and Arcite' (8 S. vii. 471; 1895).

I have frequently been reproved (I do not know why) for correcting others with unmistakable clearness. In the present case I have to thank R. R. for his clear explanation of a most absurd blunder of my own. It is only one more proof that even the most careful students fall, at times, into error[1]. Let me add that Chaucer himself furnishes an excellent example of *staves* in the sense of '*sticks*' in the following passage:—

> 'By goddes bones! whan I bete my knaves
> She bringeth me forth the grete clobbed *staves*,
> And cryeth—slee the dogges everichoon.'

### 463. Chum. I (8 S. vii. 514; 1895).

At the last reference we are told that the Latin *c* in *cum* was originally pronounced as in Italian—that is to say, the Italian *con* is pronounced *chon*. Is it, indeed? This is news for Italy. We are also informed that the change from *ch* to *k* is due to 'phonetic decay,' which simplifies and 'hardens' sounds. But in fact the change is usually the other way. Decay 'softens' sounds, if I may for once use a sadly unscientific term. It would be interesting to learn the extremely new lesson, in what language a *ch* has become a *k*[2]. We might as well expect water to run uphill.

Much nonsense is often talked about the Latin *c*. It was originally pronounced like the Greek *k* before all vowels. The easy proof is this. The perfect tense of *cadere* was formed by reduplication, i.e. by doubling the *k*-sound. Thus the perfect was *ce-cidi* (*ke-kid-i*). Those who think

---

[1] In Chaucer's *Anelida*, l. 183, we have:
> 'His newe lady holdeth him so narowe
> Up by the brydel, *at the staves ende*
> That every word, he dradde hit as an arowe.'

The metaphor is that of one who rides a horse, and, whilst tightly holding the animal in by the bridle, keeps him at the stick's end, i.e. beats him frequently with the end of a stick. As the expression 'at the staves ende' is awkwardly introduced, I had taken it to refer to the shaft of a cart; which cannot be right, as riders then rode *upon* horses, and not *behind* them.

•[2] It was argued that the Spanish *j*, once palatal, has become a guttural. But this is not really an instance of 'phonetic decay.' I believe it was due to external (i.e. Moorish) influence, which is a different thing.

otherwise have to prove that twice $k = $ double $s$; or that twice a cow is equal to two sheep.

Phonetic decay altered the Latin $c$ before $e$ and $i$ only. In Italian it took the sound of *ch* in *chin*; in Spanish, the sound of *th* in *thin*; and in French, the sound of *s* in *sin*. Only the sound $k$, and no other, can produce *ch*, *th*, and *s*, all three.

We are also informed that the original Latin $c$ is preserved in the English *chapel*! But how about the Welsh *capel*, as in *Capel Curig*? Is that pronounced with the $c$ as *ch*? Even Englishmen, with their supercilious and ridiculously ostentatious ignorance of Welsh, know better than that.

### 464. Chum. II (8 S. viii. 330; 1895).

So far as I am concerned, this is my last letter upon the present subject; and I am sure this announcement will be thankfully received.

Whether the change of $c$ ($k$) to *ch* in English words went through all its stages or not before 1066 I cannot say. It was quite a gradual process. But the preliminary stages, such as the breaking of $a$ into $ea$ in Southern words, are found quite early. I have nothing to add to Dr. Sweet's explanation in his *History of English Sounds*, p. 143; and I do not know why I need explain all over again what he has there explained so well.

The change from $c$ to *ch* only occurs in words of native origin when the $c$ is followed by $e$ or $i$, or by sounds which naturally cause palatization, such as $æ$, $ea$ for $a$, $eo$ for Teutonic $i$, and the like. If a dialect resists the change of $a$ to $ea$, then there is no *ch*. This is remarkably shown in English, where we have the Midland forms *calf, care, cold*, (A. S. *ceald*, Mercian *cald*), by the side of *chalk, chary* (adj. of *care*), and other Southern forms.

I have no doubt that whenever $ca$ became *cha* in Old French, as in *chambre* from *camera*, there was an intermediate stage, which we may roughly represent by $k(i)amera$[1]. This never happened in the Picard dialect; and I may claim to be the very person who first discovered (in 1882) the etymology of the curious word *cark*. It is simply the Picard *kark* or *karke*, a word which in Parisian and in English is spelt *charge*.

But why not consult authorities? See Sweet, *History of English Sounds*; Mayhew, *Old English Phonology*; Schwan, *Grammatik des Altfranzösischen*; Horning, Introduction to *La Langue et Littérature Françaises*, and the rest.

One parting shot at those who think that the Latin *c* was never a *k*. In the English Authorized Version we find the spellings *Kish* and *Cis* for the same person, the latter spelling being taken from the Vulgate. Are we to say that Saul was the son of *Sis*? Or, perhaps, in Italian ideas, he was the son of *Chis*!

## 465. Deficient Lines in English Verse (8 S. viii. 45; 1895).

I have shown that Chaucer frequently begins a line of five accents with a single accented syllable, and that similar lines are very common in Lydgate. I suspect they were also fairly common in our old dramatic poetry, only the editors (believing in themselves more than in the author) frequently added a sly additional syllable. Nevertheless, I just note a few that have fallen casually under my notice. In Routledge's reprint (1883) of Greene and Peele's *Works*, I find these examples :—

'Proud, | disdainful, cruel, and unjust'; p. 98.
'Mine, | and none but mine, shall honour thee'; p. 99.
'I | am she that curèd thy disease'; p. 107.

Here the editor calmly purposes to read: '*And* I am.' That is just what comes of meddlesomeness.

---

[1] How else the change could have happened we have not yet been informed.

'Fire, famine, and as cruel death'; p. 108.

Here *Fire* is a dissyllable, as usual; read 'Fi | er.'

'Gra | cious as the morning-star of heaven'; p. 168.
'Were | I baser born, my mean estate'; p. 206.

Here the editor proposes two different emendations, none being needed.

'Bow | thee, Andrew, bend thy sturdy knee;' p. 211.

So, again, in Cunningham's edition of Marlowe's *Works* I have already noted these:—

'*Tan* | *ti:* I'll first fawn [up]on the wind.'
*Edw. II*, i. 1; p. 118.

'Der | by, Sal-is-bury, Lincoln, Leicester.'
*Edw. II*, i. 1; p. 119.

Here are two consecutive lines of this character:—

'Lay | hands on that traitor Mortimer!
Lay | hands on that traitor Gav-es-ton!'
*Edw. II*, i. 4; p. 122.

''Tis | my hand; what gather you by this?'
*Edw. II*, v. 6; p. 153.

Here the editor has done well in resisting the temptation to substitute *It is* for *'Tis*.

'Mar | ry, sir, in having a smack in all.'
*Massacre at Paris*, i. 8; p. 160.

'Je rome's Bible, Faustus, view it well.'
*Faustus*, i. 1; p. 60.

'Ho | mo, fuge! Whither shall I fly?'
*Faustus*, ii. 1; p. 65.

'Frank | fort, Lubeck, Moscow, and where not.'
*Jew of Malta*, iv. 1; p. 107.

'Bá | rabas, send me three hundred crowns.'
*Jew of Malta*, iv. 5; p. 110.

Truly, times are altered since that (usually) excellent critic James Russell Lowell denied that such lines as these existed, or could exist, in English poetry, in his (otherwise) excellent article on Chaucer. The statement that they could not exist I easily refuted by a simple reference to Tennyson's *Vision of Sin*. The moral is, that editors should let the texts alone when they can.

### 466 'Parson' (8 S. viii. 65; 1895).

Perhaps the clearest old example of this word, as being a variant of *person*, is in the edition of 1555 of Lydgate's *Siege of Troye*, fol. H i. col. 2:—

> 'For eche trespasse must consydered be,
> Iustly measured by the qualyty
> Of hym that is offended, and also
> After the *parson* by whom the wrong is do.'

Probably the original MS. expressed the word in a contracted form, with the usual symbol which may be read either as *par* or *per*.

### 467. 'Wederoue' in Old French (8 S. viii. 65; 1895).

There is a queer mistake, s. v. 'wederoue,' in Godefroy's *Old French Dictionary*. He gives *wederoue* (a scribal error for *woderoue*, by the usual confusion of *e* with *o* in the fifteenth century), with the variant forms *wuderoue*, *wodruffe*, which occur in glosses to translate Lat. *hastula regia*. Hence Godefroy gives the conjectural sense: 'P. -ê. une arme de jet, lance ou autre.' But *hastula regia* was an old name for asphodel (Lewis and Short), and was translated in English by the word which we now spell *woodruff*. Hence *woderoue* is not 'a little lance,' but the English name of a plant.

### 468. Hilda (8 S. viii. 72; 1895).

\* I beg leave to dissent from the dictum at the latter reference to the effect that 'Hilda is derived from Hıldur, the war-maiden or chooser of the dead'; and I entirely decline to submit to Miss Yonge's authority as to Christian names. No doubt Miss Yonge's book is the best on this subject; but only because there is no better. It was written in the time of pre-scientific etymology; and for purposes of scholarship cannot be depended on for a moment.

The whole matter is obscured by the terrible inaccuracy of the authorities. Good English names are turned into Latin, and so disfigured as to be almost unrecognizable. For example, Æthelthryth is turned into Etheldreda, which is merely bad English without having the merit of being Latin at all. Even Audry is better than that. Again, Swithhun is not only turned into Swithun, with one *h*, rendering the word meaningless, but is even changed into Swithin. Briefly, no one will ever understand English names until he grasps the fact that they are English, and not Latin, nor yet High-German. What is the use of citing foreign forms when we can get at the native ones? And when will it ever even dawn on the English mind that the forms given in our native manuscripts are usually older, better, and altogether more primitive and original than any other 'Germanic' forms, with the sole exception of Mœso-Gothic? Possessing manuscripts of priceless authority, we often prefer modern High-German, of all languages! What can we expect from such a process but darkness?

In what language does such a form as 'Hildur' occur? In Icelandic we have the masculine form 'Hildir' and the feminine Hildr. 'Hildur' is probably an ignorant substitution for the latter.

As to *Hilda*, 'there is no room for doubt' that it is the Latinized spelling of the English *Hild*. Even Beda, though writing in Latin, uses the form Hild as the name of the Abbess of Whitby. The form *Hild-a* is a Latinism of later date. As to the sense, *Hild* does not mean 'darkness,' nor does it mean 'mercy.' The word for 'mercy' is Ger. *Huld*, which differs from *hild* just as *pull* differs from *pill*, i.e. totally. The symbols *u* and *i* are different, and the difference in the words is in the vowel. Different vowels make different words :—a golden sentence, which I recommend all readers of this article to learn by heart.

As to the sense, *hild* means simply 'battle,' neither more nor less. It does not mean war-maiden at all, but could be applied to an abbess, as every one knows. Neither has it anything whatever to do with choosing the dead. To call a girl simply 'battle' seems a strange proceeding, but this does not alter the fact. It so happens that the giving of such names to girls was a favourite habit of the English, as is well known to all students of Anglo-Saxon.

To sum up. *Hilda* does not mean 'Hildur,' but stands for *Hild*. It is neither Icelandic nor German, but a bad monkish-Latin form of a native English name. It is unconnected with 'darkness' and with 'mercy.' It neither means 'war-maiden' nor 'chooser of the slain.' That is, there are at least six mistakes in an article in which we are told that there is 'no room for doubt.'

I will merely say, to all whom it may concern, that the whole subject of English names and English place-names is in a parlous state; so much so, that nothing can be taken on trust. Verify your references, and consult the list at the end of Bardsley's book on surnames. And do not put faith in Miss Yonge; hers was a good book for its date, and that is all that can be said.

**469. 'Effrontery'** (8 S. viii. 85; 1895).

According to the *New English Dictionary* there is some difficulty as to the original sense of the O. Fr. *esfronter*. It seems worth while to suggest that it has been confused with O. F. *afronter*. At any rate, I find in the supplement to Godefroy the entry: '*Afronterie*, s.f. bravade insolente, effronterie'; and it is remarkable that all the three quotations which Godefroy cites spell the word *affronterie* with double *ff*

### 470. 'Ha-ha' (8 S. viii. 117; 1895).

This word has frequently been discussed in *N. and Q.*, but I do not remember seeing the right explanation given.

It has nothing whatever to do with A. S. *haga*, a hedge, which comes out in modern English as *haw*. Cf. *haw-thorn*. The derivation from the interjection *ha*! *ha*! is quite correct, as may easily be seen by consulting Littré and the new French etymological dictionary by Hatzfeld. But the usual explanation, viz. that the *haha* so suddenly surprises you that you involuntarily cry *haha*! (which no one ever did yet), is quite absurd. It is the *haha* itself which, as it were, cries *ha*! *ha*! that is, 'Stop! or you'll tumble in!' The very look of it is a warning, and that is all that is meant.

The English word is merely a loan-word from French. The Old French *hahé* was a hunting term, calling upon the dogs to stop, a fact which gives the clue at once. The variant *haha* similarly denotes a break in the ground, calling upon one to stop. Scarron actually used *haha* to denote an old woman of such surpassing ugliness that she came upon the gazer as a surprise! We should call her 'a caution,' which is just the sense of *haha*.

### 471. Derivation of Theodolite or Theodolith
(8 S. viii. 130; 1895).

I think I have quite a new light upon this curious word. I do not believe that it has any connexion whatever with θέα, or with ὁδός, or with λίθος. It is perfectly certain that it cannot be connected with λίθος, as is proved by the early usages of the word. The statement by Dr. H. is not merely a guess, but a very bad one, unsupported by a tittle of evidence.

My own guess at the word is quite a new one, unlike any that has ever yet been suggested. My belief is that it is derived from the personal name *Theodulus*, which, as every schoolboy knows, means 'servant of God.'

Contrary to the usual method of guessers, I have founded my guess on evidence, of a sort. In Godefroy's *Old French Dictionary* will be found an entry under 'Theodulet,' a substantive which he does not seem to be able to explain; and my notion is that *theodelitus* is merely an (ignorant) Latinized form of the same word.

Though Godefroy cannot explain *theodulet*, I think I can. It is well known that in medieval times a grammar was called a *donet*, from its author, a certain *Donatus*. Again, a certain collection of fables was called an *ysopet*, from the writer whose name we spell *Aesop*. And it appears from the quotation in Godefroy that *theodulet* was the name for some sort of book or treatise,—a treatise, namely, by a man called Theodulus. Cf. *pamphl-et*, from Pamphila.

This lands us in a track that is extremely difficult to follow up. Who was the Theodulus who, presumably, first marked the rim of a circle (used in measuring) with considerable exactitude? Remember that a *theodolite* meant at first 'a marked circular rim,' and was originally quite independent of a telescope, or any 'way of seeing'— a fact which entirely upsets the guesses hitherto current. (See the Supplement to my *Etym. Dict.*)

All that I have found out as yet is, that Theodulus was rather a common name, as there was a saint of that name. The last fact is familiar to all who have ever been to Zermatt. [And I am told that a treatise called *Theodolet* is mentioned in Rabelais (I. xiv.); where *Theodolet= Ecloga Theoduli*. This *Ecloga Vocum Atticarum* is a collection of Phrases in Attic Greek, by a medieval monk named Thomas, surnamed Theodulus; an edition by Ritschel was published at Halle in 1832. He is the same person as the Thomas Magister referred to in Liddell and Scott's *Greek Dictionary*.]

### 472. First Burning for Heresy in England
(8 S. viii. 156; 1895).

It is quite certain that there were several cases of burning for heresy in England before 1401. This question is discussed in the preface to Arnold's edition of Wyclif's *Works*, and in the Preface to my edition of the third text (C-text) of *Piers the Plowman*, p. xiii. William Sautre was the first person burnt for heresy under the new act passed in the beginning of the reign of Henry IV. All that this act did was to facilitate the process. Before it was passed, the ecclesiastics who condemned the heretics were powerless to carry out the sentence themselves; they had to hand over the criminal to the secular arm. The new act did away with this necessity, and so rendered the criminal's fate the more swift and certain[1]. And that was all the difference. Hence the popular notion, that no one was burnt before 1401, is a mere delusion.

### 473. Roadnight (8 S. viii. 166; 1895).

Under the heading 'Coincidences' (ante, p. 124), the question is raised as to the etymology of the surname Roadnight. The answer is simple enough; it certainly stands for 'Road-knight'; A.S. *rādcniht*. It does not, however, answer, in sense, to the Modern English 'knight of the road.' The A.S. *rād* was used with reference to *riding*, and *cniht* means *servant*. So that *rādcniht* was a riding retainer, a servant on horseback. The Mod. E. *road* was originally 'a path for riding,' as distinguished from a foot-path.

### 474. Foxglove (8 S. viii. 186; 1895).

The A.S. name of this plant is *foxes glōfa*, 'glove of the fox.' I make this note because the assertion is constantly

---

[1] [The words used were to the effect that the punishment might be administered 'uberius et celerius.']

being repeated that it is a corruption of 'folk's glove.' See, for example, *N. and Q.* 8th S. viii. 155. Whenever a writer uses the word 'corruption,' we may commonly suspect him to be guessing. It is the one word that is prized above all others by those who prefer assertion to fact. When any quotation can be found, either in Anglo-Saxon or Early English, for the phrase *folces glōfa* or *folkes glove*, the 'corruption' theory may be seriously considered, but not till then. Always bear in mind that during the last century, and the former half of the present, baseless guesses of this character were invented by the hundred. Only old quotations can save us from the nuisance of their tyranny.

**475. Cambridge** (8 S. viii. 265; 1895).

Every one who attempts to make any research as to the origin of Cambridge will soon find out for himself that the name of the Cam is quite modern. When any one can produce any example of the form *Cam*, either with the *bridge* or without, before A.D. 1350, we may consider the matter further; but certainly not till then.

The old name was, practically[1], Grantabridge, turned by the Normans into Cauntebridge (1142), afterwards shortened to Caumbridge (*Paston Letters*), and Cāmbridge; out of which the modern river-name Cam was wrongly evolved. I say wrongly, because it was done by help of the written word; the spoken word would have made it *Came*[2]. This shows how diligent our old writers were in evolving etymological falsities.

It is simply a question of historical research, as I have already hinted.

The A.S. name for the river was *Granta*, and it is

---

[1] Really 'Grantan-brycg'; of which I give the sense.

[2] The local pronunciation is *Kyme-bridge*, where *kyme* rimes with *time*. Those who know this fact seldom know how to interpret it.

called Granta still by the people who have not been taught better. Even educated people admit that the name is Granta at Trumpington. The A. S. name for the place was *Grantanbrycg.*

We still speak of Grantchester, for which the A. S. name is *Granta-ceaster.* For references, see the Dictionary, and the *A. S. Chronicle.* The fact that the forms *Cam* and *Cambrycg* never occur in any MS., from the year 700 downwards to 1350, is significant enough to such as are accustomed to work at etymology instead of merely guessing at it.

In an *Old English Miscellany*, ed. Morris (E.E.T.S.), p. 145, is a list of the shires and hundreds of England in the thirteenth century. Here we find *Grauntebrugge-schire* (l. 48), i. e. *Grantabridge-shire,* as the name for the county.

The first line of Chaucer's *Reve's Tale* shows the next stage; the MSS. have *Caunter-bruge, Canta-bregge, Cantabrigge*; the very late Lansdowne MS. has *Cam-brugge,* the oldest instance of the spelling *Cam* which I can call to mind. Of course the form *Cam-brugge* destroys the metre of the line, for a trisyllable is imperatively required. Hence the blunder was not the author's.

This *Cam* really stands for *Caum* or *Caam*; and the *m* is due to the following *b*; *nb* turns into *mb* as a matter of course. This is why the *a* in *Came* (so pronounced) is long; cf. E. *chamber*, M.E. *chāmbre, chaumbre.*

Spenser (*F. Q.* iv. 11, 34) calls the river the *Grant.* Drayton's *Polyolbion* makes a special study of river-names; and we there learn that the river that flows by Cambridge was called the *Grant*; Song 21, l. 51 [1]. It was my fellow-collegian who in his *Lycidas* (l. 103) spoke of *Camus*; observe that, for him, the *a* was long.

[1] Later on, at l. 107, he has 'That *Cam,* her daintiest flood, long since entituled *Grant*'; showing that he held *Grant* to be the true old name.

**476. The King's Quair** (8 S. viii. 274; 1895).

I had not intended to write a note on this subject; but I now find it necessary to do so. One of the replies at the latter reference attributes the *Complaint of the Black Knight* to Chaucer, whereas we know, on MS. authority, that it was written by Lydgate. See my note in my larger edition of Chaucer's *Works*, i. 56, or that in my edition of the *Minor Poems*, p. xlv. I may add that this poem will appear in its due place in my supplemental volume, which will contain the chief poems that have been at any time wrongly attributed to Chaucer.

The citation of the 'Icel. *kver*' (not '*kwer*') is also misleading. It is not a true Icelandic word at all, but merely the Old French *quaier* done into modern Icelandic spelling.

But now that I am about it, I may mention that 'The Kingis Quair' (formerly ill-spelt 'Quhair') is one of the 'curiosities of literature.' My edition of it, for the Scottish Text Society, was the *eleventh* in point of time; but it was, nevertheless, the *first* that was really edited from the MS. itself, and is the only one that is decently correct. I know of no parallel to this. The first edition, in 1785, was printed from an incorrect transcript made by 'an ingenious young gentleman,' who could not read the MS. correctly [1]; and the succeeding editions (except my own) were reprints from that first edition. One editor, in 1815, discovered that this original text was incorrect; but he did not discover it till too late. None of the other editors ever consulted the MS. at all; such a proceeding was, in those days, considered superfluous.

My first essay in editing Middle English was in 1865, thirty years ago, when I edited *Lancelot of the Laik* for the

[1] [This statement was somewhat too courageously denied by a correspondent who asserted that the first editor, Mr. Tytler, copied the MS. himself. However, Mr. Tytler is the very person who says the contrary!]

English Text Society. My announcement that the previous edition (printed from the same MS.) had never been properly re-read with the MS., and swarmed with errors, created quite a sensation at the time. I cited nineteen bad mistakes, and mentioned that four whole lines at a time had been omitted in two places; but I might have added that the variations from the MS. really amounted to several hundred!

Even now some ignorance remains. A gentleman who was so good as to reproduce *The Kingis Quair* after me, and to speak of my labours with some patronage, took occasion to show his knowledge of the subject by explaining the word *conyng* as 'skilful[1].' If he had but condescended to consult my glossary, he would have found out that it meant 'a rabbit.' It occurs in a list of animals at stanza 157.

### 477. 'Slubber-Degullion:' 'Strangullion' 
(8 S. viii. 353; 1895).

The etymology of this word is simple when once pointed out. The M. E. *gulion*, occurring in Gower (*Conf Amant.*, ii. 359), is a word of French origin, and meant 'a kind of gown' (Halliwell). Hence *slubber-de-gullion*, one who slubbers or slobbers his gown or robe—a dirty fellow, a paltry fellow. I do not quite understand the *de*. Perhaps (it is a guess) it should be *slubber'd-y gullion*, i. e. the pp. in *-ed*, with the adjectival suffix *-y*.

*Strangullion* is a totally different word, and the resemblance is accidental, the suffix being *-ullion*, whilst *strang-* is the base. The following extract from Cotgrave sufficiently explains it: '*Estranguillons,* m., the strangles, a disease (in horses, &c.).' It is allied apparently to *strangle*, O. F *estrangler*. Cf. 'Poir [sic] d'*estranguillon*, a choake-peare' (Cotgrave).

[1] [The MS. has *connyng*, with two *n*'s, in the senses of 'skill' and 'skilful'; and *conyng*, with one *n*, in the sense of 'coney' or 'rabbit.']

**478. 'Running the Gantlope'** (8 S. viii. 392; 1895).

The amazing and amusing quotation which derives the word *gantlope* from 'a well-known town in Flanders' is useful to me; and I am very thankful to have the quotation. If ever I write that book upon 'popular etymologies,' it will serve, though it is not quite new. One always knows the ways of the popular etymologist; he never gives his dates. So in the present case. If the word had been invented at Ghent, he could have ascertained, approximately, the date of such invention. However, Skinner, in 1671, gave it as a guess. He says—'*Gantlope*, supplicium militare. Author *Dict. Angl. putat* à Gandavo, urbe inclyta Flandriae,' &c.

**479. Welsh Place-names** (8 S. viii. 396; 1895).

It is not long since I took a railway-ticket for Llanfairpwllgwyngyll, the name of which has been humorously extended to astonish the Saxon [1]. There is no trouble about it; you simply ask for a ticket for Llanfair, which you pronounce, roughly speaking, as 'Hlanver,' with the Anglo-Saxon *hl*, and you get it at once; and you find simply 'Llanfair' on the ticket. The 'pwllgwyngyll' is superfluous in the neighbourhood, but is useful in directing letters; and then you merely put 'Llanfair P. G.,' as in Baddeley's excellent guide-book.

I wish I could impress upon my countrymen the desirability of condescending to learn the Welsh alphabet, which is extremely easy and almost perfectly phonetic (if it were not for that stupid double-sounding *y*). It would be an insult to a Frenchman to ask for a ticket for Lyons, and to pronounce it as the English *lions*. It is equally an insult

---

[1] It means 'Saint-Mary's by the white-hazel pool,' to which is added, 'very near the raging whirlpool of Llandisilio and the red rocky islet of Gogo,' all of which is, of course, superfluous.

to a Welshman to ignore the native pronunciation; and I do not see why any gentleman should stoop to such effrontery. As things are, men stay for weeks in Wales, and yet decline to pronounce the Welsh *ŷf* as a *v*.

### 480. Patriot (8 S. viii. 517; 1895).

I have shown in my *Dictionary* that the word 'patriot' occurs in Minsheu's *Dictionary*, ed. 1627; and I quote from Cotgrave's *French Dictionary* (which first appeared in 1611) the following: '*Patriote*, m. a patriot, ones countreyman.' Cotgrave also has: '*Patriot*, m. A father, or protector of the Countrey, or Commonwealth; also, as *Patriote*.' Littré shows in his *Dictionary*, that Voltaire [who ascribes the first use of the F. *patriote* to Saint-Simon, who died in 1755] made a mistake; for the F. *patriote* was used, in its modern sense, as early as the sixteenth century.

### 481. Led will (8 S. ix. 69; 1896).

Whatever 'led will' may mean now, it doubtless once meant the same as 'will led,' a phrase which occurs in a specimen of the Norfolk dialect which I have now in the press[1]. 'Will led' is said to mean 'demented,' but the original sense was 'bewildered.'

The solution is this: *Will*, in this phrase, has no immediate connexion with *will* in the sense of 'inclination,' but represents the Scandinavian form of the English *wild*, which often had the sense of 'astray, bewildered, all abroad, at a loss,' and the like. See the Icel. *villr* in Vigfusson, *wild* in my *Dictionary*, and *will* in my glossary to Barbour's *Bruce*. Ultimately *will* and *wild* are from the same root; but that is a further question.

---

[1] 'I think she is *will-led*,' explained by 'I think she is out of her mind'; *Nine Specimens of Eng. Dialects*, p. 119.

### 482. 'Charivari' (8 S. ix. 117; 1896).

In the new *French Etymological Dictionary* by Hatzfeld it is shown that *charivari* is composed of *chari* and *vari*. *Chari* is obscure, but seems to have been an interjectional cry, for which no particular etymology is either forthcoming or necessary. As to *vari*, it occurs in other words, as *hour-vari*, *boule-vari*, *zanzi-vari*, where *vari* certainly means 'noise, tumult,' and is from the O. H. G. *werren* (G. *wirren*), to confuse. The original sense of *charivari* was 'confused hubbub.' See further in the *New English Dictionary*.

It has no connexion with *chery-feire*, which means 'a fair for selling cherries,' and is well explained by Halliwell.

It is to be regretted that Prof. Morley, one of our best writers on English literature, never kept pace with the progress of modern philology, but was ready to accept any accidental resemblance as worthy of mention. Some of his statements of this character are little short of amazing. I can produce fourteen such from his *Shorter English Poems*, a book which I value highly, and (on other grounds) can strongly recommend. Thus, at p. 35, note 3, he says that *ƒare* means 'solemn preparation,' whereas it simply means 'goings-on,' from A. S. *ƒaran*, to go; and adds, that it is allied to the G. *Feier*, solemnity, which is a mere loan-word from Lat. *ƒeria*, whence the *ƒair* in *cherryƒair* is actually derived. *Fare*, in fact, is English, and *ƒair* (O. F. *ƒeyre*, G. *Feier*) is Latin; and the words are utterly unconnected. Grimm's law shows that they have not even the initial *ƒ* in common.

### 483. Anglo-Saxon Plant-names (8 S. ix. 163; 1896).

Our ancestors had a curious habit of connecting the names of plants with those of various well-known animals. Our present habits are so different that many moderns are wholly unable to understand this. To them such names as *fox-glove* and *hare-bell*[1] seem entirely senseless, and many efforts, more ingenious than well directed, have been made to evade the evidence.

Yet it is easily understood. The names are simply childish, and such as children would be pleased with. A child only wants a pretty name, and is glad to connect a plant with a more or less familiar animal. This explains the whole matter, and it is the reverse of scientific to deny a fact merely because we dislike or contemn it.

It will be understood that I can produce my evidence; but it is tedious from its quantity. I therefore refer readers to the glossary in the third volume of Cockayne's *Anglo-Saxon Leechdoms*, where the plant-names and references are given in full. Cockayne includes some names, such as *crane's-bill*, which are not found in Anglo-Saxon or Middle English, but appear in early-printed herbals. These I pass over, and mention only such as are actually found in Anglo-Saxon or Early English. The following are examples.

*Bridges nest*, bird's nest, wild carrot; *briddes tunge*, Stellaria holostea; *kattes minte*, cat-mint; *cicena mete*, chicken-meat, chickweed; *cockes fōt*, cock's foot, columbine; *cocks hedys*, cock's heads, melilot; *colts foot*, colt's foot; *cow-rattle*; *cū-slyppe*, *cū-sloppe*, cowslip; *cronesanke*, crane's shank (Polygonum persicaria); *crowe-pil*, crow-bill (Erodium moschatum); *crowsope*, crow-soap, latherwort; *dogᵹfennel*; *eforᵹfearn*, ever-fern (ever=boar), polypody; *eofor-throtu*, ever-throat, boar-throat, carline thistle; *ᵹfoxes clāte*, fox's clote, bur-dock; *foxes fōt*, fox's foot (Sparganium simplex); *ᵹfoxes glōfa*, fox's glove; *fugeles lēac*, fowl's leek; *fugeles bēan*, fowl's bean, vetch; *fugeles wīse*, larkspur; *gauk-pintel*, cuckoo-pintle (Arum maculatum); *gēaces sūre*, cuckoo-sorrel; *gāte trēow*, goat-tree, cornel; *haran hyge*, hare's

---

[1] Not found in A. S., but spelt *harebelle* in the fifteenth century.

foot trefoil[1]; *haran wyrt*, hare's wort; *haran sprecel*, (now) viper's bugloss; *heorot-berge*, hart-berries; buckthorn-berries; *heorot-bremble*, hart-bramble, buckthorn; *heort-clǣfre*, hart-clover, medic; *hind-berien*, hind-berries, raspberries; *hind-brēr*, hind-briar, raspberry plant; *hind-hælethe*, water agrimony (named from the hind); *hors-elene*, horse-elecampane; *hors-thistel*, horse-thistle, chicory; *hound-berry*; *hundes cwelcan*, berries of the wayfaring tree; *hundes hēafod*, hound's head, snap-dragon; *hundes tunge*, hound's tongue; *larkes ?ote*, lark's foot, larkspur; *lūs-sēd*, louse-seed, translating Gk. ψύλλιον; *mūs-ēare*, mouse-ear; *næderwyrt*, nadder-wort, adder-wort; *oxes eye*, ox-eye; *oxan slyppe*, oxlip; *oxna lib*, ox-heal, hellebore; *hræfnes fōt*, raven's foot; *hræfnes lēac*, raven's leek, orchis; *wulfes camb*, wolf's comb; *wulfes fīst*, lycoperdon: *wulfes-tæsl*, wolf's teasle.

Even this list is incomplete. I observe the omission of the following words, all of which are in the index to Wülker's *Glossaries*: *lambes-cerse*, lamb's cress; *hors-minte*, horse-mint; *hundes rose*, hound's rose, dog-rose; *hundes fynkelle*, hound's fennel; and there are probably more of them.

Observe, further, that the above list contains *only* such names as had the luck to be recorded. The real number must have been much greater. Thus, in connexion with the *fox*, we find, in Britten and Holland's excellent work on plant-names, that the Anglo-Saxon *?foxes clāte, ?foxes fōt*, and *?foxes glōfa* are to be supplemented by such names as the following: *fox-docken, fox-fingers* (Digitalis purpurea), *fox-geranium, fox-grass, fox-rose, ?fox's brush, ?fox's claws, ?foxtail, foxtailed asparagus, ?foxtail grass*.

[1] Cockayne omits *harebelle*, hare-bell, which occurs in Wülker's *Glossaries*, col. 715, l. 7.

# APPENDIX

### 413 (postscript). Zend 'raozha,' a lynx.

[The following 'postscript' was appended to article no. 413, on p. 341 above, but was accidentally omitted in its proper place.]

I now find that I have, unwittingly, solved a doubtful word in Zend! so I am told by my friend, Professor Cowell.

The Zend *raozha*, Pers. *rūs*, hitherto explained (by guess) as 'wolf' and 'fox,' is clearly the Russ. *ruise*, Polish *rys*, a lynx; and, by change of *r* to *l*, is G. *Luchs*, Du. *los*, E. *luce*, the same.

### 475 (postscript). Cambridge and the Cam.

[The article no. 475, printed above (pp. 384-5), was shortly afterwards much expanded, and printed (with the title 'Cambridge and the Cam') in the *Cambridge Review*, Jan. 30, 1896. For the further information of the reader, I here append a reprint of the fuller article.]

Before tracing the history of the name *Cambridge*, it is necessary to say a few words about *Camboritum*.

There is absolutely no proof as to the identity of Camboritum with Cambridge. The idea was due to Camden, who gave it as a pure guess, from the similarity of the names. All that I have to say here is, that the supposed similarity of the names is a mere illusion. It is altogether misleading to compare the form Camboritum, which occurs in an

*Itinerary* of Antonine, hardly later than the fourth century, with the form Cambridge, which is no older than the fourteenth at earliest. It is impossible to rely upon a chance resemblance of forms which are separated by an interval of a thousand years, and belong, in part, to different languages. I do not say that it may not be possible to place Camboritum at or near Cambridge on other grounds; but I decidedly affirm that it must be done for some other reason than the fact of their apparent resemblance. Note, too, that even this *primâ facie* likeness only extends to the third letter. The *b* in Cambo-ritum can have no connexion with the *b* in Cam-bridge. It is an obvious fact that the *b*, *r* and *i* in the former, are different from the *b*, *r* and *i* in the latter; and it is an ascertained fact (as will be shown) that the *Cam* in the former is different from the *Cam* in the latter. Whence it follows that the *C*, *a*, *m*, *b*, *r*, and *i* in the two words are wholly unconnected; and the external similarity is a mere coincidence, having no linguistic significance.

The history of the name of our town is quite clear. All turns upon the fact that the river-name *Cam* is modern, being wholly unknown before the sixteenth century, and being itself evolved out of the name of the town, instead of conversely. Moreover, it was a learned name, evolved out of the written word, in order to furnish a plausible etymology. Had it been evolved by the people from the spoken sound, the name must inevitably have been *Came*.

Next, if the old name of the river had really been *Cam*, the town would have been called *Cămbridge*. It is very common for vowels to be shortened, as in the case of *gosling*, the diminutive of *goose*; but I know of no instance in which the reverse process of lengthening has taken place before a combination of *three* consonants, for the plain reason that it is unnatural, giving unnecessary trouble. Every student of phonetics will see at once that, whatever was the origin of *Cămbridge*, it was certainly not *Căm*.

We can thus account for *Cam* easily enough, as being evolved from the written name of the town by a popular etymology; the next business is to account for the long *a* (as in *came*) in the name as it is spoken. This is really a mere matter of history, and only to be arrived at by the historical method.

We now come to the leading fact, viz. that the true name of the river was Granta, or Grant, a name which still exists, and can be traced back through all the centuries to British times.

The first mention of it is in Nennius, in the sixth or seventh century. In Gale's edition, p. '115' we are informed that the name of a certain British town was *Caer-graunth*. The curious spelling, with *aun* for *an*, and final *th* for *t*, is Anglo-French, the existing MS. being of rather late date; the right spelling would be *Caer-grant*. We can only identify this place by remembering that the same word, turned into Anglo-Saxon, will come out as *Granta-ceaster*, which in modern English would become Grant-chester.

The archaic form Granta-caestir occurs in the eighth century, in Beda's *History*, bk. iv. c. 19. We can hence trace the river-name downwards, through many centuries, to the present day; but I prefer to do this in connexion with the suffix *-bridge* rather than in connexion with the suffix *-chester*.

The name of our town emerges into history in the ninth century. It is spelt *Grantan-brycge* (dative) in the *Anglo-Saxon Chronicle*, under the date 875; and, under the date 1010, is the first mention of the county, viz. *Grantabrycg-scir*, i.e. Grantbridge-shire.

Domesday-book makes mention of the town as 'Burgum de Grentebrige,' the county being Grentebrige-shire.

In *Henry of Huntingdon*, where an earlier MS. has Grantebrigesyre, a later one has Kantebrigesire; see p. 9 of Arnold's edition.

*Simeon of Durham* (pp. 82, 111, Record Series) has Grantabric and Granthebrige; the MS. is of the twelfth century. He also has the phrase 'super Grentam fluvium.'

In the *Southern English Legendary* (E. E. T. S.), p. 347, l. 66, we find Grauntebruggeschire. This is about 1290.

In *Robert of Gloucester*, l. 132, the earlier MS. (ab. 1330) has Grauntebrugge-ssire where the later (ab. 1400) has Cambrugge-schire; in the same line. See Mr. Aldis Wright's index for numerous examples.

Later than 1330, I only find the form Grauntbrigge in a proper name. It came to a sudden end about 1400; for in the second year of King Henry IV, we find a reference in the *Patent Rolls*, p. 242, to a certain 'Johannes de Grauntbrigge qui obiit sine haerede.' He was a man of some mark, and his name appears frequently in various documents. See in particular the index to the *Close Rolls*. An earlier 'Johannes de Grauntbrigge' is mentioned A.D. 1283; *Abbreviatio Placitorum*, p. 275 [1].

There was much trouble with the name in the twelfth century, when the Anglo-French scribes, who were often (I suppose) Londoners, took upon themselves to turn the form *Grant* into *Cant*, and *Graunt* into *Caunt*. We still find *Grantebrigge* in the time of William II; in 1099, the coins which this king struck at Cambridge were marked with the abbreviation *Grant* (Ruding, *Annals of the Coinage*, i. 309; iii. 6). This takes us down to the year 1100.

Canon Taylor says (*N. and Q.* 8 S. viii. 314) that the earliest occurrence of the form *Cantebruggescir* is in a document dated 1142. After that date it is common. Examples are: 'Histon in Cantebrugescir,' *Rotuli Chartarum in Turri Londinensi*, vol. i. pars. 1, 80; A.D. 1200. 'Cantebrug,' *Close Rolls*, i. 381; A.D. 1218. 'Absolon de Cantebrug,'

---

[1] The title 'earl of Cambridge' occurs in 1415; the bearer of it (executed in that year) was created earl by Henry V, who began to reign in 1413.

*id.* i. 82; A. D. 1207. 'Vic(ecomiti) de Cantebrug,' *id.* i. 38; A. D. 1204; &c. It is important to observe that the name 'Johannes de Grauntbrigge' is also written 'Johannes de Cauntebrigge' in 1331; see Spelman's *Glossarium*, p. 544.

Before proceeding with the history, I must explain the variations of spelling. First, the A. S. *y* appears as *i* in the Midland dialect, and as *u* in MSS. written in the South; hence the variation between *brigge* and *brugge*. We also find *bregge*; which is Kentish.

Secondly, we must consider the Norman pronunciation of *an*. The sound of *a* was nasal, whilst the *n* was fully sounded; many scribes used *aun* to represent this. Hence the forms *Graunt* and *Caunt* are Anglo-French varieties of *Grant* and *Cant*. Unless we understand this fact, we cannot account for the long *a* in Cambridge; as will presently appear.

As far as we have gone, the chronology is as follows: The forms *Granta-brycg*, *Grentebruge*, *Grauntebrugge*, and the like, extend from the ninth century down to 1400; the spelling with *au* being Norman. The forms *Cantebrigge*, *Cauntebrugge*, and the like, extended from about 1146 to the fifteenth century. *Cantebrigge* was Latinized as *Cantabrigia*, which is frequently found in MSS. of the thirteenth and fourteenth centuries, and at all subsequent dates down to the present day.

The form *Cantabrigia* is useful; for it plainly arose at a time when the *e* in *Cant-e-brigge* still formed a syllable. There is an excellent example of this form in Chaucer; for it is well known that his *Reves Tale* begins with the line—

  'At Trumpington, 'not fer fro Cant-e-brigge.''

But, in the fourteenth century, this middle *e* was often dropped; so that Chaucer's form was somewhat archaic. The dropping of this *e* led to a new developement. The *a* was clogged by the occurrence after it of no less than four consonants, viz. *n t b r*. In nearly all such cases, the middle consonant drops out; and in this case, the middle consonant is practically *t*, as the *br* belongs to the next syllable. But this gave the dissonant form *Canbrigge* or *Caunbrigge*, which must very soon have been shifted to *Cămbrigge* or *Caumbrigge*. At any rate, *Canbrigge* is seldom found[1]. We thus see that the *m* in *Cambridge* merely resulted, by the ordinary operation of phonetic laws, from the *n* in *Granta*; so that *Granta-* or *Graunte-* first became *Cante-* or *Caunte-*, and next *Cant-* or *Caunt-*; the next step being to *Can-* or *Caun-*, and soon after, to *Cam-* or *Caum-*, because a *b* followed. And until this had happened, the coining of the river-name with a final *m* was simply impossible. This is quite clear when we can once grasp it.

I note here that the form with *Cam* actually occurs in the later MSS. of Chaucer in the line already quoted. The Lansdowne MS. (after 1400) has the hideous line—

'At Trumpington, not fer fro Cambrugge.'

We now require to know the all-important fact, that, according to the phonetic laws of Anglo-French, the combinations *am* or *an*, having a nasalized vowel, resulted in sounds with long *ā* (really the *aa* in *baa*); but the *a* was not written double, the length being understood. Yet, though we hardly ever find the spellings *aam, aan*, the slightly varying spellings *aum, aun*, are common. In modern English, the *ā* is sounded like the *ei* in *vein*. Examples with *ān* occur in the modern Eng. *angel, danger, range, change, mange*, &c., all of Anglo-French origin; whilst an excellent example with the spelling *ām* occurs in the word *chamber*, in which the *amb* is exactly like the *amb* in *Cambridge*. It follows from this, that we must expect sometimes to find the former syllable appearing as *Caum* in the fifteenth century. At this stage of the investigation I began to cast

---

[1] *Canbrigge* occurs in A. D. 1436; *Early Eng. Wills*, p. 105.

about for examples of *Caum* in the fifteenth century, and I soon bethought me of the *Paston Letters*. These examples are very striking.

In the *Paston Letters*, ed. Gairdner, i. 82, the famous Margaret Paston herself used the form *Kawmbrege* in a letter dated 1449. In the same, i. 422, Agnes Paston wrote *Caumbrege* in 1458; whilst, in the year 1461 (ii. 79), we find the most interesting form *Cawnbrygg*, being the latest form with *n* which we are likely to find.

It will now be understood that, when the form appeared as *Cam*—in the fifteenth century—the sound intended was *Kaam*, riming to *balm*: and this is why we now pronounce it as *came* or *Keim*, riming to *fame*. Most of the long *a*'s in Anglo-French have suffered the same fate, but are preserved in modern French, which has *daam* for our *dame*, and *blaam-è* for our verb to *blame*. The old *ān* (aan) is, however, still preserved before the sounds of *s* and *t*: as in *dance, lance, chance, chant, grant*, &c. All that remains is to trace the rise of the *Cam*.

It is a most significant fact that, when the name of the town was *Cantebrigge*, the river made an abortive attempt to gain the name of the *Cant!* This appears from Willis and Clark's *History of Cambridge* (i. 211), where we find an allusion to 'the common bank called Cante'; in the year 1372. We even find, from the same work (i. viii.), that, as late as in 1573, Dr. Caius alludes to 'the Canta, now called the Rhee.' But I suspect that he evolved this supposed archaic form out of the Latin Canta-brigia.

The evolution of the form *Cam* for the river seems to have been due to the revival of learning in the sixteenth century, appearing first in the Latinized form *Camus* or *Chamus*. The *Cambridge Review* for Nov. 14, 1895, quoted at p. 74 some verses by Giles Fletcher, prefixed to an edition of Demosthenes published in 1571, containing the line—

'Accipe quae nuper *Chami* flauentis ad undam.'

And again, from Andrew Melvill's *Antitamicamicategoria,* dated 1620, the line—

'Ergo vos *Cami* proceres Tamique.'

In both these examples the *a* in *Camus* is long. Hence we have *Camus* in the well-known line in Milton's *Lycidas.*

It is needless to give further details. I add a few notes, in chronological order, to show that the river-name Grant was never lost; whilst the Cam seems to have had much ado to get itself recognized. A third name was the Rhee or Ree, which I suspect merely meant 'stream,' as we find two rivers in Shropshire, both called the Rea Brook, a Ray River in Oxfordshire, and a Rae Burn in Dumfriesshire. Indeed, Willis and Clark give an example of 'le Ee' in 1447; but this merely means 'the river,' from the A. S. *ēa*, a stream.

1455. 'Le Ree'; Willis and Clark, i. 212.

1573. 'The Canta, now called the Rhee'; see above.

1576. Saxton's map of Cambridgeshire; the western branch of the river is called the Grante.—Willis and Clark.

1586. Camden says the name is doubtful; 'alii Grantam, Camum alii nuncupant.'

1590. Spenser's *Faerie Queene,* bk. iv. c. 11. st. 34, has 'the Guant,' with *u* for *r*, by a misprint. Some editions have 'Grant' correctly.

1610. Speed's map of Cambridge shows the 'Cam.'

1613. Drayton, *Polyolbion,* xxi. 51, 75, speaks of the 'Grant'; and in l. 107, mentions 'Cam, her daintiest flood, long since intituled Grant.'

1634. A map of this date in Fuller's *History of Cambridge* (1655) shows 'Granta, sive Cham fluvius.' His text only mentions 'the river Grant.'

1688. Loggan's map—'the Cam.'

1702. 'The river Cham, alias Grant'; Willis and Clark.

1831. Pigot's *County Atlas:* 'the Granta or Cam.'

The simple conclusion of the whole matter is just this · that the A.S. name *Grantabrycge* would certainly have become *Grantabridge*, or *Grantbridge*, or possibly, even *Grambridge*, if it had been developed regularly, without external influence. The changes to *Cantabridge, Cauntbrige, Caunbridge, Caumbridge*, and the modern *Cambridge* are due to French influence and to the Norman conquest; and it has been well suggested that the change from *Gr* to *C* may have arisen from a desire to avoid the repetition of *r*. And this is how the *Granta* was ultimately turned into the *Cam*; a name which, even now, has not quite displaced its original.

# INDEX

In this index, subjects and proper names begin with a capital letter. Words of which the uses or etymologies are discussed begin with a small letter.

M. E. (Middle-English), A. S. (Anglo-Saxon), and foreign words are printed in italics.

In every case, the reference is *not* to the page but to the number of the article. For example, 'charm' is discussed in articles 23 and 24 (at pp. 18, 19).

a Kempis, 318.
Accent thrown back, 2.
Adam, meaning of, 97.
Adam and Eve in the sea, 64.
adder, 27.
*æ or e* (in *archæology*), 340.
*æstel* (A. S.), 164.
*afurste* (M. E.), 401.
Age of the World, 47, 48.
Ages, the Seven, 31, 32.
Alliterative poetry, 119.
all-to, 34, 35.
Alwyne, 283.
amperzand, 83.
Angle, trisection of an, 58.
Angles, the, 307.
Anglo-French words, 120.
Anglo-Saxon, imaginary, 212, 213.
   months, 310.
   names, 363.
   numerals, 194.
   plant-names, 483.
   poem, 'the Whale,' 365.
   Translations of the N. T., 333.
Anglo-Saxons, poetic diction of the, 63.
*anlas* (M. E.), 338.
anointed, 4.

A-per-se, 83.
apple-cart, 144.
apposite, 150.
archaeology (ae *or* e), 340.
ask (a lizard), 220.
atone, 269.
*attrayed* (M. E.), 401.
auger, 27.
*aund, awn'd* (prov. E.), 113.
aWork, 234.

B to a battledore, 75.
Bagdad, 319.
bait, burning of, 238.
Baker's dozen, 52.
bálcony, 2.
baldacchino, 319.
balloon, 219.
bandalore, 267.
bane, 399.
banshee, 350.
barton, 320.
Basque, 197.
bayonet, 393.
beadle, 435.
beaker, 323.
*bear* (barley), 320.
Bede's version of St. John, 160.

beefeater, 187, 287, 410.
*begyns* (in Grimoald), 400.
bernar, 17.
bewray, 233.
Birnam wood, 156.
*blakeberyed* (Chaucer), 84.
blazer, 278.
*blyve* (M. E.), 401.
'bo to a goose,' 75.
bodkin, to ride, 315.
Boethius quoted, 145.
*boneshaw* (prov. E.), 448.
*borken* (M. E.), 401.
Brandan, St., 365.
bravo, brava, 386.
brewery, 276.
'Briga,' 96.
Buckles on shoes, 131.
buffer, 122.
buffetier, 287, 410.
*buft* (prov. E.), 122.
Bunyan illustrated, 299.
*burdes* (M. E.), 400.
Burning for heresy, 472.
by-and-by, 208.
'by hook or by crook,' 79.
*bydand* (M. E.), 66.

*c* in Latin, 463, 464.
caddy, 11.
Cain's jaw-bone, 158.
Cambridge, Cam, 475. (And see p. 393.)
*cant and keen* (M. E.), 398.
cap-a-pie, 30.
Capitals, use of, 347.
Cards mentioned, 271.
Carfax, 5, 6.
carminative, 257.
*carrefour* (F.), 5.
catsup, 293.
cater-waul, 226, 227, 228.
catty, 11.
caucus, 252.
Cavalry Curates, 429.
*ceriously* (M. E.), 374.
chair (pulpit), 331.
Chanticleer's wives, 186.
charivari, 482.
*charm* (prov. E.), 23, 24.
Chatterton's Anglo-Saxon, 78.
Chaucer: Anelida (l. 183), 462.

Chaucer: Knightes Tale, 51.
— Kn. Tale and Troilus, 69.
— Legend of Good Women (l. 16), 422.
— Man of Law's Tale, 80.
— Manciple's Tale, 42.
— Parl. of Foules (l. 363), 371.
— Parson's prol. (l. 43), 199.
— Prologue (l. 410), 246.
— *blakeberyed*, 84.
— edition by Moxon, 317.
— Stilbon, 421.
Chaucer's pronunciation, 262.
cherry-fair, 482.
Christ-cross, 21.
chum, 463, 464.
Cicero speaking Greek, 108.
claw me, claw thee, 229.
clean as a whistle, 22.
*clôture* (F.), 174.
*clubstart* (prov. E.), 427.
coat, 56.
*cælum, cælum*, 392.
*cole-prophet* (M. E.), 204.
Colours as surnames, 231
Comets, 105.
Commence to, 380.
Conrad, 1.
Coppa, a hen, 186
Copy for printers, 173.
*corsy, corsive*, 397.
cowslip, 483.
'crow with voice of care,' 371.
Crusoe, Robinson, 248.
Curiosities of Interpretation, 398, 399, 400–1.
cut away, 244.

darbies, 196.
dare, dares, 127, 128.
darkling, 270.
Davenant's English, 14.
-de (*pt. t. suffix*), 214, 215, 216.
'Dead as a door-nail,' 16.
deal board, 193.
Devonshire dialect, 192.
Dialects, English, 92.
*discure* (M. E.), 397.
Distich by Luther, 25.
Domesday Book, 425.
*drake* (M. E.), 399.

Drawing, hanging, and quartering, 369.
drunk as mice, 121.
Dryden's use of *instinct*, 258.
— use of *neyes*, 27.
*dulcarnon* (Chaucer), 147, 279.
Dunmow flitch, 191.

-*e*, final, 61.
East Sheen, 312.
Edinburghean grammar, 447.
Editions, First, 405.
Edwards' 'Words, Facts,' &c., 411.
*edyllys be* (M. E.), 124.
effrontery, 469.
*eftures* (M. E.), 210.
Egerton, 361.
*egle* (icicle), 273.
*eightetene* (M. E.), 136.
embezzle, 133.
Emendations, culpable, 165.
*emys* (M.E.), 398.
*en* pronounced as *in*, 256.
English, chronology of, 120.
— Dialects, 92.
  etymology, 101,
— Grammars, 298.
—, railway, 157.
  , sham specimens of, 295.
  without articles, 14.
English and Angle, 307.
English and German, 251, 313.
ennui, 68.
-*er* pronounced as -*ar*, 166, 167.
*ernde* (M. E.), 401.
-er-st (suffix), 326.
*ether* (prov. E.), 432.
Etymologies, ridiculous, 96, 197, 266, 302, 352, 455.
— specimens of; *aroint thee*, 455; *beadle*, 435; *Charing Cross*, 455; *Gauch* (G.), 455; *gallows*, 302; *gnoffe*, 452; *goblin*, 455; *Inkpen*, 352; *Lammas*, 455; *Pales*, 455; *Perseus*, 455; *riding*, 455; *toot-hill*, 455.
Etymology, English, 101.
Ever-, 195.
'*Exceptio probat regulam*,' 95.
expulse, 12.

Fabyan's Chronicles, error in 67.
faith, 332.
Familiarity breeds contempt, 289.
father, 432.
fathom, 432
*feabes* (prov. E.), 209.
fen, fend, 126.
Fewtarspeare, 98.
*flaskisable* (M. E.), 372.
flotsam, 445.
Fly-leaves, Notes on, 29, 33.
fod, 419.
for to, 354.
forbode, 399.
*forslinger* (M. E.), 135.
fox-glove, 203, 474, 483.
*fratry* (M. E.), 241.
French *u* for *l*, 177.
fylfot, 362.

*gā* (A. S.), 207.
*galetas* (F.), 141.
*galoches* (F.), 90.
gantlope, running the, 478.
garret, 141.
gather, 432.
*gauts* (prov. E.), 116, 117.
*gaytreberies* (M. E.), 301.
*geason, geson* (M. E.), 456.
Genders in English, 390.
genitive, form of, 89.
Genius defined, 239.
genteel dogs, 54.
Gerbertus, story of, 387.
*ghauts* (prov. E.), 116, 117.
ghost-word, 291.
— *eftures*, 210.
gill, 152.
gingham, 440.
girl, how pronounced, 341, 342.
gist, 44.
Gladstone, Mr., 300.
Glossaries, 170.
glove, 115.
*gnoffe* (M. E.), 452.
Godiva, 384.
golf, 454.
'good wine,' &c., 95.
gorilla, 134.
*gradale* (Latin), 74.

# INDEX.

grail, holy, 74.
grange, 345.
*greece* (M. E.), 398.
green-baize road, 240.
*grift* (prov. E.), 325.
*grithe* (M. E.), 398.
groundsel, 403.
gruesome, 402.
gut, 117.

H, the letter, 297.
hag, 220.
ha-ha, 470.
*halfen-dale* (M. E.), 146.
Halliwell's Dictionary, additions to, 284, 285, 286.
Hampole's psalter, 303.
handsome, 95.
hang out, 444.
harebell, 483 (footnote on p. 392).
*hauns* (Gothic), 26.
Havelok and Robert of Brunne, 65.
haw, hawthorn, 327.
Hawking, 179, 180.
hayward, 327.
Hearne's Chronicles, 170.
hedges, hedge, 327.
*hell*, v. (prov. E.), 91.
henchman, 264, 272, 415, 416, 417, 418.
Hereward, 296.
*hibiscus*, 349.
*hidels* (M. E.), 124.
Hilda, 468.
hind-berries, 483.
hither, 432.
*hoder-moder* (M. E.), 221.
hoe, 336.
hogshead, 40.
hold (of a ship), 204.
hold up oil, 153.
holt, 441.
hone (houe), hoe, 336.
*hone* (M. E.), 401.
*honi* (French), 26.
*horkey* (prov. E.), 460.
Howard, 172, 296.
*huckshins* (prov. E.), 459.
hugger-mugger, 221.
hull, 91.
hundred, 137.

icicle, 273.
'*Ictibus agrestis*,' 337.
*-ing* (A. S.), 223.
Inkpen, 352.
instinct (in Dryden), 258.
iron, pronunciation of, 451.
iron-mould, 204.

Jackdaw of Rheims, 42.
James, 343.
Jamieson's Dictionary, 148.
janissary, 236, 237.
*jeresgive* (*yeresgiue*), 72.
Jericho, to send to, 330.
jetsam, 445.
Jingo, 453.
Johnson's definition of oats, 85.
jolly, 397.

*ka me, ka thee*, 229.
Kangaroo, 247.
*ket* (prov. E.), 260.
ketchup, 293.
key-cold, 15.
kilt, 373.
*kilter, kelter* (prov. E.), 358.
King's Quair, 476.
*kittering* (prov. E.), 305.
Knot in a handkerchief, 88.
knout, 253.
Knowledge for the people, 295.

*l* and *u* in French, 177.
laburnum, 142.
lagan, 458.
Lammas, 86, 87, 254, 455.
*lathe* (prov. E.), 260.
latten, 308.
launder, v., 434.
laundress, 397.
*lea* (scythe), 260.
leary, 396.
led will, 481.
*leer* (hungry), 143.
*leet, three-way* (prov. E.), 200.
*leezing, leasing* (M. E.), 359.
legerdemain, 288.
Leighton, 382.
*lene, leue* (M. E.), 45.
Leofwine, 296.

## INDEX. 407

Letter-writing, 202.
*leue, lene* (M. E.), 45.
Liber Vitae, 363.
Limehouse, 265.
Lines, deficient, 465.
*lister* (prov. E.), 41.
*lithe*, v. (M. E.), 398.
*litton* (prov. E.), 185.
living, 19.
lobster, 103.
*lopen* (M. E.), 400.
Lord's prayer in English, 295.
— in English verse, 249, 250.
*luce* (lynx), 412, 413; *and see* p. 393.
Lucifer, 28.
lumbering, 165.
luncheon, 112.
Luther's distich, 25.
*luzern, lucern*, 412, 413.
*lytton* (M. E.), 185.

Magdalene (a boat), 246.
Man with a muck-rake, 299.
*manacus* (Lat.), 181.
Mango-trick, 450.
marigold, 436.
-mas, 86, 87.
mattins, matins, 360.
medieval, 340.
meresmen, 259.
merestones, 423.
*mete, metels* (M. E.), 400.
Metz, siege of, 76.
*miff* (prov. E.), 122.
*mill* (contest), 123.
Milton (on comets), 105.
*missa* (Lat.), 86.
mistletoe, 320.
monkey, 59.
Months in A. S., 310.
Morian's land, 304.
mother, 432.
much (i. e. great), 94.
*mustredevilliars*, 339.
mute, 368.
*mysuryd* (M. E.), 399.

*n* dropped, 27; prefixed, 27.
Ned, Ted, 328.
*neyes* (eyes), 27.

'Nice as a nun's hen,' 7.
*'nineted, 'nointed* (prov. E.), 356.
nonce, for the, 27.
North, the abode of Lucifer, 28.
Numerals in A. S., 194.
*nummet* (prov. E.), 110.
nuncheon, 110, 111, 112.
*nye* (M. E.), 400.

*oander, oandurth* (prov. E.), 322.
oats, defined by Dr. Johnson, 85.
Ockford, 425.
offal, 217, 218.
Ohthere's Voyage, 294.
Oil on troubled waters, 235.
oil, to hold up, 153.
old, 375.
*ollands* (prov. E.), 189.
'one touch of nature,' 245.
opposal, 150.
orders, to make, 292.
*orra* (Scotch), 397.
*otherwhiles* (M. E.), 99.
*oubit* (Scotch), 348.
out and out, 364.
oxhead, 40.

pair of, 151.
pam, 154, 261.
Pamphila, 154.
pamphlet, 154.
paragon, 385.
Parnell, St., 389, 457.
parson, 466.
Past tense of weak verbs, 214, 215, 216.
patriot, 480.
peas, pease, 77.
peruse, 334.
phaeton, 230.
phenomenon, 274, 275.
Pictures, two-faced, 20.
Pied friars, 53.
*pig, piggin* (prov. E.), 323.
pimple, 155.
pinchbeck, 308.
Pinkeney, 27.
Place-names, 222, 223; vowels in, 311.
Plant-names, 483.

poke, pig in a, 95.
*poortith* (Scotch), 332.
Pope, verse by the, 404.
porcelain, 46.
portress, 82.
*poudred* (M. E.), 399.
pounce, 180.
'Pound of flesh, the,' 198.
prepense, 335.
Prepositions, English, 81.
prise, 83.
Pronouns, use of, 447.
Pronunciation, 256, 262, 341, 342.
Proverb, French (*tant grate la chevre*), 13.
Proverbs: as clean as a whistle, 22; as dead as a door-nail, 16; as drunk as mice, 121; as nice as a nun's hen, 7; as right as a trivet, 22; buy a pig in a poke, 95; by hook or by crook, 79; cry bo to a goose, 75; *exceptio probat regulam*, 95; familiarity breeds contempt, 289; God sends the shrewd cow short horns, 95; good wine needs no bush, 95; handsome is as handsome does, 95; ka me, ka thee, 229; more haste, worse speed, 95; setting the Thames on fire, 205, 206.
Pseudo-Saxon, 212, 213.
punt, 255.
pursy, 397.
Putting a man under a pot, 18.
puzzle, 150.

Quasimodo, 426.
'*Qui capit uxorem*,' 33.
'*Quos anguis*,' &c., 33.

rabbit it, 39.
racoon, 408.
Railway English, 157.
*rake* (track), 370.
*raozha* (Zend), p. 393.
*rauky* (prov. E.), 178.
Reade, Reid, 231.
reave, 400.
*reckan* (prov. E.), 232.
*reckling* (prov. E.), 324.

*recure* (M. E.), 397.
*releet* (prov. E.), 200.
resplend, 9.
rhyme, 3.
rhyme nor reason, 8.
'right as a trivet,' 22.
*rim, ram, ruf* (Chaucer), 199.
rime v. rhyme, 3.
rimer, 355.
rimpling, 165.
Road knight, 473.
Robert of Brunne, 65.
robin, 290.
Robinson Crusoe, 248.
Roodee, 62.
Roses, creation of, 10.
*roun* (M. E.), 401.
Rouse, 231.
'rue with a difference,' 71.
runawaye's eyes, 431.
runnel, 316.

-*s* dropped in the genitive, 89.
sangreal, 74; sang real, 74.
*sawten* (M. E.), 398.
Saxon, etymology of, 391.
Seasons, four, 224, 225; names of, 224, 225.
Second sight, 437.
*sele* (prov. E.), 268.
*serfs* (French), 70.
*seriously* (M. E.), 374.
Shakeshaft, 98, 321.
Shakespeare: Coriol. (iv. 7. 52), 331; Hamlet (v. 1. 85), 158; Jul. Cæsar (iii. 1. 58), 420; (iv. 3. 218), 407; Merchant of Venice, 198; Troilus (iii. 3. 174), 245; Tw. Nt. (ii. 4. 45), 414; 'runawayes,' 431.
Shakespeare, Concordance to, 430.
Shakespeare's name, 98, 321.
sheen and shine, 312.
shingle, 444.
*showl* (prov. E.), 397.
shrewd cow, 95.
sidemen, 138.
*sidth* (M. E.), 171.
*sike* (prov. E.), 391.
Sindbad's Voyages, 365.
*sith* (since), 439.
*skellum*, 201.

*slare* (prov. E.), 263.
sloyd, 306.
*slubber-de-gullion*, 477.
slughorn, 280.
soc-lamb, 57.
Sodor and Man, 242.
so-ho, 461.
*sool* (M. E.), 378, 379.
sooth saw, 443.
sparable, 282.
*sparling* (M. E.), 132.
spawn, 182.
Spenser, error in, 49; his tree-list, 433.
*sperling* (M. E.), 132.
spit white, 107.
*stain, steen* (stone), 192.
stalled (sated), 383; stalled ox, 383.
*steen* (stone), 192.
-ster, *suffix*, 102, 103.
stick of eels, 100.
stoat, 427.
*strachy* (Shakespeare), 414.
*strangullion* (M. E.), 477.
stricken in years, 376.
'Strike here,' 387.
*striken* (M. E.), 376.
*styed* (advanced l), 376.
*suant, suent* (prov. E.), 395.
sulphur, 211.
sumpter, 161.
sun (gender of), 73.
sunset, 442.
Surnames, 231.
*swastika* (Skt.), 362.
Swedish and English, 406.
sweet-heart, 130.
'sweetness and light,' 309.
Swimming feat, 104.
swine, 93.
Swithin, St., 446.
*swyke* (M. E.), 401.
Syllabification, 139.

talon, 179, 180.
Tantony, 328.
*tapere* (M. E.), 162.
tarring-iron. 438.
tawdry, 328.
Ted, Ned, 328.
tennis, 190.

Tennyson: Locksley Hall, 145; metre of In Memoriam, 424; his use of *swine*, 93.
'Terra,' a root-word, 96.
tether, 432.
tetter, 106.
*th* in A. F. and A. S., 332.
Thackeryana, 449.
Thames on fire, 205, 206.
*thel* (A. S.), 193.
theodolite, 471.
Theory and Practice, 314.
-ther (*suffix*), 432.
*thethorne* (M. E.), 209.
thither, 432.
Thomas a Kempis, 318.
*three-way leet* (prov. E.), 200.
*thwitel* (M. E.), 159.
tine, 320.
to (*with infin.*), 353, 354.
together, 432.
Tooley, 328.
tooth-saw, 443.
touch (tache), 245.
touter, 329.
town, 320.
*treenware* (prov. E.), 109.
*tretys* (M. E.), 129.
tricker, 165.
Triple consonants, 381.
Trisection of an angle, 58.
trivet, 22.
trouts, 428.
*trow* (trough), 366, 367.
tureen, 109.
*turken* (M. E.), 175, 176.
*turkis* (M. E.), 175.

umpire, 27.
undern (M. E.), 322.
*unked* (prov. E.), 168.
*utas* (M. E.), 351.

*v* lost in English, 397.
*vade* (M. E.), 400.
*vant* (font), 114.
velvet, 394.
Verse, deficient lines in English, 465.
*vild* (M. E.), 204.
Vowel-shortening, 311.

Vowels in English and German, 313.

wag, 281.
wage, wages, 163.
walking width, 171.
*wallowish* (prov. E.), 377.
Walter, Water, 43.
*wappered* (Shakespeare), 135.
*warish* (M. E.), 140.
*watchet* (prov. E.), 277.
Water = Walter, 43.
watershed, 60.
*wayzgoose* (prov. E.), 344.
Weak verbs, 214, 215, 216.
weather, 432.
*wederoue* (M. E.), 467.
*welsh* (prov. E.), 377.
Welsh place-names, 479.
*welted* (prov. E.), 183.
*went* ( = he goes), 216.
*whipultre* (M. E.), 301.
whither, 432.
*whitsul* (M. E.), 378, 379.
Whitsun Day, 378, 379.
whittle, 159.
wicket, 388.
wicks (of the mouth), 125.
will-led, 481.
Wimbledon, 184.
*windlestrae* (prov. E.), 169.
Windmills, 409.
*wipple-tree* (M. E.), 301.
wither, 432.
wolf (in music), 243.
*wolwarde* (prov. E.), 36, 37, 38.
woodruff, 467.
World's age, 47, 48.
*wreckling*, 324.
wrinkle (idea), 188.
write you, 346.
Writer's errors, 118.
Wycliffe's New Testament, 149.

y<sup>e</sup> (*for* the), 55.
Year and a day, 50.
*yede, yode* (M. E.), 49.
*yeresgive* (M. E.), 72.
Yetminster, 425.
*ynly* (M. E.), 401.
Yorkshire words, 260.
you (*dat.*), 346.

Zebra, 247.

THE END.

OXFORD: PRINTED AT THE CLARENDON PRESS
BY HORACE HART, PRINTER TO THE UNIVERSITY

# Clarendon Press Series.

| ENGLISH LANGUAGE AND LITERATURE | pp. 1-6 |
|---|---|
| HISTORY AND GEOGRAPHY | p. 6 |
| MATHEMATICS AND PHYSICAL SCIENCE | p. 7 |
| MISCELLANEOUS | p. 8 |
| MODERN LANGUAGES | p. 9 |
| LATIN EDUCATIONAL WORKS | p. 13 |
| GREEK EDUCATIONAL WORKS | p. 17 |

## The English Language and Literature.

*HELPS TO THE STUDY OF THE LANGUAGE.*

### 1. DICTIONARIES.

*A NEW ENGLISH DICTIONARY, ON HISTORICAL PRINCIPLES:* founded mainly on the materials collected by the Philological Society. Imperial 4to.

PRESENT STATE OF THE WORK.

|  |  |  | £ s. d. |
|---|---|---|---|
| Vol. I. {A, B} Edited by Dr. Murray. | Half-morocco | 2 12 6 |
| Vol. II. C Edited by Dr. Murray. | Half-morocco | 2 12 6 |
| Vol. III. { D Edited by Dr. Murray . { D-Depravation | | 0 8 6 |
| | Depravative-Distrustful | 0 12 6 |
| | Disobst.-Distrustful | 0 2 6 |
| E Edited by Henry Bradley { E-Every | | 0 12 6 |
| | Everybody-Ezod | 0 5 0 |
| Vol. IV. { F Edited by Henry Bradley { F-Field | | 0 7 6 |
| | Field-Fish | 0 2 6 |
| | Fish-Flexuose | 0 2 6 |
| G To be edited by Henry Bradley. *In Preparation.* | | |

∗∗∗ One Section at least, consisting of Sixty-four Pages, is now published Quarterly at Half-a-Crown.

**Bosworth and Toller.** *An Anglo-Saxon Dictionary,* based on the MS. Collections of the late Joseph Bosworth, D.D. Edited and enlarged by Prof. T. N. Toller, M.A. Parts I-III, A-SAR. [4to, 15s. each.
Part IV, Section I, SAR—SWÍÐRIAN. [4to, 8s. 6d.

**Mayhew and Skeat.** *A Concise Dictionary of Middle English,* from A.D. 1150 to 1580. By A. L. Mayhew, M.A., and W. W. Skeat, Litt.D.
[Crown 8vo, half-roan, 7s. 6d.

**Skeat.** *A Concise Etymological Dictionary of the English Language.* By W. W. Skeat, Litt.D. *Sixth Edition.* [Crown 8vo, 5s. 6d.

B

## 2. GRAMMARS, READING BOOKS, &c.

**Earle.** *The Philology of the English Tongue.* By J. EARLE, M.A., *Fifth Edition.* . . . . . . . . [Extra fcap. 8vo, 8s. 6d.
—— *A Book for the Beginner in Anglo-Saxon.* By J. EARLE, M.A., *Third Edition.* . . . . . . . [Extra fcap. 8vo, 2s. 6d.

**Mayhew.** *Synopsis of Old-English Phonology.* By A. L. MAYHEW, M.A. . . . . . . [Extra fcap. 8vo, bevelled boards, 8s. 6d.

**Morris** and **Skeat.** *Specimens of Early English*—
Part I. From Old English Homilies to King Horn (A.D. 1150 to A.D. 1300). By R. MORRIS, LL.D. *Second Edition.* . . [Extra fcap. 8vo, 9s.
Part II. From Robert of Gloucester to Gower (A.D. 1298 to A.D. 1393). By R. MORRIS, LL.D., and W. W. SKEAT, Litt.D. *Third Edition.* [7s. 6d.

**Skeat.** *Specimens of English Literature,* from the 'Ploughmans Crede' to the 'Shepheardes Calender.' . . [Extra fcap. 8vo, 7s. 6d.
—— *The Principles of English Etymology*—
First Series. The Native Element. *Second Edition.* [Crown 8vo, 10s. 6d.
Second Series. The Foreign Element. . . [Crown 8vo, 10s. 6d.
—— *A Primer of English Etymology.* [Extra fcap. 8vo, *stiff covers,* 1s. 6d.
—— *Twelve Facsimiles of Old-English Manuscripts.* [4to, 7s. 6d.

**Sweet.** *A New English Grammar, Logical and Historical.* Part I. Introduction, Phonology, and Accidence. . . . [Crown 8vo, 10s. 6d.
—— *A Short Historical English Grammar.* [Extra fcap. 8vo, 4s. 6d.
—— *A Primer of Historical English Grammar.* [Extra fcap. 8vo, 2s.
—— *History of English Sounds from the Earliest Period.* With full Word-Lists. . . . . . . . . . . . [8vo, 14s.
—— *An Anglo-Saxon Primer, with Grammar, Notes, and Glossary. Eighth Edition.* . . . . . . . [Extra fcap. 8vo, 2s. 6d.
—— *An Anglo-Saxon Reader.* In Prose and Verse. With Grammatical Introduction, Notes, and Glossary. *Seventh Edition, Revised and Enlarged.* . . . . . . . . . . [Crown 8vo, 9s. 6d.
—— *A Second Anglo-Saxon Reader.* . . [Extra fcap. 4s. 6d.
—— *Old English Reading Primers*—
I. *Selected Homilies of Ælfric.* . . [Extra fcap. 8vo, *stiff covers,* 2s.
II. *Extracts from Alfred's Orosius.* . [Extra fcap. 8vo, *stiff covers,* 2s.
—— *First Middle English Primer, with Grammar and Glossary. Second Edition.* . . . . . . . . [Extra fcap. 8vo, 2s. 6d.
—— *Second Middle English Primer.* Extracts from Chaucer, with Grammar and Glossary. . . . . . . [Extra fcap. 8vo, 2s. 6d.
—— *A Primer of Spoken English.* . . [Extra fcap. 8vo, 3s. 6d.
—— *A Primer of Phonetics.* . . . [Extra fcap. 8vo, 3s. 6d.
—— *A Manual of Current Shorthand, Orthographic and Phonetic.* [Crown 8vo, 4s. 6d.

**Tancock.** *An Elementary English Grammar and Exercise Book.* By O. W. TANCOCK, M.A. *Third Edition.* . . [Extra fcap. 8vo, 1s. 6d.
—— *An English Grammar and Reading Book,* for Lower Forms in Classical Schools. By O. W. TANCOCK, M.A. *Fourth Edition.* [3s. 6d.

## A SERIES OF ENGLISH CLASSICS.

(CHRONOLOGICALLY ARRANGED.)

**Chaucer.** I. *The Prologue to the Canterbury Tales.* (*School Edition.*) Edited by W. W. SKEAT, Litt.D. . . [Extra fcap. 8vo, *stiff covers*, 1*s.*

—— II. *The Prologue; The Knightes Tale; The Nonne Prestes Tale.* Edited by R. MORRIS, LL.D. *A New Edition, with Collations and Additional Notes,* by W. W. SKEAT, Litt.D. . . [Extra fcap. 8vo, 2*s.* 6*d.*

—— III. *The Prioresses Tale; Sir Thopas; The Monkes Tale; The Clerkes Tale; The Squieres Tale, &c.* Edited by W. W. SKEAT, Litt.D. Sixth Edition. . . . . . . . . [Extra fcap. 8vo, 4*s.* 6*d.*

—— IV. *The Tale of the Man of Lawe; The Pardoneres Tale; The Second Nonnes Tale; The Chanouns Yemannes Tale.* By the same Editor. New Edition, Revised. . . . . [Extra fcap. 8vo, 4*s.* 6*d.*

—— V. *Minor Poems.* By the same Editor. [Crown 8vo, 10*s.* 6*d.*

—— VI. *The Legend of Good Women.* By the same Editor.
[Crown 8vo, 6*s.*

—— VII. *The Hous of Fame.* By the same Editor. [Crown 8vo, 2*s.*

**Langland.** *The Vision of William concerning Piers the Plowman,* by WILLIAM LANGLAND. Edited by W. W. SKEAT, Litt.D. *Sixth Edition.*
[Extra fcap. 8vo, 4*s.* 6*d.*

**Gamelyn, The Tale of.** Edited by W. W. SKEAT, Litt.D.
[Extra fcap. 8vo, *stiff covers*, 1*s.* 6*d.*

**Wycliffe.** *The New Testament in English,* according to the Version by JOHN WYCLIFFE, about A.D. 1380, and Revised by JOHN PURVEY, about A.D. 1388. With Introduction and Glossary by W. W. SKEAT, Litt.D.
[Extra fcap. 8vo, 6*s.*

—— *The Books of Job, Psalms, Proverbs, Ecclesiastes, and the Song of Solomon:* according to the Wycliffite Version made by NICHOLAS DE HEREFORD, about A.D. 1381, and Revised by JOHN PURVEY, about A.D. 1388. With Introduction and Glossary by W.W.SKEAT, Litt.D. [Extra fcap. 8vo, 3*s.* 6*d.*

**Minot.** *The Poems of Laurence Minot.* Edited, with Introduction and Notes, by JOSEPH HALL, M.A. . . . . [Extra fcap. 8vo, 4*s.* 6*d.*

**Spenser.** *The Faery Queene.* Books I and II. Edited by G. W. KITCHIN, D.D., with Glossary by A. L. MAYHEW, M.A.
[Extra fcap. 8vo, 2*s.* 6*d.* each.

**Hooker.** *Ecclesiastical Polity,* Book I. Edited by R. W. CHURCH, M.A., late Dean of St. Paul's. . . . . . [Extra fcap. 8vo, 2*s.*

**Marlowe and Greene.** MARLOWE'S *Tragical History of Dr. Faustus,* and GREENE'S *Honourable History of Friar Bacon and Friar Bungay.* Edited by A. W. WARD, Litt.D. New and Enlarged Edition. [Crown 8vo, 6*s.* 6*d.*

**Marlowe.** *Edward II.* Edited by O. W. TANCOCK, M.A. *Second Edition.* . . . . . [Extra fcap. 8vo. *Paper covers*, 2*s.*; *cloth*, 3*s.*

**Shakespeare.** Select Plays. Edited by W. G. CLARK, M.A., and W. ALDIS WRIGHT, D.C.L. . [Extra fcap. 8vo, *stiff covers*.
*The Merchant of Venice.* 1s. *Macbeth.* 1s. 6d.
*Richard the Second.* 1s. 6d. *Hamlet.* 2s.

Edited by W. ALDIS WRIGHT, D.C.L.

*The Tempest.* 1s. 6d. *Coriolanus.* 2s. 6d.
*As You Like It.* 1s. 6d. *Richard the Third.* 2s. 6d.
*A Midsummer Night's Dream.* 1s. 6d. *Henry the Fifth.* 2s.
*Twelfth Night.* 1s. 6d. *King John.* 1s. 6d.
*Julius Caesar.* 2s. *King Lear.* 1s. 6d.
*Henry the Eighth.* 2s. *Much Ado About Nothing.* 1s. 6d.

**Shakespeare as a Dramatic Artist;** *a popular Illustration of the Principles of Scientific Criticism.* By R. G. MOULTON, M.A. [Cr. 8vo, 7s. 6d.

**Bacon.** *Advancement of Learning.* Edited by W. ALDIS WRIGHT, D.C.L. *Third Edition.* . . . . . . [Extra fcap. 8vo, 4s. 6d.

—— *The Essays.* Edited, with Introduction and Illustrative Notes, by S. H. REYNOLDS, M.A. . . . [Demy 8vo, *half-bound*, 12s. 6d.

**Milton.** I. *Areopagitica.* With Introduction and Notes. By JOHN W. HALES, M.A. *Third Edition.* . . . . [Extra fcap. 8vo, 3s.

—— II. *Poems.* Edited by R. C. BROWNE, M.A. In two Volumes. *New Edition.* . . . . [Extra fcap. 8vo, 6s. 6d. Sold separately, Vol. I. 4s., Vol. II. 3s.

In paper covers: *Lycidas,* 3d. *Comus,* 6d.

By OLIVER ELTON, B.A.

*Lycidas,* 6d. *L'Allegro,* 4d. *Il Penseroso,* 4d. *Comus,* 1s.

—— III. *Paradise Lost.* Book I. Edited with Notes, by H. C. BEECHING, M.A. . . [Extra fcap. 8vo, 1s. 6d. *In Parchment,* 3s. 6d.

—— IV. *Paradise Lost.* Book II. Edited by E. K. CHAMBERS, B.A. [Extra fcap. 8vo, 1s. 6d. Books I and II together, 2s. 6d.

—— V. *Samson Agonistes.* Edited, with Introduction and Notes, by JOHN CHURTON COLLINS, M.A. . . [Extra fcap. 8vo, *stiff covers,* 1s.

**Milton's Prosody.** By ROBERT BRIDGES. [Extra fcap. 8vo, 1s. 6d.

**Bunyan.** I. *The Pilgrim's Progress, Grace Abounding, Relation of the Imprisonment of Mr. John Bunyan.* Edited by E. VENABLES, M.A. [Extra fcap. 8vo, 3s. 6d. *In Parchment,* 4s. 6d.

—— II. *The Holy War, and the Heavenly Footman.* Edited by MABEL PEACOCK. . . . . . . . . . [Extra fcap. 8vo, 3s. 6d.

**Clarendon.** I. *History of the Rebellion.* Book VI. Edited, with Introduction and Notes, by T. ARNOLD, M.A. *Second Edition.* [Crown 8vo, 5s.

—— II. *Selections.* Edited by G. BOYLE, M.A., Dean of Salisbury. [Crown 8vo, 7s. 6d.

**Dryden.** *Select Poems.* (*Stanzas on the Death of Oliver Cromwell; Astræa Redux; Annus Mirabilis; Absalom and Achitophel; Religio Laici; The Hind and the Panther.*) Edited by W. D. CHRISTIE, M.A. *Fifth Edition.* Revised by C. H. FIRTH, M.A. . . . . [Extra fcap. 8vo, 3s. 6d.

—— *Essay of Dramatic Poesy.* Edited, with Notes, by T. ARNOLD, M.A. *Second Edition.* . . . . . . [Extra fcap. 8vo, 3s. 6d.

**Locke.** *Conduct of the Understanding.* Edited, with Introduction, Notes, &c, by T. FOWLER, D.D. *Third Edition.* . [Extra fcap. 8vo, 2s. 6d.

# ENGLISH LITERATURE.

**Addison.** *Selections from Papers in the 'Spectator.'* By T. ARNOLD, M.A. *Sixteenth Thousand.* . [Extra fcap. 8vo, 4s. 6d. *In Parchment*, 6s.

**Steele.** *Selections from the Tatler, Spectator, and Guardian.* By AUSTIN DOBSON. . . . . [Extra fcap. 8vo. *In Parchment*, 7s. 6d.

**Swift.** *Selections from his Works.* Edited, with Life, Introductions, and Notes, by HENRY CRAIK. Two Vols. [Crown 8vo, cloth extra, price 15s. *Each volume may be had separately, price* 7s. 6d.

**Pope.** I. *Essay on Man.* Edited by MARK PATTISON, B.D. *Sixth Edition.* . . . . . . . . . [Extra fcap. 8vo, 1s. 6d.

—— II. *Satires and Epistles.* By the same Editor. *Fourth Edition.* [Extra fcap. 8vo, 2s.

**Thomson.** *The Seasons*, and *The Castle of Indolence.* Edited by J. LOGIE ROBERTSON, M.A. . . . . . [Extra fcap. 8vo, 4s. 6d.

—— *The Castle of Indolence.* By the same Editor. [Extra fcap. 8vo, 1s. 6d.

**Berkeley.** *Selections.* With Introduction and Notes. By A. C. FRASER, LL.D. *Fourth Edition.* . . . . . . [Crown 8vo, 8s. 6d.

**Johnson.** I. *Rasselas.* Edited, with Introduction and Notes, by G. BIRKBECK HILL, D.C.L.
[Extra fcap. 8vo, *limp*, 2s.; *Bevelled boards*, 3s. 6d.; *in Parchment*, 4s. 6d.

—— II. *Rasselas; Lives of Dryden and Pope.* Edited by ALFRED MILNES, M.A. . . . . . [Extra fcap. 8vo, 4s. 6d.
*Lives of Dryden and Pope.* . [*Stiff covers*, 2s. 6d.

—— III. *Life of Milton.* Edited, with Notes, &c., by C. H. FIRTH, M.A. . . . [Extra fcap. 8vo, *stiff covers*, 1s. 6d.; *cloth*, 2s. 6d.

—— IV. *Vanity of Human Wishes.* With Notes, by E. J. PAYNE, M.A. . . . . . . . . [*Paper covers*, 4d.

**Gray.** *Selected Poems.* Edited by EDMUND GOSSE, M.A.
[*In Parchment*, 3s.

—— *The same*, together with Supplementary Notes for Schools. By FOSTER WATSON, M.A. . . . . [Extra fcap. 8vo, *stiff covers*, 1s. 6d.

—— *Elegy, and Ode on Eton College.* . . . [*Paper covers*, 2d.

**Goldsmith.** *Selected Poems.* Edited, with Introduction and Notes, by AUSTIN DOBSON. . . [Extra fcap. 8vo, 3s. 6d. *In Parchment*, 4s. 6d.

—— *The Traveller.* Edited by G. B. HILL, D.C.L. [*Stiff covers*, 1s.

—— *The Deserted Village.* . . . . . [*Paper covers*, 2d.

**Cowper.** I. *The Didactic Poems of* 1782, with Selections from the Minor Pieces, A.D. 1779-1783. Edited by H. T. GRIFFITH, B.A.
[Extra fcap. 8vo, 3s.

—— II. *The Task, with Tirocinium*, and Selections from the Minor Poems, A.D. 1784-1799. By the same Editor. [Extra fcap. 8vo, 3s.

**Burke.** I. *Thoughts on the Present Discontents; the two Speeches on America.* Edited by E. J. PAYNE, M.A. . . [Extra fcap. 8vo, 4s. 6d.

—— II. *Reflections on the French Revolution.* By the same Editor. *Second Edition.* . . . . . . [Extra fcap. 8vo, 5s.

—— III. *Four Letters on the Proposals for Peace with the Regicide Directory of France.* By the same Editor. [Extra fcap. 8vo, 5s.

**Burns.** *Selected Poems.* Edited by J. LOGIE ROBERTSON, M.A.
[Crown 8vo, 6s.
**Keats.** *Hyperion,* Book I. With Notes, by W. T. ARNOLD, B.A. 4d.
**Byron.** *Childe Harold.* With Introduction and Notes, by H. F. TOZER, M.A. . . . . . [Extra fcap. 8vo, 3s. 6d. *In Parchment,* 5s.
**Shelley.** *Adonais.* With Introduction and Notes. By W. M. ROSSETTI. . . . . . . . . . [Crown 8vo, 5s.
**Scott.** *Lady of the Lake.* Edited, with Preface and Notes, by W. MINTO, M.A. With Map. . . . . [Extra fcap. 8vo, 3s. 6d.
—— *Lay of the Last Minstrel.* Edited by W. MINTO, M.A. With Map. . . . [Extra fcap. 8vo, *stiff covers,* 2s. *In Parchment,* 3s. 6d.
—— *Lay of the Last Minstrel.* Introduction and Canto I, with Preface and Notes, by W. MINTO, M.A. . . . . [*Paper covers,* 6d.
—— *Lord of the Isles.* Edited, with Introduction and Notes, by THOMAS BAYNE. . . . . . . [Extra fcap. 8vo, 3s. 6d.
—— *Marmion.* By the same Editor. . [Extra fcap. 8vo, 3s. 6d.
**Campbell.** *Gertrude of Wyoming.* Edited, with Introduction and Notes, by H. MACAULAY FITZGIBBON, M.A. *Second Edition.* [Extra fcap. 8vo, 1s.
**Wordsworth.** *The White Doe of Rylstone.* Edited by WILLIAM KNIGHT, LL.D., University of St. Andrews. . . [Extra fcap. 8vo, 2s. 6d.

**Typical Selections** *from the best English Writers. Second Edition.* In Two Volumes. . . . . . . [Extra fcap. 8vo, 3s. 6d. each.

## HISTORY AND GEOGRAPHY, &c.

**Freeman.** *A Short History of the Norman Conquest of England.* By E. A. FREEMAN, M.A. *Third Edition.* . . [Extra fcap. 8vo, 2s. 6d.
**Greswell.** *History of the Dominion of Canada.* By W. PARR GRESWELL, M.A. . . . . . . . . [Crown 8vo, 7s. 6d.
—— *Geography of the Dominion of Canada and Newfoundland.* By the same Author. . . . . . . . . . [Crown 8vo, 6s.
—— *Geography of Africa South of the Zambesi.* By the same Author. . . . . . . . . . . [Crown 8vo, 7s. 6d.
**Hughes** (Alfred). *Geography for Schools.* Part I, *Practical Geography.* With Diagrams. . . . . . . . [Extra fcap. 8vo, 2s. 6d.
**Hunter.** *A Brief History of the Indian Peoples.* By Sir W. W. HUNTER, K.C.S.I. *Eighty-second Thousand.* . . . [Crown 8vo, 3s. 6d.
**Kitchin.** *A History of France.* With Numerous Maps, Plans, and Tables. By G. W. KITCHIN, D.D., Dean of Durham. *New Edition.* Vol. I. To 1453. Vol. II. 1453-1624. Vol. III. 1624-1793. Each 10s. 6d.
**Lucas.** *Introduction to a Historical Geography of the British Colonies.* By C. P. LUCAS, B.A. . . . . [Crown 8vo, with 8 maps, 4s. 6d.
—— *Historical Geography of the British Colonies—*
   I. *The Mediterranean and Eastern Colonies* (exclusive of India).
[Crown 8vo, with 11 maps, 5s.
  II. *The West Indian Dependencies.* With 12 maps. . [7s. 6d.
 III. *West Africa.* With 5 maps. . . . . . [7s. 6d.

## MATHEMATICS AND PHYSICAL SCIENCE.

**Aldis.** *A Text Book of Algebra (with Answers to the Examples).* By W. Steadman Aldis, M.A. . . . . . . [Crown 8vo, 7s. 6d.

**Emtage.** *An Introduction to the Mathematical Theory of Electricity and Magnetism.* By W. T. A. Emtage, M.A. . . [Crown 8vo, 7s. 6d.

**Fisher.** *Class-Book of Chemistry.* By W. W. Fisher, M.A., F.C.S. Second Edition. . . . . . . . [Crown 8vo, 4s. 6d.

**Fock.** *An Introduction to Chemical Crystallography.* By Andreas Fock, Ph.D. Translated and Edited by W. J. Pope. With a Preface by N. Story-Maskelyne, M.A., F.R.S. . . . . [Crown 8vo, 5s.

**Hamilton and Ball.** *Book-keeping.* By Sir R. G. C. Hamilton, K.C.B., and John Ball. *New and Enlarged Edition.* [Extra fcap. 8vo, 2s.
\*\*\* *Ruled Exercise Books adapted to the above may be had,* price 1s. 6d.; also, *adapted to the Preliminary Course only,* price 4d.

**Harcourt and Madan.** *Exercises in Practical Chemistry.* By A. G. Vernon Harcourt, M.A., and H. G. Madan, M.A. *Fifth Edition.* Revised by H. G. Madan, M.A. . . . . . [Crown 8vo, 10s. 6d.

**Hensley.** *Figures made Easy: a first Arithmetic Book.* By Lewis Hensley, M.A. . . . . . [Crown 8vo, 6d. *Answers*, 1s.

—— *The Scholar's Arithmetic.* By the same Author.
[Crown 8vo, 2s. 6d. *Answers*, 1s. 6d.

—— *The Scholar's Algebra.* An Introductory work on Algebra. By the same Author. . . . . . . . [Crown 8vo, 2s. 6d.

**Nixon.** *Euclid Revised.* Containing the essentials of the Elements of Plane Geometry as given by Euclid in his First Six Books. Edited by R. C. J. Nixon, M.A. *Third Edition.* . . . . . . [Crown 8vo, 6s.
\*\*\* May likewise be had in parts as follows—
Book I, 1s.     Books I, II, 1s. 6d.     Books I-IV, 3s.     Books V, VI, 3s. 6d.

—— *Geometry in Space.* Containing parts of Euclid's Eleventh and Twelfth Books. By the same Author. . . . [Crown 8vo, 3s. 6d.

—— *Elementary Plane Trigonometry; that is, Plane Trigonometry without Imaginaries.* By the same Author. . . . [Crown 8vo, 7s. 6d.

**Russell.** *An Elementary Treatise on Pure Geometry.* By J. Wellesley Russell, M.A. . . . . . . . . [Crown 8vo, 10s. 6d.

**Selby.** *Elementary Mechanics of Solids and Fluids.* By A. L. Selby, M.A. . . . . . . . . . . [Crown 8vo, 7s. 6d.

**Williamson.** *Chemistry for Students.* By A. W. Williamson, Phil. Doc., F.R.S. . . . . . . . [Extra fcap. 8vo, 8s. 6d.

**Woollcombe.** *Practical Work in General Physics.* For use in Schools and Colleges. By W. G. Woollcombe, M.A., B.Sc. . . [Crown 8vo, 3s.

—— *Practical Work in Heat.* By the same Author.
[Crown 8vo, 3s.

—— *Practical Work in Light and Sound.* By the same Author.
[Crown 8vo, 3s.

—— *Practical Work in Electricity and Magnetism.* [*In Preparation.*

## CLARENDON PRESS SERIES.

**Fowler.** *The Elements of Deductive and Inductive Logic.* By T. FOWLER, D.D. . . . . . . . [Extra fcap. 8vo, 7s. 6d.
Also, separately—
*The Elements of Deductive Logic*, designed mainly for the use of Junior Students in the Universities. With a Collection of Examples. [Extra fcap. 8vo, 3s. 6d.
*The Elements of Inductive Logic*, designed mainly for the use of Students in the Universities. *Sixth Edition.* . . . [Extra fcap. 8vo, 6s.

**Music.—Farmer.** *Hymns and Chorales for Schools and Colleges.* Edited by JOHN FARMER, Organist of Balliol College. . [5s.
☞ *Hymns without the Tunes*, 2s.

**Hullah.** *The Cultivation of the Speaking Voice.* By JOHN HULLAH. [Extra fcap. 8vo, 2s. 6d.

**Maclaren.** *A System of Physical Education: Theoretical and Practical.* By ARCHIBALD MACLAREN. *New Edition*, re-edited and enlarged by WALLACE MACLAREN, M.A., Ph.D. . . . . [Crown 8vo, 8s. 6d. net.

**Troutbeck and Dale.** *A Music Primer for Schools.* By J. TROUTBECK, D.D., formerly Music Master in Westminster School, and R. F. DALE, M.A., B.Mus., late Assistant Master in Westminster School. [Crown 8vo, 1s. 6d.

**Upcott.** *An Introduction to Greek Sculpture.* By L. E. UPCOTT, M.A. . . . . . . . . . . [Crown 8vo, 4s. 6d.

**Student's Handbook** to the University and Colleges of Oxford. *Thirteenth Edition.* . . . . . . . [Crown 8vo, 2s. 6d. net.

**Helps to the Study of the Bible,** taken from the *Oxford Bible for Teachers.* New, Enlarged and Illustrated Edition. Pearl 16mo, stiff covers, 1s. net. Large Paper Edition, Long Primer 8vo, cloth boards, 4s. 6d. net.

**Helps to the Study of the Book of Common Prayer.** Being a Companion to Church Worship. . . . . . . [Crown 8vo, 3s. 6d.

**Old Testament History for Schools.** By T. H. STOKOE, D.D.
Part I. From the Creation to the Settlement in Palestine.
Part II. From the Settlement to the Disruption of the Kingdom.
[Extra fcap. 8vo, 2s. 6d. each.
Part III. *In the Press.*

**Notes on the Gospel of St. Luke, for Junior Classes.** By E. J. MOORE SMITH, Lady Principal of the Ladies' College, Durban, Natal.
[Extra fcap. 8vo, *stiff covers*, 1s. 6d.

---

\*\*\* A READING ROOM *has been opened at the* CLARENDON PRESS WAREHOUSE, AMEN CORNER, *where visitors will find every facility for examining old and new works issued from the Press, and for consulting all official publications.*

---

**London: HENRY FROWDE,**
OXFORD UNIVERSITY PRESS WAREHOUSE, AMEN CORNER.
**Edinburgh:** 12 FREDERICK STREET.

# Clarendon Press Series.

## Modern Languages.

### FRENCH.

**Brachet.** *Etymological Dictionary of the French Language*, with a Preface on the Principles of French Etymology. Translated into English by G. W. KITCHIN, D.D., Dean of Durham. *Third Edition.* [Crown 8vo, 7s. 6d.

—— *Historical Grammar of the French Language.* Translated into English by G. W. KITCHIN, D.D. . [Extra fcap. 8vo, 3s. 6d.

**Brachet** and **Toynbee.** *A Historical Grammar of the French Language.* From the French of AUGUSTE BRACHET. Rewritten and Enlarged by PACET TOYNBEE, M.A. . . . . [Crown 8vo, 7s. 6d.

**Saintsbury.** *Primer of French Literature.* By GEORGE SAINTSBURY, M.A. *Third Edition.* . . . . . [Extra fcap. 8vo, 2s.

—— *Short History of French Literature.* By the same Author.
[Crown 8vo, 10s. 6d.

—— *Specimens of French Literature*, from Villon to Hugo. By the same Author. . . . . . . . [Crown 8vo, 9s.

**Toynbee.** *Specimens of Old French (ix-xv centuries).* With Introduction, Notes, and Glossary. By PAGET TOYNBEE, M.A. [Crown 8vo, 16s.

---

**Beaumarchais.** *Le Barbier de Séville.* With Introduction and Notes by AUSTIN DOBSON. . . . . . [Extra fcap. 8vo, 2s. 6d.

**Blouët.** *L'Éloquence de la Chaire et de la Tribune Françaises.* Edited by PAUL BLOUET, B.A. (Univ. Gallic.) Vol. I. *French Sacred Oratory.*
[Extra fcap. 8vo, 2s. 6d.

**Corneille.** *Horace.* With Introduction and Notes by GEORGE SAINTSBURY, M.A. . . . . . . [Extra fcap. 8vo, 2s. 6d.

—— *Cinna.* With Notes, Glossary, &c. By GUSTAVE MASSON, B.A. . . . . [Extra fcap. 8vo, *stiff covers*, 1s. 6d.; *cloth*, 2s.

**Gautier** (Théophile). *Scenes of Travel.* Selected and Edited by G. SAINTSBURY, M.A. . . . . . [Extra fcap. 8vo, 2s.

**Masson.** *Louis XIV and his Contemporaries;* as described in Extracts from the best Memoirs of the Seventeenth Century. With English Notes, Genealogical Tables, &c. By GUSTAVE MASSON, B.A. [Extra fcap. 8vo, 2s. 6d.

**Molière.** *Les Précieuses Ridicules.* With Introduction and Notes by ANDREW LANG, M.A. . . . . . [Extra fcap. 8vo, 1s. 6d.

—— *Les Femmes Savantes.* With Notes, Glossary, &c. By GUSTAVE MASSON, B.A. . [Extra fcap. 8vo, *stiff covers*, 1s. 6d.; *cloth*, 2s.

—— *Le Misanthrope.* Edited by H. W. GEGG MARKHEIM, M.A.
[Extra fcap. 8vo, 3s. 6d.

**Molière.** *Les Fourberies de Scapin.* With Voltaire's Life of Molière. By GUSTAVE MASSON, B.A. . . . [Extra fcap. 8vo, *stiff covers*, 1s. 6d.

**Musset.** *On ne badine pas avec l'Amour,* and *Fantasio.* With Introduction, Notes, &c., by WALTER HERRIES POLLOCK. [Extra fcap. 8vo, 2s.

**NOVELETTES:—**
- Xavier de Maistre. *Voyage autour de ma Chambre.*
- Madame de Duras. *Ourika.*
- Erckmann-Chatrian. *Le Vieux Tailleur.*
- Alfred de Vigny. *La Veillée de Vincennes.*
- Edmond About. *Les Jumeaux de l'Hôtel Corneille.*
- Rodolphe Töpffer. *Mésaventures d'un Écolier.*

By GUSTAVE MASSON, B.A., 3rd Edition. Ext. fcap. 8vo, 2s. 6d.

*Voyage autour de ma Chambre, separately, limp,* 1s. 6d.

**Perrault.** *Popular Tales.* Edited, with an Introduction on Fairy Tales, &c., by ANDREW LANG, M.A. [Extra fcap. 8vo, 5s. 6d.

**Quinet.** *Lettres à sa Mère.* Edited by G. SAINTSBURY, M.A. [Extra fcap. 8vo, 2s.

**Racine.** *Esther.* Edited by G. SAINTSBURY, M.A. [Extra fcap. 8vo, 2s.

**Regnard.** . . . *Le Joueur.*
**Brueys and Palaprat.** *Le Grondeur.*
By GUSTAVE MASSON, B.A. [Extra fcap. 8vo, 2s. 6d.

**Sainte-Beuve.** *Selections from the Causeries du Lundi.* Edited by G. SAINTSBURY, M.A. . . . . . . . [Extra fcap. 8vo, 2s.

**Sévigné.** *Selections from the Correspondence of* **Madame de Sévigné** and her chief Contemporaries. Intended more especially for Girls' Schools. By GUSTAVE MASSON, B.A. . . . . . . [Extra fcap. 8vo, 3s.

**Voltaire.** *Mérope.* Edited by G. SAINTSBURY, M.A. [Extra fcap. 8vo, 2s.

## ITALIAN.

**Primer of Italian Literature.** By F. J. SNELL, B.A. [Extra fcap. 8vo, 3s. 6d.

**Dante.** *Tutte le Opere,* nuovamente rivedute nel testo dal Dr. E. MOORE. . . . . . . . . . . [Crown 8vo, 7s. 6d.

—— *Selections from the 'Inferno.'* With Introduction and Notes, by H. B. COTTERILL, B.A. . . . . . [Extra fcap. 8vo, 4s. 6d.

**Tasso.** *La Gerusalemme Liberata.* Cantos i, ii. With Introduction and Notes by the same Editor. . . . [Extra fcap. 8vo, 2s. 6d.

## SPANISH.

**Cervantes.** *The Adventure of the Wooden Horse and Sancho Panza in Barataria.* Edited, with Introduction, Life, and Notes, by CLOVIS BÉVENOT, M.A. . . . . . [Extra fcap. 8vo, *stiff covers*, 2s. 6d.

## GERMAN, &c.

**Buchheim.** *Modern German Reader.* A Graduated Collection of Extracts in Prose and Poetry from Modern German Writers. Edited by C. A. BUCHHEIM, Phil. Doc.
Part I. With English Notes, a Grammatical Appendix, and a complete Vocabulary. *Seventh Edition.* [Extra fcap. 8vo, 2s. 6d.
Part II. With English Notes and an Index. [Extra fcap. 8vo, 2s. 6d.

—————— *German Poetry for Beginners.* Edited, with Notes and Vocabulary, by EMMA S. BUCHHEIM. [Extra fcap. 8vo, 2s.

—————— *Short German Plays, for Reading and Acting.* With Notes and a Vocabulary. By the same Editor [Extra fcap. 8vo, 3s.

—————— *Elementary German Prose Composition.* By EMMA S. BUCHHEIM. *Second Edition.* [Extra fcap. 8vo, *cloth*, 2s.; *stiff covers*, 1s. 6d.

**Lange.** *The Germans at Home;* a Practical Introduction to German Conversation, with an Appendix containing the Essentials of German Grammar. By HERMANN LANGE. *Third Edition.* [8vo, 2s. 6d.

—————— *The German Manual;* a German Grammar, a Reading Book, and a Handbook of German Conversation. By the same Author. [7s. 6d.

—————— *A Grammar of the German Language,* being a reprint of the Grammar contained in *The German Manual.* By the same Author. [8vo, 3s. 6d.

—————— *German Composition;* a Theoretical and Practical Guide to the Art of Translating English Prose into German. By the same Author. *Third Edition.* [8vo, 4s. 6d.
[*A Key to the above, price 5s.*]

—————— *German Spelling:* A Synopsis of the Changes which it has undergone through the Government Regulations of 1880. [*Paper cover*, 6d.

**Becker's** *Friedrich der Grosse.* With an Historical Sketch of the Rise of Prussia and of the Times of Frederick the Great. With Map. Edited by C. A. BUCHHEIM, Phil. Doc. [Extra fcap. 8vo, 3s. 6d.

**Chamisso.** *Peter Schlemihl's Wundersame Geschichte.* With Notes and Vocabulary. By EMMA S. BUCHHEIM. *Fourth Thousand.* [Extra fcap. 8vo, 2s.

**Goethe.** *Egmont.* With a Life of Goethe, &c. Edited by C. A. BUCHHEIM, Phil. Doc. *Fourth Edition.* [Extra fcap. 8vo, 3s.

—————— *Iphigenie auf Tauris.* A Drama. With a Critical Introduction and Notes. Edited by C. A. BUCHHEIM, Phil. Doc. *Fourth Edition.* [Extra fcap. 8vo, 3s.

—————— *Dichtung und Wahrheit:* (The First Four Books.) Edited by C. A. BUCHHEIM, Phil. Doc. [Extra fcap. 8vo, 4s. 6d.

**Halm's** *Griseldis.* With English Notes, &c. Edited by C. A. BUCHHEIM, Phil. Doc. [Extra fcap. 8vo, 3s.

**Heine's** *Harzreise.* With a Life of Heine, &c. With Map. Edited by C. A. BUCHHEIM, Phil. Doc. *Second Edition.* [Extra fcap. 8vo, *cloth*, 2s. 6d.

—————— *Prosa,* being Selections from his Prose Works. Edited with English Notes, &c., by C. A. BUCHHEIM, Phil. Doc. [Extra fcap. 8vo, 4s. 6d.

**Hoffmann's** *Heute Mir Morgen Dir.* Edited by J. H. MAUDE, M.A.
[Extra fcap. 8vo, 2s.

**Lessing.** *Laokoon.* With Notes, &c. By A. HAMANN, Phil. Doc., M.A. Revised, with an Introduction, by L. E. UPCOTT, M.A.
[Extra fcap. 8vo, 4s. 6d.

—— *Minna von Barnhelm.* A Comedy. With a Life of Lessing, Critical Analysis, Complete Commentary, &c. Edited by C. A. BUCHHEIM, Phil. Doc. *Seventh Edition.* . . . . [Extra fcap. 8vo, 3s. 6d.

—— *Nathan der Weise.* With English Notes, &c. Edited by C. A. BUCHHEIM, Phil. Doc. *Second Edition.* . [Extra fcap. 8vo, 4s. 6d.

**Niebuhr's** *Griechische Heroen-Geschichten.* Tales of Greek Heroes. Edited with English Notes and a Vocabulary, by EMMA S. BUCHHEIM.
Edition A. Text in German Type. ⎱ [Extra fcap. 8vo, *stiff*, 1s. 6d.;
Edition B. Text in Roman Type. ⎰ cloth, 2s.

**Riehl's** *Seines Vaters Sohn* and *Gespensterkampf.* Edited with Notes, by H. T. GERRANS. . . . . . . . [Extra fcap. 8vo, 2s.

**Schiller's** *Historische Skizzen:—Egmonts Leben und Tod,* and *Betagerung von Antwerpen.* Edited by C. A. BUCHHEIM, Phil. Doc. *Fifth Edition, Revised and Enlarged, with a Map.* . [Extra fcap. 8vo, 2s. 6d.

—— *Wilhelm Tell.* With a Life of Schiller; an Historical and Critical Introduction, Arguments, a Complete Commentary, and Map. Edited by C. A. BUCHHEIM, Phil. Doc. *Seventh Edition.* [Extra fcap. 8vo, 3s. 6d.

—— *Wilhelm Tell.* Edited by C. A. BUCHHEIM, Phil. Doc. *School Edition.* With Map. . . . . [Extra fcap. 8vo, 2s.

—— *Jungfrau von Orleans.* Edited by C. A. BUCHHEIM, Phil. Doc. *Second Edition.* . . . . . [Extra fcap. 8vo, 4s. 6d.

—— *Maria Stuart.* Edited by C. A. BUCHHEIM, Phil. Doc.
[Extra fcap. 8vo, 3s. 6d.

---

**Scherer.** *A History of German Literature.* By W. SCHERER. Translated from the Third German Edition by Mrs. F. C. CONYBEARE. Edited by The Rt. Hon. F. MAX MÜLLER. 2 vols. . . . . [8vo, 21s.

—— *A History of German Literature from the Accession of Frederick the Great to the Death of Goethe.* Reprinted from the above. [Crown 8vo, 5s.

**Max Müller.** *The German Classics from the Fourth to the Nineteenth Century.* With Biographical Notices, Translations into Modern German, and Notes, by The Rt. Hon. F. MAX MÜLLER, M.A. A New edition, revised, enlarged, and adapted to WILHELM SCHERER's *History of German Literature,* by F. LICHTENSTEIN. 2 vols. . . . . . [Crown 8vo, 21s.

**Wright.** *An Old High German Primer.* With Grammar, Notes, and Glossary. By JOSEPH WRIGHT, Ph.D. . . [Extra fcap. 8vo, 3s. 6d.

—— *A Middle High German Primer.* With Grammar, Notes, and Glossary. By JOSEPH WRIGHT, Ph.D. . . [Extra fcap. 8vo, 3s. 6d.

—— *A Primer of the Gothic Language.* With Grammar, Notes, and Glossary. By the same Author. . . . [Extra fcap. 8vo, 4s. 6d.

---

𝔏𝔬𝔫𝔡𝔬𝔫: HENRY FROWDE,

OXFORD UNIVERSITY PRESS WAREHOUSE, AMEN CORNER.

𝔈𝔡𝔦𝔫𝔟𝔲𝔯𝔤𝔥: 12 FREDERICK STREET.

# Clarendon Press Series.

## Latin Educational Works.

### GRAMMARS, LEXICONS, &c.

**Allen.** *Rudimenta Latina.* Comprising Accidence, and Exercises of a very Elementary Character, for the use of Beginners. By J. BARROW ALLEN, M.A. . . . . . . . . . . . . [Extra fcap. 8vo, 2s.

—— *An Elementary Latin Grammar.* By the same Author. One hundred and thirty-seventh Thousand. . . . [Extra fcap. 8vo, 2s. 6d.

—— *A First Latin Exercise Book.* By the same Author. *Eighth Edition.* . . . . . . . . . . [Extra fcap. 8vo, 2s. 6d.

—— *A Second Latin Exercise Book.* By the same Author. *Second Edition.* . . . . . . . . . [Extra fcap. 8vo, 3s. 6d.

[*A Key to First and Second Latin Exercise Books: for Teachers only, price 5s.*]

**Fox** and **Bromley.** *Models and Exercises in Unseen Translation.* By H. F. Fox, M.A., and T. M. BROMLEY, M.A. [Extra fcap. 8vo, 5s. 6d.

[*A Key to Passages quoted in the above: for Teachers only, price 6d.*]

**Gibson.** *An Introduction to Latin Syntax.* By W. S. GIBSON, M.A.
[Extra fcap. 8vo, 2s.

**Jerram.** *Reddenda Minora.* By C. S. JERRAM, M.A.
[Extra fcap. 8vo, 1s. 6d.

—— *Anglice Reddenda.* FIRST SERIES. [Extra fcap. 8vo, 2s. 6d.

—— *Anglice Reddenda.* SECOND SERIES. [Extra fcap. 8vo, 3s.

—— *Anglice Reddenda.* THIRD SERIES. [Extra fcap. 8vo, 3s.

**Lee-Warner.** *Hints and Helps for Latin Elegiacs.* By H. LEE-WARNER, M.A. . . . . . . . [Extra fcap. 8vo, 3s. 6d.

[*A Key is provided: for Teachers only, price 4s. 6d.*]

**Lewis.** *An Elementary Latin Dictionary.* By CHARLTON T. LEWIS, Ph.D. . . . . . . . . . . . [Square 8vo, 7s. 6d.

—— *A Latin Dictionary for Schools.* By the same Author.
[Small 4to, 18s.

**Lindsay.** *A Short Historical Latin Grammar.* By W. M. LINDSAY, M.A. . . . . . . . . . . . [Crown 8vo, 5s. 6d.

**Nunns.** *First Latin Reader.* By T. J. NUNNS, M.A. *Third Edition.*
[Extra fcap. 8vo, 2s.

**Ramsay.** *Latin Prose Composition.* By G. G. RAMSAY, M.A., LL.D. *Fourth Edition.* Extra fcap. 8vo.

Vol. I. *Syntax, Exercises with Notes, &c.*, 4s. 6d.
Or in two Parts, 2s. 6d. each, viz.
Part I. *The Simple Sentence.* Part II. *The Compound Sentence.*

*⁂ A Key to the above, price 5s. net. Supplied to Teachers only, on application to the Secretary, Clarendon Press.*

Vol. II. *Passages of Graduated Difficulty for Translation into Latin, together with an Introduction on Continuous Prose,* 4s. 6d.

**Ramsay.** *Latin Prose Versions.* Contributed by various Scholars. Edited by G. G. RAMSAY, M.A., LL.D. . . . [Extra fcap. 8vo, 5s.

**Sargent.** *Easy Passages for Translation into Latin.* By J. Y. SARGENT, M.A. *Seventh Edition.* . . . . . . [Extra fcap. 8vo, 2s. 6d.
[*A Key to this Edition is provided: for Teachers only, price* 5s., *net.*]

—— *A Latin Prose Primer.* By the same Author.
[Extra fcap. 8vo, 2s. 6d.

**King** and **Cookson.** *The Principles of Sound and Inflexion, as illustrated in the Greek and Latin Languages.* By J. E. KING, M.A., and CHRISTOPHER COOKSON, M.A. . . . . . . . . [8vo, 18s.

—— *An Introduction to the Comparative Grammar of Greek and Latin.* By the same Authors. . . . . . . [Crown 8vo, 5s. 6d.

**Papillon.** *A Manual of Comparative Philology.* By T. L. PAPILLON, M.A. *Third Edition.* . . . . . . . . . [Crown 8vo, 6s.

**Caesar.** *The Commentaries* (for Schools). With Notes and Maps. By CHARLES E. MOBERLY, M.A.
*The Gallic War. New Edition.* Extra fcap. 8vo—
 Books I and II, 2s.; III-V, 2s. 6d.; VI-VIII, 3s. 6d.
 Books I-III, stiff covers, 2s.
*The Civil War. Second Edition.* . . . [Extra fcap. 8vo, 3s. 6d.

**Catulli Veronensis** *Carmina Selecta,* secundum recognitionem ROBINSON ELLIS, A.M. . . . . . . [Extra fcap. 8vo, 3s. 6d.

**Cicero.** *Selection of Interesting and Descriptive Passages.* With Notes. By HENRY WALFORD, M.A. In three Parts. *Third Edition.*
[Extra fcap. 8vo, 4s. 6d.
 Part I. *Anecdotes from Grecian and Roman History.* . [*limp,* 1s. 6d.
 Part II. *Omens and Dreams; Beauties of Nature.* . [ „ 1s. 6d.
 Part III. *Rome's Rule of her Provinces.* . . . . [ „ 1s. 6d.

—— *De Amicitia.* With Introduction and Notes. By ST. GEORGE STOCK, M.A. . . . . . . . . [Extra fcap. 8vo, 3s.

—— *De Senectute.* With Introduction and Notes. By LEONARD HUXLEY, B.A. *In one or two Parts.* . [Extra fcap. 8vo, 2s.

—— *Pro Cluentio.* With Introduction and Notes. By W. RAMSAY, M.A. Edited by G. G. RAMSAY, M.A. *Second Edition.* [Extra fcap. 8vo, 3s. 6d.

—— *Pro Marcello, pro Ligario, pro Rege Deiotaro.* With Introduction and Notes. By W. Y. FAUSSET, M.A. . . . [Extra fcap. 8vo, 2s. 6d.

—— *Pro Milone.* With Notes, &c. By A. B. POYNTON, M.A.
[Extra fcap. 8vo, 2s. 6d.

—— *Pro Roscio.* With Introduction and Notes. By ST. GEORGE STOCK, M.A. . . . . . . . [Extra fcap. 8vo, 3s. 6d.

—— *Select Orations* (for Schools). *In Verrem Actio Prima. De Imperio Gn. Pompeii. Pro Archia. Philippica IX.* With Introduction and Notes. By J. R. KING, M.A. *Second Edition.* . [Extra fcap. 8vo, 2s. 6d.

—— *In Q. Caecilium Divinatio* and *In C. Verrem Actio Prima.* With Introduction and Notes. By J. R. KING, M.A. [Extra fcap. 8vo, 1s. 6d.

**Cicero.** *Speeches against Catilina.* With Introduction and Notes. By E. A. UPCOTT, M.A. *Second Edition.* . . . [Extra fcap. 8vo, 2s. 6d.

—— *Philippic Orations.* With Notes, &c., by J. R. KING, M.A. *Second Edition.* . . . . . . . . . . [8vo, 10s. 6d.

—— *Selected Letters* (for Schools). With Notes. By C. E. PRICHARD, M.A., and E. R. BERNARD, M.A. *Second Edition.*
[Extra fcap. 8vo, 3s.

—— *Select Letters.* With English Introductions, Notes, and Appendices. By ALBERT WATSON, M.A. *Fourth Edition* [8vo, 18s.

—— *Select Letters.* Text. By the same Editor. *Second Edition.*
[Extra fcap. 8vo, 4s.

**Cornelius Nepos.** With Notes. By OSCAR BROWNING, M.A. *Third Edition.* Revised by W. R. INGE, M.A. . . [Extra fcap. 8vo, 3s.

**Early Roman Poetry.** *Selected Fragments.* With Introduction and Notes. By W. W. MERRY, D.D. . . . . . [Crown 8vo, 6s. 6d.

**Horace.** With a Commentary. Volume I. *The Odes, Carmen Seculare,* and *Epodes.* By EDWARD C. WICKHAM, D.D. *New Edition.*
[Extra fcap. 8vo, 6s.

—— *Odes,* Book I. By the same Editor [Extra fcap. 8vo, 2s.

—— *Selected Odes.* With Notes for the use of a Fifth Form. By the same Editor. . . . . . . . . [Extra fcap. 8vo, 2s.

**Juvenal.** *XIII Satires.* Edited, with Introduction, Notes, &c., by C. H. PEARSON, M.A., and H. A. STRONG, M.A. *Second Edition.* [Crown 8vo, 9s.

**Livy.** *Selections* (for Schools). With Notes and Maps. By H. LEE-WARNER, M.A. . . . . . . . . . [Extra fcap. 8vo.
    Part I. *The Caudine Disaster.* . . . . . [*limp,* 1s. 6d.
    Part II. *Hannibal's Campaign in Italy.* . . . . [ ,, 1s. 6d.
    Part III. *The Macedonian War.* . . . . . [ ,, 1s. 6d.

—— *Book I.* With Introduction, Historical Examination, and Notes. By J. R. SEELEY, M.A. *Third Edition.* . . . . . . [8vo, 6s.

—— *Books V—VII.* With Introduction and Notes. By A. R. CLUER, B.A. *Second Edition.* Revised by P. E. MATHESON, M.A. [Extra fcap. 8vo, 5s.

Book V, 2s. 6d.; Book VII, 2s. By the same Editors.

—— *Books XXI—XXIII.* With Introduction, Notes, and Maps. By M. T. TATHAM, M.A. *Second Edition* . . . [Extra fcap. 8vo, 5s.

—— *Book XXI.* By the same Editor. . . [Extra fcap. 8vo, 2s. 6d.

—— *Book XXII.* By the same Editor. . . [Extra fcap. 8vo, 2s. 6d.

**Ovid.** *Selections* (for the use of Schools). With Introductions and Notes, and an Appendix on the Roman Calendar. By W. RAMSAY, M.A. Edited by G. G. RAMSAY, M.A. *Third Edition.* . [Extra fcap. 8vo, 5s. 6d.

—— *Tristia,* Book I. The Text revised, with an Introduction and Notes. By S. G. OWEN, B.A. *Second Edition.* [Extra fcap. 8vo, 3s. 6d.

—— *Tristia,* Book III. With Introduction and Notes. By the same Editor. . . . . . . . . . . [Extra fcap. 8vo, 2s.

**Persius.** *The Satires.* With Translation and Commentary by J. Conington, M.A., edited by H. Nettleship, M.A. . . [8vo, 8s. 6d.
**Plautus.** *Captivi.* With Introduction and Notes. By W. M. Lindsay, M.A. . . . . . . . . . [Extra fcap. 8vo, 2s. 6d.
—— *Trinummus.* With Notes and Introductions. (Intended for the Higher Forms of Public Schools.) By C. E. Freeman, M.A., and A. Sloman, M.A. . . . . . . . . [Extra fcap. 8vo, 3s.
**Pliny.** *Selected Letters* (for Schools). By C. E. Prichard, M.A., and E. R. Bernard, M.A. *Third Edition.* . . . [Extra fcap. 8vo, 3s.
**Quintilian.** *Institutionis Oratoriae Liber X.* Edited by W. Peterson, M.A. . . . . . . . [Extra fcap. 8vo, 3s. 6d.
**Sallust.** *Bellum Catilinarium* and *Jugurthinum.* With Introduction and Notes, by W. W. Capes, M.A. [Extra fcap. 8vo, 4s. 6d.
**Tacitus.** *The Annals.* Books I—IV. Edited, with Introduction and Notes for the use of Schools and Junior Students, by H. Furneaux, M.A.
[Extra fcap. 8vo, 5s.
—— *The Annals.* Book I. By the same Editor. . . [*limp,* 2s.
**Terence.** *Adelphi.* With Notes and Introductions. By A. Sloman, M.A. . . . . . . . . . [Extra fcap. 8vo, 3s.
—— *Andria.* With Notes and Introductions. By C. E. Freeman, M.A., and A. Sloman, M.A. *Second Edition* . . [Extra fcap. 8vo, 3s.
—— *Phormio.* With Notes and Introductions. By A. Sloman, M.A. . . . . . . . . . [Extra fcap. 8vo, 3s.
**Tibullus** and **Propertius.** *Selections.* Edited, with Introduction and Notes, by G. G. Ramsay, M.A. *Second Edition.* . [Extra fcap. 8vo, 6s.
**Virgil.** With an Introduction and Notes. By T. L. Papillon, M.A., and A. E. Haigh, M.A.
[Crown 8vo, 2 vols., *cloth, price* 6s. *each, or in stiff covers,* 3s. 6d. *each.*
—— *Bucolics and Georgics.* By the same Editors. [Crown 8vo, 2s. 6d.
—— *Aeneid.* With Introduction and Notes, by the same Editors. In Four Parts. . . . . . . . [Crown 8vo, 2s. *each.*
—— *The Text, including the Minor Works.*
[On writing-paper, 32mo, 5s.; on India paper, 6s.
—— *Bucolics.* With Introduction and Notes, by C. S. Jerram, M.A.
[Extra fcap. 8vo, 2s. 6d.
—— *Georgics.* Books I, II. By the same Editor. [Extra fcap. 8vo, 2s. 6d.
—— *Georgics.* Books III, IV. By the same Editor. [Extra fcap. 8vo, 2s. 6d.
—— *Aeneid I.* With Introduction and Notes, by the same Editor.
[Extra fcap. 8vo, *limp,* 1s. 6d.
—— *Aeneid IX.* Edited, with Introduction and Notes, by A. E. Haigh, M.A. . [Extra fcap. 8vo, *limp,* 1s. 6d. *In two Parts,* 2s.

London: HENRY FROWDE,
Oxford University Press Warehouse, Amen Corner.
Edinburgh: 12 Frederick Street.

# Clarendon Press Series.

## Greek Educational Works.

### GRAMMARS, LEXICONS, &c.

**Chandler.** *The Elements of Greek Accentuation* (for Schools). By H. W. CHANDLER, M.A. *Second Edition.* . [Extra fcap. 8vo, 2s. 6d.

**Fox** and **Bromley.** *Models and Exercises in Unseen Translation.* By H. F. Fox, M.A., and T. M. BROMLEY, M.A. [Extra fcap. 8vo, 5s. 6d.

[*A Key to Passages quoted in the above : for Teachers only, price 6d.*]

**Jerram.** *Graece Reddenda.* By C. S. JERRAM, M.A. . . [2s. 6d.

—— *Reddenda Minora.* . . . [Extra fcap. 8vo, 1s. 6d.

—— *Anglice Reddenda.* First Series. [Extra fcap. 8vo, 2s. 6d.

—— —— Second Series. . . [Extra fcap. 8vo, 3s.

—— —— Third Series. . . [Extra fcap. 8vo, 3s.

**Liddell** and **Scott.** *A Greek-English Lexicon.* . . [4to, 36s.

—— *An Intermediate Greek-English Lexicon.* [Small 4to, 12s. 6d.

—— *A Greek-English Lexicon,* abridged. . [Square 12mo, 7s. 6d.

**Sargent.** *A Primer of Greek Prose Composition.* By J. YOUNG SARGENT, M.A. . . . . . . [Extra fcap. 8vo, 3s. 6d.

\*\*\* A Key to the above, price 5s. Supplied *to Teachers only,* on application to the Secretary, Clarendon Press.

—— —— *Passages for Translation into Greek Prose.* [Extra fcap. 8vo, 3s.

—— —— *Exemplaria Graeca*; being Greek Renderings of Selected "Passages for Translation into Greek Prose." . . [Extra fcap. 8vo, 3s.

—— *Models and Materials for Greek Iambic Verse.* [4s. 6d.

**Wordsworth.** *A Greek Primer.* By the Right Rev. CHARLES WORDSWORTH, D.C.L. *Eighty-third Thousand.* [Extra fcap. 8vo, 1s. 6d.

—— *Graecae Grammaticae Rudimenta in usum Scholarum.* Auctore CAROLO WORDSWORTH, D.C.L. *Nineteenth Edition.* . . . [12mo, 4s.

---

**King** and **Cookson.** *An Introduction to the Comparative Grammar of Greek and Latin.* By J. E. KING, M.A., and C. COOKSON, M.A. [Crown 8vo, 5s. 6d.

**Papillon.** *A Manual of Comparative Philology.* By T. L. PAPILLON, M.A. . . . . . . . . . [Crown 8vo, 6s.

---

### A COURSE OF GREEK READERS.

**Easy Greek Reader.** By EVELYN ABBOTT, M.A. [Extra fcap. 8vo, 3s.

**First Greek Reader.** By W. G. RUSHBROOKE, M.L. *Third Edition.* [Extra fcap. 8vo, 2s. 6d.

# CLARENDON PRESS SERIES.

**Second Greek Reader.** By A. M. BELL, M.A. [Extra fcap. 8vo, 3s.
**Specimens of Greek Dialects;** being *a Fourth Greek Reader.* With Introductions and Notes. By W. W. MERRY, D.D. [Extra fcap. 8vo, 4s. 6d.
**Selections from Homer and the Greek Dramatists;** being *a Fifth Greek Reader.* By EVELYN ABBOTT, M.A. . . [Extra fcap. 8vo, 4s. 6d.
**Wright.** *The Golden Treasury of Ancient Greek Poetry.* By R. S. WRIGHT, M.A. *Second Edition, Revised.* . [Extra fcap. 8vo, 10s. 6d.
**Wright** and **Shadwell.** *A Golden Treasury of Greek Prose.* By R. S. WRIGHT, M.A., and J. E. L. SHADWELL, M.A. [Extra fcap. 8vo, 4s. 6d.

## THE GREEK TESTAMENT.

**A Greek Testament Primer.** An Easy Grammar and Reading Book for the use of Students beginning Greek. By E. MILLER, M.A. *Second Edition.* [Extra fcap. 8vo, *paper covers*, 2s.; *cloth*, 3s. 6d.
**Evangelia Sacra Graece.** • . . . [Fcap. 8vo, *limp*, 1s. 6d.
**Novum Testamentum Graece** juxta Exemplar Millianum. [2s. 6d.
**Novum Testamentum Graece.** Accedunt parallela S. Scripturae loca, &c. Edidit CAROLUS LLOYD, S.T.P.R. . . . [18mo, 3s.
—— Critical Appendices to the above. By W. SANDAY, M.A. 3s. 6d.
**The Greek Testament,** with the Readings adopted by the Revisers of the Authorised Version. . . . . . . . [Fcap. 8vo, 4s. 6d.

**Outlines of Textual Criticism applied to the New Testament.** By C. E. HAMMOND, M.A. *Fifth Edition.* . . . [Crown 8vo, 4s. 6d.

## GREEK CLASSICS FOR SCHOOLS.

**Aeschylus.** *Agamemnon.* With Introduction and Notes, by ARTHUR SIDGWICK, M.A. *Fourth Edition.* . . [Extra fcap. 8vo, 3s.
—— *Choephoroi.* By the same Editor. . [Extra fcap. 8vo, 3s.
—— *Eumenides.* By the same Editor. . . [Extra fcap. 8vo, 3s.
—— *Prometheus Bound.* With Introduction and Notes, by A. O. PRICKARD, M.A. *Second Edition.* . . . . [Extra fcap. 8vo, 2s.
—— *Septem Contra Thebas.* By A. SIDGWICK, M.A. . [*Shortly.*
**Aristophanes.** *The Acharnians.* With Introduction and Notes, by W. W. MERRY, D.D. *Fourth Edition.* . . . [Extra fcap. 8vo, 3s.
—— *The Birds.* By the same Editor. . . [Extra fcap. 8vo, 3s. 6d.
—— *The Clouds.* By the same Editor. *Third Edition.*
[Extra fcap. 8vo, 3s.
—— *The Frogs.* By the same Editor . . [Extra fcap. 8vo, 3s.
—— *The Knights.* By the same Editor. . [Extra fcap. 8vo, 3s.
—— *The Wasps.* By the same Editor . [Extra fcap. 8vo, 3s. 6d.

**Cebes.** *Tabula.* With Introduction and Notes, by C. S. JERRAM, M.A.
[Extra fcap. 8vo, 2s. 6d.

**Demosthenes.** *Orations against Philip.* With Introduction and Notes. By EVELYN ABBOTT, M.A., and P. E. MATHESON, M.A.
    Vol. I. *Philippic I* and *Olynthiacs I—III.* . . [Extra fcap. 8vo, 3s.
    Vol. II. *De Pace, Philippic II, De Chersoneso, Philippic III.* . [4s. 6d.
    *Philippics only, reprinted from the above, 2s. 6d.*

**Euripides.** *Alcestis.* By C. S. JERRAM, M.A. [Extra fcap. 8vo, 2s. 6d.
—— *Bacchae.* By A. H. CRUICKSHANK, M.A. . . [3s. 6d.
—— *Cyclops.* By W. E. LONG, M.A. . [Extra fcap. 8vo, 2s. 6d.
—— *Hecuba.* By C. H. RUSSELL, M.A. [Extra fcap. 8vo, 2s. 6d.
—— *Helena.* By C. S. JERRAM, M.A. . [Extra fcap. 8vo, 3s.
—— *Heracleidae.* By the same Editor. [Extra fcap. 8vo, 3s.
—— *Ion.* By the same Editor. . [Extra fcap. 8vo, 3s.
—— *Iphigenia in Tauris.* By the same Editor. [Extra fcap. 8vo, 3s.
—— *Medea.* With Introduction, Notes, and Appendices. By C. B. HEBERDEN, M.A. *In one or two Parts.* . . . [Extra fcap. 8vo, 2s.

**Herodotus.** Book IX. Edited, with Notes, by EVELYN ABBOTT, M.A. *In one or two Parts.* . . . . . [Extra fcap. 8vo, 3s.
—— *Selections.* Edited, with Introduction, Notes, and a Map, by W. W. MERRY, D.D. . . . . . [Extra fcap. 8vo, 2s. 6d.

**Homer for Beginners.** *Iliad*, Book III. By M. T. TATHAM, M.A.
[Extra fcap. 8vo, 1s. 6d.

**Homer.** *Iliad*, Books I–XII. With an Introduction, a brief Homeric Grammar, and Notes. By D. B. MONRO, M.A. . . [Extra fcap. 8vo, 6s.
—— *Iliad*, Books XIII–XXIV. By the same Editor [6s.
—— *Iliad*, Book I. By the same Editor. . [Extra fcap. 8vo, 1s. 6d.
—— *Iliad*, Book III (for beginners). By M. T. TATHAM, M.A. [1s. 6d.
—— *Iliad*, Book XXI. By HERBERT HAILSTONE, M.A. [1s. 6d.
—— *Odyssey*, Books I–XII. By W. W. MERRY, D.D. . . [5s.
—— *Odyssey*, Books I and II. By the same Editor. [Each 1s. 6d.
—— *Odyssey*, Books VI and VII. By the same Editor. . [1s. 6d.
—— *Odyssey*, Books VII–XII. By the same Editor. [Extra fcap. 8vo, 3s.
—— *Odyssey*, Books XIII–XXIV. By the same Editor. *New Edition.* . . . . . . . . [Extra fcap. 8vo, 5s.
—— *Odyssey*, Books XIII–XVIII. By the same Editor.
[Extra fcap. 8vo, 3s.

**Lucian.** *Vera Historia.* By C. S. JERRAM, M.A. [Extra fcap. 8vo, 1s. 6d.
**Lysias.** *Epitaphios.* Edited by F. J. SNELL, B.A. [Extra fcap. 8vo, 2s.
**Plato.** *The Apology.* With Introduction and Notes. By ST. GEORGE STOCK, M.A. *Second Edition.* . . . [Extra fcap. 8vo, 2s. 6d.
—— *Crito.* With Introduction and Notes. By the same Editor. [2s.
—— *Meno.* By the same Editor. . . [Extra fcap. 8vo, 2s. 6d.

**Plato.** *Selections.* With Introductions and Notes. By J. PURVES, M.A., and Preface by B. JOWETT, M.A. *Second Edition.* . [Extra fcap. 8vo, 5s.

**Plutarch.** *Lives of the Gracchi.* Edited, with Introduction, Notes, and Indices, by G. E. UNDERHILL, M.A. . . [Crown 8vo, 4s. 6d.

**Sophocles.** Edited, with Introductions and English Notes, by LEWIS CAMPBELL, M.A., and EVELYN ABBOTT, M.A. New Edition. 2 Vols. 10s. 6d.
[*or*, Vol. I. Text, 4s. 6d.; Vol. II. Notes, 6s.

☞ *Also in single Plays. Extra fcap. 8vo, limp, 2s. each.*

—— *Oedipus Rex*: Dindorf's Text, with Notes by W. BASIL JONES, D.D., Lord Bishop of St. David's. . . . [Extra fcap. 8vo, *limp*, 1s. 6d.

**Theocritus.** Edited, with Notes, by H. KYNASTON, D.D. (late SNOW). *Fifth Edition.* . . . . . [Extra fcap. 8vo, 4s. 6d.

**Thucydides.** Book I. With Introduction, Notes, and Maps. By W. H. FORBES, M.A. . . . . . . . . [8vo, 8s. 6d.

**Xenophon.** *Easy Selections.* By J. S. PHILLPOTTS, B.C.L., and C. S. JERRAM, M.A. With Map. *Third Edition.* . . . . [3s. 6d.

—— *Selections* (for Schools). With Notes and Maps. By J. S. PHILLPOTTS, B.C.L. *Fourth Edition.* . [Extra fcap. 8vo, 3s. 6d.

*A Key to Sections I–III, for Teachers only, price 2s. 6d. net.*

—— *Anabasis*, Book I. With Introduction, Notes, and Map. By J. MARSHALL, M.A. . . . . . . [Extra fcap. 8vo, 2s. 6d.

—— *Anabasis*, Book II. With Notes and Map. By C. S. JERRAM. M.A. . . . . . . [Extra fcap. 8vo, 2s.

—— *Anabasis*, Book III. With Introduction, Analysis, Notes, &c. By J. MARSHALL, M.A. . . . . . [Extra fcap. 8vo, 2s. 6d.

—— *Anabasis*, Book IV. With Introduction, Notes, &c. By the same Editor. . . . . . . . . . [Extra fcap. 8vo, 2s.

—— *Vocabulary to the Anabasis.* By the same Editor. . [1s. 6d.

—— *Cyropaedia*, Book I. With Introduction and Notes. By C. BIGG, D.D. . . . . . . . . . [Extra fcap. 8vo, 2s.

—— *Cyropaedia*, Books IV, V. With Introduction and Notes. By the same Editor. . . . . . . . . [Extra fcap. 8vo, 2s. 6d.

—— *Hellenica*, Books I, II. With Introduction and Notes. By G. E. UNDERHILL, M.A. . . . . . . [Extra fcap. 8vo, 3s.

—— *Memorabilia.* Edited for the use of Schools, with Introduction and Notes, &c., by J. MARSHALL, M.A. . . . [Extra fcap. 8vo, 4s. 6d.

---

𝔏𝔬𝔫𝔡𝔬𝔫: HENRY FROWDE,

OXFORD UNIVERSITY PRESS WAREHOUSE, AMEN CORNER.

𝔈𝔡𝔦𝔫𝔟𝔲𝔯𝔤𝔥: 12 FREDERICK STREET.

PE      Skeat, Watler William
1571       A student's pastime
S57

PLEASE DO NOT REMOVE
CARDS OR SLIPS FROM THIS POCKET

UNIVERSITY OF TORONTO LIBRARY

Lightning Source UK Ltd.
Milton Keynes UK
UKOW06f1831090516

273909UK00008B/232/P